The Adams Papers

L. H. BUTTERFIELD, EDITOR IN CHIEF

SERIES I

DIARIES

Diary of Charles Francis Adams

Diary of Charles Francis Adams

MARC FRIEDLAENDER and L. H. BUTTERFIELD

EDITORS

———————— ☆ ————————

Volume 5 · *January 1833–October 1834*

THE BELKNAP PRESS
OF HARVARD UNIVERSITY PRESS
CAMBRIDGE, MASSACHUSETTS

1974

Distributed in Great Britain by Oxford University Press · London

Funds for editing *The Adams Papers* were originally furnished by Time, Inc., on behalf of *Life*, to the Massachusetts Historical Society, under whose supervision the editorial work is being done. Further funds have been provided by a grant from the Ford Foundation to the National Archives Trust Fund Board in support of this and four other major documentary publications. In common with these and many other enterprises like them, *The Adams Papers* benefits from the continuing and indispensable cooperation and aid of the National Historical Publications Commission, whose chairman is the Archivist of the United States.

Library of Congress Catalog Card Number 64-20588
ISBN 674-20402-6
Printed in the United States of America

This edition of *The Adams Papers*

is sponsored by the MASSACHUSETTS HISTORICAL SOCIETY

to which the ADAMS MANUSCRIPT TRUST

by a deed of gift dated 4 April 1956

gave ultimate custody of the personal and public papers

written, accumulated, and preserved over a span of three centuries

by the Adams family of Massachusetts

The Adams Papers

The acorn and oakleaf device on the preceding page is redrawn from a seal cut for John Quincy Adams after 1830. The motto is from Cæcilius Statius as quoted by Cicero in the First Tusculan Disputation: *Serit arbores quæ alteri seculo prosint* ("He plants trees for the benefit of later generations").

Contents

Descriptive List of Illustrations

Having seen Fanny Kemble for the first time on 17 April 1833, one day after she and her father made their initial appearances in Boston, Charles Francis Adams, together with his father just arrived from Washington, on the 19th saw her in the role in which she had made her American debut in New York: as Bianca in the tragedy of *Fazio*. By that date the Kemble conquest of Boston was complete. See p. 71, below. During the week following, Charles Francis Adams saw her in three additional roles on successive evenings. He was as faithful in attendance when she returned to Boston on a second tour in March and April 1834, her last before abandoning her theatrical career to enter upon what proved an unhappy marriage with Pierce Butler of Philadelphia. When she did return to the public platform in 1848 to do enormously successful dramatic readings from Shakespeare, which she continued through the 1850's, Charles Francis Adams' journal for the period reveals that he remained a faithful auditor to the last.

In the years between, Fanny Kemble had become a controversial figure after her frank and tactless impressions of America and Americans were published in a *Journal* in 1835 (vol. 6:132, below; Clifford Ashby, "Fanny Kemble's 'Vulgar' Journal," *Pennsylvania Magazine of History and Biography*, 98:58–66 [January 1974]) and after she became an active abolitionist following her residence on the Georgia plantation of her slaveholding husband. It was in connection with the first of these that Miss Kemble has a further place in the Adams family records. In that portion of her *Journal* relating to her first season in Boston she entered an account of a conversation on Shakespeare she had had at an evening party with a famous gentleman she did not identify, but who was easily identifiable as John Quincy Adams, and which treated the gentleman's expressed opinions with more mirth than respect. Her report of the conversation led the ex-President, under the urging of his friend Dr. George Parkman, to undertake his own account of the conversation and a fuller exposition of his views on Shakespeare in the theater. Publication of these opinions as review articles brought the matter to a close. The affair and its issues are recounted in an editorial note, p. 84–87, below.

In the first days of the Kembles' Boston success John Quincy Adams wrote that "Fanny Kemble [passes here] for a great Beauty, and a great Genius, both of which with the aid of Fashion and Fancy, she is" (Diary, 19 April 1833); and in a letter to his wife he put it that "She is very well formed—not unhandsome" (20 April 1833, Adams Papers). Initially, Charles Francis Adams, while fully acknowledging her dramatic gifts, was less taken with her appearance: "I thought her an ugly, bright looking girl," but he later acknowledged that "Her eyes give her great power" (p. 74 and 291, below). Her features would seem then to have been not conventionally beautiful but of a sort that strangely fixed the attention of the beholders. The problem of properly rendering her face must have fascinated Thomas Sully. In his "Register of Portraits" are entered ten likenesses of Fanny Kemble between 1832 and 1834 (*Pennsylvania Magazine of History and Biography*, 33:62 [January 1909]). The portrait reproduced, one of two of her by Sully in the Pennsylvania Academy of the Fine Arts and perhaps his most successful effort, has been in that collection since 1843. Oil on canvas, 30 x 25 1/2 inches, it is signed, "TS 1833."
Courtesy of the Pennsylvania Academy of the Fine Arts.

2. MRS. WOOD AND ENSEMBLE IN THE FINAL SCENE OF *La Sonnambula*   116

Mrs. Joseph Wood had made a brilliant American debut at the Park Theatre in New York on 9 September 1833 before appearing in Boston three months later. Earlier, Mrs. Wood as Mary Ann Paton and then as the wife of Lord William Lenox had, during a triumphant career at Covent Garden, won recognition as the finest vocalist in England. When her unhappy first marriage had ended in divorce, she married Wood, a handsome singer at Covent Garden but of more humble origins than hers. Together, the Woods would dominate the musical scene in New York for the four years following. See George C. D. Odell, *Annals of the New York Stage*, New York, 1927–1949, 3:657, 664; 4:63, 109; also p. 227, below.

When Charles Francis Adams first heard Mrs. Wood, he found her voice and ability worthy of comparison with those he judged best among the singers he had heard, Mrs. Malibran and Mrs. Austin (p. 227, 231, 301, below). Soon, however, her gifts won praise from him that did not look back to the performances of others: "Her complete management of her voice and powerful compass give the requisite brilliancy of execution" (p. 307, below). During the two theatrical seasons, 1833–1834 and 1835–1836, in which he had the opportunity to hear Mrs. Wood, Adams' Diary reveals that he attended twenty of her performances. He heard her in six roles: three times in the *Barber of Seville*, twice in *Cenerentola*, *Fra Diavolo*, *Maid of Judah*, and *Robert the Devil*. It was in *La Sonnambula*, however, that she became for Adams almost a passion.

Between 29 December 1835, when Bellini's new opera had its first performance in Boston (after being introduced in New York by the Woods on 13 November, preceding), and 9 March 1836, the final one of the season, Adams was at six of Mrs. Woods' appearances as Amina in *La Sonnambula.* He found the opera satisfying at each hearing until the last: "The music is sustained throughout, full of melody and character, occasionally passionate and then pathetic with some extraordinarily poetical conceptions. . . . A very delightful piece. Such a one as I love to hear. It is delicious"; "Perhaps there is in the whole range of refined enjoyments none more perfect in all respects than that of listening to the good singing of a good Opera"; "I shall remember the moments spent in hearing these notes as the pleasantest of my life" (vol. 6:297–298, 303, 345). Adams' enthusiasm was hardly greater than that of Boston's musical public: "Mr. and Mrs. Wood took the town by storm, and airs from the 'Sonnambula' were played, sung, whistled, and ground on hand-organs with persistent zeal" (Francis Boott Greenough, ed., *Letters of Horatio Greenough to . . . Henry Greenough*, Boston, 1887, p. 51).

One of the most popular of the "airs" was the finale, "Ah do not mingle one earthly feeling," which Adams pronounced "exquisite" (vol. 6:305). The front cover of the song in sheet-music form, displaying Mrs. Wood and cast before an arboreal retreat and waterfall, was executed "On Stone by J. H. Bufford corner of Beekman & Nassau Sts." and "Published at Atwill's Music Saloon 201 Broadway./Endicott, Litho." Presumably the artist was John H. Bufford and the lithographic printer was George Endicott, both well known lithographers (George C. Groce and David H. Wallace, *Dictionary of Artists in America, 1564–1860*, New Haven, 1957).
Courtesy of the Harvard Theatre Collection.

3. AUCTION CATALOGUE OF PAINTINGS FROM THOMAS JEFFERSON'S COLLECTION AT MONTICELLO FOR SALE IN BOSTON, 1833   116

The *Catalogue of . . . Choice Pictures, Being the Collection of the late President Jefferson to be Sold at Auction on Friday, July 19, at Mr. Harding's Gallery, School St.* is of eight pages and lists paintings numbered one to fifty-six. However, some numbers in the sequence are omitted, and only forty-five items were actually included. The catalogue is by subject with most of the entries bearing notes of attribution, designation as originals or copies, and averrals relating to the circumstances of acquisition by Jefferson. These last belied the claim made for all in a foreword that "The Pictures which compose this collection, were purchased in Paris by Mr. Jefferson, while residing there as minister of the United States." Of the forty-five paintings, thirteen were described as originals; the rest were entered as copies, as painted "after —," or undescribed. By subject, twenty-four were biblical, twelve were portraits, five illustrated scenes from classical literature, and four were landscapes and the like.

Most of the paintings being offered were not new to Boston. The collection had apparently been removed from Monticello after Jefferson's death and before the bulk of the furnishings and other personal property was sold at auction on the premises on 15 January

1827. The decision for early sale or removal was made by Thomas Jefferson Randolph, Jefferson's grandson and executor, who was faced with the necessity not only of meeting the indebtedness with which the estate was burdened but of protecting his mother and Jefferson's heir, Martha Jefferson Randolph, against threats of seizure of her inheritance on behalf of creditors of her impecunious and debt-ridden husband, Thomas Mann Randolph (Thomas Jefferson Memorial Foundation, *Report of the Curator, 1960*, Charlottesville, 1961, p. 12–13).

It appears that it was on the advice of Joseph Coolidge Jr., of Boston, son-in-law of Martha Jefferson Randolph, that Boston was selected as the most advantageous site for the sale of the paintings, though the collection seems to have been exhibited en route without success in New York City. In Boston, a large part of the collection was included in the Athenæum Gallery Exhibition from May to August 1828 (Thomas Jefferson Memorial Foundation, *Report of the Curator, 1957*, p. 6; *Report of the Curator, 1965*, p. 9; Mabel M. Swan, *The Athenæum Gallery, 1827–1873*, Boston, 1940, p. 85–89). The Jefferson paintings shown at the Athenæum numbered thirty-eight, and fourteen of the works listed in the 1833 Catalogue were omitted. All but two of those shown at the Athenæum—the Stuart profile of Jefferson, now at the Fogg Art Museum (Alfred L. Bush, *The Life Portraits of Thomas Jefferson*, Charlottesville, 1962, p. 76), and the portrait of Madison attributed to Robert Edge Pine—were for sale. At the close of the Exhibition only one sale, that to the Athenæum of the Greuze portrait of Franklin for $200, is recorded. However, since seven of those shown at the Athenæum, including the three already named, were not included in the 1833 sale, it seems likely that the four additional ones were sold during the intervening years, especially since six of the seven were among those listed as originals and seem among the choicest. The remainder of the collection remained in Joseph Coolidge's custody to await a more favorable opportunity for disposition.

Five years passed before another public exhibition and sale was attempted. Even then the results were not good, the public's reaction agreeing with that expressed by Charles Francis Adams that the paintings remaining "are poor enough in all conscience" (p. 128, below). Despite the brave assertion in the Catalogue that the pictures "have a value as works of art, distinct from that which they derive from their association with the names of their late distinguished owner and the venerable artist [Trumbull], whose taste directed in making the selection" (p. 2), neither associational nor aesthetic claims were given much weight in the value assigned to the paintings at the sale. Bids of thirty-five, twenty, and fifteen dollars obtained the portraits of Locke, Columbus, and Bacon respectively; and the whole sale realized a "little more than $500" (Thomas Jefferson Memorial Foundation, *Report of the Curator, 1965*, p. 10).

Although the importance of the paintings as Jeffersoniana did not immediaetly affect their value in the market place, a sufficient number of the purchasers of the paintings attached significance to their earlier locus to make possible the construction at Monticello by the

Memorial Foundation of a census of a substantial number of the dispersed works in the form of a "Paintings Locator File" (*Report of the Curator, 1959,* p. 9). A number of the paintings have found their way, some early some late, into institutional collections. Six from the 1833 sale, with two additional ones from the earlier Athenæum exhibition, have been returned to Monticello where they now hang (*Report of the Curator, 1959,* p. 22–28; *Report of the Curator, 1965,* p. 8); three—the Columbus, the Lafayette, and the Wright portrait of Washington—hang at the Massachusetts Historical Society (*Proceedings,* 2[1833–1855]:16, 23, 25); the Mather Brown portrait of John Adams, along with the Franklin, is at the Boston Athenæum (Andrew Oliver, *Portraits of John and Abigail Adams,* Cambridge, 1967, p. 49, 52).
Courtesy of the Boston Athenæum.

4. CHARLES FRANCIS ADAMS' ANNOTATED COPY OF HORACE   116
Although Charles Francis Adams had read in Horace's poetry over a period of months in 1825 just after his college graduation (vol. 2:11–19, above), and in the summer of 1831 after an extended study of his *De Arte Poetica* and other classic examples in the critical genre had concluded of Horace's essay, "I know nothing in its way superior to it" (vol. 4:109–110, above), it was not until he took up the poet again early in 1833 that he came to a full realization of Horace's powers. At the outset of this renewed effort, one of the satires so struck him that he wrote, "I wonder I never read them attentively before. How admirable. Every sentiment so just in itself, so gracefully put in. I will read Horace perpetually. Make him familiar" (p. 21, below). And after a "slow perusal" of the odes that he called "tolerably thorough," Adams concluded, "I have for the first time formed an idea of the peculiar qualities of the Poet. . . . I find him now possessed of the Power to fly high into the noblest regions of Poetry" (p. 142, below). His admiration for both the critic and the poet, Adams also recorded in his own copy of the *Opera* of Horace, London, 1824, in comments that are evident on the pages from the volume here illustrated.
The copy which Charles Francis Adams annotated has the text of J. M. Gesner but is without any scholarly apparatus. It was primarily to remedy this lack that, as Adams noted on the flyleaf, he supplied marginalia principally drawn from a consultation of the more scholarly French edition of Dacier and Sanadon, 8 vols., Amsterdam, 1735, and that of Zeunius, Leipzig, 1802 (the first of these is among John Adams' books now at the Boston Public Library; the second, along with the copy annotated, is in the Stone Library at Quincy; see p. 22 and 105, below). In addition to those annotations that compare the judgments of the critics or that undertake the elucidation of words or passages, a number of them express the reader's own aesthetic or moral judgments.
Courtesy of the National Park Service, Adams National Historic Site.

This undated document, which is without the names of those responsible for its authorship and circulation, must have been distributed in Boston on Monday, 11 November 1833, on which day the election for state offices was held. The event which occasioned it was the departure of John Quincy Adams, the nominee of the antimasonic party for Governor, from Massachusetts for Washington four days before the election. This action was seized upon by the opposition National Republican press as evidence that Adams, entertaining no hope of victory, had abandoned his supporters. On Saturday, 9 November, both the *Boston Atlas* and the *Columbian Centinel* made political capital of the departure in the passages quoted on the flier. See below, p. 209. The rebuttal from the Antimasons, evidently prepared over the weekend for circulation among the voters before they entered the polling places, expressed bitter complaint that a man of such stature, with a record of such distinguished public service, should be so vilified; sore vexation that a departure dictated by concern for his Congressional obligations should be misrepresented as an abandonment of the party leadership he had accepted.

With more anger than sagacity, the framers of the handbill, by quoting at length the aspersions of the *Atlas*, gave added currency to other charges which the enemies of John Quincy Adams had leveled at him during the campaign. The basic charge had been that John Quincy Adams supported the alleged policy of the Antimasons to "proscribe" any candidate for public office of whatever party who was a Freemason or who failed to pledge his opposition to Freemasonry. The principal evidence cited against Adams on the matter was contained in a passage from his letter to Benjamin Cowell, 28 November 1832 (LbC, Adams Papers), which the opposition press had obtained and publicized. In rebutting the charge, Adams chose, somewhat injudiciously, to have published a letter taking a position against "proscription" which he had written to John Brazer Davis (6 April 1832, MB:M. A. De Wolfe Howe Papers) without obtaining the consent of Davis' executors. In the resulting furor, in which the authenticity of the letter came into question and explanations of its provenance had to be offered, the letter became the object of fierce ridicule as the "washstand letter." On these matters, see p. 183–184, below; also *Memoirs of John Quincy Adams*, ed. Charles Francis Adams, Philadelphia, 1874–1877, 9:16–17.

However much the political effectiveness of the flier may be put in question, there is in its text a statement that goes to a basic understanding of John Quincy Adams' often puzzling political behavior: "His claims as a candidate for Governor, he leaves with his fellow citizens. His presence was not required at the election, and true to his republican principles, he will not seek to promote his election to any office, *by personal influence!*" Unstated was a second commitment made by Adams to himself and to his son Charles Francis that he would accept no elected office except one that came as a free expression of the will of a majority of the electorate (*Memoirs*, 9:21; to Charles Francis Adams, 26 November 1833, Adams Papers). Acting upon these principles, Adams had concluded, as soon as he learned that the National Republicans would not join with the Antimasons in making him their candidate against the Jacksonian party, that a majority would not likely be obtained by a vote of the people, and that in that event, even if he obtained a plurality, he would withdraw his name from the balloting that would ensue in the legislature. This decision he confided to Charles Francis long before the departure for Washington. When the results of the popular election became known, Adams' decision would be duly communicated to Benjamin Hallett, the leader of the Massachusetts Antimasons and the editor of the *Boston Daily Advocate*, and ultimately, before the legislative balloting began, to a surprised Commonwealth. See p. 188, 212, 222–223 and 239, below.

Courtesy of L. H. Butterfield.

6. ALEXANDER HILL EVERETT, AFTER A PAINTING BY GÉRARD
    IN 1825   212

The steel engraving by Henry Jordan and Frederick W. Halpin of Alexander Hill Everett (1790–1847) was published by J. & H. G. Langley, New York City, and appeared in 1842 in the *Democratic Review*, 10:facing p. 460. The engraving must have been done in the same year since it was only then that Halpin, recently arrived from England, and Jordan began to work together as a firm (George C. Groce and David H. Wallace, *Dictionary of Artists in America, 1564–1860*, New Haven, 1957). The likeness is "taken from a very fine portrait painted a number of years ago in Paris by the celebrated Girard, now in the possession of Ex-President Adams" (*Democratic Review*, 10:478). This would have been the portrait intended for President Adams for which Everett sat to Baron François Gérard (1770–1836) in 1825, when on his way to his new post as minister to Spain. Of it, Everett wrote to the President from Madrid: "In passing through Paris last August I sat a few times to Gérard for a portrait, intending it for you. My stay was so short that I could not at the time get it finished, and prepared for shipment: but I have since learned from my correspondent that it has been sent off to America. I have requested my brother Edward to deliver it to you, and venture to hope that you will do me the favour to accept it. My friends at Paris thought the resemblance pretty good, but were not much pleased with the colouring: As respects the execution, however, the name of Gérard, who stands at the head of his art in France, may be supposed to cover all defects. I informed him at the time of the destination of the portrait, and he appeared to be pleased with the opportunity of placing one of his works in your hands" (15 April 1826, Adams Papers). Whether the painting was kept by Adams in Washington or in Quincy during the years between 1825 and 1842 cannot be ascertained, nor is any information of its later whereabouts known to the editors.

The relations between the two men had long been close. Everett had studied law with Adams and had served him as private secretary in Russia, 1809–1811. As Secretary of State, Adams appointed Everett chargé d'affaires at The Hague, 1818–1824; the appointment in Madrid followed when Adams became President. At the end of the Adams administration Everett returned to Boston. In the years that followed, as Everett ventured into domestic politics on his own, there were times when the two found themselves on opposing sides, particularly since Everett, seeking to survive, seemed to follow a somewhat devious course. See, for example, p. 187, 196, and 369, below. Louisa Catherine Adams was led to say of him during such a time: "I have known [him] . . . ever since he was 19 years old and from that time I have never yet had reason to believe that he knew what a fixed principle was" (p. 208, below).

The connections between Charles Francis Adams and Everett were of a varied sort and began soon after Everett resumed his residence in Boston as editor of the *North American Review*, to which Adams was a contributor, generally unsatisfied by the treatment he received. Other points of friction developed as Adams expressed irritation on occasion at what seemed to him a lack of loyalty to John Quincy Adams and at Everett's addiction to expediency which served more often to make him vulnerable than to advance his career. See below, p. 187, 205; vol. 6:257, 261. However, the relationship underwent several transformations during the years embraced by the present volumes, as will be evident in the index. Adams was always an admirer of Everett's abilities: "As a Writer he has few equals" (vol. 3:133, above). He regarded Everett and John Quincy Adams as "the two best political writers in the State, if not in the Country" (vol. 6:198, below). In turn, Everett came to show greater appreciation of Adams' writings (p. 144, below). Further, in the tortuous course of politics, Everett, for a time at least, returned to adherence to John Quincy Adams' position, winning Charles Francis Adams' grudging approbation: "Everett is a man of whose motives of action I have seen too much within a few years to rely upon them very implicitly. He has on the whole supported my father and therefore I am disposed to do what I can to support him" (vol. 6:304, below). A respect for each other as writers and the necessities of antimasonic politics ultimately produced a situation in which the two by agreement were writing for the *Boston Daily Advocate* in tandem. See vol. 6:152–153 and 183–184, below.
Courtesy of the Massachusetts Historical Society.

7. THOMAS BAKER JOHNSON, ATTRIBUTED TO CHESTER HARDING 212
   Thomas Baker Johnson (1779–1843), only brother of Charles Francis Adams' mother, in early 1836, on leaving for Europe with the intent to remain there, carried out his earlier plan to place his financial affairs entirely in the hands of his nephew, Charles Francis. Although the hoped-for improvement in his health did not occur and Johnson returned to America in 1838, Charles Francis Adams remained his agent and trustee until Johnson's death, and thereafter under the terms of his will. Despite this manifestation of trust on the one side and magnanimity on the other, there was no intimacy between the two men. Indeed, Johnson was without any intimates, living his later life in a seclusion in Georgetown and Washington penetrated only by his immediate relatives. See below, p. 341; vol. 6:211, 339, 372; see also Thomas Baker Johnson, Will, 25 February 1842, Adams Papers, Microfilms, Reel No. 603.

As a young man Johnson had shown promise, and he was not without some mental powers even in his last years. He was a student at Harvard College from 1796 to 1798. He became deputy postmaster at New Orleans in 1810, retaining the post until 1824. During that period he was able to lay by out of his salary the $45,000.00 which he later turned over to his nephew to be invested. He seems always to have been inclined to parsimoniousness, fearing that poverty would overtake him as it had Joshua Johnson, his father.

Other fears, carried to extremes that suggest the pathological, increasingly possessed him. These included an abiding horror of Blacks, a terror that "encreased to a degree beyond remedy. . . . His Nights are destroyed by horrible visions; and the nervous suffocation and *sweats* that ensue exhaust his Frame to almost childish weakness" (Louisa Catherine Adams to John Quincy Adams, 8 November 1840; see also, same to Charles Francis Adams, 18 April 1836, 27 December 1840, all in Adams Papers). His diaries, maintained uncontinuously from 1807 to 1838 (Adams Papers, Microfilms, Reels 332–339), are revealing of this and only less so of his loathing of Jews. They show too a preoccupation with his maladies, both those which had clear and serious physiological manifestations and those which seem essentially hypochondriacal. Whether his self-absorption and self-deprivation of friends and society was the expression of a consuming indolence, or the reverse, it resulted in his retirement from all employment after 1824, seized and bound by the "great demon of Ennui" (vol. 6:16, below). Brief sketches of Johnson are at vol. 1:443, above, and in *Diary and Autobiography of John Adams*, Cambridge, 1961, 3:240; an overview of his life is undertaken by Louisa Catherine Adams in letters to her husband, 10 July 1834, and to her son, 18–21, 29 March 1838, all in Adams Papers; see also Adams Genealogy.

What significance attaches to Johnson's manifest interest in portraits of himself and of members of his family is a subject for speculation. It was Johnson who in 1816 had Charles Robert Leslie commissioned to paint the likenesses of John Quincy and Louisa Catherine Adams which he gave to Charles Francis Adams in 1836 (vol. 6:372, 386, below; Andrew Oliver, *Portraits of John Quincy Adams and his Wife*, Cambridge, 1970, p. 57–64). He also sat for at least two portraits of himself. One, done probably in 1820 and attributed to "Thomas Sully or a student," was owned in 1967 by William C. J. Doolittle of Barneveld, New York, an Adams descendant. That reproduced in the present volume of a somewhat older sitter than the other, hangs in the Old House in Quincy, the gift of Charles Francis Adams 2d to whom it had been bequeathed by Robert C. Buchanan, a nephew of Thomas Baker Johnson. A note in Adams' hand, dated 1903, on the back of the painting attributes the portrait to Chester Harding, on what grounds is not known. One of the surviving likenesses may be that for which Johnson sat to Charles Bird King in 1823 (Louisa Catherine Adams to Charles Francis Adams, 13 June 1823, Adams Papers).

Courtesy of the National Park Service, Adams National Historic Site.

8. "THE REMARKS OF MY GRANDFATHER UPON . . . THE PLAYS
[OF TERENCE], MADE FOR MYSELF AND BROTHERS MANY
YEARS AGO . . . ARE NOT PARTICULARLY STRIKING YET
SOMEWHAT CHARACTERISTIC"   212

In August 1816, impelled by word that his grandson George Washington Adams was to take part in a school production of Terence's
Phormio at Ealing near London, and that John Quincy Adams' other
two sons were studying Terence's six comedies, John Adams undertook to read them anew. Having done so, he wrote successive letters
on each of the plays to his grandsons, some jointly some severally,
accompanied by lists of passages from the plays he considered significant, translations of the passages, and, in a number of instances,
commentary on them (Adams Papers, M/JA/9.4; Microfilms, Reel
No. 188).

Charles Francis Adams, coming to a rereading of Terence in
January–March 1834 (p. 253, 279–280, below), underlined in his
copy those passages which his grandfather had noted in four of the
plays, entered the translations and observations with John Adams'
initials in the top and bottom margins, and on blank pages at the
front and back of the volume included the texts of two of the letters.
To his grandfather's opinions he sometimes appended his own comments, modifying or disagreeing with John Adams' views. The volume thus annotated, a London, 1825, edition, is one of thirteen
copies of Terence's plays now in the Stone Library at Quincy.

*Courtesy of the National Park Service, Adams National Historic
Site.*

9. THE CONVENT-SCHOOL OF THE URSULINE COMMUNITY,
MOUNT BENEDICT, CHARLESTOWN, MASSACHUSETTS   212

The view of the school for young ladies, founded in 1820 and administered by the nuns of the Ursuline Community on the crest of
Mount Benedict in that part of Charlestown which is now Somerville,
Massachusetts, is that which appeared at the top of the first page of
the four-page *Prospectus* issued by the Community. The *Prospectus*
is undated, but it was issued between 1829, when the two wings
were added to the main building, and August 1834, when the whole
structure was burned by a mob.

The building, begun in 1826, was of red brick. The central section was of three stories, the wings of two. It was located on a tract
of twenty-seven acres, two acres of which were given over to gardens.
It was said to have been the "most elegant and imposing building
ever erected in New England for the education of girls." The fee for
board and tuition was $125 annually. Courses in music, drawing
and painting, foreign languages, and cookery carried extra charges
of varying amounts. Instruction in French, Latin, Spanish, and
Italian was offered. The school's clientele was overwhelmingly Protestant. The parents apparently were satisfied that they could rely
upon the assurance offered by the *Prospectus* that "the religious
opinions of the children are not interfered with." The later testimony
under oath of Protestant students that they had been able to practice

their religion unmolested and that they had not been proselytized went uncontradicted. *"Prospectus of the Ursuline Community"*; Justin Winsor, ed., *The Memorial History of Boston*, Boston, 1880–1881, 3:240; Ray Allen Billington, "The Burning of the Charlestown Convent," *New England Quarterly*, 10:5–8 (March 1937).

Beginning about 1830 there was in Boston and vicinity a perceptible growth in the intensity of anti-Catholic feeling, fostered partly among the laboring classes by the threat posed by the rising tide of Irish immigration, among the more educated under the prodding of a substantial segment of the Protestant clergy led by Rev. Lyman Beecher. The conviction that the convent-schools, of which that on Mount Benedict was the most prominent, were part of a new papal design to undermine Protestant New England, became fixed in the minds of many. In such an atmosphere the wildest rumors were sent abroad and were believed. The ample warnings given of the mob action of 11 August were met by official indifference and inertia. Only when the tragedy had occurred, and then in the fear of retaliation by the Irish, did the "responsible" leaders of Boston meet to express their condemnation. The promise then made of a stern search and punishment for the perpetrators was fulfilled in only the most limited way. Although Charles Francis Adams' comments on the lamentable event and what it portended seemed to limit responsibility for it to "the lower part of the population," to "the ignorant and little principled," the comments carry the full sense of the larger damage done, of the way by which the concepts of "freedom" and of "justice" in America are put in jeopardy. See p. 359, 360, below; Billington in *New England Quarterly*, 10:4–24 (March 1937).

That the members of the Ursuline Community were given refuge after the fire and were able to reestablish their school in the late mansion of H. A. S. Dearborn, at Brinley Place in Roxbury, brightens the record somewhat, though a Committee of Vigilance had to be formed to protect them and a nightly patrol maintained. See Massachusetts Historical Society, *Proceedings*, 53 (1919–1920):326–331.

On Mount Benedict, the blackened ruins of the convent stood for half a century.

Courtesy of the Massachusetts Historical Society.

10. THE BALLOON ASCENSION OF C. F. DURANT FROM THE AMPHITHEATRE ON CHARLES STREET, AT "THE BOTTOM OF THE COMMON"   213

The balloonist C. F. Durant, having earlier been successful in nine ascents elsewhere, made three aerial sorties in Boston during the summer of 1834. Although no claim was advanced that Durant provided Boston with its first opportunity to observe the ascent of a balloon with a human passenger, the three ascensions in 1834, on 31 July, 25 August, and 15 September, particularly the first, occasioned widespread public interest. John Quincy Adams, reflecting still the interest in aerostatics he had shown in Paris in 1784, witnessed the event from the roof of Dr. George Parkman's house and commented later that "It made my heart ache when I saw him suspended between Earth and Heaven, to think how needlessly men will be prodigal of Life, and how wantonly they will defy the Laws of Nature." See *Diary and Autobiography of John Adams*, Cambridge, 1961, 3:xiii, 170; below, p. 353. Charles Francis Adams observed the ascension, also, noting that "it was a beautiful spectacle and the whole town and it's vicinity were alive to witness it" (below, p. 352).

It was Durant's hope, of course, that as many as possible of the interested public would, at a cost of fifty cents, witness, to the accompaniment of cannon and the music of a band, the ascension together with the various processes antecedent to it, from the large amphitheatre designed to accommodate six to seven thousand persons, which had been constructed for the occasion on Charles Street at "the bottom of the Common" (*Boston Daily Advertiser*, 31 July, p. 2, cols. 2 and 6; below, p. 352). The circumstances, perhaps, justified Charles Francis Adams' observation: "Such is the daring of man in pursuit of mere pelf, for the idea of philosophical advancement is pretty nearly given up." Indeed, half a century or more had elapsed since Cavendish's experiments made possible the pioneering ascents of the brothers Montgolfier and others, since the first attempts to gather scientific data of the free air and the first successful voyage by air over the English Channel by Jean Pierre Blanchard and Dr. John Jeffries of Boston (loyalist, physician to John Adams and his family in London); over forty years since the feasibility of ascension and safe descent had been demonstrated in the United States by Blanchard at Philadelphia. See "Aerial Navigation" in *American Magazine of Useful and Entertaining Knowledge*, 1:247–256 (February 1835); John Langdon Sibley and Clifford K. Shipton, *Biographical Sketches of Graduates of Harvard University*, Cambridge and Boston, 1873–   , 15:419–427; and *Dictionary of American Biography* under Jeffries; below, p. 352.

Following Durant's first Boston aerial voyage, which ended in the sea off Cape Ann after an hour and ten minutes, his second and third ended respectively at Mount Auburn in Cambridge and at Lincoln, fifteen miles from Boston, after an hour and forty-five minutes in the air. See *Boston Daily Advertiser*, 2 August, p. 2, col. 6; 26 August, p. 2, col. 2; 15 September, p. 2, col. 3; below, p. 353.

The wood engraving reproduced is said by the editors of the *American Magazine of Useful and Entertaining Knowledge* to have been made from a drawing "we had taken on the spot, just as the balloon was departing from the amphitheatre, amidst the peals of cannon and the shouts of the multitude" (1:254). Accompanying it (1:255) was the engraving, also reproduced, of the apparatus by which the several thousand cubic feet of hydrogen gas needed to inflate the balloon was produced in barrels in which the decomposition of water was effected with iron and sulphuric acid, and through a complex of tubes extruding from the barrels introduced into a central tank and then into the bag itself. See *Boston Daily Advertiser*, 31 July, p. 2, col. 6.

Courtesy of the Massachusetts Historical Society.

Introduction

1. CHARLES FRANCIS ADAMS, DIARIST, 1833–1836

That part of the Diary of Charles Francis Adams which begins at the midpoint of his twenty-fifth year and concludes just before his twenty-ninth birthday presents, on casual view, few variations from the journal entries made during his three preceding years and published as volumes 3 and 4 of the *Diary*. The daily routine described in the Introduction to those volumes[1] was followed in the years with which we are here concerned without any essential change or interruption. Two brief journeys, one to Cape Cod, Nantucket, and New Bedford, the other to New York, Philadelphia, and Washington, did break for the moment the physical limits which circumscribed his movements. There are, of course, a different set of familial events to be recorded and to be responded to. Two sons were born to make the continuity of the presidential line of Adamses a realizable dream; the diarist, upon the death of his one surviving brother, became the sole representative of his generation. Nevertheless, his own characterization of his diary for the earlier years as "a pretty monotonous record of the very even tenour of my life"[2] can with seeming equal justice be said of the entries which make up the present volumes. Moreover, at the conclusion of these years Adams was outwardly as much the private man, committed to his studies and to meeting his considerable family responsibilities, as he had been earlier. Evidence of change and growth is not immediately apparent.

It was with this modicum of insight that the present editors, upon cursory examination of the Diary for the period succeeding that with which they were then immediately concerned, pronounced in the Introduction to volumes 3 and 4 that in "the years covered by these volumes and for some years thereafter" there was no evidence that Charles Francis Adams would ultimately choose politics and public life as a profession. They entered no caveat to his own conclusion at the end of 1832 that "I . . . never shall succeed as a political writer. Let me turn then as soon as possible to Literature."[3] Sentiments of

[1] See vol. 3:xxv.
[2] 6 Feb. 1832 (vol. 4:235).

[3] 15 Dec. 1832 (vol. 4:421), quoted at vol. 3:xxxvi.

similar purport from the diarist are, to be sure, to be found in the pages below. And the grounds which the editors adduced for Adams' rejection of a political career for himself would, as we shall see, remain as valid deterrents: "His own temperamental unsuitability, the lack of opportunity so long as his father remained in the arena, and the unhappy experiences of each of the Adams statesmen at the hands of an ungrateful citizenry."[4]

Two political developments in 1833 and 1835, however, drew Charles Francis Adams himself into the arena without full awareness, at least in the initial stages, of the extent or depth of his commitment. They were the nomination of his father by the antimasonic party in Massachusetts as its candidate for Governor in the election of 1833 and the effort of a coalition to effect the election of John Quincy Adams as United States Senator by the Massachusetts legislature in January–February 1835. Each effort proved unsuccessful, and in each the Adamses believed decisive roles in his defeat were played by those who had been Adams' friends, allies, or political debtors. In each, because John Quincy Adams maintained his characteristic stance of non-campaigner, someone was needed who could keep the candidate fully informed of decisions and developments and who could in turn make the candidate's thinking available to those who were active in his behalf. In each, the choice fell, almost by default and certainly without formal decision, upon Charles Francis Adams.

In the gubernatorial contest of 1833, hope of Adams' success rested upon his adding to the antimasonic nomination that of the National Republicans, his nominal party. When that effort failed, in a National Republican convention torn by conflict between Adams' supporters and those who were resistant to any tie to Antimasonry, it became clear that it would be all but impossible for the nominee of any of the three dominant parties to secure a majority in the election. Adams thereupon determined that he would withdraw *before* debate and balloting on the electoral choice began in the Legislature. It became the responsibility of Charles Francis Adams to make that decision known to the Antimasons and to find the means to effect Adams' purposes with the least damage to the disconsolate party. The gain in knowledge of the ways of politics was considerable, but the experience left the diarist with no desire to prolong his participation. "I am more and more disgusted with politics. If I had not duties which my name and station prescribe to me I would forswear them altogether."[5] When

---

[4] See vol. 3:xxxv.　　　　　　　　　　　[5] 9 Dec. 1833 (5:226).

the choice of Governor had been made, despite his reflection that "I have had some moments of trial and have got through them pretty well," he concluded, "I hope this will put an end to my share in political affairs for this year."[6] When, later in 1834, he was offered the opportunity to participate further as a delegate to the antimasonic convention, he found reasons to decline.[7]

Still, the bitterness felt by the Adamses following the long struggle in the Legislature, January–February 1835, to choose between Governor John Davis and John Quincy Adams to fill the unexpired term of Nathaniel Silsbee in the Senate proved the goad required to overcome Charles Francis Adams' continuing distaste for politics and strong inclination to avoid them. During and after that protracted legislative battle, Charles Francis Adams acquired the certainty that Daniel Webster had devised the scheme which denied the election to Adams' father.[8] In opposing, during the remainder of 1835, Webster's aspirations for the National Republican nomination as President, Adams found the means to assuage that bitterness; but he also found himself ever more deeply enmeshed in politics. Under the immediate impact of his father's defeat, Adams had resolved, "I will not cultivate revengeful feeling, but it is hard in this case to restrain it."[9] As his association with the Antimasons progressed, however, he became the advocate of an alliance, earlier unthinkable for any Adams, with the Jacksonian Democrats as the means to thwart Webster. Moved by the "character of Mr. Webster and the efforts he has made to destroy or see destroyed through his friends my father's influence in Massachusetts," Adams recorded, "I am resolved upon an attempt at counteraction and for this purpose laid down what I think is the only mode."[1] Persisting, "We pretty clearly matured the plan of operations for the campaign. Thus is as I hope a nucleus formed for a party organization which shall save us from the undermining action of treacherous friends."[2] As the operation began to take effect, Adams' tone became inexorable: "[W]e must go on, and drive the party to the wall.... I shall be content if the party is punished which has endeavoured to destroy all my father's standing."[3] Meanwhile, the other voice was not stilled. "My domestic happiness is such why should I strive to shade it by dabbling in the dirty water of our political affairs. Yet I am in

[6] 9 Jan. 1834 (5:244).

[7] 4 Sept. 1834 (5:378–379).

[8] 5, 18 Feb., 14 March 1835 (6:68, 79, 138–139 and note); John Quincy Adams to Charles Francis Adams, 5 March 1835, Adams Papers, quoted at 6:74–75, note.

[9] 20 Feb. 1835 (6:81).

[1] 14, 29 May 1835 (6:138, 147).

[2] 15 June 1835 (6:158–159).

[3] 4 Aug. 1835 (6:190).

spite of warning playing with these edge tools."[4] And Adams was forced to recognize that in the pursuit, "all my studies, and occupations of every sort are stopped."[5]

The circumstances which dictated the focusing and delimiting upon politics of Adams' activities in 1835 coincided with Adams' conviction that during his twenty-seventh year (August 1834 – August 1835) he must fix upon his vocation: "It is the critical moment of my life and I am *twenty-seven years old*. Let that fact and its associations ... stir me up."[6] He elsewhere called it, "The year ... which I have regarded as the turning point of most men's lives."[7] Adams had accounted for its special significance for him on his twenty-seventh birthday:

> I have observed that this has frequently been the particular age at which men famous for talent have begun to develope it to the world. This was the age at which my father began his public career, and at which Cicero made his defence of Roscius. . . . This was the age at which Demosthenes entered upon the public business. . . . I have long been impressed with the idea that if I made no reputation at all at this age, I should never make any.[8]

Yet until the Webster challenge presented itself, a full half of that year had passed during which Adams had chided himself: "The brightest year of my life is passing. . . . I am now the only son of my father, the only representative in my generation of the distinguished branch of the name and I am vegetating in a useless hot-bed of enervating luxury."[9]

During that critical year Adams was again, by fierce loyalty to his family and its place in history, brought out of a "shell of modesty" which saw him give over to another such legal work as he had, break such political ties as he had forged in the earlier gubernatorial campaign. Nevertheless, it was also family history which had operated and would continue to operate as a deterrent to his activity in the public sphere. Absorption in the careers of his father and grandfather had brought him to an awareness of the costs of public reputation: "When I ... reflect upon the last sixty years of my family in two generations, I ask myself if distinction has not been dearly purchased. If prosperity and adversity have not been fearfully mixed."[1] Even his brother John's last years of decay and defeat, Charles attributed to "the slippery steps of the Presidential palace."[2] Such costs he had

[4] 30 May 1835 (6:148).
[5] 12 June 1835 (6:157).
[6] 7 June 1835 (6:153).
[7] 18 Aug. 1835 (6:198).
[8] 18 Aug. 1834 (5:363).
[9] 1 Nov. 1834 (6:1).
[1] 3 Oct., 5 Nov. 1834 (5:397; 6:3).
[2] 31 March 1835 (6:107).

judged unacceptable to him: "However much ... I may regret the charge [of degeneracy] which my children as well as I must endure, I would rather endure it, than pay a price for fame which would take with it all my happiness."[3]

Moreover, in the moments when Adams did contemplate a possible public career, the immediate scene which confronted him in Boston was one he judged altogether unfavorable to one of his name. He reported this without reservations in a letter to his father:

> It is a matter of regret to me here to see the extent of the prejudices against you—prejudices inherited from father to son and appearing to strike root in the very constitution of society. . . . [T]hose prejudices exist and strike root against others who are succeeding you in the same career with equal if not greater force.[4]

These prejudices which Charles Francis Adams was wont to feel disqualified him from participation were the product of the many struggles in which Adamses had asserted independence of party and had thereby incurred the wrath and distrust of party politicians generally. Whether or not one judged that honor redounded to John Adams and John Quincy Adams from these battles, Charles Francis Adams saw emerging from the pattern of the family's conflicts evidence that familial qualities were an important, perhaps decisive, element in the never-ending strife. Those qualities—"too much fury," a want of prudence, arrogance, "an overbearing disposition," and a "kind of vehement obstinacy"—Adams identified and found within himself, causing him to conclude, "We were not made for politicians."[5]

Adams believed too that beyond politics he, like his family before him, was at odds with the values and attributes that typified for him the Boston milieu—"adoration of Mammon," "religious gloom," "unbending rigidity," "the sad coloured livery" of immoderate gravity.[6] His every effort to participate in any public way in the community seemed all but impossible.

He sometimes attributed his rejection "in the place of my birth [to] the deadly coldness of hereditary prejudice and rancour," sometimes to "my own distant and reserved manners," but the City's dislike, in

---

[3] To John Quincy Adams, 23 April 1835, Adams Papers, quoted at 6:123, note. See also, on the same theme, 26 Sept. 1835 (6:229).
[4] 7 April 1835, Adams Papers, quoted at 6:121, note.
[5] 18 March 1834; 19 Feb., 13 Dec.

1835; 14 Feb. 1836 (5:280; 6:80, 281, 332); Charles Francis Adams to Louisa Catherine Adams, 24 March 1836, Adams Papers.
[6] 6 Oct., 25 Dec. 1833; 13, 27 Nov. 1834 (5:187, 234; 6:9, 25).

any event, "is closing me up like an oyster in its own shell."[7] This sense of being totally out of harmony with his surroundings made him feel often "in an enemy's Country"; made him revert from time to time and with more or less seriousness to the notion of exile.[8] "Utterly discouraged, I find nobody that thinks as I do or appears to feel any sympathy with or for me."[9]

Alternating with these feelings of frustration about the possibilities of any activity of a public sort that arose from his sense of disharmony were the feelings of discouragement and perplexity which accompanied those ventures he did undertake. A chief ground for these was the ever-present problem posed by the continual presence and prominence of his father on the political scene. To agree with John Quincy Adams on any issue was but to be thought his echo, to disagree publicly would be embarrassing to both, even to express a view on an issue on which his father had not been heard was to risk identifying him with the view or to be thought his mouthpiece. Adams put the problem succinctly: "In any public [situation] I . . . should often embarrass as well as be embarrassed by him. This will be a caution to me for future guidance. Domestic politics must be avoided. I must decline every prospect of place in which they are agitated. This is no sacrifice to me for I prefer my present independence."[1] As he here suggests, where his independence is impinged upon, it must, for the time being, take precedence over such public opportunities as might present themselves.

Privately he was free to express to his father his disagreement with him over the choice between Davis and Morton for Governor, the son preferring Morton; yet when some months later, invited to be a delegate to the antimasonic convention to nominate a candidate for Governor, he found it necessary to decline lest he have to take a public position in support of Morton, opposed by John Quincy Adams out of his anti-Jacksonism.[2] Only privately were he and his father free to differ as between Webster and Van Buren after Van Buren, seeking to court the South, softened his stand on incendiary publications and

[7] 29 Nov. 1834; 13 Jan. 1835 (6:26, 54, 318).
[8] 16 April 1833; 11 Feb. 1835; 26 Jan. 1836 (5:69; 6:74, 317); Charles Francis Adams to Louisa Catherine Adams, 27 Jan. 1836, Adams Papers, quoted at 6:318, note.
[9] 15 Dec. 1834 (6:37).

[1] 10 Sept. 1835 (6:213); see also 11 Feb. 1835 (6:73-74).
[2] To John Quincy Adams, 1–3 Jan.; John Quincy Adams to Charles Francis Adams, 9 Jan. 1834, both in Adams Papers (5:240, note; 249, note); 9 Aug. 1834 (5:357).

supported the Mexican and Florida war policies of Jackson. For John Quincy Adams these actions made Webster, despite their political differences, more satisfying than the expedient Van Buren, the candidate of Charles Francis Adams' antimasonic-democratic coalition, designed to thwart Webster in Massachusetts. For Charles Francis Adams the episode was another warning which "shows the necessity of my keeping free from party engagement," and "justifies my caution about committing my name." [3]

In point of fact, the very nature of the antimasonic party with which Charles Francis Adams was affiliated almost precluded for him public identification with it. A minority party with a distinctly middle-class membership, it could accomplish its objectives only by offering to throw its weight first to one and then to another of the major parties. In these successive coalitions sharp shifts were often necessary on basic issues. One such issue, basic to both Adamses, father and son, was that relating to the Bank of the United States, the renewal of its charter and the removal by the President of public deposits from it. As the Antimasons swung toward the Democrats in 1834 and 1835, the tendency in the party organs and among the party leaders to become anti-Bank was marked. Such an eventuality would bring to an end the Adams affiliation; even the drift brought firm remonstrances from John Quincy Adams, usually through his son. On one such occasion, when Charles Francis Adams at his father's request made objection to the journalist Benjamin F. Hallett about the articles on the subject that had been appearing in the *Daily Advocate*, the editor replied:

[H]e had been willing to consider it a dead question that he held opinions of rather a radical sort respecting banks and was opposed to the National Bank but . . . it was his design to avoid all notice of it. . . . The understanding between us therefore is that hereafter no attacks upon the Bank are to go into the paper. . . . This experience will however warn me not to go into deep water. [4]

When some months later John Quincy Adams expressed again his dissatisfaction with the Advocate's course on the Bank, the diarist wrote, "I seized the opportunity to press . . . [Hallett] that we are upon a barrel of gunpowder respecting that. This is a tender subject between us and I felt we had better pass it." [5]

[3] 17, 28 May 1836 (6:389, 397).   [5] 15 March 1836 (6:352).
[4] 11 Sept. 1835 (6:213).

The issue continued to hang in uneasy balance and was one of the considerations that made public affiliation with the party at that juncture an unacceptable risk for Adams. When a meeting at Faneuil Hall in support of Van Buren was being planned, Adams was asked to come forward and make a speech. "I explained [to the chairman] ... frankly all my difficulties.... He admitted their solidity but said he did not like to report them.... [He] desired me to assign no reasons ... but rather to put myself upon ... the unwillingness to risk my voice in Faneuil Hall." [6]

Adams' unannounced difficulties undoubtedly related in part to his reluctance to commit his father by any act of his, in part to his own uneasy alliance with the party to whose policies he only selectively adhered, and in part to his desire to avoid by any public act of his a display of the many differences in political and social beliefs that lay beneath the otherwise wholly happy relations existing between Adams and his father-in-law, Peter Chardon Brooks.

Brooks' interests were those of the manufacturing-shipping-banking community in Boston. He was a National Republican in politics, particularly close to the careers and thinking of Daniel Webster, his attorney on occasion, and of Edward Everett, husband of Brooks' daughter Charlotte. On specific issues too his position was opposed to that taken by Charles Francis Adams. Brooks was anti-Antimasonry and was among those who favored strong measures against abolitionists. [7]

By his public stand on these and related issues, Alexander Hill Everett, the Governor's brother but associated at the time in political ventures with Charles Francis Adams, had made himself "obnoxious to my Wife's relations by his political course." [8] The lesson was plain. Clearly the maintenance of harmony prevailing between the Brooks and Adams households demanded constant watchfulness and tact. Yet withholding for long periods the expression of differences on matters deeply felt was to Adams as irksome as it was necessary. After a period of months during which the Charles Francis Adams family resided with Mr. Brooks, Adams wrote, "I have lived agreeably and have received nothing but kindness and attention from ... Mr. Brooks.... But my privations are too great. I feel like a boy who has no right to utter an opinion." [9]

Adams was provided opportunity to observe the deleterious effect

[6] 11 Feb. 1836 (6:329–331).
[7] 20 Aug., 23 Oct. 1835 (6:200, 248–249).
[8] 12 April 1836 (6:369).
[9] 11 May 1835 (6:136).

upon family relations that occurred when a publicly taken position crossed what was regarded as a family interest. Such a moment came when Edward Everett as Governor was asked to participate in a Charlestown celebration of the Warren Bridge becoming toll-free. Brooks and his sons as large stockholders in the bridge corporation had fought hard to maintain the toll. "Governor Everett forgetful of his relations with Mr. Brooks ... made a speech ... which coming to Edward [Brooks'] ears irritated him so much as to make him ungovernable." As the family party that evening broke up "there were indications of a heavy thunder squall" and "Mr. Everett became the mark of some biting observations."[1] Some months earlier, when the case was still under adjudication, Adams had identified the issue as of the sort that confirmed his hesitation to risk personal relationships by entering upon public office:

> Here is a question that would come across me as a legislator in a most unpleasant manner. I would support the principle at all hazards, and yet the act would forfeit half the votes even of the best disposed towards me. I must lay it down as a rule of action to decline all invitation to take Office. . . . The rule may be laid down safely and if upon occasion the *country* should really do me the favor to call for my services in a manner perfectly unequivocal, then will be the remote day for forming an exception.[2]

Charles Francis Adams, fully sensitive, perhaps oversensitive, to the obstacles in his course toward public office, even public activity—obstacles that might be personified as Peter Chardon Brooks, John Quincy Adams, the ghosts of Adamses past, and a part of Charles Francis Adams himself—under the necessities of family loyalty and of his "critical year," yet found the means to play an effective political role while evading the obstacles. The means, earlier undeveloped, lay to his hand—political journalism.

In earlier years Adams had written and published numerous articles, mostly of a literary or historical character.[3] The few that were addressed to current problems or issues were sporadic and without cumulative effect. Their public reception, though more favorable than their author granted, left him disconsolate, and in the early months of 1833 ready to desist entirely. "I will lie on my oars"; "I lay down my pen forever"; "I begin to feel a greater doubt of my power of ever being able to apply my capacity to any serviceable end."[4]

[1] 3 March 1836 (6:344).
[2] 15 Oct. 1835 (6:243).
[3] See vol. 4, index, under Charles Francis Adams, Writings.
[4] 3, 26 Jan., 30 March, 21 May 1833 (5:3, 17, 59, 92).

The decisive moment came without preparation or full awareness. In the midst of the gubernatorial campaign of 1833, Hallett asked for "a series of political papers for the present election." Selecting the subject, "The Proscription of Antimasonry," in answer to the charge leveled at his father, Adams "wrote till midnight." When the numbers won praise from his father, Adams was "much encouraged."[5] But the flurry ended with the election, and there was no resumption of political composition until he began, during the senatorial election of January-February 1835, a series generally directed, for reasons that have already appeared, against Webster's presidential aspirations. Upon the outcome of the senatorial contest, however, Adams allowed the series to lapse. It was not resumed until May when, in the columns of the *Advocate*, Hallett asked "our able and much respected correspondent" to continue his numbers. "The crisis calls for them now."[6] As the renewed numbers continued they became more and more incisive in their attack on Webster. Newspaper comment was at last provoked. "The Newspapers are all full of allusions to my numbers which have at last roused public attention. This is the cast of the die with me."[7] Thereupon, without pause he rushed into the composition of what was to prove his major success of these years, *An Appeal from the New to the Old Whigs*, directed wholly against Webster.[8]

Thereafter, despite occasional reversions to an earlier mood,[9] Adams' commitment to political writing was firm and his output more than respectable both in quantity and quality. By June 1836, the date at which these volumes conclude, he had published since January 1835 a total of fifty-five articles, or "columns" as we would call them, in nine series on current political issues. These had achieved eighty-three known printings and reprintings in six newspapers.

In keeping with Adams' need to avoid public identification with the views he was expressing, all his writings were signed with pseudonyms. Apparently, knowledge of the authorship of the articles was possessed by a relatively limited group. Those whose names were suggested when the numbers were referred to in public discussion did not include Charles Francis Adams. When Adams confided his secret to his closest friend, one who was politically knowledgeable, the diarist records that his friend was "astonished."[1] No doubt the preservation of his secret

---

[5] 18 Oct., 1 Nov. 1833 (5:195, 205).

[6] 7, 19 Jan., 22 May 1835 (6:50, 58, 143).

[7] 12 June 1835 (6:157).

[8] On the publishing history and content of *An Appeal*, see 6:xvi–xvii.

[9] "I do not wish to give up my literary tastes in the pursuit of my political amusement. Politics are well as a condiment but they are too spicy for food" (6:209).

[1] 12 June 1835 (6:157).

in the Brooks circle was owing partly to the circumstance that the newspapers in which Adams' communications appeared were not those regularly read there. The Diary offers no evidence that Mr. Brooks became aware.

If there were advantages in keeping some unaware, there were equal advantages to be obtained from making others—notably John Quincy Adams—full partners in the secret. The articles were the means by which John Quincy Adams could be informed, without the pain that would come to both from public airing, of his son's disagreements on public issues: "[T]here are many points upon which I differ from [my father], although I do not press them at present upon public notice; it follows that my being able not to press them arises from my private situation where I can select my topics. In any public one I could do so far less."[2] Mentions of John Quincy Adams' commendations of the articles, both those that were in agreement with his views and those that were not, are frequent in the Diary.[3]

The course, then, which Charles Francis Adams had taken to resolve his dilemmas met his objectives fully. He was saved from all the complexities that would have beset him in seeking public office or in any other form of public activity; yet the body of his writing promised *reputation*. "I do not want Office at all, the labour of it would be burdensome. But I want *reputation*. I want that without which as my father's son I cannot very well get along. At least without mortification."[4] In that direction, there was the pride to be had from the attempts made in various quarters to identify the author of the articles, in that among the names advanced were those of A. H. Everett and John Quincy Adams, "the two best political writers in the State if not in the Country."[5] When the diarist looked back, he could write:

> The year has passed which I have regarded as the turning point. . . . It has not however gone without adding to me a little reputation. . . . It surely cannot be said that this life has been wasted when at twenty seven I am even momentarily compared to the most ancient and best established reputations for ability in the Country."[6]

The result is a sense of assurance and confidence in himself and his powers that is new in the Diary. Adams can now appraise a piece by him as "long on the road but good when it gets there. I think it a piece of superior writing." Again, he relishes the power the articles

[2] 10 Sept. 1835 (6:213).
[3] See, for example, 5, 19 June, 4 Aug. 1835; 12 April 1836 (6:151, 161, 190–191, 368).
[4] 5 Jan. 1836 (6:304).
[5] 7 July, 18 Aug. 1835 (6:173, 198).
[6] 18 Aug. 1835 (6:198).

confer: "I have now the right end of the Whip and mean to apply the lash. I have no favour to ask of any body and can do it if I develope the force God has given me." He responds to praise with the comment: "There are some who comprehend the value of the services I am rendering." And looking to the future, "I hope to be able to do something of value to my generation. But I am not over ambitious."[7]

The progression is not constant, nor is the confidence maintained at all times, but that a change has taken place is evident in a reversal of his attitude toward the Diary itself. At the lowest point he writes, "I am ashamed of my Diary and of myself. Never was my Diary so perfectly uninteresting and never was I so much tempted to close its pages forever.... My interest in political affairs is failing very much. Indeed I am becoming a piece of vegetation." The advance, after the demonstration of accomplishment, to a new appraisal of the Diary and, by extension, of himself is marked: "The events recorded and Opinions expressed are it is true of very little value to any body.... But they are still the materials of my life, they form the landmarks by which I can understand myself.... As such I prize them, as such I wish to continue them."[8]

2. THE MANUSCRIPTS AND THE EDITORIAL METHOD

Before the period covered by the present volumes Charles Francis Adams had settled upon an appropriate form for the entries in his journal (see volume 1:xxxix–xl). From 1827 onward he was to follow a single form that would remain essentially unchanged and to continue without any significant break until 1880.

The journal entries from 1 January 1833 to 12 June 1836, the time spanned in the present volumes, are consecutively written in three manuscript-diary volumes. In the Adams Papers serial numbering they are designated D/CFA/9, 10, and 11 (Microfilms, Reel Nos. 61–63). Adams gives to the volumes the numbers 7, 8, and 9. An explanation of the discrepancy between his numbering and the numbers assigned in the Adams Papers as they now stand is given in volume 1:xxxvii–xxxviii.

All three manuscript volumes measure 10″ x 8″, and are bound in half calf with green boards. The spine of each is missing. The volumes contain, respectively, 368, 380, and 369 pages.

[7] 3, 31 Aug. 1835; 11, 16 Feb. 1836 (6:190, 206, 329, 333).   [8] 17 Oct. 1834; 12 Dec. 1835 (5:404; 6:280).

From 1 January to 31 December 1833, the journal entries occupy all the pages remaining in D/CFA/9 following those containing the entries for the year 1832. Beginning on 1 January 1834 (below, p. 238) and continuing through 12 December 1835 (volume 6:280), the journal entries are continued through the whole of D/CFA/10. The eleventh volume of the Diary (D/CFA/11) contains the journal entries for the period 13 December 1835 – 31 August 1837, of which the entries through 11 June 1836 are included within the present volumes (volume 6:281–409).

The editorial method followed in volumes 5 and 6 of the *Diary of Charles Francis Adams* has been that followed in the first two volumes with the modifications introduced in volumes 3 and 4. That method, including textual and annotational policy, and the modifications have been explained fully in the Introductions to the earlier volumes, 1:xl–xlvi and 3:xxxix–xl.

What was said in the Introduction to volumes 1 and 2 (1:xlii) about the rendering of Adams' notation of the hour and minute of arising and retiring is not relevant here since the notation is not used during the period covered by these volumes. However, as he had done since May 1830, Adams regularly indicates for each page in these manuscript volumes a notation of place. The method employed to normalize the position of these place notations in the journal entries and to express typographically variants from his usual practice in the manuscript is explained at volume 3:xxxix–xl.

The statement made in the Introductions to the earlier volumes of the *Diary of Charles Francis Adams* (1:xlv and 3:xl) about the annotation of books and other publications mentioned in the Diary apply in Volumes 5 and 6 according to the pattern of volumes 3 and 4. The bibliographical appendix of borrowings included in volume 4 has not been carried forward in the present volumes.

Acknowledgments

The editors recognize that the editorial preparation of the volumes of *The Adams Papers* is achieved in good part through the combined efforts of The Adams Papers staff. Because various parts of the operation—transcription of manuscripts, for example—were carried forward long before the volumes being published could be said to be in the making, the list of those on the staff who have contributed significantly must include a number of former members as well as those presently on the staff. The editorial assistants and associates no longer on the staff whose work on these two volumes deserves more than general notice are Patricia O'R. Drechsler, Kate Heath, Kathleen O'Mara, and Nancy J. Simkin. During the trying period between the submission of copy to the press and the completion of the index we have been fortunate in having as our able assistants, Janet Romaine and Celeste Walker. In the late stages, a third editor, Mary-Jo Kline, has joined the Papers, not too late to make useful contributions to these volumes.

Two institutions whose ties with the Adams Papers are so close and whose contributions are so integral a part of the preparation of each published unit that they may be said to be as much a part of the Papers as we are a part of them are the Massachusetts Historical Society and Harvard University Press. The rich resources of each in able specialists have been freely available to us. The director of the Society, Stephen T. Riley, has been a valued day-by-day participant in the solution of our problems and always thoughtful of our needs. He, together with Malcolm Freiberg, as members of the Society's Publication Committee, have joined us in reading galley proofs. At the Press, to our great benefit and happiness, our Adams Papers editor and colleague, is and has been from the outset of our enterprise, Ann Louise C. McLaughlin.

From those who direct and staff the institutions whose generous help through the years has made them, in a sense, collaborators in our undertaking, we recognize for their assistance during the preparation of these volumes: Wilhelmina S. Harris at the Adams National Historic Site, Quincy; Jack Jackson at the Boston Athenæum, and a former staff member there, James E. Belliveau; Marcus A. McCorison and Frederick Bauer at the American Antiquarian Society, Worcester;

Acknowledgments

Helen D. Willard and her successor Jeanne T. Newlin at the Theatre Collection, Kimball C. Elkins and his successor Harley P. Holden at the Archives, both invaluable parts of the Harvard University Library; Joseph O'Neill at the Boston Public Library; E. Harold Hugo and William J. Glick at the Meriden Gravure Company.

For assistance, graciously given, on particular matters, words of thanks are due Richard C. Kugler of the Old Dartmouth Historical Society Whaling Museum, New Bedford; Edouard A. Stackpole of The Peter Foulger Museum, Nantucket; Paul Conley and Wilbur Raymond of the Somerville (Massachusetts) Historical Society; and Louise Ambler of the Fogg Art Museum, Cambridge.

Guide to Editorial Apparatus

In the first three sections (1–3) of the six sections of this Guide are listed, respectively, the arbitrary devices used for clarifying the text, the code names for designating prominent members of the Adams family, and the symbols describing the various kinds of MS originals used or referred to, that are employed throughout *The Adams Papers* in all its series and parts. In the final three sections (4–6) are listed, respectively, only those symbols designating institutions holding original materials, the various abbreviations and conventional terms, and the short titles of books and other works, that occur in volumes 5 and 6 of the *Diary of Charles Francis Adams*. The editors propose to maintain this pattern for the Guide to Editorial Apparatus in each of the smaller units, published at intervals, of all the series and parts of the edition that are so extensive as to continue through many volumes. On the other hand, in short and specialized series and/or parts of the edition, the Guide to Editorial Apparatus will be given more summary form tailored to its immediate purpose.

1. TEXTUAL DEVICES

The following devices will be used throughout *The Adams Papers* to clarify the presentation of the text.

[. . .], [. . . .]	One or two words missing and not conjecturable.
[. . .] [1], [. . . .] [1]	More than two words missing and not conjecturable; subjoined footnote estimates amount of missing matter.
[ ]	Number or part of a number missing or illegible. Amount of blank space inside brackets approximates the number of missing or illegible digits.
[roman]	Conjectural reading for missing or illegible matter. A question mark is inserted before the closing bracket if the conjectural reading is seriously doubtful.
⟨*italic*⟩	Matter canceled in the manuscript but restored in our text.
[*italic*]	Editorial insertion in the text.

2. ADAMS FAMILY CODE NAMES

First Generation

JA	John Adams (1735–1826)
AA	Abigail Smith (1744–1818), *m.* JA 1764

Second Generation

JQA	John Quincy Adams (1767–1848), son of JA and AA
LCA	Louisa Catherine Johnson (1775–1852), *m.* JQA 1797
CA	Charles Adams (1770–1800), son of JA and AA
Mrs. CA	Sarah Smith (1769–1828), sister of WSS, *m.* CA 1795

TBA	Thomas Boylston Adams (1772–1832), son of JA and AA
Mrs. TBA	Ann Harrod (1774?–1845), *m.* TBA 1805
AA2	Abigail Adams (1765–1813), daughter of JA and AA, *m.* WSS 1786
WSS	William Stephens Smith (1755–1816), brother of Mrs. CA

Third Generation

GWA	George Washington Adams (1801–1829), son of JQA and LCA
JA2	John Adams (1803–1834), son of JQA and LCA
Mrs. JA2	Mary Catherine Hellen (1806?–1870), *m.* JA2 1828
CFA	Charles Francis Adams (1807–1886), son of JQA and LCA
ABA	Abigail Brown Brooks (1808–1889), *m.* CFA 1829
ECA	Elizabeth Coombs Adams (1808–1903), daughter of TBA and Mrs. TBA

Fourth Generation

JQA2	John Quincy Adams (1833–1894), son of CFA and ABA
CFA2	Charles Francis Adams (1835–1915), son of CFA and ABA
HA	Henry Adams (1838–1918), son of CFA and ABA
MHA	Marian Hooper (1842–1885), *m.* HA 1872
BA	Brooks Adams (1848–1927), son of CFA and ABA
LCA2	Louisa Catherine Adams (1831–1870), daughter of CFA and ABA, *m.* Charles Kuhn 1854
MA	Mary Adams (1845–1928), daughter of CFA and ABA, *m.* Henry Parker Quincy 1877

Fifth Generation

CFA3	Charles Francis Adams (1866–1954), son of JQA2
HA2	Henry Adams (1875–1951), son of CFA2

3. DESCRIPTIVE SYMBOLS

The following symbols will be employed throughout *The Adams Papers* to describe or identify in brief form the various kinds of manuscript originals.

D	Diary (Used only to designate a diary written by a member of the Adams family and always in combination with the short form of the writer's name and a serial number, as follows: D/JA/23, i.e. the twenty-third fascicle or volume of John Adams' manuscript Diary.)
Dft	draft
Dupl	duplicate
FC	file copy (Ordinarily a copy of a letter retained by a correspondent *other than an Adams*, for example Jefferson's press copies and polygraph copies, since all three of the Adams statesmen systematically entered copies of their outgoing letters in letterbooks.)
Lb	Letterbook (Used only to designate Adams letterbooks and always in combination with the short form of the writer's name and a serial number, as follows: Lb/JQA/29, i.e. the twenty-ninth volume of John Quincy Adams' Letterbooks.)

LbC   letterbook copy (Letterbook copies are normally unsigned, but any such copy is assumed to be in the hand of the person responsible for the text unless it is otherwise described.)

M   Miscellany (Used only to designate materials in the section of the Adams Papers known as the "Miscellany" and always in combination with the short form of the writer's name and a serial number, as follows: M/CFA/32, i.e. the thirty-second volume of the Charles Francis Adams Miscellany—a ledger volume mainly containing transcripts made by CFA in 1833 of selections from the family papers.)

MS, MSS   manuscript, manuscripts

RC   recipient's copy (A recipient's copy is assumed to be in the hand of the signer unless it is otherwise described.)

Tr   transcript (A copy, handwritten or typewritten, made substantially later than the original or than other copies—such as duplicates, file copies, letterbook copies—that were made contemporaneously.)

Tripl   triplicate

4. LOCATION SYMBOLS

DLC   Library of Congress
MB   Boston Public Library
MBAt   Boston Athenæum
MH-Ar   Harvard University Archives
MHi   Massachusetts Historical Society
MQA   Adams National Historic Site ("Old House"), Quincy, Massachusetts
MWA   American Antiquarian Society
PHi   Historical Society of Pennsylvania

5. OTHER ABBREVIATIONS AND CONVENTIONAL TERMS

Adams Genealogy

A set of genealogical charts and a concise biographical register of the Adams family in the Presidential line and of closely related families from the 17th through the 19th century. The Adams Genealogy is now being compiled and will be published as a part of *The Adams Papers*.

Adams Papers

Manuscripts and other materials, 1639–1889, in the Adams Manuscript Trust collection given to the Massachusetts Historical Society in 1956 and enlarged by a few additions of family papers since then. Citations in the present edition are simply by date of the original document if the original is in the main chronological series of the Papers and therefore readily found in the microfilm edition of the Adams Papers (see below). The location of materials in the Letterbooks and in the volumes of Miscellany is given more fully and, if the original would be hard to locate, by the microfilm reel number.

Adams Papers, Microfilms

The corpus of the Adams Papers, 1639–1889, as published on microfilm by the Massachusetts Historical Society, 1954–1959, in 608 reels. Cited in the present work, when necessary, by reel number. Available in research libraries throughout the United States and in a few libraries in Europe.

The Adams Papers

The present edition in letterpress, published by The Belknap Press of Harvard University Press. References to earlier volumes of any given unit will take this form: vol. 2:146. Since there will be no over-all volume numbering for the edition, references from one series, or unit of a series, to another will be by title, volume, and page; for example, JA, *Diary and Autobiography*, 4:205.

Brooks, Farm Journal

"Farm Journal," 13 vols., 1808–1848, a diary primarily devoted to matters relevant to his Medford estate but containing some entries of family concern; a part of the MSS of Peter Chardon Brooks Sr. in the Massachusetts Historical Society.

Everett MSS

The papers of Edward Everett in the Massachusetts Historical Society. Included are a diary, 62 vols., 1814–1864; letterbooks, 67 vols., 1825–1864; and a chronological file of letters received, 18 boxes, 1819–1865.

M/CFA/3

The account book of CFA as manager of JQA's business affairs in Boston, 1828–1846; Adams Papers, Microfilms, Reel No. 297. The payment of routine agency bills, the receipt of rents from tenants, fully recorded here and sometimes alluded to in CFA's journal entries, have not ordinarily been specifically annotated in the text.

Quincy MSS

The papers of the Quincy family, in the Massachusetts Historical Society. Included are 39 vols. and 27 boxes, 1635–1886.

6. SHORT TITLES OF WORKS FREQUENTLY CITED

AA, *Letters*, ed. CFA, 1840

Letters of Mrs. Adams, the Wife of John Adams. With an Introductory Memoir by Her Grandson, Charles Francis Adams, Boston, 1840.

AA, *New Letters*

New Letters of Abigail Adams, 1788–1801, ed. Stewart Mitchell, Boston, 1947.

Adams Family Correspondence

Adams Family Correspondence, ed. L. H. Butterfield and others, Cambridge, 1963– .

AHR

American Historical Review.

Amer. Philos. Soc., *Trans.*

American Philosophical Society, *Transactions of the American Philosophical Society, Held at Philadelphia, for Promoting Useful Knowledge.*

Bemis, *JQA*
> Samuel Flagg Bemis, *John Quincy Adams*, New York, 1949–1956; 2 vols. [Vol. 1:] *John Quincy Adams and the Foundations of American Foreign Policy;* [vol. 2:] *John Quincy Adams and the Union.*

Biog. Dir. Cong.
> *Biographical Directory of the American Congress, 1774–1949*, Washington, 1950.

Boston Directory, [year]
> *Boston Directory*, issued annually with varying imprints.

Bradford, *History of Mass.*
> Alden Bradford, *History of Massachusetts*, Boston, 1822–1829; 3 vols.

Catalogue of JA's Library
> *Catalogue of the John Adams Library in the Public Library of the City of Boston*, Boston, 1917.

CFA, *Diary*
> *Diary of Charles Francis Adams*, Cambridge, 1964– . Vols. 1–2, ed. Aïda DiPace Donald and David Donald; vols. 3–4, ed. Marc Friedlaender and L. H. Butterfield.

CFA2, *Autobiography*
> Charles Francis Adams [2d], *Charles Francis Adams, 1835–1915: An Autobiography; with a Memorial Address Delivered November 17, 1915, by Henry Cabot Lodge*, Boston and New York, 1916.

CFA2, *CFA*
> Charles Francis Adams [2d], *Charles Francis Adams*, Boston and New York, 1900.

Chamberlain, *Beacon Hill*
> Allen Chamberlain, *Beacon Hill: Its Ancient Pastures and Early Mansions*, Boston and New York, 1925.

Col. Soc. Mass., *Pubns.*
> Colonial Society of Massachusetts, *Publications.*

Congressional Globe
> *Congressional Globe, Containing the Debates and Proceedings, 1833–1873*, Washington, 1834–1893; 109 vols.

DAB
> Allen Johnson and Dumas Malone, eds., *Dictionary of American Biography*, New York, 1928–1936; 20 vols. plus index and supplements.

Dangerfield, *Era of Good Feelings*
> George Dangerfield, *The Era of Good Feelings*, New York, 1952.

Darling, *Political Changes in Mass.*
> Arthur B. Darling, *Political Changes in Massachusetts, 1824–1848: A Study of Liberal Movements in Politics*, New Haven, 1925.

Dict. of Americanisms
> Mitford M. Mathews, ed., *A Dictionary of Americanisms on Historical Principles*, Chicago, 1951.

DNB
> Leslie Stephen and Sidney Lee, eds., *The Dictionary of National Biography*, New York and London, 1885–1900; 63 vols. plus supplements.

Duberman, *CFA*
> Martin B. Duberman, *Charles Francis Adams, 1807–1886*, Boston, 1961.

Edwards, *Historic Quincy*, 1954
> William Churchill Edwards, *Historic Quincy, Massachusetts*, Quincy, 1954.

Emerson, *Journals and Notebooks*, ed. Gilman
> William H. Gilman and others, eds., *The Journals and Miscellaneous Notebooks of Ralph Waldo Emerson*, Cambridge, 1960– .

Frothingham, *Everett*
> Paul Revere Frothingham, *Edward Everett: Orator and Statesman*, Boston, 1925.

Groce and Wallace, *Dict. Amer. Artists*
> George C. Groce and David H. Wallace, *The New-York Historical Society's Dictionary of Artists in America, 1564–1860*, New Haven and London, 1957.

HA, *Education*
> Henry Adams, *The Education of Henry Adams: An Autobiography*, Boston, The Massachusetts Historical Society, 1918.

HA, *New-England Federalism*
> *Documents Relating to New-England Federalism, 1800–1815*, ed. Henry Adams, Boston, 1877.

Harvard Quinquennial Cat.
> Harvard University, *Quinquennial Catalogue of the Officers and Graduates, 1636–1930*, Cambridge, 1930.

Hone, *Diary*, ed. Tuckerman
> *The Diary of Philip Hone, 1828–1851*, ed. Tuckerman, New York, 1889; 2 vols.

JA, *Diary and Autobiography*
> *Diary and Autobiography of John Adams*, ed. L. H. Butterfield and others, Cambridge, 1961; 4 vols.

JA, *Earliest Diary*
> *The Earliest Diary of John Adams*, ed. L. H. Butterfield and others, Cambridge, 1966.

JA, *Works*
> *The Works of John Adams, Second President of the United States: with a Life of the Author*, ed. Charles Francis Adams, Boston, 1850–1856; 10 vols.

JQA, *Memoirs*
> *Memoirs of John Quincy Adams, Comprising Portions of His Diary from 1795 to 1848*, ed. Charles Francis Adams, Philadelphia, 1874–1877; 12 vols.

JQA, *Writings*
> *The Writings of John Quincy Adams*, ed. Worthington C. Ford, New York, 1913–1917; 7 vols.

Madison, *Writings*, ed. Hunt
> *The Writings of James Madison . . .* , ed. Gaillard Hunt, New York and London, 1900–1910; 9 vols.

xli

Mass. Register, [year]
  The Massachusetts Register and United States Calendar, Boston, 1801–1847;
  47 vols.

MHS, *Colls., Procs.*
  Massachusetts Historical Society, *Collections* and *Proceedings.*

Morison, *H. G. Otis*
  Samuel Eliot Morison, *The Life and Letters of Harrison Gray Otis, Federalist,
  1765–1848,* Boston and New York, 1913; 2 vols.

Morison, *Three Centuries of Harvard*
  Samuel Eliot Morison, *Three Centuries of Harvard, 1636–1936,* Cambridge,
  1936.

Niles' Register
  Niles' Weekly Register, Baltimore, 1811–1849.

North Amer. Rev.
  North American Review, Boston, etc., 1815–1940.

Notable American Women
  Edward T. James, ed., *Notable American Women, 1607–1950, a Biographical
  Dictionary,* Cambridge, Mass., 1971; 3 vols.

Odell, *Annals N.Y. Stage*
  George C. D. Odell, *Annals of the New York Stage,* New York, 1927–1949;
  15 vols.

OED
  The Oxford English Dictionary, Oxford, 1933; 12 vols. and supplement.

Oliver, *Portraits of JA and AA*
  Andrew Oliver, *Portraits of John and Abigail Adams,* Cambridge, 1967.

Oliver, *Portraits of JQA and His Wife*
  Andrew Oliver, *Portraits of John Quincy Adams and His Wife,* Cambridge,
  1970.

PMHB
  Pennsylvania Magazine of History and Biography.

Edmund Quincy, *Josiah Quincy*
  Edmund Quincy, *Life of Josiah Quincy of Massachusetts,* Boston, 1868.

Quincy, *Figures of the Past*
  Josiah Quincy [1802–1882], *Figures of the Past, from the Leaves of Old
  Journals,* ed. M. A. DeWolfe Howe, Boston, 1926.

Register of Debates in Congress
  Register of Debates in Congress, 1824–1837, Washington, 1825–1837; 14
  vols. in 29 pts.

Benjamin Rush, *Letters*
  Letters of Benjamin Rush, ed. L. H. Butterfield, Princeton, 1951; 2 vols.

Webster, 2d edn.
  *Webster's New International Dictionary of the English Language, Second Edi-
  tion, Unabridged,* Springfield, Mass., 1957.

Winsor, *Memorial History of Boston*
  Justin Winsor, ed., *The Memorial History of Boston, Including Suffolk County,
  1630–1880,* Boston, 1880–1881; 4 vols.

VOLUME 5

Diary 1833–1834

Diary of Charles Francis Adams

JANUARY. 1833.

Boston

TUESDAY. 1ST.[1]

Another year. To moralize upon time is stale and old fashioned enough. Yet it has its advantages. Montaigne in the Essay I was reading on Sunday remarks that time is that of which men are always lavish upon all matters, while they grudge money and other things not half so valuable.[2] Most persons keep no account of it. Day passes after day constantly adding to the sum of human existence without creating any excepting perhaps a momentary emotion. A Diary like this which I keep forces me to more continual reflection. It reminds me of what I am, how little I have done and how much I ought to do. It brings me back to feelings of humility when I have been elated by pride, and it soothes me in moments of depression by recollection of hours sometimes well bestowed. My Diary is my companion. I unburthen my sorrows, and communicate my joys, I express my hopes and display my fears. And when days such as this intervene, I gain an opportunity of looking back to see how all these have been excited since the preceding similar Anniversary. My lot has hitherto been an extremely favoured one. I have enjoyed life without any effort. I have received benefits which no act of mine has deserved. My sense of duty has been efficient only in the passive character of a monitor of what *not* to do. If in the course of the year that now opens to me, more decided action may be required of me, I have only to hope and trust that I shall not then be found wanting. And that my Diary may assist in sustaining me through the hours of trial.

The day was warm and rainy. I went to the Office and was engaged in business affairs all the morning drawing up my books and accounts. A tedious concern but one which must not be avoided. Dependence is at all times unpleasant. The older a person grows, the less he feels disposed to submit to it, provided his temper is of the kind which mine is. Small as my opportunities are of doing any thing for myself, I yet hope to improve them to the utmost. May Heaven smile upon my

I

efforts. No walk owing to the weather. Afternoon at home.[3] Continued Anquetil [4] but finding myself drowsy, I determined to resume my Anti Masonry. So I wrote over one half of No. 8. and as I think improved it.[5] Evening for once quiet at home. Malvina, Burns.[6] Afterwards, German.

[1] The following entries through 31 Dec. 1833 derive from the volume of his diaries which CFA designated as No. 7 (Adams Papers serial listing: D/CFA/ 9; Microfilms, Reel No. 61) and which contains entries beginning at 1 Jan. 1832. For a description of this Diary MS, of the other MSS from which the printed text of vols. 5 and 6 derives, and of CFA's diary-keeping methods, see the Introduction; also vol. 1:xxxviii–xl; vol. 3:xxxix–xl.

[2] CFA had renewed his reading of Montaigne's essays the week before (vol. 4:191, 428–429).

[3] After his marriage to Abigail Brooks in September 1829 CFA's daily routine during the winter months in Boston each year was seldom varied. Mornings were spent at his office, 23 Court Street, afternoons at home at 3 Hancock Avenue (vol. 3:2).

[4] *L'esprit de la Ligue* by Louis Pierre Anquetil was undertaken on 29 Dec. (vol. 4:431).

[5] On the series of articles setting forth his antimasonic position which CFA was currently writing, some of which had already been published in the *Boston Daily Advocate* and the rest of which would appear there after a delay of several months, see vol. 4:404–431 *passim* and below, note to entry for 21 May 1833.

[6] CFA had Mme. Cottin's novel, *Malvina*, and Lockhart's *Life of Robert Burns* on loan from the Boston Athenæum (vol. 4:408, 419, 439, 441).

WEDNESDAY. 2D.

This was what is commonly called Election day. That is, the day upon which the newly elected Government of the State goes into operation. I went to the Office as usual and was occupied in settling up Affairs, making out new Accounts for the next year and finishing off old ones. It took up nearly all of my time. Took a walk. The day was lovely. If our season of last year was a cold and dreary one, that of this has been as extraordinarily mild. My walk was a very pleasant one. Gorham Brooks and his Wife dined with us. He was pleasant enough.[1] And our little dinner went off without difficulty. I should very much like to see company at my house on easy, social terms. Afternoon, passed in reading Anquetils Account of the Ligue. His is very much the same story, I have seen at second hand in Lingard.[2] Not much to the credit of the French character. Evening, quiet at home. Finished Malvina, which is a gloomy book enough. Mem. not to read any more of Madame Cottin. Burns' Life, afterwards, more of Wieland.[3]

[1] On ABA's brother and his wife Ellen, see vol. 3:259 and Adams Genealogy.
[2] *History of England*; see vol. 4:370.
[3] Probably a selection from *Geschichte der Abderiten*; see vol. 4:418.

THURSDAY. 3D.

Cloudy but very mild. Went to the Office and was engaged there very constantly all the morning. Drew my Dividends, and began the serious work of paying off all my bills which have been sent in. It is at least a gratification to me that I have been able to meet them, but it is a matter of some surprise how rapidly they accummulate. Two months ago, I had hardly any. My Summer's residence at Quincy had expunged them nearly all.

Took a walk as usual. After dinner, resumed Anquetil, but finding myself grow indolent I determined to brisk up and work away upon No. 8, the third draught of which I finished. How little good have those numbers effected. And I have slaved away at them merely to add one more to my already serious number of failures. I *will* slave no more. If it is productive of nothing but mortification, why should I voluntarily incur it at every step I take? Why should I endeavour to wriggle out a little larger hole for myself when I can move my arms and lie comfortable without stirring? After all the present jobs are done I will lie on my Oars.[1]

My Wife and I went to take Tea at Edward Brooks'. His wife is better. Mr. and Mrs. Frothingham were there also.[2] We had a pleasant evening and returned only in time for me to read the World.[3]

[1] On CFA's oft-sounded dissatisfaction with the reception given his writing, never operative as a deterrent, see vol. 3:xxxv–xxxvi.

[2] ABA's eldest brother Edward and his wife Eliza, along with Ann, sister of ABA, and her husband, Rev. Nathaniel Frothingham, are familiar figures in CFA's diary; see also Adams Genealogy.

Edward was assuming increasing control of his father's large business interests; Frothingham was the minister of the First Church, Chauncy Place, in Boston.

[3] The most recently undertaken in CFA's long-pursued reading of all the British essay-periodicals. See vol. 3:337–338; 4:405.

FRIDAY. 4TH.

Astonishing weather. No frosts and the air like April. I went to the Office. My time is very much taken up by accounts. My father's collections come in with amazing slowness, and I make up as I go both from his and mine.

In consequence of conversation last night I read the North American Review upon Mrs. Trollope. Good but as Mr. Frothingham said very coarse. I think unnecessarily so.[1] I am getting tired of censuring however. I feel more and more that in this world it is more easy to censure than to praise, that every person involves himself in cases where a double construction of his conduct can be admitted and therefore that a man should do to others as he would that others should do unto him.

Took a walk. Afternoon, I wrote more of Anti Masonry. Decided upon withdrawing my Article for the North American Review and wrote a Note to Mr. Everett to that effect.[2] That is one step. Went to the Theatre, with Gorham Brooks and his Wife. Opera of Massaniello. Music of Auber. Some pretty things but in general too noisy. Sinclair very good in a Barcarolle and leading a Chorus. One or two other Choruses also well got up. I came home on the whole very much pleased. Miss Hughes not so good. There is much of the Melodrame about the piece. On the whole, good.[3]

[1] The essay-review (vol. 36:1) of Frances Trollope's *Domestic Manners of the Americans* was by Edward Everett.

[2] CFA customarily felt that articles he submitted to the *North American Review* were subjected by its editor, A. H. Everett, to intolerable delays and postponements. His article in defense of the Puritan cause, submitted in July 1832, finally did appear after numerous vicissitudes in the July 1833 issue (see vol. 4:428).

[3] John Sinclair and Elizabeth Hughes, whom CFA had heard with no greater enthusiasm during the preceding season (vol. 4:283), were appearing with augmented chorus and orchestra in a production at the Tremont Theatre said to be "in a style of excellence hitherto unattempted in this country." *Masaniello* reached its climax in the eruption of Mount Vesuvius (*Columbian Centinel*, 1 Jan. 1833, p. 3, col. 5).

SATURDAY. 5TH.

Delicious day. I never knew in this climate, so extraordinary a week as the last, in this month. It is much more like May weather. I went to the Office. Engaged in Accounts, and paying innumerable demands that were pouring in upon me. I must stir myself or else demands will exceed the supply. Wrote up my Diary which the occupations of the week had thrown somewhat behind-hand.

At one o'clock, I had made an Engagement to return home, for the purpose of going with my Wife, Mrs. Frothingham, and P. C. Brooks Jr. in a Carriage to Medford. The road was exceedingly bad, the frost being quite touched even to it's extreme depth. We found Mrs. Everett and Miss Lydia Phillips quite well. Mr. Brooks came in shortly afterwards.[1] For myself I never care to go out in the Country during the Winter months. It looks so dreary and blank in them. But on the whole I enjoyed myself pretty well today. Returned home and took Tea quietly, after which I read Burns and wrote a little piece of a Skit.

[1] Contrary to his general practice, ABA's father, Peter C. Brooks, remained at Mystic Grove, his Medford estate (vol. 3:xviii, 10), through the winter season, 1832–1833, in company with his daughter Charlotte (Mrs. Edward

Everett), who, expecting a child, did not accompany her husband to Washington for the Congressional session (vol. 3:6). After Mrs. Brooks' death in 1830 one of the daughters of Mrs. John Phillips of Andover, Mrs. Brooks' sister, was often in attendance to share in the house- hold management. P. C. Brooks Jr., usually called Chardon, was the third of ABA's brothers currently living in Boston (vol. 3:4). On the Brookses and Everetts mentioned here, see also Adams Genealogy.

SUNDAY. 6TH.

Another fine morning. I was grieved to find this morning my child's eye affected by a violent cold and inflammation.[1] How it can be accounted for I am entirely unable to say unless it proceeds from teething. It disfigures her exceedingly. The anxieties on account of children are infinite. And I know of none so torturing. My reliance is invariably upon a higher power. What could I do without it?

Went to Meeting all day. Heard Mr. Frothingham in the morning from Joshua 10. 13. "And the sun stood still and the moon stayed." He denied the possibility of such an event. An assertion as rash as it was presumptuous. Had he confined himself to the probability of the story, I should perhaps have considered the question whether the Deity would stop the course of creation for the sake of the slaughter of a battle. But I can not and hope I never shall doubt the power of the Deity to do what seemeth to him good with the works of his hand. The rest of the Sermon was a pretty application of the idea to the various desires of Man, whether as impelled by ambition, by avarice, ⟨*money*⟩ or the various other passions.

In the Afternoon Dr. Lowell[2] took up the same subject of time as connected with the opening of the year and illustrated it forcibly in one or two familiar points according to his custom. He rarely says much that is novel. But his discourses are always calculated to affect strongly the mass. His single idea that this was the beginning of a year at the close of which perhaps many of those present would not be living created a profound silence. Yet there is no more common topic in the Pulpit.

At home, I did not succeed in reading Massillon until evening.[3] Being obliged to go for the Dr. on account of our anxiety for Louisa, our child. His report is that her sickness comes from the eye teeth. He lanced the Gums. I read some of Ruffhead.[4] Massillon's Sermon was upon the danger of falling back into Sin. Division, three causes. 1. The precautions against dangerous temptation omitted. 2. Resolutions wantonly violated. 3. The Reparations for sinful conduct not practised. Text. Romans 6. 9. "Knowing that Christ being raised from the dead dieth no more: death hath no more dominion over him." Easter day. The Text has but an indirect application. Passed an hour at Mr. Froth-ingham. Our friend Buckingham came in.[5]

[1] Louisa (LCA2), now eighteen months old (vol. 4:111 and Adams Genealogy), was the object of unremitting parental solicitude.

[2] Charles Lowell, minister of the West Church, Boston (vol. 2:395).

[3] CFA, in pursuing his study of pulpit oratory, was in the habit of reading and commenting on a sermon of Jean Baptiste Massillon each Sunday (vol. 4:97).

[4] *The Life of Alexander Pope* by Owen Ruffhead; see vol. 4:416.

[5] Joseph T. Buckingham, editor of the *Boston Courier*, was only in some senses a friend of the Adamses (vol. 3:342).

MONDAY. 7TH.

Fine morning though the Weather was colder than it had been. The child does not appear to be materially relieved. I am anxious about her. Went to the Office. Accounts and Diary took up the time. Gulliver sent and settled his Acct. by compromise. I was glad to get any thing. My Writ was the last resource and I had thought it unavailing. But it seems to have done the thing. Mr. Geitner also called in and paid on account. This gives breathing time to my money affairs.

Took a walk. Mr. Brooks and his son P. C. Jr. dined with me. After dinner, I went to a Meeting of the Directors of the Boylston Market Association. All present. Accounts looked over. Nothing done.[1] Thence to the Annual Meeting of the Proprietors of the Athenæum. Election of Trustees. Col. Perkins declines. Mr. F. C. Gray chosen. Ticknor, Vice-President. I do not admire all these People.[2]

Return to tea. The child has had a Leech applied and taken Medicine, but the inflammation continues. It is always painful to see a person suffering, but when that person is a child it is ten times increased. Finished Burns. No fire in my study so I read Ruffhead in the Parlour. Mr. Everett sent home my Article. I read it over coolly.

[1] CFA had become a director and the clerk of the Boylston Market two years earlier (vol. 3:417) to represent JQA's shares in the Association.

[2] On CFA's attitude toward Boston's men of wealth and station who, among the proprietors of the Boston Athenæum, currently filled its offices, see vol. 1:312; 3:xxx, 124.

TUESDAY. 8TH.

The weather today was clear but much more in accordance with the usual character of the Season. The Child seemed on the whole to be relieved though yet very much of a Sufferer. I went to the Office. Engaged all the morning in my usual occupations. But I obtained a short time of leisure to read more of Dr. Lingard. I seized half an hour to go and pick up a book at the Athenæum and then took my walk, first of all, calling at my Wood dealers for some fuel, and then at the Boylston Market to examine the Pantheon Hall for an advertisement.

Afternoon quietly at home. Began rewriting my Article which I read yesterday. This will perhaps be no better than the last, and I am foolish to make further attempts, yet I do not like to lose entirely all my previous labour. My mind produces nothing that satisfies me or any body else. I am in these matters pretty much discouraged.

Evening quiet at home. Read to my Wife, part of Ourika a French novel of Madame de Duras, and Pope's Eloisa to Abelard as well as the Rape of the Lock.[1] Received rather a dispirited letter from my Mother.[2]

[1] Probably in the edition of Pope's *Works* now at MQA (vol. 4:116).
[2] 3 Jan. (Adams Papers). LCA had been ill with scarlet fever which had followed hard upon an earlier illness.

WEDNESDAY. 9TH.

It snowed at day break but was afterwards a clear and mild day. The Child seems to be improving and has recovered her usual animation. I went to the Office. Occupied a little but I found myself suffering under a heavy cold and pain in my head. This with me generally paralyzes all exertion. Read Lingard. Went to the Athenæum and took a Walk—Nothing occurring of any consequence. Afternoon, I pursued the perusal of Anquetil and I wrote a little of the Article but without much spirit in either. My exertions have been so useless that I feel a total want of self confidence. I believe that it would be better for me to remain quiet and philosophize upon life. To strengthen myself by private practice without venturing upon the opinion of the world. My notions are many of them not particularly likely to catch the tone of the vulgar. Evening quiet. I did nothing. Edward Brooks came in and spent an hour, but I felt stupid and heavy. Exertion in such cases is dreadful.

THURSDAY. 10TH.

My head was relieved this morning, but I felt my cold oppress me still very much throughout the day. It was warm and rainy but I nevertheless went to the Office. I have very few interruptions there now, and have an opportunity of passing my time much more profitably than formerly. I go through every day the usual routine of Accounts, Diary, and Lingard with occasionally a mere glance at politics with which however I am at present not much engaged. This makes my morning, excepting only an hour for exercise. The rain prevented my taking this today.

Afternoon consumed at home in reading parts of Hallam's Constitutional History[1] and in writing more of my Article. I will go through this as rapidly as possible and then make a full stop in composition for this Winter. My occupations will then take some other direction— Principally to some light literature I believe.

Received a letter from my Mother. She is better and talks of nothing but the Washington outrages.[2] National affairs are in a poor condition. Evening, Ourika and the very odd Memoirs of a very odd Woman, the Margravine of Anspach.[3] I do not mention the Bible because this like the World must be always understood when we are at home.

[1] *Constitutional History of England* by Henry Hallam.

[2] Probably LCA to ABA, 5 Jan. (Adams Papers). She concludes, "Crime is tolerated, immorality publicly sanctioned and unblushing impudence is the great passport to success. We are indeed enlightened."

[3] Both *Ourika*, by the Duchesse de Duras (Paris, 1826), and the *Memoirs* of Elizabeth Berkeley Craven, Margravine of Anspach (2 vols., London, 1826), were borrowed from the Athenæum.

FRIDAY. IITH.

A severely cold morning. I went to the Office. The Child appears to be better, but my cold affects me considerably. Engaged in writing. Received a curious letter from Mr. Foord, Register of Dedham, which I answered before night.[1] I also finished Lingard's eleventh Volume which is on the whole as good as any of them. Took a half hour to read Mr. Everett's article upon Nullification. He is not powerful upon Constitutional Law. His mind embraces no great principles.[2]

Took a walk but the cold and the wind were so very intolerable, I was induced to shorten it. In the Afternoon, looked over Hallam and made considerable progress in my Article which I hope two or three more days will finish. It is totally different from the former one, perhaps better, but I do not know. Evening passed quietly at home. Read the rest of Ourika, a little trifle with but one idea in it, and more of Lady Craven's very absurd and good for nothing book.[3] Read a little of Hallam. The winter shows it's face at last.

[1] To Enos Foord (LbC, Adams Papers); the letter from Foord is missing. CFA had objected to the charges made for registering a deed.

[2] A. H. Everett's article on nullification is in the *North Amer. Rev.* (vol. 36:235).

[3] The book which CFA sometimes refers to as Lady Craven's and sometimes as the Margravine of Anspach's is the same, her *Memoirs*.

SATURDAY. 12TH.

Not so cold as yesterday although still pretty well. I went to the Office. Occupied in Accounts as usual, and finished the Article of Mr. Everett upon Nullification. Well written but superficial. Went to the Athenæum and in that manner lost my walk. My cold has disordered my system again. I have for six weeks or more enjoyed excellent health but now I suffer from my Summer difficulties. Ailing, uneasy sensations about the region of the Stomach.

Nothing new of public interest. After dinner, busily engaged in my writing which I wish to throw off and have done with. It is of no use. Mr. Everett will not publish it and he will crowd his periodical with papers which strike me as meritorious only for their flatness. That is to say they keep the juste milieu until a man is tired to death. I do not know that I ought to be discouraged, yet it seems to me difficult to prevent it.

Evening at home. Read much of Lady Craven's book which seems to be partly an olla podrida of old album reflections made by a woman who thinks herself more sensible than she is. The whole book is extraordinary enough and worthy of nobody but a lady of the noble blood of the Berkeleys. Continued my work in the evening.

SUNDAY. 13TH.

Morning cold but it moderated in the course of the day. I did nothing excepting my regular duties. Attended Divine Service all day and heard Mr. Putnam of Roxbury preach. Morning discourse from Romans 10. 10. "With the heart man believeth unto righteousness." Upon morality and religion, the difference between them and the connexion, with a discussion of the prevailing tendencies to infidelity. A very good subject, tolerably well treated. Afternoon. Ecclesiastes 3. 1. "To every thing there is a season." Subject, amusement and occupation, the business of life and it's pleasures. Mr. Putnam is on the whole a pretty tolerable thinker. He discriminates justly and though I find in him few new or very forcible ideas, he has nevertheless old ones very sensibly presented.[1]

Read a Sermon of Massillon's upon false confidence, in other words, upon trusting in faith without works. This is one of the few points in which the Catholics seem to have been right in the great quarrel with the primitive Reformers. The text of this Sermon is from Luke 24. 21. "We trusted that it had been he which should have redeemed Israel."

9

The belief of the Jews, from whence a natural transition to the existing generation. Two points—Such a trust without any labour to second it is extreme folly. It is extreme boldness. The discourse is a sensible one. Evening passed at home. I read Ruffhead, and Gardiner Gorham came in for an hour.[2]

[1] The powers of Rev. George Putnam are here rated at a somewhat higher value than on earlier occasions; see vol. 3:412–413.

[2] The three children of the late Dr. John Gorham, Julia, John Warren, and Gardner, were not only distant relatives of ABA but intimates of the household (vol. 3:55; 4:395).

MONDAY. 14TH.

Milder with the wind more from the Southward. I went to the Office. But my time was not very usefully taken up. After getting through ordinary duties, I attended the annual Meeting of the Stockholders of the Suffolk Insurance Company—My Stock there being sufficient to make it an object. The Report of the President was very satisfactory. For seven years they have never omitted a Dividend, and now they have forty five thousand dollars in crib[1] over the Capital. They have also paid seventy odd thousand dollars for losses during the last year. It seems to me that on the whole it is fair to suppose that in the run of any seven years with the same direction no worse fortune may be expected inasmuch as the losses have been twice within those seven years excessive. I am glad to hear this Account inasmuch as my investments here have been at a high rate of premium, and I was fearful I had been hasty.

Took a walk and then home. After dinner wrote on the article which I am rapidly closing. At five went to the Athenæum to a Meeting of the Stockholders about one or two motions to increase the privileges of the Reading public. I expected a debate but nothing took place. Voted against the motions and then went to the Tremont House to meet my Wife and Mrs. Gorham Brooks with whom I crossed over to the Theatre.[2] Mr. Sinclair and Mrs. Austin in Cinderella. The Music of that Opera charms me always, and I prefer her singing a thousand times over to that of Miss Hughes. The mere Spectacle went wrong perpetually.[3] We returned rather late.

[1] That is, in reserve or storage, by abbreviation and transfer from *corncrib* (*Dict. of Americanisms*). The transfer might have come equally well from the name given to the reserve pile of cards in cribbage (*OED*).

[2] On the two impressive structures designed by Isaiah Rogers and located on opposite sides of Tremont Street, see vol. 3:xiii–xiv.

[3] The singing of Mrs. Elizabeth Austin, especially in the adaptation of

Rossini's *Cenerentola*, was one of CFA's persistent enthusiasms; see vol. 4:ix, 263–264, 283. He writes of the operatic season in Boston and comments on the principal performers in a letter to LCA (27 Jan., Adams Papers).

TUESDAY. 15TH.

Coldest morning we have had. It moderated afterwards. I went to the office. Time taken up as usual. Read a Chapter or two of Lingard. Reign of Charles the second. Singular Revolution of sentiment and shows the danger of straining the human mind too high. No interruptions. Took a walk for which I felt the better. My Stomach seems to be becoming more quiet. It is but within a year or two that I have suffered from it.

Afternoon and evening engaged upon my article which I have again finished. And I read it over afterwards to myself. It has taken me a week to write it. And it struck me so deplorably poor, I was completely disheartened. I shall do no more. I have kept up my courage so far, against every species of disappointment, hoping always that at least there was some substance to redeem my style, if there was much dross. But it does seem as if there was not enough. And I must cease to write or attempt to acquire reputation beyond that of a moral and quiet member of the Community. This at least is within my power. Read to my wife from Lady Craven. Some observations are too sensible to have originated with her. She heard and copied them from others.

WEDNESDAY. 16TH.

The weather suddenly changed during the night, and it was sultry with a Southerly wind and rain in the morning. I went to the Office. A letter from T. B. Adams, in reply to my semi-annual statement and mentioning his departure from Camp Armistead to Fort Mitchell in Alabama. He seems to be likely to pass pretty thoroughly over the Southern Country.[1] I read Lingard and wrote my Diary as usual. Nothing new. Walk and home.

Afternoon, resumed the second Philippic of Cicero which I had begun some time back. It is a powerful specimen of invective although far too personal for what we should call good taste. Yet I am at a loss to know why if a man confines himself to speaking truth of an adversary he should not as well expose private as public vices. The latter are a natural consequence of the former. The only obstacle is the difficulty of avoiding slander in the mouths of the unscrupulous. In other respects, the power of Cicero is no where more visible than in this

Oration. It's vehemence is charming. That is the study for a writer who desires to assume the grand style.

Evening quiet at home. Read more of the Margravine. A curious book for trifling. Resumed my German which my studies had broken off.

[1] While Thomas Boylston Adams Jr., a lieutenant in the U.S. Army, was in service and after his father's death, CFA acted as his financial agent; see vol. 3:2, 337, and Adams Genealogy. The letter is missing.

THURSDAY. 17TH.

I cannot say that this cold morning was passed in the most advisable manner. At the Office until eleven o'clock industriously occupied upon my Accounts and occupations as usual. I then went out to pay a few bills which had been presented to me. This led me to make one or two purchases—Among others to call at J. D. Williams and buy some pretty dear Sherry Wine. I was engaged in the amusement of tasting of various kinds until my head was quite light. Thereupon I went to the Athenæum and passed the time commonly devoted by me to walking, in conversation with the Librarian.[1] As I was coming home, I met Mr. Hallet who inquired of me respecting my numbers.[2] He encouraged me a good deal about them. I told him that if he wished, I would write the rest and send them. This made me late at home. Afternoon, continued my reading of Cicero's Philippic which I shall finish tomorrow. And I began again Anquetil in whom my late occupations have stopped my progress. In the evening my Wife had a family party. Edward Brooks, Gorham, P. C. Jr. and Mr. Frothingham with their Wives, Julia Gorham and her brother. It was pleasanter than usual, broke up early and after they went I continued Anquetil.

[1] Seth Bass had been made librarian in 1825.
[2] Benjamin Franklin Hallett, editor of the *Boston Daily Advocate* and antimasonic leader (vol. 4:419).

FRIDAY. 18TH.

Morning somewhat milder. I went to the Office. Little or nothing material. Read some of Lingard's Charles the second, wrote Diary and busied myself without much interruption in my common, every day occupations. So quiet and settled is my mode of life that nothing happens commonly to interfere with it. I believe I ought to be abundantly satisfied that I am so entirely free from anxiety of any kind. I am satisfied, abundantly satisfied. When I consider how many young men there are who have no resources of mind and an overabundance of wealth, I congratulate myself upon those I have been so fortunate as to acquire.

Took a walk. Afternoon, finished No. 9 on Anti Masonry. Reviewed the three on hand and concluded to send them. Mr. Hallett seems to think they may be useful enough to collect and publish if I finish them. Certainly no indolence of mine shall stand in the way. I have done expecting much from my pen. I once was vain of it. Mortification ought to make me humble. Evening quietly at home. Finished the first volume of the Margravine's Nonsense.

SATURDAY. 19TH.

Morning extremely cold—Almost enough to take one's breath away. I went to the Office as usual. Read more of Lingard and as I find it extremely doubtful when I shall be enabled to go to Quincy, I concluded to send her Money to Elizabeth today.[1] These things always weigh upon my mind until they are over.

Took a walk as usual although my fingers were much nipped by the weather. Afternoon, enjoyed mine ease in mine inn—The first great portion of one of my tasks being completed and the other being ready for perusal and amendment. Finished the Philippic of Cicero, a powerful performance the biting severity of which was too much for the patience of Antony. Death was the only reply which he was capable of making. Brute force was to be used when mind could no longer cope with mind. That is the usual way. Read more of Anquetil, who goes over the horrible story of St. Barthelemy. Yet Lingard attempts to soften this Story and says as little as he can of the course taken by the Pope upon it. Evening quiet at home. Read a little of Caroline de Litchfield,[2] and more of the Margravine. Afterwards, German.

[1] CFA, as agent for JQA, regularly disbursed to Elizabeth Coombs Adams (ECA), daughter of TBA, her share of interest received under the terms of JA's will; see vol. 3:31 and Adams Genealogy.

[2] On returning *Ourika* to the Athenæum on the 17th, CFA had borrowed Baronne de Montolieu's *Caroline de Litchfield, ou mémoire d'une famille prussienne.*

SUNDAY. 20TH.

Milder. The first thing this morning was a tremendous fire. It was the Sugar Refinery in Atkinson Street. My morning was short. Attended divine Service and heard Mr. Frothingham preach morning and afternoon. His first was from Isaiah 45. 15. "Verily thou art a God that hidest thyself, O God of Israel, the Saviour." The incomprehensible character of the Deity, as affecting four descriptions of persons, the infidel, the superstitious believer, the curious inquirer and the men of melancholy temperament. The division was an interesting one, but it did not seem to me that the treatment of it was carried out equally well. Took a walk. Mr. Beale of Quincy dined with me, and accompanied me in the Afternoon. Having lost my usual Nap, I was so drowsy I did not catch much of the discourse. Text Romans 9. 20. "Shall the thing formed say to him that formed it, Why hast thou made me thus?" On my return home, read a Sermon of Massillon taken from Matthew 5. 5. "Blessed are the meek for they shall inherit the Earth." Subject the happiness of the just, 1. by the light of the faith which alleviates their sufferings, whilst the want of it increases those of sinners, 2. by the softening influence of grace which calms the passions when the absence of it exposes others to their unrestrained influence. This division did appear to me to be unneccessary—The ideas and treatment corresponding almost exactly. Evening at home. My Wife was suffering from tooth ach. I heard today that my father was quite unwell. Read Anquetil.

MONDAY. 21ST.

Very mild and pleasant morning. The changes of our weather are most exceedingly strange. Received letters from home, mentioning the illness both of my father and brother, and their partial recovery.[1] So that, I thank Heaven, my anxiety has not been of long duration. Time somewhat wasted today. The President has sent a Message to Congress which begins to dispel the thick Mist that hung over his course.[2] Mr. Gourgas spent half an hour at my Office. Questions about the Medford Farm. Difficulty with the Proprietors of the Railroad.[3] Mr. E. Blake also called in for a moment, to inquire about the Middlesex Canal for the second time. I told him, I was entirely ignorant.[4]

Took a walk. Met Misses Dehon and accompanied them. The eldest is sensible and conversible and I was quite pleased.[5] Afternoon, attended a Meeting of the Directors of the Boylston Market. Nothing done as usual. Might as well not have met. It is a tedious business, and I shall be very glad to get out of it. But I see no immediate prospect of doing so. Evening quietly at home. Caroline of Litchfield and Lady Craven. I afterwards attacked Wieland, but my German does somewhat lag behind hand.

[1] LCA to CFA, 16 Jan. (Adams Papers).

[2] On the Nullification issue.

[3] John M. Gourgas Jr., who had for a number of years been affianced to wed TBA's daughter, Elizabeth, upon the death of TBA had been named by the widow to administer the estate. At the same time JQA gave over to Mrs. TBA during her lifetime the rents from the Medford farm which TBA had inherited from JA but which had passed to JQA by default of a mortgage (vol. 4:266, 269–270). The productivity of the farm was currently threatened by a right-of-way acquired across the land by the newly constructed Boston & Lowell Railroad (vol. 3:xix, 236; 4:42).

[4] On the speculative interest in the Middlesex Canal Co., of which CFA was a director and his father a substantial stockholder, see below, entry for 28 Jan. (also vol. 3:150–154).

[5] The eldest of the sisters of Mrs. Sidney Brooks, married to ABA's brother, was probably Mary M., who later became Mrs. Edward Blake.

TUESDAY. 22ND.

Cloudy but mild. I went to the Office as usual and besides my regular duties, accomplished the concluding Chapter of Lingard's eleventh volume. He dilates too much upon the reign of Charles. It is in the spirit of modern history to grow dull as it has to do with Parliamentary details. Debates are generally dry because the mass of speakers rarely do more than confuse a subject or at best leave it just where it was.

Took a walk as usual. Mrs. Angier dined and spent the day with my Wife.[1] I passed the Afternoon in correcting my Article and re-writing a portion of it. I never should finish amending it. It is the last I try. Hallett does not publish any of my numbers and on the whole I do not see but my labours are pretty much at a stand still. Well, patiensia. It may come to good and if it does not, I do not feel worse situated than I was before. I worked most of the evening. One more Afternoon, and I give the very last touch I put upon that labour. Then it must go upon the waters. Mr. Beale came in and saw Mrs. Angier and spent the evening. I did nothing, but read the World.

[1] Mrs. John Angier of Medford, formerly Abigail Smith Adams, a daughter of TBA; see vol. 3:424 and Adams Genealogy.

WEDNESDAY. 23D.

A very wet, dirty day. I went to the Office but did not succeed in effecting much. As I had no other volume of Lingard at my room, I was obliged to go to the Athenæum for one, and this excursion led me to examine the Newspapers there until I had no farther time for any thing. Took my usual walk. Afternoon somewhat wasted. Mrs. Angier dined with us and went away directly afterwards. I tried to write a little of my Article but the vein was not in me. It is a little singular how unequally I feel in this respect. Sometimes my pen flows easily, at others it drags as if it was loaded with lead.

Evening, went to the Theatre, in company with Mr. and Mrs. Miller, Mrs. Angier and others. The Tempest adapted to Purcell's music, and a Pageant in honour of Walter Scott. Mrs. Austin as Ariel with Mr. Horn for Ferdinand. The music is simple, light and airy. The duett at the close of the second Act was pretty and the Chorus tolerable. But the play is dreadfully mangled to suit to the Stage, and it went off heavily. As to the other thing, it was a miserable affair.[1] We went home very much disappointed.

[1] The afterpiece, a "grand pageant" entitled "Vision of the Bard" (*Columbian Centinel*, 23 Jan., p. 3, col. 5).

THURSDAY. 24TH.

A dull drizzle and gloomy day. I went to the Office feeling excessively out of order. My indisposition of the Autumn continues and affects me constantly, not so much by any pain as by general uncomfortableness. I read some of Dr. Lingard and was engaged in my usual occupations. Time flies in this way so that I am hardly conscious of it's passage. Yet I do not know that I do quite enough to improve it.

Took my regular walk in spite of the weather, but found that my head ach was coming on notwithstanding. Afternoon, did little or nothing but finish my article. This is now out of the way, and will trouble me no more. I have laboured upon it far more than the thing is worth. I shall now lay the subject aside not to resume it. My condition was such that I could not employ myself usefully in any thing.

Miss Julia Gorham was here in the evening. At nine o'clock, my Wife and I went to a ball given at the Tremont House by Mr. and Mrs. J. H. Gray. This is a new mode for the purpose of saving private Houses.[1] It was very splendid and very crowded. But I was in any humor rather than that of enjoying it. Home quite late.

[1] "For the moderate sum of about a thousand dollars — A pretty penny to pay for seeing one's friends" (CFA to LCA, 27 Jan., Adams Papers).

FRIDAY. 25TH.

Day very dark and gloomy with rain and snow. I felt somewhat better, though with many indications of a cold caught last night. At the Office. Time taken up in writing and reading Dr. Lingard. I was unable to take my regular walk. Nothing material transpired. The gloomy weather makes me dull. After dinner, busy in reading Anquetil in whose work I made progress. I ought not to omit mentioning that I passed an hour pretty pleasantly with my friend Thomas Davis. We talk freely upon various subjects, and his mind is so fully stored with matter for conversation that I enjoy his company.[1] I put the finishing hand to my Article. Now the question is, Shall I send it again? I pause for a reply.

We were invited out for this evening, but as the weather appeared stormy, we were excused. The consequence of which was a quiet evening at home—A thing I enjoy doubly after going out for a night or two. Read Caroline of Litchfield, a very pretty little book, and Lady Craven who grows sensible all of a sudden. I expect there is a mixture here of two minds at least, and some plagiarism besides. Read Wieland.

[1] CFA seldom records a conversation with Thomas Kemper Davis except with an enthusiasm rare in the journal; see vol. 3:223–224.

SATURDAY. 26TH.

Foggy morning but it afterwards cleared away. I went to the Office and as it was a little cool I thought I would sit by the fire and read Lingard first, after which write my Journal, but I pursued my reading so steadily through the thirteenth volume that I left myself but half an hour, and that time was appropriated to another purpose—My Carpenter Mr. Ayer coming in to settle his annual accounts against me. My walk too must not on any consideration be interrupted. Met J. G. Rogers today—A man whose mind does not seem to work at all in parallell lines.[1]

Afternoon, reflected upon my Article and concluded to send it. It is a turning point in my career of that kind. If I do meet with any more mortification about it, I lay down my pen for ever so far as voluntary exertion is concerned. It is disappointing to my pride which ought not to humiliate itself before others. Occupying the situation in Society fortune has given me, if I fail in making myself deserving by my own acts why should I expose myself to the contempt of others farther than is requisite to ascertain the failure? After this, I will not blind myself. Read Anquetil and evening at home. Wieland.

[1] Judge John Gray Rogers of the Boston Police Court and a neighbor of the Adamses at 65 Mount Vernon Street (*Boston Directory*).

SUNDAY. 27TH.

Clear and wintry. Read Smollett's Independence, an ode the first Stanza of which is superior to the rest. I do not admire the genealogy he traces, as if Independence was a bastard, but many of the lines are noble, and there is vigour throughout.[1]

Attended divine service all day. Mr. Frothingham preached. Matthew 8. 29. "What have we to do with thee? Art thou come hither to torment us before the time?" The demoniacs and the swine, an allusion to the various explanations of the text and an examination of the idea prevailing among men that they were to be called before the time. I was inattentive and this explanation is lame. Habakkuk. 2. 2. "And the Lord answered me and said, Write the vision, and make it plain upon the tables that he may run that readeth it." The necessity of simplicity in matters of concernment to men. The doctrines taught by the Bible are all simple, but the ingenuity of man has perpetually attached theories to them which obscure and mystify and do injury. Theology has sprung from these theories. Theology is not Religion— As an instance the doctrine of the Atonement from the simple story of the passion of Christ.

I afterwards read Massillon. Revelations 14. 13. "Blessed are the dead which die in the Lord." The death of the Sinner and that of the just man. Contrast forcibly made. And some fine points. But the thing is rather too much laboured. And after all, the one idea is a simple one. I did little besides. Judge Hall dropped in for half an hour in the evening.[2] Political news not very important. Finished the extracts from Wieland and wrote a letter to my Mother.

[1] An earlier reading was recorded with similar pleasure (vol. 1:160–161).

[2] Judge Joseph Hall was a friend of JQA and an Antimason (vol. 2:154). Of his visit CFA wrote to his mother, "Judge Hall has been putting Abby to sleep until she feels totally unable to do any thing but lounge on the Sofa" (27 Jan., Adams Papers).

MONDAY. 28TH.

My health is not really good this winter, I am sure. Went to the Office, but a Meeting of the Directors of Middlesex Canal having been called I attended it at Mr. Chadwick's Office in Court Street. The attendance was very scanty. Yet the Report of the Agent was very favourable. A dividend of twenty dollars was declared and a balance of eight thousand more, equivalent to half as much on each share, reserved for next year. This besides an expenditure of eight thousand and more upon new works. Two years more of success would place this property on a most durable footing. It will in all probability meet with one or two drawbacks in a few years but on the whole with the present Agent, the prospect is encouraging.

My time at the Office was short, looked over Accounts &c. Walk shortened by calling at the Athenæum. Afternoon, taken up in reading Anquetil whose Catholic notions are curious. Evening, went to the public Meeting at Faneuil Hall. Speakers ordinary. J. T. Austin engrossed most of the time. On the whole a failure. Our people do not care much about the Tariff.[1] It is not true that it would ruin them. Called in for my Wife at Mrs. Frothingham's afterwards, took a little Supper and went home.

[1] At the meeting held to encourage "American industry in preference to foreign," resolutions in support of a tariff of protection were passed and forwarded to Washington (*Columbian Centinel*, 29 Jan., p. 2, col. 5).

TUESDAY. 29TH.

Cold again. Drew my Middlesex Canal Dividend, inspected books and read Lingard. On the whole pretty actively engaged. Received a short and excessively dispirited letter from my Father, mentioning the sickness of the whole family and his own.[1] I do not know how it is, but there must be something or other at the bottom of affairs at Washington. Things do not go on well there. Whose fault it is, I cannot pretend to say, but that it is some one's it does seem to me probable. My father seems to have lost his energy of character and suffers things to take their course. I hope through all the darkness that we shall see some light. My trust is always in a power above us. May his justice be administered in mercy.

Took a long walk. Afternoon, finished Anquetil's Spirit of the League. A valuable work on the whole, to study the effects of fanaticism upon the human mind. Mr. Everett sent me a palavering Note in answer to my Saturday's.[2] I was idle. Evening, went to Mrs. B. Gorham's according to invitation, stopping an hour or two at Gorham Brooks'. Conversation. Mr. Gorham has gone to Washington.[3] Several ladies, many of whom I did not know. Remained only half an hour, and wasted at home the rest of the evening.

[1] 22 Jan. (Adams Papers).
[2] Both notes missing.
[3] Benjamin Gorham, recently elected to a new term in Congress, was an uncle of ABA; see vol. 2:152.

WEDNESDAY. 30TH.

Morning cloudy and mild. I went to the Office. Received a short and exceedingly dispirited letter from my Mother.[1] She has been ill, and John and my father, and she hints at depression from circumstances which I pretty well understand. I am very fearful of events in that quarter.[2] They involve consequences which I have been labouring hard to counteract. A little more time and fortunate incidents might do so. I put my trust in a higher power.

Read Lingard and was engaged much as usual. Walk. Felt singularly. I believe it is the consequence of my present habit. It must be altered. Afternoon, lazed over Anquetil's spirit of the Fronde. I must settle down into a more regular occupation. Listlessness comes over me. This must be avoided by proposing some new subject of investigation, or continuing old ones. Evening at home, reading Caroline of Litchfield and Lady Craven. Afterwards, reviewing Wieland, I find I have made some progress.

[1] Letter missing.

[2] CFA's concerns about his mother and father in Washington were of several sorts. Their repeated spells of illness, together with the general ill-health of his brother John (JA2) and his wife and children, CFA tended to blame upon a combination of Washington's climate and poor household management. CFA also continued to oppose JQA's decision to return to the political scene in Washington. Finally, his father's and his brother's financial affairs in Washington, especially the debt-ridden Columbian Mills, seemed to CFA to offer little hope of improvement. On these matters, see vol. 3:xxxi; 4:79–80, 92, 370, 424–425.

THURSDAY. 31ST.

A snow storm and the first we have had this season. It makes a great change in the appearance of things. However severe the cold may be, there is nothing of Winter until snow comes. I went to the Office. Examined and squared my Accounts for the month.

Then read Lingard whose fourteenth and last Volume I finished. His history has on the whole been quite interesting. It is avowedly written to sustain a religious party and is therefore occasionally rather disposed to conceal the true state of the Catholic question. But apart from this it is generally candid and disposed to sustain the liberal view of the British Constitution. I believe I shall now read James Macintosh for the purpose of rectifying.[1] And if this does not give me some basis in English History I do not know what will. I have an idea of undertaking an examination of American History from the beginning to help me in any future undertakings I may meditate. But it is dimly shadowed forth before me. I know not exactly where to begin. Supposing I were to write at the same time.

Did not walk today. Afternoon, I continued Anquetil's spirit of the Fronde. Character of Mazarin. How the world has been governed, and is and will be. Evening quiet at home. Caroline of Litchfield, Lady Craven and reviewing Wieland.

[1] Sir James Mackintosh was a writer for whom CFA came to feel a peculiar affinity and from whom he frequently derived stimulation. He returned to the reading of one or another of his historical or philosophical works again and again. The *History of England*, for example, which he was to pursue for the next several months, had been part of his reading program a little more than a year earlier; see vol. 4:165, 441.

FRIDAY. FEBY. 1ST.

The cold was severe this morning. And the presence of the snow added much to the reality of the Season. It was however very clear, and being now so late, we cannot have a long continuance of cold. I went to the Office. Engaged upon business matters. Then wrote a letter to my father [1] which was not exactly what I wanted to write but as I had tried twice before without success, I was resolved it should go. This consumed my time until one o'clock. I then foolishly went to the Athenæum and thereby lost my walk. My health is now in so doubtful a state that I ought to have avoided this.

Afternoon, copied my letter and read Anquetil. The famous day of the barricades. Civil commotion. Men must fight about something. If one thing will not answer another does. Here in the midst of prosperity, we are getting by the ears. I am glad to see by the morning's Newspapers some symptoms of retracting in Carolina. [2]

Read a Satire of Horace. I wonder I never read them attentively before. How admirable. Every sentiment so just in itself, so gracefully put in. I will read Horace perpetually, Make him familiar. [3]

Evening, a family party at Gorham's where my Wife went to tea. Edward Brooks, P. C. Jr. and Wife, Mr. Frothingham and do., Mr. Franklin Story and do., Mr. F. Gray and sister. [4] Not so pleasant as usual. More stiffness owing to the presence of the Grays who have little or no conversation. The Supper was one of far more form. I indulged more than usual and was apprehensive that my head would suffer for it. Home later than usual.

[1] LbC in Adams Papers.
[2] The *Columbian Centinel* carried reports from Charleston, S.C., of new indications of moderation from the nullification forces. A public meeting on 21 Jan. had passed a resolution of conciliatory tone, and an editorial in a leading organ of nullification declared

that "South Carolina does not design ... either to use force, make war, or dissolve the union" (1 Feb., p. 2, col. 6, p. 3, col. 2).

[3] CFA entered in his copy of the *Opera* by Horatius Flaccus (London, 1824), now at MQA, copious annotations, some of which are illustrated in the present volume; see also p. xiii, above.

These annotations were generally made after consultation with the scholarly edition of Dacier and Sanadon, 8 vols., Amsterdam, 1835, which was

among JA's books and is now at MB (*Catalogue of JA's Library*); see below, entry for 12 June. Later, CFA acquired for himself another copy also with J. M. Gesner's text but with notes by Zeunius (Horatius Flaccus, *Eclogæ* [i.e. *Opera*], Leipzig, 1802), which is at MQA; see below, entries for 18, 19 July.

[4] Mrs. Franklin Story (Elizabeth), Francis A. Gray, and Henrietta Gray, were the children of Peter C. Brooks' sister, Mary Brooks (Mrs. Samuel) Gray (vol. 3:8, 107, 237).

SATURDAY. 2D.

Cold morning. I went to the Office and was occupied in writing much of my time. I also read the debate which has lately taken place in the Senate between Mr. Calhoun and Mr. Webster upon the measures necessary to be taken by the Government in the contest with South Carolina.[1] The latter seems to be assuming a very commanding position in the Nation. He now again comes forward as the supporter of the Administration, and a popular Administration I would also add. The result remains to be seen.

Took a walk. Afternoon, after dining with my Wife at Mr. Frothingham's and drinking health to his eldest son on his birth day, I returned to my room and read Anquetil.

At six, as my Wife remained at her sister's, I thought I would drop in to hear the Concert.[2] On the whole, effect of it not agreeable. Mrs. Austin however sang effectively—Especially a fine air from Masaniello, which we did not hear in the piece. Did not like Miss Hughes nor Sinclair. Horne did pretty well, but his voice fails often. Out at nine. Called for Abby and returned home.

[1] The debate took place on 28 January.
[2] At the Masonic Temple (*Columbian Centinel*, 2 Feb., p. 2, col. 3).

SUNDAY. 3D.

Cold weather all comes together. I hope the first and the last attack. Read the second Satire of Horace which is obscene, and upon a subject hardly fit to be treated in so light a manner.

Attended divine Service, Mr. Frothingham in the morning. Text. Luke 15. 14. "And he began to be in want." The parable of the Prodigal Son. Allusion to the explanations of it. Considered as the gentile world. This rather far strained, may be considered more generally to be the spendthrift soul which after exhausting itself in vain efforts after happiness, begins to turn itself in a direction towards purer sources. Upon this the Sermon rested. Afternoon, Mr. Gannett. Matthew 12. 37. "By thy words thou shalt be justified and by thy words thou shalt be condemned." A discourse upon Conversation. The sin of impure, frivolous and idle conversation. The necessity of mixing a proportion of religion and morality in the intercourse of life. I thought the Sermon a good one, directed to a good end however far short it may be of it. Mr. Gannett gives no pleasure in his delivery. But he is a worthy, zealous man and goes to his point without circumlocution. I think he touches, because he produces the most perfect silence, an infallible test as it appears to me.[1]

Returned home and read a Sermon of Massillon upon the day of Judgment. Luke 21. 27. "And then shall they see the son of Man coming in a cloud with power and great glory." Division very simple— The fearfulness of this day to Sinners because they will be exposed 1. to themselves. 2. to others. The choice of the subject is not happy inasmuch as Man's mind cannot form any idea of the nature of the trial he is to undergo. The very vagueness forms its most fearful quality. The Deity will judge, that is enough. Evening, read Ruffhead. Afterwards, Mr. Degrand passed an hour.[2]

[1] For an earlier response to the preaching of Rev. Ezra Stiles Gannett of the Federal Street Church, see vol. 3:421.
[2] On P. P. F. Degrand, a Boston stockbroker who was a long-time political supporter of JQA and sometimes an embarrassing one through his habit of purveying political gossip, see vol. 1:155–156; 3:33, 90–91.

MONDAY. 4TH.

Still cold. Went to the Office. Letter from my Mother, but not a whit more encouraging.[1] They are all sick and always sick. Wrote Diary, and at eleven o'clock attended the Meeting of the Proprietors of Middlesex Canal. Report read. Directors chosen. Votes passed and adjourned. Attendance quite thin. Had no time for reading. Accounts a little while. Took a walk. Afternoon also somewhat cut up. Read some of Anquetil and finished the second Ode of Horace. Vile subject. Evening, attended the Annual Meeting of Proprietors of Boylston Market. Officers elected, usual business done. Attendance very thin. I was chosen Clerk again. This shall be the last year I believe. Returned home at Nine. Did nothing but my numbers of the World.

[1] Letter missing.

TUESDAY. 5TH.

Clear but the weather somewhat moderated. I went to the Office, and after my usual duties attended a Meeting of the Directors of the Middlesex Canal for the purpose of organizing. Just a quorum present. Business was all performed in a very few minutes. Rest of my time taken up in reading Mackintosh's History of England, Volume 2d. He takes somewhat original views of the early reigns. And after all I do not know but what he is right. My walk as usual.

In the Afternoon, which was shortened somewhat by reason of Mr. Brooks and Mr. Frothingham dining with me, I read Anquetil. But on the whole, since I have ceased writing, I have to reproach myself with a good deal of indolence. I do not know that I can justify to myself a life in which there is a little too much of luxury and idleness. Yet I am not so far gone as to be unwilling to work whenever I may have an opportunity. My energies must still be kept up in spite of the withering influence of wealth and ease.

Evening quietly at home. Finished the first volume of Caroline of Litchfield and the second of Lady Craven's Memoirs. Afterwards reviewed some of Wieland.

WEDNESDAY. 6TH.

Snow again. Our Winter comes all together. I went to the Office. Read a little of Sir James Mackintosh's History, the philosophical character of which I very much admire. Engaged also in Diary and Accounts. The regularity of my morning life does not admit of much detail.

Called at the Athenæum and took a walk notwithstanding the weather. I have felt better within a day or two. Afternoon, read Anquetil in quite a lazy way. The History of the French people is a history of civil commotion—Intrigue going on perpetually to acquire power. It is a remarkable feature of humanity, this constant grasping of authority—As if there was happiness in superiority. True, there may be, but it must be derived from the evil passions of the heart. Arrogance, vanity, pride, are those which it nurses. Our own Country is now a prey to the most violent struggles, and may be sacrificed because we have too many ambitious men.

Evening, quiet at home. Second volume of Caroline of Litchfield and Croker's Killarney Legends.[1] Read more of Wieland.

[1] Thomas Crofton Croker's *Killarney Legends*, London, 1831, was borrowed from the Athenæum.

THURSDAY. 7TH.

Sunrise clear, but it soon changed to a driving storm from the north west with excessive cold, and was on the whole as unpleasant a day as I have experienced this Winter. I went to the Office and was occupied in writing and reading as usual. Continued Mackintosh and admired him more and more. I was also out a good deal executing commissions. Attempted to walk but found it too much.

Returned home and made ready to dine at Mr. T. L. Winthrop's. The Company consisted of Mr. S. P. Gardner and J. L. Gardner, I. P. Davis, F. J. Oliver, Mr. Brooks and P. C. Jr., Grenville and Robert Winthrop. The only two ladies Miss W. and Mrs. Grenville.[1] I was placed next to the latter and Mr. Oliver, and I had a pretty stupid time. The Company was not one of any interest to me. Nor was there any valuable or lively conversation. Returned home. Mrs. Gorham Brooks took tea and spent the evening, he came in late. Nothing but the World.

[1] Thomas Lindall Winthrop had been until recently Lieutenant Governor of Massachusetts and was one of the few of the powerful figures in Boston who continued in friendly relations with JQA. His guest lists, as on this occasion, tended to mix the generations, including when possible fathers and sons, and even the sexes. Samuel Pickering Gardner, Isaac P. Davis, Francis J. Oliver, and Peter C. Brooks were among the wealthiest of Boston merchants, insurance executives, and capitalists. Davis and Brooks, along with Winthrop, were exceptions to the generalization that the ruling families in Boston were hostile to JQA; see, for example, the entry of 18 March, below, and the references to each in earlier volumes.

FRIDAY. 8TH.

Morning clear with a North West wind but milder than it has been. I went to the Office as usual. Received a letter from my Mother[1] of a tenor rather more encouraging than heretofore. My father has nearly recovered from his sickness, and all the family are better excepting the children. I read Sir James Mackintosh, and had one or two interruptions from applicants for the empty house. Called on T. Davis and Blake to ask them to dine with me tomorrow. I was then engaged on one or two Commissions. Thus passed the morning, terminated as it usually is by a walk.

After dinner Anquetil and the intrigues of Cardinal de Retz. Evening read at home, Caroline de Litchfield until nine, when my Wife and I went to a party at Mrs. A. H. Everett's.[2] A great many there and a very mixed assemblage. Few whom I ever knew. I endeavoured to make my bow to every body whom I did know. And to find something or other to say, but it is hard work. Mr. Gannett speaks the truth. The conversation of an evening party is disgraceful to intelligent beings. Returned home late and read the World.

[1] 3 Feb. (Adams Papers).
[2] On Mrs. A. H. Everett, the former Lucretia Orne Peabody, and her husband, see vol. 3:57–58.

SATURDAY. 9TH.

Cloudy and mild. I went to the Office and was engaged in my usual occupations. These were however somewhat interrupted by Commissions, as also by my endeavours to get a Company to dine with me. One or two of my acquaintances have declined and the consequence is that I am very much at fault. It is a little singular that in a place like this I should have so few friends. I believe the only intelligible explanation is to be found in my own character. The morning passed away and I had not made sure of filling my table of five guests. E. Blake, E. Quincy, T. K. Davis and Dr. E. G. Davis came[1]—Young men whom I know and of whom I entertain a very good opinion. It was the first dinner of any pretension that I had given and it passed off extremely well. My things were all pretty good and appeared to be very well relished. And the company sat more than three hours conversing very pleasantly. Evening quiet at home. I read to my Wife more of Caroline of Litchfield, a very prettily told Story. Afterwards, I wasted an hour, and read the numbers of the World.

[1] For CFA's views on Dr. Edward G. Davis, see vol. 3:240; on CFA's kinsman Edmund Quincy, see vol. 3:3, 96, 141, and Adams Genealogy.

SUNDAY. 10TH.

Mild and cloudy. A thaw seems to be taking place as if to remind us of the passage of the Winter. I passed an hour looking over the engravings of the Galerie de l'Hermitage de St. Petersbourg.[1] Some of them are very good. Attended divine Service all day and heard Mr. James Walker of Charlestown preach.[2] In the morning from Hebrews 12. 22. 23 and [2]4th. The Text is too long to extract. The subject was the immortality of the social affections. A pleasing idea, very pleasingly managed. Afternoon. 139 Psalm 23–4. "Search me, O God, and know my heart, try me and know my thoughts." "And see if there be any wicked way in me, and lead me in the way everlasting." Upon purity of thought. I remember distinct portions of this discourse, but have no idea of it as a whole. Mr. Walker is an agreeable as well as a sensible Preacher. I know few of the Clergy who rank above him. I afterwards read a Sermon by Massillon from Matthew 11. 6. "Blessed is he, whosoever shall not be offended in me." It was upon the utility of afflictions. He considered the natural effect of them as injured by three excuses prevailing in the world. 1. That people were too weak to bear them, which arose from the want of resolution in themselves. 2. That the afflictions themselves were excessive which is an injurious charge against the Deity. 3. That the incapacity to bear them excused all purpose of improvement. This Sermon shows conclusively what I have so often said, the bad effect of a perpetual division in heads. The same general idea runs through the whole. Evening quiet at home. Read Ruffhead, and afterwards Wieland.

[1] A copy of Musée Imperiale de l'Hermitage, *Notice sur les tableaux*, St. Petersburg, 1818, remains at the Athenæum.

[2] Rev. James Walker, whose wife was a cousin of ABA, was later President of Harvard College; see vol. 3:113.

MONDAY. 11TH.

Morning mild and cloudy. Snow fell during the night but the days are warm. Went to the Office. The news from Washington remains much the same. This Winter is verifying the fears which I have all along entertained in respect to my father's situation in Congress. His temperament as well as his situation very much unfit him for that body.[1] But it is useless for me to worry myself upon a subject over which I cannot have the least control. My anxiety can be shared by no one. I feel perhaps too sensitively the unfortunate effect upon his reputation, and also the very injurious operation which it reflects upon myself. Indeed as to me, my best way is to court retirement, to turn my attention as much as possible to literature. My course would become necessarily involved with that of my father, if I was at all in a public situation, the difficulty of which would be that I should have to differ or agree—Neither of which might suit my feelings. I must therefore seek private life. I must abandon any hope I may have entertained to keep up the reputation of my family, and must attempt by building up the reputation of a respectable man to give that feature to our character which perhaps it most wants, dignity. In this as in all things, I rely for support upon a higher power, who guides and governs us according to his will.

Dr. Phelps called upon me this morning. He came with a subscription paper for the Antimasonic Newspaper. It does not sustain itself. He wants me to subscribe to the Stock.[2] I considered of it and concluded to grant more than I was able, fifty dollars. It appears that he expected double the sum. I do not think that is reasonable. A case of this kind is a trial, and one must throw one's self completely upon one's own judgment. I took my ground and the Dr. left me to try one or two more with a promise of returning. My income for a year past has been large. But it depends somewhat upon the legislation of Congress how long it may continue—And other contingencies which are but too likely to turn out unfavourably. I feel it a most urgent duty to guard as far as I may against them, and I have therefore saved a portion of each year's receipts. As yet my endeavours have been crowned with success, and appear to be likely to ward off partially any blow, but they must not be remitted. I this day made an investment, but I know not how judiciously.

Short walk. Afternoon, Anquetil. And evening read Caroline of Litchfield, a very pretty tale, and Wieland.

[1] The immediate occasion for CFA's observations here would seem to be the debate on the tariff in which JQA was currently embattled. The morning papers reported *in extenso* JQA's speeches in the House on 31 Jan. and 1 Feb. (*Columbian Centinel*, 11 Feb., p. 1, cols. 5–7). The larger issues (adverted to here in the lines which follow) raised for CFA by JQA's insistence on remaining active in the political sphere are discussed at vol. 3:xxxi–xxxvii.

[2] Dr. Abner Phelps' appeal was in behalf of the *Boston Advocate*.

TUESDAY. 12TH.

A very bad day with rain which froze as it reached the ground and made the walking intolerable. I went to the Office and after regulating my Accounts as usual, and writing Diary, I sat down and read Mackintosh. I am really delighted with this Volume. It appears to me the most philosophical history I ever read, and at the same time loses none of the high moral and religious character without which it is not worth studying. How poor all my own thoughts and efforts seem to me in comparison. They appear to be the vapouring of an empty head in comparison with the rich store of a highly cultivated natural intellect. I am in despair as to myself. This is one of the very few books which produces upon me the effect which the works of the old masters have been said to upon painters.

After dinner Anquetil who writes well and is yet tedious. The truth is, his subject has no relief in it. A monotony of struggles, for selfish interests and the passions of a moment. No aspirations breathed out from the impulse of the higher principles of our nature. Evening quiet. Caroline of Litchfield and Wieland. I make very slow progress in German.

WEDNESDAY. 13TH.

More snow with a high wind and most unpleasant. I went to the Office where I now enjoy uninterrupted quiet and read Sir James Mackintosh whose book from the spirit in which it is written is charming. I sit down to it as to an intellectual treat of the first class and have only to regret that he did not accomplish his purpose of writing out in extenso the whole of the British History. I most of all admire the heroic moral tone by which the historian judges of human action. Calm, decided, yet benevolent in general. I could not walk again today.

Afternoon—Reading Anquetil which is a totally different history and yet drawn up with no little of talent. I am also engaged in assorting Pamphlets for the Bookbinder. They do accummulate immensely fast upon me.

Evening, finished Caroline of Litchfield, a pretty little trifle with a good deal of human nature and some pardonable romance. I begin to look at these things more mildly than I used to. Afterwards Wieland, the extracts from whom I finished. My time is perhaps not passed to the best advantage, and yet it goes quietly, happily, and not altogether unprofitably, I hope.

THURSDAY. 14TH.

A clear day at last. But the streets presented the appearance of winter with the quantity of ice in the streets and the immense icicles pendant from almost every house. Went to the Office and pursued quietly the study of Sir James Mackintosh whose book, I am sorry, is nearly finished. My quiet is perfectly preserved. I have not a soul to see me. This though it argues me unknown and unheeded is yet an exceedingly pleasant thing, for it avoids all the roughnesses of life which I see so thickly spread around more distinguished characters.

Walk, partly with Edmund Quincy. Afternoon, Anquetil, and Voltaire's History of the Parliament of Paris,[1] which I take up to understand the nature of that body and to explain some parts of Anquetil's work. The History of the Fronde is highly interesting.

My Wife went out to tea, and I took up a MS volume of my Grandfather's upon the negotiation of 1783, containing the copies of all the Papers.[2] That is a great subject in itself. I believe I must take it up in a scientific methodical way. Went to P.C.B. Jrs. Family and nobody else. Pleasant time. Home at ten.

[1] A copy of the 2-vol., Amsterdam, 1769, edition in French is at MQA.

[2] Probably one of the letterbook volumes in which were entered copies of the correspondence and papers of the 2d Joint American Commission, and which bear on their covers the words, "Peace 1782 1783": Adams Papers, Lb/JA/15, 20, 21 (Microfilms, Reels 103, 108, 109).

FRIDAY. 15TH.

Morning cloudy but it was pleasant afterwards. I went to the Office and finished the volume of Sir James Mackintosh. The closing sketch of the order of Jesuits is beautifully drawn up. I have expressed my opinion so repeatedly upon the merit of this work that nothing remains for me further to say.

I went to the Athenæum and looked over the Newspapers. An extraordinary union is taking place in Congress between Mr. Calhoun and Mr. Clay for the purpose of settling this question.[1] What the result will be in the Nation, and the fate of the parties, it is impossible to foresee, but I am somewhat fearful that we have reached the brazen age of our Nation.

Took a walk. Afternoon, reading Anquetil. My Wife went to Medford, and I dined alone. Read some of Voltaire's History of the Parliament. Abby returned to tea. Evening at home. Mr. Beale called in and passed an hour. Dipped into Montaigne.

[1] Calhoun had given his assent to Clay's proposal to modify the tariff to achieve an end of the crisis.

SATURDAY. 16TH.

Morning cloudy but it afterwards cleared away. I went to the Office and passed my time in Accounts. I was also engaged in reading the Newspapers, but on the whole I cannot say that my morning was profitably passed. Went to the Athenæum for the purpose of obtaining a new subject to read at my office but I did not succeed. I believe that my proper course would be now to commence my investigations into the history of our own Country. My principal difficulty is to know where to begin. The field is a tolerably wide one. And a vast deal of it is unknown to me. I must go over it faithfully.

Took a walk. In the afternoon read Anquetil finishing the third

Volume. Evening, read to my Wife some of Croker's Legends of Killarney, so poor a book that I do not think I shall be able to get through with it. Afterwards, read German. The little fables of Herder, which are pretty and easy.

SUNDAY. 17TH.

The snow now begins to disappear. A considerable body of it has been collecting gradually. Read Montaigne for an hour. His Chapter upon human inconsistency is admirable. I have not generally seen the merit of this Author, but that Chapter contains a deep insight into human nature.

Attended divine service all day. Mr. Frothingham preached, from John 9. 2. "And his disciples asked him, saying, Master, who did sin, this man or his parents, that he was born blind." He took upon himself to confute the idea that the Deity could be considered as punishing in the various dispensations which men in this world experienced—An idea which, he said, was familiarly cherished by the Hebrews and was even now somewhat entertained in the Christian world. With respect to the punishment of children for the faults of their fathers, I do not pretend to believe in it, although there is something in the apparent government of the Universe to cherish the idea. It would be exceedingly difficult however to convince me, that according to the laws governing man, he is not often made to pay the penance of his sin by his own suffering corporeal or mental, in this world. Even the hereditary complaints which are the consequences of vicious conduct most frequently, however they may seem to fall upon the innocent, fix no little mortification and suffering in the minds of the guilty persons. For myself, I must candidly confess that my own experience has shown me strongly the fact that I can not do wrong with impunity. Whatever intentional misconduct I may have been guilty of, has left no little of the suffering which has fallen to my share to atone for it. And on the other hand, the happiness of my life has invariably dated from the quiet performance of duty, not fully perhaps, but then not unwillingly.

Afternoon. Matthew 9. 8. "But when the multitudes saw it, they marvelled, and glorified God, which had given such power unto men." Text relates to a miracle, the performing of which has ceased. But the Sermon related to the power conferred ordinarily by the Deity upon man and divided it into five parts, the power over the productions of the earth, that over inferior creatures, that over the elements, over events and lastly the power of men over themselves.

31

On my return home, which was somewhat delayed by a visit at Mrs. Frothingham's, I read a Sermon of Massillon's for the occasion of the day of commemoration of the Virgin. Subject, Fidelity as exemplified in her, to be secured by measures of precaution, and by those of correspondence as he styles it, which I take to mean merely perseverance. The dangers of Fidelity under the first division are stated to be self weakness, the opinion of the world and the forgetfulness of grace, the measures of precaution are seclusion from and indifference to the judgments of men, and gratitude to be constantly cherished; under the second division, the dangers are from not pursuing as well as straying from the path of grace, both which must be avoided by perseverance. Quiet evening at home, finished Ruffhead and read Herder.

MONDAY. 18TH.

I went to the Office this morning but had scarcely got there before I perceived I had left my keys with the child to play with. The consequence was that I could do nothing. I therefore went down to the Athenæum to read the Newspapers and try to make up an opinion upon the speech and bill of Mr. Clay. On reflection, I think the speech is worse than the other. It is unstatesmanlike, and unsound. It gives no views that are either just or generous. It stamps the man.

I read or rather skimmed Henry Lee's publication in answer to the Memoirs of Jefferson. It falls into the very vice it blames. It is abusive to Jefferson, my grandfather and father, and lauds Hamilton. Mr. Lee has erred extremely. He might have made a strong case against his adversary if he had only been careful to avoid that kind of crimination which shows a partisan. His hostility to my father is excessive, considering that the latter has generally thought rather favourably of him. His moral character is so bad that no little pains ought to be taken by him to avoid unnecessarily aspersing those of others.[1]

Walk, and dined with Gorham Brooks at the Tremont House. Mr. Brooks, Mr. and Mrs. Frothingham and Abby. His wine is good. I returned home for half an hour which was wasted, and went down again to tea and the Theatre. Masaniello again. It was well done, home late. Read the World.

[1] Major Henry Lee of Virginia, for whom JQA entertained respect as a writer and whom he had appointed early in his Administration to a minor position in the Post Office Department, had while in that office been engaged in political writing for Calhoun. Upon resigning in 1826, Lee became a pamphleteer and newspaper propagandist for Jackson. Jackson had rewarded him with an interim appointment as consul general at Algiers but when his name was pre-

sented in the Senate, confirmation was denied on grounds of his profligacy and personal morals. His *Observations on the Writings of Thomas Jefferson*, N.Y., 1832, was the second book in which he undertook to defend his father, "Light-horse Harry" Lee, from what he judged to be unwarranted attacks. JQA, *Memoirs*, 7:180–182; 9:346–347; *DAB*.

TUESDAY. 19TH.

A mild day causing the streets to flow with the melted snow. I went to the Office and was engaged in writing and Accounts much of the morning to make up for the time lost yesterday. I stole an hour however to skim over Mr. Sparks' book upon Gouverneur Morris. Some of the letters are memorable. They go far to sustain the famous charge made by my father for which he has incurred so much of the enmity of the gentlemen here. I am glad they were published as historical memorials.[1]

Took a walk. Afternoon Anquetil in whose work I am progressing gradually. I also go on with Voltaire's History of the Parliament of Paris. As my Wife was out to take Tea, I took up by way of relaxation Johnson's Preface to Shakespeare. I have read it half a dozen times, and each time with renewed admiration. I went down to Mrs. Frothingham's at eight. Mr. and Mrs. Gorham Brooks, Miss Dehon and a sister, and my Wife. We remained until ten.

The Community here is quite moved by a case of suicide in a young couple, which was discovered yesterday.[2] The usual morbid curiosity is displayed upon it, in hunting up details and causes. For my part, I think such things had better be kept out of sight. After the circumstances are once known and the misfortune regretted, it serves no purpose to go farther.

[1] The publication of a portion of Gouverneur Morris' correspondence (Jared Sparks, *The Life of Gouverneur Morris, with Selections from his Correspondence*, 3 vols., Boston, 1832) provided substantiation for the view that Morris and the Federalists of the Essex Junto, between whom there were close ties in their effort to combat Republicanism from 1804 to the Hartford Convention of 1814, did indeed look to and advocate the dissolution of the Union. JQA, against whom the Federalists in Boston had maintained an unrelenting opposition since his term in the Senate during which he had supported the Louisiana Purchase and the Embargo Bill, had aroused them to a new fury and to new denials by charging in the *National Intelligencer* (21 Oct. 1828) that the Junto in 1807–1808 had been "engaged in a plot to dissolve the Union and re-annex New England to Great Britain" and thereafter by maintaining his ground following the pamphlet-publication of their defense. For the definitive justification which JQA had prepared but not published, the Adamses sought just such evidence as was supplied in Morris' correspondence with Timothy Pickering and others of the faction. On the long history of the quarrel, see vol. 2:297, 311–312, 317, 343–344, 350–351; 3:63; Bemis, *JQA*, 1:195, 575–576; 2:161–176; HA, *New England Federalism*.

[2] The bodies of John Carter, twenty-three, and Mary Bradlee, twenty, were

found suspended by their necks in her father's store on Washington Street. Parental consent had been withheld to their marriage, which would have been followed by the couple's moving to New Orleans (*Columbian Centinel*, 19 Feb., p. 2, col. 6).

WEDNESDAY. 20TH.

Another mild day. Office. Diary and Gouverneur Morris. Many good points about him, but he was an intriguer as there have been few. He wanted to bring out General Washington against my Grandfather on account of the course of the latter in regard to the French treaty. I think it is to be regretted that General W. did not live to answer his application. Of that however I do not know. How much is it to be desired that the papers of General Washington should be published. Mr. Sparks has the care of that too.[1]

Walk. Afternoon, Anquetil continued—Intrigue, Mazarin, de Retz, Condé, three men perhaps of equal ability though of unequal honesty. Three men who put France to the torture for many years merely to gratify their own selfish purposes. Went on with Voltaire. I have done writing. Who is the gainer? Certainly, I am. Perhaps every body.

Evening, Miss Julia Gorham and Thomas Frothingham took tea, the former went in with us to see Mrs. Jos. Quincy. Quiet evening. Returned at ten.

[1] See vol. 4:xii–xiii.

THURSDAY. 21ST.

A change of twenty degrees in the atmosphere made us feel as if we had not absolutely bid good bye to Winter. I went to the Office as usual and divided my time in the way I commonly do. Pursued the reading of Gouverneur Morris. There is just enough published to show what remains behind. I would give a good deal to be able to read the letters to him of which those published are the replies. Mr. Sparks has exercised considerable caution in his selections. Yet another might have done worse.

Took a walk. Met Judge Rodgers, a singular mind. Afternoon, Anquetil whose account of de Retz's escape from death at the meeting of the Parliament is extremely interesting. He was an extraordinary genius.

In the evening went to Gorham Brooks'. Mr. and Mrs. J. Gardner and Mr. N. Silsbee Jr. Supped there and returned home late. I am becoming so tired of this way of life which is altogether new to me, that I hope the time is not distant when we may be allowed to change it for a more quiet and domestic one. Above all, my studies suffer exceedingly.

FRIDAY. 22D.

A beautiful day. I went to the Office later than usual, having been engaged by Conant from Weston who came at last with some Wood, and he also paid me a sum of Money.[1] Time taken up in writing and reading.

Made a little progress in Gouverneur Morris. It is to his credit that he was opposed to the miserable expedient resorted to by the Federal party to prevent the election of Mr. Jefferson. His subsequent conduct is not in accordance with that beginning.

I walked earlier than usual to accompany Mr. Peabody.[2] Dined at Mrs. Blake's with a few young men invited by Edward. R. Sturgis, W. E. Payne, N. Silsbee Jr., a Mr. Baker from Northampton, I believe, S. P. Blake and the ladies. Conversation tolerably pleasant—A good deal of it political. How difficult it is for a man to talk much and be prudent. Yet if he does not talk, he is voted a bore. I endeavour always to be guarded but my tongue now and then outruns my reason. We got up from table at about seven o'clock and I went home.

Quiet evening with my Wife. Read to her a little more of the Legends of Killarney which are poor enough. I afterwards looked over the Introduction to Alison on Taste.[3]

[1] Silas (or Amory) Conant remained as lessee of the farm and woodland at Weston bequeathed to JQA by W. N. Boylston. See vol. 2:228; 3:17, 20; 4:294.

[2] Oliver William Bourn Peabody, brother-in-law of A. H. Everett and his assistant at the *North Amer. Rev.*, occupied the office just across from CFA's at 23 Court Street and was a frequent walking companion (vol. 3:336, 378–379).

[3] The reading of Archibald Alison's *Essays on the Nature and Principles of Taste* (1790) marked a renewal of CFA's continuing interest in 18th-century treatises on the principles of art.

SATURDAY. 23RD.

Another delightful day. I went to the Office. Read my father's Speech[1] and pored over the Intelligencer until I was weary. Then read more of the letters of Gouverneur Morris. I find I appropriate only an hour or at most two of the morning in any reading. Another, for walking, and the rest divides itself into writing, Accounts and Newspapers. Is this working to the best advantage.

I walked and went to inquire about Wood, but found it high. Returned home and thence to dine at P. C. Brooks Jr.'s with my Wife. Nobody else. Returned at four and read Anquetil. This is a book that does not require much study, but I began Alison on Taste which cannot be read superficially to any purpose. Returned in the evening to bring back my Wife. Supper. I did little afterwards.

The last week has been given up far too much to dissipation. It unsettles my mind and disorders my body. It injures my taste for that simplicity of life which is after all the great end of human existence, or rather I would say, the true means, by which the great ends are accomplished.

[1] On the tariff, delivered in the House on 4 February.

SUNDAY. 24TH.

The day was cloudy with mist, rain, hail and finally snow. I passed the morning in reading Alison on Taste. A correct idea of the principles of taste is essential to good writing. I think I have not got it. Mr. Alison resolves it into a train of simple emotions occasioned by the association of certain qualities with certain objects or subjects, in the imagination. Why is it that any such association takes place? I must read Mr. Burke's Essay over again.[1] It is wonderful how little I gain by reading.

Attended divine worship. Prof. S. Willard. Genesis 2. 3. "And God blessed the seventh day and sanctified it, because that in it he had rested from all his work which God created and made." Upon the institution of the Sabbath, the importance of sustaining it, and the medium to be drawn between the rigidity of Puritanic observance and the laxity of that of the Catholics. We are such regular observers of the Sabbath that upon this subject time is almost thrown away. Certainly so, so far as the arguments brought forward in this discourse are concerned. For the rest, the Sermon was dull enough.

Afternoon, Mr. Frothingham. James. 1. 27. "Pure Religion." The words are taken arbitrarily from their connection. A short discussion of what it really is, not theology, not a dogma or ecclesiastical ceremony, but a belief in the superintending government of a divine being. It is true that men often err in their ideas of the true nature of religion. There are extremes on each side, and that which totally decries the usefulness of the external ceremony is far the most dangerous. Read a Sermon of Massillon. Text, John 1. 23. "I am the voice of one crying in the wilderness. Make straight the way of the Lord." Subject, the pretexts for delay in conversion: 1. the want of grace which is making the Deity assume our fault, 2. the indulgences of self, the pleas of youth, the violence of the passions, the difficulty of a change of life. I was not struck with the Discourse.

Evening. Read a little of a British History of the United States [2] and Alison on Taste. My German again lags.

[1] CFA had read Edmund Burke's essay on taste in 1824 and again in 1828; see vol. 1:383; 2:285-295 *passim*.

[2] In Lardner's *Cabinet Cyclopædia*, vols. 103-104; see vol. 4:108; below, entry for 17 March 1833.

MONDAY. 25TH.

A sudden change in the weather which has brought down the Thermometer again quite low. At the Office. I get no News from home. My father's last Speech seems to have been quite a successful one.[1] I hear of it from several quarters. Engaged this morning in writing and reading Morris as usual. He had made up his mind to a dissolution of the Union. And he was not afraid to say so.

Took a walk and ordered a further provision of fuel for the winter. It is extraordinary what an amazing amount of this I am in the practice of consuming. Nobody can live in this climate without considerable resources. This is the cause of the high price of labour, provisions &c. Afternoon, Anquetil whose book is drawing to a close—Not much to my regret for I am tired of intrigue.

Evening with my Wife and Mrs. G. Brooks to the Theatre. The White Lady of Avenel. Music of Boieldieu. "No" and the last Act of the Tempest for the benefit of Mrs. Austin.[2] The Opera is pretty, the music is light and airy and in character with the Scotch scene to which it is adapted, the combined pieces are however of considerable difficulty and above the powers of the performers. The Auction Chorus at the close of the second act requires far more practice to give it, it's full effect, and one or two trios entirely failed owing to the difficulty of the singers. Sinclair and Mrs. Austin sustained the piece. For the rest, it has neither the brilliancy of Masianello, nor the ringing melodiousness of Cinderella. After all, Rossini is my favourite.

Returned very late. We heard to day of the death of Mrs. Everett's new born infant.

[1] " 'Il n'y a qu'heur et malheur dans ce monde' says Jean Jacques Rousseau. Little did I imagine that my *chiffon* of a Speech upon the Southern Machinery, would have been the most popular thing I ever did or said. I never spoke upon any important topic, with so little preparation. I was too unwell to make any suitable preparation. I had given up the idea of speaking upon the Subject at

all. . . . I had commenced it at an early period of the Session and had been obliged to lay it aside half finished despairing of being able to bring it to a close before the close of the Session. I was urged however by some of my Colleagues to say something" (JQA to CFA, 13 March, Adams Papers).

[2] The program at the Tremont Theatre consisted of *The White Lady, or The Spirit of Avenel* in which Mr. Sinclair, Mrs. Austin, and Mrs. Barrymore sang; *No*, a farce, sung by Mr. Sinclair and Miss Hughes; and Mrs. Austin as Ariel in the last act of *The Tempest* (*Columbian Centinel*, 25 Feb., p. 3, col. 4).

TUESDAY. 26TH.

Weather quite cold. At the Office after another business delay with Conant, the Tenant at Weston. Received by Mail, a copy of Mr. Appleton's Speech from Mr. Everett. Affairs at Washington still remain in a very doubtful state. I studied the Intelligencer and finished the volume of Gouverneur Morris. On the whole, so far I have derived a very mixed idea of his character. That he had a great deal of talent is I think quite clear. That he was an intriguer is also pretty evident. Above all he had a very great idea of his power in political foresight which events will not fully justify. A man of common observation after considering attentively the course of events will hazard half a dozen distinct conjectures as to results, and the probability will be that in some of them he will be right. If it does so turn out, he forgets those in which he has failed, and forthwith sets up as an oracle, on the strength of his success. Morris predicted a military Government for France, but he also insisted upon the weakness and exhaustion of the Revolutionary government. He foretold the result of the French struggle, but he was outrageously mistaken in regard to our own. With him the United States were ruined when the Judiciary bill was repealed, the new Bank was to throw every thing into confusion, and Mr. Madison had destroyed our prosperity. These are the dreams of a party visionary. Seventeen years have shown their utter futility.

Athenæum and a walk. Afternoon Anquetil. Evening at home. Tried two or three books but disliked them all. Alison on Taste. Glad to have a quiet evening.

WEDNESDAY. 27TH.

The Child has not appeared well within a few days. She shows sickness almost immediately. I know no anxiety equal to that which any symptoms of that kind in her create. My trust is always in a higher power, and yet I feel as if I was almost too deeply attached for this world. It brings it's own punishment in the care it occasions.

Mild weather in the morning, but it cleared off cold at night. Went to the Office but my time was wasted. I had not my regular work, so I began a letter to my father but did not go on with it. Somehow I cannot write as I used to. The rest of my time was passed in destroying the remainder of the loose papers which had been in a box in my other room, and which I perceived today had been ransacked in all probability by some of my Office boys. A troublesome set which would joyfully be dispensed with by me if I could hit upon any other mode of getting my work done. Poor George. He had many, many good qualities. And when I remember what he might have been, it makes me feel more deeply the singular weakness of humanity.[1]

Walk. Afternoon, Anquetil. I find he was a Catholic priest which dissipates my wonder at his notions about religious liberty. Voltaire. And Alison. He lays it down that nothing in this world is *in itself* beautiful. Is this true? And if it is, does it not fundamentally destroy the argument of the existence of a deity from his works, or in other words, natural religion? To say that things are beautiful or sublime merely because the mind of man associates certain qualities with certain things, leaves every point to the decision of human caprice. If there is nothing beautiful or sublime in the material world but what is arbitrarily pitched upon by the fancy of man, it will be hard to deny the same assertion when applied to the moral universe. And where will this lead? But I am plunging deep into metaphysics.

My Wife took tea out. Family party at Mrs. Frothingham's. P.C. and Gorham Brooks and ladies, Edward, Miss C. Dexter and Wife and myself. Tolerably pleasant. Returned at ten and got upon Architecture and building.

[1] The destruction of the mass of papers left in the Court Street office by his brother George (GWA) was an occupation to which CFA frequently returned, and almost always with melancholy reflections on GWA's unrealized talents. See, for example, vol. 3:xxxi–xxxii, 6–7, 217, 219, 347, 364.

THURSDAY. 28TH.

Our changes of weather are abrupt enough. It was severely cold this morning. I went to the Office where I pursued my common avocations. Read a little of Mr. Sparks' Memoir of Gouverneur Morris which is flat and dry enough. The fashion of unadorned prose is very prevalent in the present day but I cannot say that it strikes me as particularly charming. I want something to stir people up. I want to see the higher kinds of style.

Went to the Athenæum and was therefore very considerably abridged of my walk. N.B. Never to go there at or near one o'clock.

Afternoon, Anquetil. Account of the murderous conflict in the suburbs of Paris, between the armies of Turenne and Condé. Very interesting. Read more of Voltaire. The Parliament of Paris. He hardly is distinct as to the present constitution of it. He wrote for such as were familiar with it. Evening quiet at home. My Wife was suffering with a head ach and the Child has hardly been well all day. Read Alison whose argument is ingenious but hardly convincing.

MARCH. 1833
FRIDAY. 1ST.

Heavy snow for the first Spring day. I went to the Office and was pretty well occupied all the morning. Had a call from Mr. George W. Pratt who came to pay a sum of money on Acct. of a final Dividend of Bird & Savage's Estate in London. I received and deposited it although it belongs to the Estate of my Grandfather.[1] Edward Blake also paid a short visit to talk about the passage of Mr. Clay's bill. One of the singular manœuvres that at times occur in public bodies has driven it through both houses. This Country has never witnessed a baser dereliction of principle.[2] I can take to myself the credit of having foreseen it. Read a little of Gouverneur Morris and omitted my walk on account of the weather. Afternoon, Anquetil, and Voltaire. I took some time to write to my father whose engagements will cease before my letter reaches him.[3] Evening quiet at home. Read a little of Madame de Genlis' "Parvenus" and Mrs. Child's Mother's book, which is a good practical view of education.[4]

[1] The failure of the London banking house of Bird, Savage, & Bird in 1803 had imposed severe financial strain at the time upon both JA, whose funds were temporarily on deposit there, and JQA, whose decision it had been to place them there. Receipt of the dividend noted here constituted repayment in full of the debt which had been liquidated in installments during the intervening years (JQA, *Memoirs*, 1:262-264).

[2] The maneuvering by which the compromise effected in the tariff bill by Clay was adopted in House and Senate is deplored in an editorial in the *Columbian Centinel*, 1 March, p. 2, col. 4.

[3] LbC in Adams Papers.

[4] Both *Les Parvenus* by Stéphanie Félicité Ducrest de St. Aubin, Comtesse de Genlis, and the *Mother's Book* by Lydia Maria Child were borrowed, as were several others of the works CFA was currently reading, from the Athenæum.

SATURDAY. 2ND.

Snow and a feeble Shine alternated, but towards evening the wind rose and produced a degree of cold greater than any thing we have had this winter. I went to the Office and was engaged most of my time in bringing up all my Accounts for Agency as well as on private matters for the last month. This is a business necessary but hardly agreeable.

Attempted a walk with Mr. Peabody, but it was so unpleasant we shortened it considerably. Political affairs at Washington look gloomy. There is very little confidence to be put in any body or in the permanence of any thing. The wild anarchical principle is a little too powerful by this system of our's.

Afternoon, copied my letter to my father and read more of Anquetil. His book is a history of the passions of the human race. By a process of induction gained from such experiences as those and which are to be found in almost every Country, you could almost make up a book of formulas, representing the course of men upon certain contingencies. Patriotism in its noblest and purest form is a very scarce plant. Our world is too cold for it.

Evening quietly at home. Read Madame de Genlis, and Mrs. Child's book after which I made progress in Alison's book. I subdivide my occupations a little too much for my own advantage.

SUNDAY. 3D.

Excessively cold, with a sharp wind which makes it intrude into houses through every crevice. The suffering of cold is much increased by wind.

I finished Alison on Taste, this morning. There is a good deal of ground for his principal position that objects are only the signs by which we express certain qualities or affections of the mind, but I cannot assent to it entirely. Because we must say that the beauty of the Created Universe is a mistake, there is no beauty in it any farther than the idea of fitness to arouse certain emotions of men. *I* must still believe that there is beauty in itself—That the Divinity created the Universe not for man's faculties, any more than he created Man for the Universe. The whole was framed upon one great plan which could have been regulated on no plan but one that embraced sublimity and beauty. I mean if we admit a Deity at all.

Attended divine service and heard Mr. Frothingham from Romans. 6. 5. "If we have been planted together in the likeness of his death, we shall be also in the likeness of his resurrection." A Sermon in some sort preparatory to Communion. In the afternoon, Mr. J. O. Sargent, a young man [1] discoursed from 1. Kings 19. 12. "After the fire, a still small voice." It was a young man's production, upon a text he justly called sublime. It considered the account as representing the modesty of power, it's unostentatiousness. True enough. But without the knowledge of the power that existed, the voice would strike one but little. The voice was accompanied by all the signs of the most exalted strength, and it is the contrast which makes the sublimity.

At home in the Afternoon. Read Massillon. Luke 3. 4. "Prepare ye the way of the Lord, make his paths straight." Subject, the disposition suitable for Communion, requiring faith, 1. of respect which distinguishes good from evil. 2. of prudence which submits to trial 3. of love which inspires ardor 4. of generosity which meets sacrifices. Evening passed quietly at home. Conversation, not of a very profitable kind. Afterwards, began Burke on the Sublime over again.

¹ John Osborne Sargent, Harvard 1830.

MONDAY. 4TH.

This is the day upon which General Jackson is inaugurated a second time. The People have made him President, and for once they have in their blindness done better than if they had tried to see. This Country seems to be under divine protection though I cannot say that I see it's merits. We are a very sinful People in many respects.

At the Office. Read the Intelligencer and a copy of Mr. Arnold's Speech sent to me by my father.¹

Surprised exceedingly by the appearance at my Office of T. B. Adams. I thought him at Pittsburgh. He has a furlough for a couple of months and has come to see his mother.² We conversed a great deal upon affairs at Washington where he was lately, and upon the condition of the various members of the family. His accounts are on the whole favourable. Read a little of Morris and took a walk.

¹ Thomas Dickens Arnold, Representative from Tennessee.
² Mrs. TBA, a widow since March 1832, continued to live in Quincy but with only one of her six children still at home (vol. 3:29; 4:259). Her eldest son, lieutenant in the U.S. Army, was a principal stay in adversity.

TUESDAY. 5TH.

If one should judge of the month by the weather, one might readily suppose that we had committed an error in calculation, and that February was just beginning. The Thermometer was at zero this morning.

I went to the Office and was engaged as usual in accounts, diary and a little of Gouverneur Morris. Mr. Sparks is again at his tricks about the negotiation of the French Treaty. He seems determined to exalt Franklin and Deane at the expense of my Grandfather. Such is history. Even posthumous fame depends upon the miserable conceits of this or that prejudiced brain.[1] I reflected upon this during my walk, and upon the stormy life led by my father and grandfather. They sacrificed much for the benefit of the Country, and the Country has in return held them to a far more severe account for their private faults than it has felt gratitude for their public services. That such a man as Jefferson should be an idol and my Grandfather detested—That Jackson should be lauded to the skies and my father persecuted is perhaps a hard measure of justice between the merits of the men.

Afternoon, finished Anquetil without regret. Began the Memoirs of Cardinal de Retz.[2] There is a vast deal of knowledge of the world and profound remark in his book. Evening quiet at home. Burke on the Sublime.

[1] On the Adams view of Jared Sparks' bias revealed in his edition of the *Diplomatic Correspondence of the American Revolution* and elsewhere, see vol. 3:160–161; 4:xii–xiii, 214–215. For JA's accounts of his controversies with Franklin, his fellow commissioner, and with Silas Deane, his predecessor, see JA, *Diary and Autobiography*, 2:304 ff., 345–350; 4:43, 68 ff. See also *Adams Family Correspondence*, 3:xxiii–xxv, 186–188, 229, 232, 394–395; 4:165–168, 173, 175, 180, 183–184, 189–190.

[2] JA's copy of *Mémoires, contenant ce qui s'est passé de remarquable en France pendant les premières années du regne de Louis XIV* by Jean François Paul de Gondi, Cardinal de Retz, 4 vols., Geneva, 1777, is among his books now at MB. See *Catalogue of JA's Library*.

WEDNESDAY. 6TH.

I was detained all the morning in the Supreme Court Room because I wished to obtain admission as a Counsellor, not that I have any object in it. My practice is nothing, but I wish at least to retain my standing in society.[1] A cause upon the nature of the liabilities of a master for his servants' acts was interposed so that I was not released until one o'clock which is my regular time for walking.

Met E. Quincy. He informed me of the death of young Joy which I was very sorry to hear, although he was only an acquaintance.[2] Afternoon, reading Cardinal de Retz whose book is in many respects charming. He was an accomplished rascal, and a dangerous one inasmuch as he had many merits which concealed and palliated his faults. He writes in a way to show his fairest side, yet a little reflection will show that his foundations are all rotten.

My Wife went to Medford in the Afternoon, and she and I went to a party at the house of Mr. and Mrs. F. C. Lowell.[3] It was handsome. I enjoyed myself about as much as usual and returned home before midnight.

[1] Although CFA did have a client or two from time to time, he made no effort to pursue an active legal practice. He was assiduous, however, in observing the formalities required to advance through the several classes into which the Massa-chusetts bar was divided (vol. 4:1–2).

[2] Joseph Barrell Joy died in Matanzas, Cuba, on 15 Feb. (*Columbian Centinel*, 11 March, p. 2, col. 5).

[3] At 53 Beacon Street (*Boston Directory*).

THURSDAY. 7TH.

The Season just begins to show signs of moderating. It is somewhat late in the month of March to do so, but in this as in many other things it may truly be said, "better late than never." The preceding is a very silly remark.

I went to the Office. No news from home. Occupied as usual. Mr. Sparks gives me more of a trial of patience than he deserves. He is dry and hard in his manner. Took a walk. Afternoon somewhat shortened by having Mr. Brooks dine with me. He appears to enjoy life more than ever. He has been a prosperous as well as an industrious man. He has gone through life upon principles which ensure success to a certain extent, though he has gone by the assistance of fortune far beyond it. Read Cardinal de Retz. Passages are dry. They contain details of intrigues in the Parliament of Paris. Finished Voltaire's Account which is the least interesting work of his that I have ever read.

Evening, Mrs. Adams and I paid a visit to a bride, Mrs. J. T. Stevenson. He is the Dr. S's brother and looks very much like him. A good deal of company. We remained half an hour and upon our return stopped in at our neighbour Fullerton's. A musical party. I went in because we had been several times invited and declined.[1] Mr. and Mrs. Sinclair and several other singers. I knew but few of the people. Mr. and Mrs. W. Lee, Miss Mary Otis and the Dixwells.[2] The singing was good, and we did not return until nearly midnight.

[1] J. J. Fullerton's interests included painting as well as music; see vol. 4:305–306.
[2] These acquaintances are identified at vol. 1:269; 3:355; 4:427.

FRIDAY. 8TH.

A mild and pleasant air in the early part of the day although the wind went round to the Eastward afterwards. The walking very bad from the melting of the snow. I went to the Office. Read the President's Inaugural Address—A very prudent performance which expresses enough of each side to be perfectly safe. Did some business with Mr. Degrand and made an investment on my father's Account of some surplus Money that was lying in my hands. I accomplished a good deal of Gouverneur Morris. This with my walk finished the morning.

Afternoon at home. P. C. Brooks Jr. came in to tell us of the fears entertained of the fate of Mr. Dehon, the father of Mrs. Sidney Brooks. She has come from New York with her husband in consequence.[1] The poor man has been in the utmost embarrassment in his affairs for some time, and it is feared he may have made away with himself. It is a week since the family have had no tidings of him. How much suffering there is in this world.

Read more of de Retz. Evening quietly at home. Read to my Wife. After which finished Burke on the sublime, and the World. This is the most indifferent of the Essayists that I have yet read. The tone is too light to be useful and yet too heavy to be amusing. There is much coarseness in many of the Papers under the idea of Wit, and the ironical is altogether too profusely general. I am glad to have finished it.

[1] Sidney Brooks, brother of ABA, had lived in New York since his marriage five years earlier; his wife Frances was the daughter of William Dehon (see vol. 3:4, 36, and Adams Genealogy).

SATURDAY. 9TH.

Fine morning. I went to the Office and passed my time pretty industriously there. Read more of the life of Gouverneur Morris and of his intriguing disposition in France. He was an Aristocrat in feeling. His connections were Tories and although he emancipated himself from their bondage, he retained through life the marks which had been printed in early life.

Went to the Athenæum to read the comments that the principal Newspapers make upon public affairs. Mr. Clay comes out rather brighter than has been anticipated. Success is the great rule by which public men are tried. It saved my father in his critical position of last year, and it will probably extricate Mr. Clay now. The principles which produced both measures, will remain open for discussion in future years.

As my Wife went to Medford, I dined at P. C. Brooks Jr's. Salt fish and Mr. and Mrs. with the two Miss Olivers.[1] Nothing peculiar. Returned home and read De Retz. My Wife got back to tea. Quiet evening at home. Sidney Brooks called in and sat an hour. He told us more of

Mr. Dehon's absence. The better opinion seems to be that he was in a state of the utmost mental anguish and on a stormy night of last week wandered away and was frozen under some snow bank.

[1] Probably the Francis J. Oliver family, relatives of Mrs. P. C. Brooks Jr., who was Susan Oliver Heard.

SUNDAY. MARCH 10.

A lovely day. I read some of the History of the United States this morning. A feeble book. Attended divine service and heard Mr. Frothingham preach from 1. Corinthians 15. 26. "The last enemy that shall be destroyed, is death." It was an attempt to treat the subject of death in connexion with two or three losses that have happened in the Society lately, more especially that of young Joy. I thought it a little heavy. Discourses of that kind must distress a Clergyman greatly. There is no room for any particular eulogy, and common places are tiresome.

Mr. J. D. Green in the Afternoon from Romans 12. 2. "Be not conformed to this world." Public opinion as a standard of moral conduct. Its fluctuating character and innate defectiveness. A common subject, simply treated. It is a prevailing vice among us. The judgment of the public is not the proper rule, but it is rigidly imposed as such in this Community. On my return home I read Massillon. Luke 2. 10–11. "I bring you good tidings of great joy, which shall be to all people. For unto you is born this day a Saviour, which is Christ the Lord." On the Nativity, considered as having produced 1. Glory to God, 2. peace to men. The sermon was a good one.

Evening quietly at home. Resumed my German and read the Connoisseur,[1] being the next of the Essayists in order.

[1] CFA's copy of *The Connoisseur*, 2 vols., London, 1822, is at MQA.

MONDAY. 11TH.

The Winter will not leave us. This morning we had snow and sleet and weather altogether disagreeable. I went to the Office. Nothing new. Wrote a good deal and made some progress in Sparks, the latter part of whose book is very cautiously worded indeed. He says but little respecting the violent days of the embargo and the war.

Took my usual walk. In the afternoon, I attended a meeting of the stockholders of the Boylston Insurance Co. for the purpose of learning something in regard to their Affairs. Found them not so well off as

I anticipated. The amount of business is so trifling that any loss comes hardly. They have no means of setting aside a reserve to meet it and make Dividends too. I crossed over and then attended a Meeting of the Directors of the Boylston Market. Nothing material done. A good deal of talk about that stock. Mr. Williams[1] would give 130 for it. He will drive every body out of the Market literally.

Quiet evening. Read Madame de Genlis and Mrs. Child. Afterwards, Herder.

[1] John D. W. Williams; see vol. 3:150–151.

TUESDAY. 12TH.

Morning mild but cloudy and rain. I went to the Office and was occupied as usual. Finished Mr. Sparks' book. He is a writer who has gained reputation by the absence of every thing that can interest any body. He is not a bit more attractive than an old Almanack. Yet having got hold of the subject of the American Revolution, he interests people through that and makes money. Gouverneur Morris lived a life which might have been made vastly amusing.

Went to the Athenæum. Learnt that the body of Mr. Dehon had been found in the harbour. Poor man. Life's fitful fever is over. He is before another and a final tribunal.

Afternoon read Cardinal de Retz. He is composing a Manual for an Intriguer. He affects a candour in judging of himself which he does not feel, and claims a merit which he does not deserve. His principle was a sham. His life a disgrace.

Evening, finished the first volume of Madame de Genlis' "parvenus." I wonder what could have given her books so much success. To me they are intolerably tedious. A letter in the life of Gouverneur Morris gives some insight into her own character. Another intriguer. Finished Mrs. Child's book. Afterwards, Read German which continues exceedingly difficult.

WEDNESDAY. 13TH.

Morning wet and mild but it afterwards cleared away with a North Wester. I went to the Office and was somewhat occupied. Mr. Curtis came in with General Towne from Worcester County. And they wished me to draw up a Deed and Mortgage for the purpose of selling the remainder of the land owned by Mr. Boylston at Princeton in the homestead, with the exception of the 600 Acres reserved.[1] They wanted it done by noon tomorrow, so that I worked pretty steadily until one and finished all but the description, which for the present, I merely put into a rough draft.

Took a walk. On my return home found Miss Elizabeth Phillips who has come to spend some days with my Wife. She has altered much since I first saw her. Her spirits have not yet recovered from the shock experienced by the behaviour of her lover.[2] Afternoon, reading de Retz whose book does not hold on perfectly from its containing a little too much of the same thing. Evening, read one of Horace's Satires, though they are misnamed, and then went to a little party given to the bride Mrs. Stevenson—Only forty or fifty people and a little fatiguing. We got home at half past ten.

[1] Upon the death of Ward Nicholas Boylston of Jamaica Plain and Princeton, Mass., JQA and Nathaniel Curtis of Roxbury, appointed by his will as coexecutors, made CFA conveyancer for the estate. General Salem Towne had been the purchaser of several parcels of the extensive land holdings. See vol. 3:5, 78, 85–86.

[2] Elizabeth Phillips, a cousin of ABA's from Andover, had, a few months earlier, been jilted on the evening intended for the wedding; see vol. 3:146; 4:416.

THURSDAY. 14TH.

Clear, bright day. I was engaged most of the morning in finishing off the deed and Mortgage, in comparing the description of the bounds with General Towne and in talking over the matter with Mr. Curtis. Ayer, the Carpenter then came in and we talked over the repairs necessary to be made upon the House lately occupied by Mr. Brackett.[1] He gave me an estimate which I found too high, and I then appointed him to go down there tomorrow at ten o'clock. Not much time was left me, and I went to the Athenæum to get a book on Architecture. Found nothing less than the Encyclopedia. From thence, I went to consult Dr. Hayward, a Surgeon of some eminence.[2] For two or three years past I have found myself troubled with wens which have been increasing in number as well as in size. How or why they come I cannot divine, but as the prospect of their disfiguring me was very unpleasant, I have made up my mind to have them extracted. The Operation was short and not painful. So that I went to dinner as usual. Afternoon I felt easier because I was disembarrassed of three in my head. I am afraid I have more.

Read de Retz as usual. I also read the sixth Satire of Horace, some of the History of the United States, and some German. I accomplished thus much because I declined going to Mrs. B. Gorham's where the ladies went.

[1] The rental property at the corner of Tremont and Boylston streets (No. 105) had been vacant since the removal of Rufus Brackett in November (vol. 3:188).
[2] Dr. George Hayward of 154 Tremont Street (*Boston Directory*).

FRIDAY. 15TH.

Morning mild. I went to the Office as usual. From thence at ten o'clock I went according to my agreement with Ayer the Carpenter and looked at the house at the corner of Boylston Street. Made my estimates and gave my directions. I hope and trust the repairs cannot be very large. Those Houses have cost a great deal of money. I have been endeavouring to improve them ever since my Agency and I think the effects now begin to appear. Returned to the Office, thence to the Athenæum and a walk.

Quiet dinner at home. Miss Phillips out. Afternoon, read de Retz. Felt uncomfortably from the violent drawing of the plaster upon one of my wounds. Towards evening it increased and the rapid formation of matter produced violent shiverings for two hours of the evening that disabled me from any exertion whatsoever. This was followed by a profuse drenching perspiration. I had sent to Dr. Hayward to give me relief but from some mistake he did not come. The throbbing was so great, my suffering in the night was intense.

SATURDAY. 16TH.

As soon as I could get through with my breakfast I went down to see Dr. Hayward. He looked at and dressed the wound and pronounced it to be in a good condition notwithstanding the collection of matter formed in it. This relieved me a little but I was very good for nothing during most of the day. The throbbing in my head continued. I took Medicine and remained at home in my study, a very useless personage to all intents and purposes.

I received the report of my father from the Minority of the Manufacturing Committee. It is an eighteen Column Report,[1] but I managed to read it through and it was the only thing I did for the day. It is one line of public policy, that of a statesman, but it is not the line by which this Country can be governed. They are too much in the hands of political Jugglers—General Jackson et id genus omne who have no basis but the popularis aura. Retired to bed early and in pain.

SUNDAY. 17TH.

I obtained some rest during the night and felt better all day, though my head throbbed very much and my stomach felt out of order.

Remained quietly at home most of my time and read in the morning the Account of the History of the United States in the Dr. Lardner's Collection, and in the Afternoon, a long Sermon of Massillon's upon the Divinity of Christ. Text Luke 2. 21. "His name was called Jesus, which was so named of the Angel." His argument is that the Divinity is proved by the brilliancy and the general spirit of his Ministry on Earth, for supposing him to have been only a Man. The first would have naturally led men to idolatry and the Deity must have been by his attribute as Creator, responsible. The second would have spread a fatal snare for our innocence. This is a doctrinal point and it is treated by him with all the zeal which the Catholic sect entertain. I do not pretend to say any thing certain upon the point. Some of his views on the first division of the discourse are very powerful. And I believe they may be said to be convincing in regard to his earthly character. But I do not know that they go far enough to justify idolatry.

I took a short walk this morning. The air was cold, the wind being from the raw East. Evening quiet. Gardiner Gorham passed an hour. I was sleepy and dull. Read a little upon Architecture.

MONDAY. 18TH.

Mild though cloudy. I went to the Office and received a letter from my father at last. It is a sort of review of the state of things at the last of the Congress. I think he himself is rather depressed, he speaks of his own and the health of the family as bad, and intimates not the most agreeable things as to the state of his property.[1]

My time was taken up in writing, attending to applicants for the House in Tremont Street and looking over the Intelligencer. Mr. Webster's Speech[2] is too long to read at once. I went to the Athenæum to pick up scattering opinions upon my father's Report. Walsh as usual praises it. The Boston papers are calm as death.[3] Masonry *is* powerful, who can doubt it.

Isaac P. Davis came up to see me. We talked and I read to him parts of my father's letter. They are about to print the Report for circulation. He came to inquire as to the correctness of it as reported by the Intelligencer, for which I told him, I thought I could vouch, such reports being generally corrected by himself.

Walk and home to dinner—Miss Lydia Phillips spending the day. Afternoon, read de Retz whose Accounts are somewhat sickening of the intrigue and nightly consultations to regulate the hypocrisy of the day. Evening at home. Visitors to see Miss Elizabeth Phillips. Mr. Charles Bartlett of Charlestown and Miss Elizabeth Parks. Cousins of my Wife. William G. Brooks also came in soon afterwards.[4] Not late to bed.

[1] JQA to CFA, 13 March (Adams Papers). The family's transfer from Washington to Quincy, usually effected upon the adjournment of Congress, was to be delayed for a month because of the weather, LCA's health, and the need for JQA to make arrangements about his debts. See also, above, entry for 25 Feb., note.

[2] On Nullification, delivered 16 Feb. in the Senate.

[3] Robert Walsh, editor of the *National Gazette* in Philadelphia, as well as of the *American Quarterly Review*, was one of JQA's firmest journalistic supporters (see vol. 4:175, 214–215). When CFA came to prepare the Report for pamphlet publication he included the comments from the *Gazette* of 13 March on the inside front cover: "The Report of ... Mr. Adams ... is the product of his athletic and capacious mind.... The performance is altogether one of extraordinary strength and momentum; equal in masculine sense and argument, sustained impetus, intrepid candor, and importance of general maxims and conclusions, to any one of the antecedent state papers from the same pen.... Its length is as great as that of Mr. Calhoun's dissertation; but in every other respect it forms a contrast like that between true dialectics and the most artificial sophistry, wisdom and error, nutritive aliment and vitiating drug. Mr. Adams ... exhibits, with original traits, all the spuriousness and evil tendencies of the claim of nullification.... That part ... in which the relations between the slave-holding and non-slave-holding States, and the conduct and tone of the South toward the North, are treated, is particularly racy and impressive. In the art of *exploding absurdities*, Mr. Adams is, indeed, consummate."

CFA is not altogether accurate in his comment on Boston newspapers. On the day of the present entry the *Columbian Centinel*, in printing lengthy excerpts from the Report (p. 1, cols. 3–7), called it "one of the most able documents that has been published during the whole session of Congress" (p. 2, col. 5).

[4] The mothers of ABA, Charles Bartlett, and Elizabeth Parks were sisters; the fathers of ABA and William G. Brooks were brothers; see vol. 3:70, 113, 132, 324.

TUESDAY. 19TH.

Lovely morning but the wind got round soon after. I went to the Office and passed my time making up Diary and looking over Mr. Webster's Speech. It is a good, solid but rather dry law argument upon the theory of Nullification. Isaac P. Davis called up to see me again. He asked me to correct the proofs and make up a caption for the edition of the Report spoken of yesterday.[1] They print five thousand at East-burn's Office.[2] I went down to see about it, and Eastburn agreed to send a proof tonight but he did not.

Walk. Reflections upon the present State of things and unaccountable and irrepressible low spirits. Afternoon, tried to write but without any success. Read Cardinal de Retz. Evening at home. Sidney Brooks called and was amusing for an hour. Mr. Beale and his Son came in to take leave. He goes to Quincy in a day or two.

[1] The Report had been ordered printed by the House of Representatives. However, because "the documents are much delayed in the printing" (JQA to CFA, 13 March, Adams Papers), a Boston pro-tariff group had decided to publish at once. The report was also circulated in pamphlet form elsewhere. In Phila-delphia, for example, Robert Walsh, after printing the report in full in the *National Gazette*, issued it as a supplement in an edition of 9,000 copies (JQA, Diary, 12 April).
[2] John H. Eastburn was the printer for the *Daily Atlas*; his office was at 18 State Street (*Boston Directory*).

WEDNESDAY. 20TH.

Morning mild and cloudy with Easterly Winds. I went to the Office and was engaged in writing my Diary most of my time. Took a walk at noon with Mr. Peabody and went home quite fatigued. I waste a good deal of valuable time and perhaps this may be one cause for my low spirits. Afternoon, wrote to my father.[1] My letter was a poor and a lame one but I have tried anew so often that I am in fact discouraged. I finished this at a venture. Received one sheet of proof which I corrected immediately.

Evening, Rain. We went out notwithstanding to a small party at Mrs. J. Quincy's. About fifty and generally selected from the upper crust, as it is called. A very handsome Supper, but the thing was on the whole quite dull. I do not know why I should go into Company for I take little pleasure in it. The mere idea of duty is perhaps as strong as any thing. We returned shortly after ten. I read the Connoisseur.

[1] LbC in Adams Papers.

THURSDAY. 21ST.

Morning cloudy and cool. I went to the Office as usual but must plead guilty to a great deal of idleness. At the Athenæum, where I read the English Newspapers and Magazines. I think the alteration in the British mode of thinking is one of the most surprising incidents of the present age. They talk democracy more than I ever expected to hear them. Query, Is this for the better? I fear not. My doubts as to the durability of our Government lead me to hope that others will be aware in time of the danger to be incurred in adopting our principles.

Took a walk. Afternoon, busy copying my letter which engrossed nearly my whole time. I read a little of Retz finishing the second Volume. My Wife and Miss Phillips took tea out so that I spent my Evening studying Architecture. It must be a delightful pursuit but then it is an enormously expensive one. Our little fortunes in this quarter would vanish in a trice before it. For myself, I do not know that I shall ever want to exercise myself practically in it, but at any rate, it is a useful branch of refined acquirement.

Went in the Evening to Mrs. Frothingham's. Found there, Gorham Brooks and his Wife, William G. Brooks and our families. Nothing material took place. I returned home with the ladies at ten. The Wind had come round to the South and it was warm.

FRIDAY. 22D.

The day was a lovely one. I went to the Office and from thence to the Athenæum after lounging round idly at various places. Read several Articles in the Quarterly Review, done in the blackguard style of that periodical. One upon Coaches amused me a good deal.[1] The perfection to which riding has been carried in England is very surprising. In this Country we have great facilities through our water communications. We improve also, every year.

Intended a walk this fine day, but an engagement or two disappointed me. Dined with Mr. Frothingham, my two ladies being there. Conversation with him afterwards upon the Brooks family and the prospects of some of the Members. We agreed in wishing them well.

Returned home and did nothing but draw up a Caption to my father's Report. Evening quietly at home. Mrs. Trollope's second volume.[2] She does tell a good deal of truth. We ought to see ourselves and take advantage of even such corrections. The style of self puffing is rather ludicrous. Architecture afterwards.

[1] An essay-review of *The Traveller's Oracle* by William Kitchener and *The Horse and Carriage Oracle* by John Jervis (*Quarterly Review*, 48:346–375 [Dec. 1832]).
[2] *Domestic Manners of the Americans*, borrowed from the Athenæum.

SATURDAY. 23D.

Another beautiful day. I went to the Office and was engaged there part of my time in writing, partly in reading a little of the History of the United States and partly in correcting proof of my Father's Report. I drew off the final copy of my Caption, and took it to the Office to be referred to Mr. Davis. Thus went the morning with a long walk in consequence of the beauty of the day.

After dinner I was engaged in drawing off the last of my Sherry Wine purchased some time since from Mr. Williams. In consequence of my want of confidence in my Man, I did the whole of the work myself. Afterwards, I read a good deal of Cardinal de Retz. Felt interested in the account of the Meeting with the Grand Condé, but on the whole, as Voltaire observes, there is a very great inequality in the style. Some portions are decidedly heavy.

Evening quietly at home with my Wife and Miss Phillips. This is almost the first evening since her stay that we have been domestic. Her spirits require company and variety. And I think her stay with us has improved them. Read Mrs. Trollope. She did not see the best Society. But she judged well of what she did see. An American could judge equally well of England. It is all nonsense. Architecture and the Connoisseur.

SUNDAY. 24TH.

A fine day although an easterly wind took from it the delightful balm which we enjoyed yesterday and the day before. I finished the Article Architecture in the Encyclopedia previous to attending Divine Service as usual at Chauncy Place. Mr. Frothingham preached all day, first from Psalms 34. 19. "Many are the afflictions of the righteous, but the Lord delivereth him out of them all." A discourse of a consolatory kind apparently. The reasons why the righteous are afflicted are not to be known by Man. He can merely assign some plausible conjecture with which to satisfy himself. But they present to him the strongest argument he has short of Revelation for the belief of a future State. They throw him upon the Justice of a creating and governing Deity, who will make all things result in good. Second, from the book of Leviticus 19. 14. "Thou shalt not curse the deaf, nor put a stumbling-block before the blind." The Spirit of this passage may be taken to be, that you injure not the physically maimed, nor those who may morally be included in the class. Not the really deaf only but those who are absent and cannot hear, not merely the blind, but the ignorant and uninformed are within the scope of that benignant law which watches over the defenceless.

I afterwards read a Sermon by Massillon upon the Epiphany. 2 Matthew 2. "We have seen his star in the east, and are come to worship him." The Star in the East may be considered as the light of truth, which was adored by the Magi, avoided and concealed by the Priests and persecuted by Herod. Hence the division. 1. Few receive truth. 2. Many endeavour to evade and conceal it. 3. Many openly betray and oppose it. There is a great deal of soundness in the discourse. The world is not easily open to new truth. It exerts itself to avoid it at first, and nothing but the force of habit and the brilliancy with which it continues forever to shine produces the conviction that at last settles down in Society.

William G. Brooks, my Wife's cousin dined with us today. In the evening the ladies went down to Mr. Frothingham's, and I joined them there at nine. A large Company. All the Wales family,[1] Mr. Thayer, Dr. Fisher and many others. We remained a little while and returned home before ten.

[1] Perhaps the family of William Wales of Dorchester. Mrs. Wales, before her marriage, was Elizabeth Quincy, great-granddaughter of Justice Edmund Quincy.

MONDAY. 25TH.

Foggy rainy morning but it afterwards cleared away. I went to the Office and was engaged most of my time in correcting proof for my father's Report. It goes on slowly. Nothing of any particular consequence occurred. Took my walk. Received a letter from my Mother stating the probabilities of their coming.[1] According to this my father is to be here directly and her coming is postponed until May. So it is.

My spirits were on the whole, better today. Afternoon, read Cardinal de Retz's Memoirs who flags as he goes on.

My Wife and Miss Elizabeth Phillips proposing to go to the Theatre, we took tea at the Tremont House. From thence a whole party proceeded, consisting of Mrs. Gorham Brooks, Mrs. Frothingham and 3 children, two Miss Phillips' and my Wife. Much ado about nothing, and an Afterpiece called Free and Easy. Mrs. Barrett as Beatrice, it being for her benefit. Barrett as Benedick.[2] It was better supported than I expected. The other piece was absolutely good for nothing. Yet it made us laugh.

[1] Letter missing.
[2] On George H. and Mrs. Barrett (earlier Anne Jane Henry), actors in the theater for many years, see vol. 1:92, note, and Odell, *Annals N.Y. Stage*, 3:121, 123.

TUESDAY. 26TH.

Morning clear and cool. I went to the Office as usual and finished correcting the rest of the proof of my father's Report. It makes a Pamphlet of forty pages close printing. A good deal of time was also consumed in a variety of little commissions of various kinds. Attended to the repairs to be made to my Gig, and various other small matters, besides taking my regular walk.

Mr. Brooks and Mr. Everett dined with me. I did not much relish it. Mr. Everett is to me one of the most unpleasant men in private society that I ever met with. He strikes me as artificial, rarely expressing a sentiment of any kind and never one from his heart, and covering every thing with a perpetual tone of persifflage. I do not like him.[1]

Afternoon quite cut up. I read a little of Cardinal de Retz and but a little. Miss Elizabeth Phillips left us today to spend a week at Mrs. P. C. Brooks'. She appears to have revived considerably since she came to us, and I think it probable with good management, she may safely get over the mortification that presses her down.

We went this evening with Mrs. Gorham Brooks to see the work of the blind who have lately excited much sympathy. The Institution is a good one, although I could not see them with any pleasure.[2]

[1] A restatement of a view of Edward Everett long held by CFA; see vol. 3:9–10, 295; 4:127.

[2] A performance in which the pupils of the New England Institution for the Education of the Blind displayed their proficiency in reading, writing, arithme-tic, &c., together with an exhibition of their handiwork, was held at the Masonic Temple on 19 March, but so heavily oversubscribed that this second performance was scheduled; see *Columbian Centinel*, 15 March, p. 3, col. 2; 21 March, p. 2, col. 4.

WEDNESDAY. 27TH.

Our usually quiet habits have been so exceedingly disturbed of late that I confess I looked with great pleasure to the moment when we might get back to them again. I confess I am not made for a gay, dissipated life. I have tastes of home, which absence from it only makes more sensibly felt.

Went to the Office. Felt unwell and feverish all day. Received a letter from my Father[1] inclosing the Conveyance made the other day in which I had made an important omission. Sat down immediately and drew up another which I sent off at once.[2] A long walk with Mr. Peabody and then home. Afternoon, Cardinal de Retz of whom I finished the third volume. His escape from France was on the whole a surprising one—Though I should have supposed Mazarin would not have been sorry for it. My eyes and head pained me so much I was not diligent. These wens still continue to trouble me. Evening, Mrs. Trollope who is biting enough, but her book is after all a very small concern.

[1] 23 March (Adams Papers).
[2] CFA to JQA, 27 March (LbC, Adams Papers).

THURSDAY. 28TH.

The North West wind makes our weather exceedingly cool, but it keeps it clear. I went to the Office. Read the History of the United States, the first volume of which I finished. It is a poor superficial affair. A good deal of time taken up in little Commissions of various kinds. To the Athenæum and thence to walk. Went to South Boston which is a dreary walk. Home to dine.

Afternoon, finished the Memoirs of Cardinal de Retz. On the whole, they present no pleasing picture. He makes himself out a man of not very agreeable character to that of his profession, and he no doubt varnishes his case as far as possible—At least so says his Companion Guy Joli, whose memoirs come next. I do not know what has induced me to take to this line of reading. Perhaps I should do better to drop it. I have a hundred other things to learn of more consequence.

Evening at home. Read the Bible, Mrs. Genlis' second volume of les Parvenus, and Mrs. Trollope. The latter is really too absurd. After-wards I resumed German but being tired of Dr. Follen's German Reader which I am satisfied is a very poor book for beginners, I took up at once Schiller's History of the Thirty years war which I found easy.[1]

[1] A copy with JQA's bookplate of the *Geschichte des dreyssigjährigen Kriegs*, 3 vols., Leipzig, 1793, is at MQA.

FRIDAY. 29TH.

Another cool fine morning. I went to the Office and passed my time principally in Accounts, bringing down those of the Quarter to the close of the month. I also went out to purchase a copy of the Report of my father which I found selling very cheap.[1] The Edition at this rate must circulate.

Passed an hour in looking at Haydon's Picture of Christ entering Jerusalem.[2] I was on the whole disappointed. The canvas is too much crowded, it takes away all feeling of unity in the composition. Had the crowd been represented more distant this would not have been so striking, the face of the Saviour is totally unworthy of him. A gigantic figure of the Canaanitish Woman is disgusting both from its bold prominency and from it's ugliness. Even the Penitent girl which the Painter tells us he considers as his best composition, is a great masculine figure with her back to the Spectator and without expression from her face being covered. I confess I was most pleased with the face of Joseph of Arimathea and the Ass.

Took a walk at one. Afternoon, the Memoirs of Joli.[3] He is dry and uninteresting. There is none of that philosophical observation of human character that help one out so much with De Retz. Evening at home, finished Trollope, Les Parvenus, and Schiller's Thirty years war.

[1] John Quincy Adams and Lewis Condict [of New Jersey], *Report of the Minority of the Committee on Manufactures, Submitted ... February 28, 1833*, Boston, 1833 [37 pages]. On the inside front cover, along with Walsh's comments (entry for 18 March, above), is a preface, unsigned [by CFA?], giving the background and circumstances of the preparation of the Report and estimating its significance beyond the immediate issues: "Under the guise of a Report, Mr. Adams enters into a full exposition of the domestic policy of the country, taken as *one connected system*, and he explains the principles which for forty years guided us in our unprecedented career.... The peculiar character of this paper is to be found in the ... complete issue it makes up with the President, and the whole race of what are called 'strict construction' politicians, nullifiers, and all who would stop the prosperity of the nation on a cavil for a ninth part of a hair."

[2] The painting had been on exhibition for some months at Harding's Gallery on School Street. It was described as 15 feet long and 12 high, six years in the painting, and the only work by Benjamin Robert Haydon in America (*Columbian Centinel*, 1 Jan., p. 3, col. 2).

[3] At MQA is a copy of the *Mémoires de Guy Joly*, 3 vols., Geneva, 1751, the third volume of which contains the *Mémoires* of Claude Joly and of the Duchess of Némours.

SATURDAY. 30TH.

Clear morning, but the wind so very high as to be unpleasant. I went to the Office and was occupied in taking off the Quarterly Account. This with a stroll which I took with Mr. Peabody to look at the improvements going on at the North end of the town consumed much of my time, and I did not omit my regular walk. Dinner as usual. Afternoon, Mr. Joli whose work does not interest me at all. Is it not time lost to work upon it. Evening, Les Parvenus, and Schiller's Thirty years War.

My time is pretty regularly filled up, but not very beneficially, and as I grow older, I begin to feel a greater doubt of my power of ever being able to apply my capacity to any serviceable end. Yet it is not quite fitting that I should despair. I am almost too young. Perhaps with the same powers, I cease to feel the same degree of confidence that I did. A young man can very often do more with assurance than an old one with substantial talent.

SUNDAY. 31ST.

The day was a pleasant one with the wind at the Southwest. I passed an hour in reading the Account of the French Revolution as given in the little Library of Entertaining Knowledge.[1] It is a little confused from its declining to adopt the style of Narration and using the various testimony which has been elicited, according to the words of the Witnesses.

Attended Divine Service, but my Wife being taken faint in the morning,[2] I left the Church with her in the Prayer. And as I could not well return, I took a walk. Afternoon, went alone and heard Mr. Bigelow. Text from Psalms. 37. 37. "Mark the perfect man and behold the upright, for the end of that man is peace." I heard the same discourse at Quincy on the 29th of last July. His manner has not improved since then.[3]

On my return home, I read Massillon. A Sermon upon the Anniversary of the purification of the Virgin. Luke 2. 22. "And when the days of her purification according to the law of Moses were accomplished, they brought Jesus to Jerusalem to present him to the Lord." He considers this as a striking example of submission to the will of God whence comes his whole discourse. The difficulties in the way of this submission he calculates to be, 1. A degree of vain glory which leads all men to question what they cannot understand. 2. An impression that all objects are to be referred to self as the object of creation 3. A false estimate of virtue which substitutes certain duties agreeable to the individual for such as properly belong to him. On the other hand, he holds the benefit of submission to be found in the relief it gives from the pains of life. These he classes thus, 1. Anxiety for the future. 2. Distress for the present. 3. Regrets at the past. On the whole a good Sermon, particularly in the third point of the first and the whole of the second division. But the system of division is bad in itself as may be seen in the first part where nearly the same idea prevails in the parts, the presumption of man. Evening quiet at home. Read a little of the French Revolution.

[1] A continuing publication (51 vols., 1829–1838) of the Society for the Diffusion of Useful Knowledge, London. CFA's set is in MQA.
[2] ABA would give birth to a second child in September.
[3] Vol. 4:337.

MONDAY. APRIL 1ST.

A most delicious day, the air as mild as it is in Summer. I went out with little Louisa to enjoy the air and give her a little of the freshness of the Spring. She is just able to walk alone and she takes great pleasure in it.

Went to the Office where I received a long letter from my father.[1] He proposes to come on soon. My time was taken up in drawing up Accounts, balancing books and the like until my usual hour for walking. But the day was so warm I did not get my usual distance. Afternoon at home, reading Joli whose account of the escape of Cardinal de Retz is rather the other side of his own picture. So it is in this World. Le grand Condé made an honest remark when he said no body was a hero to his Valet. Evening quietly at home. Les Parvenus and a little of Shakespeare's Merry Wives. Schiller too, but German is hard.

[1] 26 March (Adams Papers).

TUESDAY. 2D.

Morning fine although the wind was a little Easterly. I went to the Office after walking a little while on the Common with my Wife and child. At the Office time taken up in Accounts and in listening to Applicants for the house at the corner of the Common. A Mr. Fuller came and took it rather against my Will.[1] I then went out and was busy in giving various orders for the purpose of getting it ready. I must however inquire a little about Mr. Fuller. Went to see about my Horse and found he had arrived—So that I can now begin my expeditions to Quincy.

Walk as usual. Afternoon at home, reading Mr. Guy Joli. I am tired of him, he does however expose some curious things and he teaches one great moral lesson, of how debasing to the finest intellect the slavery to any sensual passion in a course of years becomes. Old age loses all it's dignity when it clings so to the flesh. Evening quiet at home. Shakespeare's Merry Wives and Schiller, but the night is not the proper time to read German.

[1] Elijah Fuller was to prove a punctual tenant of 105 Tremont Street for four years (M/CFA/3).

WEDNESDAY. 3D.

Out early this morning to make arrangements and draw Money from the Bank in order to go to Quincy. Started at ten and got there in an hour—My horse being very lively. Walked to Mrs. Adams'. Settled Affairs with her though Elizabeth being out, I did not see her. Then back to the old Mansion where I saw painter and carpenter, and gave the necessary orders for the little Repairs which I contemplate executing this Spring.[1] Saw Carr the Tenant and endeavoured to be looking out after a man.[2] On the whole I did as much today as I expected, and even more, for my time was very limited.

Returned home to dinner. The ride out had been delicious, but my return was in one of the Easterly breezes which are cheerless enough. After dinner, finished Gui Joli and was glad enough so to do. I shall stop here with that pursuit. What to take up next is the question? Evening quiet at home. The Merry Wives. Omitted German and read the Account of the French Revolution. There is nothing new in it, excepting the statement of the utter ignorance in which the King and the Ministers appear to have been of the public feeling. If not so clearly vouched it would appear utterly incredible.

[1] Among CFA's responsibilities as JQA's agent in managing his properties in Boston and Quincy was maintaining the Old House in good repair and preparing it each year for occupancy by the family upon their return from Washington.

[2] In addition to the Old House, JQA's lands in Quincy, inherited from JA, included the farm at the foot of Penn's Hill and a tract at Mount Wollaston. John G. Carr was the latest in a series of tenants (see vol. 3:38, 186; 4:249, 261).

THURSDAY. 4TH.

Rain with Easterly breezes. This was the day appropriated for the regular Fast—A custom of Puritan origin which has gone somewhat to decay.[1] It being observed far more as an occasion for feasting and excess.

I finished the Account of the French Revolution. Attended divine service at Mr. Frothingham's where the collection of persons was somewhat small. Mr. F. preached from Proverbs 20. 1. "Wine is a Mocker." His subject was Intemperance, which he announced to be peculiarly appropriate to the day, as probably this of all the year was the occasion of the greatest excesses. A singular though perhaps a correct assertion. He considered it as the prominent National vice. Much had been done to check it, though occasionally with a somewhat injudicious zeal. "Wine is a mocker" because it deceives in every respect. It presents itself in the attractive form of social enjoyment until it destroys the spirit of society. It promises strength and gives weakness, it seems to sharpen while it actually dulls the faculties. It is the purpose of this day to amend by the consideration of one's faults. Let every man reflect upon this and so regulate his conduct. A very good Sermon and I am sorry there were not more to hear it. Afternoon, Mr. Parkman.[2] Psalms 106. 3–4. "Remember me, O Lord, with the favour that thou bearest unto thy people. That I may see the good of thy chosen, that I may rejoice in the gladness of thy nation, that I may glory with thine inheritance." The Preacher reproved us a People, for a somewhat excessive self-complacency, for a tendency to worldliness and for slander and party spirit. All of which is true and fair enough.

I remained at home afterwards, reading Voltaire's Correspondence which is the luxury of idleness. But not being satisfied, I began Botta's account of the Revolution.[3] My Wife took tea at Mrs. P. C. Brooks Jr. Mr. Degrand called in for half an hour. I went for Abby at 9. Supper. Gorham Brooks and his Wife there. Return at ten.

[1] On the custom in New England, see vol. 3:208–209.

[2] Rev. Francis Parkman, on whom see vol. 3:51, 204–205.

[3] CFA was reading Charles Botta's *History of the War of the Independence of the United States of America* in a version in English by G. A. Otis (below, entry for 6 April). In MQA are JQA's copies of two editions of this translation (3 vols., Phila., 1820; 2 vols., Boston, 1826) as well as one in French (4 vols., Paris, 1812–1813). The copy of the 1826 edition had been GWA's.

CFA returned from time to time to Voltaire's correspondence. The 16-vol., 1785, edition in MQA, which in the note at vol. 1:139, above, is said to be of the *Œuvres complètes*, is of the *Correspondance* only.

FRIDAY. 5TH.

I did intend to have gone to Quincy this morning, but the weather being misty and the roads wet, I also having a pretty bad cold, the design was abandoned. Went to the Office. Engaged in various occupations, of Accounts, writing &c. all my time. With not much apparently to do, I yet find that I have no time to read. This always was a great puzzle to me. Took my usual walk. The weather became warmer and the afternoon was clear.

I began my Afternoon on a new plan. Read Botta for two hours,

and German for one, and found that it answered infinitely better.
Evening. Read to my Wife, part of the Parvenus and the close of the
Merry Wives. It is rather a mediocre play. Evening, I became interested
in a guide book of the City of Paris. The Account of the Rogues and
thieves there is extraordinary. But it was rather wasting time. Architecture or Painting will do far better.

SATURDAY. 6TH.

Fine weather. I went to the Office and was engaged in writing and
Accounts most of the Morning. Received a letter from my father[1]
together with the Deed returned to the purchasers of the Boylston
Property. I forwarded it directly to Mr. Curtis. Looked over my Affairs
carefully, then drew up a Lease to settle with Mr. Fuller the new
Tenant, and then went up to the House to examine it. The workmen
were in it. From thence I went to an auction sale of Wines which
consumed half an hour. And I had no time for my regular walk.

After dinner, read for two hours in Botta's History translated in a
pretty bald manner by Mr. G. A. Otis. I filled another hour with
Schiller. The days having grown so much longer, I have to improve
a morning hour, with which I read Horace's Satires. On the whole
my present distribution of labour pleases me.

Evening quietly at home. Read to my Wife. My cold was tolerably
uncomfortable, and My Wife seemed to be following the example.
Evening, not yet having regular labour, I commenced the Account of
the Excavations at Pompeii, in the Library of Entertaining Knowledge.

[1] 1 April (Adams Papers).

SUNDAY. 7TH.

Morning delightful. But the East Wind set in cold and harsh at
Noon. I read part of the Account of Pompeii before attending divine
service. Mr. Frothingham preached all day. Job. 5. 26. "Thou shalt
come to thy grave in a full age, like as a shock of corn cometh in his
season." A funeral Sermon upon Mr. Morril late a Deacon in the
Church who died last week at an advanced age.[1] It was on the whole
happily done, for the subject was one of those whose services to the
world are not of a noisy character, and who pass through life satisfied
with the performance of the honest but limited duties of their sphere.
A good man is as the world goes, as fair a spectacle as it can present,
but there is no great room for the vehemence of rhetorical eulogy, nor

for the exercise of any extensive philosophical reflection. Mr. Frothingham did every thing that was possible. He alluded to his long life and his death as a uniform Christian and to the performance of his duties social and moral. The afternoons was a discourse commemorative of the day, Easter. John 20. 20. "Then were the disciples glad, when they saw the Lord."

I read a Sermon of Massillon's from the same text as last Sunday's, the subject was the proper disposition for a holy life, exemplified in the text through 1. the spirit of self devotion or sacrifice in the Saviour 2. in the spirit of fidelity of Mary. The first branch included a view of the Atonement which I do not meddle with as it is one of the knotty points of doctrinal theology. A short walk with my Wife who is suffering from a cold. Evening at home. Read Pompeii.

[1] James Morrill had been an officer and deacon of the First Church from 1789 to his death on 3 April. A lengthy extract from Mr. Frothingham's funeral sermon, together with a likeness of Morrill, is printed in Richard D. Pierce, ed., *The Records of the First Church in Boston 1630–1868*, Col. Soc. Mass., *Pubns.*, 40 (1961):724–727.

MONDAY. 8TH.

Heavy rain all day with the wind high from the Eastward. I went to the Office. Nothing very material in the way of business. I wrote, and read some portions of the North American Review for April. This periodical seems to be assuming a new species of character. It is the vehicle of brilliant, superficial Essays without much attempt at criticism. The writers for it seek to dazzle the public for the time without aiming to leave much which can be looked upon as sterling matter for reference.

My article has now been postponed a year, and I think I see in one of those of the present number, some thoughts springing from it's perusal. I think I shall never write for that Review again so long as it continues under it's present auspices. My mortification in connection with that publication has been greater than I think I deserve, and I have brought it upon myself by endeavouring to do something when it is the decision of a superior power that I must at least for the present remain entirely idle.

I went up in the rain to the South end to look at some furniture, but could find nothing to suit me. Afternoon, I intended to have attended a Meeting of the Directors of the Boylston Market, but it rained so hard, and having wet my feet before dinner, I concluded to remain at home. Read Botta, and Schiller. Evening quiet. Les Parvenus and Pompeii. My Wife still suffering much with her cold.

TUESDAY. 9TH.

Morning cloudy but it afterwards cleared away. I went to the Office and was engaged in my usual series of avocations. Of these it is not often that reading can be said to make any considerable part. Money Affairs consequent upon the commencement of the Quarter, Accounts to be regulated, Dividends to be obtained and money to be deposited take up time. I was also today engaged in finishing the Leases of the House 105 Tremont Street. I have succeeded in advancing the Rent. My labours in this may have brought me back considerably from the very depressed condition in which the Property was shortly after I assumed the management. I can confidently affirm, that in point of paying character in the Tenants, and condition of the Houses in regard to Repair, my father's Estate is really more valuable by twenty per Cent than it has been for many years.

Instead of walking, I was obliged to go down to see a Wardrobe which my Wife was in treaty for. This consumed the whole hour. After dinner, Botta and Schiller. My Wife though still sick with a cold, went to Mrs. Frothingham's to tea. I made up for my morning's omission by reading the second Satire of Horace's Second book, comparing Pope's imitation.

Went down after my Wife at a little after eight. Gorham Brooks and his Wife there. They go to Mr. Brooks' at Medford tomorrow, to spend the Summer. He has sold his own pretty Estate obtained by her.[1] Returned home by ten.

[1] The home which the Gorham Brookses had owned in Watertown was probably a gift to Mrs. Brooks from her father, Resin D. Shepherd of Watertown; see vol. 3:259; 4:185, 433.

WEDNESDAY. 10TH.

Fine clear morning. I walked for an hour on the Common with my child. Met my old classmate Lothrop.[1] He is a Clergyman at Dover in N.H. We left Cambridge with some little clouds between us on Account of certain reports stated to have been set in motion by him. I never took the trouble to ascertain their correctness. We were stiff and civil.

I went to the Office. T. B. Adams called in and spent an hour.

Conversation various. He leaves this quarter on Tuesday for Pittsburgh. I wrote, and read part of the American History. Walk as usual. Went round by Sumner Street to look at a range of new Houses. Their fronts are very pretty.

T. B. Adams and Louisa C. Smith[2] dined with me. The afternoon was by this means exceedingly shortened. I read Botta. Evening at home. Idle. Read more in relation to Pompeii. A very curious subject.

[1] After an early intimacy, CFA and Samuel Kirkland Lothrop quarreled over matters not entirely clear. Thereafter CFA was never more than correct toward him and maintained a low opinion of his integrity. See vol. 1:170, 249–250; 2:170; below, entry for 16 Sept. 1834.

[2] Louisa Catherine Smith, a spinster niece of AA, had resided at the Old House since her childhood, and during JA's later years had devoted herself en-tirely to his care. Later, she returned to the Old House to take charge of it for JQA during periods when LCA was absent. Still later, after TBA's death, she boarded with the widow and was her consolation (JQA, Diary, entries for 5 Oct. 1826, 14 Aug. 1832, 14 Oct. 1833; CFA to ABA, 18 April 1827; to LCA, 30 Oct. 1829; both letters in Adams Papers; see also Adams Genealogy).

THURSDAY. 11TH.

I made ready to go out of town this morning, but the weather on the whole looked so threatening that I concluded to remain At the Office—Having a morning somewhat uninterrupted I was able to make good progress in reading the Account of the United States. Reached the close of the War. The Account is superficial with little of the spirit of philosophy and rather calculated to interest than to improve.

Took a long walk with Mr. Peabody. Early after dinner, as it cleared away, I concluded I would not lose the day, so I rode to Quincy. Found the workmen at the house busily occupied and promising to finish this week. Walked up to Mrs. Adams' and saw Elizabeth. She looked better than I expected to see her. Difficult to get a man. High time now.[1] I remained looking round until 6. Then returned. Tea and quiet evening at home. I was much fatigued.

[1] It had become apparent that the long engagement, now of four years' duration, to John M. Gourgas (vol. 2:387) was not likely to lead to marriage; see below, entry for 31 May.

FRIDAY. 12TH.

Cloudy with rain. Weather altogether unpleasant. I went to the Office after reading a portion of Horace. Got a couple of hours to read the American History besides going to the Athenæum and calling on Mr. Lothrop. The work is in the latter part of it full of gross errors.

The Writer had but a very indistinct idea of the operation of our system.

After dinner, was obliged to go down and attend a Meeting of the Directors of Boylston Market. No Quorum. Went over to the Insurance Office where I looked at the plan for widening the Street— The object of a Meeting to advise further expenditures. Decided to call one for Monday. Mr. Baldwin[1] talked away for a couple of hours. He strikes me as a very unpleasant man to have any thing to do with. I do not like the whole business.

Returned and read a little of Botta. Evening quietly at home. Les Parvenus, and one Act of Twelfth Night. Afterwards Pompeii.

[1] Perhaps Aaron Baldwin, on whom see vol. 3:303.

SATURDAY. 13TH.

Fine morning. I went to the Office and was occupied there in reading the North American Review—All the principal Articles of which I went through with. On the whole I did not derive much profit from any of them. This work contains little of any value to any body. A few young men are admitted to try their unfledged wings, and the rest of the matter is supplied by old ones who have other views in life and therefore cannot write independently. My Office boy had run away with my History.

Did business with Mr. Degrand and bought of him shares of the Merchant's bank to make up a round sum. This is on Agency Account. Walk and home to dinner.

I had intended to have gone to Quincy but from some cause or other felt unwilling to. Afternoon, Botta but did not read any German. Evening quietly at home. Les Parvenus and an act of Twelfth Night. Finished Pompeii.

SUNDAY. 14TH.

Clear morning and fine day. I occupied part of yesterday Afternoon and this morning in pasting in the rest of the labels in my possession into my father's books. It is now some years since I received them, and only now have I finished the work.[1] Many books still remain without them.

I attended divine Service all day. Heard Mr. Frothingham. Morning from 1. Thessalonians 5. 19. "Quench not the spirit." A view of the danger to a religious spirit in the three ages of youth, manhood and age. I did not catch the Text of the Afternoon's though a better discourse.

Read Massillon. The book I now am upon is entitled Mysteries, being Sermons upon those Anniversaries which commemorate the supernatural and inexplicable incidents in the history of the Saviour. This discourse was upon the Incarnation. 1. Corinthians 2. 7–8. "But we speak the wisdom of God in a mystery, even the hidden wisdom, which God ordained before the world unto our glory: Which none of the princes of this world knew." Three characteristics he thinks are to be found in man. A disposition to judge of all things by the palpable distinctions of this world, which forms his pride. A reference of every feeling to the pleasures of the senses and an inclination to bring his reason up as the infallible and universal judge. These points he considers to be affected by the mystery of the Incarnation, first in the humility of the Saviour's worldly situation, second, in the total disregard of all the objects of human desire, third, in the incomprehensible mystery of his birth. On this last point, there is some strong reasoning. Thus passed my day. Gardner Gorham passed the evening with us.

[1] The bulk of JQA's extensive library was at the Old House (vol. 3:55–56); however, upon the death of GWA, JQA had acquired, largely as an offset against his assumption of his son's debts, GWA's large collection of books. These remained in Boston in CFA's possession (vol. 3:324–325; 4:283–284). Affixing JQA's bookplate in each volume and cataloging the collection were the means adopted to maintain the identity of the books after they were shelved along with CFA's own books in his home and at his office. The task had been carried on intermittently since March 1830 (vol. 3:176).

MONDAY. 15TH.

Morning clear but extraordinarily cold for the Season. I left home early for the purpose of attending a meeting of the Directors of the Boylston Market. Question as to the Appropriation for widening the Street. A discussion of two hours followed which was wound up by a recommendation to appropriate two thousand dollars in aid of the object. The sum required is five. Mr. Child dissented.[1] I consider the appropriation as rather heavy. But I was surprised to find the value attached to Property up here.

This delay was a serious one to me as I had designed an early day at Quincy. Determined however upon not being put off, I started at ten and reached the house about eleven. Found the Painter gone. My time being short, I employed it to the best of my ability and returned to town just by dinner time.

Afternoon, T. B. Adams called and conversed upon subjects of business &c. He leaves tomorrow. I find him vastly improved. Evening passed quietly at home. Began the Itineraire of Chateaubriand.[2]

[1] R. Child (below, entry for 27 April). He is erroneously identified at vol. 3:220 and thus in the index (1968 edn.) as Joshua Child.
[2] CFA's copy of *Itinéraire de Paris à Jérusalem et de Jérusalem à Paris*, 2 vols., Paris, 1812, is in MQA.

TUESDAY. 16TH.

Clear day but the weather is cold and comfortless. I know of no deception greater than our month of April. We have a fine air and clear Sun. The face of nature seems to invite to enjoyment, but suddenly we are cut in two by a keen, sharp Easterly wind that dispels every agreeable expectation. The Child is now ailing too, and on the whole there is a weight upon my spirits. Besides this, I experience a most unaccountable apathy which paralizes all exertion. Is this a natural or a healthy state of mind? I answer No, and would correct it if I could, but the die is cast. I would leave the Country and attempt to revive my energies in Europe but I have not the means apart from my occupations.

Finished the History of the United States which is a poor thing— Unworthy of its high company. Walk as usual. Afternoon, Botta and German. Very hard. I think I shall devote my Summer to the acquisition of this language and Spanish and Italian. I shall have four months in the Country in which time I think I can make considerable progress. Evening at home. Twelfth Night, Les Parvenus, and above all the affecting book of Job, to my Wife. Afterwards, Chateaubriand.

WEDNESDAY. 17TH.

The morning was so cloudy that I concluded not to go to Quincy. The Newspapers announce my father's arrival at Philadelphia, but we hear not a syllable about him by private communication. At Office where I read some of Sir James Mackintosh's third volume of the History of England. I also went to the Athenæum and passed an hour. Nothing of any consequence happened. Afternoon quietly at home. Read Botta and one hour of German.

Went to the Theatre to hear and see Charles Kemble and his

daughter. The piece was the Stranger. She performed Mrs. Haller. There is something so affecting in that play that it affects me deeply even with poor acting. That on this evening was chaste, suitable, and yet exceedingly touching. I could not resist a few tears, and the house was generally affected.[1] But to feel it thoroughly a person must be a parent. I recognize here a difference in the effect upon me tonight and formerly independently of the superior performance. Farce called the dumb Belle. Exceedingly comic. Mrs. Barrett and her husband. Something was necessary to change the current of feeling and this did it. Home by eleven.

[1] William Dunlap's adaptation of Kotzebue's *Menschenhass und Reue* became a favorite in the theatrical repertory immediately upon its presentation in America in 1798 (Odell, *Annals N.Y. Stage*, 2:43–45). CFA had seen it at least once before, in 1825 (vol. 1:456). During the engagement of the Kembles, which began on 16 April and ended on 17 May, the Adamses attended the theater more frequently than was their custom.

THURSDAY. 18TH.

A lovely morning. I thought I would ride to Quincy and observe the progress which was making besides the chance that my father might arrive. My ride was delightful. I followed the most picturesque of the smaller roads which winds and winds in many ways, but I enjoyed the air and the breeze which for once was not decidedly east. Found the house but not it's master. Engaged in arranging engravings as well as I could, and distributing them in the various rooms.[1] Progress not very rapid however. Looked upon the garden. On the whole, I had far less than usual of the cheerless feeling which seems to spread itself round the old Mansion in Quincy.

Returned home in good season for dinner. Miss Julia Gorham dined with us. Afternoon I read Botta, but was interrupted by Conant who came to pay money on Acct. at Weston. Our settlement is usually long, and it was this day longer from the fact that all my Papers were at the Office. However we accomplished our purpose, and I received a sum of Money which does something to set up my funds again. Evening not being able to obtain Tickets for the Theatre we remained very quietly at home. Read a little of Twelfth Night. Afterwards, Chateaubriand.

[1] Upon their removal from the White House in 1829, JQA's and LCA's belongings such as engravings, prints, paintings, chinaware, &c. went into storage. They were sent to Quincy for placement in the Old House in late 1832, but when many objects arrived in bad condition CFA sent them to be cleaned and repaired (vol. 4:399).

FRIDAY. 19TH.

Morning clear, but a cold, raw wind which as usual destroys all it's charm. I went to the Office and was so much engaged in accounts that I did not read any thing. Mr. Degrand called in about the sale of some Stocks. Mr. Tilden about some shares in the Stock of the Daily Advocate to which I subscribed.[1] This is in the nature of a joint Stock though not incorporated. It was a sum greater than I could afford to give, but I concluded it was better if possible to avoid the responsibilities of a partnership of this sort even at some sacrifice. I accordingly paid the money for the shares and immediately transferred the Certificate to the Directors.

Took a walk and did some Commissions. Among other things, bought some Burgundy. Just as we finished our dinner, my father came in just from Washington. He looks, I think somewhat weatherbeaten from his Journey and rather thin from the illness of the Winter. But his health is better.

The Afternoon was taken up in Conversation and in the evening we went to the Theatre. The performance was Fazio, a play of Milman's. Bianca, Miss Kemble. Fazio, her father. She did well, although the impression made by her was not nearly so great as in the Stranger. The piece is one of pretension, there is much straining for tragic effect without complete success. The auditor does not go with his [endeavours?]. The last scene however was good. Afterpiece, the Boarding House—A poor thing.[2] We were at home in good Season. And I retired at my usual hour.

[1] Perhaps Henry Tilden, printer (*Boston Directory*).

[2] Boston, by this date, was in a fever over the Kembles (*Columbian Centinel*, 22 April, p. 2, col. 3), who were experiencing a repetition of the ecstatic receptions they had had in New York, Philadelphia, Baltimore, and Washington since their American debut in Sept. 1832 (Odell, *Annals N.Y. Stage*, 3:598–609). JQA, clearly animated by a desire to see this new constellation rather than by any fondness for the play, put aside the fatigue of his journey to become a member of the party: "Saw Milman's Tragedy of Fazio; which I should not have thought anything could have tempted me to see. Charles Kemble performed the part of Fazio; and his daughter Fanny Kemble that of Bianca. They both pass here for first rate performers.... The Tragedy of Fazio, is very dull and flat; but yet much more supportable than I could have thought possible. The farce was called the boarding house—laughable; without much wit." (Diary, 19 April.)

Of Miss Kemble's Bianca on this occasion, a Harvard undergraduate remembering it sixty years later had a different impression: "We went out, transfixed with horror and fascination, into uttermost darkness, as when one passes an arc light on the road" (Henry Lee, "Frances Anne Kemble," *Atlantic Monthly*, May 1893, p. 664). A portrait of Fanny Kemble as Bianca is reproduced in the present volume; see also p. ix–x, above.

SATURDAY. 20TH.

Warm morning. I went to the Office, leaving my father at home with Mr. Degrand. Engaged in writing and Accounts but had time to be able to accomplish one or two Chapters of Mackintosh's third volume. He treats of Mary of Scotland without any of the chivalrous spirit which has led so many to defend her. I think he is right. The woman who could marry her husband's murderer in a few short months after the deed can have had no moral sense, and the excuse of a Queen's violation is merely adding one crime to another. It is a very false notion of honor to defend such acts let a female's beauty plead ever so strongly. What is the moral influence of palliating these crimes? Are women more chaste, when they see an excuse of force readily admitted? Every female will plead force.

Paid a visit to Mrs. Sidney Brooks but was not admitted. After dinner, my father went to Quincy in my Gig with me. He proposes to make an experiment of the residence for a day or two. If too lonely, he will come in to see us. I remained with him until six when I returned home. Quiet evening.

SUNDAY. 21ST.

Fine morning. I did not attend Divine Service today, but went with my Wife to Medford to Mr. Brooks'. Found the family consisting of himself, his son Gorham and his Wife very well. Dined and spent the day. The house seems to go through as many phases as it has new Tenants. They were pleasant. Took a walk down the bank of the Canal.[1] It is picturesque, but the Country still has a bleak look. Not a leaf to be seen and the grass barely turning. Mr. Shepherd and P. C. Brooks Jr. came in the Afternoon. We left just after tea and got home shortly after Sunset.

I read a long Sermon of Massillon's upon the Passion of the Saviour. John 18. 37. "To this end was I born, and for this cause came I into the world, that I should bear witness unto the truth." He considered it, 1. as a manifestation of the obstinacy of the world to oppose the truth, 2. as the greatest evidence of that truth. His divisions are again subdivided. I think the first portion of the Sermon exceedingly powerful. It shows a keen insight into the weakness of human nature, and the precious sophistry which is perpetually employed to cover its indulgence. Nothing else but the Connoisseur.

[1] On the Brooks estate in Medford and the Middlesex Canal, which passed through and along it, see vol. 3:xviii–xix, 236, 249.

MONDAY. 22D.

The weather continues fine. I read a Satire of Horace and then to the Office where I made some progress in Sir James Mackintosh's History. On the whole this comes more nearly up to my own idea of what it ought to be than any thing I ever read. He is perhaps a little partial to Elizabeth, but I do not know whether, after reviewing the circumstances in which she was placed, it is fair to say so.

I took a walk with Mr. Peabody. Nothing material. After dinner read Botta and Schiller. Evening my Wife being out, accomplished a few Chapters in Bigelow's Technology—A book so useful I have a great mind to buy it, which is a rare thing with me.[1] Went for my wife at Mrs. P. C. Brooks Jr's. Several persons there. Mrs. Frothingham and Miss Lydia Phillips, Mr. and Mrs. Story, Francis Gray and W. G. Brooks. Returned at ten. Finished the first volume of Chateaubriand's Itineraire.

[1] CFA had borrowed from the Athenæum Jacob Bigelow's *Elements of Technology*, Boston, 1829.

TUESDAY. 23RD.

Weather cloudy with a few drops of rain. I went to the Office and passed my time in reading far more usefully than I have been able to do hitherto. I finished all of the third volume of the History of England which remains of the composition of Sir James Mackintosh, and I think it is deeply to be regretted that he died precisely when he was treating of the most important point in the whole history. The continuator is more positive and less philosophical. I think I see an immediate difference. Perhaps my acuteness may be somewhat aided by my consciousness of the fact.

Walk. I had Gorham Brooks and Mr. Tenny to see me this morning.[1] The first about the Theatre. His Wife wishes to go from Medford. I volunteered to ride out for her. Letter sent in by my father to copy. Did it, and rode to Medford and back before six o'clock, brought Mrs. Brooks in with me.

Evening, Theatre. Much Ado about Nothing. Benedick, Mr. Kemble, Beatrice, Miss Kemble. His performance was very good. I cannot speak in so unqualified a manner of her's. She had a restlessness and excess of motion especially with her head which was tiresome, and a mannerism which after a person has seen her several times is rather satiating. Her conception of the part was tolerable and yet not exactly mine. Beatrice is a Wit and a humourist, she has not much of the girl about her. Her speeches are those of a matured woman. Quick, and independent, haughty and reflecting. Such a character requires considerable dignity. And here was the failing. I think the Masquerade Scene was the best thing on her part.

We left the Theatre to go to a party at Mrs. T. W. Ward's given to Miss Kemble. She has attracted much attention here in private circles. And much mutual misunderstanding has taken place. I thought her an ugly, bright looking girl.[2] We returned home at eleven.

[1] William Tenney, tenant of the house at the rear of 23 Court Street since 1830 (vol. 3:128).

[2] Mrs. Thomas W. Ward (vol. 3:288) was but one of many Boston matrons entertaining for Miss Kemble, a situation not usual for persons in the theater. But she was no ordinary figure: "Miss Fanny Kemble is the *Lion* at Boston now; and it is as dangerous not to worship her there, as it is to doubt the infallibility of the Italian Opera at New York. . . . Miss Fanny Kemble is for an actress just about what her father is for an actor—quite *passable*. . . . The Ladies of fashion at Boston visit her—but she goes to Church and it is understood does not receive visits on Sundays." (JQA to LCA, 20 April, Adams Papers.) For a later social event for her, attended by JQA, see below, entry for 11 May.

WEDNESDAY. 24TH.

Clear day. I went to the Office after reading an hour of Horace. My time taken up much as usual. Made some progress in the continuation of Mackintosh although I could not say that I felt the spirit in reading that I have done heretofore. The writer has not the same philosophical mind, he leans more upon authority, and he has not the sharpness of discrimination.

Walk as usual, and I called in at the Athenæum. Afternoon quietly at home. Read Botta and made some progress in reading over German but I am very slow.

My Wife and I went to the Theatre again tonight, the Play of Venice Preserved. Jaffier, Mr. Smith. Pierre, Mr. Kemble. Belvidera, his daughter. The first man ruined his part, an essential one to the effect of the piece. Kemble's conception of the character of Pierre was good, but it seems to me that it wanted the full force of the character. He is a jealous, vindictive, haughty character, concealing his private griefs under the mantle of public spirit, and at the same time high spirited, full of sentiments of honor according to the world's definition of the term. She was rather cold at first. I did not wonder at it. For to lavish the prodigality of married love upon Mr. Smith, is not easy for a young single woman of any delicacy.[1] Afterpiece, Blue Devils, poor enough. We got home early.

[1] To find even such minor faults in the performances of the Kembles was currently judged churlish in Boston: "They are of that captious race, who labor under the impression that it argues the quintescence of taste and judgment to find fault. Such morbid beings would imagine blemishes in perfection itself, and the best efforts are lost upon them. It would be well for such persons to reflect a moment, whether the imperfections which haunt their imaginations, are not rather the spectres of their own diseased faculties, than the defects of these accomplished performers." (*Columbian Centinel*, 24 April, p. 2, col. 4.)

For most of the audience in the theater, apparently, the impact of the performance was so great that the critical faculties were overwhelmed. One in that audience, sixty years later recalled that "When [Miss Kemble] as Belvidera, shrieking, stares at her husband's ghost, I was sitting in front, in her line of vision, and I cowered and shrank from her terrible gaze." (Henry Lee, *Atlantic Monthly*, May 1893, p. 664.)

THURSDAY. 25TH.

Fine day. I was quite occupied all the morning, first in Commissions, then I went to Quincy. This being my dear Wife's birth day, I remembered it by presenting her with a little trifle. Found my father very quietly situated and apparently very well contented. I had an hour's conversation with him upon a variety of subjects and then returned to town. Arrived at home exactly in time for dinner.

Mr. Brooks and his son Gorham dined with me and upon the special occasion I treated them to a bottle of Burgundy. The former was a little indisposed today but the latter sat until five o'clock.

I could not read to any purpose after such a day, and I therefore concluded as my Wife was not at home to try my luck at the Play. Obtained a seat in the second range of Boxes, and sat quiet and incog. The Provoked Husband. Lord Townley, Mr. Kemble, Lady Townley, his daughter. The piece wants spirit in the performance. Johnson, and the rest who are very good where the conception of parts has been taught them, fail here in a piece not for a long time since represented here.[1] I came home but slightly gratified.

Called at Mrs. Frothingham's for my Wife and found Mr. F. returned from his trip to New York. Chateau-briand a little.

[1] In referring to "Johnson" CFA evidently means "Smith" (of whom he had expressed reservations a day earlier), who took the role of Manley (*Columbian Centinel*, 25 April, p. 3, col. 4).

FRIDAY. 26TH.

Morning cold and easterly. As My Wife proposed to go to Medford to pass the day, I thought I would not remain at home alone, so I rode to Quincy. Found my father quietly ensconced in the Study, and I passed the morning with him in conversation. Discussion of the meaning of the word Orphan, as connected with Mr. Gerard's trust in Philadelphia. Is it confined to those deprived of both parents, or the father, or one of them indifferently?[1] Quære de hoc. As he was about to dine at Mr. Danl. Greenleaf's, I had nothing to do but to accompany him. Mr. and Mrs. Daniel vegetate in the same quiet way with their trees. He examines the genealogy of the Greenleaf while falling into the sear and yellow one. Mr. Thomas his brother was also there.[2] At three, they went to a Parish meeting, and I returned to the House where I was occupied hanging pictures. Returned home late. Found Abby had already got back. Read a little of Chateau-briand, but the weather makes me exceedingly drowsy.

[1] Nicholas Biddle, chairman of the trustees of Girard College, had requested JQA's assistance in the preparation of a system of instruction and discipline for the school for orphans which would soon open its doors (to JQA, 9 March, Adams Papers). JQA, according to promise, extended his stay in Philadelphia on his way from Washington to Quincy to have conversations on the questions (to Biddle, 31 March, LbC, Adams Papers; JQA, Diary, 13, 15 April). Pursuing those conversations, Judge Joseph Hopkinson, who had participated in them, had written to JQA (20 April, Adams Papers) asking his opinion on the construction the trustees, in fixing admissions policy, should give to the word *orphan* used in Girard's will. Was an orphan a child without both parents, a child without a father, or a child without one parent? In Hopkinson's view the definition covered only the first two of the three situations.

JQA, when CFA arrived at the Old House, was consulting authorities in preparation for a reply to Hopkinson. They included "The Greek Lexicons, Latin Dictionaries, that of the French Academy, the Epistle of James in the New Testament, Calvin's Lexicon Juridicum, Euripides and the French Don Quixot" (Diary, 26 April). When he did reply (8 May, LbC, Adams Papers), he opted for a child who has suffered the loss of either parent, arguing that "at least for all beneficent purposes a motherless child, must be an Orphan. . . . I have the greater satisfaction in coming to this conclusion because it seems to me that the principle of limiting the sense of the word to persons who have lost their *fathers*, carries with it something of discourtesy and even of injustice to the female sex. . . . The distinction countenances a pretension of superiority on the part of our own sex which would be peculiarly misplaced in the relations between Parent and Child."

Biddle's address a few months later at the laying of the cornerstone (printed in the *National Gazette*, 8 July, and attached to Biddle to JQA, 10 July, Adams Papers) suggests that JQA's view did not prevail.

[2] Daniel and Thomas Greenleaf were brothers of John Greenleaf, who was married to AA's niece, Lucy Cranch, on whom see Adams Genealogy. Daniel was an apothecary and doctor, owner of the wharf on Quincy Bay used by JQA for swimming. His wife Elizabeth was his cousin. Thomas, a justice of the peace, was a supervisor of the Adams Temple and School Fund (vol. 2:153; 3:57, 90).

SATURDAY. 27TH.

Cold and Easterly. Our weather gives no pleasure to the Spring. I was exceedingly engaged all the Morning. Mr. Tenney notified me that he was about to quit the house he has occupied for three years. I regret this as he has been a good and punctual tenant. Mr. R. Child and J. H. Foster [1] called upon the subject of the Boylston Market. The Directors are divided in opinion upon the propriety of an addition to the amount recommended for widening the Street. I am to call a Stockholders meeting to decide upon it. I was in various ways kept running all the morning. So that no reading could be done.

Afternoon pursued Botta, and omitted German. My mind is so distracted, I can make little or no progress in so desultory a pursuit. Evening quietly at home. We declined a party at Mrs. A. H. Everett's given to Miss Kemble. I made some progress in the Itineraire.

[1] On James Hiller Foster, a canny merchant, see vol. 3:13, 92, 136, and Adams Genealogy.

SUNDAY. 28TH.

Fine day. I passed the early part of the morning in reading a Sermon of Massillon upon the resurrection. Romans 4. 25 "Who was delivered for our offences and was raised again for our justification." He considers this event as furnishing, 1. the motive. 2. the means for perseverance in grace. In the first point I agree with his reasoning. In the second I am hardly so willing. One position of his strikes me painfully. He describes the condition of Christians as utterly miserable if the truth of Revelation is not real. That is to say, that the privation of all the sensual gratification the world affords is a serious and tremendous evil unless it is compensated by a state of future happiness. I think the philosophy of many of the ancient heathen sects is superior to this, and the practical effect of the doctrine is far worse than the theory. That a future existence operates as a powerful superinducing motive to good conduct is certain, but without it, it is by no means true that a state of sensual indulgence would be a state of happiness. Virtue in many respects is its own reward. And it should always in public be so inculcated. For the passions are quite strong enough to require every possible obstacle to their indulgence.

We went to Quincy at eleven o'clock—My Wife and I. Found my father quietly settled at home. Dined with him, and in the Afternoon I attended Divine Service with him. Mr. Whitney preached upon Reform. Text Jeremiah 13. 23. "Can the Ethiopian change his skin, or the leopard his spots, then may ye also do good, that are accustomed to do evil." Sermon commonplace enough. The old Church is in serious peril on account of the pressure of the debt and the incompetency of Mr. Whitney to sustain himself.[1] It is impossible to tell what the result is to be. Returned to the house, took tea and then back to Boston. The Country looks cheerless yet. W. G. Brooks passed half an hour with us.

[1] Rev. Peter Whitney was in his thirty-third year as minister of the First Church in Quincy (vol. 1:157). Both because of his age and as a result of recent over-expenditure by the parish, a special committee of inquiry had been recently constituted with JQA as its chairman (JQA, Diary, 22 April and following entries).

MONDAY. 29TH.

My man servant has left me and the consequence is that we are put to some inconvenience. This comes of these frequent removals. At the Office—Some applications on account of my house but none that I liked. Engaged in a variety of Commissions on my father's account as well as my own. The day was sultry and oppressive to a most excessive degree. I felt excessively incommoded by a severe cold in my head caught on one of the chilly days of the last week.

After dinner read Botta. We had intended to have gone to the Theatre or to a party at Mrs. Crowninshield's,[1] but we could get no tickets for the one and I felt unequal to the other—So that we passed the evening quietly at home. I read a little more of Chateaubriand. The Itineraire has not much interest. It displays an amiable man, and an enthusiastic one.

[1] That is, Mr. and Mrs. Benjamin Williams Crowninshield (vol. 1:30).

TUESDAY. 30TH.

Morning sultry but the Wind afterwards veered and it became quite cold. I walked with the child previous to going to the Office. My cold however still so very troublesome, that I could do little or nothing with comfort.

I was obliged to go upon several pieces of business which took up time and fatigued me also. Called at the Boylston Market, made up the Record and made the arrangements for the purpose of calling a meeting of Stockholders to authorize the Appropriation contemplated as I mentioned heretofore. These various occupations engrossed all my time until dinner. Afterwards, I read Botta.

Evening walked out with my Wife and paid a visit at Mr. Frothingham's. Conversation upon the Theatre, Miss Kemble and Francis the first.[1] We returned early and I continued Chateau-briand.

[1] Fanny Kemble was the author of a tragedy, *Francis the First.*

WEDNESDAY. MAY 1ST.

Col. Perkins has lately made a splendid donation of his dwelling House to the Asylum of the blind. This has carried to it's height the enthusiasm of the public for this charity. And this day was the one fixed upon for the fair by the Ladies to assist it. A fair is an appeal to the mixed passions of human Nature. Its ultimate purpose is Charity, but the means which it uses are the common ones of barter and value. Many will be found willingly to pay a high price for an article when they would not elsewhere be reconciled to buying the same article for less and giving the difference right out of pocket. After a hurried call at the Office, I accompanied Mrs. Frothingham and my Wife. The crowd was great and the arrangement not very convenient.[1] I remained until my patience was wearied out and then went to the Office where I was busy the rest of the morning. Afternoon, Botta. We are about moving and therefore in confusion. Miss Julia Gorham and her brother Gardner came in for an hour. I afterwards finished Botta and enough of Chateaubriand's Itineraire.

[1] The wide current interest in the possibilities of education for the blind (see entry for 26 March above) had found handsome expression in Col. Thomas Handasyd Perkins' gift for the establishment of the Perkins Institution for the Blind. The gift carried with it a requirement for matching gifts of fifty thousand dollars. A Fair at Faneuil Hall was conceived as a major means toward the realization of this sum. Twelve thousand people attended during the four days the Fair was open. Nearly thirteen thousand dollars was raised, of which "two dollars only were counterfeit." Mrs. Harrison Gray Otis Jr. (Eliza Boardman), an energetic widow, took conspicuous leadership in the fund-raising effort. Later in the year her efforts and those of the Boston ladies associated with her were subjected to merciless satire in a volume issued anonymously in New York under the title *Scenes at the Fair*. It later became known that the author was Fanny Inglis, afterward Mme. Calderón de la Barca, who is better known as the author of the letters to William H. Prescott published as *Life in Mexico*, 1841 (vol. 4:185; *Columbian Centinel*, 30 April, p. 2, col. 4; 11 May, p. 1, cols. 1–4; 22 May, p. 2, col. 5; Morison, *H. G. Otis*, 1969, p. 491–492, 547).

Boston–Quincy

THURSDAY. 2D.

I was much occupied this morning in making final preparations for quitting our house for the Summer months. This is quite a business, as it takes place also at the season of cleaning. Went to the Office. Engaged there for some time in Accounts and writing my Diary which had fallen in arrear for a day or two.

At 1/2 past twelve, I started to go to Quincy in my Gig with Dr.

Parkman who almost invited himself to accompany me.[1] I was glad to have him. We arrived there before two and I found my Wife and child quietly housed. The day was a fine one, and I felt on the whole grateful that we had so many assistances to get over the unpleasant part of the change. The worst thing is to my Wife in losing her Nursery Woman for the Summer. Such little evils we must learn to submit to.

Afternoon passed in the garden sowing seeds. Evening quietly passed at home. Conversation with my father. Pursued none of my usual occupations, excepting the numbers of the Connoisseur.

[1] Dr. George Parkman (vol. 2:158). For Dr. Parkman's purpose in going to Quincy and for its outcome, see below, entry for 11 May, note.

FRIDAY. 3RD.

Morning clear but the wind remarkably sharp from the North. I rode into town very much to my own discomfort, having been indiscreet enough to forget my coat. Occupied in the various little ways which I have so often mentioned when living out of town. Went to my House and found it very well taken care of. Then several Commissions besides persons at my room about the House, to be let, and Mr. T. K. Davis who sat and talked a couple of hours.

Returned to Quincy and after dinner busily occupied in the Garden. Tried to sit down and read Horace, but I am not sufficiently settled to be able to do it. I have always found that when at Quincy I do not make one half the progress in study that I do at home. Yet the Library is larger, and the conveniences for reference are consequently so much better. One difficulty however is that nothing is in its right place. If ever so good, it is of no value when you cannot easily lay your hands upon it. Evening quietly at home. Mr. Beale came in for a little while.

SATURDAY. 4TH.

Morning cool. I rode to town and was busy most of my morning in the various commissions which residence here seems to impose. A great deal of time was taken up in the various applications of Tenants for the house that is vacant, as well as directions for the alterations and repairs which I wish to be made. I was obliged to go to the House for sundry purposes, and I there obtained several books &c.

Dined at Mr. Frothingham's. Conversation about Col. Perkins' donation. I have subscribed very far beyond what it seems to me I ought to have done. But when others hold back, it seems to me not right to countenance their higgling.

After dinner I attended the meeting of the Stockholders of Boylston Market. A considerable number present. Much discussion upon the expediency of an appropriation. Some dissatisfaction expressed and opposition to any large sum. $3000 failed almost unanimously. $2500 failed by two to one. 2000 succeeded by a few votes. I believe the change of my votes produced it. Am I justified in my course. *I* think so or I would not do it. Yet I hope nothing will be done. The minority is too large. Returned home to tea. Quiet evening.

SUNDAY. 5TH.

Morning cool with an Easterly wind. I was occupied part of the morning upon a labour which will probably take up most of my Summer, arranging and putting into the Catalogue all the books of the last arrival. Attended divine service and heard Mr. Gannett of Cambridge. He is a man of rather effeminate mind and not capable of struggling with the difficulties of the present day.[1] His morning discourse was from 2 Peter 1. 16 and embraced the leading evidences of the truth of Christianity. He dined with us and seemed to be melancholy. I have forgotten the Afternoon text.

Read a Sermon of Massillon's. Text 1. Corinthians 2. 12. "Now we have received, not the spirit of the world, but the spirit which is of God." He argues that the spirit of the world is totally inconsistent with and opposed to the spirit of God, because the latter requires 1. abstraction and seclusion, 2. penitence and amendment, 3. energy and courage. There is much worth meditating upon in that Sermon.

My father's Coachman, Kirke arrived this afternoon with the Carriage and horses but without my Mother. She was not well and therefore delayed her Journey after having sent the Carriage forward. I am quite anxious about her. In the evening we sat quietly at home. Conversation with my father. Afterwards I read the Connoisseur.

---

[1] Earlier comments on Rev. Thomas B. Gannett were to the same effect (vol. 3:249). JQA was more discursive: "Mr. Gannett dined with us—he is a young man of intelligent, but I think of anxious and melancholy disposition. He has difficulties with his Parish and is much alarmed at the rapid progress of infidelity.... Mr. Gannett appears to be under great discouragement, and dejection of Spirits. He told us that he had asked for a dismission from his parish; but did not say whether they had agreed to the proposal" (Diary, 5 May).

MONDAY. 6TH.

Clear but cool morning. Rode to town. Occupied in my usual little round of trifling commissions, and in conversation with Ayer the Carpenter and others. My house plagues me exceedingly. I am not here enough to see the Applicants. And many come whom I do not want to see and do not know how to treat. I was detained in town until quite late, which was not material as my father and wife had an early dinner to attend the funeral in Weymouth of Cotton Tufts who is dead at last.[1]

Afternoon occupied in the garden pruning and training. The weather is extraordinarily dry. No rain has fallen to speak of for many weeks. I worked a little upon the Catalogue. Evening, Conversation about Francis the first. My father read the Prefatory Memoir to this piece of Miss Fanny Kemble's—Extravagantly laudatory.

[1] Cotton Tufts Jr. was a cousin of AA and continued to live all his life in the family seat at Weymouth, where he became postmaster. He married Mercy Brooks (cousin of ABA's father), who survived him. JQA wrote of him as "a man who has lived nearly to the age of fourscore; having had a liberal education, but never emerged from obscurity and retirement. He was entombed, in the same yard, and near the spot, where fifty-six years ago, I followed my mother's mother to the grave" (Diary, 6 May 1833). See Adams Genealogy.

TUESDAY. 7TH.

I remained out of town today to do business here. The weather was exceedingly warm and terminated in the evening with a slight shower. I walked to the Houses at the foot of Payne's hill for the purpose of collecting the rents which have been due there for some time. Saw one of the Tenants and obtained a little, the others I did not see. From thence, I went to the Canal stopping on my way at Mrs. Adams' to pay a short visit there. Mrs. Greenough a sister of her's is with her.[1] My business at the Canal was to inquire what would be the cost of Stone steps for the house in Court Street,[2] which having ascertained I went on to Mount Wollaston. The Orchard looks barely alive, and the Tenants seem to do every thing they can to destroy it. I am still hoping however that in this case some good may yet come from my suggestions. The view from the hill as lovely as ever. I should delight in a house on this spot, but my means and my disposition are unequal to the thing.[3] Returned home pretty well fatigued. Afternoon, Catalogue and a little of Horace. The time passes here very rapidly and yet very quietly. Conversation in the evening.

[1] Mary Harrod of Haverhill was the second wife of William Greenough (*NEHGR*, 17 [1863]:168).
[2] Shipment of granite from the Quincy quarries was a principal element in the commerce of the Quincy Canal Wharf.
[3] The charm and the temptation exerted by Mount Wollaston on CFA and on other Adamses were deeply rooted; see vol. 3:268, 309–310; 4:362–363.

WEDNESDAY. 8TH.

The morning was bright and the weather continued exceedingly warm. I went to town, and my time was taken up in writing at my Office. I was more quiet today and yet no Applicants for the house came. Such is my fortune always. Mr. Tenny came and settled with me.

I called upon my cousin once Mrs. S. B. Clark now Mrs. Treadway. She is a bride at present on a visit here. I have not seen her for eight years[1] and there seems no great prospect of it now for I have twice failed.

Returned to dinner. Afternoon, taken up with the Catalogue and copying for my father. Read one or two of the Epistles of Horace. Evening quiet conversation at home.

[1] Susanna Boylston Adams, daughter of CA, was for fourteen years the widow of Charles Thomas Clark. Late in the preceding month Susanna had married William R. H. Treadway. For a time in JA's last years she had lived at the Old House to care for him (vol. 1:32). On her and her husbands, see Adams Genealogy.

THURSDAY. 9TH.

Weather moderated and one of our Easterly winds. I rode to town. Busy at the Office. Mr. Treadway called to see me and spent half an hour. He is a law publisher in New York, and comes here partly as a Journey of pleasure for his bride and partly with views of his own.

Application for my house. I was so tired of it that I concluded to let it go although not much to my satisfaction. Returned home to dinner.

Afternoon, read an Epistle of Horace and was engaged in restoring some order to the chaos which my fathers books are in. This is likely to be a business of some length. A Letter from my Mother renders it probable that she may be here tomorrow.[1] Evening at home. Our time goes on in so undiversified a manner that my dull record becomes supremely dull. There is no relief in it whatever.

[1] Letter missing.

FRIDAY. 10TH.

I had intended to remain quietly at home all day but a notification of a draught upon my father from New York made it necessary for me to go to town.[1] I did the business and passed the rest of my time in writing. Nothing of any particular consequence occurred and I returned to dinner.

Afternoon occupied in work upon books which progressed faster than I expected. We looked out for my Mother and she finally came, but much later than we had anticipated. She looks thin and feeble. I was glad she was through the Journey safely. She came, attended by only one woman, her former Servants having all left her. There are some advantages in clearing the House of a few dependents although the inconvenience of it may be momentarily felt.

Evening, Conversation. I think my Mother's spirits are somewhat better than I had been led to suppose. Read the Connoisseur.

[1] JQA had authorized John Adams Smith of New York, a son of AA2, to draw upon him for $960, the balance due him under the will of JA (JQA, Diary, 10 May). On Smith, see Adams Genealogy.

SATURDAY. 11TH.

I remained at home this morning as my horse by his week's work is very considerably fagged. Excepting an Epistle or two of Horace and some work in the garden, I did little or nothing but work upon the Catalogue and dispose of the books. This is the first and most necessary thing, but I am afraid that I ought to accuse myself of indolence from the habit of desultory reading that I form when living at Quincy. There are too many books. I cannot fix my attention to any given point. Perhaps to a man of literary taste there is no greater luxury than this of miscellaneous dipping, but it entirely destroys any thing like continued reflection. My father went to town to dine, and did not get home until late.[1] Evening quiet. Sat up later than usual.

[1] The dinner at Dr. George Parkman's had been planned with care to bring together for the occasion, two lions— JQA and Miss Fanny Kemble. Dr. Parkman had called at Quincy on 2 May to make certain of JQA's presence: "His principal object seemed to be to ascertain whether I would accept an invitation to an Evening party at his house to meet Mr. and Miss Kemble. He said the young Lady was desirous of being introduced to me. And I could but say that it would be very pleasing to me. . . . As a sort of personage myself, of the last century, I was flattered by the wish of this blossom of the next age, to bestow some of her fresh fragrance upon the antiquities of the past, and I answered Dr. Parkman accordingly" (JQA, Diary, 2 May). Both parties have left records of the dinner conversation. JQA entered in his journal: "I had much conversa-

tion with Miss Kemble, chiefly upon dramatic Literature; but it differed not from what it might have been with any well educated and intelligent young woman of her age. I spoke to her of some of her own poetical productions, but she did not appear inclined to talk of them. What she appeared chiefly to pride herself upon was feats of horsemanship. She said she had rode this morning about thirty-miles, and leaped over many fences and stone walls. She said they expected to remain in this country till about this time next year. I asked her if she had ever seen her Aunt Mrs. Siddons upon the Stage. She had not—but had heard her read Shakespear. She had known her only as a very good woman." (Diary, 11 May.)

Miss Kemble's recollection of the conversation centered upon one aspect only, that which related to JQA's views on Shakespeare: "Last Saturday, I dined at ——'s; where, for my greater happiness, I sat between —— and ——. . . . Presently, Mr. —— began a sentence by assuring me that he was a worshipper of Shakespeare; and ended it by saying that Othello was disgusting, King Lear ludicrous, and Romeo and Juliet childish nonsense: whereat I swallowed half a pint of water, and nearly my tumbler too, and remained silent; for what could I say?" (*Journal by Frances Anne Butler*, 2 vols., London, 1835, 2:205-206.)

When the published *Journal* reached Boston readers and became a topic of general conversation (see entry for 5 May 1835, below), Dr. Parkman requested JQA to record his response to her remarks in Parkman's copy of her *Journal*. JQA entered a lengthy defense: "Miss Kemble appears to have misapprehended the purport of my remarks upon the plays of Shakespeare. I said that my admiration of him as a profound delineator of human nature and a sublime Poet was little short of idolatry, but that I thought he was often misunderstood as performed on the stage.

"The character of Juliet, for example, was travestied almost into burlesque, by the alteration of the text in the Scene where the Nurse with so much precision fixes her age (Act 1, Scene 3). The Nurse declares she knows it to an hour:

and that next Lammas eve . . . she will be *fourteen*. Upon this precise age, the character of Juliet, her discourse, her Passions, and the deep Pathos of the interest that we take in her fate very largely repose. . . . As the play is performed on the Stage, the Nurse instead . . . says she will be nineteen.

"*Nineteen!* In what Country of the world was a young Lady of nineteen ever constantly attended by a Nurse? . . . Take away the *age* of Juliet and you take away from her all . . . the consistency of her character, all that childish simplicity, which blended with the fervour of her passion, constitutes her greatest charm. . . . [T]hat which in her mouth is enchanting would seem but frothy nonsense from a woman five years older. Miss Kemble is mistaken when she says she remained silent at these and similar observations. She dissented from them. She thought the love of Juliet and her discourse were suited to any age. . . . I inferred that having been accustomed to personate Juliet as a young woman of nineteen, she saw no incongruity. . . . From the discolouring of my remarks in her journal, it is apparent that she did not understand them. . . . Miss Kemble . . . singularly misstates the fact when she represents me as saying that Romeo and Juliet was childish nonsense. That there was childishness in the discourse of Juliet I did say; and the Poet has shown us why—because she had scarcely ceased to be a child, the nonsense is not in Shakespear; but in the alteration of his text upon the Stage.

"I observed also that there were several of the most admired plays of Shakespear, which gave me much more pleasure to read than to see performed upon the Stage—As instances of which I mentioned Othello and Lear, both of which abounded in beautiful details in poetical passages, in highly wrought and consistently preserved characters. But the pleasure that I take in witnessing a performance upon the Stage depends much upon the sympathy that I feel with the sufferings and enjoyments of the good characters represented and upon the punishment of the bad. I said I never could sympathise much with Desdemona or with Lear; because I never could separate them from the estimate that the Lady was little less than a wanton, and the old King nothing less than a dotard. Who can sympathise with the love of Desdemona? . . . She falls in love and makes a run away match with a Blackamoor for no better reason than that he has told her a braggart story. . . . For this she not only violates her duties to her father, her family, her Sex, and her Country, but she makes the first advances. . . .

"The great moral lesson of the Tragedy of Othello, is that black and white blood cannot be intermingled in marriage without a gross outrage upon the law of nature, and that in such violations Nature will vindicate her Laws. . . .

"Whatever sympathy we feel for the sufferings of Desdemona flows from the consideration that she is innocent of the particular crime imputed to her, and that she is the victim of a treacherous and artful intriguer. But while compassionating her melancholy fate I cannot forget the vices of her character. Upon the Stage, her fondling with Othello, *is* to me disgusting. . . .

"The character of Desdemona is admirably drawn, and faithfully preserved throughout the play—It is always deficient in delicacy. . . . This character takes from me so much of the sympathetic interest in her sufferings, that when Othello smothers her in bed, the terror and the pity subside immediately into the sentiment that she has her deserts.

"I further observed to Miss Kemble, that I felt a similar want of interest in the character and fortunes of *Lear*, as represented upon the Stage. . . . The dotage of an absolute Monarch, may be a suitable subject for a Tragedy; and Shakespear has made a deep Tragedy of it. But as exhibited upon the Stage it is turned into a Comedy. Lear the dotard and the Madman is restored to his throne and Cordelia finishes with a wedding. What can be more absurd! . . . [T]he restoration of a dotard from old age to his senses, is as much out of nature as the restoration to his throne is preposterous. . . .

"This was the purport of the remarks which I made at your Table to Miss Kemble, and with which it would seem from the notice of them in her journal, she was not only displeased but shocked. . . . Miss Kemble had herself written a Tragedy not destitute of merit; and I thought the most respectful manner of treating her would be, not by complimenting her upon her own performances, nor even upon her writings, but by conversing with her upon subjects with which she must necessarily be familiar, and upon which in acknowledging some impressions of my own mind, I hoped to elicit from her, either her assent to them, or some observations which might have served me to rectify my opinions." (Parkman's copy of the *Journal* has not been located; JQA, however, had his remarks copied into his letterbook, dated 5 Nov. 1835, Adams Papers.)

JQA expatiated further upon his views of Shakespeare and reflected upon a lifetime of witnessing his plays upon the stage in a letter to Parkman following the return of the now annotated copy of Kemble's *Journal* to him (19 Nov. 1835, LbC, Adams Papers). Parkman, in reply (23 Nov., Adams Papers), expressed his admiration and reported that he had made JQA's inscribed remarks available to the editor of the *New England Magazine*. They appeared, with the omission of the sentences relating to Miss Kemble, in the December issue of that journal (9:435–440) with the title "Misconceptions of Shakespeare upon the Stage" and signed "Q." In Jan. 1836, the *American Monthly Magazine* published JQA's letter to Parkman of 19 Nov. 1835 under the title "Personations of the Characters of Shakespeare," unsigned, and again with references to Miss Kemble deleted (7:38–40). Both articles were also circulated in tear-sheet form with separate pagination; copies are in MHS. A third article, with the title "The Character of Desdemona" and signed "J.Q.A.," followed in the March issue of the *American Monthly Magazine* (7:209–217), but whether this was written under the same provocation as the other two or at a different time is not certain.

Most surprising in the *contretemps* is the failure of the knowledgeable Miss Kemble to recognize that the main thrust

86

of JQA's remarks, however otherwise confined, was directed against theatrical practice already under challenge in London. "Improving" Shakespeare's text in staging his plays had been the accepted and generally followed practice for a century and a half. However, objections to the rewriting of Shakespeare's plays for stage presentation were commonplace in literate circles in the 18th century, if unheeded in the theater. Moreover, the theater managers and directors themselves had at last, within the preceding decade, begun to move toward the restoration of the original text. Kean at Drury Lane in his production of *Lear* from 1823 onward had discarded Nahum Tate's version of Act V, in use since 1681, in which Lear is restored to his throne and Cordelia marries Edgar, replacing it with the original ending. Macready was already preparing for his 1834 production of a *Lear* still further stripped of Tate, and in 1838 would achieve a presentation of *Lear* faithful to Shakespeare's text. C. B. Young, "Stage-History," in George Ian Duthie and John Dover Wilson, eds., *King Lear*, Cambridge, England, 1960, p. lvi–lxiii.

SUNDAY. 12TH.

A cloudy day with a few drops of rain and now and then a misty dampness in the air. I occupied an hour or two in work upon books and attended divine Service all day. A gentleman preached whose name I do not know. His first text was from Acts 20. 24 upon fortitude, the other from Luke 17. 21 the kingdom of God. They were neither of them remarkable and both quite respectable.

Read a Sermon of Massillon's for the Anniversary of the Assumption of the Virgin. Text from the Song of Solomon, 1. 6. or rather 7 as it stands in our translation. "Tell me, O thou, whom my soul loveth, where thou feedest, where thou makest thy flock to rest at noon." He considered the death of Mary as affording her 1. consolation. 2. glory —Consolation for the indifference expressed towards her by Jesus, for the slights and injuries received by him from the Jewish People, for the length of her stay upon earth, glory as a compensation for her abasement on earth, by her state of privation, of dependence and of disgraceful suspicion. This is one of the Sermons which I do not admire. It gives such mournful ideas of the state of a religious man. It expresses such a conviction of his miserable state of unhappiness in this world, that I wonder how any man can think well of his God who believes it. The Saviour expresses no worldly affections because he had none. Mary was like all other women, a sinful being and the attempt to make her more so arises from the natural infirmity of humanity which lays stress upon the ties of birth. The Saviour in this as in every thing else must be excepted from the general rule. The mystery of the birth of Christ is one of those things I never pretend to rest upon. Inexplicable as it is in every point of view, I prefer to let it remain so, satisfied with the divine nature of the mission and its beneficent purpose. Mr. Degrand was here all day. Evening quietly at home.

MONDAY. 13TH.

Fine day. I rode to town. Weather quite warm. Time taken up all the morning in Commissions. Went to the House to see that every thing was safe and in order there. Found that the Painters had been both curious and negligent—Opening windows &c., but no harm done. Then to the Athenæum, to write Diary at Office, and to make a purchase or two. Such is the outline of the morning.

I remained in town to dinner and went to the Tremont House, the table thin and not so good as usual. Thence to Boylston Market calling on the way to see one or two Tenants and to dun for money. There was no meeting of the Directors of the Boylston Market as I had expected, so I remained in town for nothing.

Returned to Quincy by five and read an Ode or two of Horace. Evening very quiet. Upon going to bed however, we found the child exhibiting symptoms which from their suddenness and similarity to the croup alarmed us exceedingly. She got through the night however, though not without constant anxiety on our part. Indeed, I have never before experienced what emotion was. I love that child perhaps too much. If so, may God in his mercy look tenderly upon me.

TUESDAY. 14TH.

It looked misty and rained occasionally so that I did not go to town. My morning taken up principally in reading Horace and in working upon the Catalogue. I make progress but as yet rather slowly. I hope to get things so arranged in a day or two as to make a final disposition of most of the books. To this purpose I had the Office cleared away this morning and effected a transfer of those volumes which I designed to go over. Some discrimination must be exercised as the mould has made serious inroads even upon the books of value.[1]

In the Afternoon, notwithstanding the rain, I was obliged to ride down to Mount Wollaston to see the farmer and buy some hay. The late dry weather has materially raised the price of this article.

The child appeared so hoarse today, that she was subjected to some severity of Medicine. I perceive now the value of so careful a Nurse as Mrs. Fields if I had not known it before.[2] Some exposure has produced this effect. Evening quiet at home.

88

¹ "The Office," located on the grounds at the Old House, was on the second floor of the old farmhouse. Until after JQA's death, the books which JA had given to the town of Quincy remained there subject to "the injury of time, of damp, and mice, and utter neglect" (vol. 4:139, 389–391).
² On LCA2's nurse, Mrs. Field, see vol. 4:314.

WEDNESDAY. 15TH.

Rainy and warm. I was busily at work at home in effecting the transportation of the books to the Office, which for the most part I did—And relieved my father's study from a great load. They overrun all receptacles however. I became much fatigued from my labour. With the assistance of the two men, I managed to do pretty nearly all that was necessary for the present.

The day was sultry with clouds. My time slips away in the variety of my little occupations without a possibility on my part of turning it to better advantage. After dinner, I was busy in putting a preparation upon my trees which are under my particular care. Mr. and Mrs. Frothingham however came out and stopped me. They took tea and were quite pleasant. Evening very quietly at home.

THURSDAY. 16TH.

Misty, easterly, disagreeable day. I went to town and my time was taken up in a variety of ways, so that I was at the Office but a very little while.

Made purchases at several places, and bought at Auction a number of trees for the further improvement of the Quincy house. They come from Maine and their success is somewhat problematical. One or two calls from a Tenant or two consumed the remainder of my time. Returned to dinner. Afternoon taken up in the garden and superintending the preparation in digging necessary for the new purchases.

The child has been better although she is still very much troubled with her cough. Anxiety about her is mingled with all my feelings, now the nurse has gone. We have not had rain enough materially to wet the ground. Evening quietly at home. Conversation without any particular interest.

FRIDAY. 17TH.

Misty again but it cleared away towards the Afternoon. I passed my morning in reading Horace and attending to the Catalogue until my trees came out of Boston which have been unreasonably delayed. After that, my whole time was taken up in giving the directions necessary to transplant them. My space is but limited, and I was compelled somewhat to crowd it. But by diligence, I effected the placing of the greater part of them. Whether any of the forty will take is very doubtful, but I always calculate that the number of chances of success is greater than the price given for the whole, that is, that though many should die, yet enough would remain to compensate. I have ten Maple trees, ten Firs, ten spruces and ten white cedars. I consider the second, the most and the first the least promising. Evening, quietly at home.

SATURDAY. 18TH.

The weather was clear and very warm this morning. I went to town accompanied by John Kirk my father's man. Our principal object was to see about purchasing a Carriage which had been advertised at Auction today. I examined it and fixed a price in my own mind, but it sold for twenty five dollars more. My Mother is in want of a vehicle. Other occupations consumed my remaining hour so that I returned with little success.

My residence at Quincy is to gratify my father and in that light it satisfies me, but it causes the neglect of my Agency here more than I should wish. A great many things are to be attended to at places widely distant from each other, and I am not here long enough to be thorough with them.

After dinner, I went up to Payne's hill on a general dunning expedition but did not find a single Tenant at home. It cost me a long and a hot walk. Whatever my way of earning my Compensation in Boston may be, that at Quincy is much more laborious in proportion. I have had a great mind to give it up. Deacon Spear would probably do it and more thoroughly for half the money.[1]

Returned home and read a little of Horace. The Child is, we think, better, but she still has the cough which does not yet seem decided enough to pronounce it Whooping Cough. Evening at home.

[1] Deacon Daniel Spear had preceded CFA as JQA's agent in the management of the Quincy properties (vol. 3:180, 185–186; 4:249).

SUNDAY. 19TH.

An exceedingly warm morning, but in the Afternoon we had light showers and before night the wind changed until it became really cold—One of the extraordinary variations of our Climate. I read a good deal of the Letters of Madame de Sevignè.[1] A brisk letter writer, but rather coarse. This was the fashion of the age. We have changed all that. Our day is a pure par excellence.[2] We admit no bad words, or ideas.

Attended divine Service. Two Sermons from Mr. Whitney, 1. John 1. 46. and 1 Corinthians 14. 40—The last upon propricty of behaviour and the decencies of life.

Read a Sermon of Massillon's being the last of the Mysteries, upon the visitation of Mary. Text. Luke 1. 39. "And Mary arose in those days and went into the hill country with haste into a city of Judea." He considers this conduct of Mary as furnishing an excellent moral for our day. 1. In her superiority to worldly proprieties and judgments 2. in her contempt of hardship and difficulty 3. in her *thoroughness*. These he considers as the obstacles which self love most successfully raises against man's progress in grace. The last he treats by considering that class of persons who wish to unite their duties to God and to the world. I confess I do not see the strength of his reasoning. I am of the latter class, so far as to say that God made us mortals to perform duties in this world and duties which require time and attention.

Mr. and Miss Beale passed an hour. Read Sevigné. I have done the Connoisseur, and from my engagements was unable to get at my house the Observer.[3] As a consequence I intermit two days. The Connoisseur is decidedly at the bottom of the Essayists, I have yet read.

[1] Among JQA's books in MQA are two sets: *Lettres de Madame de Sévigné à sa fille et à ses amis*, 12 vols., Paris, 1812, and *Recueil des lettres de Madame la Marquise de Sévigné*, 4 vols., Leyden, 1736. Perhaps because of CFA's interest, JQA also shortly took to reading the letters. His comments are somewhat more incisive than CFA's (JQA, Diary, 24, 25, 27 July 1833).

[2] Thus in MS.

[3] CFA's copy of Richard Cumberland's *The Observer*, 3 vols., London, 1822, is at MQA.

MONDAY. 20TH.

The weather was misty and cold today. I went to town accompanied by my Mother's woman Mrs. Kirk.[1] Went to the Office and from thence to the House in quest of some books and papers. Did some business also and made up Accounts. A person called upon me respecting the building of a Carriage for my father. I went up to see one of his patterns, which I was not altogether pleased with. It was too showy, and not in the very best of taste. I had not time nor inclination to come to a decision about it before leaving town.

In the Afternoon, I read a little of Horace, and worked for some time in the Garden setting out the remainder of the Trees obtained the other day. Several of them begin to give significant indications of death. I doubt whether I save many.

Read Madame de Sevigné. She gives all the interest of her letters by lively phrases and happy turns of expression. Such things cannot be translated, nor are they in themselves of value. Such a book is rather a mode of lounging away time. Began this evening Cumberland's Observer.

¹ Elizabeth Kirk (vol. 3:253) was the wife of JQA's servant and coachman, John.

TUESDAY. 21ST.

Heavy rain for the first time. The wind from the eastward, but it became gradually warmer notwithstanding. I passed my morning at home and somewhat idly. Part of it was devoted to thinking over the remaining portion of the task respecting Anti-Masonry. The Advocate has resumed the publication of my numbers.¹ And I feel as if the hand once put to the plough, the whole field ought to be finished. Yet the success of the pieces is not such as to make one feel particularly desirous to continue. I have failed in all my attempts. I have written carefully and laboriously, far more so than most young men of my age, yet I have found no one disposed to allow me credit for it, and all throwing obstacles which act in my mind as a delicate hint that I am not wanted. Is inaction under such circumstances a reproach? Do I make it an excuse for indolence, or is it really a justification. That is a question to consider. Afternoon, Read a little of M. Burtin upon Painting, whose theory I do not quite like,² and worked in the Garden. Quiet evening at home.

¹ Of the nine antimasonic articles which CFA had written for the *Boston Daily Advocate* in late 1832 and early 1833, six had been published in December and January under the title "A Brief History of the Masonic Outrages in New York" (see vol. 4:404–431 *passim*, and above, entries for 1–18 Jan. *passim*). The *Advocate* had resumed publication of the series on 14 May with No. 7, No. 8 on the 17th, and No. 9 on the 21st (each occupying cols. 1 and 2 of p. 2), all bearing the title "History of the Morgan Abduction" and the signature "F" (see vol. 4:350).

² *Traité théorique et pratique des connoissances des tableaux* by François Xavier de Burtin, 2 vols., Brussels, 1808, is in MQA.

WEDNESDAY. 22ND.

Morning clouds but on the whole a very delightful day. I went to Boston. Time engrossed by Accounts of various kinds and Commissions. Drew up the Acct. of T. B. Adams for the last six months. Called upon Mrs. Frothingham on account of my Wife and was overtaken by a Coachmaker who saw me on Monday. He took me to see the Carriages of Mr. Welsh and Mr. I. Thorndike both of which are his. I liked them partially. They are built far too ornamentally for my taste. In this Country simplicity and richness are the only things persons of the better class of beings in worldly situation, can resort to. I gave him my ideas upon what my Mother wanted and told him to come out to Quincy this Afternoon and see what he would allow for the old Carriage. Thus went my whole morning.

After dinner, I made the final bargain with him, agreeing to allow him five hundred dollars Cash and exchange Carriage with harness. He goes on directly to make it.

Worked in the Garden for some time, and then finished a Letter to T. B. Adams to accompany his Account.[1] Consulted my father upon the propriety of finishing my Numbers, which are now published as far as they go. He speaks well of them and encouraged me in regard to their character, although he did not decidedly advise continuing just now. I think at present I shall give them up. Evening quiet at home.

[1] To Lt. T. B. Adams Jr. (LbC, Adams Papers).

THURSDAY. 23RD.

Mild but the weather very cloudy and a few drops of rain. I went to town accompanied by my Wife. We hesitated on the way about turning back but finally decided to go on. My time was pleasantly taken up. I first did business and then stopped in at a sale where I purchased for my Wife a Psyche glass[1] once the property of Mrs. J. Russell who goes to Europe. Thence I went to the Exhibition of Pictures at the Athenæum which has lately opened.[2] A large number of old pictures, some of which seemed to me uncommonly good. My time passed rapidly in looking at them.

Dined at Mr. Frothingham's. He brought out some of *his* Burgundy purchased of the same lot with mine. It has turned. I am mortified and sorry for mine. This Wine is dangerous. At four we started for home and arrived in good season having had a pleasant day. Worked a little in the Garden. Evening fatigued. Retired early.

[1] A full-length mirror swinging in a frame; a cheval-glass (*Webster*, 2d edn.).

[2] The Gallery of the Athenæum, forerunner of the Museum of Fine Arts, housed the nucleus of a permanent collection and since 1827 had held periodic exhibitions (vol. 3:xv, 235). The current exhibition opened on 15 May (*Columbian Centinel*, p. 2, col. 7).

FRIDAY. 24TH.

Clear but cool. I remained at home all day. My morning passed without due improvement. I worked in the garden, read a little of Horace's second book of Epistles and arranged the Office. My disposition of time is not methodical, neither is it in any degree profitable. And the interruptions which are very constantly taking place worry me. I believe that for the purpose of avoiding this I shall endeavor to transfer my place of labour to the room over the way. A habit of unsettled life is the worst thing for the mind of one who wishes to be a Student.

Afternoon, I walked up to Payne's hill and obtained but little more satisfaction than usual from my walk. The Tenants are always out, or they do not feel ready to pay. The air was not unpleasant however, so that my health if not my purse was benefitted. Evening at home.

SATURDAY. 25TH.

I went to Boston today. My first object was to get the Glass purchased the other day safely lodged at the house, which I did. But the anxiety and trouble attending the process was not trifling. I then went to the Office and was engaged in various little occupations of business for some time. Then called at Mr. Brooks' where I had a pleasant chat for nearly an hour, then attended a wine sale and bought some wine for my father, and then went out of town.

At dinner, we tried my father's Burgundy. It is as good as ever it was. Mr. Frothingham can only blame his ill fortune.

Afternoon, Read Horace and Mr. de Burtin, whose taste in Pictures is not of the most exalted kind. He deals in technicals rather than in the spirit of the Art. I was indolent as is too often the case nowadays. Evening quietly at home.

SUNDAY. 26TH.

Rainy, cold, disagreeable day. I attended Divine Service in the morning but missed in the Afternoon from the drowsiness which has of late overcome me so much. Mr. Whitney preached, and really if I did not make it a point to pay a little attention to the Minister I do not think I should ever gain any thing from him. As it is, today, I must confess myself exceedingly deficient.

Read a Sermon of Massillon's upon the spirit in which works of charity ought to be performed. Galatians 5. 25. "If we live in the spirit, let us also walk in the Spirit." He prescribes three rules by which it will be possible to judge 1. first, that they should be considered as belonging to the duties rather than the merits of men, 2. second, they should be performed as a counterbalance to the sin committed, 3 thirdly, they should have no mixture of human views. A tolerably good practical Sermon.

The remainder of my time was passed either in reading Horace or some of Madame de Sevigné. Evening at home. Mr. Beale and his Son George came in. The former leaves tomorrow on a trip to Niagara Falls and quits his house to take up his abode when he returns home at Mrs. Adams's.

MONDAY. 27TH.

Morning clouds with rain and occasionally openings of dry, clear weather. I remained at home all day. Read part of the first and second Epistles of the second book of Horace and worked quite hard morning and afternoon upon some improvements in the garden. I am not accustomed to handle the spade and hoe. It blisters my fingers, yet the exercise is very good. Indeed it is here that I feel the principal benefit of my present way of life. Intellectually it does me very little service. Physically it aids me. I was so fatigued in the evening that I could attend to nothing.

TUESDAY. 28TH.

Rode to town. Went to the Gallery for an hour and to the Athenæum. I sat for an extremely large proportion of the time looking at the picture said to be by Guido of Judith with the head of Holofernes. The expression of her face is admirable, decision, religious heroism, masculine daring in her attitude. Such a picture as that gives me some idea of the excellence of the Ancient Painters. I also greatly admired a warm landscape of Gaspar Poussin.

At the Office, I did little or nothing but prepare a draught of a letter to Mr. J. Angier. He does not keep his books precisely.[1] Returned home. Afternoon read M. de Burtin. A mere Hollander who talks about *his* Collection, and looks down upon the far nobler efforts of the Italian Schools.

In the evening, read Madame de Sevigné. Her letters are the merest whip syllabub[2] that ever was frothed, and yet they are pretty. Their little apt phrases and gentle expressions give them to readers a charm, far more substantial books never possess. I find a good deal of satisfaction in Cumberland's Observer.

¹ The letter to John Angier, husband of TBA's daughter, Abigail, and Medford schoolmaster with whom TBA's son, John Quincy, was enrolled, was finally written and sent on 3 June (LbC, Adams Papers). Angier's bills for schooling, for which JQA had assumed the pay-

ment, were a recurring source of irritation to CFA (vol. 4:170).

² Ordinarily written as "whipped" or "whipt" syllabub. See JA, *Diary and Autobiography*, 2:127: "whippd Silla-bubs."

WEDNESDAY. 29TH.

The weather was so doubtful that I did not go to town. Time occupied partly in reading some of Horace and partly in attention to my gardening and planting projects. This is, all of it, vanity and vexation of spirit. But I have persevered through all sorts of discouragement until at last I have a little prospect of success. My principal difficulty here in Quincy consists in the desultory character of my occupations which prevents all pursuit of any definite purpose. Residence here is the most quiet thing in the world. We have no interruptions from abroad, and live almost as much to ourselves as any family can be supposed to do. The monotony of existence is such that my Journal can barely be kept along. Yet I waste my time just as much as if I was in the middle of dissipation and tumult.

Afternoon, read Mons. de Burtin. I believe I continue with him because I have no other subject to turn to at present. I do not admire his taste or his doctrines which flow from it. Evening Madame de Sevigné and the Observer.

THURSDAY. 30TH.

Dull morning but it afterwards cleared away. I remained at Quincy. In the hope of improving my time better, I this day moved my place of study to the Office, and devoted a considerable portion of the morning to reading the first Chapter of Neale's History of the Puritans.¹ My winter's examination of English History has given me a pretty good idea of the subject of this book. Yet I may here pick up bits.

I take up the work as preparatory to a general view of American History which it is highly necessary for me to take. The very extraordinary slowness of my father in doing any thing with the Papers which were a legacy to him for the purpose of using, and his perceptible advance in age warn me of the necessity of gathering what I may for some distant occasion.[2] My present leisure could not be better employed.

I have finished the Epistles of Horace and begin the Epodes. Afternoon, a walk to Payne's hill in quest of rent. I pick it up by driblets. It is hardly worth the trouble—I mean my Commission for which I do it. Evening, Madame de Sevigné and the Observer.

[1] Daniel Neal's *History of the Puritans ... to 1688* is in MQA in an edition in 5 vols., Newburyport, Portsmouth, and Boston, 1816–1817.

[2] Upon his retirement from the Presidency, JQA had projected as an occupation for himself the writing of a biography of JA and had in a desultory fashion, under CFA's persistent urging, composed some of it. However, he never summoned the necessary enthusiasm for the task and was drawn ever farther away from it by his return to the political arena (see vol. 3:257; 4:175, 352).

FRIDAY. 31ST.

Fine morning. I went to town. My time was consumed at the Gallery, in my performance of Commissions and at the Office. I met at the first several acquaintances and did not enjoy myself as much as when I am entirely alone. Pictures require a perfectly quiet, contemplative mood. They call for the exercise of imagination. I might sit and enjoy some single pictures for hours. One thing however strikes me, which is the disagreeable contrast between the old and the new pictures. There is a want of tone in most of these which is manifested very much. A fury of colouring that regards little but the most unpractised eye. We are behind in Painting in this Country.

Saw Mr. Frothingham for a moment, and called at Mr. Brooks'. Then out of town. Afternoon, reading Horace. Interrupted by a visit from Miss Julia Gorham and her brother. In the evening also Mr. Whitney with his two daughters were here.

Finding that according to my present mode of life my Journal is interrupted, I brought it to Quincy with me and was engaged in bringing up the Arrears of it. Elizabeth C. Adams spent the day here. She looks better than I expected to see her. But she seems to be in a bad way. Her situation is one of an unpleasant character. Contracted in marriage for many years, and likely to remain so indefinitely.[1] Read Madame de Sevigné and the Observer.

[1] To ECA's other problems was added the threat of tuberculosis. "She is in a very bad way. She has been ordered to ride on Horseback and stays with Mrs. Miller to ride at the manage. Mrs. M. has been a Mother to her. Gourgas goes on as usual. He has not been near us" (LCA to JA2, 25 May, Adams Papers).

JUNE 1833.

SATURDAY. 1ST.

This is the first very fine day we have had for some time. I did not go to town. But my time was taken up not unprofitably. I read several of the Epodes of Horace, one Chapter of Neale's Account of the Puritans and made some progress in Hutchinson's History, Volume the third, which I read over carefully—My former perusal having been a tolerably negligent one.[1] How many books, we skim over in this way with little better than complete waste of time.

I took a note of the Account of the meeting at Albany in 1754 and Franklin's project of a union. This is one of the dates. It is a little singular that Government originated the idea, but that neither this, nor the separate Colonies at all favoured the mature project. Here is the same feeling that has been at work with us for so many years and is now.

Afternoon walk to Mount Wollaston and examine the Orchard. It has survived the effect of the winter before last, but it bears the scars of the Struggle. I sat down and looked at the scene. A more beautiful prospect is seldom to be found. Mused most philosophically. Evening, the ladies having gone to tea at Mrs. Adams' my father and I walked up for an hour. Mr. and Mrs. Angier and Mr. Edward Miller[2] were there.

[1] CFA had read in the third volume of Hutchinson's *History of the Colony of Massachusetts Bay* briefly in 1828 (vol. 2:253, 256).

[2] A Quincy resident and a Supervisor of the Adams Temple and School Fund; he is characterized sharply in vol. 1:303.

SUNDAY. 2ND.

The day was warm and cloudy. I read a little of Horace at the Office and attended Divine Service both morning and afternoon. Mr. Whitney discoursed from 23. Luke 46 and 13 John 23. In the morning his aim seemed to be principally to put in a small plea in favour of Judas Iscariot—The most original as well as effective mode of preaching Christianity that can well be conceived. What will not men think of next. His afternoon was a strong call upon his hearers to partake the Communion which as it was Sacrament day, it is pretty fair to conclude he meant to have delivered in the morning.

I read a short Address rather than a Sermon by Massillon in which he holds up to imitation the example of the primitive Christians. It is short and has no artificial divisions being nothing more than a simple exhortation to a single point. Text from Hebrews 10. 32. "Call to remembrance the former days." This closes the volume of Mysteries so called.

Mrs. J. Angier and Miss Elizabeth C. Adams called in and took tea in the Afternoon. As the wind seemed to be setting in to blow with rain, they returned home early. Conversation afterwards. I read a few letters of Madame de Sevigné and the Observer.

MONDAY. 3D.

Fine morning. It became cooler at night. I rode to town, the roads in very fine order. My time was principally taken up in writing and copying a Letter to Mr. Angier on the subject of J. Q. Adams.[1] I was glad to find the workmen engaged upon the steps of the house behind my Office.

Called to see Mr. Brooks. He is worried about a pain in his knee. Such uninterrupted health as his spoils a man for sickness. He gave me a Check with an increased sum of one fourth part.[2] This is voluntary on his part and entirely unnecessary on mine. I have had fortune enough already to see that all over the necessaries of life make man little happier. I hope I shall not feel dazzled by the prospect of wealth. My wishes are for independence and comfort for myself and my children. I have no wish to look down upon others or to be looked up to merely on this account. Yet I am conscious that much of the respect paid to me springs more from this accessary than from any quality which may belong more properly to me. Men are wrong to condemn so severely the purse proud. For too often they are Idols of their own raising. And the very loudest levellers of the mob will fawn obsequiously upon the man for whose destruction they are crying. All this is moral of no flattering character. I wish for my own peace to remain unassuming and grateful to God for all my blessings.

Returned to Quincy. Afternoon not very usefully occupied. Read some of the Epodes of Horace which are vile. Evening quietly at home. Sevigné and the Observer.

[1] See note to entry of 28 May, above.
[2] The payments Peter C. Brooks made quarterly to each of his daughters represented interest received on sums he set aside, augmented, and invested for them as advances against their "portion." ABA's check in the amount of $400 was an increase over the $300 received in each earlier quarter (vol. 3:95).

TUESDAY. 4TH.

Day clear but uncommonly cool for the Season. Not having any thing particularly to call me to town I remained quietly at home. Pursued my regular avocations, which are now, first my Diary, then a few Odes of Horace, a Chapter of Neal's History, and the rest of the time upon Hutchinson.

This is a tolerably good employment of the morning, but I have still to call myself to Account for my Afternoons. This was taken up partly in reading the maxims of William Penn [1] from which it seems to me Franklin has borrowed much of his worldly wise system without adopting the highly religious tone which accompanies and moderates it, partly in drawing up Indexes to my Father's Pamphlets,[2] a never ending business. His Library has cost me an immense deal of toil. Will it ever repay me? That is a question.

In the evening Mr. and Mrs. Danl. Greenleaf called and paid a visit. The latter has just been in town to the wedding of a niece and returns full of talk. I read only my numbers of the Observer.

[1] JQA's copy of Penn's *Fruits of Solitude in Reflections and Maxims Relating to the Conduct of Human Life*, Phila., 1792, is in MQA.

[2] In the Adams Papers (M/CFA/30) is a 28-page list in CFA's hand with the heading "Catalogue of Pamphlets." The date of the latest imprint entered, 1833, suggests that the list was made in or just after that year. It seems likely that it is the "Index" to which CFA here refers. In the Adams Papers, Microfilms, Reel No. 326, however, on the evidence of the handwriting and the lack of any statement of ownership by another, the list is mistakenly identified as a catalogue of CFA's own collection. CFA's low opinion of the value of such ephemera (below, 7 June) makes it unlikely he would have formed such a collection himself.

WEDNESDAY. 5TH.

Morning fine but it changed soon after to quite cold. I remained very quietly at home. Read the Carmen Seculare which is a beautiful specimen of the Religious Lyric Poetry of the Ancients. Ben Jonson has done something in the way of successful imitation. I also read over the first Satire and the first Ode—In which many of the ideas are similar. My next study was Neale of whom I read about one half the first Chapter in the reign of Elizabeth. I also read some of Hutchinson's History and was just in a train of interesting research upon the first principles of the division between the parties at the Revolution when the call for dinner intervened. One thing is to be noticed, how much my Grandfather's statements made at an advanced age are corroborated by Hutchinson's third volume, printed since but written at the time.

Afternoon, I cannot yet bend my mind to occupation. But I have effected much in thus employing my mornings. My character is now so formed that my happiness depends greatly upon the occupation of my time in a satisfactory manner. Evening quiet at home. Madame de Sevigné and the Observer.

THURSDAY. 6TH.

My father accompanied me to town today. I was engaged in running round upon a variety of little Commissions for the greater part of the time, the remainder being taken upon in the never ending business of Accounts. I brought mine up to the present date and settled them to my satisfaction. Went to my House after several things and finally spent an hour at the Gallery.

Dr. Parkman hearing my father was in town came in quest of him to dine at his house and I was of course asked, not being easily left out. Great urgency prevailed and so we went. It was a small family party to a certain Mr. and Mrs. Jackson from Philadelphia, consisting of Judge Thatcher and his Wife, Daniel Parkman and his Wife, and Mrs. Parkman.[1] The three ladies Mrs. G. and Daniel Parkman and Mrs. Thatcher are sisters and cousins of Mrs. Jackson. We had a tolerably pleasant time, although I was under the embarrassment of feeling myself a supernumerary all the time. Returned home before Sunset. Dr. Parkman is a very great and very constant admirer of my father and is profuse in his civilities towards him. He is also to all appearance exceedingly disinterested for he asks nothing but his company.

I did little or nothing in the evening, as I felt unusually fatigued. Read my numbers of the Observer—A book I am much pleased with, as both in morality and tone it is far superior to its predecessors the World and Connoisseur.

[1] JQA identifies Mrs. Parkman as "old Mrs. Parkman the mother" (Diary, 6 June 1833). The Parkman men are identified at vol. 2:158.

FRIDAY. 7TH.

Morning cloudy but the day was clear with an unpleasant easterly wind at noon. I remained at home all day. Visit from Mr. Harvey Field who came for himself and a Neighbour to settle the rent that was due to my father. Conversation upon the late Representatives Election. He evidently thinks himself perhaps not without Justice the cause of my father's great success. He says the Masons here were his most violent opponents. Yet Masonry has no influence any where.

I was rather delayed about my work, yet succeeded in accomplishing a Satire and an Ode of Horace, the remainder of the Chapter of Neale begun Wednesday and some of Hutchinson. My share in the latter being a little of the smallest.

In the Afternoon, I pursued my work upon Indexing Pamphlets. A large Collection of many good ones and many very flat, stale and unprofitable. Perhaps it is one of the most singular subjects we have to speculate on, the feeling with which one examines the effusions personal, political and miscellaneous of past times. All dead and buried in the tomb of the Capulets. All the evidences of the restlessness of the human mind. Quiet evening at home. I read Madame de Sevigné and the Observer.

SATURDAY. 8TH.

Morning fine. I find the air for the season unusually cold. I went to Boston and was engaged there in a variety of ways. My time passes always very rapidly without my ever having a chance to look at a book. Is this useful employment of my life. Called at Mrs. Frothingham's, then to the Gallery and Athenæum.

As I was walking today I came across one of those very unpleasant circumstances which give us a chill in the midst of life and prosperity. A poor man as he was starting his handcart loaded with a barrel of something or other, slipped and fell, the barrel falling upon his head All this happened a few feet from where I was walking. He seemed not to have been very severely hurt for he was able to get up but he bled freely. A crowd was collecting so rapidly and there being persons to take the necessary measures I went away but the incident was a touching moral lesson to me which I hope to recollect.

On my return home I found the child drooping. These changes of weather affect her. I read a part of Henderson's History of Wines a book obtained from the Athenæum which gave me a great deal of new information upon the subject.[1] Indeed before this, my ideas were not a little confused. All the French Wines were in my mind mixed up together, without much reference to the spots where they grow. Evening quietly at home. Read a little of the book of Prince Puckler Muskau[2] and the Observer.

[1] Alexander Henderson, *History of Ancient and Modern Wines*, London, 1824.
[2] Although CFA borrowed Prince Pueckler-Muskau's *Tour in England, Ireland*

and France in 1828 and 1829, 4 vols., Phila., 1833, from the Athenæum along with Henderson's book, there is a copy in MQA.

SUNDAY. 9TH.

A most extraordinary day for weather, first, a chilly East wind, then a sudden change to West, then North with a most furious gust of wind, and a very little rain. I passed my morning in the room with the child who seemed very sick. These violent and sudden attacks occur so regularly that it seems to be part of the system of the child. They create in us much anxiety.

I attended Divine Service and heard Mr. Motte of Boston who also dined with us.[1] His discourses were from Ephesians 6. 24 and 1 John 2. 25. The morning was taken up in a view of the character of a Christian which he considered a name distinguishing only such as are followers in faith and practice of Christ, so that according to him an infidel might be nearly a Christian—The divinity of Jesus being the only thing in the way. He also fell into the same train of reasoning about Judas Iscariot that we had last Sunday. His Afternoon discourse was upon the light of natural religion. He is a thinker, although perhaps wanting in basis. This idea of saying fine things of Judas is most preposterous.

Read a Sermon from Massillon being the first on the Anniversary of a Saint. The Volume I now begin consists of ten Sermons of this kind. This was a eulogy of Saint Agnes, one of the martyrs of the Church. He drew from her life the following moral, 1. the superiority of the truely pious over all the temptations of the world 2. the victory which they can also achieve over suffering and death. Men are not to plead their situation in life or circumstances for sin, nor should they excuse themselves because of the difficulty of virtue. The same general subject makes the greater part of the Sermon read by me on the 24th of February last. This is a youthful, that was the mature effort. Evening at home. Read Puckler Muskau.

[1] Rev. Mellish I. Motte was a classmate and college friend of GWA; see vol. 3:110–111.

MONDAY. 10TH.

Morning cold with occasional showers through the day. I went to town for the purpose of voting, and attending the regular Meeting of the Directors of Boylston Market. The first was soon done and the other being for the Afternoon, I am afraid I must stand responsible for a very considerable waste of time.

Passed a little while at the Athenæum and also at the Gallery. How much better I could have done in the little study I have made for myself at Quincy, to which I am becoming somewhat attached. I was caught at dinner time at the Gallery in a shower of rain and I found Mrs. Dexter and Mrs. Barrell in a similar predicament. Having been offered an umbrella, I persuaded them to take it and was barely in time for dinner at Mr. Frothingham's.

Attended at Boylston Market but found no Quorum and therefore no meeting. Took the time to make up the records of the Association. I then called at the houses of two or three Tenants in the Neighborhood and then returned home. I had an hour of work after I got back. Evening, finished my volume of the German Prince, the second volume of Madame de Sevigné and the Observer. The Child seemed decidedly better today for which I am duly thankful.

TUESDAY. 11TH.

Our Season is very extraordinary—High winds and cold with an unusually small proportion of rain. Altogether quite comfortless. I remained at home to improve my time. Read over some of Horace—One of the Satires and one of the Odes. His Poetry is certainly splendid. His imagery is powerful, but his was not the spirit of an ancient Roman. I read also a Chapter of Neale which goes very far to confirm me in the opinions formerly entertained by me. A little also of Hutchinson, in which I go on slowly from my desire to compare all the Papers of the day. This mode of reading has already cleared my mind prodigiously of the mists which surrounded it. I now have a definite conception of the immediate origin of our Revolution. But after all, it is manifest that the question was one of natural boundary between two energetic Nations. Let our's only remain a Nation and it is invincible.

Afternoon, Read Henderson's book upon Wines. How many new subjects there are for the human mind. The growth and produce of the vine connects itself with the whole history and Geography of the world. It gives new ideas upon many collateral questions. And so it is with almost every thing in existence. And yet men die for want of occupation, or what is worse they sink into vices of the most degrading character. Evening, Madame de Sevigné and the Observer. The child was better today.

WEDNESDAY. 12TH.

Cold day. I remained at home. Read as usual beginning with Horace. My practice is to read over the Notes of the Edition of Dacier and Sanadon and to compare the Text of my edition which is Gesner's. I then note down in the Margin all that occurs to me as worthy of remark especially in cases where local allusion occurs. My Copy has no Notes. As soon as I shall have gone through the whole Volume in this manner I propose to have it bound up with perhaps an occasional blank leaf and make it my book of reference whenever I desire to consult the Author.[1] Read a Chapter of Neal and some of Hutchinson with occasional reference to the Prior Documents.[2] Thus my morning had gone before I was sensible of it's passage.

In the afternoon I read Henderson and walked up in quest of Mr. Field, the Tenant who provokes me so much.[3] I could not find him. I never can. He is a slippery good for nothing and such men are more trouble than value. I have one or two now on hand.

Evening at home. We heard today of the death of Mr. J. S. Johnston of Louisiana by the explosion of a Steamboat on the Mississippi.[4] He was an amiable and a worthy man, and his loss is to be felt as well by the Country as his immediate circle of acquaintances and friends.

[1] CFA's procedure in reading Horace is discussed above, entry for 1 Feb., note.

[2] That is, John Almon's *A Collection of Interesting, Authentic Papers*; see vol. 4:155.

[3] F. W. Field, sometimes confused in the Diary with Harvey Field, also a tenant but of a different sort; see vol. 4:286, 292–294.

[4] Josiah Stoddard Johnston, U.S. Senator from Louisiana, perished when the steamboat *Lioness* blew up (JQA, Diary, 12 June 1833).

THURSDAY. 13TH.

The day was tolerably pleasant notwithstanding a cold Easterly wind that prevailed for an hour or more. I went to town. My time engrossed as usual. Called twice upon Mrs. Frothingham on my Wife's account, dropped in for a moment at an auction and engaged upon Accounts. Collected some Dividends, among others that of the Columbian Office which turns out remarkably well. This is about the sum total of the Account that I can give.

Returned home at my usual time but the Afternoon was not profitable. Mr. J. H. Foster and daughter made a short visit to the family. I made a little progress in Henderson but I want a Map. In the evening, my father and I went up to Mr. T. Greenleaf's—A strawberry party of

Quincy people. The fruit was good and we got along on the whole amazingly well. Returned early and I read the Observer. Not a very profitable day.

FRIDAY. 14TH.

This is the first really pleasant day we have had for a considerable time back. I staid at Quincy and occupied myself in my usual way. Read Horace, the Journey to Brundusium, which has no claim to be called a Satire. I then made some progress in Neale although his Account is uninteresting from its sameness. Hutchinson to the close of Bernard's Government. He had more than his match. The power of the British Government had little or no support when support was of consequence. And perhaps the mode of treatment was not quite decided enough.

Afternoon, finished Henderson's book upon Wines which I consider as a very valuable work and supplying a void in literature. I have received many new and cleared many formerly received ideas. He has not gone sufficiently into the modes of preserving and improving wines, situation &c. which would have added a practical value to his work.

The public is now expecting the visit of the President here for which many preparations are making. General Jackson conquers every thing.[1] I read a few of Madame de Sevigné's letters, but on the whole was idle.

[1] On Jackson's visit to Boston, see notes to entries of 26, 27 June, below.

SATURDAY. 15TH.

Fine morning. I went to town. My time divided between my house which I visited to get a book, my Office and the Athenæum. To read seems to be a thing out of the reach of common probabilities in a morning, and the consequence is a considerable waste of time. But I find myself far more callous to the neglect than I ever was before. My exertions have resulted so very little to my satisfaction, that I am now content to swim with the stream.

Returned home to dinner. Afternoon rather wasted. I read an Account of the state of Knowledge in England in the earliest times, being the preface to the New Annual Register in one of its early volumes. This is not doing much.

The ladies went out to tea, and in the evening my father and I called at Mr. John Greenleaf's to see Judge Cranch who has just arrived from Washington. He was out. We saw Mr. Greenleaf and Mrs. Dawes.

This house is just as it was. Not a sign of improvement. Every thing going to ruin. The family lift up their hands, helpless and submissive. Energy is a plant of tender growth, but for success in life it is absolutely indispensable.[1]

We went from here to Mrs. Adams' where we found Judge Cranch and his Wife, Mrs. Greenleaf, Mrs. Angier and Joseph, her brother, Miss Miller and Miss Beale. Passed an hour, and return. Began the second volume of the Observer.

[1] Judge William Cranch of the federal Circuit Court of the District of Columbia (vol. 1:24, 39), a son of AA's sister, Mary (Smith) Cranch and Richard Cranch, JA's gifted friend, was exceptional among the current members of that family line in attaining any distinction of place. His wife was the former Anna Greenleaf. Judge Cranch's sister Lucy had married his wife's brother, John Greenleaf (vol. 1:434), and they apparently shared with other Greenleafs a want of industry (above, entry for 26 April). Moreover, the Judge's daughter Elizabeth in marrying Rufus Dawes (vol. 1:36–37, 39) had allied herself to a family which offered still another example for CFA of the ease with which families that had had position could suffer deterioration (see vol. 4:91). He adverts once more to the theme of decay in connection with the Smith family of Weymouth in the entry for 9 Aug. 1833, below. For most of the persons mentioned in the present note, see also Adams Genealogy.

SUNDAY. 16TH.

Fine day after a brisk shower in the morning. I attended Divine Service all day. Heard Mr. Jos. Angier preach.[1] Texts from Philippians 2. 12–13. and Psalms. 2. 11. The subject, man's free Agency under the impulse and guidance of the divine being, and the reasons why we are directed to serve the Lord with *fear*. He accounts for it from the very fact of free agency which leaves man the choice and the risk between good and evil. Mr. Angier writes with some beauty and he has a considerable fund of thought to begin upon. His manner was very considerably embarrassed and he did not give to his delivery all the impulse of enthusiasm which might have fully developed the powers of his style.

Mr. Degrand was here all day but without bringing from Boston any thing particularly new. The fact is that we are now in a state of profound quiet in this Country. Whether this is the fore runner of a storm of no trifling fury remains to be seen.

I read a Sermon of Massillon's in honour of St. Francis, 2. Corinthians 12. 10. "When I am weak, then I am strong." He draws from this matter the following moral. 1. The apparent weakness of the instrument by worldly aid. 2. The great strength of the same through faith in God, all to exemplify the supernatural aid which God has always given to the spread of the Christian faith. The Sermon is feeble. Mr. Jo. Angier and Mrs. John A. called.

[1] Rev. Joseph Angier (Harvard 1829) had graduated from the Divinity School in 1832.

MONDAY. 17TH.

The vegetation of the year which had promised so fairly begins to suffer from the want of moisture. We have not for two months had one day's settled rain. I remained at home and read Horace, Neale and Hutchinson, devoting nearly equal portions of my time to each. The latter becomes more interesting as he proceeds to give accounts of his own experience as Governor. He was a man with a good deal of selfishness of character himself and therefore willing to attribute the same to others. There is an affectation of candour which makes rather against him than for him.

In the afternoon, I read a work of Mirabeau's which has been hid until lately. It consists of a collection of Letters to many individuals unknown.[1] They are many of them very characteristic and amusing. Mirabeau was one of the most extraordinary men of the last age. A monster of iniquity with a brilliancy of talent which smoothed all things to the outward eye in such a manner as to fascinate. Evening quiet at home.

[1] Mirabeau's *Letters during his Residence in England*, 2 vols., London, 1832, had been borrowed from the Athenæum.

TUESDAY. 18TH.

Fine day though exceedingly cold. I went to Boston. Finding that my time was much wasted by my way of life, I went to the Athenæum and got the second Volume of Marshall,[1] which I propose to look over for the political events of the period after the close of the war. The History of the course of Washington is among the astonishing Romances of life. There never was a man before in such a situation to do good to the world and never one before so much disposed to improve it. Patriotism may derive a shining and a warming light from his example. It teaches that all is not hollow pretence, that there can be public virtue and that the world will appreciate it. I was very much struck with his address to the army officers, notwithstanding the very dry style of the biographer. Mr. Curtis called on me for a moment, about a paper to be drawn up for Mr. Boylston's Estate.

I returned to Quincy, and passed my Afternoon reading Mirabeau's

Letters. A singular genius of whom I must learn something more. What a diversity of human character is to be found in this world. No two persons are alike when you see them in history, and although the common mass of mankind resemble each other sufficiently to pass together in a general view, yet a careless observer will note the differences between the individuals who compose it. Mirabeau was a genius and a rascal, an active and an indolent man, quick to see beauty and fitness, dull to practise it. Unprincipled and yet full of sentiments the most exalted. What a contrast to Washington. Passed the evening at home. Read a few of Madame de Sevigné's letters and the Observer.

¹ John Marshall's *Life of George Washington*, probably in the revised edition, 2 vols., Phila., 1832.

WEDNESDAY. 19TH.

The day was fine. All the family drove into town this morning, in the Carriage. I went first to the Office and spent an hour without doing much. The remainder of my time was taken up with the ladies at the Athenæum. It is a pleasant and a profitable thing to spend time studying the efforts of genius in one great line of art. There is nothing more striking than the decline of art as exemplified in the ancient and modern pictures. The colours which in the one seem laid on with singular truth and propriety, look patched from droppings of the rainbow in the other. I passed an hour in the reading room, and thence to Mr. Frothingham's where we all dined. Mrs. Gorham Brooks was there, and Mr. Brooks came after dinner.

We returned to Quincy safely after a tiresome day. In the evening, we went by invitation to Mrs. E. Miller's, a Quincy party with no variety to mention. Home by ten. We saw Mr. Beale who has returned quite pleased from his tour.

In conversation with my father today, I obtained more information respecting his property, which very materially altered my ideas upon the subject. Instead of gaining ground, it seems he has been able barely to hold his own. And judging from the prospect I should expect that my former impressions were justified. This must rouse my slackened attention to my former plan. It must warn me not to trust too implicitly to present indications of wealth, and to look hardly and sharply to the future. But my father, his futurity I do not like to look forward to.

THURSDAY. 20TH.

Fine day although cloudy. I remained quietly at Quincy as much to get over the fatigue of yesterday as to do something in the way of literary occupation. I read Horace, the remainder of Neale's Account of the Reign of Elizabeth, and a little of Hutchinson. These are all exercises of the mind but they are hardly as active as they should be.

I ought to be writing to keep my hand in practice. The Account of Hutchinson ought to inspire me with a subject than which I hardly know a finer. At any rate, I ought to meditate it. My father who is the person to do what is requisite seems to hang off from the undertaking, and to be disposed to plunge into any thing else which will give distraction to his mind.

In the afternoon, I read the second volume of Mirabeau which is not so interesting as the first. It has far more of the appearance of bookmaking. This with a little Indexing engrossed my time. Evening read some of Madame de Sevigné. And two very good numbers of the Observer upon the truth of the Christian Religion and the character of the Moral it inculcates. Conversation also with my Mother about General Jackson.

FRIDAY. 21ST.

Morning cloudy with an occasional dropping of rain which did not amount to a shower. I rode to town and passed my morning indolently, part of it at the Athenæum Gallery where I was present at the sale of Doughty's pictures.[1] They did very well on the whole. Paintings are things which require a very highly cultivated state of Society and a long established taste in the wealthy. We are as yet but little advanced in these matters. Money has not been long in any hands. I also passed some time in finding one of my father's Tenants, out of whom I extracted his rent. This is at least something for my visit.

The whole town was alive with the expectation of seeing the President of the United States. General Jackson has been prodigiously successful in his excursion this Summer from Washington. His Popularity has appeared unbounded even in the strong holds of opposition. There is a cause for this. But where it lies I do not know. He has served his Country no more usefully than a thousand others, but he has the prestige of military glory which dazzles all mortal minds. The art of killing is prized higher than the art of vivifying. My father who was his competitor for the Presidency and a man of incomparably superior character, yet carries with him perpetually a load of unpopularity. He knows none of the arts of conciliating. And he relies too much upon the extent of his own powers to flatter by reposing confidence in others. These are useful lessons to the mind that will improve them. Public favour is a very fascinating thing, but what wise man would place his happiness in it. How much better to resort to less stimulating pleasures.

My Afternoon was passed in reading Mirabeau whose book I finished. It would have been as well, if closed with the first volume. I must now do something more useful. Threatened today with head ache and indigestion, but it passed away. Evening at home. Read two more admirable papers by Cumberland upon the Christian Revelation.

[1] Thomas Doughty, of Philadelphia, the well-known landscapist and lithographer, had taken up residence in Boston in 1832. Sixteen landscapes by him were offered for sale (Groce and Wallace, *Dict. Amer. Artists*; *Columbian Centinel*, 21 June, p. 3, col. 7).

SATURDAY. 22ND.

When passed at home, my days have so much uniformity that I think it hardly of use to sit down and record them. Indeed to a man not engaged in great affairs, it is rather absurd to keep a Journal. He has nothing to write about but the reflections of a solitary whose influence on the world is next to nothing. The principal advantage resulting from the habit is derived in early life when habits are forming. We learn method and facility in composition. In these respects I am very sensible that I have been greatly benefitted. But the time has gone by. And I now do from the force of habit which has been formed. Such is man always, and hence the origin of a thousand customs which long survive the causes that created them.

I read Horace, Neal's Second Volume, and finished Hutchinson's book. On the whole I feel for the Author. His career was that which many men pursue. Begun with brilliant prospects and ardent hope, continued in the belief that views of personal interest and public convenience could be combined and when the moment of being undeceived came, choosing conscientiously perhaps but not fortunately, he passed the remnant of his life in melancholy exile from the scene of his early promise. He has left a book as little tinged with bitterness as could be expected, but yet disclosing in every page the rankling of the arrow in the wound.

Afternoon, read one or two miscellaneous papers of d'Alembert.[1] One upon Rhetoric and Oratory describing what so many learn and teach, yet so few practise with success. Another upon Christine of Sweden, a singular character. I was thinking why it was that she and Charles 5th. never received much applause for their resignation of their Crowns, while Washington's retirement has been so much lauded. The world will look into *motive*. In the former they assign as cause, caprice, in the latter, patriotism. Perhaps this might be further examined. Evening quiet at home.

[1] No copy of d'Alembert's works survives in MQA nor among the Adamses' books at MB and MBAt.

SUNDAY. 23RD.

The day was clear but quite cool. I attended divine service and heard Mr. E. Q. Sewall preach two sensible, tolerably well written Sermons. One from 6. Matthew 6. the other text I did not catch, but the discourse was far the best. It was upon the exercise of religion producing joy.[1] I can understand this better than the melancholy, discouraging tones which Massillon is so fond of indulging. To be innocent is surely to be happy, the more a man makes himself innocent by the conscientious discharge of all his duties, the more happy he ought to be. Sin is misery, whereas Massillon's doctrine reverses the whole process and makes man miserable in proportion as he becomes more religious, and happy as he brings his mind to indifference. What views of the Creator!

Massillon's Sermon for today was in honor of St. Benedict the ascetic. Hebrews 11. 7. "By faith, Noah being named of God of things not seen as yet, moved with fear, prepared an ark to the saving of his house, by the which he condemned the world." Benedict by the light of faith discovered the vanity of the hopes and security of the world. 2. He condemned the vacillation and despair of man by his activity in securing the means of eternal safety. And all this how, because he went into the forest and lived like a brute, because he deprived himself of God's best gifts for fear he might abuse them, because he set an example which deprived the world of thousands of useful beings. I do not comprehend such religion. The Apostles did not do so. The Saviour set no such example. Evening quietly at home.

[1] Edmund Quincy Sewall (Harvard 1815) was Congregational minister of Scituate. JQA noted of his performance, "His voice is not good and his articulation is indistinct; but the composition of his Sermons is very good, and his afternoon discourse was occasionally pathetic. Religious sentimentalism is the most common characteristic of the writings of the young Unitarian Sons of Harvard University." (Diary, 23 June 1833.)

MONDAY. 24TH.

The day was wet and foggy with wind from the Eastward so that I did not stir from home. Indeed while the town is making a holiday of General Jackson's visit, it is waste of time for me to attempt to do any thing there. Read Horace and Neale. The latter gives an Account of the first settlement of Plymouth Colony and the admirable address by Robinson which is interesting. I ought to have read this history before I wrote upon the subject.

Engaged also upon the controversial papers between Hutchinson and the General Court. They are exceedingly well done and strong on both sides although I think the reasoning leans against the Governor. Indeed, had it not been for the consent to the authority of the Long Parliament, I should be clear. To this it can only be answered that times of civil commotion are not the best from which to draw precedents to settle great principles.

My afternoons require more easy reading, and I think I earn the privilege when my mornings are so well spent. Read the Letters of St. John the Pennsylvania Farmer, which are very pretty.[1] Evening quietly at home. Mr. Beale called in and spent an hour.

[1] A copy of *Lettres d'un cultivateur américain* by Michel Guillaume Jean de Crèvecoeur (who used various forms of his name on the titlepages of his books), 3 vols., Paris, 1787, is in MQA.

TUESDAY. 25TH.

It rained so very heavily nearly all day that I did not pretend to execute my intention of going to Boston. The time was passed far more profitably in my Office which is becoming quite an agreeable place to me from it's quietness and from my having it entirely to myself. I read Horace's Art of Poetry, which the more I go over the more I admire, Neale who becomes interesting as he progresses in the Stuart Reigns, and Tudor's Life of James Otis.

Reading Hutchinson has given me quite the spirit of investigation into our early times, and I have already cleared my notions wonderfully by the exercise. James Otis was an uncommon man. He certainly did much to excite the popular feeling and bring forward the Revolution. Mr. Tudor has written a book which posterity will value. It was made up partly from reminiscences by my Grandfather which might have been lost if it had not been for its composition.[1] Our Revolution is becoming more and more, daily, matter of history. Contemporaneous testimony is now to be found only in the books. I must study out the history fully.

Afternoon, Read more of St. John's Letters. There is a very pretty style of sentiment running through their composition. Alas! that in the rough features of this world one can hardly recognize the resemblance. Suffering so often treads upon the heels of pleasure that one cannot ever feel over confident even of the happiness of the moment. If it were not so, the world would be too fascinating. Mad. de Sevigné and the Observer.

[1] In *The Life of James Otis*, Boston, 1823 (two copies of which, each with CFA's bookplate, are in MQA), William Tudor made use of the letters of reminiscence JA had written him in 1817 and 1818 and which were published in 1819. See vol. 3:334, 388; below, entry of 12 July. CFA later took a more measured view of Otis and of Tudor's *Life* of him than he does at this time when he was accepting without question JA's estimate. See the discussion by L. H. Butterfield in *An American Primer*, ed. Daniel J. Boorstin, 2 vols., Chicago, 1966, 1:236–238.

WEDNESDAY. 26TH.

The morning was so bright that I expected a pleasant day to go to town, but it did not so turn out. The wind was quite cold, with occasional threats of rain. The first thing that met me upon my arrival in town was the loss of the key to my Office. How this has happened I am not at present able to divine. I went to Mrs. Frothingham's to deliver a Note and hoped to find the key returned when I got back but it was not so. I luckily found at a machine shop, a key ready made which with a little doctoring was made to answer. My visit to town was therefore not lost, as I passed my time in copying out a power of Attorney for the Executors of Mr. Boylston which has been in my hands since last week.

Returned to Quincy to dinner. General Jackson has been sick and therefore delayed two days but he proceeds on his Journey today.[1] Read a little of Horace, but my afternoon was shortened by my Wife who wished me to accompany her to walk. Evening Cumberland's Observer—A series of numbers upon Shakespeare, Johnson and Milton which are extremely instructive as well as interesting.

[1] JQA recorded the events of the President's visit and the circumstances of his illness more fully: "The President, must hasten back to Washington, or he will be glorified into his grave. They fagged him by their reception on Friday, and their presentations and Addresses on Saturday. . . . Monday Morning there were to be two exhibitions; one putting the Constitution Frigate in the new Dry Dock at the Navy-yard, Charlestown—the other was an Address delivered to him on Bunker's Hill by Edward Everett; and in the afternoon, he was to receive his scientific honours at Harvard University. He was sick in bed the whole day, under the care of Dr. Warren. . . . The Bunker's Hill and Harvard University decorations are postponed." (Diary, 25 June.)

THURSDAY. 27TH.

Fine morning but it clouded up, and we had occasional heavy showers through the day. After doubting a little while, I concluded to go to town, and accomplish what I had left undone. Accordingly I passed my time in finishing the draught of the power of Attorney begun yesterday, bringing down my Quarterly Accounts to this time, and copying out the draught of an Account Current for Monday. I also had a little time for Judge Marshall's last volume. If I always passed my hours in Boston as usefully, I should be more content to go there. Returned home without having experienced any interruptions in my labours, excepting Jackson the Painter, and Mr. Kuhn to collect my heavy subscription to the blind Asylum.[1] I am glad it is paid, and I hope I can say it was done cheerfully.

Found Dr. Waterhouse here upon a visit to dine. He grows old.[2] To day his conversation was principally upon the reception of General Jackson at Cambridge and the conferring upon him the degree of L.L.D. This is a step taken by the College rather from the spirit of worldly compliance than from a sense of right. My father is somewhat indignant at it, which is not surprising although in him the motive is very liable to be misunderstood. It wanted only this to fill the climax of absurdity in General Jackson's elevation.[3]

I read the rest of Horace's Art of Poetry, which is sound throughout with perhaps only two or three trifling exceptions. No single Essay that I know of has done more to exhaust a subject. Subsequent writers have been content to follow. Evening, St. John, the ladies took tea at Weymouth. I read the Observer. Not quite well.

[1] The successful campaign concluded, Col. Perkins had deeded his home to the Institution (*Columbian Centinel*, 15 June, p. 2, col. 7). Kuhn was probably George H. Kuhn (vol. 4:388).

[2] Dr. Benjamin Waterhouse, approaching eighty, had been a close friend of JA and of JQA for more than fifty years. A man of wide learning, he had earlier been professor of physic at Harvard and at seventy-nine had importuned JQA to support his appointment to the chair of Natural History there. CFA had earlier found pleasure in listening to the conversation of the old friends that was likely to touch on a variety of literary or scientific subjects (vol. 4:90, above, and *Adams Family Correspondence*, 4:xiii–xiv, 32–34; see also, Waterhouse to JQA, 17 April 1833 [Adams Papers]; JQA, Diary, 18 June 1833).

[3] During President Jackson's visit to Boston and to Cambridge JQA and CFA had resolutely absented themselves from all events planned in connection with it. JQA's self-exile in Quincy indicated no lack of interest in all that occurred during Jackson's stay, and Waterhouse's account of the ceremonies in Cambridge elicited a warm response. JQA's account in his diary of that part of the conversation with Waterhouse is included in John Spencer Bassett's "Notes on Jackson's Visit to New England, June 1833" (MHS, *Procs.*, 56 [1922–1923]:244–260).

JQA's opposition to the award of the honorary degree had earlier been vigorously expressed to President Quincy of Harvard when he had come to the Old House to inquire of JQA's willingness to attend: "I said that the personal Relations in which President Jackson had chosen to place himself with me were such that I could hold no intercourse of a friendly character with him.... And independent of that, as myself an affectionate child of our alma Mater, I would not be present to witness her disgrace in conferring her highest Literary honours upon a barbarian, who could not write a sentence of Grammar, and hardly could spell his own name." To Quincy's account of the Corporation's reasons JQA reacted, "I was not satisfied with these reasons, but it is college ratiocination and College Sentiment. Time serving and Sycophancy are qualities of all learned and Scientific Institutions. More than 50 years since the College gave this degree ... to a Frenchman by the name of Valnais, about as fit for it as Andrew Jackson ... I had some good humoured discussion with Mr. Quincy upon this occurrence, but adhered to my determination to stay at home" (Diary, 18 June; later repeated in similar language in the letter from JQA to CFA cited below).

Reports of the incongruities of the occasion were relished in the Adams household, particularly those relating to Jackson's behavior and response: "I understand he behaved with great dignity during the Latin Oration and never moved a muscle of his face during the recital, an excellent proof that he relished the striking and complimentary parts of it to the satisfaction of Mr. Q. and the Learned Body. I send John a Squib in the form of an Improvisation which I wrote ...

Discerning old Harvard presents the degree
Old Hickory asks pray *what means LLD?*
The Corporate Sages afraid of excess
Reserve for themselves that of A.S.S."
(LCA to Mrs. JA2, 6 July, Adams Papers)

Outside the family, too, a good deal of ribald comment was provoked, especially from the pen of Major Jack Downing (for example, *Columbian Centinel*, 19 Aug., p. 1, cols. 5–7).

The award of the degree, however, produced more serious consequences for President Quincy. At an Overseers' meeting early in 1834, J. T. Austin and A. H. Everett sought to embarrass the President by raising the question whether the Overseers had been given proper and timely notice of the meeting set to confirm the action of the Corporation. A committee of inquiry was appointed, and the matter was not finally disposed of until 13 February (*Columbian Centinel*, 13 Jan., p. 1, col. 6— p. 2, col. 1; 14 Feb., p. 2, col. 5; 19 Feb., p. 2, cols. 1–3). In the interim the *Centinel* printed on the authority of the *Charlestown Aurora* a rumor that "it is not improbable that Mr. Quincy may retire from the Presidency of Harvard College" (3 Feb., p. 2, col. 1). These actions would seem to have provided part of the basis for Quincy's conviction that the Everetts had sought to oust him, probably with the hope that he would be replaced by Edward Everett (see below, entry for 23 Aug. 1834, note).

JQA, opposed as he had been to the action taken in the matter of the degree, nevertheless rose to Quincy's defense, as he would again later in the year in the matter of the student riots: "I see with great concern that another stream of disputation has opened from a fountain bitter as wormwood and gall. The discussion at the Board of Overseers upon the Diploma which has polluted the Catalogue of our Alma Mater with the name of Andrew Jackson, is reported in the Daily Advocate and has deeply afflicted me. The more so, because the debate discovers the spirit of chicanery against President Quincy, assailing him, not on the really questionable ground of his conduct on that occasion, but on the mere omission of the formality of giving due notice.... His real error was in consenting to confer the degree upon a man every way unworthy of it. He gave me notice of the meeting personally, and I told him I *would not* be present to see ... that prostration of Learning at the feet of Power.... And through the whole of that Presidential tour, where was there one single voice of remonstrance heard against the baseness of that servility and adulation, cringing while its object, like a skunk, scattered his stench as he went ... continually alternating between the visit to the close stool and the reception of some fulsome address?" (JQA to CFA, 18 Jan. 1834, Adams Papers.)

1. FANNY KEMBLE, AS BIANCA IN MILMAN'S *Fazio*,
BY THOMAS SULLY, 1833
See page ix–x

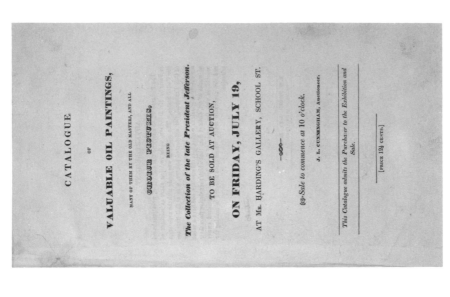

2. MRS. WOOD AND ENSEMBLE IN THE FINAL SCENE OF
La Sonnambula
See page x–xi

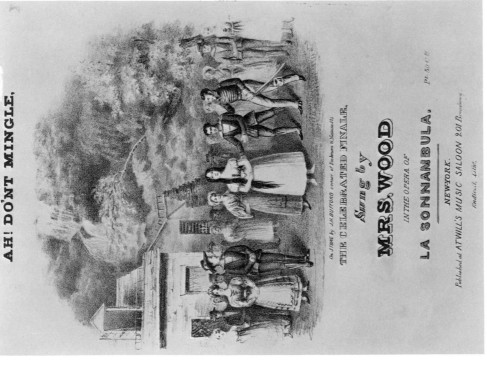

3. AUCTION CATALOGUE OF PAINTINGS
FROM THOMAS JEFFERSON'S COLLECTION
AT MONTICELLO FOR SALE
IN BOSTON, 1833
See page xi–xiii

QVINTI HORATII FLACCI

OPERA.

AD FIDEM EDITIONIS

I. M. GESNERI.

R. Westall, R.A. inv.   Gul. Finden fc.

CARM. LIB. III. Od. IV.

HARDING, MAVOR, ET LEPARD.
LONDINI.
MDCCCXXIV.

It would be difficult to comprise more of the art of style in an equal number of lines and do it so very greatly withal.

This is one of the few human beings which have exhausted a subject.

Q. HORATII FLACCI

DE ARTE POETICA

LIBER.

August 8. 1833.

I this day have finished this volume after a slow perusal of several months. And I can say with truth that it is the first time I have formed any idea of the true character of the Poet.

Charles Francis Adams.

N.B. This text is from the edition of Gesner. I have compared it with the improved copy by Zeunius, Leipsic 1803 as well as with the editions of Dacier and Sanadon. No English should read the editions... noted, until perhaps the fourth or fifth time. I have put in the margin such as appeared to me valuable for the elucidation of the studies.

4. CHARLES FRANCIS ADAMS' ANNOTATED COPY OF HORACE

See page xiii

INFAMOUS ABUSE
Of Mr. Adams,—by National Republicans !!!

FELLOW CITIZENS : JOHN QUINCY ADAMS twice received your votes for President. When he retired from that office, he accepted a seat in Congress. His services there will form a bright page in history. He saved the "INDUSTRY OF FREEDOM," and preserved the integrity of the Union. He was always *first* at his post and *last* to leave it. The next Congress will meet early in December. Mr. Adams, with his usual punctuality, left Quincy a few days since, to travel by easy stages and be in Washington in ample time to take his seat. His claims as a candidate for Governor, he leaves with his fellow citizens. His presence was not required at the election, and true to his republican principles, he will not seek to promote his election to any office, *by personal influence!* Should Mr. Adams be elected Governor, he could not go into office until January, so that his duty to his constituents would require his attendance in Congress for several weeks. Under these circumstances Mr. Adams has taken his departure for Washington, and you find him *insulted, villified* and *abused* for this attention to business, as if he were *a runaway slave,* by the organs of the National Republican party, who support John Davis against John Quincy Adams !

Fellow Citizens, read this infamous and scurrilous assault upon your late favorite President, the first Statesman in the Nation, and then say if you will countenance a party that seeks to gain its ends by such *infamous means.* If there is a moral sense of decency left among us, this insult will be *rebuked!!!*

[*From the Boston Atlas of Saturday.*]

"Lost, Strayed, or Stolen!"

"Missing, the Antimasonic candidate for Governor! He was last seen oñ the road to Providence, on *Sunday* last, mounted on a pacing grey horse, dressed in a blue coat, metal buttons, light nankin pantaloons, silk stockings and pumps. It is supposed he is on his way to Washington.

Whoever will return the said candidate to the Antimasonic Committee Room, in Merchants' Hall, shall receive the thanks of his deserted and disconsolate friends, an entire file of the Boston Advocate, one thousand of the "Cowell letter," and as many more of the "Washstand correspondence."

N. B. No charges paid."

[*From the Centinel of Saturday.*]

"Mr. Adams, the file leader of the political Antimasons, despairing of success as their candidate for Governor, has left Quincy and gone on to Washington to take his seat in Congress."

FRIDAY. 28TH.

Fine morning although the Northwest wind made the air still quite cold. I staid at home all day today. My time passed in my usual avocations. Horace's Odes, Neale and Tudor's Life of James Otis. Upon reading the history of the Puritans, there is a great deal of matter which I regret I did not know when I wrote my Article for the North American, which I see by the Newspaper, is to be published on Monday, after so long a delay.[1] There are points which might have been stated more strongly, and others perhaps a little softened. But these regrets would probably always recur upon reading a book on the subject, as every writer has to present some new or singular view of some point or other. I was interested in Mr. Tudor which is a valuable series of reminiscences.

In the afternoon, I walked up to Payne's hill to see Mr. Field for the last time. As usual, he was not at home. On my return I felt so indisposed that I did not do much. Evening quiet at home. My father went into town to dine with Lieut. Gov. Armstrong and did not return until late. Read Cumberland's criticism of Congreve's Double dealer.

[1] See vol. 4:428, and note to entry for 4 Jan., above.

SATURDAY. 29TH.

Fine day and more like Summer than any thing we have had. My Wife received a Note[1] in answer to a proposition of her's, by which this was the day fixed to begin a contemplated visit to her father's at Medford.

I went into town earlier for the purpose of going to my house. I examined my Parlours and was pretty well satisfied that it would be necessary to do more to them than I had contemplated. I was therefore busy in taking down the Pictures to put them in greater security. Having done all that I deemed necessary, I went to the Office and was very busy there in finishing off Accounts and balancing my books. The results are quite favourable. Attended a Stock sale at Noon but purchased nothing—The only Stock which I wanted going for more than I had designed to pay for it. This took up nearly all my remaining time.

I returned to Quincy but not to see my Wife and child. And I wandered about the House feeling as if I did not know what to set about doing. God forgive me, if I love them too well. Walked up to Mrs. Adams' to see and settle with Elizabeth, in anticipation of Monday when she and I both propose to leave town. She was unwell and lying down. She is threatened with pulmonary disease, and I am fearful she is not prudent enough to get over it. Returned home and read St. John. I have myself felt a little indisposed for the last day or two. Quiet evening. Conversation with my father. Cumberland's Observer.

[1] Missing.

SUNDAY. 30TH.

The morning was fine and the day warm. I was occupied partly in attendance upon Divine Service all day and partly in my ordinary occupations. Texts from John 5. 68. and 8. 12. by Mr. Deane the Minister of Scituate. It is a long time since I have heard him, but I confess I liked him better than my previous impressions would seem to have authorized.[1] He discoursed upon the argument of the skeptic that the Christian religion wants dignity, and upon the influence of revelation upon the character of mankind, more especially in the female branch of it.

I also read a Sermon of Massillon from John 1. 7. "The same came for a witness to bear witness of the Light" omitting "that all men through him might believe." A Commemoration of John the Baptist, whose testimony to the light and truth condemned the world while he was condemned by it for doing so. This testimony was borne in his mode of life which displayed his austerity, his humility and his zeal. Some parts of this discourse appeared to me remarkably good, but it did not strike me so much in its general power and the singularity of the contradiction to the whole in the omitted portion of the verse is not a little remarkable.

In the evening, we all went to pay a visit to Mr. and Mrs. Quincy who have just moved out of town.[2] They seemed to be as yet much at sixes and sevens, so that we stayed but a short time. A Country place for the first day or two is generally comfortless. Mr. Deane dined here.

[1] It had been nine years since CFA had heard Rev. Samuel Deane and recorded his impressions (vol. 1:155).

[2] Col. Josiah Quincy IV, son of President Quincy of Harvard, regularly brought his family to Quincy for the summer (see vol. 3:29 and Adams Genealogy). As military aide to the Governor, he had just completed his duties as the State's host and guide to President Jackson during his visit to Massachusetts (his recollections of the events associated with that visit are in his *Figures of the Past*, p. 296–316).

[*Medford*]

MONDAY. JULY 1ST.

The day was excessively warm. I went to town and was engaged pretty actively, first, in finishing off my Quarterly Accounts, second in *my* affairs. Purchased of my Broker, Mr. Degrand, a four month's Bank credit for a considerable sum which made it necessary for me to be active in the collection of my Dividends and putting all my affairs in train. The Dover Stock has done very well[1] and my residence out of town enables me to spare more of my money than I could otherwise readily do without. This with two or three small interruptions consumed the remainder of my day.

I rode to Medford and found my Wife and child whom I was glad to see. The Afternoon was passed with little or no regular occupation although I did not quite pass it without reading—One or two Articles in the Monthly Review the most interesting of which was upon Mr. Jay's late work.[2] The Writer is not a Convert to Mr. Sparks' new doctrine.

In the evening, we all went down to Mrs. Angiers for the purpose of paying a visit to Judge Cranch and his Wife who happened to be there. By we all, I mean Mr. Brooks, Mrs. Gorham Brooks, my Wife and self. After stopping some time we returned home and found our child quite sick with pukings which we did not understand. She had been unusually fretful which with her is an unerring sign of indisposition. From the want of an experienced person in the house, I had an anxious and sleepless night.

[1] Shares in the Cocheco Manufacturing Co. of Dover, N.H., given to ABA by Mr. Brooks (vol. 4:129).

[2] A review of William Jay's *Life of John Jay* in the *American Monthly Review*, 4:35–79 (July 1833).

TUESDAY. 2D.

It is not easy to say how much I suffered during the night and morning—The child taken so suddenly, my Wife in no condition to bear so much anxiety and compelled to rely upon our own resources for a remedy. In a strange house so far as all the assistance we required was concerned and giving trouble, I felt quite unhappy. Then there is such a change in the house that I hardly know Medford again. Mr. Brooks himself appears to me depressed by his own difficulty, a recurrence of a complaint in his knee which arose from an injury received some years ago, as well as from the changes about him. I accompanied him to Boston as the child had taken medicine and seemed somewhat better. Little Peter, Mrs. Gorham Brooks' child had been affected in just the same way.

My hours in Boston were anxious, and the weather was very warm. I was engaged in a number of little occupations relating to money affairs and had an hour's conversation with Mrs. Frothingham in which I spoke very unreservedly of matters as I viewed them. Such is the vanity of human expectation. The plan which I had supposed would fix the comfort of Mr. Brooks' declining years, turns out the least eligible of any that he has pursued.

I returned to dinner with Mr. Brooks, the child had seen the Dr. and he had relieved very much all our apprehensions. The Afternoon was quietly passed. I looked over the North American Review, more especially my Article which I find much less altered from the original than was the preceding one. It must now take its chance with the public. My expectations of literary success have been humbled to such an extent that I expect little praise, and my peculiar views together with my name lead me to anticipate some little censure. To counterbalance this I have nothing but a clear conscience. Evening, there were visitors. Mr. and Mrs. Stetson and the Misses Osgood.[1]

[1] Rev. Caleb Stetson, Congregational minister at Medford, his wife, and the Misses Lucy and Elizabeth Osgood are briefly characterized at vol. 3:76–77.

[*Quincy*]

WEDNESDAY. 3D.

The child had an excellent night so that she appeared quite nicely this morning. As I had written to my Mother what was calculated perhaps to alarm her[1] if I should not go to Quincy and as Mr. Brooks was to be absent all day tomorrow, I concluded to go to Quincy instead of returning. Went first, however, to Boston. Occupied there in the usual manner with me at Quarter time—Drawing up Accounts &c. Mr. W. Lovering called upon me with respect to an Interest in land in High Street, possessed by my father, for which he makes an offer.[2] I told him I would let him know. The day was showery so that I could not be in the Streets much. Rode to Quincy and found the family much as usual. My Afternoon was spent in making up the Arrears of my Diary as well as reading. Quiet evening. I went to bed early.

[1] 2 July (Adams Papers); the subject of the letter was LCA2's indisposition.
[2] On JQA's interest in property on High Street, Boston, see vol. 3:210.

THURSDAY. 4TH.

It is now so many years since the Declaration of Independence that the vigour of its celebration is rather slackened. The City of Boston still holds on to its accustomed forms and here and there is to be found some place where the festival is held, but noise is not to me a necessary concomitant of rejoicing. I hope I felt duly grateful for the enjoyments of the day which were to be found in a profound quiet.

My time was taken up in writing, and reading Horace, Neal and the Life of James Otis. I compared the latter with Hutchinson and detected him in some want of candor. If I should again review anything I think it would be this book.

Quiet dinner at home. My father seemed unwell from a severe cold. In the Afternoon I rambled down to the Orchard at Mount Wollaston and spent an hour gazing at the view which was in great beauty today. The men were mowing exactly as if it was not a bit of a holiday. The trees of the Orchard look very stationary although they have gained this Season considerably. Returned home. Mr. Jo. Angier of Medford made a visit and took tea. He came over with his Mother and Mrs. Angier Jr. After tea we went up, and found Mr. Beale, Miss Louisa Smith and a whole room full. Returned and read some of Mr. Rush's late publication upon England.[1]

[1] Probably *Memoranda of a Residence at the Court of London* by Richard Rush, Phila., 1833.

[*Medford*]

FRIDAY. 5TH.

I went to town this morning and was engaged at my Office in my usual way. Read some portions of the North American Review as well as a little of Marshall's Life of Washington. In the first I was much pleased with the article upon Phrenology.[1] Without being very sound it is yet amusing and pointedly written. The science, like many others which have been struck out bears witness to Man's ingenuity, and to his passion for novelty. It is in some respects very dangerous, as it gives room for materialism as well as for the belief of the fatalist.

I went to Medford and found the child and my Wife pretty well. After dinner I amused myself as well as I could with one or two of the late periodical publications. But my principal difficulty in passing time here is the not feeling capable of devoting it to useful purpose. Books are wanting, place is wanting, and above all the spirit that presides over literature.

I walked down to the Grove and sat there in a kind of a reverie made up too much of views of perhaps too personal a nature. But these have a moral with them, to an understanding mind. They are empty, vain dreams, exposing our weakness to ourselves. I thought of writing again, selecting Hutchinson as the subject. Evening, quietly at home, reading and Conversation. I think Mr. Brooks seems very much depressed with his leg.

[1] Considerable interest in phrenology had been generated in Boston during the preceding year, largely through the presence of Dr. Johann Gaspar Spurzheim, whose death in November had been widely lamented (vol. 4:397, 401). The article in the *North Amer. Rev.* (37:59-83 [July 1833]) by Gamaliel Bradford was essentially a review of three of Dr. Spurzheim's books.

SATURDAY. 6TH.

Fine day. I accompanied Mr. Brooks to town. At the Office, then the House and a call at Miss Oliver's, which was returned by her soon afterwards with the amount of her Rent. Mr. Lovering also called in and after a little conversation, I concluded the bargain with him in regard to the Property in High Street.[1] This is advantageous to both parties. My father could do nothing with the small share he had in the Estate, and Mr. Lovering pays for the Piece only what would induce him to take the trouble of acquiring it in the little divisions which are made of it.

Returned with Mr. Brooks to Medford. Mr. Shepherd came out and dined. We had a pretty dinner, and I lazed away the whole of the remainder of the Afternoon. Such is life at Medford. Mr. Shepherd was less noisy than usual. He is a self made man, with some vanity about wealth and a little fondness for the things of this life—Not perhaps more, however, than have we all.

We went to Mrs. N. Hall's to take tea. Mr. B., Mrs. Gorham Brooks, Wife and myself. Mr. and Mrs. Nat. Hall, daughter, niece, Miss Gray and a certain Mrs. Amory whom I did not know.[2] Talked miscellaneously with Mr. Hall.

[1] William Lovering, whose home was on High Street (*Boston Directory*).
[2] Peter C. Brooks' sister, Joanna, was the wife of Nathaniel Hall of Medford. Their daughter was Mary Brooks Hall. Henrietta Gray was the remaining unmarried daughter of another sister (see vol. 2:155; 3:70, 107, 123).

SUNDAY. 7TH.

The Morning was drizzly but it became clear and warmer as the day advanced. I attended Divine Service all day, and heard Mr. Stetson. The morning's was a Communion Sermon in which he did not hesitate to introduce the powerful rhetorical figure of the supposed presence of the Saviour and this in a voice and manner just as cold as if he was saying that the weather was fine. In the Afternoon he endeavoured to discuss the doctrine of final retribution as the support of Christianity. This is an important subject in this day. Mr. Stetson is on the whole somewhat above the ordinary run of Clergymen, although his delivery is as usual very indifferent and subtracts from his influence.

Read a Sermon of Massillon's though not so thoroughly as I could wish. It was upon the Anniversary of St. Magdalen. Luke 7. 47. "Her sins which are many are forgiven for she loved much." Magdalen had loved the world, the same love when penitent she directed to the Saviour, a love which softened the bitterness of all her undertakings, a love which knew no limits in the extent of its sacrifices. That love which had been misdirected, when it took its proper course, was the means of her salvation.

I was quite unwell all day, from having indulged somewhat too much in fruits yesterday. A rigorous system of starvation for the greater portion of the day, effected the restoration of my comfort. Quiet evening.

[*Quincy*]

MONDAY. 8TH.

The morning was cloudy with occasional showers of rain. I went to town and was occupied much of my time first in a walk to my House, next in business and accounts at my Office, third in an hour wasted at the Athenæum. I also read a Chapter or two in Marshall.

As it was my day to stay in town, I dined with Mr. Frothingham very quietly. Afternoon. Attended a Meeting of the Directors of the Boylston Market Association. There was a Quorum for once and they passed upon two or three bills that were presented. The rest of the time was taken up in conversation. These are good men to talk.

We had a thunder shower during the time. After it was over, I rode to Quincy and found my father somewhat better and my Mother not very well. Solitude and want of amusing occupation are a little too much for them. I hope, I may find not so much stimulus in the active scenes of life, as to lose all enjoyment in those that are passive.

The evening was passed in conversation and reading aloud the Article in the North American Review upon Phrenology. It is by Dr. G. Bradford. He resisted the fever very imprudently, when it was at it's height.[1] Read the numbers of the Observer.

[1] Presumably the "fever" over phrenology.

[*Medford*]

TUESDAY. 9TH.

My purpose in coming here last Night was to obtain of my father the necessary Deed of the Estate in High Street. I had written [it?] as long since as Saturday in order to get it done before I came, but my Father was so languid he did not finish it until this morning. He went up after breakfast to get an acknowledgment of Mr. Greenleaf, but forgot me when he got there and kept me nearly two hours dancing attendance.[1] At last I went up myself and perhaps upon meeting him, lost my patience a little too much.

My father is in many respects an altered man. Age has relaxed his energies, and the extremes of hot and cold in which his mental system is exercised by his present mode of life are far too trying. Yet on the other hand my business character must be sustained—For I do not know that I shall have any thing else upon which to found myself. A smart pace got me to Boston at the time I had myself appointed for the delivery of the Deed. And the business was settled.

Received a Note from Mrs. Everett requesting me to dine at her house in Charlestown today. After passing my morning as usefully as I commonly do, which is not saying much, I accompanied Mr. Brooks to Charlestown. We found Mrs. G. Brooks and my Wife who had come from Medford. Our dinner was a very genteel one, and we divided after it to our respective destinations, i.e. the rest of the party to go to tea at Mr. Pratt's at Watertown, while I drove Mr. Brooks' gig to Medford. I found my little child glad to see me and passed the remainder of the day in idleness and solitude.

Mr. Everett was rather more gracious than usual to me today. It is unfortunate for me that I always suspect in him a motive of some kind or other for all the acts of his life. Mrs. E. looks better than she has done although still not well. The party returned at eight, and we retired early. In my hurry I forgot the Observer this morning but shall make it up.

[1] It was Ezekiel Price Greenleaf, the son of Thomas, the notary, who so absorbed JQA's interest on this and other occasions. The younger Greenleaf was an expert on horticultural matters and was so recognized by JQA. Examination of Greenleaf's nursery of seedling plants, "a work truly stupendous," generated the excitement which caused him to forget CFA (vol. 2:156, 229; JQA, Diary, 9 July 1833).

[*Quincy*]

WEDNESDAY. 19TH [10TH].

I left Medford with Mr. Brooks, and my Wife was to follow in the Carriage. My stay here this time has been less agreeable than ever, from the absence of occupation and of the company which I have always had heretofore. Mr. Frothingham has been there and generally some others of the family. Add to this, a change in Mr. Brooks himself from the effect upon his spirits of his knee.

Time wears insensibly enough, but when I take a jump of five years back, what a difference there does appear to be between things then and now—A difference in Mr. Brooks' family, in our own, and in the world at large. These are matters for the Philosopher, for the moralist, who would turn the small incidents of life to account.

I was engaged in Boston partly in Accounts, partly in reading Marshall. Rode to Quincy to dine and found my Wife and child there before me. The Afternoon was passed in making up my Arrears of Diary, and in taking a Salt water bath, the first this Season.

THURSDAY. 11TH.

Fine day. Having been to Boston a great deal of late, I concluded I would try the comfort of a day or two in quiet and study. Remained at Quincy and returned to the whole series of my ancient occupations. Read an Ode or two of Horace, a Chapter of Neale and instead of continuing directly the life of James Otis, I compared about one half of the second volume of Minot's History of Massachusetts with my Grandfather's copy. My object was to copy the Marginal Notes which were after all of little importance. But he conveyed away from the family his books, and I thought I might at least retain in mine some symptoms of the action of his mind.[1] The work itself is an exceedingly superficial one and very wordy.

In the afternoon I walked to Payne's hill after my usual business of dunning the Tenants and with usual success. I then strolled over to Mount Wollaston and took a bath at the beach of that farm. It was charming. There are some Lime trees which are the relics of a former age. I sat in their shade some-time and mused. Then home pretty well fatigued. Evening quiet at home. Read a little and but little. My father's birthday—66 years old.

[1] JA's copy, with marginal notes in his hand, of George Richards Minot's *Continuation of the History of the Province of Massachusetts Bay, from the year 1748 . . . to 1765*, 2 vols., Boston, 1798–1803, was among the books which JA had given to the town of Quincy, which remained in the "Office" at the Old House, and which are now in MB. The second volume of CFA's set still in MQA, which bears the notes copied in CFA's hand and identified as JA's (vol. 3:334), reflects the action taken for the reasons he states.

FRIDAY. 12TH.

The Season is at present delightful—Not too warm and yet comfortable. I passed another day in the quiet enjoyment of life at Quincy. Although drowsy from my fatigue of yesterday with broken sleep last night, I read two or three Odes of the second Book of Horace, a Chapter of Neale, and executed the rest of the comparison with Minot. I have gained from it but little.

My mind has been floating uncertainly upon a scheme for reviewing the third Volume of Hutchinson. I do not as yet imagine any thing definite. A sketch of the man is what I want to begin with. But for this I must look after materials.

In the Afternoon, I finished the first volume of Crevecœur, and read over my Grandfather's Correspondence with Tudor about James Otis which is among his best and most characteristic things.[1] I then went down to the Water and took an agreeable bath. This is the third in succession. And I feel as if it had done me good.

My father spent the day at Cambridge on College duty. He did not get back until evening. Read the Observer.

[1] In MQA are two copies of *Novanglus and Massachusettensis* (Boston, 1819) containing as an appendix "Letters from the Hon. John Adams, to the Hon. Wm. Tudor . . . on the Events of the American Revolution" (see vol. 3:387–388).

SATURDAY. 13TH.

The day was still fine although increasing in heat above those preceding. I rode to town this morning and was mainly occupied in Accounts and little Commissions besides a visit to the Athenæum where I found nothing. My mode of spending time is somewhat useless in the City, and yet my neglect of going exposes me to considerable censure. Having just enough of business to do, to bring many persons to see me who not finding me at my Office, are provoked, while I have so little when there as not to pay me for consuming the most valuable hours of the day.

Returned to Quincy to dine. Afternoon, I read several of my Grandfather's letters upon James Otis, and made up the rest of my Diary. But the time after dinner particularly in Summer is not the Season for application. It goes without any means of turning it to much account. After tea, I took a bath which was as pleasant as any of the preceding. Then home where I read several Articles in the North American Review, one upon the Blind apparently from Dr. Howe which is somewhat curious.[1] The philanthropy of the Age is well directed in this case, although one may well be doubtful whether it can go so far as the most sanguine appear to anticipate.

[1] "Education of the Blind" by Samuel Gridley Howe, *North Amer. Rev.*, 37:20–58 (July 1833).

SUNDAY. 14TH.

A very hot day with a Southerly wind, more oppressive than any thing I have felt this Summer. My morning was not very actively employed. Read an Ode of Horace and wrote my Diary.

Attended Divine Service all day. Mr. Smith, the Preceptor of the Hingham Academy,[1] preached, in the morning upon the immortality of the Soul as the Christian doctrine, 1. Thessalonians 5. 6. and in the Afternoon Titus 3. 9. upon the absence of divisions. He was quite brief and had little of substance in his discourses. But he was good looking, and his manner was quite tolerable.

I read a Sermon of Massillon's upon St. Bernard. Text Ecclesiasticus 46. 16–17. [(] our version makes part 13. 14. 15. [)] "Beloved of his Lord, he established a kingdom and anointed princes over his people. By the law of the Lord he judged the congregation. By his faithfulness he was found a true prophet." A parallel between Samuel and Bernard, considering them in three lights, as religious men, as Apostles and as teachers of truth. I know little of Bernard's history, and am not willing to take my knowledge implicitly from this authority.

Mr. Degrand passed the day here. Nothing new. Mr. Beale and his son were here in the evening. There was a shower.

[1] Increase S. Smith was the preceptor of the Derby Academy in Hingham, 1826–1844 (Thomas T. Bouvé and others, *History of the Town of Hingham*, 3 vols. in 4, Cambridge, 1893, vol. 1, pt. 2, p. 141).

MONDAY. 15TH.

The weather promised to be warm so that I concluded to remain at home. It was in fact however quite tolerable the wind coming out from the North West. I went to the Bath and enjoyed a very agreeable plunge. My way is not to remain long enough to fatigue myself and yet to obtain the benefit of the freshness. I read a little of Horace and also some of Neale and Tudor's life of Otis, but I do not advance much in my project. I want energy to begin.

The Afternoon was passed in reading St. John de Crevecœur. He gives some statistics which for that period were no doubt quite valuable, and some account of customs which are curious and to me in a great degree new.

Mr. and Mrs. Wm. Lee came out and paid a visit this Afternoon. Mrs. A my Mother was too unwell to see them. She is suffering severely from her old complaint the Erisypelas. In the evening I went out in the Carriage with my Wife and the Children. Little Louisa, our child was taken sick and gave us some trouble. She is in the process of cutting teeth and gives us much anxiety. We did little or nothing. I read the Observer.

TUESDAY. 16TH.

Fine day and as cool as need be. I rode to town by way of the Neck for the purpose of seeing the improvements going on there. Roxbury is receiving a great deal of the surplus population of the Capital and bids fair itself to become quite a City. The peculiar situation of Boston insulated as it is, prevents the possibility of an indefinite increase, and the progress of the building mania has already taken up most of the vacant spots. The price of land is so enormous that I do not wonder so many people prefer to avoid it. An admirable house might be built for the money that a small one costs with the land in the centre of the City. Boston has unquestionably been under an impulse within a few years which makes one wonder at the remembrance of what it was.

My morning was not very usefully spent. I hardly know what I did with it, excepting to pay a few bills and make up old accounts. Stopped in at a second hand book store where I purchased a nice copy of Grahame's History of the United States.[1] I also went in to see the collection of Pictures belonging to the late President Jefferson, which are poor enough in all conscience.[2]

Home. My Mother was quite ill all day but more particularly in the Afternoon. Dr. Holbrook came over and seemed to comfort her more by his mildness of manner than by his medicines.[3] I read an Ode or two of Horace and some of St. John. Quiet evening.

[1] CFA's copy of the 1827 edn. of James Grahame's *History* is in MQA. He had earlier given careful study to the work and had published an essay-review of it (vol. 3:27, 204, 213, 226).

[2] The paintings from Thomas Jefferson's collection were on exhibition at Chester Harding's Gallery on School Street and were to be auctioned on 19 July. They were said to have been acquired by Jefferson in Paris with the assistance of John Trumbull, then living there (*Columbian Centinel*, 13 July, p. 3, col. 1). The titlepage of the catalogue of the collection issued before the auction is reproduced in the present volume; see also p. xi–xiii, above.

[3] On Dr. Amos Holbrook, see vol. 3:287.

WEDNESDAY. 17TH.

The day was cool. I remained at Quincy and occupied myself in reading according to my usual way. An Ode or two of Horace, a Chapter of Neale who becomes more and more prosaic as we go along. Tudor's Life was more interesting. He gives sketches of three of the leading men of the day, Hawley, S. Adams and Hancock, which I compared with those drawn by Hutchinson. Considering the difference of the source, I think the likeness is tolerably kept. While Tudor either does not mention at all or softens away the unfavourable portions of character, Hutchinson makes them a little the strongest, but both admit the correctness of each other, the one by confessing the faults, the other by allowing the virtues. This is as much as can be expected from history.

Poor Hutchinson. Dr. Holbrook was only yesterday telling a Story of Dr. Jeffries visit to him three days before his death. He then regretted his house on Milton hill, and his old habits in his native State.[1] Such is the fate of Man.

Afternoon reading St. John who was a little dry and uninteresting. I called in the evening at Mrs. T. B. Adams. She has gone to Medford. Saw E.C.A. her daughter with whom my little business was. Saw there Miss Smith, Mr. Beale and Mr. Gourgas. Returned home at nine. My Mother was much better today.

[1] Dr. John Jeffries, a Bostonian and a loyalist, afterward practiced in London, where, in addition to attending former Governor Thomas Hutchinson, he was present for the birth of JA's first grandchild, William Steuben Smith, in 1787 (JA, *Diary and Autobiography*, 3:203). Hutchinson built his celebrated countryseat on Milton Hill in 1743 and resided in it, mainly during the summer months, with pride until 1774, when he left Massachusetts for England. The history of the estate is to be found in Malcolm Freiberg, *Thomas Hutchinson of Milton*, Milton, Mass., Milton Historical Society, 1971.

THURSDAY. 18TH.

Cloudy with occasional thunder showers round about us but no rain of any consequence here. I rode to town and spent my morning in rather an idle way. Went to the Office, the Athenæum, and dawdled an hour at the second hand Book Store where I purchased a copy of Gesner's Horace for the sake of comparison with my copy and those of Dacier and Sanadon.[1] I have little or nothing else to say in excuse for nearly four hours. Commissions however took up some time.

In the Afternoon I was engaged in copying a long Antimasonic Letter from my father to a Committee in Vermont. He rather overdoes this business. Mr. Everett has lately written a letter however, which has transferred a large portion of the Hornets to his person. He is less easy in the traces. I do not know how he will get through.[2] Read an Ode or two of Horace. Evening with my Mother who is better. Read the Observer.

[1] See above, entry for 1 Feb., note.

[2] Edward Everett, in a letter of 29 June to H. W. Atwill printed in the *Concord Gazette*, had come out strongly against Freemasonry. National Republican newspapers were severely critical of him for thus inflicting damage on the party of which he was a leading member (*Columbian Centinel*, 15 July, p. 2, col. 5; 20 July, p. 2, col. 1). The plan of Everett and his brother Alexander Hill to effectuate a union of the National Republicans with the antimasonic forces through the nomination by both parties of JQA for governor, presenting a common front against the Jacksonian Democrats (A. H. Everett to JQA, 11 July 1833, Adams Papers), would presently appear.

FRIDAY. 19TH.

I remained at home all day and pursued my usual occupations with tolerable industry. Read a little of Horace and was pleased at the acquisition which I made of Gesner's edition yesterday. The notes are not so long as those of Dacier and Sanadon while they contain quite important matter. I finished the second volume of Neale, and am at present somewhat in doubt whether to go on with it or not. I also pursued my reading of Tudor with interest. He has embodied many of the anecdotes of the Revolution, which without him, would probably have perished. And his Judgment upon facts is generally sound. His sketch of Franklin is a very good though perhaps rather a favourable one. He touches the points of his character which are weak tenderly. Perhaps this is due to a man whose services have been so great as to compensate for his faults. But Mr. Sparks at the present day is attempting far more than this. He is for setting up Franklin at the expense of every body else.[1] Afternoon, finished the second volume of St. John which is dull enough and read one or two Articles in the North American Review. Evening in my Mother's room. Conversation. Observer.

[1] On the impact upon the Adamses of Jared Sparks' interpretation of American diplomatic history from a strongly pro-Franklin position, see vol. 4:xii–xiii.

SATURDAY. 20TH.

Clouds but no rain. I rode to town and passed my time in a very desultory way. Read a little of Marshall however. Went to see Mrs. Frothingham and sat with her half an hour. This engrosses pretty much all that I did.

Much newspaper discussion of Mr. Everett's letter. The National Republican Presses are out against him very generally. Yet what is National Republicanism at this day? A splinter of a party—Containing not a Majority of any State in the Union. The fact is that just at present there is a centripetal force in parties which brings the mass together previous to new divisions.

Afternoon, I did little or nothing more than write my Diary and read an Ode or two of Horace. Mrs. Frothingham and her Son Thomas came out to pass the Afternoon. Passed the Evening in my Mother's room who continues to improve, and read the remainder of the North American Review for July. I have not gone through a number for a long time before. It is pretty good. The Observer—Numbers upon Greek Literature.

SUNDAY. 21ST.

The day threatened great heat, but clouds and an East wind prevented. I read an Ode or two of Horace and attended divine Service all day. Mr. Brooks from Hingham preached and much better than when I have heard him on former occasions.[1] His texts were Revelations 22. 3. on the existence and worship of a God, and Hebrews 13. 9. on the character of Jesus Christ.

I also read a Sermon of Massillon 1. Corinthians 6. 2. "Do ye not know that the saints shall judge the world." It was the occasion of the Anniversary of St. Louis or Lewis the 9th. of France. He proposes thus. Piety is deemed by the world incompatible with heroic greatness. High rank is held to Apologize the relaxation of rigid morality. The example of Louis overthrows the two ideas. He was a noble King by being a pious man. His station made him more rigorous in the performance of his duties. The Sermon is good, but St. Louis was not the less fanatical, for he exhausted his kingdom and threw away his life in the pursuit of a very trifling object. Jerusalem could not make men more pious nor add to the glory of the Saviour, yet how much blood was lavished to acquire and to keep it.

Evening Mr. Simmons[2] and Mr. Degrand were here. I passed the time in my Mother's room.

[1] JQA praised Rev. Charles Brooks both for his sermons and his delivery, but he admitted that Brooks was "not a favourite with others" (Diary, 21 July 1833). For the other view, see vol. 3:318.

[2] David A. Simmons, attorney, who at one time had had his office in the 23 Court Street building (vol. 3:2).

MONDAY. 22D.

The day was exceedingly warm. I went to town, according to agreement for the purpose of collecting rent, but was disappointed, as I was also at Payne's hill where I called before starting.

I remained very quietly at my Office all the morning reading Marshall's Life of Washington, and I could not help being astonished at the vast amount of difficulty to be overcome to get our present system of Government into action. Nobody but Washington could have started the vessel. It is hard enough for others to keep it afloat. Returned to Quincy—My horse suffering more from the heat that I ever knew him to do for the five years that I have used him.

Afternoon, wrote my Diary, read an Ode or two of Horace finishing the second book and began copying some of the Letters to my Grandfather. I have been reflecting that as there seems no immediate prospect of a continuation of my father's proposed biography, there is very great probability many of the valuable evidences may be lost which are exceedingly important as testimonials. I have concluded to take copies of them, without saying any thing to any body.[1]

The Evening was bright and warm. Mr. T. Greenleaf and his two daughters were here for an hour. It is the first time for two years that the Portico has been delightful to sit in, which always puts me in mind of former days. Read the Observer—Cumberland's peculiar view of Harmodius and Aristogiton.

[1] In the Adams Papers is a volume of 115 pages, mainly in CFA's hand (M/CFA/31; Microfilms, Reel No. 327), consisting of transcripts from the letters of JA and AA and also reminiscences of JA by others. Most of the work was done during 1833. The first page bears a note:

"Quincy. July 23, 1833. The Manuscript papers of the late John Adams are in a state of confusion and liable to destruction from a variety of accidents that might happen. As this state of things does not at present seem to be likely soon to be remedied, I have thought it expedient to copy into this book, such Letters as from their nature are most liable to be lost, while at the same time, they are valuable as testimonials in the hands of his posterity. As I go on in my investigation, it is possible I may find other papers, copies of which I shall be glad to embrace in my present plan. I hope thus to form a volume which will be of value to myself at least, even should events show my labour to have been a useless public precaution. Charles Francis Adams."

TUESDAY. 23D.

The day was quite cool with an Easterly wind which to the feeling was very pleasant after yesterday's heat. I was occupied all day pretty busily. Read Horace and finished Tudor's Life of Otis besides copying several Letters into my book.

My new scheme may lead me into an extensive examination of the papers remaining which will not be without its uses to me hereafter, I hope. I read this afternoon a portion of the correspondence of my Grandfather with his Wife about 1780–82 which is exceedingly characteristic.[1] I do not know a part of his private MS. which are calculated to be more amusing. There is nothing in them but the high toned honesty which prevails in all his actions throughout his Life. But the gentler tones of affection are constantly to be found in them, and here it is that the public understands him very little.

Elizabeth C. Adams spent the day here. She is better since her return from the Journey lately taken with Mrs. Miller. Evening quiet at home. I was exceedingly drowsy, but managed to copy a letter for my father [2] besides [reading?] a couple of the Observer.

[1] The letters of this period are contained in vols. 3 and 4 of *Adams Family Correspondence.*

[2] JQA's reply (LbC, Adams Papers) to A. H. Everett.

WEDNESDAY. 24TH.

Another day of extreme heat terminated by a flurry accompanied with a very little rain. I remained at home and was very busily occupied in writing off the correspondence of my Grandmother with Mr. Jefferson in 1804.[1] Letters of great power and in a tone and temper which are exceedingly creditable to her. Mr. Jefferson has rather the worst side of the argument although such as it is, he maintains it stoutly.

I read two long and beautiful Odes of Horace and in the Afternoon went through a considerable number of old papers. This was my afternoon's work. Went down and took a short bath, but was hurried away by the blackness of the surrounding clouds. Dipped into the fourth volume of Prince Puckler Muskau—A curious book, somewhat entertaining and graphic in respect to the present manners of the British nobility. Luxury seems to have crept over the nation—And present appearances seem to indicate another example of the uniform course which takes place with empires.

Mr. Beale was here in the evening for an hour but had nothing new. The night was sultry.

[1] CFA included AA's letters to Jefferson of this period in his *Letters of Mrs. Adams,* both in the 1840 and later editions.

THURSDAY. 25TH.

A cool day. These alterations of our weather are very relieving to the feelings. For the air is chilled before it gets to be so heated as to afford little support.

I went to town and inasmuch as I picked up the rent from a Tenant, did not lose my time. Continued reading the second volume of Marshall and the account of Washington's last days. Perhaps it was fortunate for him that he died exactly as he did. The storm that came on immediately afterwards would not have proved agreeable, nor would he have felt comfortably under the appeals of Hamilton and many other of his friends to avert it by personally coming forward again.

Returned to Quincy without seeing any acquaintance. Afternoon passed in writing and reading, finished the Jefferson Correspondence. And went down to the Wharf where I took a very agreeable bath. Mrs. Ed. Miller with L. C. Smith and Elizabeth C. Adams paid a short visit in the evening. Read some of Puckler Muskau who has a kind of dry humour, that is very amusing. Conversation and the Observer.

FRIDAY. 26TH.

Morning fine and day cool. I remained quietly in my study, writing, reading some Odes of Horace and looking over old Papers. This last engrossed most of the time.

I have been led by my examination into an idea of methodizing most of the Correspondence of my grandmother at least so far as related to herself and her husband. Much that I find is useless and valueless yet I do not feel myself authorized to destroy. This it is that gives the excessive tedium to this duty, for the chaff is constantly re-appearing and embarrassing. My examinations have disclosed to me the days of prosperity and those of adversity in about equal proportion—Some periods of public and others of more bitter private suffering, some hours of great elation for success produced by individual exertion for the public good and others of as much for the rewards which were reaped for it. Such is man's life in every scene in which you may place him. The hewer of wood and drawer of water has his sorrows just like the rest of us, but no man will take the trouble to lay open the record of it. Events sustain men, yet events themselves are just the same when once you understand the art of discriminating their grades. Love, Hatred, Virtue and Vice are developed with the same certainty that sounds will come when you touch the keys to which they belong. A truce with further morality today.

My Afternoon was passed in the same occupation until I was summoned to go to Boston with my father and the ladies. We stopped to take tea with Mrs. Frothingham prior to going to hear the French Opera Company which is performing for a few nights. The piece was Zampa, a kind of Don Juan story; the hero, a Pirate gets possession of an old rich man's castle and forces the daughter to marry him. But at several periods, a marble statue of a girl this man had seduced gives signs of animation, particularly as this fellow in jest at a banquet, puts a ring on its finger in token of marriage. Just as he is to consummate his marriage, his bride in marble carries him off. We returned by midnight.

SATURDAY. 27TH.

As the day was likely to prove a hot one and I had no leading object to carry me to town, I passed my time very quietly looking over old Papers. A packet which I opened contained the love letters of the old gentleman in 1763–4, just before his marriage.[1] They were mostly written during the period of three or four weeks when he went up to Boston to be inoculated for the small Pox—At that time considered as a great exertion, not without much of personal hazard. The subject of course is an odd one for lovers, but they both seem to be so honest and simple hearted in discussing it, that after all these letters are far more true to nature than the sophistications of studied refinement. I do not find much to answer my particular purpose.

As I lost so much sleep last night, it was made up this afternoon, the rest of which was wasted in reading Puckler Muskau. I finished the volume. It is far better than the other one which I read and not wanting in reflection of a profitable kind. Some of his predictions appear not unlikely to prove true.

I was not quite well in the evening, and the child gave us another night like that passed at Medford on the first. I was not quite so uneasy from the fact that we had more assistance at hand. Slept a few hours on the bed in the study.

[1] The first volume of *Adams Family Correspondence* includes these letters (never printed by CFA) as well as those noted in the following entry.

SUNDAY. 28TH.

Morning warm, although a high wind dispelled all the inconvenience one might otherwise have experienced from it. I attended divine service all day and heard Mr. Whitney preach but without much benefit to me as one of his hearers. I rarely find any thing in his Sermons which is not a repetition of the most commonplace popular notions. Mr. Whitney is a worthy man in his life and conversation I believe, but it is difficult to pay him that degree of respect which he perhaps deserves.

Read a Sermon of Massillon's upon St. Stephen. Acts 6. 10. "And they were not able to resist the wisdom and the spirit by which he spake." His uniform mode of treating these subjects is by urging the example. To be a defender of the truth requires that a man should be enlightened, intrepid, and full of the spirit of charity. St. Stephen became so from the possession of such qualities. This is cause to exhort others. I think Massillon understands reason far more than most panegyrists.

A considerable period of time was passed in reading some of the letters of J. Adams to his Wife 1774–6. Many of them are admirable and richly merit publication. I have a great mind to make a collection. At any rate, the more valuable ones I must copy. Evening at home. I read a little of Captain Hall's book of travels,[1] and a couple of Observers which I did not like.

[1] Probably Basil Hall's *Travels in North America* or his *Fragments of Voyages and Travels*, in both of which CFA had read earlier; see vol. 3:116; 4:355.

MONDAY. 29TH.

Cool morning with a gradual clouding up as if at last it was likely to produce Rain. I went into town and was busy most of my time in a variety of Commissions which my Wife wanted performed. Went to the House and from thence to Mrs. Frothingham's. After that I stepped into a grate factory and was so much pleased with one or two patterns that I ordered one to supersede mine in my sitting parlor. This is perhaps an extravagance, but I have deluded myself into the notion of it's being economy, first, by preventing the necessity of such frequent repairs, second, by the lower price of Anthracite fuel.

At the Office, I read a little of Marshall. Returned home and passed the Afternoon quietly in my usual way, first, writing my Diary, second, reading Horace, third, looking over old Letters. This last was not so interesting today.

Evening at home. It began to rain. I read a little of Basil Hall's travels, copied part of a letter of my father's to Mr. Rush, and read the Observer. Cumberland has done something for literature in his account of the writers of the old Comedy in Greece. But he has done injury by depreciating the character of Socrates. No satisfactory evidence of his bad character exists while much of a noble philosophy remains under his name. This makes one point. Another is, that his personal character should not be traduced from the abuse of malicious enemies even though it might not have been perfect, at this time of day. The influence of *that* was upon his own age, that of his doctrines has been eminently beneficial upon every subsequent one.

TUESDAY. 30TH.

A hard rain in the night with occasional showers through the day. Having made an appointment with the maker of the grate to take his measures at my house I went to town. My time was passed in a pretty useless manner with the exception that I finished Marshall's Life of Washington. It is a work written without much pretension to style or interest, containing a good deal of valuable matter of fact but none of the speculative philosophy which might in this case have worked to great advantage. At the same time, it must be confessed that the use of it is not without danger.[1] Perhaps the part of discretion is to avoid it.

Returned home and passed the Afternoon in my usual occupation— Horace three or four of whose Odes I endeavour to read daily and some of the old letters. They are in such a state of confusion that the endeavor to reduce them to order seems absurd. Yet who will ever do it? If I am to judge from the indications of the past five years, certainly not my father. Evening, read aloud some of that amusing book, Humphry Clinker.[2]

[1] Because of its Federalist bias, perhaps.
[2] On returning Marshall's *Life of Washington* to the Athenæum in the forenoon, CFA had borrowed Smollett's *Works* ("Entry of Books Borrowed," MBAt archives).

WEDNESDAY. 31ST.

Morning cool and pleasant without a cloud in the sky. I remained quietly at home. My time with the exception of what was taken up by Horace, was entirely devoted to reading and assorting the old Correspondence. With what a mixture of feelings do I look over these old papers. They contain the secret history of the lives of a single couple— Joy and sunshine, grief and clouds, sorrow and storms. The vicissitudes are rapid, the incidents are interesting. Happy are those who pass through this Valley with so much of innocence. Vice stains no one of these pages. Occasionally there is fierceness of passion, but it commonly grows out of public events and has no accompaniment of bitter remorse and self upbraiding for the contamination of guilt. I think the gloomy predominates, and yet there have been few persons whose story altogether comprises so much of what the world calls prosperity. Look at the persons in a similar station with John Adams. Washington had no children and twenty years less of life. Jefferson died a bankrupt with bitter private griefs and nothing to compensate for them. Madison is childless though time has dealt mildly with him, and Monroe died a bankrupt after long years of pecuniary distress and mortification. Not one of these have had the closing consolations of John Adams. All of them have had their sceptres wrenched by an unlineal hand, no son of their's succeeding. That pride was reserved probably to John Adams alone in this world. Who can believe there is not a beneficent though a just Deity, who measures out even in this life our portions of reward and retribution. Afternoon, read St. John. Evening, Humphry Clinker.

THURSDAY. AUGUST 1ST.

Fine day. I passed it in my usual occupation. I am making out a pretty complete set of the Letters of my Grandfather and Grandmother to each other. The former are amusing from the short, concise and yet humorous style in which they are written. The latter interest from their gravity.

My Grandmother was a thorough politician. She passed her life in the midst of one of those crises in Society, when the old work was pulled down and the new one put up. These papers are all that remain of a very extraordinary woman. There is a maternal pride peeping out constantly which has as much charm in it as any thing—A disposition to press forward her Son because she thought him really the first man in the Country, and for once she was not much in error. Her penetration was not that partial fondness which invests its object with merely imaginary qualities. It was the result of Judgment.

Read a little of St. John. Evening, no reading as my Mother was upstairs still troubled with the Erisypelas flying about her.[1]

[1] That is, the "flames" of "St. Anthony's fire."

FRIDAY. 2D.

My day was passed very quietly here in the pursuit of my usual occupations. I went to the Office, where after reading one or two fine Odes of Horace I pursued my business of reviewing old Letters. I came today, across a most remarkable file written from Philadelphia during the year 1776. Among them, is that extraordinary one which speaks of the 4th of July in such terms.[1]

My Grandfather was a very great man, with man's imperfections

138

clinging about him. He had more of the moral sublime about him than any hero of the Revolution without excepting Washington. His private Letters display tastes equally strong for the enjoyment of private life. In this he differs from my father who still is agitated by the restless worm.[2] These are very valuable papers.

Afternoon, I read St. John who has become in the 3d. volume exceedingly dry. Evening quietly at home. Humphry Clinker. My Mother was better.

[1] *Adams Family Correspondence*, 2:27–33.
[2] Political ambition.

SATURDAY. 3D.

Fine day although somewhat cool. I went to town. By appointment I was to meet the Painter for the purpose of deciding upon what was to be done at my house and how. My rooms look badly enough and require an outlay which if to be repeated at such short intervals would exceedingly alarm me. And the tenure of the house is of so precarious a kind that I feel little satisfaction in it. After discussion and settlement, just as he went, my Wife and Mrs. Frothingham came in—The former having come to town with my Mother in the Carriage. After passing an hour and settling several things, we all left the house—They to return to Quincy and I to my Office. I passed a little while in Accounts, attended a Sale of Stocks and saw Mr. Brooks, then returned to Quincy.

The Afternoon was spent in writing, looking over Letters and reading Horace, the fourth book of whose Odes I began. Quiet evening at home. Humphry Clinker.

I afterwards finished the Observer. On the whole, the perusal has given me pleasure. It is a book full of sound morality, Christianity and valuable literature. It's merits are far above the miserable productions which I have been reading for some time before such as the World and Connoisseur. And if I cannot approve his treatment of the character of Socrates, I am willing to concede something to his reasons for so doing. It was a mistake and not a fault.

SUNDAY. 4TH.

Morning hazy with clouds of vapor, and excessive heat—All which terminated in the sharpest thunder shower we have had during the Season. I was occupied in the morning with my Diary and an Ode or two of Horace. Attended Divine Service and heard Mr. Whitney, first upon the Communion and in the Afternoon upon Death. My attention wandered very much in spite of myself.

Read a Sermon of Massillon upon St. Thomas Aquinas, 1. Esdras 8. 7. "He omitted nothing of the law and commandments of the Lord, but taught all Israel the ordinances and judgments." His division is simple, first, respecting the desire of acquiring knowledge, second, the right mode of using it. There is a good deal of sensible matter in his discussion of both sides of the subject. But Thomas Aquinas in another Century will be totally forgotten. And his innumerable productions rather argue at the present day against the imitation of his example. Who reads them excepting here and there a book-worm or a meta-physician.

Evening, Humphry Clinker aloud, after which I began the Mirror.[1] We have been for a week past expecting the arrival of my brother John and his family from Washington.

[1] CFA's copy of *The Mirror*, 2 vols., London, 1822, is at MQA.

MONDAY. 5TH.

Foggy with an occasional Easterly puff of wind which kept us quite cool. I remained very quietly at home pursuing my usual studies and reading more letters. The number of separations which took place in the lives of the pair was considerable—As many as six or eight, and each interval is filled up with letters twice, thrice and oftener per week. The collection is consequently very considerable. And although I have been industrious and picked up a great many it is very clear to me that more remain behind. The whole, if ever I can get them together will form a very valuable mass of history, and parts of it might be published to great advantage. Other parts will tell truth not to be spoken at all times.

Read an Ode or two of Horace whose powers until now I never appreciated. A student at Cambridge forms no valuable idea of any thing in the way of literature. He gets crude notions of a Classic, is discouraged with the difficulties and want of helps he experiences in reading the mere sense, and leaves off disgusted with learning. That is to say, if he is ambitious of *rank* as a Scholar, he will delve through, but the moment the incitement is taken off, he flies to other and more congenial pursuits. How many of my class are precisely in this predicament.

Evening, Humphry Clinker, and the Mirror.

TUESDAY. 6TH.

Cloudy with occasional drops of rain. I went to town. Engaged for some time in Commissions. Called at Mrs. Frothingham's and talked a little with her. Then to the Office where I read a little of Hudibras with more pleasure than I have commonly derived from the book.[1] The thing should be taken as a condiment, a little at a time and the flavour of it dwelt upon.

Stopped in at a sale of wine and could not resist the temptation of a sale of some Hermitage which I bought. My Stock insensibly increases. It must be diminished. I shall purchase no more in heavy quantities. And on my return I hope to begin actively upon consumption.

Called to see Mr. Brooks and then returned home. Afternoon. My usual occupation—Discovered the file of 1780 which makes up as I imagine nearly the whole series. I must now collect the other side which is my Grandmother's. An Ode or two of Horace and Humphry Clinker in the evening.

My father has been drooping for some time past. His health is bad and his spirits are worse. The great misfortune of his life, I still continue to believe was his return to public life after having once gracefully though involuntarily retired. It subjects him to alternations which his Constitution as well as the past habits of his life render exceedingly trying. What the end of it will be, God only knows, and he will direct, but to our blind vision it will go hard to shorten his days. If this is the close of a life passed in so much of worldly success, a less brilliant is certainly a more happy one. Read the Mirror.

[1] On CFA's copy (in MQA) of Samuel Butler's mock-heroic *Hudibras*, see vol. 1:xii–xiii; its titlepage is reproduced in the same volume.

WEDNESDAY. 7TH.

It was quite a warm day although early and at noon there were showers. I remained quietly ensconced in my Office. Read some Odes of Horace, and looked over a mass of old papers.

I derive a great deal of advantage from this occupation in the way of fixing dates of the events of the Revolution, and a good deal of the private history which gives the clue of mysterious public affairs. I made a discovery today of two or three additional private Journals of John Adams, and a curiosity in some old coins of the time of the English Commonwealth, 1649. These were inclosed in a letter from T. Brand Hollis,[1] though this has no notice respecting them.

Little occurred that is worthy of particular notice. My father seemed better today, and in the evening I had an interesting conversation with him upon the old Massachusetts history, James Otis, Hutchinson, Bernard, Sam. Adams and the actors of that day. Afterwards, a little of Humphry Clinker. Mirror.

[1] Thomas Brand Hollis, heir of Thomas Hollis, benefactor of Harvard College, was an English antiquarian, dissenter, and political radical whom JA visited in July 1786 and with whom he maintained a correspondence for eight years thereafter on a variety of subjects; see JA, *Diary and Autobiography*, 3:188, 196–200. CFA's expression of interest in the coins is apparently his first in a subject that was to absorb him for most of his life.

THURSDAY. 8TH.

My day passed in the quiet pursuits which render my Diary so exceedingly monotonous. I finished the Odes of Horace which completed my perusal of the book. It has been tolerably thorough this time, and I have for the first time formed an idea of the peculiar qualities of the Poet. Heretofore I was under an impression derived from some of his Anacreontic Poems, that he was a pleasant, Jovial, Epicurean Poet, but I find him now possessed of the Power to fly high into the sublimest regions of Poetry. He has also one great attribute of a Poet which supplies a wonderful charm to his verses, the faculty of happy application of epithets. This forms the superiority of Byron's muse over that of all modern Poets and it goes a great way to make the fascination of Shakespear. A single adjective will very often form a picture out of the sentence, and the mind has the pleasure of filling up the outline with as much additional colouring as suits the particular taste of each reader.

The remainder of my time was filled up with my common occupation, examining letters of which I found many additional files. They contain much of the gloomy. My Grandmother's trials were severe indeed. War, her husband absent a rebel with certain danger to himself of death if he should be taken, her Mother dying, her child very ill, a Servant in the house in the last and most dreadful stage of dysentery which at that time pervaded the Country. She was a wonderful woman to go through it so well—The Country too in an extremely poor condition and depressed by an unequal war. I cannot imagine any thing much more gloomy.[1]

Evening, My brother John, his Wife and child arrived having been two weeks at Long Branch. He looks out of health, although he has grown stout and fat since I saw him which is now three years.[2] Conversation and the Mirror.

[1] The references are to AA's letters to JA of Sept. 1775 (*Adams Family Correspondence*, 1:276–288 *passim*).

[2] Some account of JA2 appears in vol. 1:xxvi; a likeness of him is in vol. 3 along with further observations, p. xv–xviii, xxxi. Since his last visit to Quincy in the summer of 1830 (vol. 3:277) JA2 had been in progressively poorer health, suffering especially with failing eyesight (vol. 4:414, 417; LCA to ABA, 11 Jan. 1833, Adams Papers). Accompanying him and his wife, Mary Catherine, was their daughter Georgeanna Frances, aged two. The older daughter, Mary Louisa, now five, had preceded them to Quincy, coming with LCA (JQA, Diary, 10 May). On all, see Adams Genealogy.

FRIDAY. 9TH.

I had intended to go to town today but it was a cold day with an Easterly wind and heavy rain. The consequence was that I remained very quietly at home pursuing my regular and usual occupation.

Read over a large file of my Grandmother's letters which I discovered today. She has more of grief than of Joy in her correspondence, and yet she was a cheerful woman. But one remarkable feature in her grief is to be found in the occasions of it. I do not know whether vices are hereditary in families, but it would almost seem so from the number of examples which one meets with. The Smith blood seems to have had the scourge of intemperance dreadfully applied to it. Yet the first example of the race whom I know of, was an exemplary clergyman. A Son, Grandchildren in two branches, and great grandchildren have defied all the efforts of the most careful education.[1] Here have been the causes of the bitterest sorrows of our family. Public misfortune and pecuniary losses have been nothing to the wearing sorrow occasioned by deep mortification from personal misconduct. My father was telling me of the family of the Warrens of Plymouth, and we have before us the case of the Everetts. It is not without cause that every member of such families should feel in constant alarm lest an unwary moment plunge him into the vortex which he sees so ready to engulph all about him. This is not out of my mind.

The family here is now quite large. John was not well all day and appeared to be suffering from the weather. I felt cold but otherwise in unusual health. Evening, reading Humphry Clinker to the ladies. It is not without occasional embarrassment, for the style of writing in that day was a little of the coarsest.

[1] CFA elsewhere says in even stronger terms, "Our family has been so severely scourged by this vice that every member of it is constantly on his trial," below, entry for 2 Sept. 1834. In referring to those in the Smith of Weymouth line so afflicted, CFA doubtless had in mind, among others: William Smith Jr., son of Rev. William Smith and brother of AA, and presumably one or more of his sons; CA and TBA, grandchildren; JA2 and GWA, great-grandchildren

(Mary Smith Cranch to AA, 25 April 1785; Mrs. William Smith Jr. to AA, 26 Oct. 1785, both in Adams Papers; AA to Mary Cranch, 10 Feb. 1788, MWA; AA to JQA, 1 Sept. 1800, Adams Papers; to Mary Cranch, 10 Nov. 1800, AA, *New Letters*, p. 255; JA, *Diary and Autobiography*, 3:234; CFA, *Diary*, 1:xxiv, 158, 161, 164, 169; below, entries for 28 Oct., 18 Nov., 31 Dec. 1834; on all those mentioned, see also Adams Genealogy).

SATURDAY. 10TH.

The day was fine, and I went to town accompanied by Sarah, the child's nurse for the Summer, whom I also brought out again. My time was very much taken up in performing Commissions entrusted to me by various members of the family.

My father who seems badly in body and mind, being disabled in his hand, requested me to call and deliver messages verbally in answer to two Letters he received this morning. One was from B. F. Hallet upon the subject of Dearborn's election. Degrand has been exercising a little of his French impudence by getting inserted indirectly what he could not procure directly, my father's opinion in favour of Dearborn. The Antimasons, seeing a statement in the Centinel to this effect, are desirous of counteracting it. The business is one of great delicacy.[1] I had other political conversation also.

From thence I went to see A. H. Everett—My purpose to tell him, my father would try to see him on Wednesday.[2] He then spoke of my last Article and it's success. He referred to notices of it in the New York American and Montreal Paper. I have seen neither, but I have met with one in the Morning Post which was unexpected and therefore the more agreeable.[3] This is a virulent Jackson Newspaper. It is a little encouraging to me and God knows, I need it. But the greatest sign of my success is to be found in a request to write again upon Hutchinson's third volume for the January number. I said I would endeavor to be ready although at present in the midst of my Grandfather's Papers. This gives me occupation at the same time that it sustains me as a descendant of a brilliant family in the public estimation. Here is the rub upon my spirits. Although I can have no hopes of any public success like that of my fathers, yet at least I can desire to stand as a worthy descendant so far as my own conduct can affect me.

I made two or three other calls and then to the House where I could not get in. On the whole, I was walking all the morning. Returned to dinner. Afternoon quiet, reading over Letters, and Evening, finished Humphry Clinker.

[1] In July JQA had been importuned by Degrand to endorse the candidacy of Gen. H. A. S. Dearborn for reelection to Congress from the Norfolk district on the grounds that the Antimasons were alleging JQA's opposition to his candidacy. Despite his good opinion of Dearborn and his conviction that Dearborn had been honorable in maintaining his neutrality on the Masonic question, JQA persisted in his refusal to become embroiled in a contest outside his district (JQA, Diary, 21 July). Nevertheless, in the newspapers thereafter, apparently by Degrand's design but without ascription, there appeared a squib that "Much as Mr. John Quincy Adams has written on the subject of Masonry, he is decidedly in favor of the re-election of Gen. Dearborn" (*Columbian Centinel,* 7 Aug., p. 2, col. 5). On the same day B. F. Hallett wrote to JQA (Adams Papers) seeking a disclaimer for publication in the *Advocate*. His letter, however—and thus JQA's reply—was delayed. Hallett, without waiting, printed a denial, though JQA's reply went no further than reaffirming his determination to endorse no candidate (10 Aug., LbC, Adams Papers). Each of the parties continued to claim him, however (see *Columbian Centinel,* 16 Aug., p. 2, col. 3). No majority was achieved through nine elections. Dearborn was finally defeated by the antimasonic candidate on 3 March 1834.

[2] To A. H. Everett's letter on behalf of himself and his brother urging JQA's consent to allow himself to be run for Governor by a coalition of Antimasons and National Republicans (see above, entry for 18 July, note), JQA had replied as he did to two visitations from Hallett and other Antimasons, refusing without any reservation on the ground that his election could result only in "a turbulent administration and a furious renewal of the contest at the end of the year" (JQA, Diary, 10, 30 July; to A. H. Everett, 23 July, LbC, Adams Papers). Everett had replied asking for an opportunity to discuss the question further (to JQA, 8 Aug., Adams Papers).

[3] In its review of the July issue of the *North Amer. Rev.,* the *Boston Morning Post* said of CFA's essay on *Memorials of the Stuarts*: "This is an excellent article, because it dares to render a little justice to [Cromwell] . . . whom many generations . . . have considered it an exalted merit, to damn. . . . We thank Heaven we have lived to see the time when there is some chance of his coming out of purgatory" (17 July, p. 1, col. 2).

SUNDAY. 11TH.

Morning clear and warm although the air was sufficiently elastic to prevent any inconvenience from it. I laboured to finish the assorting of the Letter files today, and completed it so far as I know of any at present. I have found some dating as early as 1762, two years before their marriage, and coming down through 1774, 5, 6, 7, 9. 80, 1, 2, 3, 4, 6, 9. 92, 93, 4, 7, in each of which years there was a considerable separation. There is much valuable matter in the Correspondence, and it richly merits to be preserved and bound up into volumes. But I do not know whether at present I feel willing to undertake the responsibility of it.

Attended divine Service and heard George Whitney in the morning upon the difference between Morality and Piety, and in the Afternoon upon the beneficial influence of Christianity. George always looks to me oddly in the Pulpit. His manner is dashing and wants solemnity, and the man is too perpetually peeping through.[1]

I read in the Afternoon a very short and the closing Sermon in the volume of Panegyric—Upon a holy martyr, patron of a church not named. Text. Acts 1. 8. "Ye shall be witnesses." He considers the testimony *now* necessary to be three fold: 1. A testimony of sacrifice or suffering, 2. of submission, 3. of desire for another world. This is the martyrdom of the present day. I cannot enter into the spirit of these doctrines. I wish to avoid all evil and sinfulness, I wish to submit as far as I am able to all the dispensations of divine Providence, but I cannot convince myself that the proper use of the enjoyments this world has to afford was to be denied us by a beneficent Creator. It is the province of the reasoning faculty to discover what this proper use is, and the neglect or disregard of its admonitions appears to me to constitute sin. Evening, Mr. and Mrs. J. Quincy Jr. and Edmd. paid a short visit.

[1] Rev. George Whitney of Roxbury, son of Rev. Peter Whitney, spent his boyhood in Quincy and was one class ahead of CFA at Harvard. JQA thought that he "improves as he advances in years, and if he perseveres with industry and vigilance in his studies, will make a shining character" (vol. 4:68; JQA, Diary, 11 Aug. 1833).

MONDAY. 12TH.

I went to town and passed the day. Time very much taken up in Commissions and exercise of various sorts. I went to my House to attend to the setting of the grate which the man was doing. This is the first piece of business. I then went to the Athenæum and passed nearly an hour idling, dined at Mr. Frothingham's who treated me to some very nice wine, of that which we bought Tuesday. I am well content with my purchase. No news of any kind. Attended a meeting of Directors of Boylston Market. Things begin to look brighter in this Quarter. We have wiped off our Notes. No business. Got into idle conversation with these Directors, and staid till quite late so that I was not at home until eight o'clock. The riding was very pleasant. Warm evening.

TUESDAY. 13TH.

The morning began with very heavy showers and wind from the South. It afterwards cleared away and was hotter than was at all comfortable to the feeling, which a shower again qualified to tolerable.

I was occupied in looking over and attempting to discover some papers among the general mass of my Grandfather's. I found but one, the original of the Letter to Webb which I copied. This has been published over and over again, but I thought a copy would not be useless from the genuine paper.[1] I spent an hour in comparing copy of the old Journals with my father, a work intermitted since last Autumn.[2] I also began reading over Virgil critically, and finished the first Eclogue.[3] This gives pretty much the sum total of my day, the labour of which was shortened by the very enervating effect of the South wind. I am as yet doing little for Hutchinson.

On this day my child completed her second and entered upon her third year. She has enjoyed very good health during the year and has given us full as little trouble as any little thing of her age could. May I be thankful ever to the Divine being for having dealt so kindly to me, and blest my lot with a degree of happiness I know not how I can deserve. May he continue it to me, and I will endeavour at all times to turn the lesson of prosperity to the true account, my own amendment, in feelings, temper, vices &c. The cares and anxieties of life are so great that they require a mind well disciplined to bear them. Mine although I know that they are in themselves comparatively trifling to those of the mass of men, I am ashamed to say, sometimes unduly worry me. I must bear it in mind. Evening, I tried to read aloud, but my book was dull. Mr. Aug. Whitney and his Sisters[4] called to see Mrs. J. Adams.

[1] CFA appended to his transcription of JA's letter to Nathan Webb, his cousin, "Play fellow at the Grammar School in Braintree, and . . . contemporary at Colledge" (12 Oct. 1755; fair copy with JA's note, 22 April 1807; both in Adams Papers), a memorandum, "This letter was first published in the [*Monthly*] *Anthology* for [May] 1807 and many times since" (M/CFA/31). He continued to attach significance to the letter, characterizing it in terms unusual for him when he came to print it: "Perhaps there never was written a letter more characteristic of the head and heart of its writer. . . . It was the letter of an original meditative mind . . . formed, by nature, for statesmanship of the highest order. . . . The ken of the stripling schoolmaster reached far beyond the visible horizon of that day . . . But it is not in the light only of a profound speculative politician that this letter exhibits its youthful writer. It lays open a bosom glowing with the purest and most fervid affections of friendship" (JA, *Works*, 1:23–26, with text of letter to Webb).

[2] In Sept. and Oct. 1832, JQA and CFA had begun to collate sections of JA's diary with transcriptions which JQA had had made by amanuenses (vol. 4:365–384 *passim*; see also Introduction to JA, *Diary and Autobiography*, 1:xli–xliv).

[3] CFA returned to the study of Virgil periodically, most recently during the preceding year (vol. 4:247–279 *passim*). He would pursue his current reading of the poems until 21 Jan. 1834 in his copy of the *Opera*, London, 1824, now in MQA and with his annotations throughout. On the day he finished he noted the fact in it with an explanation of his procedure: "This text is from the edition of Heyne, Leipzig 1798 with which I have compared it. The Notes were too voluminous to transfer with any success." The edition of Gottlieb Heyne which CFA names is not among the numerous editions in MQA nor among JA's books in MB nor JQA's in

MBAt; however, among the last named is JQA's copy of the edition by Heyne, 4 vols., Leipzig, 1767–1775.

⁴ Children of Rev. Peter Whitney (JQA, Diary, 13 Aug.).

WEDNESDAY. 14TH.

I went to town, accompanied by my father. The day was warm but not oppressive. I was occupied in the various little ways which consume so much time. First, went to the House where I found the workmen had been careless enough to leave the windows and doors open, and that with such a rain as we had yesterday. This is the consequence of trusting people. But what can a man do? The Grate is changed and thus is one of the Jobs out of the way. I saw the Carpenter, the Painter and the Whitener today and gave to each of them their several directions.

Called in accidentally to see some Statuary now exhibiting and was quite agreeably surprised. It is a group composed of four separate figures each in a single block of stone representing Tam O'Shanter, Souter Jonnie, the Land lord and Landlady from Burns' famous little Poem. They are all seated on large chairs and all expressing a different particular and yet the same general character. I was charmed with the effect. The material is the hard Ayrshire reddish stone. And the artist, a common Scotch Stone Mason who knew nothing by science of the human anatomy. Under these circumstances, the effect is wonderful.[1]

My father was quite punctual, and we returned home to dine. Afternoon short. I passed it in writing, and reading the second Eclogue of Virgil. After tea, the Ladies went out to see Mrs. Quincy, and I had a conversation with my father upon the moral character of our nation as influenced by it's politics. I cannot but think that we are driving here a very dangerous political experiment. And what is worse, the world is becoming involved in it's success. Mirror.

[1] The pieces by J. Thom had occasioned great interest earlier in New York City, an interest being repeated in the exhibition at Harding's Gallery (*Columbian Centinel*, 23 May, p. 1, col. 6; 29 July, p. 2, col. 2).

THURSDAY. 15TH.

Fine day. I remained at home and occupied myself in my usual way interrupted only in the morning once for the sake of taking a sea bath. Sat down to Hutchinson and wrote off without stopping a very considerable quantity of matter. But my process of composition is very laborious from the way I have got into of not maturing things in my mind. Writing is foolish without great reflection, and this should be managed without the aid of pen and ink. I now think I can make a good thing out of this.

Spent nearly an hour in comparing text with my father. The old Journals are sometimes tedious and they were so today. Afternoon, read Virgil's third Eclogue which is very pleasing. And looked through the trunks for the old Papers I wanted, but without success. Found incidentally some scattering letters of my Grandfather's Correspondence. Quiet evening.

The intention was to have gone on a party today to Nantasket with some of the Quincy family but the various members of the family felt indisposed to go, and we excused ourselves. Mr. Beale and his eldest daughter called in the Evening.

FRIDAY. 16TH.

Clear with a cool Easterly wind. I worked today with considerable effect upon my review of Hutchinson. I find the matter flows in upon me abundantly. The great difficulty is to know what to choose. I leave that for hereafter and strike now while the iron is hot.

I took a bath with my brother at the Wharf and found it quite pleasant. Read Journals with my father for a short time. But they want Interest just at present. Afternoon began copying the material Letters of the Correspondence I have been assorting out. Finished one and a half and read the fourth Eclogue of Virgil, the Pollio, a burst of poetry which is wonderful but the cause of which I find no satisfactory explanation of. Our Commentators are fond of twisting every thing into an announcement of the coming of the Saviour. I own I see no foundation for it. Virgil appears to have been unacquainted with the Hebrew Prophets who foretold his coming.

Evening. Conversation with my father upon the subject of the early Revolutionary War. Afterwards with the Ladies. My father's health concerns us all very deeply.

SATURDAY. 17TH.

Foggy with the Wind from the Eastward but it did not rain. I rode to town and was moving about some time. Went to the House and found that they had accomplished the business of whitening which is so much more done, but the Carpenter had not been. He is always the one behind hand. The Painter begins Monday or Tuesday, and his work is the principal business. I hope this will be all over in a week's time, as I begin to feel anxious to get the house inhabitable.

Called by Appointment at Mrs. Frothingham's, to meet my Mother who came in with Mrs. J. Adams. Found the former and agreed to meet her at noon at the Harding rooms. I then called upon Miss Julia Gorham with a Note from my Wife.[1] The object was to explain her not writing sooner. Thence to the Office where I could stay but little. At Harding's room where the Tam O'Shanter Statues are, we found many Ladies of our acquaintance. They and the Statues engrossed all the time until one o'clock.

I was grieved to hear of the dangerous illness of Henry Brooks at New York.[2] His father left town this morning to see him. Home to dinner. Afternoon Virgil and copying Letters. Quiet evening. President Quincy took tea here. Legends of the Library at Lilies.[3]

[1] Missing.
[2] Henry and Horatio Brooks were ABA's unmarried brothers. Both had early been apprenticed in foreign trade and spent many of their years abroad. Henry in 1830 had returned after four years in Europe and resumed residence in New York City where he worked with

his brother, Sidney, in the firm of Davis & Brooks. See Adams Genealogy.
[3] George Nugent Grenville, Baron Nugent, and Anne Lucy Grenville, Lady Nugent, *Legends of the Library at Lilies*, 2 vols., London, 1832; borrowed from the Athenæum.

SUNDAY. 18TH.

On this day I complete twenty six years of my Life. Another year has been added since I recurred to the self examination which the occasion creates, and that year has been full of mercies to me. I was then under the feeling of awe which the visitation of a new and fearfully pestilential disease created in the Community, and attempting to reason myself into calmness for the event.[1] The disease passed over us lightly. I was then feeling much anxiety as to the prospects I had before me in life. My uneasiness has diminished. I have done but little to deserve my prosperity, it is true. I am no further advanced in the estimation of the world than I was, yet my morbid sensitiveness about it has diminished. My worldly prosperity so far as it depends upon pecuniary matters has increased again in a most extraordinary and unlooked for degree, yet I hope I am not unduly elated or excessively rejoiced. The causes of my anxiety upon this subject are now to a considerable extent removed. I feel in hopes that futurity will not be quite so serious as I had thought it, yet such creatures of the dust as we are, I know that the only rational foundation for such hopes is not to be seen in the exertions we may make, but it must be traced in unerring faith in the benevolence of a supreme being who builds up as he destroys from motives as inscrutable as they are just. I will do as I have done. I will endeavour in all humility to deserve my blessings. I will try to fulfill the duties for which I was created. While my conscience can seem to my examination tolerably void of offence in serious matters, I shall be little anxious as to the decision of the world. And while I am so bountifully provided with the goods of this world, I will not seek to repine for any thing that may have been denied me. Indeed I know not what more I ought to desire.

The day was fine. I attended divine Service all day and heard Mr. Whitney from whom I derived but little benefit. He has not mind enough to make his discourses interesting. And he has a particular tendency in his doctrines which he does not perceive but which does not make me relish them the more.

Read a Sermon or rather a Eulogy in the French style upon the Arch-Bishop of Vienna, M. Villars. Ecclesiasticus 51. 15 and following. "My foot went the right way, from my youth up sought I after her, earnestly I followed that which is good and my heart was troubled, therefore have I gotten a good possession." It is not in the style of the Panegyrics. These are exhortations to the living drawn from the examples of the Dead. The Eulogy is strictly in praise and honor of the dead. It appeared to me that in many respects this was a very fine example. He considered him in three lights, as a man of unblemished moral purity, as a good churchman in his responsible capacity, as the beneficent dispenser of his worldly goods. Much especially in the second division was calculated to thunder in the French Pulpit and Ecclesiastical world.

Evening quiet at home. The Ladies went out to make a visit or two. I read the Mirror.

[1] The journal entries of Aug. and Sept. 1832 which refer to the epidemic of cholera in Boston are merely factual, revealing nothing of the agitation here spoken of. See vol. 4:341–361 *passim*.

MONDAY. 19TH.

Fine day. I went to Boston and passed my morning in a variety of occupations. Went to the house where I found the Carpenter at work in preparing for the arrival of the Painter. Tomorrow the latter begins. I also spent a little while upon 'change and a little upon Bradford's History which I am sure I find more dry than any thing I have yet examined.[1] Thus passed my time until the hour of return. One thing lightened my heart considerably and that was the news from New

York of Henry Brooks which was quite encouraging. Poor fellow. I hope he will be able to weather it this time. After dinner, I had time only to write my Diary, read an Eclogue of Virgil and copy a very little of my task. In all this, Hutchinson does not progress. I am not without reflecting a good deal upon it, however. Evening quiet at home—Reading a little.

[1] CFA had borrowed Bradford, *History of Mass.*, from the Athenæum.

TUESDAY. 20TH.

Fine day. I rode to town accompanied by my brother. Time taken up in my usual variety of ways. I went first to my House where I found the Painter had set his men to work in earnest. The day is exceedingly favourable. Finding they needed no further overseeing I went away. At my Office a Note sent me down all the way to 135 Ann Street after a pump maker to repair 105 Tremont Street, and from thence I went to the Athenæum for the purpose of obtaining one or two volumes.

Hearing that Mr. Sergeant of Philadelphia was here, my brother and I concluded that it would be proper to call.[1] We found him at home, as well as Mrs. and two Miss Sergeants. He looks somewhat altered in his face during the six years since I have seen him. He said the same of me. After sitting fifteen minutes, we started off on our road homeward.

Afternoon, an Eclogue of Virgil, my Diary and copying. It was interrupted somewhat early by a summons to get ready to attend the Wedding of Miss Caroline L. Whitney the daughter of the Minister of our Parish married to a Mr. Charles Hill of Roxbury. Most of the people of Quincy were there. One or two pretty faces, but it was extremely dull to me at least. I have learnt to look upon these things as the taxes we pay to Society, and therefore submit to them patiently. Return at nine.

[1] John Sergeant was several times a Representative from Pennsylvania in Congress and had been appointed during JQA's administration as envoy to the Inter-American Congress; see vol. 1:83–84.

WEDNESDAY. 21ST.

Fine day though cool. I remained at home all day, and it was tolerably fortunate that I did, for I found myself unexpectedly quite indisposed. This lasted throughout the day and materially diminished the amount of my labor.

I did effect something nevertheless upon Hutchinson. I find my ideas flow fast enough but they want methodizing. I propose to write all I think of first, then to read Hutchinson's book carefully over again and digest the material before I begin, in the finish. I wish I had the facility which distinguishes some. Yet I do not know whether I ought to do so.

Several visitors were here, but I did not go in to see them. Afternoon Virgil and Copying, which with a little comparing Journal with my father must account for the time. Evening, Sir Jonah Barrington[1] and the Mirror.

[1] *Personal Sketches of His Own Times*, 2 vols., Phila., 1827, borrowed from the Athenæum.

THURSDAY. 22D.

Day fine although there was a Sea fog hanging over us all the morning. I rode to town. Time a good deal taken. First came a man to procure a transfer of the Boylston Market share, which I had not more than effected when Mr. Conant from Weston came in to pay money long since due. This business settled I had an application of a man for a place, and one or two other incidental visits. I went to my House but found it so shut up that I was unable to get in. The rest of my time was employed in finishing a Deed for Mr. Boylston's Trustees. Returned to Quincy having had an uncommonly busy period.

My afternoon was taken up in my usual occupations. Read the ninth Eclogue of Virgil, wrote my Diary and copied a little into my book of choice things—A letter of my Grandmother's giving a curious account of an alarm during the Siege of Boston from a foraging party on one of the Islands.[1] My father went into town to dine with Mr. Alex. H. Everett, and did not return until late. Evening quietly at home. I read to the Ladies a little of Sir Jonah Barrington which is more dull than I thought. Afterwards the Mirror. I was better today.

[1] To JA, 24 May 1775 (*Adams Family Correspondence*, 1:204–206).

FRIDAY. 23D.

The morning was foggy with a North Easter and a little rain. It cleared away however before night. I remained at home all day.

Finished during the morning my first draught of the Hutchinson Article, and read it over, the substance of it I am pleased with and by remodelling, transferring in some parts and amplifying in others, I think I shall be able to make it do. This is a pleasant occupation and a creditable one. And I do not know that for the present I want any more. My moments of mortification have somewhat passed away. I do not now feel that sense of wounded feeling from disappointed exertions which depressed me once so much. To be sure, I have gained but little from my exertions, but that little whatever it may be is something, and at least evinces my disposition, not to rely upon my position alone for my character.

I compared a little old Journal and in the Afternoon read the tenth Eclogue of Virgil and copied more of the Correspondence. The Account of an alarm I finished and began a Letter from my Grandfather announcing the election of Washington.[1] Evening quietly at home.

[1] As commander in chief of the Continental Army; to AA, 11–17 June 1775 (*Adams Family Correspondence*, 1:215–216).

SATURDAY. 24TH.

Fine day with a cool Easterly wind. I went to town accompanied by my brother. My time was very much taken up in doing little commissions for my Mother who was to entertain company today. I went also to my House where I found the Painters engaged upon the second coat. One of the rooms was done and upon looking at it I did not know whether to be pleased or displeased with it. I do not think it can be called ugly. But it does not equal my expectation. I had time enough to read a Chapter of Bradford's History, and I engaged my man servant for the first of next month. This I believe completes my family.

After a good deal of walking to and fro, I went to the Stable and meeting my brother we returned to Quincy. My father entertained a small company to dinner. Mr. Sergeant, Mr. Crowninshield, I. P. Davis, Lieut. Gov. Armstrong, Edward Brooks and Josiah Quincy. The party was quite a pleasant one, and they went away in good season. On the whole, it was far better managed than I thought possible. We all retired quite early.

SUNDAY. 25TH.

Morning fine although the dry weather still continues. I attended divine service in the morning and heard Mr. Capen of South Boston preach upon the character of Balaam. He is not very interesting although his sermon did not want sense.

Nothing material until an occurrence at dinner which materially affected the remainder of the day. In conversation a remark together with a gesture of my brother's at table produced in me an excessive burst of passion and a scene ensued which was quite of an unpleasant character. It is due to him however to say that he did not return the violence. It is needless for me to explain the reasons why I was so agitated. It grows out of feelings on my part which have always been peculiarly sensitive to the peculiarly captious, overbearing, contemptuous tone that appertains to his manners. Accustomed to little of it in my intercourse with others, it galls me beyond expression when I find myself constantly under it's action in a domestic circle. It makes me after a time, jealous, uneasy, restless and liable to anger. The stronger curb I apply, the more liable I am to a greater extent of violence when I break it. I know that it is my brother's misfortune in better days to have contracted these peculiar ways which result from want of reflection rather than premeditation, yet it is not always in my power to consider it. The incidents of the past ten days and even from the night of his arrival had put me under a most unpleasant restraint. Is it to be wondered at that my patience failed? Any body who knows what I am will not wonder. My fear of such an event has always occasioned my dislike to be under the same roof with him for any length of time, yet the injudiciousness of my parents has brought on what I fear will not be healed soon. I was far the greatest sufferer because I had the whole family against me as well as my own conscience for an act which I foresaw might happen and did not guard against. Had I been wise enough to persist in my rule of not being led into temptation, all might have been well. I read a Sermon of Massillon's twice over aloud to cool myself with partial effect, though my state of mental excitement was I think greater than I ever knew it and not far from madness. All the sore feeling of years seemed to be working up a convulsion in my frame. I reasoned myself into a state to be willing to apologize for the offence committed by me to each member of the family, but I could not think of his manner with any calmness at all.[1]

Massillon's Sermon was upon Villeroy, Archbishop of Lyon. His Division was simple considering his character, first as a great Statesman second, as a Churchman. A union in those days more common than it is now. Text. Ecclesiasticus 50. 5. Too long for insertion.

My evening was not much more quiet than my afternoon, and my Wife who was much affected by this incident gave me additional and still deeper anxiety. All this was quite punishment enough for my offence, and perhaps even more. I am in the habit of thinking such

155

things are a kind of set off to qualify the tendency in my head to turn at my prosperity and happiness.

[1] In JQA's Diary are two passages which seem likely to relate in whole or part to the unpleasantness: "My ardent desire to abstract myself more and more on this day from the cares and troubles and contentions of this world meets continual obstacles and disappointments" (25 Aug.). "I have this day been in much agitation of mind from sorrows which must be confined to my own bosom. In a life of vicissitudes I have had much prosperity; but as life draws towards its close, anticipation has no ground for hope; all is dark and gloomy. Night is no longer a Season for repose. Morning brings with it no refreshment. It is well for me to prepare the mind for the conviction which cannot fail to be realized that Old Age is the Season of Adversity" (26 Aug.).

MONDAY. 26TH.

After a restless night, I arose and breakfasting, went to town. My determination was to endeavor in future to avoid occasions upon which to come here and incur the risk of difficulty. The amount of occupation which my house and the preparations to enter it furnish, gave me plenty of justification for absence, so I remained in town until late in the evening.

I was much engaged all day—In the morning by business matters, in the afternoon by reading in my study. Mr. Greene[1] called upon me to transfer Shares of the State bank to me which business was accomplished. This makes a sum out upon interest considerably beyond what I can permanently invest. Yet I have a repayment in November of the loan July 1st. and my income accrues in equal portions on the first of the two preceding months so that I consider the proceeding perfectly safe. My expenditure upon the House is considerable, but most of it will not be due for some time. On the whole my finances stand pretty fair. This is to me an important subject—Important from the fact that my father goes backward almost as fast as I advance. Collected a little Rent, made a settlement with Dr. Parkman on my brother's Account and saw Mr. I. P. Davis. Thus the time passed.

Read a little of Hutchinson in the Afternoon, and seventy lines of the first Georgic. The Painters did not finish until after sunset, and I staid them out. The Accounts from New York[2] are not encouraging. Returned to Quincy quite late.

[1] Simon E. Greene, stockbroker; see vol. 3:296.
[2] Concerning Henry Brooks.

TUESDAY. 27TH.

Morning warm with a South west wind. My father accompanied me to town. I was engaged at the House where the Painters were doing a little more outside work, and in various commissions which kept me going most of my morning. Dr. Parkman came in to get my father to dine with him.

I had made a sort of half engagement yesterday to P. Chardon Brooks that I would dine with him so that this left me free to fulfil it. Nobody there but Henry Dalton[1]—A very pleasant dinner and some very nice Bordeaux. Conversation detained me until five. No news from New York. As this was one of the purposes of my stay I called at Edward's and then at Mr. Frothingham's. He went out with me to the Post Office, where we found a Letter from Mrs. Sidney Brooks. I thought as far as it went, it was decidedly for the better, but there was no indication of any permanent improvement. This poor fellow has been struck down in a manner which I can hardly realize.

Called for my father at Dr. Parkman's and we returned about sunset. My Wife talked with me, and gave me reasons for altering my plan.

[1] Henry Dalton of Baltimore was a cousin of the Brookses. Gorham Brooks was at the point of moving to that city to enter business under the firm name of Dalton & Brooks; see vol. 2:235; Brooks, *Medford*, p. 453.

WEDNESDAY. 28TH.

I said that my plan was to be altered. This is in consequence of a disposition on the part of my brother to conciliate, by his manner to my Wife and by his postponing his departure. As this manifests an inclination which is certainly uncalled for by the circumstances, I feel it to be my duty to reciprocate it. So far as I can, I will do so. This will depend entirely upon him. If I am not subjected to any galling sense of inferiority unjustly and unnecessarily pressed upon me in matters of daily intercourse we shall do well. If I am again, I must leave the scene before my temper gets the better of me. I wonder what pleasure a man can feel in piquing himself upon always gaining little victories in boasting. What is there which raises more sharp angles in the whole progress of life?

I started early this morning to be present at a meeting of the Class called for nine o'clock, Commencement morning. Reached Cambridge shortly after that time and upon looking round found nobody. A more thorough examination discovered Fay, Dillaway, Allen, Sherwin, and I heard of two more.[1] But the purpose for which the meeting was called the removal of the Cenotaph or monument of the Class, was not accomplished. Our Graveyards are not sacred places so that our little memorial is suffering in its present position. The idea is to put it in Mount Auburn. I went to look at it as well as at many of the

old scenes of my College life. Many things are changed. Much building and ornamenting gives a different look to the place. I cannot account for the desolate feeling which came over me while I was there.
Nothing came back to me that I valued. My friendships formed there
have been none of them permanent. Poor Sheafe too, the inscription
to whom on the Stone did nothing to diminish my melancholy, he has
gone to a better world.[2] This world has made all the rest uncongenial
to me. I live in my own family and my own thoughts. The rest is a
blank. Part of my feeling may also be attributed to the coldness of my
instructors with whose names I have not a single warming association.
They might have made me love the Institution. Is not this difficulty
at the bottom of the present decaying condition of the College? For
on this day the marks of decay struck me forcibly. No Graduate of
modern times whom I have met entertains any enthusiasm for the
place of his education. Few of them contracted any of the spirit of
literary research. Indeed this which I did not acquire and which I
weakened there is the only tie that holds me to it.

I hastened from the spot, and returned to town, where my avocations restored the general tone of my thoughts. In consequence of the
reasons assigned above, I returned home to dinner. Afternoon passed
in writing Diary and reading a little. Quiet evening.

[1] None of the classmates mentioned, Richard Sullivan Fay, Charles Knapp Dillaway, Phineas Allen, and Thomas Sherwin, had been of CFA's circle during their undergraduate years (vol. 1:374; 2:273).

[2] George Sheafe, with whom CFA had been on terms of some intimacy, had died in 1826, the year following their graduation (vol. 1:12, 374; 2:22). A search has failed to reveal the location or fate of the class monument with its memorial inscriptions.

THURSDAY. 29TH.

As I had been going for so long a time I concluded it would be
better to remain quietly at home today and turn my attention to wind-
ing up the principal things I was occupied about. In consequence of
this I did little more than copy diligently morning and afternoon. A
business for which I have no conveniences here and which affects my
breast a good deal. I have got engaged in copying out the principal
Letters in the Correspondence between my Grandparents and my
principal difficulty has consisted in the difficulty of limiting my selection. They are all so good it is very hard not to copy all, yet this is
more than I can or ought to do.

Hutchinson is all this while falling into the background. Nothing
else of particular interest. I omitted to mention that my father started

yesterday on a little trip to the mountains of New Hampshire, in company with Mr. and Mrs. I. P. Davis. This is in consequence of the urgency of the family who are concerned at the languid state in which he has been for some time past.[1] In the evening, quiet at home. Gov. Knight[2] and another man called. Nobody recollected him in time.

[1] The ten-day trip through the White Mountains was accomplished with no more than minimal curtailment of program because of ill health (JQA, Diary, 29 Aug.– 7 Sept.).
[2] Nehemiah Rice Knight, U.S. Senator from Rhode Island and former Governor.

FRIDAY. 30TH.

Cold morning. The Easterly winds have prevailed of late very much although the drought has become exceedingly severe. I went to town and was occupied at my house and in a variety of little ways all my time. I have now finished with workmen and am waiting for the moment to call my people [*i.e.* servants] together, which I have arranged for Monday next.

Saw Mr. Brooks who has returned from New York. His Account is exceedingly doubtful. The chance for life and death seems to me to be about equal, and nothing but the decision of the divine being can be expected for him now. Henry has some advantages in a good constitution unimpaired by excesses.

I dined at Mr. Frothingham's and settled with his wife about the house. The Cook whom she has had for a couple of months comes to us, and leaves her just at present without. I regret but do not know how to avoid this. Went up to my House for the purpose of doing something, but a good dinner had destroyed my power of mental exertion. Remained there until six when I started upon my return. Quiet evening at home.

SATURDAY. 31ST.

The morning was cloudy with slight rain. I remained quietly at home, and my time was very quietly engrossed by my occupation although it is of such a nature as to leave me but little to record. I copied several letters coming down to the two famous ones which have been made into one and with an altered date have figured away as a prophecy of the 5th of July 1776.[1] They are very remarkable Letters but not much more so than the whole series of which they make a part.

It is pretty clear to me that during my stay here I can do very little more in the way of copying these very valuable papers, and as I feel unwilling to leave them to take their chance again in old trunks and damp rooms, I have concluded to draw up Indexes and get them bound up in Volumes. In this way their chance for entire preservation will be better and I can extract from them at my leisure.[2] The remainder of my day was taken up in the work of Indexing.

Evening at home. Read a considerable part of Dumont's Recollections of Mirabeau.[3] My Wife was not well all day.

[1] Following his transcription of JA's two letters to AA of 3 July 1776, CFA appended a note: "A compilation from them with some changes has been published as a single Letter, and is in general circulation" (M/CFA/31). On the early publishing history of the two letters, see *Adams Family Correspondence*, 2:31–33.

[2] The enterprise embarked upon in consequence of the decision to bind the loose letters of JA and AA was the first major effort to organize and preserve the family's correspondence. So bound the letters (and numerous other series) remained until they were deceased by the staff of the Adams Papers in 1955–1956 and placed in archival boxes in the course of arranging a single chronological file of all materials in the family's papers that were unbound in their original state.

[3] CFA's copy of Pierre Etienne Louis Dumont's *Souvenirs sur Mirabeau et sur les deux premières assemblées législatives*, Paris, 1832, is in MQA. However, a day earlier he had borrowed from the Athenæum a translation (Phila., 1833), and it was this that he was reading during the following days (below, entry for 10 Sept.).

SUNDAY. SEPTEMBER 1.

The morning was cloudy with a shower, but it afterwards cleared away quite cool. I was occupied all day that was not taken up by my regular duties in indexing the letters and concluded two Volumes to take into town tomorrow.

Attended divine service and heard Mr. Whitney preach. One Sermon upon doctrinal points and one commonplace upon death. I cannot interest myself at all in his discourses and therefore do not often pursue them.

Read a Panegyric of Massillon's upon the Prince of Conty which is exceedingly happy. He considers his subject first as a military hero, second as a private citizen, third, as a learned man, coupled with religion. How far Monsieur le Prince deserved his exalted character, it is not for me to determine. Perhaps there is as much necessity to look behind the scenes in death, as at any other time of mortal history. His text which I do not insert from it's length, was from the Wisdom of Solomon 8. 10.11.13. In the evening, Mr. Beale and his daughter came in to spend an hour.

MONDAY. 2D.

The North wind was almost a gale this morning. I went into town with it blowing in my face very violently and scarcely recollect having had a more disagreeable ride. My time was very much taken up between my house and Office. Found the Cook there this morning, but was disappointed in the man who did not come at the time promised. I accidentally found him afterwards and as he appeared to be an idler without any adequate excuse I dismissed him on the spot. This disarranges me very considerably. I do not at present know what to do.

Called to see Mr. Brooks and Mrs. Frothingham. The latest accounts from Henry are very distressing and I am sorry to say tolerably decisive of his fate. This is deeply unfortunate, particularly at this time to me. I can only trust in a merciful Providence who guides and guards all our destinies. Our fate is in his hands. Mr. Brooks appeared to me exceedingly depressed.

I returned home to dinner and passed my Afternoon in writing Index for the third Volume of the Papers which I completed. I was quite fatigued and unable to do any thing in the evening. The night was quite a cold one.

TUESDAY. 3D.

I went to town this morning for the purpose of attending to my household which yesterday's accident had disarranged. At the house I found Mrs. Field, and not very long afterwards I procured a man so that this thing was off my mind. My time until one o'clock passed I scarcely know how.

I then went to see Edward Brooks for further news from New York. He handed me a letter from Sidney decisive enough in its character and advised me to remain in town until the afternoon Mail so that I might prevent my Wife from feeling any farther suspense. He asked me to dine which I did, he and his Wife being quiet and alone. She looks to me pretty much as she used to, before she was sick, although she still remains in a very feeble condition. After dinner we went down to his Office and found there a Letter giving the final intelligence. Poor fellow, he was just about my age and as amiable, good-hearted a man as I ever knew. I have seen but little of him owing to his various and continual absences, but I know none of my brothers in law for whom I have felt greater regard. But such is the destiny of man. What shadows we are, and what shadows we pursue.

He had every thing to live for, but God in his infinite wisdom pronounced his decree, and the reasoning of mortals upon it is made foolishness.

It remained to me to disclose the fact to my Wife, for which I started directly on my return. But I did not effect it entirely. She received such intelligence however as to make his recovery hopeless to her, and I reserved the last until the morning. She was much affected, but bore it as well as I could expect. Quiet evening alone with her.

WEDNESDAY. 4TH.

I this morning made the final disclosure to my Wife and although much affected, she bore it on the whole remarkably well. Went to town and had my time engrossed as usual by the cares of my house. I progressed very much this day and looked more as if I was in a state of preparation for our move. Nothing of particular consequence took place.

On my return to my Office yesterday from receiving the news of poor Henry Brooks' death, I found on the table a notice of my election as a delegate from Boston to the Anti Masonic Convention which meets here next week for the purpose of nominating a Governor and Lieut. Governor. The contrast between the two subjects which thus presented themselves in connection in my mind was painful. There is nothing additional to be said after the touching words of Burke upon a like occasion at the hustings of Bristol,[1] but if there is a moment when the bustling nothingness of our political electioneering comes most strikingly across the mind, it is when our ideas are drawn to the solemn appeal of a voyager to a silent world. This subject as well as the incident that gave rise to it must be reserved for more serious consideration.

I was engaged some time in Accounts and returned to Quincy only after an hour or more passed in wandering about to procure my winter's supply of fuel. Prices are somewhat reduced which is a great comfort. My afternoon was taken up in preparing the remainder of the Volumes of the Correspondence, for which purpose I neglected every thing else. The family went down to Mrs. Quincy's to a party given in commemoration of the Anniversary of the arrival of their family to this Country two hundred years ago. My Wife and I remained quietly at home.[2]

[1] In his speech at Bristol on 9 Sept. 1780, when he stood forward on the hustings, Burke referred to the death on the preceding day of Mr. Coombe, another candidate: "The melancholy event . . . reads to us an awful lesson

against being too much troubled about any of the objects of ordinary ambition. The worthy gentleman who has been snatched from us . . . has feelingly told us, what shadows we are, and what shadows we pursue" (*The Works of Edmund Burke*, 9 vols., Boston, 1839, 2:286).

² The Quincy family was given, too much given in the Adams view, to expressions of its consciousness of the distinction conferred by the antiquity of its marks of gentility (vol. 1:311–312; 3:11–12, 411). On the arrival of the first Edmund Quincy in America in 1633 and of the first Henry Adams at roughly the same time, see *A Pride of* *Quincys*, Massachusetts Historical Society, 1969, p. [1].

The manner of marking the two-hundredth anniversary was described by President Quincy's son Edmund: "The whole family being assembled we all signed a record of the occasion written on parchment and intended to be kept in the archives of the family for the benefit of future generations. . . . We had singing and dancing and a very elegant supper in the West parlor. Mrs. John Quincy Adams was there too. Pres. A. was absent on a journey." (Journal, 4 Sept. 1833, Quincy Family Papers, MHi.)

THURSDAY. 5TH.

Went to town accompanied by my brother. The day was cloudy and very sultry indeed. I passed much of my time at the House and at an Auction sale of the furniture of Mrs. H. G. Otis who being about to cross the Atlantic winds up here. I attended for the purpose of purchasing a small dining table, instead of which I got a large one at a price not much greater so that I did very well.¹ This and some Commissions wore away the day until time to return. Afternoon again passed in a similar way. Finished the Index work for the whole making five Volumes, and got all but one in readiness for binding. This has been a labor voluntarily undertaken, but I hope it will prove somewhat of a security. After the binding is done I shall proceed with my copying. It is high time if I intend to begin at all to think seriously of Hutchinson. Evening quietly at home.

¹ The auction held at 8 Somerset Street, the home of the widow of Harrison Gray Otis Jr., included a "set of Grecian dining tables" (*Columbian Centinel*, 5 Sept., p. 3, col. 7). On Mrs. Otis (Eliza Boardman), see vol. 4:185 and entry for 1 May, above.

FRIDAY. 6TH.

I went to town again this morning and was occupied in the closing directions for the house, which has at last resumed it's natural appearance. I was obliged to attend to a thousand little things which go into the sum total of starting a household, as my Wife is not able to attend to any thing, and Mrs. Frothingham upon whom I much depended has been called away to New York. She returned yesterday, and I saw her this morning. She looks very much fatigued. My time passed without my noting it until my usual hour for return.

Poor Henry Brooks was brought here and thus closes the scene with him. It appears that he has been diseased in his liver for upwards of a year, and that no human aid could have effected his restoration. It is a very extraordinary case. His complexion was exceedingly sallow, but I never should have dreamed of his being unsound. This circumstance is a relief against all doubts of his medical treatment.

My Afternoon was a clearing up one. I finished off all the work that remained, and restored things as much as I was able to their places. The family went to town to see Miss Kemble as Julia in the Hunchback[1] so that we had a very quiet evening of it. Nothing material.

[1] *The Hunchback* by Sheridan Knowles had become a fixture in the repertory (see vol. 4:413–414). With this performance the Tremont Theatre, redecorated and with gas lighting substituted for oil, began its new season (*Columbian Centinel*, 4 Sept., p. 2, col. 4).

[*Boston*]

SATURDAY. 7TH.

This was the morning for our move. Accordingly after seeing to every thing, I went off leaving my Wife and child to follow in the Carriage with my Mother. On my arrival in town I found myself occupied with a multitude of the little things necessary to be done as I stated yesterday. The whole family arrived safely at about eleven, and we were again safely installed in our establishment.

This while it relieves me of much of the peculiar anxiety experienced now at Quincy, is attended with cares of it's own. I would endeavor as far as possible to shake them off. For in this world, I am pretty well satisfied that man makes little for his own happiness who extends his anxiety to subjects that little deserve it. I propose from the present time to devote myself more to literature, to do every thing that I may be able to find, and to waste as little as the constant and inevitable calls of life will permit.

I went to the Office, and from thence to the Athenæum. Afternoon at home. My Mother left us at five, despairing of finding the President. But he arrived nevertheless about an hour afterwards. His health and spirits seem to have been improved by the trip. He staid with us the evening. Mr. and Mrs. Frothingham also called. Thus ended our first Boston day.

SUNDAY. 8TH.

Morning cloudy with a few drops of rain. My father returned to Quincy after breakfast, Kirk having come in a Gig to take him out. I attended divine service at the Meeting house in Chauncy place all day. Heard Dr. Gray of Roxbury preach in the morning upon the proper use of time as a preparation for death, in the afternoon upon the pure in heart, Matthew 5. 8. I am no great admirer of the personal character of the preacher, so that in the pulpit I have no faith in the persuasion of his lips.[1] I hope this is not uncharitable.

At Meeting I saw Sidney and P. C. Brooks Jr. who came in to see my Wife. Miss Julia Gorham dined with us. After service in the Afternoon, I accompanied Sidney to Charlestown for the purpose of seeing Mr. and Mrs. Everett. We found the latter at home, and he came in before we returned. I took the opportunity to consult him as to his intention to be a candidate for the Antimasonic nomination of Governor next week. He declines, as I think, wisely.

We took tea and returned. I found Miss Julia and her brother Gardner sitting with my Wife. The child seems a little unwell. One anxiety follows hard upon another. I am fixed in Boston to relieve myself from one and this gives me another. My trust is always in a much higher source.

Read a Funeral Oration of Massillon's upon the Dauphin, son of Louis 14th. A disease of some kind in one year swept through the family of this King and left him in his old age desolate. How different from his outset in life. One of the Greek sages pronounced the truth that no man could be reckoned happy until after he had ceased to live. Time has added or taken away nothing from it's simple warning. The text was from the Wisdom of Solomon. 9. 12. "So shall my works be acceptable, and I be worthy to sit in my father's seat." He is a negative character in history, though he shines in panegyric.

[1] CFA's earlier comment on Rev. Thomas Gray (vol. 4:382) was the same.

MONDAY. 9TH.

Morning damp and cool. I went to the Office as usual and passed the greater part of my time in accounts. Several persons came in— Mr. French upon the subject of the Boylston Market, but he turned to Antimasonry.

I took the opportunity to ask several questions as to the proposed convention, for the purpose of assuring myself of the intentions of the party previously to my committing myself. This is a subject upon which I have endeavored to reflect and have also consulted with my father. I do not feel any great desire to go forward and make myself conspicuous in this business, because it would at once deprive me of the quiet which I have and do enjoy. Yet there are public duties which every citizen should perform whenever the crisis is such as he deems to call for his exertion. I certainly consider this question a deeply important one to the welfare of the Community, and if I can probe my heart to the bottom, I find nothing in it upon this occasion but a wish merely to do my duty. I am sensible that the first charge which persons so disposed will make against me, will be an ambitious desire to advance myself. The real truth is that if I had such a desire, my own judgment would lead me to court another party far more powerful in this place and disavow all connection with the Antimasonic. I believe myself to be for the present destroying all my views of political advancement by taking any such course as I propose to take. My purpose is not to enter into these matters at all any farther than is absolutely necessary for me and yet acquit myself of the duty which I think is incumbent upon every citizen. My conclusion from the whole is this, that I will attend the Convention, perform my duty, but do nothing more. I am not called upon to go out of my track as a private citizen.

In the afternoon I resumed my reading of Hutchinson and went into collateral researches in Minot, the Massachusetts State papers, Bernard's Letters and Novanglus. Evening quiet. Edward Brooks came in and passed an hour pleasantly.

TUESDAY. 10TH.

My time now begins to be more at my disposal, and I enter again very quietly upon my ancient occupations. This produces a monotony in my Diary which is after all a sign of tolerable content.

At the Office I read Bradford's History, examined accounts and finished Dumont's Recollections of Mirabeau. I have read this work in the translation which is evidently great injustice to it. The egotism of an old Frenchman (for although Genevese, he appears to have much of the French manner) is not unpleasant in his own language, but when you show it off in another it is intolerable. A greater defect is it's shallowness, for he had great opportunities and little has come of it. The illustrations of Mirabeau's character are meagre but yet the most valuable portion of the book.

I went to the Athenæum to investigate one or two historical points, without success. Afternoon, Hutchinson and the Massachusetts State Papers. Quiet evening. Sidney Brooks spent it with us.

WEDNESDAY. 11TH.

As my Wife expected some of the family from Quincy, I took the trouble to go down to Market. She was disappointed after all, my father and brother's wife being ill and unable to come.

At ten o'clock I went up to the Representatives Chamber in the State house to attend the Antimasonic Convention which met there. A very considerable number of persons from various parts of the State attended, and they appeared to me to be generally of the respectable but middling class of the Community. Mr. Bailey was made President,[1] with four Vice Presidents and three Secretaries. The morning was consumed in the various modes of organizing the portions of the body into managing Committees, reading Reports &c. A vote was passed referring the nomination of Candidates to 4 o'clock in the Afternoon. Shortly after one I returned home and attended again at 3. The canvassing then began. And it was soon found that the time before the election would be far too short to allow of a full consideration of the matter. It was postponed until ten o'clock in the morning. The remainder of the time was taken up in reading a report upon the influence of Masonry upon the districting the State. It is in many respects a curious developement.

I did not attend the adjourned meeting at Faneuil Hall in the evening. Thus I have embarked in the ship of the party, and this day have acted exactly according to my plan. My name has not been concerned in any forward participation in the movements, while I leave no shadow of doubt upon my opinions. Evening quietly at home.

[1] John Bailey, later to be the antimasonic party's candidate for governor, had served as clerk in the State Department during JQA's whole incumbency as Secretary of State and been Representative from Massachusetts during JQA's term as President (*Biog. Dir. Cong.*).

THURSDAY. 12TH.

Fine clear morning. I went to the Caucus which was called to consult upon a candidate for Governor, immediately after breakfast. It sat from eight o'clock until one and was at times agitated pretty violently. The parties appeared to me about equally divided between Mr. Lathrop and Mr. Shaw, of Lanesboro—The former being the favourite of the old school, the latter sustained by the young men, more particularly those from the interior Counties. I thought I saw plainly a great jealousy of the State Committee which is located in Boston and which has for the most part dictated to the Country party. Things were fast tending to a division when a private current was set in motion in favour of the nomination of my father which very soon took the place of every other sentiment, and I left the Hall to start for Quincy and announce to him the state of the case previous to the arrival of the Committee who were to announce it.

I arrived just at dinner time. Found him looking extremely unwell and recovering from a very severe attack. I stated the matter to him and after consideration he seemed disposed to adhere to his resolution to decline. The Committee consisting of Col. Pliny Merrick, of Worcester, Mr. H. Gassett of Boston and Mr. Whitmarsh from Bristol County came out and brought such resolutions as put a new face upon the matter. He seemed much agitated but deferred giving any positive opinion until ten o'clock tomorrow morning. They accordingly withdrew. He did not however remain long in suspense. The appeal was so direct to him as an individual and to the principles which he has been always supporting, that he could not withstand it. He wrote a brief answer which I brought with me.[1]

It rained lightly much of the afternoon. I got home soon after six and spent a perfectly quiet evening.

[1] The resolution of the "State Antimasonic Convention for the Commonwealth of Massachusetts, In Convention at Boston Sept. 12, 1833," together with a retained copy of JQA's reply of the same day, in CFA's hand, are in the Adams Papers. The resolution was couched in terms best calculated to break JQA's defenses: "We recognize as a sound republican principle, which ought to govern nominations and acceptances of nominations for office, that in a free Government, no citizen, standing prominent for public service, is at liberty to reject a nomination upon personal considerations, alone, when tendered to him by a large body of his fellow citizens, acting as a party, whose principles he approves, especially where the citizen so nominated is best qualified to concentrate public sentiment, in favor of those principles, and to heal the divisions of party. . . . Relying upon the patriotism of John Quincy Adams, as evinced, through a long life devoted to the advancement of truth, and the best interests, of our Free Institutions, regardless of mere popularity; and having the utmost confidence, in his eminent abilities, and sound principles, his uniform regard for public policy, rather than personal politics, the Antimasonic Convention, do Unanimously tender to him their nomination . . . and ask his acceptance of the same, as a personal sacrifice on his part, required by the existing State of parties, in this Commonwealth and the Union." JQA's reply was in kind, and he recorded in his journal under the same date: "I had done every thing in my power to prevent this [nomination], which is an exceedingly unwelcome movement to me: but it was placed upon grounds which left me no honourable option of declining. . . . I accept the nomination, which casts me again upon the stormy ocean of political electioneering when I hoped and believed I was snug in the Port. If there be a fatality that pursues me, there is a Power above by whom it is guided."

FRIDAY. 13TH.

At an early hour I went out for the purpose of putting into the hands of Col. Merrick the answer which last night I brought with me. After considerable search I found him at the Hall of the House of Representatives. The Convention stood adjourned to the hour of half past nine o'clock. I waited and in the mean time conversed with many of the delegates whose names I did not know. The feeling seemed to be quite warm for the nomination, and the announcement of the acceptance was enthusiastic. Now the thing is done. For myself I feel perfectly indifferent as to the issue, and only desirous that there may be a graceful end to his public life whenever it may please Heaven to guide my father's mind to that conclusion.

The Convention proceeded to nominate a Lieutenant Governor. And here another contest took place, the present incumbent Samuel T. Armstrong was supported by the greater number, but the stiffer party sustained Mr. William Reed of Marblehead. The objection to Armstrong arose from an expression in his letter to the State Committee dated two years since by which he questioned the right of making a political question of Antimasonry. It was a little curious to see the party who supported the nomination of Mr. Shaw yesterday without any public pledge, and quoting the authority of Mr. Webster whose course to the party has been any thing but explicit, now turning round zealously to insist upon a downright committal. Such is the inconsistency natural to the human mind. The difference was only settled by the passage of a resolution in fact pledging all candidates who accept nominations to the peculiar doctrines of the party, after which Mr. Armstrong was unanimously nominated. My own opinion was in favor of the nomination without any such resolution. It is peculiarly ungracious to threaten a man with a condition at the same time that you offer him a present. A Committee was sent to see him and in the afternoon he sent an answer natural enough in his circumstances but which fell into the error of want of decision. If he had Antimasonic opinions he should have expressed them, if not he should have positively declined the nomination. I think in his situation I would have written them a letter which would have made them tingle and feel ashamed. The Convention voted his answer unsatisfactory and proceeded to nominate Mr. Reed.[1] I then left it.

Three days have passed in this business, my apprenticeship in political electioneering. The more I see of it the more I am satisfied of the inaptness of my peculiar character to this sort of thing. I cannot assent to the discipline or the doctrines of mere party. I love my independence of thinking and acting too well. At the same time however I must admit that in this Assembly I thought I saw an attachment to general principles very creditable even though it might be excessive, and less of the mere electioneering spirit of the day than I had anticipated. My own conduct has been throughout satisfactory to me. I have done my duty, and now dismiss the subject of politics from these pages.

In the evening, Sidney Brooks was here. My Wife was a little unwell.

¹ Subsequently Reed also declined the nomination (*Columbian Centinel*, 18 Sept., p. 2, col. 3). The ultimate candidate was Samuel Lathrop.

SATURDAY. 14TH.

Fine morning though cool. I went to the Office and passed most of my time there, but could not resist going to the Athenæum for an hour. The Masonic newspapers are out very violently against the nominations.¹ This is no more than was to be expected and will do no great injury. But what the result of all these things is to be, remains as yet much in the dark. Judge Hall called but I felt a little head-achy from indigestion and rather irritable so that I wished his dissertation upon the mullein poultice indefinitely postponed. Read some of Bradford's History which is most terribly dull. I fear I shall fail in my undertaking from nausea at the materials at which I am to work.

My head being still a little troublesome I thought I would ride it away so directly after dinner I started for Quincy. Passed my mother on the road, who was coming in to see my Wife, and consequently missed her, but found my father and the remainder of the family somewhat better. Conversed with him upon the events of the day, and found him disposed if possible still to get rid of his threatened honor. He says that if the National Republican party will pitch upon any person who is satisfactory to the Antimasons he will yet withdraw. There are many obstacles to this proceeding. He seems still however to cling to public life on a different stage. So long as this feeling lasts, it is a matter of perfect indifference to me where his lot is cast. The great objection still exists. Took tea and returned to town but it was quite late first. My head was cured by the remedy.

¹ A collection of such editorials from the State's newspapers is carried in the *Columbian Centinel*, 20 Sept., p. 2, col. 3. The *Centinel*'s own editorial blast was reserved to its issue of 25 Sept., p. 2, when in a lead editorial occupying almost the entire first column, JQA's whole political career is reviewed to show that "an inordinate thirst for office and power predominates in him, over every other principle." Representative of an even more unfriendly current attitude is one of a series of letters on "Political Parties" by Thomas Filmer of Salem (*Columbian*

Centinel, 30 Sept., p. 1, col. 5) in which of the antimasonic party he writes: "Men who seek distinction, join such parties, and foment their bad feelings in hope of profiting themselves. Thus Mr. Adams. . . . But Mr. Adams having no popular qualities, and being naturally a selfish and repulsive man, shows . . . the truth, that his movements are only one more form of the self-advancement, which has marked his whole life. Such men are the pests of republics."

SUNDAY. 15TH.

Fine day although yet very cool. I have caught a severe cold which makes me feel it somewhat more than I probably otherwise should. Attended Divine service at Mr. Frothingham's and heard him in the morning from Ecclesiastes 2. 20. "Therefore I went about to cause my heart to despair of all the labour which I took under the sun." It was against despair as being unjustifiable both from the changes which are constantly occurring in the world, and from the deeper reasons drawn from our religious duties. Mr. Lunt[1] in the afternoon from Romans 2. 14 "For when the Gentiles, which have not the law, do by nature the things contained in the law, these, having not the law, are a law unto themselves." A discussion of the obligations of law prompted by mere nature, which was very dry and not particularly striking in any way.

Read a funeral Oration from Massillon upon the "Grand Monarque" Louis 14th. Ecclesiastes. 1. 16–17. He considers him as a King and a Christian. The age of this Louis was one of great glory to the French, but it is difficult to bestow unqualified praise to him on account of it. His wars were all of them unjustifiable, and his domestic administration was one of cruel oppression. His religion was bigotry, and his generosity, injustice. Few Monarchs of late times have undergone greater vicissitudes of fortune, and perhaps the hour when he was greatest was after adversity had made him feel almost every variety of disappointment.

In the evening, at home. The child and her nurse are both unwell with the complaint of the season.

[1] On Rev. William Parsons Lunt and his later connection with the Adamses and Quincy, see vol. 4:48–49.

MONDAY. 16TH.

Clear and cool. I went to the Office and was occupied in reading Bradford's History in which I made considerable progress. The difficulty with me is that I desire to be at the same time writing. I cannot reflect to much purpose without reducing my ideas to some definite shape—A circumstance that makes writing to me far more of a labor than it need.

A short walk. Afternoon reading Hutchinson and the Massachusetts State Papers, the blunders of Governor Bernard, who was a very indifferent Agent for the execution of the schemes of the British Ministry. He was an Englishman coming here for the sake of money, with no strength in the affections of the people, and with a disposition to arbitrary doctrines which he had not the judgment to conceal. Joined with this was an open and rather irritable temper, which he had not very much under his control. He was thus almost at the mercy of the popular party—The leaders of which knew their business.

Resumed my reading of Virgil today with the first Georgic, and in the evening wrote a considerable portion of my Article. Thus I have at last fallen pretty thoroughly into the regular course of life which is customary to me in town.

TUESDAY. 17TH.

The day was fine but somewhat cool. I passed an hour at home in writing upon my Article and then went to the Office. Mr. Peabody called in and asked me to take a walk with him to see the Lowell Railroad at its termination upon Craigie's bridge which I did. We had some incidental conversation upon the Governor's election during which I communicated to him my father's remark made to me last Saturday and authorized him to mention it to Mr. Everett or any other confidential person who might be supposed likely to have influence at Worcester.[1]

Read a good deal of Mr. Bradford's whose history does not strike me as better as I proceed. There is no philosophy, no general view of human nature, nothing but facts and those not very fairly developed. I cannot read much at a time. Afternoon at home. Read Hutchinson who is almost as dry but in politics the Antipode to the other. Continued my study of Virgil's first Georgic and in the evening after sitting with my Wife, continued my writing. One day is so like another now that my diary is dull even more than it's wont.

[1] At the National Republican state convention.

WEDNESDAY. 18TH.

The day was cloudy with rain. I went to the Office and passed the greater part of my morning in reading Bradford. He fails more as he goes into the more important period. His views are narrow and his arguments little or nothing. The poor man was eaten up to a great degree by party feeling. He had worked himself into a frenzy so that he thought old political disputes should be made to bear upon new ones. Neither should be treated by the historian with any violence of feeling.

I went, notwithstanding the rain, to see the collection of fruit for the Anniversary dinner of the Massachusetts Horticultural Society. It was generally handsome. But a good deal of the finest especially in Peaches was from New York. This vicinity shone particularly in grapes and pears. The Apples also were very enormous and fine. The crowd was not great. I felt no temptation to dine, having generally an aversion to that sort of public celebration.[1]

On returning home, found my brother John's wife and children had come in to spend the day. She is still unwell with her cough. My mother was so much indisposed as not to be able to come in. They went out early in the afternoon. I read Hutchinson and the State Papers of Massachusetts getting through the documents of minor importance. I must bend my attention to the main question until I feel secure that I can grasp it. Evening at home very quietly. Read a Chapter of Scott's fair Maid of Perth to my Wife. Virgil and the Mirror as usual.

[1] The Massachusetts Horticultural Society was celebrating its fifth anniversary with an exhibition of fruits and flowers at Concert Hall and with a public dinner and address by A. H. Everett (*Columbian Centinel*, 18 Sept., p. 2, col. 6).

THURSDAY. 19TH.

Morning very warm and sultry. I awoke feeling excessively heated and feverish, and this settled into a nervous head ach for the day. At my Office in the morning where I continued to read Bradford whose book I finished, at least so far as is necessary to me at this time. It is highly improbable that I shall ever touch it again.

Looked over my Accounts, balanced my books and then endeavoured to better myself by taking a walk. But the attempt did not succeed. Since my return to town I have felt excessively languid, probably caused by the season of the year and my change of life. This particular kind of dog-day heat is also a very unpleasant thing to the feeling.

Afternoon, continued Hutchinson though not with much vigor. Read all his complaints and did not much wonder at them. To struggle with popular feeling, hard as it is every where, becomes twenty times harder in a Community in which there is so rigid a compliance expected with public opinion. My Grandfather and my father have done it all their lives. The consequences have reflected upon me, who am myself exactly such another in disposition although not in talent. I have the spirit to be independent without the capacity to keep myself above water. I am therefore doubly unfortunate. Quiet evening.

FRIDAY. 20TH.

Another excessively sultry day. I felt better however. Morning at the Office. Read all the State Papers previous to the famous Message of Jany. 6. 1773.[1] They relate principally to the place of Session of the General Court.

I was about to continue when Mr. T. K. Davis came in and discussed political affairs. The dissension in the National Republican party is very great. Mr. Webster has expressed his opinion in favor of coming in to my father's nomination, Mr. Gorham the reverse. The Masons are of course not merely hostile but furious. And the National Republicans are in their nature so supine a party as to be easily led by the nose by half a dozen active individuals. What is this thing called the National Republican party? A matter of threads and patches.

After dinner I remained at home very quietly and read the rest of Hutchinson's volume. I have taken this time an impression from it, different from any preceding one. There is more malice in it than I thought, more of the disposition to complain, yet after all, much allowance must be made for the poor man's situation.

My mother and brother's Wife came in to take tea, and remained here until after a shower. They left a little before nine o'clock in the evening. At eleven we had far the most severe thunder storm I have experienced this season.

[1] That is, Gov. Hutchinson's speech in which he took the position that Parliament had "a Right to make Laws for Us in all Cases whatsoever." For JA's views on the significance of this message, see *Diary and Autobiography*, 2:77–78.

SATURDAY. 21ST.

Morning cloudy but much cooler. I went to the Office and passed my time in reading the controversial papers which took place between Hutchinson and the Legislature. I accomplished the Message of the Governor and the reply of the Council. The first appears to me an ingenious argument, but it wants bottom—The bottom of sound principle. My time passed so rapidly that the number of pages accomplished was very small. I look upon the labour bestowed upon these points as the substance of my proposed article.

In the afternoon, as my Wife seemed anxious to know how the ladies got through their trip yesterday evening, I rode to Quincy. Found them safe and sound at home, they just escaped the storm. My father had gone to Randolph to look after some land, which has been sold for taxes. A Note which I brought to my Mother from my Wife was so pressing,[1] that she concluded to come in with me, so that we returned and got home by seven o'clock. Quiet evening at home. I read the remainder of the first Georgic.

[1] Note missing.

SUNDAY. 22D.

I sit down to write the record of a trying day to me. We were just seated very quietly to take breakfast as well as usual, when my Mother as she was putting a piece of bread to her lips, suddenly rose, staggered three steps to the folding door and then fell insensible upon the floor, not without striking her head against the table in the corner. We raised her and sent for the Dr. Stevenson. It was three hours before we succeeded in restoring animation completely. She was also very sick at her stomach and complained of coldness.

This event, bad at any time, was twenty times more so in the fact that my Wife was on the eve of confinement. Her condition was such that I made up my mind to go out of town to Medford and bring back the Nurse engaged for the occasion, Mrs. Reed, this took just two hours of the morning, and at one I went home and found my Mother slightly better. There being no cause for immediate uneasiness I went to Meeting and heard Dr. Lowell preach from Hebrews. 11. 1. "Faith is the substance of things hoped for, the evidence of things not seen," upon faith as a means of support.

Returned and read Massillon's funeral Oration upon Madame, the Dutc[h]ess of Orleans, mother of the famous Regent. Text. Proverbs. 31. 28–31. It was a panegyric upon her, in the three great relations of life, first, in her duty to society, second, her domestic life, third, her religious obligations. There is a panegyric upon the Regent which sounds oddly from the pulpit—No more infamous debauchee being known in the annals of modern history. It may admit of question at all times how far parents are responsible for the vices of children, and most especially in the case of Royal families. The Dutchess of Orleans certainly kept herself quite pure, and that is something. I have her

Journal which I read some years since. It is spiced with scandal and not over moral, though tolerably amusing.

My Mother was better in the evening though unwell all the afternoon. But my Wife then felt herself becoming rapidly sick, so I went for Mrs. Frothingham who had agreed to be with her. The Dr. came at ten. At about Midnight she was delivered of a Male child.[1]

[1] There would seem to have been no question that the first-born male of the fourth generation in the Adams family would bear the name John Quincy; in *The Adams Papers* he is designated as JQA2. Among the brothers who would follow, he was the least given to writing. Independent in his thinking and possessing a winning personality, he was five times Democratic candidate for governor of Massachusetts and all his life active in the affairs of Quincy. His qualities are best revealed in a sketch by his daughter Abigail Adams Homans in her *Education by Uncles*, Boston, 1966, p. 25-38. See also Adams Genealogy.

MONDAY. 23D.

I slept but about two hours, for my anxiety about my Wife kept me uneasy. She was exceedingly exhausted by her labour and in a critical state all night. The Dr. remained with her all night and left only in the morning. She was however somewhat better on his return at ten o'clock. My mother had passed an agitated night but was on the whole as well as I could reasonably expect. On the whole, I felt as if I had great occasion to be grateful to God for dealing thus tenderly with me in a day of so much trial. Another relation is imposed upon me, my utmost wishes have been gratified.[1] May it impress me with a further sense of my own unworthiness, and with a resolution still farther to exert myself in a becoming and proper manner, that I may be a real father to my children.

Rode to Quincy as well to notify the family of these occurrences, as to get Mrs. Kirk to come in with me for the purpose of aiding in the care of the invalids, especially my mother. The family seemed pleased. Returned home by one o'clock and found my people doing well.

Afternoon, I went out to attend a Meeting of the Boylston Market Directors. Little or no business beyond declaring a Dividend. At last after the lapse of eighteen months, we make out to pay a sum of two dollars on the share. I hope hereafter we may do better.

Returned home and passed the evening in my study working upon my article, which now again makes progress. Feeling much fatigued, I was glad to retire to my little room to rest.

[1] To the gratification of CFA's "utmost wishes" was added JQA's deep satisfaction in the extension of the line to still another generation: "There is no Passion more deeply seated in my bosom than the longing for posterity worthily

to support my own and my father's name. I trace my ancestors in the grave-yard and on the town Books to Henry Adams one of the first Settlers of the town of Braintree at Mount Wollaston. All I know of those of my fathers name untill him is that they were born, were married and died. He was eminent, and my desire has been that his name and his possessions here should continue in his and his descendants' name. For this I have done my part. My sons must do theirs. There is now one Son of the next Generation, and my hopes revive." (Diary, 30 Sept. 1833.)

TUESDAY. 24TH.

My Wife had a good night and seemed to be on the whole much on the recovery. The boy is a stout little fellow, and seems quite tolerably. Thanks be to God for all his mercies. My mother begins to feel her weakness and the severity of the blow she received in her fall. But she is on the whole tolerably well.

I went to the Office and was engaged most of my time in Accounts as well as making up my Diary which has been backward for a few days. Prepared a list of Boylston Market Proprietors and took quite a longish walk to get rid of an impending head ach. My system has been so sub-ject to wearing anxiety for some time past that I should not be sur-prised to have it disordered, it is not yet diminished entirely. But I feel great relief from my reliance upon a higher power than this world contains.

Afternoon, reading the Massachusetts State Papers over without profit. I never gained much from repeating after a certain time. Evening, Mr. Degrand called in for a few moments. Kirk came in with the Carriage, but as Madame was not strong enough he went out again. Evening, writing.

WEDNESDAY. 25TH.

Beautiful weather. My Wife was tolerably today. My Mother not quite so well, but both on the whole still comfortable. It was the day of general muster, and the noise of guns was somewhat trying, es-pecially in the Afternoon, but they got over it pretty comfortably.

I went to the Office and was engaged there some time in Accounts and the &c. of business. Mr. Knowles called upon me at last to let me know that the Carriage was to be in today. It is a little more than four months since he engaged to make it, which is double the period con-tracted by him to deliver it in. He has been to Washington and has had a fever.

I went to see a collection of Pictures for sale,[1] and took a long walk.

Exercise is a thing I find absolutely necessary since my removal to town. The ride has a beneficial effect upon my health which I should hardly be able to realize if I did not find the contrast directly. But my regular quantum of exercise restores things.

Afternoon reading, but lazily. I finished in the course of the evening, my Article, and upon reading it over am less satisfied than ever. The positions are loosely stated and the argument disjointed. There is besides a superfluity of words. I must go over it with the file. Virgil and the Mirror.

¹ The paintings being shown at Cunningham's Auction Room included, according to announcement, works by Carrachi, Barrochio, Sassoferato, Poussin, Titian, Holbein, Ostade, Teniers (*Columbian Centinel*, 25 Sept., p. 3, col. 7).

THURSDAY. 26TH.

Very fine weather. My wife was tolerably and my Mother somewhat better. The Carriage came in from Quincy, bringing with it my father. He looks quite unwell and appears to want interest in political affairs excepting always Anti-masonry. I was busy some-time with Mr. Knowles and the Coach. A change was effected, I paid him the balance and so the whole matter was settled. At the same time, I must confess that I wasted a good deal of my time this morning—Owing to my having finished my old labour and not at present possessing a definite occupation to succeed it.

Walk as usual. My father and little Louisa dined with us and returned to Quincy shortly afterward. I read a little of the Correspondence of Voltaire with d'Alembert—A little vanity and the spirit of proselytism—Resistance against authority without steadiness to settle the force of the blows. Poor France felt deeply the consequences. I read also, a part of a publication of the Library of Entertaining Knowledge, the habits of birds—Some curious information in it.

FRIDAY. 27TH.

Fine day. My Wife seems to be slowly but gradually improving. My Mother on the other hand does not recover decisively. She thought change of air might do her good, so she concluded to go to Quincy today accompanied by my child Louisa and her Nurse. She is somewhat unwell from the process of teething. This did not however take place until afternoon.

I went to the Office. A short visit from Mr. A. H. Everett. He talks politics, is in a difficult situation and can foresee nothing. The Masonic

Interest is unexpectedly predominant in the elections to the Worcester Convention. By unexpectedly I mean more than was expected, for that it would be very strong nobody with common sense could doubt. The consequence is in all probability a distracted election. This is not a ground of dissatisfaction to my father.

I went to the Athenæum and accidentally took up a book called a Sunday in London.[1] The picture is not a pleasing one and might be used to advantage in considering the virtuous horrors of Mrs. Trollope or the civil sneers of Hamilton.[2] Walk as usual. Afternoon, Voltaire and d'Alembert—A very bad spirit in these letters. Yet there is sprightliness. Domestic Habits of birds.

My wife seemed better after she had been relieved from the anxiety about my mother's condition. Quiet evening. Call from Mr. C. C. Woodward a polite beggar. I would have assisted him if I had not lately seen in the Newspapers something which earns for him the addition of swindler. Finished the last numbers of the Mirror.

[1] London, 1833. Primarily a collection of George Cruikshank's illustrations of high and low life in London, there is accompanying satiric text by John Wight.

[2] Thomas Hamilton, whose recent book on the United States was the subject of much adverse comment but which CFA would not read for another six months. See entries for 22, 23 March 1834, 22 Jan. 1835, below.

SATURDAY. 28TH.

Fine day. I went to the Office and amused my leisure time in reading the Records of my Life by J. Taylor[1]—One of the most superficial works of a superficial age. This is not the way I should pass my time. I must begin a volume of Bacon or one of Milton's prose. I want to fill my ear with the nervous style of the older writers.

Made a call or two without success. At one I started to go to Quincy as my father had asked me to dine there with Messrs. St. Clair Clarke and Peter Force from Washington.[2] I found the family tolerably and my little Looly lively although not with her accustomed looks. Discussion turned principally upon the late publication by the President respecting the deposits in the Bank of the United States.[3] General Jackson is realizing all that was foretold of him. And there is no help for it. The people sustain him. Politics are rather a sickening occupation. There is so much of false in it, that I do not wonder they have [been] made the theme of abuse in all ages. A great statesman is to be sure an admirable spectacle but how few deserve the title. Certainly General Jackson does not.

Returned home at sunset, and found my Wife and baby nicely. When I reflect upon the incidents of the past week, I feel more and more for how much I have reason to be thankful—My Wife preserved to me after a very trying confinement and my child a fine one. My mother prevented perhaps by a wise providence from adding to the danger of the scene both by her own weakness and by the agitation it might have caused. Certainly, my trust has not been in vain. Began the Lounger[4] and read several of the numbers published by my Grandfather in 1809.[5]

[1] John Taylor, *Records of My Life*, 2 vols., London, 1832, borrowed from the Athenæum.

[2] Matthew St. Clair Clarke of Pennsylvania had at the last adjournment of Congress completed his service as Clerk of the House of Representatives, an office he had held since 1822 (*Biog. Dir. Cong.*). Peter Force had begun and maintained his *National Journal* (1823–1831) in support of JQA and his policies (see vol. 1:25, 244); his publication of original materials in American history and of reprints of rare pamphlets was still in the future. Clarke and Force had formed or were about to form a printing partnership for the publication of *American Archives*, which Congress had authorized in 1833 and the first volume of which would appear in 1837.

[3] The President's statement announcing the removal of public deposits from the Bank of the U.S. was read to the Cabinet on 18 Sept., published in the *Washington Globe*, 23 Sept., and reprinted in *Columbian Centinel*, 26 Sept., p. 1, cols. 3–7.

[4] CFA's copy of *The Lounger*, 2 vols., London, 1822, is at MQA.

[5] During 1809 JA was led to send to the *Boston Patriot* a series of autobiographical letters designed to justify his public actions on a number of matters that had been put in question many years before and had been recently resurrected. Although the letters continued to appear until 1812 and reached a total of 134, most of them were written in 1809. A substantial number of those which had been printed were reissued in ten serial parts in 1809[–1810]. These were perhaps the "numbers" which CFA was beginning and would continue to read. He published a selection from them in his edition of JA, *Works*, 9:239–330, with an explanation of their genesis. See also JA, *Diary and Autobiography*, 1:liv, lxxi–lxxii.

SUNDAY. 29TH.

Fine day though cloudy and warm. My Wife looked better than she has yet done. Her colour begins to revive. The child is well and hearty. I begin to realize a new state of feeling—One which will, I hope, turn my attention more to my duties as a man and a citizen. The continuance of the family in a male branch renders it more necessary for me not only to support myself by prudence but to guide to the utmost of my feeble abilities the course of the future successors. May God in his mercy look with favor upon my efforts.

I attended divine service all day. Heard Mr. Frothingham. John 7. 17. "If any man will do his will, he shall know of the doctrine, whether it be of God or whether I speak of myself." Upon the liberty of construction often taken without proper attention to the obligations imposed by positive injunction. Matthew 6. 30. "Wherefore, if God so clothe the grass of the field which today is, and tomorrow is cast into the oven, shall he not much more clothe you, O ye of little faith?" A beautiful text and a beautifully written discourse, upon the truth of the figure alluded to as well as the reliance upon Providence which it inculcates. For myself I become every day more and more satisfied of the fact. In the storms as in the sunshine of life there is nothing for man to look to but the support of a divine being. I have sometimes thought Mr. Frothingham not willing to go far enough in this notion.

Read a Sermon of Massillon upon the choice of a Religious profession by a Nun. Text from Psalms 17. 17–20, or according to our version which is in many places differently divided from that of the Septuagint. 18. 16–19. "The Lord sent from above, he took me, he drew me out of many waters. He brought me forth also into a large place, he delivered me because he delighted in me." His division was threefold although he managed to accomplish but two parts of it. He considered her as obtaining the part of election and of preservation. She had been elected from the earliest time for heaven, and preserved from the dangers of the world. Her consecration, the third head, was omitted. I cannot adopt the idea of election, because it involves the monstrous extreme on the other side. Nor can I admit the duty of Monastic seclusion in any of God's creatures. There is something fascinating in the idea but not consistent with the purposes of man so far as we understand them. Quiet evening.

MONDAY. 30TH.

I make it a point as far as I can to avoid any share in the political agitations of the day. But I cannot help feeling the harshness with which my father is treated by most of the Masonic party. It is far beyond any thing he experienced while engaged in the canvass for the Presidency. The National Republican party has quailed under the threats of this portion of it and will proceed to make an independent nomination with almost the certainty of failure.[1] My own judgment has always led me to condemn his return to public life, especially as I foresaw these evils. Yet in itself as avoiding the situation I have no regret that things should result in this manner. My only wish now is that his own friends will not desert him, and leave him in a small minority. If he can come out as the first with a plurality, it will save him much mortification and perhaps in the end serve the cause.

My Wife sat up a few minutes today. At the Office engaged in Accounts as tomorrow is Quarter day. Drew up my Quarterly statement and my own books, which took up most of my time. Called to see Mr. Clark and went to the Athenæum. Afternoon, reading My grand-father's letters, and Voltaire with d'Alembert. Evening, Shakespeare's Henry 4th. 1st. part. I waste my time in little things.

[1] Any hope that the National Republi-cans in convention beginning 3 Oct. would nominate JQA as their candidate for governor would seem to have been doomed by the violent tone of the attacks on him in the National Republican press since his announcement of candidacy. The *Columbian Centinel* on 30 Sept., p. 2, col. 3, printed a letter from a cor-respondent calling upon all good National Republicans to resist the effort to effect the nomination of "the most un-popular man that could be mentioned in the whole State of Mass.... If there is anyone among your number who means to support him at the Conven-tion, *he has no right to go there.*"

TUESDAY. OCTOBER 1ST.

The day was fine though cooler than it has been. I went to the Office after passing an hour in reading part of the third Georgic. My Wife still appears quite tolerably, and the child thrives. My time was so much taken up in attending to my Accounts, that I could not read. Went to see my Mother and John's wife who were at my house for an hour. Renewed at the Mutual Ins. Office four policies of Insurance upon different buildings in Boston and Quincy. The average of the last seven years has been very favorable, as I should have had not more than three or four dollars to pay on the whole, if I had not increased the amount of one of them a thousand dollars. I also settled my Quarterly payment to Mr. Foster.[1]

My walk was shortened. Afternoon quietly at home. I read the Cor-respondence of my Grandfather which is too voluminous. He did not select his materials with sufficient attention to the taste of the public. The result was that his defence in itself quite satisfactory was not read. The people read but partially. Evening, Racine's Iphigenie en Aulide,[2] Voltaire and d'Alembert, picking scraps for my article. Lounger.

[1] Phineas Foster, brother-in-law of Mrs. TBA, was, since TBA's death, guardian of his minor children to whom quarterly payments were due under JA's will; see vol. 3:27; 4:269, 399.
[2] CFA's copy of the *Œuvres* of Racine is at MQA; see vol. 4:49.

WEDNESDAY. 2D.

Morning cloudy with occasional showers. I went to the Office and was busily occupied most of my morning in Accounts, which I brought completely up. Mr. Curtis called in about a Lease to be drawn up for the Trustees, and I drew up a sketch for the same. I also read an Article in the last number of the North American Review upon Mr. Fidler which is very well in it's way.[1] But it is hardly worth the time to notice such a creature.

Afternoon quietly at home. Read a considerable portion of the last publication of the Library of Entertaining Knowledge upon the Elgin Marbles. This with two acts of Iphigenie en Aulide and a little of Voltaire made my whole labour for the day. I must add about one hundred lines of the Georgics.

This is a quiet mode of life and vastly different from the turbulence of the political world. My father has always loved to ride the whirl-wind, but he is not happy. His enjoyments are but one mode of in-toxication. And however great the ideas may be connected with them, the man sinks under their weight. My objects in life must be different. I have literary tastes and talent enough to turn them to respectable account. I have now children to educate and to maintain. These are occupation enough. Politics have become of a kind which drive men like myself out of active participation in them. Besides which I have at present insuperable obstacles to encounter in the course which my conscience has prompted me to take. For this I feel no regret.

[1] A review by A. H. Everett of Isaac Fidler's *Observations on Professions, Litera-ture, Manners and Emigration in the United States and Canada* in North Amer. Rev., 37:273–314 (Oct. 1833).

THURSDAY. 3D.

Fine day. I went to the Office. Occupied in Accounts. My brother John came in for a little while. He mentioned to me a transaction that has occurred, involving considerable difficulty. Col. Quincy has fool-ishly made a publication about a letter published by A. H. Everett the other day to J. B. Davis by which a shadow of discredit has been thrown upon the genuineness of it. My father is of course much provoked, and has written to Quincy who is in a flurry about the matter.[1] I went down to see Mr. Hallet, editor of the Advocate and learnt at his Office, that the Worcester Convention had nominated Mr. John Davis of Worcester.[2] This saves the party from present annihilation—And re-leases my father from the very critical situation he held.

I went to Quincy to dine. John and his Wife had returned from their visit to town. My purpose was to see the Tenants in which I did not succeed. I conversed with my father upon this subject of the letter, and concluded it would be advisable for me to take some steps in it.

This must be done. I thought over it and after my return home in the evening, drew up something in the nature of a reply.[3] How disgusting such sort of political warfare is. John and his Wife left Quincy on their return home.

[1] Ten days earlier there had appeared in Boston newspapers extracts from a letter from JQA to B. Cowell which seemed to justify the charge that JQA advocated support only for candidates who could certify their antimasonry. Everett asked for permission to publish the entire letter to show the charge false, but JQA instead turned over to Everett for publication, copy of a letter JQA had written in April 1832 to John Brazer Davis, since deceased, assuring him that in a letter to Gov. Lincoln JQA had supported Davis in his effort to gain appointment as county attorney for Suffolk, and stating unequivocally his belief that "Your Masonic degrees, do not in my mind form the slightest disqualification to the fulfilment of every duty public or private to the performance of which you may be called. My Anti-Masonry is earnest, ardent and deeply rooted — but it is to the Institution, as at present existing — to its Oaths — its Penalties — its Obligations, and their practical operation as disclosed to the world. It applies to no Individual, understanding and acting upon Masonic principles as I am very sure you always have done, and will do. If there be in the Spirit of Antimasonry, any thing of persecution, I disclaim all participation in it."

In publishing the letter, Everett stated incorrectly that the letter had been found among Davis' papers after his death. Col. Josiah Quincy, Davis' executor, upon inquiry from Davis' heirs, asserted in a letter he turned over to the newspapers despite an explanation to him from JQA, that he had not seen such a letter among Davis' papers. The effect of Quincy's letter, which he stoutly maintained was contrary to his intent, was to cast doubt upon the authenticity of JQA's letter to Davis. JQA in his letter to Quincy offered the explanation he had earlier given him that contrary to Everett's assertion, the letter had been found in a writing desk of Davis' that had been sold after his death, and that the purchaser had returned the letter to JQA, its sender. In the press the writing desk came to be referred to as "wash-stand," and the letter became known as the "wash-stand letter." It was the occasion for much ribald comment in the National Republican papers, of which lines from a long poem, "The Washstand," will serve as example:

"Ye anxious crowds who struggle to obtain
Your highest hopes, but struggle on in vain,
Write letters — private — secret — confidential —
Then make them public, should it be essential.
'Tis well to finish what is well begun,
And wise, most wise, to look to *number one*.
Should ugly spots of conscience hang about,
GO to thy WASHSTAND — TRY TO WASH THEM OUT."

The complicated course of the story can be traced in JQA, Diary, 23, 26, 29 Sept., 2 Oct.; A. H. Everett to JQA, 23, 25, 28 Sept., Adams Papers; JQA to Josiah Quincy Jr., 2 Oct. 1833, MHi: Quincy Autograph Coll.; JQA to J. B. Davis, 6 April 1832, MHi:Quincy Autograph Coll.; *Columbian Centinel*, 1 Oct., p. 2, col. 1–2; 2 Oct., p. 2, col. 1; 1 Nov. 1833, p. 2, col. 3. On John Brazer Davis, see vol. 3:63; 4:140–141, 208.

[2] The National Republican nominee for governor was John Davis of Worcester; for lieut. governor, S. T. Armstrong of Boston (*Columbian Centinel*, 4 Oct., p. 2, col. 1).

[3] What seems to be a draft of CFA's reply in his hand, addressed to the Editor of the *Boston Daily Advertiser*, undated, and setting forth the circumstances attendant upon the writing of JQA's letter to Davis, its return to JQA after Davis' death, and its publication, is in MHi:Quincy Autograph Collection.

FRIDAY. 4TH.

Morning fine. I amended and altered my draught of last evening, and then called upon Quincy for the purpose of procuring his assent to the facts relating to J. B. Davis. After some conversation, he inclined to the opinion that he should make the statement and I accordingly left him to assure himself of the necessary facts, to write them in a letter to me for publication.

At the Office. Accounts. Mr. Edward Everett called upon me. His purpose to converse in consequence of the statement made by me of my father's sentiments as expressed to me on the 14th of last month.[1] He and his brother are placed in an extremely critical situation between the two nominations, and his object was to procure if possible the withdrawal of my father. He said that the Boston Antimasons would resist it violently but that the Country members of the party would listen to any recommendation my father would make. I repeated to him my belief of my father's disposition to withdraw, provided he could obtain satisfactory assurances of it's being agreeable to the party. He left me with a request that I would ask my father not at present further to commit himself. This incident is among the curious things of the day. I reflected upon it and bethought myself how it would answer for the Antimasonic party to go for Morton.[2]

I rode to Quincy in the Afternoon and conversed upon the Subject, stating at length Mr. Everett's communication to me. His answer with which I was charged was this, that he acknowledged having said to A. H. Everett and to me, what he understood me to say, that in accordance with it he would do every thing consistent with honor and honesty. And that he would receive any distinct proposition on the subject, either in writing or verbally from Mr. Everett.[3] Of all things in the world to try to break the Anti-masonic party up is the very worst policy in this gentleman.

My mother seemed cheerful and my child quite lively. I took tea and returned although not until very late. Read a little of the Elgin Marbles and the Lounger. My Wife is yet nicely.

[1] That if the National Republican nomination went to someone acceptable to the Antimasons, JQA would withdraw as antimasonic nominee.

[2] Marcus Morton, the Democratic candidate for governor, was personally opposed to freemasonry, though not a political opponent. For JQA, Morton's support of Jackson made him unacceptable when alliances were repeatedly proposed (Darling, *Political Changes in Mass.*, p. 95–120 *passim*).

[3] On the following day A. H. Everett visited JQA in pursuit of his plan (JQA, Diary, 5 Oct., and see entry for 7 Oct., below).

SATURDAY. 5TH.

Fine day, but I rose with a head ach from some difficulty in digestion, and it did not leave me until night, and sickness at my stomach. Went to the Office. Quincy called upon me in regard to the business. He has again changed his plan and adresses a letter to the public. I gave him the remainder of the evidence and asked him to submit his paper tomorrow to my father. Occupied in drawing up two leases for Mr. Curtis which I completed, and then went to the House to see my Mother who had come in with the Nurse and my Child from Quincy. I much regret that she cannot remain longer, but we live in a Country where servants must be humoured.[1] My Mother seems unwell, and is affected by the political hurly burly.

I took a walk. Afternoon read the Correspondence in the Patriot, of 1809. My Grandfather was decidedly prosy and senile. Thus it is with man ever. One little error or other is always occurring to mar the very best meant efforts. I lazed away the time, as the operation of my headach is always to destroy all my energy. It is a little singular that my return to town should be productive of such an effect. Lounger as usual.

[1] Mrs. Field, the nurse, had been "homesick" in Quincy (JQA, Diary, 5 Oct.).

SUNDAY. 6TH.

I arose feeling better and devoted my day to quiet and meditation. As this is in its true nature a religious day, I purpose as well as I can to make it so. I attended divine service and heard Mr. Frothingham preach in the morning from Luke 23. 44-45. "And it was about the sixth hour and there was a darkness over all the earth, until the ninth hour. And the sun was darkened, and the veil of the temple rent in twain." The agitation of nature at the passion of our Saviour. Mr. F. tries to ascribe the phenomena to natural laws, while he urges the cause of it to be the act of the Deity. With me, this appears immaterial. God can alter the laws of the Universe at what time or to what extent he pleases. The veil is rent as typical of the opening of the Christian faith to the Gentiles as to the Jews. The Sermon was beautifully written, but did not please me so much as that of the Afternoon from Acts 8. 20. "Thy money perish with thee, because thou hast thought that the gift of God may be purchased with money." Upon simony, and from thence to the general subject of attachment to money, and an undue estimate of it's value. In this community, this subject needs often press-

186

ing. The great vice of this New England people is their adoration of Mammon. And rooted as it is in the character, the tree has now attained immense luxuriance and bids fair to overshadow us all.

I read Massillon's second Sermon upon a nun's profession. Psalms 83 (84). 1–2. "How amiable are thy tabernacles, O, Lord of Hosts! My soul longeth, yea, even fainteth for the courts of the Lord." He considers a life of seclusion as liable to temptation of time, of disgust, of example, and he sets against them the consolation that the degree of temptation is less, that of comfort greater, more pure and more abundant. Of course I cannot assent to the justice of the foundation which makes life selfish and destroys society.

Quiet evening. Finished Iphigenie which is a beautiful poem. I pass my time quietly at home. I hope I pass it usefully but at any rate I pass it in a way that money could not improve.

MONDAY. 7TH.

The morning was delightfully pleasant. I give no daily account of the state of my family because I thank Heaven that as yet they are well. And the incidents of the past week have been so numerous, I have said nothing of my brother's departure which we regret. Since the difficulty his manner to me has been changed to so great an extent, that I have felt a return of my ancient good feeling which time and haughty treatment had as I thought destroyed. He and his Wife have also treated mine in a way which I shall not soon forget. They have been kind and obliging to her at a moment when such conduct was essential. I hope the time may come when I can do something to show my grateful feeling.

Office. Mr. Hallett called upon me—A long political conversation. The plot thickens, but nearly all my father's political friends have deserted him. And the fire of Masonic hatred is opened upon him with a fury that baffles conception. The course of Mr. Webster, A. H. Everett and his brother, Governor Lincoln and others will be worth remembering. What a situation this puts me into here! But inasmuch as I cannot help myself, my way is to grin and bear it. Only basing myself upon the broad ground of principle and taking care to justify every one of my acts by some suitable motive in my own mind.

Rode to Quincy to dinner. Found my father and mother pretty well. I was surprised to hear A. H. Everett had been here, and stated a piteous case to my father. He says he must leave the State. Is this true? or is it for effect upon my father's compassion? Time will disclose this.

I went with my Mother to Mrs. Adams' on business. Finished what I had to do and returned. Conversation. Informed by my father of his political plan of action,[1] also of Quincy's affair which is the turning point of the canvass. Returned home. Evening, copying a letter for my father.

[1] "I desired Charles to suggest to the Anti Masonics in the event of a failure of election of Governor by the People, when the selection of the two Candidates comes to be made by the House of Representatives, to drop me altogether, so as to have their whole strength to give to two out of three Candidates instead of four" (JQA, Diary, 7 Oct.). The fourth candidate was S. C. Allen of the Workingmen's Party. That JQA's plan, which was the one he ultimately followed, was formulated so early has not been generally noted.

TUESDAY. 8TH.

Morning cloudy with heavy rain in showers throughout the day and night, yet very warm. I went to the Office, where my time was very much taken up in Accounts and the various little items attending particularly upon this Quarter day. Mr. Peabody called in for a few minutes but without saying much of importance. He inquired when Quincy was to be forthcoming with his publication. I told him he had written to Govr. Lincoln with a strong probability that it might delay him. Collected Dividends at the several Banks and on the whole my time went so rapidly that I was late home. No reading again. Afternoon reading the Letters of my Grandfather.

I this day received payment for my July Article in the North American Review. Better late than never. My other one makes no progress. I began but became dissatisfied directly this evening. My critical reading of Virgil continues, as also does dipping into Voltaire. This last however grows tiresome. Read two Acts of Racine's Brittanicus. I think I may indulge in a few observations presently. My only objection that they take too much room.

WEDNESDAY. 9TH.

It rained when I arose and there was a rainbow in the West which Sailors generally would consider a forerunner of bad weather. The day was nevertheless clear and mild as if it was September. I went to the Office. My whole time again taken up in Accounts and paying bills. Mr. Curtis called and I delivered to him the leases. It is not a little remarkable that when I bring down a valuable book here to read, my time appears immediately to be so taken up that there is not an instant to attend to any thing of the sort. However as the Quarter time passes, my leisure will increase, and I am quite determined I will not waste so much of it as I have been in the habit of doing.

Called upon Mr. Hallet to disclose my father's plan to him, but he was not at home. Took a walk. My mother and Elizabeth C. Adams came in, the latter to see me but I had given up all idea of seeing them so that I was out of the way.

Afternoon engaged in copying a long Letter to Mr. G. A. Otis from my father. I also finished the volume of Letters, which my Grandfather did not complete. By trying to get in too much he failed in getting enough. The State Papers he inserted would have been preserved in other shapes. The remarks in self defence which he would have made are now lost. So it is with fate. Read the remainder of Brittanicus together with La Harpe's Commentary upon it.[1] Lounger as usual.

[1] Probably contained in his *Lycée ou cours de littérature ancienne et moderne*, a set of which is in MQA; see vol. 3:12–13.

THURSDAY. 10TH.

Much of my morning time was taken up in delays at my house and afterwards in Accounts. At the Office I pretty nearly closed up the business of the beginning of the quarter. Then called upon my friend Thomas Davis and had a pleasant conversation with him. He is the only young man I know who has any character in a degree similar to my own. I do not know whether he will meet with much success in the world, but he deserves it.

On my return to my Office, found Mr. Conant from Weston. He came to talk about the Weston farm, his lease of which expires next spring. It seems he and his brother agree well enough, but the wives do not agree so well—A common case. They propose to separate and he wishes to know the terms upon which he may have the farm again. I told him I had never thought about it at all but would reflect and let him know as soon as possible.

Deprived of my walk, but I made it up in the Afternoon. Read Bacon's fragment upon the colors of good and evil. A wonderfully clear mind he possessed. His smallest rag has as much substance in it as the whole suit of many others.[1] Evening, final draught of my new Article. Lounger.

[1] CFA's reading in the *Works* of Francis Bacon which he was to pursue until the end of January was clearly in the 12-vol., London, 1807, edition now in MQA. For other editions at MQA of some or all of Bacon's writings, see vol. 1:23; 3:201.

FRIDAY. 11TH.

Morning clear and cool. After my usual quantity of Virgil I went to the Office and was occupied there in writing and Accounts. Called to see Mr. Hallett at the Advocate Office and had some conversation with him respecting political Affairs. I communicated to him my father's plan, and he said the party had hesitated about Shaw's nomination already. He intimated that they wished John Welles to take it. He it seems is trying to resist the current of Boston Masonic Gentry.[1] I suggested the circulation of scattering votes for the former person as Governor where the Antimasonic party do not take much. Mr. John Bailey whom I met there informed me of my being appointed Chairman of a Committee at the late Convention, of which fact I knew nothing until this moment. It is not an unimportant duty either, the draughting a Memorial for the next Legislature.[2]

Took my walk as usual. Afternoon, read over Bacon's colors of good and evil. I wish I could make myself master of this little piece. Of what wonderful use it might be in argument. Copied a letter to Governor Lincoln, from my father. It seems likely that he is dealing in a little of the littleness that is going about.[3] After all, what does the whole thing amount to? A place of Governor in a State containing 600,000 persons with a Council controlling every act. Evening, at home, working upon my Article in which I made considerable progress. This must be got out of the way.

[1] Henry Shaw of Lanesboro and John Welles of Boston (vol. 1:333–334) were the latest entries in the continuing search by the Antimasons for a candidate for lieut. governor who could be agreed upon and who would accept; see above, entry for 13 Sept., note, and JQA, Diary, 10 October.

[2] A memorial asking that there be instituted an examination into the nature of the masonic institution in Massachusetts (JQA, Diary, 14 Oct.).

[3] To quiet the raging controversy over the authenticity of JQA's letter to John Brazer Davis (above, entry for 3 Oct.), JQA had urged upon Josiah Quincy that he ask Gov. Lincoln to verify receipt of JQA's letter to him supporting Davis' appointment as county attorney (JQA to Josiah Quincy, 2 Oct., MHi:Quincy Autograph Coll.). Upon the Governor's refusal to Quincy to be drawn in, JQA himself requested Lincoln to say whether he had received the letter, at what date, and if still in his possession to return it or a copy of it to JQA (JQA to Levi Lincoln, 10 Oct., MHi:Levi Lincoln Papers).

SATURDAY. 12TH.

Morning warm with clouds, but the wind became easterly and very uncomfortable. I went to the Office and was occupied in Accounts. The time becomes so short that these with my Diary and an occasional interruption make up all I can do.

I intended to have gone to Quincy but the Carriage came in with my Mother. She appears exceedingly depressed. Her lonely way of life is not calculated for her at all. She dissuaded me from going to Quincy so I took a walk. My Wife and child are doing nicely. I thank Heaven for all mercies.

Afternoon, I read Lord Bacon's New Atlantis, a singular fragment, and afterwards some other of his little detached works. Not one of them is without value. There is thought and that very profound in most of them. His observation of nature was clear and if he had meddled less with the profligacy of the times he lived in, how much more his mind could have done for the benefit of the World. The older I grow, the more I admire the powers of intellect and the less I see of them round and about me. Mediocrity is the stamp of almost every thing with us. My father is the only one of the great men of our day who appears to me to have any thing durable, and he has wasted his powers. Evening my article.

SUNDAY. 13TH.

The storm set in last night and it rained heavily in showers throughout the day. I attended Divine Service all day and heard my friend Mr. George Whitney preach. Texts John 20. 29. "Jesus saith unto him, Thomas, because thou hast seen me, thou hast believed, blessed are they that have not seen and yet have believed." Matthew 21. 30. "And he came to the second and said likewise. And he answered and said I go, Sir, and went not." The first discourse upon faith, the necessity of which he maintained from the limited faculties of man which disable him from comprehending the purposes of God, from the control which any direct evidence would necessarily have over man's will purposely left free by the Deity, and from his weakness which fails him at once under the pressure of a revelation from a superior world. The other sermon was upon good resolutions, the failure of which arises from their originating in momentary remorse, or personal fears or from a want of knowledge of their nature and the force necessary to execute them. The two were good and creditable to Mr. Whitney who would do very well if he had a little better manner, alias more Modesty. This is somewhat of a deficiency in a Clergyman.

I read Massillon. Third Sermon upon a nun's taking the veil. 1. Thessalonians 4. 3. "For this is the will of God, even your sanctification." The subject, the three vows of the nun as means of regeneration, that of perpetual virginity a victory over the body, of perpetual poverty a victory over the temptations of the world, and obedience a relinquishment of that pride of character so common and so dangerous. To all this I would submit one question in answer. Which has the most merit, a nun or a woman in the world of equal purity of character? I am not positive that some places of the description recommended are not expedient in every community. As a resort for the afflicted in mind, for the despairing in fortune, for all who have passed through the hope of futurity in this world it strikes me as useful, but not for young women who are formed for active life. Evening continued writing. Lounger.

MONDAY. 14TH.

Cleared off with a sharp air from the Northwest. I went to the Office and passed my time much as usual. It is a little singular that I do not get along any better with my reading.

I went out rather early to Quincy and dined. Found my father and mother quite tolerably and had a conversation with him upon politics and otherwise. He gave me some hints respecting the Memorial which I propose to consider. After dinner, I went up in town and visited two or three Tenants without much success. Called at Mrs. T. B. Adams and saw Elizabeth as well as Mrs. Angier, the former goes soon to New Orleans. I wished to know what arrangement to make respecting her Interest &c.—All which was settled.

Miss Smith returned home with my Mother to spend a week with her. I left about dark and reached home quite fatigued. Indications of an incipient head ach. I could not write, it was so cold.

TUESDAY. 15TH.

My indications were not ill understood. I had another head ach of indigestion. These now occur so frequently as to alarm me. Some thing must be done to save me from being a slave to medicine.

I was busy in affairs all the morning. Called at my Carpenter's and went with him to see the house in Hancock Street which I propose to fit up and rent at a higher rate. The amount of repair must be considerable, but I think I can raise more than enough to compensate for it. My first and most difficult job is to obtain an outlet to the yard. This may be done in three ways—One by purchasing a right of way behind, or one at the side, or making a passage way underneath through the cellar. The modes are various and the adoption of either must depend upon the difficulties which I have to encounter. On my return to the Office, I found a Tenant about Rent, and soon after Mr. Plumer of New Hampshire who came to see my father, alias to inquire if he should find him. It did so happen that almost while he was speaking, my father came in, and I left them to talk it out together as I had much business.[1] Thomas B. Adams has sent me one half of the sum due on his Note,[2] and so I transfer one share of the collateral. This with Dividends &ca. made me quite busy.

My father dined with me as well as my Mother. He talked of his Poem of which another edition is to appear. This is rather a delicate subject and one upon which I have always been cautious. I said more today than perhaps I should have done. But candor is perhaps the best policy. I endeavoured to avoid injustice as well as hurting feelings, I know to be sensitive. How I got out of the scrape, God knows, but I meant well.[3] My Parents left town at about five and me to my head ach which disabled me from useful exertion.

[1] William Plumer, former U.S. Senator from New Hampshire, was JQA's principal support for the charges he had leveled against the Massachusetts Federalists; see vol. 2:350; 3:332, 418; and note to the entry for 19 Feb., above.

[2] Lt. T. B. Adams had borrowed $200 in Oct. 1831 (vol. 4:154).

[3] A third edition of JQA's *Dermot MacMorrogh*, his romantic-satiric "epic," would appear early in 1834. For that edition JQA had made some changes in the text and added stanzas (JQA to Melvin Lord, 17 Oct.; to Benjamin Waterhouse, 21 Oct. 1833, both LbC's, Adams Papers). Whether CFA's expressed reservations about JQA's further involvement with the poem were based entirely on his estimate of its worth as poetry or partly upon his view that the anti-Jacksonism implicit in the satire had lost its bite is not clear. He does seem to have been successful, however, in expressing his opinion without damage to JQA's sensitivities: "Charles . . . gave me his own candid opinion of Dermot MacMorrogh. That it excites no interest. The freedom with which he expresses this opinion, deserves my respect and is a pledge of the goodness of his heart as well as of the firmness of his temper and of the sincerity of his filial affection" (JQA, Diary, 15 Oct.). On the poem and its publication, see also vol. 4:390–391.

WEDNESDAY. 16TH.

Morning cloudy and damp. A Southerly wind with sultry weather. I went to the Office and was occupied in various ways, writing my Diary &ca. I had a short time to read an Article upon the Life of C[hief] J[ustice] Jay which was indescribably tame.[1] If Mr. Everett thinks he can maintain a Review with this sort of fence riding twaddle, I should think the best thing to happen would be it's failure.

Owing to the state of the weather I did not walk. In the Afternoon at home. My Wife dined downstairs for the first time today. She seemed much fatigued by the exertion. I read a part of the Legislative Investigation into Masonry as published by the Antimasonic party.

This is for the purpose of digesting the ground of the Memorial I shall perhaps have to prepare. It is as well to begin early and go over all the ground often. Evening, my Article which I am spoiling at least for the taste of the North American Review. Lounger. On the whole, I do not improve enough my time.

> [1] The review of William Jay's *Life of John Jay* (*North Amer. Rev.*, 37:315–340 [Oct. 1833]) was by O. W. B. Peabody.

THURSDAY. 17TH.

Morning foggy with easterly wind. I began reading Virgil's Æneis having finished the Georgics. A peculiarity of the ancient works is that one never tires of reading them. The same beauties stand out in bolder relief every day. I find the Poetry of the Georgics more exquisite than ever. The high polish, the ease and facility with which the versification is conducted, and the beauty of the thought are now and must remain unequalled monuments of ancient mental exertion.

At the Office, read an article upon Homer from the North American Review.[1] There is a good deal in it. Parts of it remind me of Mr. E. Everett's Lectures upon that subject, but it is more decided in the expression of opinion. I took a walk but did not feel the full glow of health. If that is going to desert me, then shall I suffer a real evil.

Afternoon reading over the Legislative Investigation, which to be sure puts an odd face upon affairs. This subject of Masonry is one of the most distressing that has arisen in our times, principally from the palpable truth it contains conflicting as it does with men's habits and prejudices. I have taken my side. The result must be that my personal prospects are destroyed. But it was not possible for me after once I had examined to balance. Luckily my pecuniary circumstances are not liable to suffer extensively from this cause. Even they however are not out of danger.

Evening, writing on Hutchinson. Paid a Wedding visit of fifteen minutes to my friend Edmd. Quincy's bride.[2] He has passed the Rubicon. I hope the chances of life will turn to him favorably. There was much company. I did not stop.

> [1] The article on Homer in the current issue (vol. 37:340–374) was by A. S. Packard of Bowdoin College.
> [2] Edmund Quincy's marriage to Lucilla Pinckney Parker in Boston was reported in the *Columbian Centinel*, 17 Oct. 1833.

FRIDAY. 18TH.

Morning fine and tolerably warm. I read some of the first book of Virgil's Æneid and went to the Office. Mr. Peabody called in and asked me to take a walk with him. We went over Craigie's bridge to Charlestown and home again. Nothing particular—Conversation about politics and general subjects.

On my return found Kirke in with the Carriage and my Mother. I started to see her, but as I wished to call for a moment at the Advocate office, Mr. Hallet stopped me to talk upon several points of importance. The consequence that on reaching home I found her just starting. She informed me of the death of Thomas J. Hellen, in Fairfax County Virginia, of brain fever after two days illness.[1] Poor fellow— His life was thrown away in nothings. His mind was constituted so peculiarly that the ordinary considerations which act upon men very feebly influenced him. The world will bear no traces of his existence and his friends will feel no grief at his loss. He had been in life a cipher.

I took a ride in the afternoon to improve my digestion. On my return, sat down and put the finish to my Article upon Hutchinson. I then commenced a series of political papers for the present election. Mr. Hallet wished me to take up some subject and I selected the one of Antimasonic Proscription.[2] Wrote till midnight.

[1] Thomas Johnson Hellen, a nephew of LCA and a brother of Mrs. JA2, died at twenty-four. Along with his brother and sister, he had for a number of years after the death of their parents lived in the JQA family in Washington. He had attended Phillips Exeter Academy and had been a student at Harvard for two years, but seems never to have been able to overcome the extreme indolence that characterized others of his family. The fullest account of JQA's efforts, long expended and unappreciated, on behalf of Thomas and his elder brother Johnson is in JQA, Diary, 20, 23 March 1830. See also Adams Genealogy.

[2] In anticipation of the state election on 11 Nov., the *Boston Daily Advocate* published CFA's four unsigned articles "The Proscription of Antimasonry" (22 Oct., p. 2, cols. 3–4; 25 Oct., p. 2, cols. 2–3; 30 Oct., p. 2, cols. 2–3; 1 Nov., p. 2, cols. 3–4), defending Antimasons against the charge of blacklisting candidates from the simple fact of their being Freemasons. A promised fifth and concluding article was never finished (entry for 6 Nov., below).

SATURDAY. 19TH.

Morning clear and cool. My Wife took advantage of it and rode out for the first time. Our course hitherto has been exceedingly prosperous, she having recovered very gradually and without any material drawback.

Finished my first number upon Proscription and a little specimen of a skit about which I have my doubts. At the Office engaged all the morning with visitors. First, Mr. Ladd who is the Tenant of the house 103. Tremont Street and wants repairs done. He sat a great while, Conant from Weston coming in and after him Judge Hall, the latter about nothing, the former about his lease. Conversation was kept up until the bell rung one, and my whole time appeared to have gone like a flash.

Rode to Quincy to dine. Found the family much as usual—My father perhaps in not quite so good spirits from the answer of Governor Lincoln to him.[1] I think he has lost his diplomacy as he [has] advanced in life. No longer having objects to gain, he has indulged in the expression of private opinion to persons in whom he could as he thought confide. The consequence is that when they have a mind to, they become snakes and bite him. So it is with Governor Lincoln. One great rule with politicians should be to treat friends as if they might one day become enemies, and enemies as if they might become friends. And a difficulty in my father's bold and energetic style is that it puts positions in so striking a shape as to be used by enemies against himself as decisively as it can be for him. A passage in one of his previous letters to Lincoln of which the latter reminds him is one of these and if published at this crisis would hurt him confoundedly.[2] He has committed an error also of which he is aware, in trusting any thing to Alexander H. Everett.

Returned home after visiting the Tenants again uselessly. My Wife had a bad tooth ach.

[1] Levi Lincoln to JQA, 14 Oct., Adams Papers. This lengthy reply to JQA's request for confirmation that he had recommended John Brazer Davis in a letter of 6 April 1832 and that the Governor had received that letter (see above, entries for 3 and 11 Oct., notes) was accompanied, in conformity with JQA's request, by a copy of the letter of recommendation. In his reply, however, Lincoln indirectly warned that publication of the recommendation might require him to bring to public notice passages in other letters he had received from JQA indicative of a belief in proscription of those who had taken the Masonic oath and anomalies in the recommendation itself that had caused him to judge the recommendation at less than the value JQA had assigned to it in his letter to Davis.

[2] The passages which Lincoln quoted were from JQA's letter to him of 18 Dec. 1831 (MHi:Levi Lincoln Papers): "A gang of two hundred thousand Masons from every nook and corner of the Union, are joining in one concerted yell of persecution! persecution! and certifying and swearing that *they* never took an Oath incompatible with their duty to their Religion or the Laws of the Land"; "The denial of the Royal Arch oath is a miserable prevarication. The entered Apprentice's Oath and penalty is itself a violation of all Religions and of the Constitution of our Commonwealth. To say that such an Oath is not to affect Religion or Politics is to unite impossibilities"; and from another of 1 Feb. 1832 (same): "I do hold as disqualified for an impartial Juror, at least between a Mason and an Anti Mason, any man who has taken the Masonic Oaths and adheres to them."

In replying to Lincoln, JQA reserved until later a full discussion of "my consistency with myself on the subject of Masons and Masonry, [and] the purity of your Administration from 'the reproach of Masonic influence upon Executive Appointments.'" However, in the meantime, in view of Lincoln's belief that publication of JQA's letter to him about Davis would involve Lincoln in the controversy, JQA offered assurance he would not publish it: "It is sufficient for me to know your unwillingness to give this testimony to deny myself the benefit of it, were it even more necessary for my justification than I suppose it to be." (19 Oct. 1833, same.)

SUNDAY. 20TH.

Cloudy with heavy rain all day. I copied several Letters for my father and prepared them to go in the Mail. Attended divine service at Mr. Frothingham's and heard him preach two Sermons on one Text. Genesis 27. 34. "And when Esau heard the words of his father, he cried with an exceeding bitter cry and said unto his father, Bless me, even me also, O my father." He began by considering the question of the superior purity of the early ages of mankind—Denied it and held it to be discouraging to the honest efforts of the present generation. Considered the history of the Patriarchal period and selected the incident of the birthright of Esau—Commended him and severely reprehended Jacob. Considered the passages in Hebrews and the Prophets which looked otherwise, explained them and closed by a comparison between the narrow birthright of the Jews, and the universal spiritual birthright of the Christian dispensation. *I* did not go with these Sermons. It is clear to me that Jacob was the chosen of the Deity and that the character of Esau though fair in seeming represents the halfway morality and religion which would sacrifice much it most values for considerations of a temporary nature. At the same time I do not justify Jacob, but the wisdom of the Divinity is never to be questioned by me, even though I can not see the mode in which it is exercised. Jacob no doubt met with strict Justice, tempered with mercy. Occasionally these discourses occur in which I find myself at issue with Mr. Frothingham. His mind is not so stern and stiff as mine.

Read a Sermon of Massillon's from Hosea 2. 19–20, the last upon the monastic vows. "I will betroth thee unto me forever, yea, I will betroth thee unto me in righteousness and in judgment and in loving kindness and in mercies. I will even betroth thee unto me in faithfulness, and thou shalt know the Lord." The division follows the Text. 1. An Alliance of righteousness, 2. of judgment and kindness, 3. mercies, 4. faithfulness. It appears that this woman left her Mother, being an only child, her friends, her station, to become a Nun, against the consent and wishes of them all. This may be Christianity, but it is not the form of it which ensures my confidence and worship.

The baby was unwell today and made us uneasy. In the evening, I wrote a short letter to Mr. Brooks[1] and read Bacon's physical mythology of the Ancients explained.

[1] Letter missing.

MONDAY. 21ST.

Heavy rain. I was up late and went to the Office. Occupied in reading the rest of the number of the North American Review. It deals in a variety of matter, but the whole is rather superficial. And there is a namby pamby sort of style about it which may be admired by the writers but which will never circulate the publication. Amiability is a beautiful thing in private life, but the world requires something of sterner stuff.

Our public here is deeply interested in the present reception of Mr. Henry Clay who has come on here to make up a little popularity for the ensuing Session of Congress. A procession was to have taken place but the rain prevented, at least a large part of it.

I could not walk. The baby was so unwell that Dr. Stevenson was consulted. He appeared better in the Afternoon. My time was taken up in reading Bacon's Mythology of the Ancients explained. It is rather ingenious than solid. I came across an opinion of Cato which agreed remarkably with my idea as expressed in the last Article upon Vaughan.[1] Read over the Proceedings of the Anti-masonic Convention, and endeavoured to put into form my ideas upon the Memorial to the Legislature. These political matters have put me in the midst of business—Yet I find great pleasure in recurring to my classical studies and the flexible verses of Virgil. Bacon's Historical characters and the Lounger.

[1] The essay-review by CFA of Robert Vaughan's *Memorials of the Stuart Dynasty* in the July issue of *North Amer. Rev.*, 37:164–189; see vol. 4:428.

TUESDAY. 22ND.

Rain continues. This will be of great service this day in replenishing the Wells. We have not had so much at a time since the month of April I think. I went to the office and was engaged in business and in writing. I have effected a sale of a considerable quantity of Stock in the Massachusetts Fire and Marine Insurance Co. for my father and propose with it and the proceeds of Merchants' Bank Stock as well as the Bank Deposit to make up a sum sufficient to redeem his Note at the American Ins. Office, on the 21st. of December next. This off his shoulders and perhaps I. Hull's payment in the Spring will materially relieve his affairs.[1] Hallet publishes my first number today. I made a sketch of another.

No walk, and consequent head ach, or nearly. Afternoon hard at work, Bacon's Character of Elizabeth and beginning of a history of England. O, the evidence of the servility of a noble mind, and the imperfection of human nature. Copied a letter for my father and wrote No. 2 of Proscription. My style improves by practice. This exercise of it will polish the periods and push out the sense. Read two hundred lines of the first book of the Æneid. Lounger.

[1] CFA's efforts had long been directed toward the reduction of JQA's interest payments through the sale of securities and consequent reduction of JQA's heavy bank loans and through outright payment of his obligations to JA's heirs as those obligations became due. See vol. 4:259, 425. One such legacy of $3,000 would become due in May 1834 to Isaac Hull Adams, son of TBA, when he reached twenty-one; see Adams Genealogy.

WEDNESDAY. 23D.

Fine clear day. I was very much occupied most of my time in executing a business operation. Having gathered together all the sums I could well spare, I have been negotiating to put them all on interest so as to be payable on the precise day on which the Note to the American Insurance Office becomes due. I applied to the Cashier of the Tremont Bank but he was not disposed to accommodate, nor very civil in his manner about it. I therefore consulted with Mr. Degrand and made an arrangement as advantageous as I could wish. I deposited the whole Sum together with 6 per cent Interest received in Advance, in the Commercial Bank, withdrawable on the 21 of December, with the exception of $400 which I retain on Interest myself.

I paid a visit to Mrs. Clay, as I felt bound to, particularly as he had the magnanimity to go out yesterday and see my father. She looks much as ever.[1]

In the Afternoon, I rode to Quincy. I forgot to mention that I went to Faneuil Hall to hear Mr. Clay speak to the people.[2] The crowd was great and he said a few words of no material consequence. The feeling in his favor is considerable. Conversation with my father—Political. He disclosed to me his intention respecting the election, to be kept a profound secret for the present.

Took tea and returned late. Found my Wife and children comfortable, but I was so fatigued that I did not work very actively the remainder of the time.

¹ CFA attended Mrs. Clay's parties in Washington while her husband was Secretary of State in the Adams Administration (vol. 2:92). Of Clay's visit during his swing through the Northeast preparatory to another Presidential campaign, JQA wrote: "This fashion of peddling for popularity by travelling round the Country; gathering crowds together; hawking for public dinners, and spouting empty speeches, is growing into high fashion. . . . Mr. Clay has mounted that hobby often, and rides him very hard. . . . Mr. Clay had two deputations sent to him from Boston, at Providence — One, of the tough Seignors to invite him to a Public Dinner, and one of the tender Juveniles to escort him into the City" (Diary, 22 Oct.).

² Meaning is clear but overwriting in MS has made the reading of "to the" uncertain.

THURSDAY. 24TH.

Very lovely day. I went to the Office and was engaged much of my time in Accounts. Settled up all my books and found myself likely to be pretty hard pressed for Money for two months to ensue. My father also is likely to make severe draughts upon his Account so as to leave little or nothing. I called at Mrs. Procter's to receive her rent, which is nearly the last at present due. My clearance has been pretty thorough.

My father and Mother came in. I went up to see the latter about the christening of my Child before they went away. But accidentally striking some wrong chord, we were unable to come to any decision. I talked on the subject also with my father, and settled upon having it done here in Boston on Sunday next.¹

In the afternoon I had a call from Josiah Quincy about his Letter; he publishes tomorrow, but I think the probability to be rather harm than good from it.² I read a little of Bacon's Novum Organum. Copied a paper for my father and wrote a draught for the Memorial to the Legislature. In the evening, I finished the first book of Virgil's Æneis and read the Lounger.

¹ From LCA's letter written the following day and received by CFA on the 26th (Adams Papers), it would appear that LCA had voiced strong objection to the idea that the christening of JQA's namesake take place other than at the First Church in Boston and at a Sunday service, feeling that the suggestion reflected an unworthy sensitivity to the public controversy then raging around JQA.

² The *Columbian Centinel* (26 Oct., p. 2, col. 1) reprinted Col. Josiah Quincy's letter to the editor of the *Daily Advertiser*, in which Quincy detailed the circumstances that had caused him to become convinced since he wrote his earlier letter that the letter from JQA to J. B. Davis was genuine, was written at the time asserted, and had come into JQA's possession through the agency of Stephen Bates in the way alleged earlier. He reiterated, however, that existence of the letter had not been known to him or to Davis' family earlier. In the *Centinel's* editorial comment following, the accusation was repeated that JQA, in publishing a private letter not his property for political profit, was guilty of an impropriety.

FRIDAY. 25TH.

Morning cloudy but it afterwards cleared away quite pleasant. I went to the Office and was busy as usual. My multitudinous occupations make the time pass with me with very great rapidity.

My second number appeared in the morning's Advocate. I called to see the Editor but did not succeed. This business of politics engrosses too much of my time. The appearances now are that the hostility to my father takes another and more artful direction. Finding the abuse he has encountered [may] do him good, they now direct a more covert battery against his Anti-masonic doctrines. This is much better calculated to touch him.

My regular exercise has been all interrupted of late, and I do not know when it will be resumed. Afternoon, read Lord Bacon, wrote some little upon my next number upon Proscription, and copied for my father. This took up much of the Afternoon and Evening. Copied part of my father's letter to Govr. Lincoln.[1]

[1] CFA would be engaged until 4 Nov. upon copying this promised response to Gov. Lincoln's charges against JQA of inconsistency on proscription. It occupies thirty-three pages in JQA's letterbook (Adams Papers), and, as JQA noted there, was never sent. For it, a much briefer reply was substituted on 5 Dec. (MHI:Levi Lincoln Papers).

SATURDAY. 26TH.

Fine day. I went to the Office. Received a letter from my Mother in regard to the affair of the other day. I shall endeavor to think no more of it. I was occupied for an hour or so in looking up authorities for facts which were requested of me by my father. And after I had succeeded my next move was to start for Quincy. As my father is going away soon I thought it advisable to call again upon all the Tenants who owe Rent. But my success was as indifferent as it has been. I got nothing out of them but promises.

On the road out I met my Mother coming in. She seemed depressed. She went in to see my Wife and returned to dinner. Conversation with my father. Consulted him respecting my draught of a Memorial and generally upon the course of political affairs. He is writing a letter to Lincoln which will probably make something of a stir. He proposes to publish it for pamphlet circulation. He remains here longer than he purposed to complete it. I returned to town rather early. Worked upon my several jobs in the evening.

I was gratified to find it a fair day and that nothing would prevent the taking place of the ceremony of my child's baptism. My father and Mother arrived at about half past 9 o'clock. And my Wife being well enough proceeded at the proper time to the Meeting House. Dr. Stevenson's child and mine were christened at the same time—The latter receiving the name of his Grandfather John Quincy. I hope in the support of the Deity for him throughout his life, without attempting to divine any modes in which it may externally be manifested. My wishes or my fears weigh for little, but my acts so far as they may influence his destiny are proper subjects for care and consideration.

My father, mother and Miss Smith dined with me. The former addressed a letter to me, with the seal used by his father on the occasion of the signature of the Treaty which established our Independence.[1] This is only given to me in trust with a successorship in this child or any other I may have at my election. Of course I feel without exulting in it the responsibility these things impose upon me. My trust can be only in a divine providence that has never yet deserted me, nor will while I strive to deserve it's support.

I did not attend divine service in the afternoon as I had engaged to take Mrs. Reed the Nurse home to Medford. As we rode along I could not help feeling how much my heart was relieved since I passed the same way with her exactly five weeks ago. My Wife was then about to go through a trial the severity of which I then feared but hardly anticipated, and my Mother was just recovering from a fearful convulsion of nature. She is now, I thank God, better, and my Wife bids fair to regain her usual health. How much have I to be thankful for. We sat together in the Evening and conversed as I trust in no unprofitable manner. Afterwards, I wrote the rest of a paper upon proscription and copied for my father.

Of Mr. Frothingham's Sermon in the morning I have as yet said nothing. It was from 1. Corinthians 1. 27. "God hath chosen the weak things of the world to confound the things which are mighty." He instanced the truth of this in the choice of David, in the rise of the gospel, in the dispersion of many of the greatest historical enterprises, in the ascendency of the mind over brute force, in the disposition by which meekness gains over violence. Some portions of the discourse were very eloquent.

Having finished Massillon after a persevering perusal of years, I began this day the Sermons of Atterbury.[2] The first was from the 50th Psalm 14. "Offer unto God thanksgiving." It began with some Account of the Psalms and proceeded to consider the general duty of man to praise God, 1. as an absolute 2. as a relative duty, then he went over the advantages of doing so. It is quite striking to perceive how different a course is taken by a French and English divine. The one is brilliant, the other plain. The one seeks to operate upon the feelings, the other upon the reason. The one is elaborate, the other simple.

[1] "The Treaty Seal" used by JA in signing the treaties with Great Britain on 30 Nov. 1782 and 3 Sept. 1783 was the Boylston family seal and was inherited by JA from his mother Susanna Boylston. It is now at the Old House in Quincy. In the letter to CFA which accompanied it (27 Oct., Adams Papers), JQA wrote "It is my desire that . . . [it is] to be transmitted down . . . so long as it shall please Heaven to continue the family, and the name, as an admonitory Memorial of John Adams, one of the Chief founders of American Independence." On the seal, see also *Adams Family Correspondence*, 4:xv–xvi, 202.

[2] The Sunday reading of sermons by Bishop Francis Atterbury would continue until the end of August 1834. A copy in 2 vols., London, 1820, is in MQA with CFA's notations dating his reading of each sermon.

MONDAY. 28TH.

Fine day although the morning was cloudy and threatened snow. I went to the Office. My Wife being now without a Nurse, and one of her Women being taken sick, begins to feel her weakness. The necessity of an exertion coming at the moment when enough was already to be made, reminds me of the trying times of the Autumn of 1831,[1] and makes me feel more disposed to learn patience.

I was occupied most of my time in drawing off my Proscription No. 3, which I accomplished and then called upon Mr. Hallett. With him I had much conversation upon political affairs. I wish if possible to prevent the contingency likely to take place if they row one way and my father another. It is difficult to do so without disclosing my secret.[2]

The Afternoon was taken up in riding with my Wife. She is very feeble and requires constantly air and exercise. After my return, I was busy in making the copy of the letter to Lincoln and the No. 4 of Proscription.

[1] ABA made a slow recovery after the birth of LCA2; mother and daughter were unwell in September and October of 1831 (vol. 4:136–157 *passim*).

[2] See entry for 7 Oct., above.

TUESDAY. 29TH.

Day clear but cold. My family in a state of disarrangement from sickness. I went to the Office and occupied myself as usual. Milton has not yet been touched. Such is the vanity of human resolution. Returned to the House to see my Mother who came in this morning to take leave. She proposes to start on Thursday.[1]

I had also intended to take my Wife to ride but she could not go. My morning was thus in a great degree lost. After dinner she found time and I accordingly rode for one hour. This shortens my time for occupation and I accordingly had not leisure for much. My principal work was copying the letter to Governor Lincoln upon which I made considerable progress. I also found time for the fine narration of the fall of Troy in the second book of the Æneid.

[1] For Washington.

WEDNESDAY. 30TH.

Day cloudy and wind very raw. I went to the Office, from thence to a sale of pictures at Cunningham's rooms[1] and to the Athenæum. Returned home at noon and notwithstanding the weather took my Wife to ride. The wisdom of this I am not confident about, but the exercise of the two preceding days having done her much good, I thought it best to try.

After dinner my father came in for the purpose of supplying himself with money, to start my Mother off tomorrow. I regretted my change of determination as to going to Quincy since it had been the means of obliging him to come in. Conversation, he appeared rather dull. He returned to Quincy before tea.

Evening, I was sitting down to copy, when a visit from Mr. T. Davis was announced. I took him into my study, and we sat until ten. Conversation, mostly political—Mr. Clay's views, and the attack upon the Everetts. I thus passed my day without doing much.

[1] Said to be represented in this auction sale were oils by Salvator Rosa, Poussin, and lesser known artists (*Columbian Centinel*, 30 Oct., p. 3, col. 7).

THURSDAY. 31ST.

Morning cold and clear. I went to the Office and was able to effect something in the way of reading before dinner. I began Milton's Defence of the People of England against Salmasius[1]—A curious specimen of the mode of supporting a controversy in those times. We have become more polite without changing at all the current of human feeling which does remain and must remain very bitter. Milton's style is strong. He wrote in Latin and this though it gives us none of the idioms of language which characterize each species, yet is favorable to the energy of composition.

I walked an hour on the common with my child. The breeze was clear and bracing. My mother could not have a finer day to start.

Afternoon at work copying. Evening the same, excepting a little of Virgil. The Child keeps us so much awake nights that I have to make up my sleep in the day time.

[1] A copy of *The Prose Works of John Milton*, 7 vols., London, 1806, is in MQA.

FRIDAY. NOVEMBER 1ST.

The day was cold and clear, and in all respects favorable for the progress of my Mother's Journey. I went to the Office and passed my time not very profitably, being engaged all the time in hunting after a woodsawyer, after all without success; this is comic.

At one, I went to Quincy. The ride was quite a cold one. My father seemed well and glad to see me. There is a quiet heartiness about his welcome and an apparent desire to please that I enjoy exceedingly. He alluded to the numbers upon Proscription with so much of compliment that I felt much encouraged by it. But as he says, nobody will read them but the Anti-masons because it is a principle to read nothing. The allusion to Mr. A. H. Everett, he appeared to regret, but I could not help it, for his windings ought to expose him to contempt. It seems that the Atlas, one of their factions Newspapers has come out also with an attack in it's own virulent manner. The probability seems to be that he will be crushed. I regret it for him though he has not altogether deserved any different fate.[1]

After much desultory conversation, I returned to town. Evening, my Wife was down for the first time. I copied more of the Letter to Lincoln.

[1] Although A. H. Everett is not named in the published version, the reference to him in "The Proscription of Antimasonry," No. 4, is clear. Having completed a destructive analysis of the Address framed by the leadership of the National Republican convention which contained a violent attack directed at Antimasons in general and seemingly at JQA in particular, CFA turns to a consideration of Everett: "And —— was willing to affix his name to a paper he never wrote, filled with such miserable trash. A good reasoner, an amiable man, and fitted to honor a far better party than that which now dishonors him;

... surely he might have abstained from sanctioning with his name so atrocious a libel upon thousands of his fellow citizens.... The thing is done—and regret is unavailing. The hand of retributive justice cannot however be far away, when such newspapers as the Centinel and the Atlas can have the insolence to threaten the independence of his judgment, and to dictate to him, notwithstanding all his attainments, notwithstanding all his great services to his party—the course he must pursue" (*Boston Daily Advocate*, 1 Nov., p. 2, cols. 3-4).

SATURDAY. 2D.

The day was milder than it had been and looked cloudy but it soon after became quite clear. I went to the Office and was engaged most of my time quietly at work upon my Accounts. Nothing of material consequence.

The political world is in a state of commotion about a very small matter—This election of Governor. The prospect for the future is not very clear, and I do not like much to look upon it. So far as I myself may be concerned, my course seems to me to be tolerably clear before me. I have nothing to expect and nothing to wish in a life of so much turmoil. My father has had too much of it not to show me how uncomfortable it is. I shall however persevere and do my duty.

Went to the Athenæum and from thence home stopping to see a copy of Titian's Venus lately brought from Europe for Exhibition. The original is in the Dresden Gallery. It is very pretty, but not so voluptuous as I had imagined. There was also a picture of Diana sleeping, an original of Corregio which I did not admire. Afternoon engaged in copying Lincoln's letter. It is too harsh.

SUNDAY. 3D.

Clear and cold morning. Passed an hour in copying, after which I attended Divine Service at Mr. Frothingham's and heard him from John 6. 27. "Labour not for the meat which perisheth, but for that meat which endureth to everlasting life." I was not quite so attentive as usual from the fact of my being drowsy in consequence of broken rest. The subject seemed to me to distinguish the exertion described in the latter portion of the text, and the necessity not to forget the former but to make it secondary.

Mr. Ripley preached in the afternoon from John 17. 17. "Sanctify them through thy truth, thy word is truth." An endeavour to prove that all sin is falsehood, or in other words that sinners in pursuing vicious indulgences put themselves in a false position both as to this world and the next. Mr. Ripley was a College Scholar. There was hope and promise in his University success. He is a respectable though quite a dull preacher.[1] Such are the changes of this life.

I went home and read the second Sermon in the Collection of Atterbury, preached upon the occasion of some meeting of a Charitable Institution in London. 1. Peter 4. 8. "Charity shall cover the multitude of sins." There is a great deal of admirable sense in it—Strong practical merit which after all is better than flash. He first discusses the meaning of the words, maintains his own construction, justifies it from objection and draws his inferences from it. He in fact maintains the doctrine of works which was then unpopular in England against the Presbyterian idea of grace. And I confess I agree with him. Evening, conversation and copying the Letter to Govr. Lincoln.

[1] On Rev. George Ripley, later prominent in Transcendentalism, see vol. 3:149.

MONDAY. 4TH.

Fine clear day. I went to the Office and passed my time very quietly reading the small talk of Mr. Taylor's book. There is something amusing in it, just as there is in a panorama of moving figures. The motion and variety pleases even where we take no interest whatever in the individuals. What a view of human nature. He praises few and censures many yet without any malice, for he is evidently a Courtier and has been a Legacy hunter.

Walk and home. I finished the copy of Lincoln's letter this afternoon, but I mean to try after an alteration before it finally goes. Read part of the profound work of Lord Bacon, the Novum Organum. A wonderful mind. My Wife now sits for two hours of the evening with me, but retires early on account of the fatigue of the child. The election rages.

TUESDAY. 5TH.

Fine morning but quite cold. I went to the Office. Time taken up in Accounts as usual and in writing Diary. Instead of employing my time as I ought to have done, I amused myself with Taylor's trashy miscellany. He is one of those numerous writers of the present day who do little or nothing for the literary world and yet who deal in chat that is quite amusing for literary loungers.

Went to the Athenæum, thence to walk. Afternoon occupied in copying a letter to Mr. Otis for my father, then Bacon's Novum Organum, and I tried to write in the evening but without success. I am reading aloud to my Wife in the evening Scott's Fair Maid of Perth. He has great powers of description, and a charming flow of style.

WEDNESDAY. 6TH.

Pleasant morning. My father came in to town this morning preparatory to his going away. As Mr. Everett wished to see him I invited him to dine with him, and after a battle with Judge Hall who had accidentally caught him up in the Street, I secured my point. The remainder of my morning was passed at the office.

My father came in and we had much miscellaneous Conversation—Principally political—At times touching upon Lincoln's letter,[1] at times upon the elections now pending, and afterwards upon affairs of money. I was thus disabled from doing any thing and shall be obliged to give up writing my No. 5 upon Proscription. I do not know that this will be any great loss.

My dinner was a tolerably pleasant one, but Alex. H. Everett seemed to be awkward and not able to reconcile himself to his situation. He has been trimming, and is ashamed of it.[2] Judge Hall came in afterwards, and in the evening Degrand. They none of them seem able to foresee the event of the election but as I think incline to the belief that Davis will be elected. It may be so, but the dullness of my optics is such that I am unable to discover the place to show it. Should this happen, however, it will make some difference in the general course of events. My father retired early in order to be ready for the morning's departure.

[1] CFA took the occasion to urge upon JQA the omission of parts of his letter to Gov. Lincoln, which he "readily promised to do." JQA packed the letter in his trunk to take with him to Washington for revision (JQA, Diary, 6 Nov.).

[2] "Alexander H. Everett . . . assured me that he did not write the part of the National Republican Convention Committee's Address which concerned me. He said it was very much debated and he disapproved it. But he thought it would bear a different construction from that which I applied to it. There has been a great struggle to strike off Everett from the [state] Senatorial ticket this year" (JQA, Diary, 6 Nov.). Whatever were JQA's feelings about Everett after the meeting, LCA continued to share with CFA, at least for a time, a bitterness toward him derived from the feeling that he owed his whole career to JQA: "I have known the Gentleman . . . ever since he was 19 years old and from that time I have never yet had reason to believe that he knew what a fixed principle was. . . . He is one of the ephemeral class whom your Grandfather thoroughly read and despised and who owes all the standing he had attained to by basking in the smiles of your Fathers early partiality which had set his judgment in this as many other instances to sleep." (LCA to CFA, 17 Nov., Adams Papers.) CFA's attitude toward and relations with A. H. Everett during the next few years would undergo substantial changes, which can be traced through the Index in vol. 6. A likeness of Everett appears in the present volume; see also p. xv–xvi, above.

THURSDAY. 7TH.

My father left us this morning at 1/2 past 6 o'clock. I regret his going although in the present disturbed condition of our political affairs in this State, it cannot be disagreeable to him to be out of the State.[1]

I went to the Office and read some of Milton. He is coarse but nervous. His style is not genuine English, because he had written in Latin and this is a translation. Notwithstanding all of this, he can furnish us very clever hints.

Took a walk. Afternoon and evening, engaged in a review of my Article upon Hutchinson asked for by Mr. Everett again yesterday. I wrote over two pages and revised all but the close. I think I could do better if I were to write anew. But the labour is too much for these times. Who thinks of doing so much as I commonly do in this way? I read a little of the Fair Maid of Perth, but my Wife was fatigued from the child's restless nights.

[1] The *Columbian Centinel* (7 Nov., p. 2, col. 2) reported JQA's departure on the eve of the election as indication of his awareness that "he has not the slightest prospect of being elected Governor." By the 9th it reported further that his departure was said to reflect his "despairing of success" and, on the authority of an "intimate" friend, that JQA did not *wish* to be elected Governor (p. 2, col. 2). A broadside issued by partisans of JQA in answer to the deductions unfavorable to his candidacy drawn from JQA's departure is reproduced in the present volume; see also p. xiv–xv, above.

FRIDAY. 8TH.

A cloudy morning but it cleared away and became a very fine Indian Summer day. I went to the Office and passed my time in reading Milton's Defence of the People of England. One or two persons came in. Mr. Knowles, the Carriage maker who did not seem pleased with my objections to his tufts, and other parts of his work. I doubt very much whether he will be able to maintain his reputation if he does not pay more attention to thoroughness of detail. Mr. Hayford the Mason called in at my request and I gave him directions. P. C. Brooks Jr. called about a Pew at Mr. Frothingham's Church. I authorized him to make an arrangement to suit himself.

Walk—Then home. In the Afternoon, I finished my revisal of the Article upon Hutchinson and to get rid of it, inclosed it to Mr. Everett. Perhaps I may have to send back for this also in consequence. Copied some letters left by my father and despatched several of the Packets he left, so that by night I found my work to be done considerably lessened. Leisure hereafter for the Winter, I hope.

SATURDAY. 9TH.

Fine morning, but it afterwards clouded over and by night was very gusty with rain. I went to the Office and passed my time in reading Milton, but his work is so coarse and so little English that I skipped to some treatises as they originally came from his pen. Several small papers upon the best mode of a Commonwealth interested me much and were in far more English taste. As I was threatened with a recurrence of head ach, I took a long walk and only with partial benefit.

I this day sent to Mr. Everett my Article upon Hutchinson. I cast it upon the waters—Hoping and believing that it contains principles of which I ought not to be ashamed. My afternoon was passed in writing and copying a letter from me to my father about the Lincoln letter,[1] which together with the copies made yesterday, I sent away by the Mail. Evening, reading the Fair Maid of Perth, Virgil and Lord Bacon.

[1] CFA to JQA, 9 Nov., LbC, Adams Papers. Pursuing their conversation on revising JQA's reply to Gov. Lincoln, CFA recommends modification in these particulars: (1) by eliminating such phrases as "carotid artery cutting" and "brotherhood of butchery" so as not to "startle the weak brethren" among the antimasons; (2) by curbing the attack on Gales and Seaton of the *National In-telligencer* on the ground that despite their weakness on the Bank and on Masonry, "upon matters of general politics their principles are correct," and "they do not truckle to Jackson and do resist Nullification"; (3) by omitting the attack on Jackson and the kitchen cabinet as having a divisive effect on the antimasonic forces.

SUNDAY. 10TH.

Fine day. I attended divine service and heard Mr. Frothingham preach an excellent Sermon from Malachi 3. 14. "Ye have said, what profit is it that we have kept his ordinance, and that we have walked mournfully before the Lord of Hosts." It was upon the doctrine of utility, as at present advanced in politics, the greatest happiness of the greatest number and, showing it's selfishness, its utter inconsistency with true principles and its folly. I was much struck with the decided character of the Sermon and it's aptness to the present state of the political world. To be sure, nothing ever was more contemptible than the doctrine advanced in these times, but it is the march of the democratic principle which in this Country is sweeping every thing before it. I am always glad to hear a Clergyman like Mr. Frothingham proclaim aloud his principles.

I did not attend divine Service in the afternoon, but as the weather was fine thought it better to take my Wife to ride for her health which is yet very delicate. We went along that pretty road by Jamaica pond and Brooklyn. I got home in time to read a Sermon of Atterbury upon the miraculous progress of the Gospel. Isaiah 60. 22. "A little one shall become a thousand, and a small one a strong nation: I, the Lord will hasten it, in his time." He considered first the fact of the progress of the Gospel, next that it must have been miraculous, he then refutes those who attempt to explain it upon ordinary grounds and refers the remainder of the subject to another discourse. This is characterised by the same qualities which belong to the others which I have read, good sense, simplicity, and practical views.

In the evening, I read to my Wife, but Edward Brooks came in and passed some time. I this day heard through Mr. Peabody of an accident which happened on the Railroad between New York and Philadelphia by which my father was brought into very great danger. The Car in which he was broke an axle tree, and the one next in order coming up struck and overturned. My father was in the first and escaped unhurt.[1] We have great cause to thank the Deity that he has preserved to us a life valuable on more than private accounts. The tempests of politics are nothing to the manifestation of the Divine will, and the nothingness of human power before it.

[1] In a brief note on the day of the accident JQA announced his escape unhurt. He followed this with a detailed description (to CFA, 8, 10 Nov., both in Adams Papers) and also recorded the circumstances fully in his Diary (8 Nov.). In reporting the accident on the day of the Election, the *Centinel* used as headline: "OMINOUS. *John Q. Adams upset*" (11 Nov., p. 2, col. 2).

MONDAY. 11TH.

This is the day appointed by law for the election of State Officers. The result is with a higher power. I went to perform my duty by voting for the whole of the Antimasonic ticket with the exception of my father for Governor, in whose place I substituted Henry Shaw, and of myself for Representative, for whom I put T. K. Davis. This once done, I set about my usual occupations of reading and writing. Took a walk.

Afternoon, I finished Bacon's Novum Organum—A work which will require many more than one deliberate perusal before I can be said to be master of it's wisdom. Lord Brougham has made a valuable analysis of it.[1]

In the evening at home very quietly with my Wife. Finished the first volume of the Fair Maid of Perth, and the third book of the Æneid. Read also, Racine's delightful little Comic piece of the Plaideurs—Singular that the French critics set this down so low. La Harpe scarcely speaks of it. I laughed heartily several times.

[1] See vol. 4:7.

TUESDAY. 12TH.

The returns come in this morning and manifest one thing decid-edly—The total prostration of the National Republican or till now dominant party. Even in their head quarters in this City, they have failed in electing one man on their own strength. And their Senatorial tickets have failed in all the surrounding Counties. The Country votes come in very heavily for my father and show a falling off only for the Nationals.[1]

I went to the Advocate Office where they were in great glee. I re-joice at it on account of the inhuman attempt to crush my father by those who professed once to be his friends. It has recoiled upon them-selves with a force they will long have cause to remember. But the election devolves upon the Legislature, and a new and difficult ques-tion presents itself—One upon which I conversed with Mr. Hallett for some time. I hope that yet my father may be able to withdraw him-self from the caballing of a Legislative assembly.

In my absence from my Office, I missed several persons whom I should have seen. Walk before, and after dinner. Began a second time the Novum Organum. Evening, the Fair Maid of Perth and Racine's play of Berenice.

[1] In final returns, JQA and the anti-masonic ticket polled 18,274 votes or 29 percent of the votes cast. The National Republicans polled 25,149, the Democrats 15,493, the Workingmen 3,459. The Antimasons carried 100 of 301 towns and five counties (Bristol, Franklin, Middlesex, Norfolk, and Ply-mouth). In the gubernatorial election of 1832, in which the National Re-publicans had won a clear majority, the Antimasons had been third; the National Republicans had polled 8,797 more votes, and carried 100 more towns, the Antimasons had polled 3,519 fewer votes and won 34 fewer towns than in the contest just concluded (Darling, *Political Changes in Mass.*, p. 104, 115).

WEDNESDAY. 13TH.

The weather very fine today, although growing quite cool. The returns still come in very unfavourably to the National Republicans. The running is quite close between the three Candidates and mani-fests the indisposition of the People to sustain this wreck of a party any longer. There must be new divisions. But the prospects of the Nation are not good. God only knows what may become of us. I am half dis-gusted with the Republican principle, although if we analyze truly such feelings we shall find too often that they grow out of dissatisfied personal consequence. The Government is yet dispensing it's blessings

7. THOMAS BAKER JOHNSON, ATTRIBUTED TO CHESTER HARDING
See page xvi–xvii

6. ALEXANDER HILL EVERETT, AFTER A PAINTING
BY GÉRARD IN 1825
See page xv–xvi

8. "THE REMARKS OF MY GRANDFATHER UPON . . . THE PLAYS [OF TERENCE], MADE FOR MYSELF AND BROTHERS MANY YEARS AGO . . . ARE NOT PARTICULARLY STRIKING YET SOMEWHAT CHARACTERISTIC"

9. THE CONVENT-SCHOOL OF THE URSULINE COMMUNITY, MOUNT BENEDICT,
CHARLESTOWN, MASSACHUSETTS
See page xviii–xix

10. THE BALLOON ASCENSION OF C. F. DURANT FROM THE AMPHITHEATRE
ON CHARLES STREET, AT "THE BOTTOM OF THE COMMON"
See page xix–xx

Mr. Durant's apparatus for making Gas

and though the worm of corruption is making it's way in the interior, it yet looks fair on the outside.

I spent an hour or two with Mr. T. Davis in conversation and took a long walk. My health troubles me. After dinner, I read Virgil but was not so much occupied as I ought to have been. Evening, the Fair Maid of Perth, and Berenice. I wrote a letter to my father upon the political state.[1]

[1] 13 Nov. (Adams Papers). He reported the Antimasons sanguine that JQA would emerge successful; however, he opposed assent by JQA to election by a "legislative cabal," more particularly in a legislature composed of a majority from the opposition party.

THURSDAY. 14TH.

I enjoyed the brightness of the day by taking a long walk. I went also to the Office and was occupied some time there in reading and my common avocations. Collected some Dividends and studied upon my Accounts. My pecuniary affairs have been uncommonly prosperous during the last year, which is among the many things I have to be grateful for.

Called at the Athenæum and looked at the political papers. The other parties than the National Republican are quite in exultation, and the bitterness of this in defeat is exhaled in the most rancorous and malignant fury against my father.

Afternoon, I read Bacon's Novum Organum and Virgil's affecting story of Dido. I do not greatly admire his hero in this business. His coldheartedness is a vice past defence. Evening, the Fair Maid of Perth. I copied the letter to my father upon political matters and sent it.

FRIDAY. 15TH.

The rain set in after sunset last evening and continued until morning when we had a fog so thick one could see but a yard off. I had fixed this time to go to Weston and arrange matters for a sale of the wood. I accordingly started at 1/2 after 8 o'clock and reached the Farm in two hours. It looked much as usual. I sent for Mr. Jones the Auctioneer, and we had a short conversation upon the time &ca., but as it was coming on to rain again I felt it necessary to hurry home. Accordingly, I started and reached Boston before three o'clock. The day had become clear, but heavy clouds again rose in the southwest and we had a clap or two of thunder with hail. Afternoon, Bacon. Evening, the Fair Maid of Perth and Racine's play of Bajazet.

SATURDAY. 16TH.

Fine day although growing much cooler. I went to the Office and was occupied much of my time in Accounts. Mr. William Spear came in from Quincy and settled with me for the Wood which was sold last month. He reports another sale to have taken place and the whole to have done very well. Upon these sales we must depend finally to disengage my father from his embarrassments. I went through T. B. Adams' semi annual accounts, drew one up to send to him and deposited in the Saving's Bank his balance, all which kept me pretty thoroughly engaged.

At one, I took a walk. Mr. Brooks, Gorham and his Wife dined with us. The latter go away next Thursday to his new destination, Baltimore. He seems to have revived since he has the idea of an occupation. His mind is too active for indolence. They left us at four, and I passed the short remainder of the Afternoon in reading Virgil, whose fourth book I finished. The fair maid of Perth, and Racine's Bajazet which I finished.

SUNDAY. 17TH.

Fine morning and the weather far more in character with the Season. I passed an hour in reading Chalmers on the adaptation of the mind to external nature, being the first of the Bridgewater treatises.[1] A book written with too much of a flourish of trumpets constantly going beforehand but still not without it's value. There is an affectation of a dignified, antique style about it which I do not admire, and a use of words and phrases which appear in these days quaint.

I attended divine service this morning and heard Mr. Barrett[2] preach from 1. John 4-5. "They are of the world: therefore speak they of the world and the world heareth them." An attempt to distinguish the worldly man from the man of the world, him, who makes it his object from him who keeps it in subjection to higher duties and purposes. There was nothing remarkable in it.

I did not attend in the Afternoon as my Wife went to ride with me. There is a difficulty now that Mr. Brooks comes into town about a Pew. I must get one at all hazards. Read a Sermon of Atterbury's finishing the subject discussed last Sunday. The fourth point of which was to show the advantage of the miraculous spread of the Gospel, and the last, when and how and why it stopped—As sensible as usual.

I finished in the Evening the Fair Maid of Perth and also began reading one course after closing another—I closed the last number of the Lounger. This is also the last of the periodical Essayists included in my course began not less than three years since. With little intermission I have in that time regularly read two papers daily and each twice over, and in this manner have accomplished the Tatler, Spectator, Guardian, Adventurer, Rambler, Idler, World, Observer, Connoisseur, Mirror and Lounger. I now undertake a far more necessary study, that of the Bible in the same manner. I begin with Genesis and propose to take Hewlett's Commentary to aid me,[3] two Chapters nightly to be read once with the Notes and once without. May God prosper the undertaking.

[1] Thomas Chalmers, *Power, Wisdom, and Goodness of God, in the Adaptation of External Nature to the Moral and Intellectual constitution of man*, 2 vols., London, 1833, was borrowed from the Athenæum.

[2] On Rev. Samuel Barrett, see vol. 4:297.

[3] A copy of *Commentaries and Annotations on the Holy Scriptures* by John Hewlett, 5 vols., London, 1816, is in MQA.

MONDAY. 18TH.

Cool and clear. At the Office, studying out Accounts, and with two or three Country visitors. Mr. Adams from Quincy with a bill, and Col. Jones from Weston with an advertisement for a Wood sale. After accomplishing matters with them, I took a walk, calling upon Mr. Jas. H. Foster about the matter of the Pew.[1] There is difficulty about it.

Afternoon, reading Bacon and Virgil's fifth book. I accomplish very little. Since the election which is now very calm, I have little to put me out of the even tenor of my way. I go on even more secluded than ever from society and contented in the belief of the general innocence of my course and the hope that I may improve my time and myself to the utmost without the injury which must result to me, if I give way to the paths of stronger temptation.

[1] J. H. Foster, in addition to his mercantile activities, was deacon in the First Church and had in his charge the church's management; see vol. 3:92.

TUESDAY. 19TH.

The cold now begins to make us sensible of the approach of Winter. I went to the Office and passed my time in reading the remainder of

Milton's answer to the publication made under the name of the King called Eikōn Basilikē, in modern character. There is roughness and yet vigor in his manner of controversy. I should prefer some more polished weapons. There is one merit however in his style worthy of imitation. There is no surplusage in his style. No superabundance of words to represent ideas.

Took a walk as usual and in the afternoon, read Bacon's Novum Organum which I find I have mastered pretty well. Here is an author who has more ideas than words, whose style becomes involved because he is so cumbered with them. Yet his page is one a man will return to again and again, while the mass of works of the present day pass to be forever forgotten. I read my usual portion of the fifth book of Virgil.

In the evening, read to my Wife from Tom Jones [1]—A mine of sense and feeling but unfortunately alloyed with immorality and with disgusting ideas. Delicacy seems to be unnatural to the native English mind. All its vigorous productions of an original character are coarse.

[1] Broken sets of the, London, 1789 and 1795 editions of *Tom Jones* are in MQA, along with JQA's set of Fielding's *Works*, 12 vols., London, 1766.

WEDNESDAY. 20TH.

Very cool indeed. I went to the Office and was busy in reading Milton although not with a great deal of profit. Called upon Mr. Hallet and had a conversation upon political affairs. I asked him to withdraw my name from the Antimasonic list of Representatives. He demurred. I told him how I was situated, that I did not wish positively to refuse but that if it was a matter of indifference to the party, I would rather have it taken off. He said he would see how the thing was received and if he could do it easily, my request should be complied with, but that they wanted names and especially Lawyers. My Law is a vast thing to be sure.

Received a letter from my father with a caution about the Post Office. It seems, one of my packets came quite open, but whether forced open or merely worn through, I cannot say.[1]

Miss Julia Gorham dined with us. Afternoon continued Bacon, and read three hundred lines of Virgils fifth book. Evening, Tom Jones, and Racine's Andromaque. I have now finished all Racine's best tragedies. I admire them as fine specimens of versification, and strong personation of passion and character, but I regret the clogs which the stiffness of the French taste has embarrassed him with. All plays in

French are alike. They all turn upon love, and they all have heroes and heroines out of nature, with each a confident or confidente to work out the plot with. And this in the face of the fact so often stated by the "Grand Condé," that no man is a hero to his Valet de Chambre. They use no bigger words than the mass of mankind. What call is there to elevate them out of nature?

[1] JQA to CFA, 16–17 Nov. (Adams Papers). JQA was less willing to suspend judgment: "It had been broken open . . . I suppose they will do the same by this. So write me nothing by the mail which you are not willing to see published. . . . Look to your Jackson-Masonic Post-Office, but make no complaint. The Post-Office here is in the very lowest depth of corruption, insolvency and swindling, and so are others if not all the Departments of the Government." Having vented his wrath, however, in a postscript he had second thoughts, noting that the broken cover *was* of flimsy material.

THURSDAY. 21ST.

Morning milder and more pleasant. I went to the Office and passed an hour in occupation. Mr. Peabody came in and asked me to walk with him. I accordingly went, and on my return went to the Athenæum to select some book for my morning's exercise. I find some difficulty in selecting a suitable subject for my morning meditations. I picked up a volume of Parliamentary debates of the time of the American War, which I thought might clear my ideas a little as to those times. But I must turn my attention more definitely to that subject if I take it up at all.

Walk. Afternoon, having received a letter from my Mother, I answered it and wrote one also to my father [1]—The subject generally political. There is a clue yet to be unravelled which I do not understand. Evening quietly at home. I began the Account of the life of Racine prefixed to his works. A man killed by the critics, which is bad enough to be sure. When he probably was worth all the critics together that ever touched his works. There is much to profit by in this Account. Hewlett and the Bible as usual.

[1] LCA's letter (17 Nov., Adams Papers) reports the illness of herself, John, and Mary. CFA's letter to JQA is in the Adams Papers, but his letter to LCA is missing.

FRIDAY. 22D.

Cloudy with a heavy rain through the most part of the day. I went to the Office and passed most of my time in reading the account of the Parliamentary debates upon the American affairs. The difference in the mode of reporting and speaking since that time is prodigious.

The public is the Auditor now and the consequence seems to be harangues of great length and very moderate substance. I do not perceive that the Orators of the British Parliament very much excell our's. Perhaps the taste of the Speakers is better, but their productions have not so much matter.

Walk in the rain as I was suffering again from slight indigestion. Afternoon, busied in copying my Letter to my father, which I executed and sent. Evening, Tom Jones and the Life of Racine. Heavy rain in the night.

SATURDAY. 23D.

I spent an hour at market this morning making purchases, although I did not think that the display was as great as I should have expected so soon before our thanksgiving day. Then at the Office where I received a call from Mr. William Spear and a settlement for some Wood sales at Quincy.

Walk. I had a small company to dine. Mr. Thomas K. Davis, Edmund Quincy, Edward Blake and Thomas Dwight.[1] It was tolerably pleasant, but not one of my most agreeable dinners. We drank abundance of wine and rose from table a little before seven o'clock. The rest of the evening quiet at home. I did little however excepting my regular work of the Bible and Hewlett.

[1] Thomas Dwight, Harvard 1827, was an attorney.

SUNDAY. 24TH.

Since Mr. Brooks has taken possession of his Pew, I have to go to some other and my efforts to procure one have been hitherto pretty unsuccessful. My Wife and I concluded to go to Meeting at any rate, and try one of the Gallery Pews, which an acquaintance of her's had just left. I was much pleased with the situation although the world of fashion pronounces them not to be tolerable. They command a view of the House and are admirably situated both as respects the preacher and the Music.

Mr. Frothingham preached all day. Texts, Phillipians 4. 8. "If there be any virtue." Considering the three classes of reasoners who doubt the existence of virtue—The sceptic by profession, the sceptic by the illusion of his passions and the sceptic by the operation of the world, and the apparently unequal dispensations of prosperity. The other from John 8. 7. "He that is without sin among you, let him first cast a stone." Upon the duty of gentleness in judgments of others, and the difficulty of claiming to be immaculate one's self. The discourses were both moderately good and with pretty simplicity.

I read also one of Atterbury's Sermons describing the Scorner. Proverbs 14. 6. "A scorner seeketh wisdom and findeth it not." The person mentioned in the text he defines as impelled by pride or suspicion, and given to false wit or sensuality by which all his opinions are twisted from the right way. Quiet evening at home.

MONDAY. 25TH.

Snow and the first arrival of winter. I went to the Office. Mr. Conant from Weston came in and passed a considerable time in talking about the lease of the farm there and many other matters appertaining to it. He demurred also about taking my horse which has puzzled me extremely. The expense of keeping him here is very great.

I went to vote for the remainder of the Representatives to be elected from Boston, and put in the whole Antimasonic ticket excepting myself in whose room I put T. K. Davis. I do not know what the probabilities are. Read more of the Parliamentary debates in 1774. Afternoon at home. Lord Bacon, and Virgil 5 and 6 books. Evening Tom Jones and Smith's Moral Sentiments.[1]

[1] A copy of the London, 1792, edition of Adam Smith's *Theory of Moral Sentiments* is in MQA.

TUESDAY. 26TH.

Snow continues with pretty warm air. I went to the Office as usual and passed my time in reading the Parliamentary Debates. Came to the famous speech of Mr. Burke on Conciliation with America which is a jewel. It is a pity that two or three coarse yet strong figures rather depress the general tendency of the style. When I read productions like these, I feel the full [weight?] of my own vanity and insignificance. They are Orations indeed.

I did not take a walk today. Afternoon, Lord Bacon, Novum Organum. Evening, Tom Jones, and writing. I was a little depressed today. I know not why. But at this season, it will be so sometimes. Read some of the Psalms which relieved me.

WEDNESDAY. 27TH.

I went to Market as usual upon the morning preceding Thanksgiving day and found the price of Poultry by the extortion of the venders who attempt a monopoly so high that I declined buying any at all. And my general purchases were very slight. Occupied some time in running about to procure a pew at the Meeting house in Chauncy place and finally succeeded in taking one in the Gallery, which I occupied last Sunday.

The remainder of the morning passed in reading the Parliamentary Debates. I find nothing satisfies me after the speech of Mr. Burke. Afternoon, Lord Bacon, Novum Organum, and in the evening, besides Virgil I began Smith's Theory of Moral Sentiments. Read to my Wife from the Psalms and Tom Jones.

THURSDAY. 28TH.

This was the day set apart as usual for Thanksgiving. It was quite pleasant, and I read in the course of the morning a considerable quantity of Chalmers' Treatise. He introduces a long argument against the Tythe system and the poor laws not very judiciously I should think in a general dissertation. These matters would put people to sleep in the next Century.

Attended divine service and heard Mr. Frothingham from Isaiah 9. 3. "Thou hast multiplied the nation and not increased the joy; they joy before thee according to the joy in harvest." An historical Account of Thanksgiving day from the earliest days of the Colony—A festival after harvest. The discourse was excellent and some passages extracted from the early records of the General Court very interesting.

I took a walk and then went to dine with my Wife at Mr. Brooks'— Mrs. Everett who is Mistress of the House, Mr. and Mrs. Frothingham, Edward Brooks, and several of their respective children. Pleasant enough. My Wife returned before tea and we passed a quiet evening at home.

FRIDAY. 29TH.

Morning cloudy and raw. I went to the Office and finished the Parliamentary History, for 1774—A record of great importance in American Affairs. Little else. I called at the Athenæum and procured another Volume of a better collection. Afternoon, Lord Bacon, and the beautiful 6th. book of Virgil, Smith's Moral Sentiments, Tom Jones. Nothing material happens to enliven the monotony of the daily duties.

We have heard and with deep regret of the death of Mary E. Roberdeau in Philadelphia. She had recommended herself much to us here by her good nature and pleasing manners, two years since, and we had hoped to have seen her again, although she has been for some time announcing her decline. So it is in this world. Every step we make brings us nearer to the pitfalls.[1] There is a deeper moral in every death, particularly after persons become parents. Mr. B[rooks].

[1] On Mary E. Roberdeau, long-time friend of LCA, see vol. 4:131. News of her death was contained in a letter from LCA to ABA (25 Nov., Adams Papers). In the same letter she reported Mrs. JA2's convalescence from scarlet fever, but John's condition no better: "Long suffering and anxiety concerning the health of his Wife with the succession of uneasiness which has assailed him for the last two years have produced a nervous irritation of mind which contributes much to retard his recovery."

SATURDAY. 30TH.

Morning cloudy with heavy rain throughout the day. I went to the Office and sat very quietly reading the Parliamentary History. The papers relating to the breaking out of the disturbances are full of interest. They show the decisive tone which was taken from the first. There was no working up. The simultaneous rising throughout the Country is a very strong indication of the State of the question.

Afternoon, read Lord Bacon de Augmentis Scientiarum and finished the charming book of Virgils Æneis containing his Descent. Evening quiet. Tom Jones, Racine and Boileau's Correspondence.[1]

[1] A collection of the correspondence of Racine and Boileau had first appeared in vol. 2 of the *Mémoires de J. Racine*, ed. Louis Racine, Paris, 1747–1750. CFA was perhaps reading the letters between them contained in vol. 6 of Racine's *Œuvres complètes*, ed. L. Aimé-Martin, 7 vols., Paris, 1825, a copy of which is at MQA.

DECEMBER. 1833.
SUNDAY. 1ST.

I read a little of Mr. Chalmers' book before I attended Divine Service and heard Mr. Frothingham preach all day. John 19. 25. "Now there stood by the cross of Jesus, his mother." The duty of firmness in cases of trial, and of active interposition. Afternoon, John 5. 3. "In these lay a great multitude of impotent folk, of blind, halt, withered, waiting for the moving of the water." Upon the morally sick and infirm, those who suspected not their own condition, those who could stand when there was no trial. The discourses were good but not very interesting.

Read Atterbury—A Funeral Sermon upon the death of the Lady Cutts. Eccles. 7. 2. "It is better to go to the house of mourning, than to go to the house of feasting, for that is the end of all men and the living will lay it to heart." Of course a panegyric. She was but eighteen and according to him a model of excellence. The style is simple and the praise moderate, perhaps it may have been just.

Received a letter from my father which I sat down directly to answer.[1]

[1] To CFA, 26 Nov., Adams Papers; to JQA, 1 Dec., LbC, Adams Papers.

MONDAY. 2D.

Morning cloudy and mild. I went to the Office and was occupied there in reading the Parliamentary History. Only one or two interruptions. Dr. Brown, the Quack who wants my house 103 Tremont Street in connection with the other,[1] and Mr. Peabody. Nothing else material.

Politics are not pleasant. Mr. Rush has come out against the Bank and the question seems likely to become Antimasonic. If so, of course I am out of my element. Took a walk. Afternoon, writing and copying my answer to my father. Tom Jones and Smith. Correspondence, Boileau and Racine.

[1] John A. Brown, "botanic physician," lived at 105 (*Boston Directory*, 1833). In the entries below for 20 and 26 Dec., CFA refers to Brown as "the Steam Doctor," and in that for 10 Feb. 1834 calls the house he occupied, "the Infirmary."

TUESDAY. 3D.

Morning cloudy. I went to the Office. Mr. Conant the younger called on me from Weston about the Farm and discussed the subject of the Lease. I told him of what I proposed to do. It seems both these brothers want the Farm, and very probably will bid upon each other for it. I do not much relish the idea but see no way clearly to help it. After he had gone, I called to see Mr. Hallet and had a long conversation with him. I communicated to him my father's determination[1] and heard his objections which were neither few nor gentle—To all which I tried to reply as well as I could. He said he would write to my father, which I urged him to do.[2] I suppose he suspects me a little of partial statements. I am not radical enough. We discussed the Memorial also. Quiet afternoon. Walk. Lord Bacon de Augmentis Scientiarum. Virgil seventh book. Tom Jones and writing to my father. Correspondence Boileau and Racine.

[1] In letters to CFA of 19–21 and 26 Nov. (both in Adams Papers), JQA was unequivocal in his determination to withdraw his name when the choice of governor came up for consideration in the Legislature. "If I were certain of

being elected and if I had the highest popular vote (short of a Majority) I should still withdraw. I never would be Governor of Massachusetts, but by the voice of the People." He further granted CFA permission to communicate his in-

tent at CFA's discretion. Public announcement of the decision would be made at the proper time in a letter JQA would write to the *Advocate*.

[2] Hallett's letter to JQA (7 Dec.) is in the Adams Papers.

WEDNESDAY. 4TH.

Morning the same kind of cloudy weather we have had for some time back. I went to the Office and was engaged for some time in Accounts, then called upon Mr. Hallett and had another conversation with him, which ended in his bringing out a Memorial. I have been all along surprised at the singular mode of proceeding he has adopted, and today I found out the secret. My being put at the head of the Committee was an unexpected stroke to him as he intended to draw up the Memorial, from the first. The delays are accounted for as my Draught embarrassed him. It *now* turns out, that the Committee has met without notifying me and adopted his and rejected my draught which in its present shape was never intended to be submitted to the Committee. I am not a little mortified at the position in which I have been in spite of myself placed. Nevertheless I must take it as the first lesson of my political experiences. I took a walk. In the Afternoon, looked over his draught, made some alterations and sent them back with a letter to Mr. Hallett.[1] Evening at home. Tom Jones, and finished the letter to my father.

[1] 4 Dec. (LbC, Adams Papers); enclosure missing. In the letter, CFA asked for the return of his draft as he was without a copy. He later entered it in his Letterbook (following item No. 16214, Adams Papers, Microfilms, Reel 158).

THURSDAY. 5TH.

The weather continues mild. I went to the Office. Received an apologizing letter from Mr. Hallett,[1] returning me the draught with a request I would remodel it. I replied very briefly declining to do so, in this stage of the business and intimating to him in reply my utter dissatisfaction with his proceeding.[2] In his letter, he says both draughts were read to the Committee, and with the State Committee present. Now this was totally against my will, but what is more singular Mr. Bailey happening to come in, I find that it is not true. He made a representation to the Committee that his was the result of joint consultation, giving them the impression I had seen it, while he suppressed my draught, and now he tells me this is the result of consultation with the Committee upon both drafts. This want of honesty in so trifling a transaction has shaken my faith in his political character and principles. I have therefore written to my father to be guarded towards him.[3]

Mr. Bailey conversed much with me, and I communicated to him my father's intention that he might reflect upon it. I gained no time to walk. After dinner engaged with Mr. Chadwick and Mr. Eddy upon the last year's Accounts of the Middlesex Canal.[4] It took us about two hours to go over them very superficially and check them with the book. The rest of the day and evening with the exception of a little while to finish Tom Jones was devoted to copying a letter from my father.

[1] Letter missing.
[2] To B. F. Hallett, 5 Dec. (LbC, Adams Papers).
[3] To JQA, 4–5 Dec. (Adams Papers). In his letter CFA reported Hallett's reception of JQA's proposed step and, without detailing his reasons, warned

JQA against placing trust in Hallett, and cautioned him about communicating with Hallett in any confidence.
[4] Caleb Eddy was superintendent and treasurer of the Canal company, Ebenezer Chadwick a director; see vol. 3:153, 247.

FRIDAY. 6TH.

Morning a little cloudy but it afterwards cleared away and became very pleasant. I went to the Office. Time passed in looking over Accounts which from my negligence have gone considerably wrong. I went to the Athenæum for an hour to read the President's Message and other documents.[1] This is a flimsy performance.

The City is in commotion about a local election for Mayor—A miserable affair in which there is not a sixpence choice between the three candidates. I shall vote for the weakest to defeat the others.[2]

Afternoon quietly at home. Read Lord Bacon de Augmentis Scientiarum. Virgil. In the evening Byron's Corsair to my Wife,[3] and after it, Smith's Moral Sentiments a book valuable for it's acute observation if not for it's moral system.

[1] The President's annual Message to Congress, delivered on 3 Dec., was printed in the Boston newspapers on the 6th.
[2] The leading candidates were William Sullivan and Theodore Lyman,

both political enemies of JQA. The third and antimasonic candidate was George Odiorne.
[3] On CFA's periodic returns to the reading of Byron and on copies of his *Works* in MQA, see vol. 3:41, 185.

SATURDAY. 7TH.

Morning cooler but fine weather. I went to the Office and was engaged in rectifying my Accounts which I finally succeeded in doing—

So that instead of finding myself nearly two hundred dollars deeper than my Accounts show for, I find a few dollars against me which exceed my actual expense. This is far the best error. It is not worth going over the accounts again to correct it, but I intend after new year to begin upon a new and a more accurate system.

Had one or two visitors. Mr. Walsh, an Applicant for the Office opposite and Mr. William Spear from Quincy. Walk. Afternoon Bacon. Virgil. Received a long political letter from my father and a short business one from T. B. Adams.[1] Quiet Evening. Finished Byron's Corsair to my Wife, and began an answer to my father.[2]

[1] JQA to CFA, 2 Dec. (Adams Papers); the letter from Lt. Adams is missing.
[2] To JQA, 8 Dec. (Adams Papers).

SUNDAY. 8TH.

Cloudy and raw. I read some of Mr. Chalmers in the morning prior to attending divine service. Mr. Gilman of Charleston, S.C. preached[1] in the absence of Mr. Frothingham to New York. Ezekiel 97. 2. "Clouds and darkness are round about him: righteousness and judgment are the habitations of his throne." The inexplicable character of the Deity, yet the impossibility of reasoning from the creation to any other than the attributes here ascribed to him. 16. Luke 31. "And he said unto them, If they hear not Moses and the prophets, neither will they be persuaded, though one rose from the dead." The argument against the authenticity of the scripietal [scriptural] account of Christ. The discourses were remarkable for nothing, but were clear expositions of the more ordinary views of Christianity.

Read a discourse by Atterbury, delivered at the period of the Anniversary of the Restoration. Ezekiel 37. 3. "And he said unto me, Son of man, can these bones live? And I answered, O Lord God, thou knowest." The wisdom of providence manifested in Revolutions of Government, subject divided in four parts, 1. as displaying marks of his attention to the affairs of the world, 2. as ordering a sort of justice by distributing reward and punishment in this world which could not be done in the next, 3. as discovering the folly and vanity of men, 4. as inciting to national piety. I had heard Mr. Frothingham some time since on the same text to a different purpose. I hardly consider the Restoration as so great a blessing. Evening quiet. Read Chalmer's.

[1] Rev. Samuel Gilman, Harvard 1811, minister of the Second Independent Church in Charleston, and poet, who would be best remembered, perhaps, as the author of "Fair Harvard" (*DAB*).

MONDAY. 9TH.

It rained and blew a hurricane last night, but this morning the weather was as fair and mild as October. I went to the Office and after my usual occupation went down to see Mr. Hallett. We had another conference. He apologized and explained. I did not see his card until this morning requesting this interview. He urged me to make the draft, and I was not taken into the snare. He explained to me the facts as Mr. Bailey told them, without reflecting that his own letter to me was thereby proved a falsehood. He finally suggested the calling the Committee together and deciding upon the draft tomorrow, to which I consented. We had much further conversation upon the proposed withdrawal of my father. He is opposed to it in every shape, but assents *if* my father will pursue the course he suggests. This is the dictation of party. This is the arrogant fancy of the Newspaper press which is scourging this Country with a rod of Iron. We broke up by my promising to write to my father.

I have lost my confidence in Mr. Hallett, and will try to be prudent as it respects him. I am more and more disgusted with politics. If I had not duties which my name and station prescribe to me, I would forswear them altogether. Attended a Meeting of the Directors of Boylston Market, and after my return, copied a letter to my father. To day, the election for Mayor took place.

TUESDAY. 10TH.

Fine morning. I went to the Office as usual. Engaged in Accounts &ca. Called on Mr. Oliver about the Note of my father due on the 21st instant. And called to receive the Dividend upon the New England Insurance Stock which relieves my borrowing materially. Yet I shall be pressed to make up the sum.

Walk. Afternoon read Chalmer's and attended a Meeting of the Committee on the Memorial. Dr. Phelps, Mr. Gassett and Mr. Hallett present. The latter read his rough draught and we criticised it. I found how it was and took part to show that I was not offended, but I was not entrapped by his complimentary style to suggest any thing in writing myself. We passed upon it and report to the State Committee for it's publication. And there is an end of it.

In the evening Mrs. Frothingham with her son Thomas and Miss Susan Phillips came up to spend an hour with my Wife.[1]

[1] On Susan Phillips, a cousin of ABA, see vol. 2:279.

WEDNESDAY. 11TH.

Fine day although the weather is growing colder and more in accordance with the season. I went to the Office, and into State Street to collect Dividends. Heard of the suicide of A. Richardson, Grocer and man of property. This spirit of selfdestruction is growing very prevalent in the Community and displays the existence of something wrong. Is it not that we are straining the cords too high. We are too grave a people. I believe that man's mind cannot stand long the pressure which unintermitted attention to any single pursuit whether money, religion, education, or any other good thing brings upon it.[1]

Mr. Bailey called upon me and read a letter he had written to my father. He suggests a middle course, not to decline but to affect to decline, and that not until the selections have been made.[2] I told him my objections which appear to me to lie on the face of the plan. I had no walk. Afternoon, Bacon and Virgil. Evening finished Smith's Moral Sentiments. Racine to his son, very good.

[1] Capt. Asa Richardson, fifty-one, hanged himself in his home on Montgomery Place (*Columbian Centinel*, 12 Dec., p. 2, col. 4). For further reflections on suicides in New England, see below, entry for 25 December.

[2] John Bailey to JQA, 10 Dec. (Adams Papers).

THURSDAY. 12TH.

Cloudy and cold today. I went to the Office and read very uninterruptedly for about an hour in the Parliamentary. I thought that I would then amuse myself and accordingly called to see Mr. Davis with whom I had much conversation. I remained so long as to lose my walk. Afternoon quietly at home reading Bacon de Augmentis.

Evening, my Wife never having seen the Opera of the Barber of Seville, and Mr. and Mrs. Wood, good singers being here, I went with her and Miss Julia Gorham to see them and hear them. The piece is a charming one. I have seen it often but never should be tired of it.[1] Mrs. Wood is a fine performer though her natural voice is not so pleasing as Mrs. Austin's. His is a fine man's voice without any great pathos in it.[2] Afterpiece, My Aunt. Returned home early.

[1] For CFA's delight in Rossini's music, see vol. 2:60, 277, 321; also, below, entry for 2 Oct. 1835. A different response, following CFA's acquisition of greater operatic sophistication, is in the entry for 15 March 1836, below.

[2] The voices of Mr. and Mrs. Joseph Wood had first been heard in America at the Park Theatre in New York in the September just past. Their success was instantaneous and maintained over the next three seasons during which they dominated the musical scene.

Mrs. Wood's voice was hailed by the influential music critic of the *Mirror* in New York as "one of the most extraordinary ... we ever remember to have heard" and he saluted her as "the first English singer of the day. We say *English* ... recollecting Malibran." For Mr. Wood there was praise as "a good actor and a very fair singer." Odell, *Annals N.Y. Stage*, 3:657, 664; 4:63, 109.

Although CFA came, during this first Boston season of the Woods, to sense more fully the extraordinary vocal gifts of Mrs. Wood (see the entries for 19 Dec. 1833; 24 April and 5 May 1834, below), it was when he heard them again during the 1835–1836 theatrical season that his enthusiasm for Mrs. Wood's singing and for opera reached its fullest expression. During the Woods' three Boston engagements in that season his Diary shows that he attended sixteen of their performances, especially those of *La Sonnambula* (see note to entry for 29 Dec. 1835, below). A sheet-music cover of Mrs. Wood in the role of Amina in that opera is reproduced in the present volume; see also p. x–xi, above.

FRIDAY. 13TH.

Cloudy day and cold. Went to the Office as usual and was occupied for some time in reading and writing. One or two persons came in— Mr. Degrand and others on business, but I had on the whole a remarkably quiet time.

Took my usual walk. Afternoon writing a letter to my father, which I was engaged also in copying, a task of considerable fatigue.[1] My Wife had some of her friends to tea and pass the evening—Miss Julia Gorham, Miss Carter[2] and Miss Sarah Tilden.

I procured Mackintosh's Progress of Ethical Philosophy from the Athenæum and was much interested in the charming style which distinguishes it.[3] I also find a great subject opened before me, the nature and value of which I had very little idea of until lately. It must be extensively explored before I write again upon any subject.

[1] To JQA, 13–14 Dec. (Adams Papers).
[2] On Anne Carter, see vol. 2:158; 3:2–3.
[3] See vol. 4:354.

SATURDAY. 14TH.

Morning at the Office. Received a letter from my father[1] with a copy of the report of the Bank Directors and a request to me to touch the elbow of the Editor of the Advocate. I called but he was not at home. The state of political affairs at Washington seems at this moment to be fearful. I do not know how the termination will be, but the Country seems to me in danger.

Walk. Afternoon, continued and finished my letter. Made a little progress in Mackintosh, but this correspondence with my father swallows up vast quantities of my most useful time. Evening, Mr. Brooks was here.

[1] 8 Dec. (Adams Papers).

SUNDAY. 15TH.

The weather keeps cloudy but does not positively rain or snow. I read Mackintosh and attended Divine Service. Mr. Robbins.[1] Job 37. 21. "And now men see not the bright light which is in the clouds: but the wind passeth and cleanseth them." A dull Sermon upon the moral government of the Universe as a means of reliance and cheerfulness. Some thought the reference to the fashion of suicide now prevalent pretty close upon the family for whose consolation the Discourse was intended, the Richardsons. Mr. Frothingham, Proverbs 28. 1. "The wicked flee when no man pursueth but the righteous are bold as a Lion." Moral courage necessary to man, with an examination of the Ancient Stoical doctrine which denied the existence of pain. Sermon of Atterbury upon the Anniversary of Queen's Anne's accession. 1. Timothy. 1st, 2d and 3d. "I exhort, that 1st of all supplications, prayers, intercessions and giving of thanks be made for all men; for kings and all that are in authority; that we may lead a quiet and peaceable life in all godliness and honesty: for this is good and acceptable in the sight of God and our Saviour." Division follows the text, 1. *duty* of supplication &ca., 2d. *reasons*, that we may lead a quiet life, 3d. *motive*, that it is acceptable in the sight of God. Evening quietly at home. Mr. Blake passed a couple of hours with us.

[1] Rev. Chandler Robbins, recent graduate in divinity at Harvard and at the point of assuming his long pastorate at Boston's Second Church.

MONDAY. 16TH.

Morning cloudy. I went to the Office where I received a letter from my father and the Address to the People which accompanied it.[1] In consequence of it, I called upon Mr. Hallett and had a long conversation with him at my Office—Remonstrating in the first place about the Bank and afterwards conversing upon the matter of the Address. I had read this carefully over twice, and though I did not show it to him, yet I brought forward it's main features for discussion. He remonstrated against two parts, and I think reasonably, the recommendation of a plurality in Congressional elections, and the opinion in favour of Davis. He sat three hours. I returned home, and in the afternoon wrote a letter in reply urgently against these two points with half a dozen other trifling ones.[2] The writing and copying took my whole time without finishing. Went to Mr. Frothingham's to spend an hour, as Sidney Brooks and his Wife were there from New York to spend a day or two. Returned at ten. Dr. Stevenson there.

¹ JQA to CFA, 11 Dec. (Adams Papers). The accompanying Address is missing. However, there is in the Adams Papers, filed under date of 1 Jan. 1834 (Microfilms, Reel No. 498), JQA's retained copy (31 p.) of that Address. On it he has entered changes, including alterations which CFA suggested in his letter referred to in the note following, and other corrections which JA2 had suggested. In a letter to CFA of 24 Dec., received on the 27th (see note there), JQA instructed him to enter all corrections on the copy JQA had sent earlier and turn the corrected MS over to the *Advocate* for printing. Should the *Advocate* decline to run it, he wished to have it submitted to the *Daily Advertiser*, and if declined there, to have it published as a pamphlet. The *Boston Daily Advocate* did carry the Address on 10 Jan. 1834 (p. 2, col. 1— p. 3, col. 3) and appended to it JQA's letter to the Speaker of the House of Representatives, dated 21 Dec., on which see below, entries for 27 Dec. and 1 Jan., and accompanying notes. The Address was later printed in JQA, *Letters on the Masonic Institution*, Boston, 1847, p. 219–274. A draft-fragment (11 p.) filed in the Adams Papers with JQA's retained copy of the Address seems to be an earlier and incomplete version.

² To JQA, 16 Dec. (Adams Papers). CFA concentrates on JQA's statements of his preferences which he had incorporated in the draft of his Address announcing his withdrawal. These statements, on some counts gratuitous, were that in his judgment, and he hoped in that of his supporters (i.e. the Antimasons), John Davis, who had won a plurality in the first canvass, should be elected; and further that the election laws should be changed to permit election by a plurality rather than by a majority of the votes cast. On the inclusion of these issues, CFA sided with Hallett and the antimasonic committee for which he spoke. CFA's other objections to the draft related to JQA's usual pithiness and tactlessness in phraseology.

TUESDAY. 17TH.

Morning clouds, it began to rain in the Afternoon and to blow almost a hurricane. I was seriously anxious for the safety of my chimney tops, which however went safely through the night.

I went to the Office, but did nothing. Discomposed by a head ach from indigestion. I eat too fast. This is a fault of all Americans and springs from hurry of habit. Most of the dyspepsia for which the Country is peculiar springs from it.

Walk. Afternoon felt better and completed my letter. Sent it. At home very quietly. Read Mackintosh. This book will lead me I don't know where.

WEDNESDAY. 18TH.

The rain and wind continued through the day. I went to the Office. Engaged in my usual occupations—Writing and Parliamentary Debates. Nothing of consequence. Could not walk.

Home. Afternoon, Bacon de Augmentis and Walpole¹ and Virgil and Mackintosh. Thus I give in brief my various pursuits. But they all fill me with despair. Walpole alone is a small literary fop. The rest are masters of their Art. What a dog am I, to think of publishing to the world my thoughts after such as these.

[1] Horace Walpole's *Letters to Sir Horace Mann*, 3 vols., London, 1833, had been borrowed from the Athenæum.

THURSDAY. 19TH.

The weather cloudy but the wind has ceased. I went to the Office and was engaged in reading and writing. Received a letter from my Mother by which being informed that she had sent some Curtains to me,[1] I had them [insured?] at the Columbian Office for their presumed value here. Received from my father a letter for Mr. Hallett.[2] He called for it, and we had a conversation which kept me from my dinner. He is in great distress from my father's course. And he urged me to impress upon him the necessity of changing some features of the Address. I am satisfied myself that it would be expedient.

I wrote all the Afternoon.[3] In the evening my Wife and I to the Theatre. Mr. and Mrs. Wood. Der Freyschutz. Weber's music. The choruses with one exception failed. Mr. Wood's voice is as a whole the best I have heard here. It is not so well trained as Garcia's. She sings very well but I do not relish her *style*. Too much dashing and not that delicacy which struck me in Mrs. Austin, nor the deep intonations of the Signorina.[4] Yet it is decidedly pleasant to hear such music. Comer fails in serious parts. The Orchestra pretty good. Music wild and wonderful. Home and to bed early.

[1] LCA to ABA, 11–14 Dec., written in journal form at ABA's suggestion, and continuing an earlier letter, 8–10 Dec., in the same form (both in Adams Papers).

[2] To B. F. Hallett, 16 Dec. (LbC, Adams Papers). Principally a defense of JQA's proposed course against the charge that Hallett had predicted would be raised: that once again JQA had shown disregard for the claims of party.

[3] To JQA, 19 Dec. (Adams Papers). A renewed plea to that made in CFA's earlier letter of the 16th that JQA remove from his address any mention of election by plurality and any endorsement of Davis. The same points were further urged in two letters of the 19th from Hallett to JQA (both in Adams Papers).

[4] On CFA's recollections of Manuel Garcia, his celebrated daughter, Signorina Maria Felicita (Mrs. Malibran), and Mrs. Elizabeth Austin, see below, note to entry for 24 April 1834.

FRIDAY. 20TH.

Fine morning. I went to the Office and passed my time very quietly reading and writing and making up Accounts. Mr. Ladd called in and we had a talk. He is the least punctual of my Tenants, and the most requiring in repairs. I talked to him plainly and he promised much better. I should like to get rid of him as a Tenant, and would let the House to the Steam Doctor if he would take it.

Walk. Quiet afternoon copying my letter which is a critical one. Then read more of Bacon's admirable Treatise. Evening at home— Mackintosh his account of Hartley, Tucker and Paley. Read Walpole to my Wife.

SATURDAY. 21ST.

Beautiful day. I was very busy all the morning in money affairs. After coming from Market, I called at the Commercial Bank and took up the Deposit made there two months since. The pressure for money is such here that the Cashier offered to guarantee seven and a half per cent for one year upon the sum. I afterwards had Mr. Degrand in chase for me to pay the note due at Mr. Oliver's Office that he might have the money. I did so before twelve o'clock and felt gratified that I had been able to put a stop to so large an amount of Interest. My father goes backward at Washington, I believe, but I have the satisfaction of pushing him a little forward here.

Walk. Afternoon. Finished Bacon de Augmentis—A wonderful sketch, showing the vastness of the original mind which could embrace it. Evening at home, quiet, Walpole, and Mackintosh.

SUNDAY. 22D.

Heavy rain and the Streets in such a condition from its freezing on the bricks as to be dangerous. I went to Meeting nevertheless. Mr. Frothingham, 1 Mark. 1. 3. "The beginning of the gospel of Jesus Christ, the Son of God, the voice of one crying in the wilderness." An eloquent Account of the origin and progress of Christianity with a happy allusion to it's first starting on this shore and the anniversary of it today. Mr. Emerson [1] from Colossians 1. 9–10. Too long to quote, but the substance in the closing words, "increasing in the knowledge of God." The destruction of Idolatry, and sacrifice, and the cherishing of the immortal principle within us, he considers as the great results of Christianity. His Sermons are always interesting though often paradoxical. Atterbury. Matthew. 7. 12. "All things whatsoever ye would that men should do unto you, do ye even so to them, for this is the law and the prophets." The explanation of this maxim on the Anniversary of the 5 November. On the whole the poorest Sermon of his I have read. Finished Mackintosh. Walpole in the evening to my wife.

[1] Ralph Waldo Emerson during the year before had severed his connection with the Second Church in Boston. Now returned to Boston after an eventful period in Europe, he continued to preach in many pulpits but did not resume a formal connection with any congregation.

MONDAY. 23D.

The day was beautiful. I received from my father a long letter upon politics. He does not print his Address until after the election of Governor which avoids one great difficulty I had apprehended, influence upon the Electors. In other respects I must wait for his decision. His account of affairs at Washington and especially Mr. Rush's course is unpleasant enough.[1]

Read the remainder of Burke's speech upon conciliation with America, and took a walk. Afternoon, Bacon, Sylva Silvarum, a collection of subjects for experiment. Read several passages pointed out by Mackintosh, one in Pascal, one in Montaigne and Sir Samuel Romilly's Essay on Codification in the Edinburgh Review.[2] Evening, Walpole. My Wife suffering under a severe cold.

[1] JQA to CFA, 19 Dec. (Adams Papers). By giving his support to Jackson's attack on the Bank of the United States, Richard Rush had created consternation in JQA and confirmed for him the indications he had observed in the *Boston Daily Advocate* and other antimasonic organs of a developing adherence among Antimasons to the policies of Jackson and his party. The immediate effect upon JQA was to make his opposition to the election of the Democratic candidate in Massachusetts, Marcus Morton, absolute. However, contrary to the earlier impressions of his intentions held by CFA and by Hallett, JQA in the present letter, and again in another to CFA on the 21st (Adams Papers), gave explicit directions that the Address stating his support of Davis in preference to Morton was not to be published until *after* the Governor had been chosen by the State Senate: "My declared preference then will have had no effect upon the election. But afterwards, if Davis is elected it will shew that my opinion was in his favour, and if Morton is elected it will shew why I was opposed to his election. The chief reason is at least of no partial or temporary character; but such as I am willing to stand and abide by, under any possible event. You will understand that this determination is the result of my own convictions."

[2] For 1817 (vol. 29).

TUESDAY. 24TH.

We have within a week or ten days experienced prodigious alternations of weather. Today brought with it another Easterly rain which with the snow which fell in the night put the Streets under water. I went to the Office and passed my time quietly enough in reading and making up Accounts. No walk. Afternoon, Bacon, Silva Silvarum, and in the evening I was busy in reading over Mackintosh's main positions together with the comments of the North American Review and looking over the first Alcibiades of Plato.[1] What a field.

[1] In MQA there is a copy of the *Dialogues* in French, 2 vols., Amsterdam, 1770, as well as editions in English and Greek of his collected writings.

WEDNESDAY. 25TH.

Christmas day. The desire to consider it as a day of celebration is increasing very fast in this Community.[1] I think if it would tend to amusing and innocent relaxation and social intercourse, it would be beneficial. The tendencies here are too grave. Religion is at all times a subject of such portentous magnitude to mortals that unless mingled with much cheerfulness it oppresses the intellect. Money the other great pursuit strains the faculties in a different manner. Is not the increasing number of suicides in some measure connected. It might be a subject of very useful inquiry to look back upon the ostensible motives of those who have lately committed the act. How many are led to it from religious gloom? How many from the pursuit of money? How many from dissipation and extravagance?

Office. Drawing up Leases for the Boylston Executors. Athenæum. Afternoon, reading Bacon, and Plato's Alcibiades. Began some sketch of a new Essay, upon the History of the United States.

Supper party at Mrs. Samuel Gray's, family—Mr. Brooks and three daughters. Mrs. Ward, Mrs. Henshaw,[2] the daughter of the first and son of the second, Mr. and Mrs. F. Parkman, Mr. and Mrs. Story and Miss Henrietta Gray of course. Pleasant enough. We returned a little before eleven.

[1] "Nearly every newspaper in the city, in course of the present week, has had an article recommending a more marked observance of Christmas day" (*Columbian Centinel*, 25 Dec., p. 2, col. 3). Characteristic was a communication printed in the *Centinel* endorsing the idea "that this interesting anniversary should be suitably commemorated" and suggesting that the "Congregational Churches may be opened and services be performed the same as they are on the annual Thanksgivings" (20 Dec., p. 2, col. 3).

[2] Mrs. Thomas W. (Lydia) Ward was a daughter of Samuel Gray by his first wife; the identity and relationship of Mrs. Henshaw to the rest of the group are not known to the editors.

THURSDAY. 26TH.

Fine day again. Office. I was about to go to work, when Mr. S. Conant from Weston came in about his Lease. He was followed by

Brown the Steam Doctor on a Lease also, Mr. Nathl. Curtis came in upon a similar subject, and then Mr. John Bailey with whom I had conversation upon politics. I read to him my father's letter, and conversed with him upon the state of the case.[1] No conclusions however. My walk was in this manner shortened.

Afternoon, Bacon Silva Silvarum. He discusses the force of imagination not only upon persons themselves but upon those upon whom it may be directed. This is one of the most curious and least investigated of mental phenomena. Evening at home.

We were wakened in the night by the child, which seemed to be labouring under heavy oppression of the lungs. It took an emetic and kept us up.

[1] JQA in his letter to CFA of the 19th (above, entry for 23 Dec., note) had specifically excepted John Bailey from those Antimasons he charged with allying the movement to Jacksonism, "Of this new conspiracy, I am very sure that Mr. Bailey has no suspicion. . . . I still place unlimited confidence in *him*." He authorized CFA to show his letter to Bailey.

FRIDAY. 27TH.

Fine clear day. I went to the Office. Engaged in copying out my Accounts for the close of the year. Mr. Peabody called in and asked me to walk, we accordingly went round the new street which is opening from Broad to Purchase Street—A very great improvement indeed.[1] The city is in the full tide of prosperity, but it's progress seems now likely to be impeded by the embarrassments into which our currency is ⟨likely⟩ to be plunged. Thus it is, that man spoils his fairest blessings by his own wilfulness.

Afternoon, Mr. Price Greenleaf called and spent an hour. Read Bacon and Virgil. Evening, received a letter from my father No. 10 which informed me of his having sent his letter to the Speaker with No. 9 on the 21st. *This has not come to hand.*[2] And it is now too late to send and return before the Legislature meets. My position is excessively embarrassing. I sent a letter notwithstanding.[3] Corrected the Address.[4]

[1] The new street around Fort Hill had a length of 2,000 feet, had been constructed at a cost of $11,320, and had involved the destruction or removal of a number of dwellings and shops but permitted the construction of two wharves (*Columbian Centinel*, 2 Jan. 1834, p. 2, col. 3).
[2] JQA to CFA, 24 Dec. (Adams Papers). CFA's concern over the missing letter and its enclosed letter to the Speaker of the House of Representatives of the Commonwealth was of short duration. On the following day he received both (21 Dec. and enclosure, Adams Papers).
[3] No letter from CFA of this date has been found.

⁴ JQA's letter of the 24th set out in
detail the corrections he wished made
in the Address, making it possible for CFA to enter those changes in the draft
he had received on 16 Dec. (see the
note there).

SATURDAY. 28TH.

Fine day. I was at the Office all the morning, occupied in drawing
out my Quarterly Account. Mr. Walsh called in, my new Tenant who
succeeds Mr. Peabody—Otherwise quite uninterrupted. Walk. Dined
by invitation today with P. C. Brooks Jr. Mr. Brooks, his son Edward,
and Mr. Frothingham. Pleasant enough.

Returned home, and was gratified to find the missing packet had
arrived. I am now prepared. But I never in my life was more at a loss
to know what the probable operation of this measure will be. I trust
in the support of a higher power through all the trials it may bring
upon me, or upon my father.[1] He now stands quite free from the
effect of consequences personal to himself, and he ought not to regard
them at any time.

Evening, reading to my Wife from Miss Edgeworth's Harrington.[2]
Her style is fascinating. Plato's second Alcibiades.

[1] JQA, in the letter CFA had just received, had expressed his awareness of CFA's apprehensions: "I am giving you a great deal of trouble, and Masonry and Anti-Masonry are putting your virtue to a severe trial at an early age. But it is good for a man to bear the yoke in his youth. Stand to your arms, that is to your principles, and do not ... flinch from your Post, and shrink into your shell, at the first approach of the peril which could test them by trial." (21 Dec., Adams Papers.)

[2] The regular evening readings in the novels of Maria Edgeworth would continue through April, doubtless from CFA's set of her *Works* now in MQA; see vol. 4:160.

SUNDAY. 29TH.

Fine day. I attended divine Service all day. Heard Mr. Frothingham
from Luke 1. 78–79. "The day spring from on high hath visited us,
To give light to them that sit in darkness and in the shadow of death,
to guide our feet into the way of peace." An account of Christmas,
how the nativity came to be fixed on the 25th. His idea was that it
was owing to the change of light from the Sun in the Winter solstice.
A poetical idea enough. Afternoon, Acts 4. 32, pt. "Neither said any
of them that ought of the things which he possessed was his own." The
community of property of the Apostles, it's operation in their case,
extended to us only in the beneficial tendencies of the faith, which
makes the ability to practise virtue a common blessing. Atterbury
Matthew 14. 23. "When he had sent the multitude away he went up

into a mountain apart to pray." The duty of religious retreat and meditation, considered in two views, 1. the limitations. 2. the benefits. Quiet evening. Harrington.

MONDAY. 30TH.

Fine day. I went to the Office and finished most of my business for the present quarter. Called upon Mr. Mason and received the balance due upon the Estate in High Street and drew up my inventory for the year which gives a tolerably favourable result. Thus business matters being settled I took my walk.

Afternoon reading Bacon, finished the first volume of the Silva Silvarum, and wrote to John,[1] and in part to my father. Read Harrington to my Wife. The style is very charming. My boxes arrived from Washington.

[1] CFA to JA2, 30 Dec. (Adams Papers), an acknowledgment of receipt of curtains purchased from John and his wife, also of a letter from JA2 (22 Dec., missing) relative to the terms of sale and settlement. CFA also comments generally upon the political and economic issues in Washington and Boston.

TUESDAY. 31ST.

Fine after clouds. I went to the Office, drew up all my Accounts and settled my balances. Very quiet and undisturbed all day. Walk. Afternoon, wrote to my father but a blot coming down upon my Paper accidentally prevented my being able to send it.[1] Sent my letter to John and Quarterly Account. Evening, Mr. T. K. Davis called in and talked a couple of hours. I retired late and had a restless night.

The year 1833 closed, and when I look back upon it, I feel my unworthiness of so many and such continued blessings. I have prospered in my affairs. I have been blessed with another child and a son. I have striven and not entirely without success, to make myself useful and respectable in society. None of these things come without the direction of a divine dispenser. While I continue my faith in him, while I labour to deserve the share of benefits which is so bountifully granted me, I must pray for his support and his guidance in all the paths of life, and that my failings and errors may be judged rather with the charity of his mercy than the rigor of his Justice.

[1] CFA did send a brief note to his father (31 Dec., LbC, Adams Papers) acknowledging receipt of JQA's letter of 26 Dec. (Adams Papers) and reciting the accident which befell his reply begun the preceding day.

No. 8   Diary

1 January 1834

12 December 1835 [1]

Stat monitis contraria virtus
Ovid Met. 10. 709

[1] Titlepage of D/CFA/10 (Adams Papers, Microfilms, Reel No. 62), which begins where D/CFA/9 ends and contains all the journal entries CFA made between the terminal dates indicated here. In the MS the epigraph is on the page preceding the titlepage.

An explanation of the discrepancy between CFA's numbering of his Diary volumes and the Adams Papers serial listing is given at vol. 1:xxxviii–xl. For a description of this Diary MS and of the other MSS from which the printed text of vols. 5 and 6 of the present edition is derived, see the Introduction.

JANUARY. 1834.

Boston

WEDNESDAY. 1ST.

The first page of a new volume on New Year's day—A day which to the young brings all the elastic vigor of hope into activity, and to the old presents only the recollections, the pictures of mingled colours as providence has ordained it through the past. I am now reaching that middle stage of life when certainty is gradually taming down the luxuriant imagination, while prosperity has not removed the enjoyments to be derived from the sober reality of life.[1] If I am not so much as my fancy ten years since might have painted me as now to be, yet I am more, far more than an unprejudiced observer would at that time have ventured to have prophesied. My own share in producing this situation has been vastly small. I cannot look back and say, this and this, my energy and virtue bought about, therefore I ought not to calculate upon doing in future any more that I have done in times past. The days of my greatest activity in forming character have passed. Yet I do not repine. My mercies have been innumerable. The Deity has looked with eyes of favour upon my efforts, small as they have been. He has compensated them very far beyond their value. This is the highest encouragement for me to persevere. My trust is in his guidance and protection. With that, the future is to me more of a picture of hope than it was in my early days. Then all was dim and indistinct, and I was eager to know. Now that it is clearer, I hope not less, but trust more.

The day was uncommon for the Season of the year. Bright and yet mild. It was the day of the assembling of the Massachusetts Legislature and consequently the one upon which my father had directed me to attend the House of Representatives and immediately after the election of their Speaker to send in the Letter which had been sent to me. After waiting nearly three hours and being elbowed by the five hundred and fifty Legislators who were called to take care of the Commonwealth of Massachusetts, I succeeded in giving the Letter. The Speaker, Mr. Calhoun read it aloud,[2] and the annunciation of the signature created a murmur of surprise through the Hall. I immediately left it but had only time to take a walk and make purchases of some trinkets as New Year's Presents to the members of my family. This is a day always celebrated in this manner, and we have so few of a festive sort that I am very glad to keep up the custom.

I passed a quiet afternoon at home. But at six o'clock, Mr. Hallett sent a Note requesting to see me and I went down in the Evening.[3] His purpose was not distinctly explained, but I gathered it to be, to inquire how far my father's course and published Address would conflict with the proposed junction with Jacksonism. I did not explain it to him in any but general terms. I told him that it would be disapproved, but that they had better act without reference to him. He seemed very much depressed and a little disposed to kick at my father. He has had so much sway here, that it has a little turned his head. I left him, saying that I would give him the Address in a day or two. Evening, remainder of it reading Sir James Mackintosh.

[1] At the place in the MS to which this note is subjoined an asterisk has been inserted. On the blank page opposite, in CFA2's hand, dated "May 29/93," and preceded by an asterisk, appears the sentence: "This middle-aged moraliser was at this time just 26 years, four months and 18 days of age!"

[2] The letter which the newly elected Speaker, William B. Calhoun of Springfield, read was dated at Washington, 21 Dec. 1833 (retained copy in Adams Papers), and asked that the House, in choosing two names to send to the Senate for election from the four who had received the largest number of popular votes, consider JQA's name "withdrawn— as in the possible event of my election by the Senate, I should deem it my duty to decline accepting the appointment."

[3] Note missing.

THURSDAY. 2D.

The New Year brings with it several duties among which the most important is in a social point of view to redeem one's engagements. I was busy much of my time in settling accounts and in bringing up my books. Received the dividends upon my stock in the Manufacturing

Co. which was considerable and also the Atlas Insurance. It rained and I was hurried, but I got through with Mr. Foster's payment notwithstanding a long visit from my new Tenant opposite, Mr. Walsh. He got upon Masonry, the Grand Lodge having this day surrendered their civil charter.[1] He is a Mason. Fortunately, I asked him the question before I began—So that I was enabled prudently to regulate my conversation. He declined signing the famous Declaration, so he says, he is between fires, so are all men who halt between right and wrong. His defence of Masonry was curious. Afternoon I was very busy writing to my father. Finished and copied a long letter, but did not have time to send it.[2] Miss Edgworth's Harrington aloud to my Wife.

[1] The Massachusetts Grand Lodge, upon building its new Masonic Temple, had asked the Legislature to amend its corporate charter to permit it to own real estate to the value of $60,000, but the petition had been denied. Through the surrender of its charter as a corporation the Lodge would be enabled to retain title to its building. Taking this course did not affect Masonic activities and prerogatives (*Columbian Centinel*, 3 Jan., p. 2, cols. 2–3).

[2] To JQA, 1–3 Jan. (Adams Papers). CFA reports the effect of JQA's withdrawal as insuring the election of John Davis. He makes explicit his own opinion, contrary to that of JQA, that, despite his Jacksonism, Marcus Morton was to be preferred to Davis as governor.

FRIDAY. 3D.

Morning colder. Office. Time as much taken up in business affairs as ever. I brought up my private Accounts. From some cause or other, I feel this year unaccountably hurried. I *would* read my Article in the North American Review however.[1] It disappoints me on publication. I must strive to do better.

Walk. Nothing of great interest excepting that the National Republicans have carried all the Senate. This was not quite expected. A paragraph appeared in the Daily Advocate, stating the fact of the existence of a letter similar in purport to my father's, from Mr. Davis.[2] I called to find Mr. Hallett and tell him I should retain the Address a day longer in my hands in order to wait for alterations in the Address contingent upon such a course—One or two passages in it being likely to become inappropriate by means of it.

Afternoon after despatching my letter and waiting for the Mail which as my man said brought me nothing, concluding from the present state of things that if Mr. Davis had written such a letter, it would be suppressed, I sent the Address.

Evening, a visit from Mr. T. W. Cross about my brother's Note.

At such an unseasonable hour, it put me very much out of temper. This I record for my future amendment. I paid him however. Quiet evening. Finished Harrington.

¹ CFA's review of the third volume of Thomas Hutchinson's *History of the Province of Massachusetts Bay* appeared in the January issue (38:134–158). There are two drafts in CFA's hand in the Adams Papers (M/CFA/23, Micro-films, Reel No. 317).

² The *Advocate* alleged in addition that Davis' friends were holding the letter back until the Senate membership had been determined (3 Jan., p. 2, col. 3).

SATURDAY. 4TH.

Morning tolerably clear. I was occupied an hour in my weekly visit to Market, after which I passed my time at the Office very quietly. Did not think of calling for my Letters until noon, when I found one from my father inclosing another to Mr. Hallett.¹ I called upon him to deliver it, and found him in no amiable mood. He seemed disposed to make alterations in the Address. I felt somewhat provoked with him for this, and it was with some effort I kept my temper. He had been the means of bringing my father out by a very unusual series of resolutions, and once out, he seemed to imagine he was tied forever. I told him at once, that his resolutions and not my father were to blame for this state of things, and that if as he threatened, he became Jacksonian, the only result would be that the penetration of my father would be justified. I imagine these views had some effect. We parted goodnaturedly, but neither of us pleased.

I took a short walk. Mr. Brooks and Edward dined with me—But little or no interesting conversation. Short afternoon, Lord Bacon. Evening, Miss Edgeworth's Ormond.

At eight o'clock, Mr. Hallett was announced, and he sat with me in my study until nearly eleven. His tone was entirely changed. Instead of Jacksonism, he professed to consider my father's suspicion as very unjust and more than hinted that as I had raised it, I ought to put it down. He read me my father's letter to him and then opened his business. He had read the Address to Messrs. Bailey and Whitmarsh, [who?] had liked it much better. Their remarks however had been directed to certain passages, and he would proceed to submit them for my consideration. They were disposed to say nothing against the main points. I thought but did not say, that he had usurped authority in showing it to them, and that it was not a little imprudent in him to come to me for alterations under the cover of their names which he had already been refused under his own. However it would not do to slight them. I listened to them all, assented to some, doubted of others, and refused the rest. The condition was to be the restoration of harmony, and as the changes were not material, I thought them worth the object.

¹ To CFA, 31 Dec. 1833; to B. F. Hallett, same, LbC (both in Adams Papers).

SUNDAY. 5TH.

Morning snowy and quite cold. I attended divine Service all day. Heard in the morning Mr. Frothingham. Psalms 55. 14. "We took sweet counsel together and walked into the House of God in company." A review of Parish history for the year—Baptisms, Communicants and Deaths: 13, 2, and 24. Some remarks of a very excellent practical character upon the custom of private Baptism. As this list includes these cases, it is very apparent, that the number of those never baptised at all must be considerable. He added some observations upon the Communion which I took for consideration. My opinions upon that subject are not slightly formed, and the experience of the last year has strengthened them. My passions are too strong yet, to risk the double damnation of violated vows.

Afternoon. Mr. Gilman again. Psalms 57. 7. "My heart is fixed, O, God, my heart is fixed." Upon steadiness of purpose fixed upon firmness of principle. He is not a very attractive preacher. His manner is effeminate.

Atterbury, at home. 1. Corinthians 15. 19. "If in this life only we have hope in Christ, we are of all men, most miserable." This was a discourse preached at the Funeral of Mr. Bennett a rich bookseller in London. It seems to have given rise to some critical hostility at the time and not without reason. He endeavours to justify it in a Preface longer than the Sermon. The points are these—That without the belief of a future state, men are in a worse condition than brutes, and Christians the most miserable of men. Now the first is a doubtful point as it impeaches the economy of the divine government. The second as it gives a gloomy look to Christianity. He justifies himself pretty well from the charge of novelty in his doctrine in the Church but no farther.

Evening, my wife and I went to Mr. Frothingham's. His choir were practicing there—Miss Woodward his only female singer, but she was not in voice tonight. Some others there, Miss Wallach, a sister of Richard Wallach of Washington, and Mr. J. E. Thayer, a Jacksonian broker. We returned early.

MONDAY. 6TH.

I find my mornings much shortened from a lazy practice I have of remaining over the fire at my House dipping into the Newspaper. To-day my stay was to superintend the putting up at last of the Curtains.

At the office, finally where I was busy as usual in Accounts. My receipts come in very slowly, but I busy myself paying off my debts as fast as I can. Walk.

Afternoon quietly at home. Read Bacon, and in the evening began a Letter to my Father. The last act of the Play is now performing, and I am to describe its close. In a few days, we shall know what the effect of the series of events of the last year will be. I endeavour in my communications to my father to be perfectly impartial, to keep him informed of the true state of things here and to guard him as well against the measures of his friends as those of his enemies.

TUESDAY. 7TH.

Cold weather. I went to the office where I pursued my occupation of Accounts. Nothing of any consequence happened.

The political affairs of the day are at last settling down into quiet. Mr. Davis will be chosen one of the Candidates to send up to the Senate, the vacancies having all been filled by the National Republicans, the Senate will by a large vote elect him as their Governor. Home. Afternoon, wrote more of my Letter to my father.

I was sincerely grieved to hear today of the death of Dr. Stevenson's only remaining son.[1] This is a severe blow to him, and it made me feel gloomy all day. Every parent must in some measure have an affliction of this kind brought home to him. Read in the evening from Miss Edgeworth and Mackintosh, whose work I am going over.

[1] John Gorham Stevenson, three years of age (*Columbian Centinel*, 10 Jan., p. 2, col. 7).

WEDNESDAY. 8TH.

A very beautiful day. Our weather this season has been uncommonly mild and open. I went to the Office. The Editor of the Advocate sent me a proof of my father's Address this morning and in going over it without the MS, and afterwards with it I was taken up nearly my whole time. It engrossed three hours morning and afternoon and after all I did not look over the whole. Mr. Davis was not elected today so that it became necessary to put off the publication until Friday.

Mr. Frothingham dined with me, for the first time for a very long while. He talked much of Dr. Stevenson and of his affliction. Miss Julia Gorham took tea and spent the evening here so that I was disappointed of my promise to go to see Mr. Brooks. J. W. Gorham her brother came in afterwards. I read a little of Mackintosh and copied the letter to my father.

THURSDAY. 9TH.

I was again engrossed the whole morning in correcting proof. Mr. Davis was this day elected Governor,[1] and the Address will appear tomorrow. I finished at about one o'clock. My Accounts, Diary and every thing else have gone backward in the mean time. I hope this will put an end to my share in political affairs for this year. I have had some moments of trial and have got through them pretty well.

Walk. In the Afternoon, read Bacon and Virgil. Finished and sent my letter to my father and felt as if I might now begin anew.[2] My own prospects however are mortified. My article in the North American has sunk without a struggle, and I am to make no literary or any other sort of reputation.[3] Well, if it must be so, it must. Evening, Miss Edgeworth's Ormond, and Sir James Mackintosh.

[1] In the Senate Davis received thirty votes, Morton four, and there were three abstentions (*Columbian Centinel*, 10 Jan., p. 2, col. 3).

[2] To JQA, 6–9 Jan. (Adams Papers). CFA's sense that his political antimasonry had come to its end was echoed by his father: "I have now taken my leave of them as a party. There is perhaps nothing that makes it desirable that they should continue to exist as a party excepting to prevail upon the Legislature" (to CFA, 18 Jan., Adams Papers).

[3] Such discouragement was recurrent following the publication of each of CFA's articles, irrespective of manifestations of reader interest of some sort that were almost always forthcoming. In this instance, appreciative notice was to come from his father: "I have been reading your review ... with great satisfaction. ... Your severity consists in your moderation. I should have handled him more roughly and perhaps not have done him so much justice" (to CFA, 31 Jan., Adams Papers).

FRIDAY. 10TH.

Mild day. I went to the Office and passed my time in making up the arrears of the last few days. My fathers Address appeared this morning in the Advocate[1] but it did *not* appear in the Advertiser. I did not suppose it would.

Walk. Then I went according to invitation to dine with Mr. Brooks—

Company, Mr. John Parker, Mr. Dudley Hall, R. D. Shepherd, R. D. Tucker, P. C. Brooks Jr. and myself. Tolerably pleasant but nothing remarkable. I returned home at dark and passed a quiet evening reading Ormond to my Wife. Lord Bacon.

[1] See above, entry for 16 Dec. and note.

SATURDAY. 11TH.

Day mild. I went to the Office. Engaged in accounts and in reading the North American Review. This Journal is carried on with a good deal of ability, yet when one looks back to reflect what reputation it has added permanently to itself, what sort of a work it is to refer to and read over, one is apt to cry out vanity of vanities. The matter is pleasing and now and then interests but there are no profound views. None of that wisdom of ages which will come down from the book shelf a hundred years hence oftener than it does now.

Walk. Looked into the Newspapers and was amused with the manner in which my father's Address is treated by the Masons.[1] Afternoon reading Lord Bacon whose Sylva Sylvarum is rather dull. There is much of loose experiment in it and all of the unfinished discovery of a powerful mind divided into too many channels. Such a giant few have seen in the mental world before or since. Evening. Virgil, and Miss Edgeworth's Ormond which is moral as well as charming. Mackintosh.

[1] The view taken in the *Centinel* of the Address published in the *Advocate* was that it was "of great length, . . . a gratuitous offering, and has a tendency to perpetuate animosities" (11 Jan., p. 2, col. 6). Occasional sniping was followed in the *Centinel* for 29 Jan. (p. 2, cols. 1–3) by a five part "Address . . . done into English," in the style of *Hudibras*. It concludes with the speaker (JQA) saying:
"But there's one path both safe and clear, Make me your Governor next year. But do your best or do your worst, I'm John the son of John the I."

SUNDAY. 12TH.

Day stormy, with snow, rain and frost. I attended divine Service all day and heard Mr. Frothingham in the morning. 1 Corinthians 7. 29,30,31. "But this I say, brethren, the time is short: it remaineth that they that weep be as though they wept not, and they that rejoice as though they rejoiced not, and they that use this world as not abusing it, for the fashion of this world passeth away." A discourse moral and consolatory. A very refined and yet simple view of human duty under all the dispensations of Providence, more particularly directed to Dr. Stevenson and his family under their recent affliction.

Afternoon, Mr. Young.[1] 1. Samuel 4. 21. "And she named the child Ichabod, saying the glory is departed from Israel; for the ark of God is taken." The doctrine of original sin, followed up by a discussion of the effect of Parents sins upon children. The Jewish Law contains the well-known and fearful passage declaring children to the third or fourth generation to be the sufferers for the sins of the parents. Mr. Young explains it by the moral consequences. Every action has its consequence. Disgrace or infamy has its consequence by the stain it leaves upon a family, which is generally got over at about the fourth generation. It may be so. It is certainly a mystery which no Commentator satisfactorily explains. And I know no better view of it than his.

Read Atterbury. Luke 16. 31. "If they hear not Moses and the Prophets neither will they be persuaded, though one rose from the dead." Subject, a standing Revelation the best means of conviction, 1. to whom the text alludes, 2. the truth of the application, 3. inferences to be drawn from it. A slight performance. Evening, finished Ormond.

[1] On Rev. Alexander Young Jr., see vol. 3:49.

MONDAY. 13TH.

The children give us considerable uneasiness in different ways. And fear and anxiety respecting them are the only troubles that I have. If I did not rely upon a higher power, I do not know what I should do.

Clear and cold morning. I went to the Office and looked over my Accounts which are not closed so rapidly as usual from the delay which has taken place among the Tenants. Read some of the Parliamentary History—Debates upon the American war and errors of the Ministers.

Walk. Afternoon. Wrote and despatched a letter to my brother John, inclosing his Note.[1] Read Lord Bacon and finished the Sylva Sylvarum. Read part of Patronage to my wife and finished my second perusal of Mackintosh. I have been benefitted by this book. It has opened my eyes and enlarged my understanding. It has warmed my heart, and exalted my feelings.

[1] LbC, Adams Papers. The note paid was that owed to T. W. Cross. CFA assumed the note in exchange for the curtains.

TUESDAY. 14TH.

Morning clear and cold. The rain and frost immediately following have made the Streets a sheet of ice. At the Office. Mr. Fuller one of my Tenants came in and we had a long talk about his House. He wants to keep it and protests he does not know that he committed a mistake in not informing me of the use to which he put it. I think I remember some things not quite so clear to prove the point. I told him I had engaged with Brown, or at least had gone so far upon the supposition that he Fuller would certainly leave the House, that I should have to see him again. Brown certainly ought to have acted more openly. I have a difficult part to play between them. I wish and hope to act honestly and fairly. I wish to see justice done to my father, and to improve his income as far as possible. Mr. Hurlbert came in about the House in the rear. I offered to take down the rent for a good Tenant.

Walk. Afternoon at home. The children sick. Louisa looks heavy and feverish. She took medicine but refused it so as to injure its effect. Evening, Patronage and a reperusal of Smith's Moral Sentiments.

WEDNESDAY. 15TH.

Morning clear and cold. I went to the Office. Time taken up in Accounts and making up my Diary. The mornings now are short and I do as I have always done, waste them. My mode of life is not favorable to my own improvement, I feel sensible. The best and most valuable time in the day is precisely that which I do not make use of.

Called for my Wife and we took a walk. Afternoon. Read the remainder of the volume of Bacon's Letters. These display him such as he was, with a mind far above all his contemporaries, and yet willing to abase himself by compliances which would dishonor the meanest. Perhaps his is a striking illustration of the character of man even in his best estate. Read Virgil also and in the evening Patronage. The children continue to give us uneasiness although they are better. Instead of reading from which my attention wavered I wrote, part of an Essay.

THURSDAY. 16TH.

Fine day. I went to the Office. Time passed very uninterruptedly reading the Debates. Mr. Curtis called in to pay me his Account, and I went down to do two or three little matters of business. Walked with my Wife. The children seem better although they both appear troubled with coughs. Received a letter from my Mother.[1] She seems much more cheerful this winter than I have known her for a long while to be.

Afternoon Lord Bacon, History of Life and Death. Virgil. I have reached the twelfth Book—And as a Poem have relished it more upon this than upon any preceding perusal. We went down to pay a visit to Mr. Brooks and Mrs. Everett in the evening. Mr. Shepherd was there. Mr. B. not, till 9. Conversation. Returned at ten.

[1] Letter missing.

FRIDAY. 17TH.

Very mild with a Southerly wind and rain. I went to the Office and passed my time in reading and Accounts. Read the second part of Mr. Binney's speech upon the Bank question, and it seems to me that I have not lately seen a finer specimen of statesmanlike skill and manner.[1] To be sure, his subject was fruitful. Conversation with my new Tenant, Mr. Walsh. No walk, owing to the weather.

Afternoon. Read the Tract upon the conspiracy of 1825 in Russia, published by the Court constituted under the orders of the Government. It's exposition of the connexion it had with Freemasonry is curious. Virgil.

Evening, I was invited to go and meet a party of young gentlemen at the house of my friend Blake. There is a sort of club consisting of W. E. Payne, H. B. Rogers, C. C. Tucker, Jon. Chapman, Henry G. Chapman, F. Shaw, Edward Blake and his two brothers who meet at each other's houses. They play Whist and have a Supper. I do not exactly understand my position in this business. I was received and treated with very great civility by all the members. But I should not wish to belong permanently to any such association. The character of the conversation did not appear to me to be particularly exalted nor even profitable. I nevertheless enjoyed the evening and could not help feeling sensible of the very kind manner in which I was treated. I did not return home until nearly twelve o'clock, not wishing to break up a party at which I was only a guest.

[1] The *National Intelligencer* had begun the publication of the speech on the Deposits Question by Horace Binney, U.S. Representative from Pennsylvania, on 8 Jan., and had printed the second part on the 14th (p. 2, col. 1 – p. 3, col. 3). The concluding part was printed the following day (p. 2, cols. 1–5).

SATURDAY. 18TH.

The day was more like May than January. The baby makes us very uneasy. He has a cold which distresses us—The perils incident to children, and the misery of parents when they are ill.

I went to the Office—Reading and other incidental occupation. Then a walk. Home. Afternoon, reading but not to much purpose. Continued the 12th book of Virgil and came almost to the end. The vigor of the poet sustains him to the last. Read Patronage in the evening. Afterwards sat up in my room reading and writing an answer to my father's last letter.[1]

The child was so restless and uneasy that I preferred sitting up to troubled sleep. As the amusement of occupation of any sort is better than the restless fancies of inaction, I endeavour to console myself with prayer and trust.

[1] In his letter to CFA of 9 Jan., answered by CFA on the 19th (both in Adams Papers), JQA reasserted his position that anti-Jacksonism took precedence over anti-masonry in the determination of his course of action.

SUNDAY. 19TH.

The weather continues particularly mild, and probably produces this tendency to colds. I attended divine service all day and heard Mr. Frothingham. Ezekiel 33. 26. "Ye stand upon your sword." A too confident reliance upon power, which is the foible of mankind, exemplified in the text where the Lord reproaches the Jews for leaving him, claiming their lands by the right of inheritance and of possession.

I preferred the more practical though perhaps more common discourse of Mr. Parkman in the afternoon from James 1. pt. 19–20. "Wherefore let every man be slow to wrath. For the wrath of man worketh not the righteousness of God." To *me*, this came with a voice of real instruction. My great sin is the violence of my temper, and this upon occasions when really there is neither call nor adequate justification. I have endeavoured to amend. And I do, but the difficulty of the task is hardly conceivable to one of milder nature. Mr. Parkman alluded to the duty of self government in the domestic circle where men oftenest fail, and I laid up the advice he gave for future thought. *Here* he was not full enough.

Read a Sermon of Bishop Atterbury. Job 29. 14. "I put on righteousness and it clothed me: my judgment was as a robe and a diadem." Preached before the Lord Mayor of London—The blessing of a good Magistrate to whom honour is justly due when he maintains the character described in the Text. An indifferent discourse. I think less and less of them as I read on.

Evening Mr. T. K. Davis took tea with us and sat an hour after which Mr. Degrand came in. We were very anxious about the child who seemed feverish and with his Lungs excessively oppressed. He was a little better towards night.

MONDAY. 20TH.

The child was not so well this morning. His voice was almost gone. The Dr. calls it a catarrh on his Lungs of a very severe character.[1] I went to the office quite anxious about him.

Time taken up in Accounts, reading the rest of Mr. Binney's Speech which does not quite equal the first and second parts, but on the whole Congress rarely furnishes such specimens. Walk. Afternoon, attended a meeting of the Directors of the Boylston Market Association. Nothing was done however. The distress continues here, and is very likely to continue if I may judge by the indifference with which it is viewed by the Majority at Washington.

Home, the child better which was a source of great comfort to me. Finished and dispatched a letter to my father. Col. Josiah and Mrs. Quincy called and passed a couple of hours. General but not interesting conversation. Tried to read Smith but could not fix my attention.

[1] "Poor little Johnny is as unwell with a catarrh as his grandfather ever was" (CFA to JQA, 19 Jan.).

TUESDAY. 21ST.

The weather changes to much cooler. The child was pronounced better this morning much to my relief. I went to the office and was busy in Accounts which I find now assuming a little more of ease. The pressure has operated and seems likely to operate upon my receipts. I am now just getting rid of embarrassment. Drew the Dividend at the Life Insurance Co. which is improving.

Short walk. Afternoon at home but my late nights prevented a very good employment of time. Read Lord Bacon's History of Life and Death, a work of singular character and full of imaginations with many valuable ideas. Finished the Æneid of Virgil. I have read it with pleasure though not with the critical accuracy of Horace. I find repetition of a Classic only shows me how much I let escape before. Evening quiet. My wife retired early. It was cold.

WEDNESDAY. 22D.

This was the first morning which has occurred this winter, of extraordinary severity. I went to the Office and found that my Office boy had deserted me. Thus it frequently happens. I made my fire and sat down to my occupations. But the morning was so short as hardly to allow of any such thing.

I went about to pay all the small Accounts which I could get rid of, from a twofold consideration, to relieve my own mind and to aid so far as I was able others who might want the money more, in this time of great pressure.

Afternoon at home without doing much. My time is now very lazily spent. Read Bacon and wrote a letter to my Mother.[1] Evening, Patronage and Adam Smith.

[1] Adams Papers. LCA answered promptly on the 27th (Adams Papers).

THURSDAY. 23D.

Morning still colder. I went to the Office. Occupied in Accounts. I have no time for the Parliamentary Debates. Completed the payment of my little bills and took a walk.

Dined at Mr. Frothingham's—Mr. Brooks, P.C.B. Jr., my Wife and myself. We had a very pretty and a very pleasant dinner. Little or no restraint. Returned home notwithstanding an invitation to Mr. Brooks' in the evening—It being too cold to remain out late.

Evening Patronage and Adam Smith.

Governor Davis has arrived and made his Speech[1]—A string of common places with some very false, incorrect notions about the currency. So it seems to me. I said so at dinner perhaps very imprudently. Many men might suppose it the result of pique. The truth is he is a much overestimated man. He has conducted himself with discretion and he is thought a genius. My father is a genius, and he is not prudent. He is therefore undervalued.

[1] Following his election as governor, John Davis resigned his congressional seat and returned to Boston to take the oath of office and deliver his inaugural address on 21 Jan. (*Columbian Centinel*, 22 Jan., p. 2, cols. 3–6).

FRIDAY. 24TH.

The third cold morning. I went to the Office quite late and found every thing so cold and cheerless that I left in disgust without making a fire or sitting down to work. I went to the Athenæum and amused myself in conversation with Mr. Walsh upon the present distress in the money department. Our majority seems to have gone mad, and they have the power. A democracy has it's evils. In the mean time, I suppose I should feel myself as less exposed to absolute suffering from all these events, than any body, or at least than the great number.

Afternoon, Lord Bacon. I want some definite occupation and yet if I had it, I do not know how I could manage to pursue it. Evening quietly at home. Patronage, which is not so interesting. The idea of a perfect female character it is very well to define, but it's improbability destroys the illusion of a tale of real life and brings us down at once to a moral treatise. Adam Smith.

SATURDAY. 25TH.

Weather moderating. The Dr. finally assured us this morning that our children did not need his services further at this time, and the idea is charmingly comfortable. The baby gives us some care, but we hope he will now be less uneasy.

I went to the Office and endeavoured to make up arrears, but what with a visit from Mr. Ladd and one from Mr. Walsh, I executed but little even though I remained until two.

We were invited to dine at Mr. Brooks' with a company—A. H. Everett, R. D. Shepherd, Mr. Peabody, Messrs. Walker, Magrath, and Seaton, young men at Cambridge, from the South, Mr. Frothingham, my wife and self. Edward Brooks and the family made up the table. The dinner was very pretty although the rooms were too cold to be perfectly comfortable. We returned home by six and I read as usual. Patronage, and a volume of Entertaining Knowledge.

SUNDAY. 26TH.

My record of Sunday is now little else than that of my religious exercises. A few years since I could hardly have expected that I should so easily have fallen into the performance of a regular train of duties. Mr. Frothingham preached, though a fall of snow very seriously prevented attendance. Mark 7. 11. "Ye say, if a man shall say to his father or mother, It is Corban, that is to say, a gift, by whatsoever thou mightest be profited by me, he shall be free." The unrighteous reservations which are for special purposes to the neglect of the familiar charities of life—A practice somewhat common in these days of ostentatious generosity. There is great justice in censure of this. Yet the heart must not be allowed to swing back to selfishness.

1 Timothy 2. 4. "Who will have all men to be saved and to come unto the knowledge of the truth." I will not undertake to state the

substance of this discourse. The reason why is that if I understood the starting proposition, I doubt it's foundation. If not I do nothing but misrepresent.

Read a Sermon of Atterbury's upon a Fast declared for some national losses. Psalms 3. v.6,7, and 8. "In my prosperity I said I shall never be moved. Lord, by thy favour thou hast made my mountain to stand strong, thou didst hide thy face and I was troubled. I cried to thee, O Lord, and unto the Lord I made supplication." The subject was the intoxicating effect of prosperity and the moral to be drawn from reverses. I can not say that I think the Sermon worth discussing—Mere performances of specified duty. Atterbury had too many other and worldly schemes in his head. Quiet evening.

MONDAY. 27TH.

Fine day. I went to the Office rather earlier than usual and was engaged in writing up my Arrears of Diary as well as drawing the Lease for Mr. Ladd. He has given me a great deal of trouble and at last got me so indifferent that I threatened to turn him out. This brought him to reason and he has taken the House on a Lease of three years, which he executed today. He kept [me] so long that I could not take my walk.

Afternoon, reading Bacon and Adam Smith—The former in the History of Winds, a collection of observations formed into system, with his peculiar power of induction. Began the Andrian of Terence, a new walk of classical Literature for me.[1] Mr. French called upon me with some of the French papers relating to Masonry, and requested me to translate them. I did so this afternoon. It is a little curious that one of them relates to a female Masonic Lodge in Paris, the nature of which is not very completely defined. Evening, Patronage, and Adam Smith.

[1] CFA had borrowed from the Athenæum the *Comœdiæ* of Terence in Latin and in a blank verse translation by George Colman. However, from the thirteen copies of the plays at MQA (eight belonging to JQA, three to CFA, and one to GWA), he also had by him for use his copy of the London, 1825, edition; see below, entry for 17 March 1834.

TUESDAY. 28TH.

Mild, winter day. I went to the Office. Engaged in writing and had a visit from Mr. Walsh, who conversed as usual upon the troubles of the money department which seem to be growing greater instead of less. Took a walk. Nothing else of material consequence. Walk. Afternoon, Bacon History of Winds, Adam Smith and Terence.

My time slips away so very quietly now that I hardly perceive its passage. Its uniform course leaves little to remember and therefore little to record. Evening. J. W. Gorham came in and spent an hour. He is studying medicine here but does not seem to have much foundation. Patronage and a few pages of Adam Smith.

WEDNESDAY. 29TH.

Pleasant winter weather. The children appear now to be pretty well and my heart is easy. I went to the Office and occupied myself in arrears. Mr. Conant, the Farmer from Weston came in, and he talks more than enough. His present subject, the Lease and some requests. Mr. Kauffer, a Tenant applied for delay. The pressure pervades all classes.

I dined by invitation with W. E. Payne—The same club, H. G. Chapman, J. Chapman, E. and S. P. Blake, H. B. Rogers and myself, C. C. Tucker. I talked more than I ought and not so prudently as I ought. I am sensible that in this circle, I am liable to be misunderstood and yet know not how to avoid it. We left at seven, and I returned home to pass the evening. But did nothing. Must I return these civilities.

THURSDAY. 30TH.

Mild, agreeable weather. I received a short Note from my brother at Washington, though without any thing material in it.[1] My day was wasted in dancing attendance at an Auction where after all I bought nothing. Perhaps there is no greater waste of time than this. Mr. Alfred Welles an importing Jeweller was selling part of his Stock, and although the cry is so loud of hard times, I should hardly imagine it had much foundation if I was to judge from the sales here. Not [that] there was no sacrifice, but it was not greater than usually happens. At the Office only for a short time. Nothing else material. Afternoon quietly at home. Lord Bacon and Terence. Evening, Adam Smith and Patronage aloud. Nothing particular.

[1] Letter missing.

FRIDAY. 31ST.

A delightfully mild day. I went to the Office and from thence to a Meeting of the Directors of the Middlesex Canal. The purpose was to declare a Dividend which was done. The gross receipts were over $56,000—A sum which enabled us to give thirty dollars a share. This is a blessed thing for my fathers affairs[1] and will probably enable me to redeem another portion of debt due in May to Isaac Hull Adams, he being then of age. And if this should be done, the funds here will in the course of one year have been released from an annual tax[2] to the amount of $500, nearly a sixth part of the usual receipts.

Walk and home. Afternoon. Finished the last volume of the works of Lord Bacon in the edition which I have, and went on with the Andrian, the text of which is easier than I had expected.

I was grieved to hear of the illness of little Edward Everett whose case was to night very critical. We went to P. C. Brooks, but the supper party of the family was damped by the intelligence from this child. Returned at ten.

[1] On JQA's holdings in the Middlesex Canal Co., see vol. 3:151.
[2] That is, annual interest payments to JA's legatees so long as the legacies remained unpaid.

FEBRUARY. 1834.

SATURDAY. 1ST.

We were anxious to hear of the little child and at last had an account which promised favorably. My wife went out early this morning for the purpose of riding on horseback at the Circus[1] which exercise has been recommended to her.

I went to the Office as usual. Engaged on money affairs. Made an arrangement for a sum in amount about half of what will be necessary, to become payable with interest in the month of May. I have Notes payable on the first of that month for about a third of the balance. The rest I must squeeze somehow or other.

Walk. Afternoon, reading Adam Smith. I tried to write to my Father but failed for lack of subject. Quiet evening at home—Read Patronage to my wife. Continued Terence and Smith.

[1] In the Roman sense, and probably the name of a Boston riding academy or the like.

SUNDAY. 2D.

A lovely day as I have ever seen at this season of the year. We attended divine service all day and heard Mr. Frothingham. Matthew 22. 39. "The second is like unto it, Thou shalt love thy neighbor as thyself." An examination of this passage which condenses the whole of theology into Love of the Creator and the created, which gives little that is new but thoroughly refines and purifies the old.

Luke 12. 16–22. The parable of the rich man accummulating his gains, the question, what his offence? not his wealth, not his industry, but his presumption, in imagining that *he* was the director and ruler of all his prosperity. Adam Smith has much to say upon the subject of Fortune. Plutarch tells us Sylla relied much upon his Fortune. We know Julius Cæsar's speech to the Boatman. Lord Bacon says it is productive of failure to attribute events too much to one's own agency. Addison has remarked the frequency with which acts you anticipate as certain will not happen. Why are not all these manifestations of the same presumption which cost the rich man in the parable his life? I believe in my fortune, or in other words in the divine care of a superintending Providence, which has done for me what my own agency never could have brought about.

Read a Sermon of Atterbury. Matthew 25. 40. "Verily I say unto you, inasmuch as ye have done it unto one of the least of these my brethren, ye have done it unto me." He considers first how it is that acts of mercy are decided to rank first at the day of judgment. Secondly, why, when done to the poor they are said to be done to the Saviour himself. A charity Sermon, but it is not filled out at all. Evening, Mr. and Miss Beale called in and passed an hour. She looks quite sick.

MONDAY. 3D.

Another delightful day. I went to the Office. Engaged as usual in making up my arrears, which is about the only occupation of my morning. I lounge away too much time at the Post Office reading the Newspapers. I do nothing and ought to be ashamed. The money pressure still continues, and the accounts from Washington are that it will not cease. The Administration party is determined to do nothing. Heaven help us.

Took a long walk, invited by the beauty of the day. Afternoon reading Stewart Essay on the cause of beauty,[1] and the Andria. Afterwards I went to the Boylston Market to attend the annual Proprietor's meeting. Nothing done but the election of Officers and the usual organization for the year. I tried to vacate my post but did not succeed. Afterwards, I went to Mrs. Frothingham's, where she had a party of children, it being her eldest son Thomas' birth day. A few grown persons of the family, but it was very fatiguing. Returned home by ten o'clock.

[1] Probably Dugald Stewart whose philosophical essays had been acclaimed by Sir James Mackintosh.

TUESDAY. 4TH.

The weather holds on mild although it was cloudy today. I passed my time in no better manner than usual. Accounts and Newspapers. Mr. Degrand called in and gave me his speech to read which was quite tolerable—Two or three very good points.[1] I took a long walk. Reflected upon the present state of things and upon the possibility of writing something to affect the people. But the press is overloaded already, and I have no means to communicate my opinions even supposing they were worth any thing. Began and gave it up.

Afternoon at home, finished Smith's Moral Sentiments from which in the second reading I have gathered much. Mine is about the time of life when such inquiries are valuable as they aid in fixing conduct upon some permanent foundation before times of severe trial commence. Col. Jones from Weston called and made a settlement with me for Wood. He was frightened by the decided tone of my yesterday's Letter.[2] This is opportune. Evening quietly at home. Patronage.

[1] Probably the speech on the "Money Market" which he had delivered at Faneuil Hall on 11 Jan. and which had been printed in the *Columbian Centinel* on 1 Feb., p. 1, col. 6 – p. 2, col. 4.

[2] To Col. John Jones, 3 Feb. (LbC, Adams Papers). The sale of wood from the Weston property had taken place in December.

WEDNESDAY. 5TH.

Mild but cloudy. I went to the Office and passed my time in reading the debate in the Senate between Mr. Webster and Mr. Wright.[1] This is of some consequence as it lays open the future operation of parties. The former is driven to the Wall and now takes his course while the latter daringly proclaims that the party he represents will persevere to the end. Now comes the tug of war.

Attended a meeting of the Proprietors of the Middlesex Canal being the annual one for the choice of officers. Nothing new excepting the substitution of Abbott Lawrence as a Director in the place of J. B. Joy deceased. Walk with my Wife to order some things for a dinner I propose to give, tomorrow.

Afternoon at home. Began Mr. Gallatin's Essay upon Banks and Currency which requires very fixed attention to comprehend, yet which conveys a great amount of valuable information.[2] Terence. Evening quiet. Patronage.

¹ The speeches in the Senate on the New York Resolution relating to Deposits by Silas Wright Jr., of New York, and Daniel Webster were printed in the *National Intelligencer* on 31 Jan. (p. 3, cols. 1–3) and 1 Feb. (p. 2, cols. 1–6).

² Albert Gallatin's influential essay first appeared in Dec. 1830 and March 1831 in the *American Quarterly Review*. It was afterward revised and expanded and published as *Considerations on the Currency and Banking System of the United States*, Phila., 1831. For an earlier reading by CFA, see vol. 4:36.

THURSDAY. 6TH.

Fine morning but it afterwards grew cloudy. I went to the Office and I believe for the first time since New Year devoted an hour or two to Parliamentary Debates. Read the progress of the Ministerial fears during the period when a combined resistance displayed itself of the extent of which the actors had formed no conception. The parliamentary opposition appear gradually gathering courage and strength. Took a walk.

Had company to dine with me, Mr. Slocum, Josiah Quincy Jr., W. E. Payne, Dr. E. G. Davis, T. K. Davis and P. C. Brooks. Nothing remarkable happened. Things went on pretty well and the company did not all leave until nine o'clock. This is the largest and most expensive entertainment I have given. Its nature is that of a tax on property. Retired early to bed.

FRIDAY. 7TH.

A snow storm. Such are the alternations of our weather. I went to the Office as usual. Nothing particular. Mr. Degrand called and I executed the money transaction contemplated. Interest at 12 per cent which is enormous and grows out of the political war between the Bank and the Executive. This sum belongs to my father and will, I hope make a moiety of the payment to Hull in May next. Attended a meeting of the new Board of Directors of the Middlesex Canal. The usual organization. William Sullivan talks like a depressed man. He is pretty distant to me. General politics about the same. Read a good deal of the English Debates and felt as much interested in the squabbles of that day as in those of this. What a world of perpetual commotion it is. And how often does the mountain produce a mouse.

Short walk. Afternoon, I did little but finish the Andria—A curious specimen of domestic life among the ancients. Terence borrowed from Menander. The pictures are all therefore drawn from Grecian manners. The French have done little more than imitate, with the addition of their own peculiar habits.

Quiet evening at home. Finished Patronage which after all, I consider the most heavy of Miss Edgeworth's productions. The character of Lord Oldborough is nevertheless one of her best. The Percys are too perfect to be interesting. Wrote a letter to my father, being my third attempt.[1]

[1] 7–8 Feb. (Adams Papers).

SATURDAY. 8TH.

Fine day though cool. I went to the Office and purposed to pass my time industriously in reading. But Mr. Conant the Tenant from Weston came in and consumed much of my time. He is fond of talking. I was afterwards obliged to go in quest of a person to make a demand of and nevertheless failed in seeing him. My Cash department is small. Lost my walk for the most part. Afternoon, wrote to my father and engaged in copying the Letter which took up most of my disposable time. Evening quietly at home. Began reading the Absentee, another of Miss Edgeworths Tales.

SUNDAY. 9TH.

Weather cloudy. Attended divine service all day. Mr. Putnam. Ecclesiastes 1. 14. "I have seen all the works that are done under the sun and behold, all is vanity and vexation of spirit." A moral common place. John 14. 6. "I am the truth." These discourses did not keep my attention whether it was that they were dull or I was, I did not decide. Sermon of Atterbury. Job 22. 21. "Acquaint now thyself with him and be at peace." 1. What is acquaintance with God. 2. Its use to be at peace. 3. The time *now* i.e. with Job a moment of affliction. Hence the general subject of the relief of piety in times of trouble. Subject good, treatment slight. Evening quiet. Mr. Degrand called in to spend an hour, but had nothing to say.

MONDAY. 10TH.

I have rarely known a time when my existence was more monotonous than at present. Even my literary occupations which usually give some variety to my Journal have dwindled so much as to be scarcely perceptible. I vegetate and am likely so to do. This is an incident of my condition from which I must not start. In a Community like our's where all classes are in eager pursuit of wealth, and can spare no time for other purposes, he who by circumstances is relieved from the pressure, is in some degree thrown aside from the current of affairs.

Office, where Mr. Brown kept me the whole morning in argument about the Infirmary.[1] He had taken advantage of the Tenant and got a Contract for it from me in April next. The Tenant came to complain and I thought him aggrieved. I have endeavoured in consequence to rectify my mistake. I kept my temper perfectly throughout.

In the Afternoon, read Stuarts Essay upon the Beautiful in which he endeavors to refute Burke and substitute a new theory. I do not think him perfectly satisfactory. Mr. Brooks took tea and spent a couple of hours, though he had not much to say. I read a little of the Absentee. Afterwards, took an incidental direction in my reading and examined Buffon's Natural History of the Ass.[2]

[1] See the note to the entry of 2 Dec., above.
[2] In the *Library of Useful Knowledge*.

TUESDAY. 11TH.

Beautiful day. I went to the office. I find my new acquaintance in the room opposite takes up full as much of my time as the former one Mr. Peabody did. Indeed he seems less busy and more talkative.

Read the Intelligencer which contains the last debate, in Congress. The scale seems to be balancing now pretty even. In the mean time there is great distress. A certain amount of Bankruptcy and nothing else will relieve the Community.

Walk. Afternoon, Stewart on the sublime. He derives the beautiful from sight and the association of ideas by which the terms descriptive of impressions on the eye are gradually transferred to other objects of different senses and mental observation. The sublime he likewise draws from elevation. Terence, the Eunuch. Afterwards, read Plato's Apology of Socrates, with the Account of Socrates in Enfield's History of Philosophy.

WEDNESDAY. 12TH.

Cold again. I went to the Office but executed little excepting a Lease of the Tenant at Weston, and studied a little the returns of the Massachusetts Banks. I judge from them that our currency is in a pretty dangerous condition. There is considerable difference among the Institutions, but the oldest Institutions do not in all cases appear strongest or best managed. In the mean time the public distress is not diminishing nor likely to be diminished. The effect will probably be felt by us all only after the lapse of months. The Manufactures of the Country must depress wages, and this will operate far and wide.

Short walk only, in consequence of some Commissions. Afternoon, read Stewart on Taste. His power of illustration is greater I think than his original matter. Terence, the Eunuch. In the evening Miss Edgeworth's Absentee. Finding myself without purpose, I intend now to go back to my German.[1] Began again today.

[1] CFA had at least twice before, in the winter months of 1830 and of 1832–1833, undertaken the study of German through the use of the grammar and reader compiled by C. T. C. Follen (vol. 3:357–377 *passim*; 4:403–431 *passim*). Despite his abandonment of Follen earlier (entry for 28 March 1833, above), it would appear from the selections read over the succeeding weeks that he had returned to the same text.

THURSDAY. 13TH.

Fine day. I went to the Office and executed the remainder of the Lease to the Farmer at Weston. Attended the sale of things belonging to Mr. A. Welles, which did not go off quite so briskly as before. The smaller things however sold well. The heavier ones showed (and it is the first private indication I have found) the present state of pressure in the Community.

Short Walk. Afternoon, read Ricardo upon the question of Currency which was at one time much agitated in this Country. Public affairs present daily a more gloomy aspect. The People are at last realizing the election of Andrew Jackson. He is making them feel that they like the frogs in the fable have got for their ruler a devouring and inflexible being. The worst of it is that in the punishment, the innocent are involved with the guilty. We must wait for events.

Read more of the Eunuch which has more wit and character in it than the Andrian. Evening quiet. Had a pleasant visit from T. K. Davis who sat till ten o'clock.

FRIDAY. 14TH.

Morning passed at the office occupied in the same series of nothingness which distinguishes so much of my time. My spirits are a little affected by this state of things. I feel as if I was not doing any thing worthy of myself and as if I should not ever be more than one of the idle drones of Society. I know that this is wrong, that I *ought* to think how greatly favoured I am in life to be put above the necessity of labour. Perhaps this is one cause of my uneasiness. To be a mere liver of a life of luxury is not fully to my taste. To be a hanger on upon the popular favor is still less so. I cannot *court* any body. And my talents however much I may prize them, are not of that transcendent description which secure admiration in a moment.

Walk. Afternoon. Read Ricardo's Pamphlet on the Bank of England which gave me some new ideas upon that subject. Terence, the Eunuch—A description of a rape which would be rather harsh for our ears. Evening quiet at home. The Absentee. I afterwards began Du Bos Reflections upon Poetry and Painting.[1]

[1] JQA's set of Jean Baptiste Dubos' *Réflexions critiques, sur la poésie et sur la peinture*, 3 vols., Paris, 1719–1740, is in MQA.

SATURDAY. 15TH.

Mild but cloudy. I went to the Office and spent an hour in reading the Parliamentary Debates. In the present disturbed state of our own Country it is a great relief to go abroad and look at the state of things in foreign countries and in history. Yet wherever one looks, there is an appearance of solidity which comforts. Here the example is lost every twenty years.

I took a walk. Afternoon, reading Dubos Reflexions upon Poetry and Painting—A pleasing book upon a pleasing subject. On the whole, I take more pleasure in these studies than in all the noise of politics. Were it not, that the present measures press upon the industry of the Country and consequently upon our resources, I should make myself tolerably indifferent to the state of things.

Evening. The Absentee, a pleasing work, and La Fontaine's Fables which are charming.[1]

[1] Three editions (1769, 1777, and 1797) of the *Fables* of Jean de La Fontaine are in MQA.

SUNDAY. 16TH.

The day was pleasant. I attended divine service and heard Mr. Frothingham preach from Psalms. 4. 4. "Commune with your own heart and be still." The sermon was directed against the fashion of theological controversy in the present day. He combated what he considered two leading popular errors—The first, that all subjects could be perfectly submitted to the test of argument and reason, with a view to elicit all truth. The second, that this truth could be made evident by the agency of popular discussions. The immediate occasion of this discourse was the scheme of lecturing upon the evidences of Christianity devised by a combination of orthodox and episcopal Clergymen to combat the much dreaded heresy of the Fanny Wright School.[1] I am somewhat doubtful in my own mind what can be right in this case. That Mr. Frothingham is perfectly correct in his positions seems to me undeniable. But the misfortune is that he consults only the feelings of the educated classes who can be content with moderate religion to guide their reason and affections. The large mass with whom religion must be a passion or nothing, require excitement, require the strong emotion which controversy and nothing else can give. Our Community is a very moral one, but it cannot live in the dead calm of all the exciting passions. Pleasure is thought wicked because it can rarely be tasted in that moderation which preserves from sin. The love of strong liquors is perhaps the most dangerous of all this sort of temptation among us. To preserve from this, resort is had to one of two things—The accummulation of money which is a pretty complete security, or the zealous pursuit of religious faith. The two latter are not unfrequently united, but the first does not often combine with either. Of the three, the first is undoubtedly the most injurious in it's effects upon society, and hence it is, that though I cannot approve of them, yet I do not look with quite so much dislike upon their various modes of manifestation. For the rest, Mr. Frothingham was as polished as usual, and his manner not often so animated, became decidedly eloquent.

Afternoon, Mr. Sargent preached. Text. 1. Kings 18. 28. "Elijah came unto all the people and said, How long halt ye between two opinions? If the Lord be God, follow him, but if Baal, then follow him." A discourse deprecating controversial fury in the pulpit and lukewarmness in the people. It was well conceived and in parts not badly executed, but the young man has no idea of the mode to carry out his plan. It was written with a view to attack boldly. It was preached so very much under this daring tone, that the figures seemed out of place and the apostrophes mere nonsense. Such is always the result, when an Orator does not keep the feeling of his auditors on the same pace with his own. The effect upon those who analyse little was unfortunate for the poor youth. And coming so directly after the morning, the condemnation fell the more heavily.

Read a Charity Sermon of Atterbury. Luke 10. 32. "He came and looked on him and passed by on the other side." An examination of the usual objections made to giving. 1. Inability, 2. public distress or hard times, 3. delay or a distribution by legacy, 4. that charities multiply poor, 5. badly managed. There is no new view of these questions. I long to begin some better thinker. Evening quietly at home. Young Gardiner Gorham passed a short time. I wrote to my father.

¹ On the threat to established religion posed by Frances (Fanny) Wright, see vol. 4:76.

MONDAY. 17TH.

Cloudy day. I went to the Office and was engaged the whole morning with Tenants. Finding my finances now alarmingly low, I made a sweep around the Tenants on Saturday and they answered the call bravely. Mr. Conant came in and we were for a considerable time engaged in getting through the terms &ca. of the new Lease for five years—After which it was signed and sealed and that business finished.

Walk. Afternoon, copied and despatched the Letter to my father.¹ Finished Terence's Eunuch. Its close is not happy. It seems to fall short in the character of the boaster, but there are more original strokes of humour and vigor of thought in it than in the Andrian. The parasite is admirably drawn. His double meaning in every speech construed by his patron as a compliment and by others as a sarcasm is very well done.

I went to the Theatre this evening with my Wife. Rule a Wife and have a Wife. Miss Kemble as Estefania and her father as Leon.² The play is one of the most licentious of those very licentious authors Beaumont and Fletcher, and in order to make it tolerable about one half is taken out of it in the representation. Still there is a deal of wit in it and that sort of dramatic action which keeps attention fixed. The first character in it, Michael Perez was performed by Mr. Smith who though tolerable was not as good as he might have been. Miss Kemble as Estefania performed with great spirit, and there were fewer of her drawling airs than I have seen in any of her parts. He is admirable in this line. The poets have left it doubtful what Estefania is, but the course of the action betrays her to be totally destitute of all moral principle and of shame. In those days morality was not the fashion, wherein it must be admitted we have improved. I must give as my general conclusion that I came away pleased, without inquiring narrowly into causes. Afterpiece a new one called Woman's worth and Woman's ways, written to show one performer in several characters. Miss A. Fisher who has spirit and animation went through well, but she overexerts herself, loses the ease which is all important for effect in an Actress, and gives the auditor an impression of pain for her suffering. We returned home before ten o'clock—An arrangement which I think very well of. Read a little more of Dubos.

[1] 17 Feb., Adams Papers. Stimulated by JQA's favorable comments on the review of Hutchinson's *History*, CFA reflects on the difficulties facing one who would write on the country's history: "American History cannot be written very fairly in this Century because . . . no man is brave enough to encounter the opposition which a fair judgment of individual character would probably create. Any qualification of praise towards Otis, Hancock or S. Adams would yet be regarded as enmity in this State, and the same would happen elsewhere upon touching Jefferson, Hamilton or Franklin. Mr. Sparks is filling the Country with eulogies for the simple reason that he compiles for the popular taste. . . .

There is no going a step among the original papers without observing that . . . the passions worked as vehemently in those days as they do now. . . . A concealment under the garb of general perfection at once removes the age from us into the regions of Hercules and Theseus."

CFA also reports on the current economic distress in Boston, and discourses on A. H. Everett's difficulties in the Harvard Board of Overseers, with the *North Amer. Rev.*, and on the political scene.

[2] This renewal of Kemble appearances at the Tremont Theatre was begun on 4 Feb. and was to conclude on the 18th (*Columbian Centinel*, 17 Feb., p. 3, col. 4).

TUESDAY. 18TH.

Weather singularly mild and pleasant. Our whole month of February has been quite uncommon. I went to the Office and was engaged for some time in affairs and in writing my Diary. A little of the Parliamentary Debates, some talk with Mr. Walsh and a walk made up my morning.

Afternoon, reading Dubos, whose critical reflexions are very excellent generally, but who nevertheless manifests his French notions now and then. The fact is not a little singular that the French people who generally are not so remarkable for method and rule in small affairs, are yet perfect slaves to ideas of convention in all matters of thinking. The English, perhaps the most exact business men in the world, are bold and irregular in their intellectual exertion.

Began the Heautontimorumenos [1]—A Latinised Greek compound. The Romans were in their Literature prodigious borrowers. Evening, being disappointed in getting tickets for the play, we sat at home and I finished the Absentee. I resumed the study of German this evening.

[1] Of Terence.

WEDNESDAY. 19TH.

My morning was wasted in reading over some English Newspapers. There is something quite charming in the appearance of comfort and solidity which one finds in them. I should like exceedingly to live in England, provided I had a very large fortune and no *roots* in this Country. America is a fine Country and to people of middling circumstances a paradise, but the spirit of change is too active, the blast of unlimited democracy too furious to make it agreeable to the classes who happen to be exempted by circumstances from labor. In a regular democracy there should be no property. I can imagine no state of things in which any thing like equality can otherwise be secured. And this would prove an equality of misery.

At the Athenæum, nothing particularly new. Walk. Afternoon, Dubos, who manifests his French opinions more and more as he goes on. I cannot imagine why people should be so anxious to put the human intellect into a strait Jacket. Fiction is fiction, and it matters little whether we regard it one way or another provided it touches the heart. *That* is the true test of the good. That is the point from which to start in investigating causes. Terence. Evening, Emilie de Coulanges. Miss Edgeworth understands the heart. German.

THURSDAY. 20TH.

A very lovely day. I went to the Office and occupied myself in writing and reading. Made some progress in the Parliamentary Debates. These were at that time acrimonious enough and remind me much of the state of things at Washington. This is not becoming one particle better but the excessive pressure is going off from the commercial men. Perhaps this will have an effect upon the decision of the present question. What ever that may be, the General will do nothing to aid the distressed community. He relies for his popularity upon far different people.

Took a walk and dined with Mr. Brooks. Nobody there but my wife and myself. Tolerably pleasant. Returned home to tea. Evening Emilie de Coulanges, and German. I translate into English each Fable of Lessing in the German reader. The Child is as restless, and uneasy as ever. Our nights are disturbed.

FRIDAY. 21ST.

Fine day. I went to the Office, but did not spend my time as profitably as I might have done. Received a letter from my Mother not in very good spirits and describing a very heated state of things at Washington.[1] Our Country is doomed to go through a perpetual agitation under the influence of individual passions. Ambition when beyond a certain limit is a terrible scourge.

I took a walk to the North part of the City to see the changes and improvements going on there which are certainly very great. But a check must now come upon the prosperity of our people.

After dinner, read Dubos, and Terence. In the evening I went to Mr. J. Sumner's in Chesnut Street—A family party, Mrs. Gray and her Daughters, Mrs. Story and Miss Henrietta, Mr. Brooks and his three daughters, Mr. F. Coffin. We played one game of Whist. Returned at ten more amused than I expected to have been.

¹ 17 Feb., Adams Papers.

SATURDAY. 22D.

Fine day. Office. I had two or three persons made application to me upon various subjects. Mr. E. Fuller came in upon the subject of the Lease of the House; I preferred drawing new ones to renewing the old. Accordingly I filled up a blank and executed it upon the spot. Mr. W. Spear from Quincy came in to pay me a short balance of money. Mr. Harrington with a recommendation of W. Spear for Coroner at Quincy which I signed although with some doubt of the propriety of my doing so, being a resident and citizen of another County. I took a walk.

Regretted to hear of the death of Mr. Wirt at Washington.¹ He has been much of a sufferer all his life and my wonder is he should have gone on so long.

Afternoon read Dubos and continued Terence. In the evening, finished Miss Edgeworth's Emilie de Coulanges and began Vivian. Judge Hall came in and spent half an hour. Nothing material took place. German Fables of Lessing.

¹ William Wirt died on the 18th. JQA's sentiments on Wirt and the means he took to have them incorporated in the House Journal are reported in the *Columbian Centinel* for 26 Feb. (p. 2, col. 1).

SUNDAY. 23D.

Dull rainy day. I arose late from the disturbed night caused by the child. Attended divine service all day and heard Mr. Frothingham preach. Ephesians 2. 12. "Having no hope and without God in the world." The discourse seemed directed at the present inclination towards the infidel principle. It touched upon the distressing nature of a state without hope, and the absence of support in a God. My thoughts wandered in spite of me. Proverbs 16. 25 and 14. 12 the same words being contained in both. "There is a way that seemeth right unto a man but the end thereof *are* the ways of death." A startling text, but a true one. It may seem curious that what a man does from the belief that he is right is not innocent, but as in this world's affairs a person fails of success for want of judgment to conduct prudently, so in those of the other, one can err from neglect of or opposition to that knowledge which guides to safety.

Read a sermon of Atterbury. Romans 11. 16. "If the first fruit be holy, the lump is also holy; and if the root be holy, so are the branches." This was a discourse delivered to the sons of the Clergy upon a day of commemoration. It touched upon the advantages and corresponding obligations of their condition. But it touched lightly upon the disadvantages of the English Church system which makes the toil and the pecuniary benefit and honor fall to different persons, and frequently gives the latter to the least worthy. Quiet evening at home.

MONDAY. 24TH.

Cloudy day. I went to the Office, but my time was much taken up by Mr. Walsh who came and conversed three hours. This is a little too much although I like his conversation because it is not frivolous. His subjects are generally literary, political or historical—So that my time is not so completely lost. Walk. The relief in the money market which was felt last week does not hold on. There was a great pressure Saturday and an extensive bankruptcy.

Afternoon, Dubos—A long section upon the Music of the Ancients. A curious idea of his to resolve the ancient theatrical representation into something resembling our modern operatic performances with the remarkable addition that while one man sung or spoke in recitative, the other did the gestures. What more ridiculous idea can present itself to the mind, yet this is justified by our author, who is all alive for the unities of the French Stage and talks of the necessity of keeping up the illusion. Such are the curious workings of the human mind. Evening. Vivian, a very moral Story, and continued my labours upon German.

TUESDAY. 25TH.

Snowy morning and an appearance of recurring winter. I went to the Office but did very little. Mr. Walsh came in and conversed upon

English History so long, that my leisure was pretty much taken up. I do not think such use of time absolute waste, and I felt gratified today that I could remember so clearly the succession of British Ministries from the time of Anne.

Walk was short as I went to see some of Mr. Cogswell's books. He is selling his Library having made a bad business of his Round hill School.[1] I do not however propose to buy. Afternoon passed at home reading Dubos. Finished the account of the ancient Stage. Finished also the play of the Self Tormentor. The characters of Menedemus and Chremes are strong delineations of human nature. I do not perceive that husbands adopted a different tone then from that which they often assume now. Evening at home, Vivian, and German.

[1] Joseph Green Cogswell in 1823 at Northampton with George Bancroft had established Round Hill, an experimental school remarkable in a number of ways, but which had been at various times beset by troubles including a revolt of students during which they had consigned their masters to a dungeon while they themselves went on a week-long spree at a Northampton hotel (Charlotte Everett to Edward Everett, 10 March 1830, MHi:Everett Papers).

Cogswell's distinguished career, however, earlier and later was largely concerned with books. He, along with George Ticknor and Edward Everett, had studied at Göttingen in 1817. He traveled widely in Europe, met and corresponded with Goethe. When he returned to Harvard in 1820 to become librarian and professor of mineralogy and geology, he brought for the College library the Ebel-

ing collection of 3,000 volumes and 11,000 maps and charts. It was in discouragement at the lack of interest there in the development of the library that he left to found Round Hill. Much later he was to become John Jacob Astor's adviser in establishing for the public the Astor Library in New York City, its superintendent, and the compiler of its printed catalogs 1848–1861 (*DAB*; Morison, *Three Centuries of Harvard*, p. 266). His own book collection must have been a substantial one. The *Columbian Centinel* gave the sale notice in its news columns, an unusual procedure, recommending it to "the attention of scholars. . . . These books were selected by Mr. Cogswell when in Europe, and a large portion of them are works which can rarely be purchased in this country" (25 Feb., p. 2, col. 2).

WEDNESDAY. 26TH.

Morning clear and cooler than for some time past. I went to the Office and from there to a sale of Mr. Cogswell's books. I did not go to purchase, nor yet from curiosity but rather from the sense of nothing to do. I met there W. E. Payne and Dr. E. G. Davis with whom I had much amusing conversation. But this is wasting precious hours. Alas, my regrets lead to no reformation. Lounged over the Newspapers and lounged at Office.

Walk. Afternoon, Dubos, upon Genius, the difficult question of *natural* powers. A man who admits his definition must deny one of

Jefferson's dogmas that all men are born free and equal. Began the Adelphi. The first Speech of Micio is admirable. Evening at home. Vivian, a very strong exhibition of the truth of the assertion that all wickedness is weakness. Began the German of Wieland.

THURSDAY. 27.

Fine day. I went to the Office and from thence to Mr. Cogswell's sale, but got no books. Did little or nothing as usual. Lounged at the Athenæum. Came across a number of the Eclectic Review for December, reviewing my number upon Vaughan in the North American of last July. He does little more than quote with approbation.[1] It is a little singular that this Eclectic has fallen upon both of my Articles—Although as they relate to English works of interest to the liberal portion of the English Community it is not perhaps so surprising. I feel flattered by this sort of distinction. It encourages me when I have my moments of depression. Yet after all, what is it? I am not sensible of gaining estimation by my labour. The world moves on here, and pays little attention to efforts which do not impel their immediate interests. A speech upon the present distress with sufficient confidence and not half the basis would make a man's fortune.

Walk. Dined at P. C. Brooks Jrs., his father, Mr. Slocum and my wife. It was middling. I returned home and read an article in a French periodical upon the death of Princess Borghese—A disgusting exhibition of vanity in the last hour made with the belief in the author of the Account that there was something grand in it. Evening at home. Vivian. German.

[1] The subjects of the essay-review in the *Eclectic Review* (3d ser., 10:462–479) are the *Memoirs of the Court of King Charles the First* by Lucy Aiken and the article by CFA in the *North Amer. Rev.* on Vaughan's *Memorials of the Stuart Dynasty*. A substantial quota- tion from CFA's article is introduced as representing "sensible and temperate re- flections" (p. 477) and is followed by the judgment that "The Reviewer does justice to the value and merit" of Vaughan (p. 479).

FRIDAY. 28TH.

Our weather is perfectly delightful. Mr. Walsh took up the whole morning in conversation excepting a short time when I was at Auction purchasing books. Procured a copy of Constant's book upon Religion which is a standard.[1] I propose to read it. Politics still prevail and money and Bank affairs.

Walk. Miss Julia Gorham dined and spent the day with us. Afternoon, Dubos, and Terence, Adelphi. Evening I read the Annual Register and went with my wife and Miss Gorham to visit Dr. and Mrs. Stevenson. They wish for visitors to enliven them since their misfortunes. Returned home after ten.

The Dr. is a very singular man. He forms opinions and feels little hesitation in expressing them. Those opinions are of the most monarchical tendency in politics. There is much of that sort of opinion in this part of the Country, but it is kept down in secret.

[1] CFA's copy of Benjamin Constant's *De la religion, considerée dans sa source, ses formes et ses développements*, 5 vols., Brussels, 1824–1825, is in MQA.

SATURDAY. MARCH 1ST.

Beautiful day. I went to the Office. Occupied in reading the Debates in the British Parliament and in our Congress. It is not without profit to compare them. Great Britain survived all the predictions and became more flourishing and powerful than ever. I hope we shall get through in the same manner. Great Britain however never experienced what it is to have the property of the Country and it's power get into different and opposing hands. The whole of the working of the system becomes irregular. And the people suffer, not the wealthy for then is the opportunity for the oppression of these.

Walk. Afternoon, reading Dubos. Disquisition upon the rise and decline at particular times of poetry and painting. Afterwards, Terence, the Adelphi. I read for about an hour and commonly finish one Act. Evening at home—Quiet reading. Vivian—This is one of the most masterly sketches Miss Edgeworth has drawn. The evils of weakness, of that sort of procrastination which avoids the present danger without reflecting, or without regarding future consequences are admirably exhibited. How many more men are ruined in this way than by decided wickedness. Continued my German which is now the same old Ass's story of Wieland, which I hammered upon so long, once before.[1]

[1] Vol. 4:417–427 *passim*.

SUNDAY. 2D.

Snow, clouds and wet weather. I passed my morning hour in reading the Annual Register for 1832, being the account of the Reform bill. The Author is evidently a decided tory and slides in his impressions in favor of that side throughout the debates.

Attended divine service. Mr. Frothingham preached. Exodus 20. 17. "Thou shalt not covet." A disquisition upon the tenth commandment as the foundation of the moral law, regulating society. In the Afternoon John 13. 12–14. "So after he had washed their feet and had taken his garments and was set down again, he said unto them, Know ye what I have done to you? Ye call me Master and Lord, and ye say well for so I am. If I then your Lord and Master have washed your feet: ye also ought to wash one another's feet." The general subject may be gathered from the text to have been the idea of humility conveyed as a charge to Christians. But I was absent and unable to fix my attention enough to follow the train of reasoning in the discourse.

Home. Read a Sermon in Latin by Atterbury. A concio ad clerum from the Text Romans. 13. 1. "Let every soul be subject unto the higher powers." An argument in favour of passive submission to Kings and the divine right of these to rule. It considered, 1. who were meant as higher powers, 2. how far the subjection was to go, 3. the reasons for the injunction, 4. to whom it was addressed. I have not often come across the well known doctrine of the English Church nor do I admire it when I do. It is not a little singular that the Bishop was soon after banished for intriguing against the reigning family. Evening very quietly at home. German.

MONDAY. 3D.

Cooler than it has been. I went to the Office, and passed my time as usual not to much purpose. I have been meditating some change by which I could appropriate my time to better profit but as yet can hit upon nothing. I spend some time after breakfast now in reading the Annual Register for 1832. It is very interesting from its describing what may fairly be considered as having been a moment of crisis in Great Britain. Walk. Afternoon, made progress in Dubos and the Adelphi of Terence.

My Wife went down to her father's and I joined her in the evening. It was a little birth day notice for Mrs. Everett's eldest child Anne. Several children and Mr. and Mrs. Frothingham with a Mr. Bierly an Englishman seeking his fortune in business among the crowd at New York. The evening from the noise and bustle was not agreeable. I moreover had a head ache—An unpleasant reminiscence which I have escaped from for a considerable time. Returned home very early.

TUESDAY. 4TH.

Lovely morning. The fine weather this season decidedly predominates. A person disordered in his stomach takes very little notice of the beauties of nature, and today I did not enjoy myself. Attended an auction and walked a good deal but I did not feel much better. I wish I could be sure my system was not disordered, somehow or other. Felt relieved after dinner.

Read Dubos and had a visit from Mr. Frothingham and talked of books. Terence. Mr. Brooks took tea with us, and we went to the Theatre to see Mr. Power the Irish Comedian.[1] St. Patrick's Eve, a piece of his own writing to describe an Irish Gentleman, and Teddy the Tiler, an afterpiece to show a vulgar Paddy. He does not overdraw. His Irish is characteristic and highly amusing. His own piece is not bad in effect though it has little in its substance of particular merit. He has taken advantage of Stage effect and sentimental places. We came home on the whole, quite well pleased, But my head ach had returned.

[1] Tyrone Power, the first of that name celebrated in the American theater, had made his New York debut in the preceding August (Odell, *Annals N.Y. Stage,* 3:655).

WEDNESDAY. 5TH.

Another very beautiful day. I went to the Office and occupied myself as well as I could with the Parliamentary Debates. As I find however that these are rather heavy and that I can get the cream of them in the Annual Register, I conclude to return this work to the Athenæum and get the other.[1]

Received a letter from my father[2] which is not in very good spirits upon the subject of the Bank, and upon public affairs generally. He thinks the votes of the House of Representatives will sustain the President and that commotion in the principal cities will be the consequence.

Walk. Afternoon read Dubos, and finished the Adelphi of Terence. The close of this play is abrupt and disappointing. The character of Micio is suddenly changed and becomes a mere nose of wax. Began the Hecyra. My wife took tea at Mrs. Frothingham's and I went in the evening. A family party, W. G. Brooks and his wife with her sister. Mr. Bierley was the only stranger. It was *to me* decidedly dull. Returned at ten.

[1] By "this work" CFA means the *Parliamentary Debates,* by "the other" he means the *Annual Register* for the same year. On the 5th, he borrowed from the Athenæum the volume for 1776.
[2] 27 Feb. (Adams Papers).

THURSDAY. 6TH.

Hazy and clouds. A few drops of rain from time to time but it cleared away in the evening. Office, where I was not regularly occupied but still managed to make a little progress in the Annual Register. Went home and passed much time in making up a party to go to the Theatre. But failed in the party though I got tickets for myself and wife. There is always much vexation in getting any thing which depends upon others, to take. I never did any thing of the sort without cause to regret it.

Walk. Afternoon copied a letter to my father which I wrote yesterday,[1] and read a part of the Hecyra of Terence. After tea went to the Theatre, accompanied by my wife and the two Frothingham boys—Mr. Power in Ettiquette run Mad and Born to good Luck. The first piece by himself. His genuine humor was visible most clearly in the latter, but I came away sated with laughing and Hibernianism. It is not an amusement which with me would endure as there is little variety in the humour and no wit. An Irishman is after all a very ordinary body. The Actor inclines too much to *gentility* too, and his Paddy O'Rafferty changes too easily from a rough Kilkenny boy to a Neapolitan Marquis. His dancing especially belied his brogue. Returned after ten.

[1] 5 March (Adams Papers).

FRIDAY. 7TH.

Fine day. I went to the Office. Time taken up by Diary and progress in the Register. I am going over the ground of the volume of Debates I have been reading in order to keep hold of the thread. The Account gives more of a party tinge to the proceedings for which allowance must of course be made.

Walk. Fell in with Chapman and talked with him. I perceive a gradual revival of the old federal secession and new Southern nullification doctrines in this Community. Thus it is that opposition in this Country always precipitates itself into ultra measures. Afternoon, Dubos and the Hecyra of Terence. Even quietly at home. Our days are so monotonous as hardly to need a Journal. German.

SATURDAY. 8TH.

My Ink is so pale today, I have great doubts whether I can write. Went to the Office—Weather being very stormy with wind and rain. Read the remainder of the volume of the Annual Register. I carried it back to the Athenæum but did not take out a new volume from doubt. The book is hardly interesting enough to fix my attention. Cannot I get something that will do it more effectually. Got hold of a book at the Athenæum upon Wines. It is more manageable than Henderson's although not so satisfactory. The author is too compendious and talks too much of measures. His information is however valuable. His name is Cyrus Redding.[1]

Home. Afternoon, finished Dubos and the Hecyra of Terence. The former has not quite filled my expectations. Upon the latter there have been great debates. It was not successful in representation, and Colman gives his opinion of the causes why it was not so. He attributes the failure to its being dry. I think it wants the observation of human nature and the great *sketchiness* of his other plays. Evening quiet at home. Began reading Miss Edgeworths story of Ennui. German.

[1] The volume was *History and Description of Modern Wines*, London, 1833.

SUNDAY. 9TH.

Clear and pleasant day. Began Benjamin Constant's book upon Religion which I bought the other day. I am charmed with it's beginning.

Attended divine Service and heard Mr. Frothingham from Job 28. 12 and 28. "But where shall wisdom be found? and where is the place of understanding? Behold the fear of the Lord, that is wisdom, and to depart from evil is understanding." A sermon maintaining that knowledge though it may be power is not in itself either a true guide of morals nor a rule of faith; and directed at the present outcry for education, without regard to religion. Matthew 6. 14. Mr. Pierpont[1] "If ye forgive men their trespasses, your heavenly father will also forgive you." Repentance and amendment. Mutual forgiveness. Mr. Pierpont defined what resentment might be indulged, and what was his view of Christ's doctrine of forbearance. He seemed to have forgot the injunction to present the other cheek when the one had been slapped.

Atterbury. Volume 2.—A supplement. Acts 26. 26. "This thing was not done in a Corner." The evidence of the truth of Christianity from the publicity of its miracles. Short. Evening quiet at home.

[1] Rev. John Pierpont; see vol. 3:129.

MONDAY. 10TH.

Cool but pleasant. Went to the Office and from thence to the Athenæum where I spent nearly all my morning. Read the remainder of Mr. Redding's book upon Wines which is pleasant enough. He recommends strongly the French products but displays such a scene of cheatery of Foreigners as to discourage any one from buying them. The English from their love of strong liquor are however more apt to be deceived than any other Nation—And we through them. Read an Article or two in the Periodicals and found my morning gone.

Walk. In the Afternoon, copied a letter into my book commenced last Summer, of the correspondence of J.A., but since I have had these letters bound and put into a durable shape my zeal flags. Wrote a short letter to my mother,[1] sending one of her commissions by Mr. Oliver who goes tomorrow morning to Washington on the Committee to take the Memorial.[2] Evening at home, the story of Ennui and German.

[1] Adams Papers. "The children are pretty well. John keeps his size, though his Mother does not think his beauty half so *inexpressible* as Louisa's was. This latter personage is getting to the age when the trials of patience come, and we find her by no means the amiable personage we had flattered ourselves. N'importe. We must call it proper spirit."

[2] The Memorial to Congress, signed by more than 6,600 Boston citizens and adopted at a meeting in Faneuil Hall on 6 March, urged effective action by the Congress against the "recent usurpations" of the President in fiscal matters, especially as they related to the Bank (*Columbian Centinel*, 8 March, p. 2, col. 2).

TUESDAY. 11TH.

Dusty. Office as usual. I brought down a volume of Jefferson's Memorials to read but did not open the book. I had several Commissions in different places which took up my attention. Waste. Waste. Shall I ever do any thing more? Walk with Edm. Quincy who for a wonder talked politics. There must be something of an excitement to do this.

Home. Afternoon, Benjamin Constant upon Religion. A great deal of good with some questionable matter. But the style makes the reading a charm. Began the Phormio of Terence, the last of his six plays. I have gone through them fast. Read a speech of Lord Castlereagh in a volume of British Pamphlets, my Wife being out at tea. Evening quiet. Went down to Mrs. Carter's for my Wife at eight, Miss Julia Gorham and her brother Gardner. Returned at ten.

WEDNESDAY. 12TH.

Fine day and mild as May. I went to the Office. Occupied in my Accounts and paying off as many of my engagements as possible. This took me some time. I had some to spare for Jefferson's Life which I began. I wish to read this with attention and observation.[1]

Walk. Afternoon, Constant who begins his system while he attacks the habit of system making. Phormio of Terence and as my Wife was out a Speech of Mr. Canning upon the Congress of Verona. It is on many accounts very remarkable. There is some prophecy in it. A person in considering the present state of things feels almost sick at heart. The democratic principle is sweeping with such ravages over us. Mr. Canning foresaw it.

Went to Mrs. S. Gray's in the evening—The family, and Mr., Mrs. and Miss Sumner. Cards and light supper. On the whole we got through the evening very well. Home by ten.

[1] The reading here begun of Thomas Jefferson Randolph's 4-volume edition of the *Memoir, Correspondence, and Miscellanies* of Jefferson had been preceded by the reading of numerous reviews of it, conversations about it, &c., since its appearance in 1829. See above, vols. 3 and 4, *passim*.

THURSDAY. 13TH.

A very fine day. I went to the Office and was occupied in my usual manner. Made some progress in the Life of Jefferson and was much struck with his Account of the Debates in the first Congress. It is quite a pity that he had not continued them more fully. Was engaged in several commissions which consumed some of my morning.

Walk and home. I did not accomplish much this afternoon, as my wife wanted me to give directions and superintend the table she proposed to entertain her guests with this evening. We have been invited out this Winter to the houses of every member of the family and this was designed as a general return for the civilities. Mrs. Everett, Mr. Brooks, Mr. and Mrs. Frothingham, Mr. and Mrs. P. C. Brooks, Mr. and Mrs. Story, Miss Henrietta Gray, Mr. and Mrs. W. G. Brooks, and Edward Brooks made the company, being the largest I have ever entertained. We had a very pretty light supper, and tolerably agreeable time until ten o'clock when they all arose and dispersed. On the whole, I was glad to get rid of this kind of engagement at once.

FRIDAY. 14TH.

Fine day but cool. I went to the Office, but was not very industrious. Read the National Intelligencer for the Debates and was somewhat surprised at Mr. Webster's tone which intimates pretty decidedly a refusal to adjourn during the present unsettled state of the times.[1] Of course, this will make us a summer residence here—A thing hitherto untried.

Mr. Walsh came in and consumed some time. He is lengthy when he comes. Walk. Afternoon, Benjamin Constant, but he did not interest me. Continued Terence's Phormio, to the last Act. Evening quiet at home, which is agreeable as a variety from the past. Ennui and conversation. Afterwards I read German.

[1] Webster's speech touching adjournment, along with Henry Clay's, appeared in the *National Intelligencer* on 10 March (p. 3, cols. 1–4).

SATURDAY. 15TH.

Our Season is fine but uncommonly dry. I went to the Office, and read the Volume of Jefferson's Memoir with the single interruption caused by Mr. S. Burril from Quincy on a *promising* expedition for his rent. Nothing important transpired. The Market for Money is said to be easier, but the distress and consequent loss by forcing sales is still great.

I dined at P. C. Brooks Jrs. with Mr. Brooks, Mr. Story and Mr. Frothingham. Nothing interesting. Conversation flagged. Returned home but did little or nothing. Evening quiet at home. Read part of Ennui, and afterward German.

SUNDAY. 16TH.

Fine day. I read Benjamin Constant. Divine Service all day. Heard Mr. Frothingham from Genesis 2. 17. "The tree of the knowledge of good and evil." He gave to it a figurative meaning which I did not fully take and which I did not much admire. That experience gives a knowledge of good and evil is true, that man should be forbidden to touch experience seems to be only reasoning in a circle, for experience must come from something and it is necessary to explain what that was— Apple or something equally palpable.

Mr. Gannett in the Afternoon. Matthew 6. 13. "Lead us not into temptation but deliver us from evil." This is a text of some difficulty at all times. Mr. G. makes it to mean trial in order that we may avoid evil. The common view is, Suffer us not to be led into temptation, and I think it just and reasonable. "Deliver us from evil" then means exactly what it says. The Lord's Prayer strikes me as a perfect formula. One which supersedes all Prayer excepting that which may arise from special occasions of distress. Afternoon, Atterbury, Matthew 11. 3. "Art thou he that should come? or do we look for another?" The Message of John the Baptist and the manner as well as matter of the reply. A very slight composition.

Evening, we went down to pass the Evening with Mr. Brooks, Mrs. Everett. Mr. and Mrs. J. Bradlee came in and passed a part of it. Conversation general and not particularly interesting. We returned home at ten, but I do nothing afterwards, excepting my regular Chapters.

MONDAY. 17TH.

Fine morning. I went to the Office after a visit from Mr. Stephen Whitney. This is a member of our House of Representatives from Deerfield. He is one of the leading Antimasons in that body, and came to me to get a draught of a bill copied which the Committee were to offer as *their* measure to suppress Masonry. This bill like all the other Papers on this subject was drawn by Mr. Hallett. Although the humble business of copyist was not very flattering to my vanity, I yet thought it prudent not to decline the offer, and consequently spent two hours of my morning in executing a copy. As Mr. Whitney had at the same time requested any Comments I might make, I added some and sent them to him.

Walked down to see some furniture and a House designed for Mrs. Ritchie, but not occupied by her. Mr. Otis wishes to sell it, far above its value. I was not struck with either, though the situation is pleasant.[1] Afternoon, finished the first Volume of Benjamin Constant, and also the Phormio of Terence. I have been much pleased with this author. His Comedies appear cold to us, but there is every difference in reading and acting. I was struck with that in Rule a Wife and Have a Wife. My Grandfather has written Notes to accommodate us which I have transferred into my copy though I do not think them quite just.[2]

My wife went out to Tea. Mr. T. K. Davis called for an hour. I then went to Mrs. Frothingham's. Family, part, and the Sumners and Miss Julia Gorham and Miss Anne Carter. Home at ten.

[1] Harrison Gray Otis, who lived at 45 Beacon Street (the third of the great Boston houses he built) from 1806 until his death in 1848, in 1831–1832 built next door at No. 44 a house for his daughter Sophia, Mrs. Andrew Ritchie (at the time the two houses bore the numbers 42 and 41 [*Boston Directory*, 1834; *Columbian Centinel*, 17 March, p. 3, col. 6]). Apparently Mrs. Ritchie never lived in the house but let it. Otis did not succeed in selling the house, leasing it to a succession of tenants including Francis C. Gray and Samuel Austin. When sold by the Otis heirs, the purchaser was Robert Gould Shaw Jr. The house is now owned and occupied by the Meteorological Society of America (Morison, *H. G. Otis* [1969 edn.], p. 193–196, 533, 547–548; Chamberlain, *Beacon Hill*, p. 177–178).

[2] The letters JA wrote to his three grandsons in 1816 about the plays of Terence are in the Adams Papers (M/

JA/9, Folder 4; Microfilms, Reel No. 188). The copy of the plays into which CFA transferred JA's comments (London, 1825) is in MQA and is illustrated in the present volume; see also p. xviii, above.

TUESDAY. 18TH.

Weather clear and pleasant. I went to the Office and was occupied in making up my Diary, and reading the Debates in the Intelligencer which are active enough. As usual my Father finds it difficult to keep his temper.[1] We were not made for politicans. We have too much fury about us.

Mr. G. A. Otis called to thank my father through me for the loan of books for his translation of Cicero's Offices. He thinks he has now got something very superior. He cannot publish because the booksellers are embarrassed. He talked as an Author often talks and as *all* writers think. Some are wise enough to know that such language is usually disgusting to hearers.

Walk. Afternoon, reading Benjamin Constant and began to read over Cicero's Tusculan Disputations. My next Classical study is to be Ovid but until I can get to Quincy for the purpose of looking over the copies in my father's Library I can do nothing, in that line. Cicero is always charming. And his Tusculans I did not pay sufficient attention to. My wife was not at home to tea, but came in shortly afterwards. Ennui. I afterwards studied Wieland.

[1] JQA's temper had been aroused by thrice being refused permission to present resolutions from the Massachusetts legislature and as many times losing an appeal from the Chair's decision (*National Intelligencer*, 12 March, p. 3, cols. 4–5; 13 March, p. 3, col. 1; 15 March, p. 3, col. 1).

WEDNESDAY. 19TH.

Uncommonly warm for the Season. I went down to the Office. My time passed quite unprofitably. My good resolutions produce little benefit of any sort. What with lounging at Insurance Offices, and conversation with Mr. Walsh, and reading Newspapers, and accounts now and then, I am making useless my most valuable time. Walk, after stopping at the Athenæum where I saw nothing new.

Afternoon reading Benjamin Constant. His Account of the Jewish History remarkable and not unworthy of attention. Tusculan question whether death is an evil. The elegance of the style always pleases— Even when the argument is inconclusive or the reasoning fanciful. Some of the ideas have abundant force particularly in the mouth of

the Pagan. Evening quietly at home. Finished Ennui and began Almeria. German which begins to come easier.

THURSDAY. 20TH.

It rained last night but was clear in the morning. I read some of
Constant, and went to the office. Most of my time was taken up by the
Conants who came in to settle the Lease. One of them found me more
decided than I have been accustomed to be upon the article of rent.
He brought me in his usual account for labour which I did not admit,
as the provision of the Lease was that it was not to be asked for unless
they should not clear themselves upon the farm. Hay is the great
product of the farm, and it is perfectly absurd to imagine that with
hay at its present and ruling price within the year they should not have
cleared themselves. It is true on the other hand that labour was high
and the corn failed. Yet Silas Conant did not affirm he had not cleared
himself, and his brother when appealed to was totally silent. I put
off the day of settlement by agreement to Monday.

Walk. Benjamin Constant. His book fails occasionally in interest,
and I read it at the very worst time in the day for my benefit. Cicero's
Tuscdan which as my Wife was out I continued in the evening. It is
very charming. I wish I could possess myself of half his elegance of
style. Went for my Wife at Mrs. Frothingham's. Miss Mary and Miss
Ann Dehon with their brother. The first sung several songs with little
or no expression, but as I thought, correctly, not being an exact judge.
Home at ten.

FRIDAY. 21ST.

I spent most of my morning at the Athenæum reading in the English Periodicals and amusing myself as well as I could. The English
as well as ourselves grow dismally heavy. There is nothing to do, and
no genius to produce any thing. Literature is at a stand, yet the press
groans under the efforts of the writers for bread. Walk. Benjamin
Constant after dinner, then Cicero. Evening, Almeria. My days are
monotonous enough.

SATURDAY. 22D.

A cold and very windy day, much in character with the month. I
amused myself this morning with reading Baron d'Haussez upon the

manners and Institutions of England. He treats Great Britain pretty much as Hamilton does America.[1] He pushes forward the unfavorable side. There is truth in each picture but it is overcharged.

Office. Read a good deal of Jefferson but not interesting. His early correspondence is flat compared to my Grandfather's. He had more judgment and less genius than my grandfather, yet he was less sound in his theories which is remarkable.

Walk. Dined with a party at Mr. Brooks—Messrs. Shepherd, W. Wells, Kirk Boott, G. Bancroft, Palfrey, Story, Col. Baldwin, Edward, P. C. Brooks Jr. and myself. A very handsome dinner and tolerably pleasant, but not remarkable. I returned home at sunset. Quiet evening. Finished Almeria. Read d'Haussez.

[1] On the preceding day CFA had borrowed from the Athenæum, *Great Britain in 1833* by Charles Lemercher de Longpré, Baron d'Haussez, 2 vols., London, 1833, and *Men and Manners in America* by Capt. Thomas Hamilton, 2 vols., Edinburgh, 1833.

SUNDAY. 23D.

Cool. Continued and finished d'Haussez whose book has diverted me much. He is satirical enough. He strips the glitter off English Society and exposes the nakedness as well as the pretensions which belong to it. His opinion of English women however is very flattering and perhaps not undeserved. The domestic character of the British female is unexceptionable. We are beneath them however only in one point, extent of cultivation.

Attended divine Service all day. Dr. Lowell in the morning. Psalms 55. 19. "Because they have no changes, therefore they fear not God." A very sensible practical discourse upon the vicissitudes of life, the dangers of prosperity and the probability of changes to try the Christian. Dr. Lowell has much in his favour in manner. He looks the Clergyman, which is much, and he never acts in a way unbecoming to him. Afternoon. Mr. Frothingham. Matthew 14. 25. "And in the fourth watch of the night Jesus went unto them, walking on the sea." A Sermon of beautiful phrases and generally of ideas highly refined which seldom actively interest. Mr. Frothingham used to indulge much in this style, but of late he has entered occasionally upon a bolder and a better one.

Read a Sermon of Atterbury's. Matthew 11. 6 "Blessed is he whosoever shall not be offended in me." On the incarnation of the Saviour, refuting the silly objections of the impossibility and unreasonableness of the account. Such a man of straw is hardly worthy of a blow. Evening. Read Hamilton's book on Men and Manners in America. Thomas B. Frothingham passed the evening.

MONDAY. 24TH.

Mild. Read Mrs. Jamieson's Memoirs of Female Sovereigns,[1] Christina of Sweden—A curious and interesting personage. Office. Time pretty much engrossed by the Conants who came to make a settlement. I heard no more of the claim for labour but as a silent compromise admitted an Account of Collection for about five dollars more than usual. The business was finished in the course of a short time and much to my relief.

Short walk. Afternoon wrote a letter to my Mother upon the subject of our Summer Arrangements.[2] Mr. Brooks has invited us to Medford, but our acceptance can only depend upon the probable length of the Session. Read Constant and Cicero's Tusculan Question, Nr. 2. Evening quiet at home. Madame de Fleury by Miss Edgeworth. Afterwards, German.

[1] Mrs. Anna Jameson, *Memoirs of Celebrated Female Sovereigns*, 2 vols., London, 1831, borrowed from the Athenæum.

[2] 23 March (Adams Papers); a reply to LCA's letter to CFA (19 March, Adams Papers) inviting his family to spend the summer at Quincy. The question of summer residence was left unresolved pending further word on the probable adjournment date of Congress.

TUESDAY. 25TH.

Cloudy with occasional showers of hail and rain. Read the Account of Queen Anne by Mrs. Jamieson. I was not aware before that she became latterly intemperate. Office. Mr. Walsh came in and spent much time. I therefore executed very little. Walk. Afternoon read Benjamin Constant but without that degree of attention which it requires. Continued Cicero's second Tusculan Question—Whether pain is an evil. He had too much mind to fall into the Stoic subtlety. Evening at home. Mr. T. K. Davis came in and passed an hour pleasantly. Nothing new.

WEDNESDAY. 26TH.

Cool but clear. I went to the Office after lounging some time over Mrs. Jamieson. Her account of Maria Theresa is very interesting. The Austrian Princes have seen great reverses. And even now they cannot be free from anxiety. Office. Jefferson. His Early Letters want interest.

I find only one upon the subject of the Cincinnati deserving of notice.

Walk. Afternoon, Benjamin Constant. Mr. Price Greenleaf came in and spent an hour. He had little news from Quincy excepting that the distress had extended there. I suppose we shall know more of this hereafter.

My wife and I went to the Theatre, to see Miss Kemble and her father. The piece was modern—The Wife or a Tale of Mantua.[1] It turns upon a wish to undermine a wife in a husband's affections. In order to do which, recourse is had by the villain to the force of suspicious circumstances. The result is defeated by the fact that the man selected to effect the object turns out to be her brother. Her part is not much. That of the brother is very well and Kemble performed it in his best style. We returned home early and much gratified.

[1] The engagement of Miss Fanny Kemble and her father at the Tremont Theatre had begun three days before and was to continue until 11 April. *The Wife* is by James Sheridan Knowles.

THURSDAY. 27TH.

Fine morning. I went to the Office and was occupied part of my time in Accounts and part of it in reading Mr. Jefferson's Letters, then I went to the Athenæum where I wasted time in looking over the Athenæum Newspapers and English Periodicals. They have little in them that is not flimsy and yet they amuse me.

Walk. Afternoon at home. Benjamin Constant and Cicero. Finished the second Tusculan Disputation.

In the evening, my wife and I went again to the Theatre. The Gamester [1]—Mr. Beverley by Mr. Kemble, Mrs. Beverley by his daughter. The tragedy is of the most gloomy description. An amiable but weak man led on to his own destruction by the arts of a treacherous friend who works upon his passion for gaming, first to enrich himself, next, to seduce the Wife. The performance was good. He certainly suited me better than Cooper in the same part.[2] After piece "Turning the Tables." Home rather late.

[1] By Edward Moore.
[2] CFA had seen *The Gamester* in 1825 with Thomas Abthorpe Cooper in the role of Beverly (vol. 1:437, 448).

FRIDAY. 28TH.

The season is uncommonly clear and dry. I went to the Office and occupied myself as well as I could, not however without reading Newspapers an undue portion of the time. The state of public affairs is becoming daily more critical. The Bank of Maryland has failed, and the Governor of New York has sent a Message to the Legislature which looks very much as if the Safety fund was in the most imminent danger. Yet there is not a symptom of relenting on the part of the Government.

Walk. Afternoon Benjamin Constant—The Age of Homer which he construes to please himself. Began Cicero's third Tusculan Disputation upon the Stoical doctrine of endurance. We passed a quiet evening at home quite alone. Finished Madame de Fleury. I pursued German.

SATURDAY. 29TH.

Lovely day. I was so much tempted to be out that I did not execute much at home. Walked to the Boylston Market to make up the record of the annual meeting which took an hour or two. Mr. Kirke called in to see me from Quincy. My Mother has, I presume dismissed him and he has come for his wife.[1] This will probably have some influence upon our Summer arrangements. The idea of a totally new batch of Servants is comfortless enough. I have been very much inclined to accept of Mr. Brooks' invitation for this year and yet when I reflect upon it, I scarcely know what the result would be. I never yet could get through a week there, how could I manage six months? We must await the decision from Washington. Afternoon, Benjamin Constant and German in which I think I get on. Cicero.

[1] John Kirk, the Adamses' coachman, was periodically intemperate. Mrs. Kirk regularly lived in the Old House while her husband was employed in Washington. See LCA to CFA, 19, 28 March 1834 (Adams Papers); vol. 4:330, 398.

SUNDAY. 30TH.

The Weather yesterday terminated in a shower and subsequent fall of the temperature more than forty degrees to this morning. It was today unusually cold. I amused myself with Benjamin Constant, but I think his latter volumes do not correspond to the first. They partake too much of system-mongering.

Attended divine Service on this being Easter Sunday. Mr. Frothingham was suffering from so severe a cold he could scarcely speak. His Sermon was from Hebrews 2. 15. "That he might deliver them who through fear of death were all their lifetime in bondage." Upon death, the mode in which various people view it. The fearful ideas entertained of it by Christians, more than others, and that in direct opposition to the superior hope they have through the revelation of Christ in his resurrection. This is a curious subject for inquiry and observation.

In the afternoon a Mr. Kent supplied Mr. Frothingham's place.[1] His Text was from 1 Corinthians 10. 13. "God is faithful, who will not suffer you to be tempted above that ye are able, but will with the temptation also make a way to escape." No, I am wrong. This was the subject of the Sermon by Atterbury which I read afterwards, and which I liked. His position was that temptations are always beneath the *power* of endurance, that this is proved both by experience and by reason and that it is a text full of comfort and exhortation to the Christian.

Mr. Kent's discourse was from Matthew 25. 29–30. "For unto every one that hath shall be given, and he shall have abundance: but from him that hath not shall be taken away that which he hath. And cast ye the unprofitable servant into outer darkness: there shall be weeping and gnashing of teeth." The duty of moral exertion. By moral exertion, a distinct duty is presented from the physical or intellectual efforts which are always impelled sufficiently by selfish motives. Perhaps this idea was rather developed than directly expressed. The illustrations all looked to it. The preacher was neither correct in delivery nor in style, but his substance was practical and sound. Afternoon occupied as mentioned. Evening quietly at home. Nothing of particular consequence. Mr. G. Gorham came in and passed an hour in conversation—After which I read German, and my usual occupations.

[1] Benjamin Kent had taken his degree in divinity at Harvard in 1823. His pulpit was in Duxbury (*Mass. Register*, 1833).

MONDAY. 31ST.

Fine day. I went to the Office and was occupied very busily in making up my Account for the last Quarter. This took three good hours work, and I felt glad that I had such full occupation. I accomplished the Account at the exact time I generally leave my Office for my Walk. Afternoon I wrote a letter to my father to accompany it and copied it,[1] thus forwarding the Packet today. Received a Letter from my Mother which dispirited me much.[2] She has indulged in her usual melancholy strain which has affected my Wife and me. I do not know what to do.

Postponed thinking of it for the purpose of seeing Miss Kemble in Isabella. This is a play in which Mrs. Siddons is said to have been very great, and I had much expectation raised from this fact. But I found the two first Acts decidedly heavy, and she seemed to me tame in the others. I do not admire the piece.[3] Its groundwork borders upon the ludicrous. To marry two husbands is not so very terrific an idea as to make the former one kill himself. Yet upon this expectation the whole villainy of Carlos and management of the plot depends. In short I was as much disappointed in this piece as I was more than pleased with the Gamester. Home immediately afterwards.

[1] LbC, Adams Papers.
[2] To CFA, 28 March (Adams Papers).
[3] *Isabella or the Fatal Marriage*, a tragedy built on a plot by Mrs. Aphra Behn, was adapted by Garrick from the play by Thomas Southerne.

TUESDAY. APRIL 1.

The weather was blustering with occasional rain. I went to the Office as usual and was occupied in making out a list of Stockholders of the Boylston Market for the use of the Treasurer and his semi-annual Dividend. I forgot to notice yesterday in it's proper place the meeting of Directors which I attended in the afternoon in which they declared this Dividend to be four dollars on the share and at the same time voted to go into the building of a new fish Market. This spirit is the bane of the productiveness of that property yet from the characters of the Directors and their stake in it I cannot help believing they are doing well for it. A Mr. Curtis came in to transfer some shares and expressed an inclination to sell them, upon which I made him an offer without much judgment I confess. He retired to think upon it.

I was engaged in business. Called upon Mr. P. Foster and settled with him as to the Quarterly Interest. No walk. Afternoon at home. Benjamin Constant, and Cicero's Third Tusculan. Evening to Mr. Brooks. A family party and Supper. Mr. and Mrs. Jackson, a new married pair with her Mother and Aunt.[1] Mr., Mrs. and Miss Sumner, Mr. Coffin, W. G. Brooks and wife. I was dull and did not relish it.

[1] Elizabeth, the widow of Nathan Bridge, was a sister of Mrs. Henshaw, and the mother of Susan A. Bridge, who had been married to Charles T. Jackson for just a month (*Columbian Centinel*, 1 March, p. 2, col. 6; Brooks, Farm Journal, 1 April 1834, MHi).

WEDNESDAY. 2D.

The weather cloudy and dull. I was myself in but indifferent spirits. The answer of my Mother has operated so much upon Abby that I am afraid she has undone all that I have been striving to do. She has declined her father's invitation on the ground that my friends wish her to be with them. Thus matters now stand. She has offered to spend the intervening time before their arrival with him, and his answer was not decided, but *I* thought declining.

Office. Occupied in Accounts—One or two applications on a change of Tenants in the House 23 Court Street which was much to my satisfaction. The former Tenant has not disappointed my fears. Called on Mr. Robinson at the Gas light Office to inquire into Slader's (the new applicant's) character. He gave a good one but doubted his ability to pay so heavy a rent. Afternoon, wrote to my Mother.[1] Constant and Cicero. Evening quiet at home. Read Miss Edgeworth's Dun, and afterwards German.

[1] The letter is in the Adams Papers.

THURSDAY. 3D.

This was the regular day appointed for Fast according to the custom of this people.[1] I remained at home in the morning and read Constant until the time for Divine Service when I attended and heard Mr. Frothingham from 12 Luke 19–20. "And I will say to my soul, Soul, thou hast much good laid up for many years, take thine ease, eat, drink and be merry. But God said unto him, Thou fool, this night thy soul shall be required of thee: then whose shall those things be, which thou hast provided." A very good Sermon upon the appropriateness of the occasion to the Season when man casts his seed upon the land with all the hopes and fears which necessarily belong to the support of his existence.

The day was fine. There was no service in the afternoon, owing to Mr. Frothingham's cold. I read Benjamin Constant. Walk. I was a good deal surprised to find how much changed the spirit of this Institution had become. The Streets bore far more of the appearance of a holiday and festival than on any other day in the year. The Common was crowded and the Streets filled with Coaches. There appeared to me far more of what I should consider a pleasant recreation among the people than I ever see on our Jubilee days, when there is drinking and riot but no pleasure, or cheerful appearance.

Read Cicero, finishing the third Tusculan Disputation. And to divert my mind with a little light reading, I took up the Mille et une Nuits[2]—One of the most amusing of all works. The mixture of Eastern manners with their peculiar mythology, the marvelous combining with the beautiful, the power of invention, of description and of narration make this work infinitely charming. My Wife went out to Medford with her sisters. This evening Mr. Brooks was understood to have renewed his invitation for the intervening period to the close of the Session. Read Miss Edgeworth. Mr. Degrand came in for an hour.

[1] On the observance of Spring Fast Days in Massachusetts, see vol. 3:208–209; 4:23.

[2] A set of the 6-volume, Paris, 1774, edition is in MQA.

FRIDAY. 4TH.

Fine morning. I went to the Office but not until after I had occupied myself in reading some time.

My memory is so treacherous that I forget to put things in their right places. It was not today but on Wednesday that a gentleman called upon me and spent two hours about a scheme to purchase Monticello for Mrs. Randolph.[1] He said his name was Hart from New York. He gave no account of himself but talked with the utmost freedom of all the principal persons in the Country—My friend this and my friend that. He was shrewd though exceedingly discursive in his remarks. His Account of his success and the various modes in which he had been received was laughable enough. He did not ask me to subscribe probably gathering my opinion from my conversation.

Time at the Office in Accounts. Walk. Afternoon, Benjamin Constant and Cicero. Evening for a wonder, quiet at home. German.

[1] After Jefferson's death in 1826, Thomas J. Randolph, the executor of Jefferson's will, sold Monticello to Dr. James T. Barclay in return for Barclay's properties in Charlottesville. Barclay lived in Monticello until 1834, when he sought to dispose of it. Efforts at that time to reacquire it for Jefferson's descendants failed, and it was sold in 1836 to Uriah P. Levy, then a naval lieutenant, later commodore. Levy's intent to have Monticello pass to the Nation at his death miscarried, and it remained in the ownership of the Levy family for nearly ninety years until the Thomas Jefferson Memorial Foundation was organized in 1923 to acquire it (Paul Wilstack, *Jefferson and Monticello*, N.Y., 1939, p. 213–223).

SATURDAY. 5TH.

Fine day. Office. Mr. William Spear called upon me to let me know that William Field one of the Tenants had run away from Quincy after having embezzled and forged to no inconsiderable amount. Loss to my father of half a year's Rent and House vacant. At the same time here the Tenant has gone from the House in Court Street without paying his last month's due. These are losses resulting from the state of the times. I gave Spear a general power to collect the remaining rents for fear of loss.[1]

Accounts. Walk. Afternoon reading Constant and Cicero. Mr. Brooks came in by request to see my Wife and they settled it between them that we are to go out on the tenth of May to Medford. In the mean time there seems to be a probability of the adjournment of Congress. I never was more in doubt in my life.[2] Evening quietly at home, reading Miss Edgeworth's Manœuvring and German.

[1] The defections of Field and CFA's employment of Spear in his own stead as JQA's agent in Quincy are reported in CFA to JQA, 18 May (LbC, Adams Papers).

[2] CFA reported the tentative arrangements in a letter to LCA (5 April, Adams Papers). ABA would remain at Medford in charge of Mr. Brooks' household for two months. CFA's stay was to depend upon the adjournment of Congress, he to go to Quincy whenever the family arrived.

SUNDAY. 6TH.

Fine day but cool. I attended Divine Service all day and heard Mr. Frothingham and Mr. Ripley. The first from 6. John 57. "As the living Father hath sent me and I live by the father: so he that eateth me even he shall live by me." A Sermon upon the Communion, explaining the common understanding of the words with us and the effect of them in their operation upon that ceremony. The other from 4. Amos 12. "Therefore thus will I do unto thee, O Israel: and because I will do this unto thee, prepare to meet thy God, O Israel," upon death and deathbed repentances. Mr. Ripley is no doubt a good thinker and a fluent writer, but I can never feel much pleased with his discourses, nor do I admire in any degree the sort of character which my College associations invest him with.

Read a Sermon of Atterburys. Text. Matthew 27. 25. "Then answered all the people and said, His blood be on us and our children," the curse of the Jews, its fulfilment and the justice of God seemed to be the leading topics of it. I think Atterbury's second set of Sermons not so good as the first. Indeed with the exception of a few of the first, they are all indifferent. Evening quietly at home. Read Miss Edgeworth.

MONDAY. 7TH.

Morning pleasant. I went to the Office and passed my time very easily. My office boy has deserted me and consequently half the time I make no fire. My Office is dirty and on the whole very disgusting. I wish I could make some arrangement by which to give it up, and make one at home, but this is not possible while I live in my present house.

Walk and Newspapers. Athenæum. What an idle life! After dinner finished Benjamin Constant whose book has not held out equal to my expectation. His theory is a doubtful one, but I like his incidental criticism. Cicero, fourth Tusculan upon the Passions. He argues in favor of perfect apathy, and I do not know but he may be right.

Evening. Theatre with my Wife. The Hunchback. Sir Thomas Clifford by Mr. Kemble, Julia, Miss Kemble. This piece I saw performed about eighteen months since and then gave my opinion of it in this Diary. The inferior parts were then better cast than now but Miss Vincent though thought by some equal appeared to me inferior by far to Miss Kemble. The former wanted ease, she spoke too fast, and had not so much expression. Indeed, this is the great point of the latter. Her eyes give her great power. Mr. Barry though respectable did not equal Mr. C. Kean.[1] Home. Half an hour to the Mille et une Nuits which are charming.

[1] CFA's response to *The Hunchback* by Sheridan Knowles and to its earlier performance is at vol. 4:413–414. The Kembles' engagement, announced as their "farewell," was to end on 11 April (*Columbian Centinel*, 11 April, p. 3, col. 4). CFA's final verdict on Fanny Kemble, as is suggested in the present passage, was a highly favorable one: "I cannot help thinking that with all her mannerism and affectation she has points which I have not seen elsewhere equalled" (CFA to LCA, 2 April, Adams Papers).

TUESDAY. 8TH.

Morning cloudy without rain. Went to the Office and from thence to collect Dividends. This with Accounts and lounging consumed my morning. Thomas Doyle called upon me to apply for a situation as Gardener and Coachman at Quincy. I could not give him much of an answer but promised to write to Washington and get word from there in a week.

Walk and home. Mr. Brooks and Mrs. Everett, Mr. and Mrs. Frothingham dined with us, and we had a pleasant time. I afterwards wrote to my Mother[1] and as I could do nothing, sat down to the luxury I do not often allow myself, of reading the Mille et une Nuits. I remember the Stories distinctly but I enjoy them far more than I did from the greater relish my not often reading works of a similar description gives[s] me. Evening quietly at home. Read Manœuvring and afterwards instead of German went on with the Arabian Tales.

[1] The letter (Adams Papers) is concerned chiefly with the possible employment of Thomas Doyle.

WEDNESDAY. 9TH.

Rainy morning with clouds. I went to the Office but did not spend my time to much advantage. Mr. Walsh came in and consumed an hour. I had two or three other interruptions of various sorts from Tenants and persons wishing for Houses. But nothing else particular.

The Account of the closing votes upon the Bank question came and have manifested so determined a spirit in the House of Representatives that nothing is to be done but appeal to the next elections.[1] The Country is in a bad way.

Home to dinner. Afternoon, finished the fourth Tusculan of Cicero and read the Arabian Tales. What a life of luxurious idleness mine is. Evening at home, finished Manœuvring and read German.

[1] The House of Representatives voted to concur with the recommendations of the Committee of Ways and Means that the Bank not be rechartered and that the public deposits not be restored to it (*National Intelligencer*, 5 April, p. 3, col. 4).

THURSDAY. 10TH.

Morning fine weather. I went to the Office and occupied myself as usual but not to much profit. Mr. Jones came in and paid me his Note which with other collections makes a considerable sum. The time for the payment is soon approaching.[1] I collected several of my own Dividends and found them favourable, but the account of a late loss affects very much some of the Insurance Companies in which I am interested. I imagine it will abridge my expected receipts a little. The vessel was run down at sea and was insured for more than a hundred thousand dollars.[2] To set off this, the National Insurance made a Dividend today. Walk. Afternoon, the Arabian Nights, and Cicero's fifth Tusculan. Evening my wife had been to Medford but returned late. German.

[1] That is, to Isaac Hull Adams.
[2] The ship *Pagoda* nine days out of Boston for Valparaiso with a cargo worth $100,000 was sunk by collision with the ship *William Pitt* from Liverpool on 12 March (*Columbian Centinel*, 10 April, p. 2, col. 7).

FRIDAY. 11TH.

I had one of my unpleasant headachs today. Thinking it arose from indigestion I thought I would walk it off, but I found this only made the matter worse. My day was wasted. In the Afternoon, however I took a little Carbonate of Soda and it cured me which makes me see at once my complaint is an acid stomach.

I read the Arabian Tales which are too fascinating for me to leave off and Cicero's fifth Tusculan that wisdom is happiness. A dispute of words, which would be remedied by a definition. Now, is it possible for me to say that I feel perfectly happy with a headach such as I had this morning? Let my moral qualities, my virtues and merits be what they may, there is the physical evil which prevents enjoyment.

Quiet evening at home, being unable to procure tickets for Miss Kembles farewell benefit which took place this night. Began Miss Edgeworth's Belinda which is the most sprightly of her works. German.

SATURDAY. 12TH.

A very lovely and very warm day. I could not keep much at the Office. Mr. William Spear came in from Quincy and paid me a sum of money on his Note, the counting and entering which took up much time. The present disordered state of the currency is one of the beauties of Jackson's rule, and its inconvenience is now practically felt by the increasing demands of the brokers. The public is now exceedingly interested in the results of the New York election which has been going on for three days in this week. It has been made a test by both parties, although the mere choice of Mayor is not a political question of much moment. The whole place has been given up to the most violent excitement, and bloodshed has taken place.[1] It is the first instance of popular violence we have had, but I very much fear, not the last, we shall see in our generation. My faith in a democratic government is becoming weaker.

Miss Louisa C. Smith dined and spent the day with us. I read the Arabian Nights and Cicero's fifth Tusculan. Evening, did nothing. German.

[1] For the first time the mayor of New York was to be elected directly by popular vote rather than by vote of the Council. While the Whig candidate, Thomas Verplanck, was narrowly defeated by the Democrat, Cornelius Laurence, because the Whigs elected a majority of the Council the results were interpreted in Boston as a Whig victory.

The riots and bloodshed centered in New York's 6th Ward where more than a hundred "infuriated wretches," said to be Jacksonians, stormed the anti-Jackson headquarters. "A great number of respectable citizens were knocked down and cut in a shocking manner. For a considerable time the polls were in possession of the rioters." (*Columbian Centinel*, 11 April, p. 2, col. 2; 12 April, p. 2, cols. 3–6; 14 April, p. 1, cols. 6–7; 16 April, p. 2, cols. 2–3.)

SUNDAY. 13TH.

A summer's day. I walked out upon the Common for an hour after breakfast with my Wife and child and took the benefit of the balmy air. Attended divine service and heard Mr. Walker of Charlestown preach all day from Ezekiel 18. 25. "Yet ye say, The way of the Lord is not equal, Hear now, O house of Israel: Is not my way equal? Are not your ways unequal?" He laid down the position that all sin and evil was the consequence of misconduct proceeding from the inequality of man's nature—That the Deity was the Judge but not the capricious cause. The other text was 2. Corinthians 5. 4. "For we that are in this tabernacle do groan being burdened; not for that we would be unclothed, but clothed upon, that mortality might be swallowed up of life." The nature of death. How much more influence man exerts after his death than is commonly supposed, the fear of it should not regulate the course of human action because we can look to a future state with hope and confidence. My abstract is very lame, but the preacher was eloquent and touching.

Home. Read Atterbury. Text [*blank line in MS*] A sermon to prove that Christianity must be a state of suffering, and the example of the Saviour a precept and exhortation to endure it. This is another shape of the argument in Mr. Bennets Funeral Sermon. I do not assent to it because although I cannot agree that bodily pain is consistent with happiness, yet I do maintain that happiness must arise from virtuous conduct and a virtuous mind and can spring from no other source. Quiet evening at home.

MONDAY. 14TH.

Fine day. I went to the Office and was occupied in Accounts to some extent. Conversation with Mr. Walsh and lounging at Insurance Offices. The interest taken in political affairs is now much greater here than usual and the result of the New York election though not decisive is sufficiently so to inspire confidence into the opposition forming against the Government.

Walk. P. C. Brooks Jr. dined with me and in the afternoon I went down to the Boylston Market to a Meeting of Directors but none was held. Returned home and finished the fifth Tusculan of Cicero. Evening, Mr. Davis passed an hour or two.

I received from Washington my father's speech which he did not deliver upon the subject of the Bank of the United States and Mr. Taneys reasons. He has published it nevertheless. It eclipses all other Speeches yet made, and breathes the same tone of fearless invective which has always distinguished his writings.[1]

[1] The *National Intelligencer* for 12 April printed in eighteen columns a speech which JQA had intended to deliver in the House on 4 April but had been prevented from doing by a parliamentary maneuver. It bore the title, "Speech ⟨Suppressed by the Previous Question⟩ ... on the Removal of the Public Deposites ..." and was prefaced by a statement recounting the circumstances of JQA's unsuccessful efforts to gain recognition to speak to the Resolution of the Massachusetts Legislature on the state of the currency, the removal of public monies from the Bank of the United States, and the reasons alleged in justification by Secretary of the Treasury Taney. Having been "compelled to resort to the Press, to make Public the remarks," JQA was quick to arrange for pamphlet publication as well. On the 13th he revised the text and was notified by Joseph Gales of the *Intelligencer* that an order to print 50,000 copies of the pamphlet had been received (JQA, *Memoirs*, 9:127). It was widely reprinted. The corrected printer's copy, 63 pages of text in JQA's hand and 23 pages of supplementary material partly in the hands of amanuenses, is in the Adams Papers.

TUESDAY. 15TH.

The children seem to be a little disordered which makes us uneasy and unhappy. I trust as I ever do. The day was excessively and unnaturally warm. I went to the Office. Two or three visits from Tenants &ca. I went into State Street where a meeting had been called of the people to notice the *"triumph"* in New York.[1] These things seem here to be under a species of guidance which I can neither admire nor approve. The mob seem to be acquiring an ascendency even in this most settled of grave places.

It was too warm to walk. Afternoon at home. I began Sir James Mackintosh's History of Maritime Discovery in the Cabinet Cyclopedia.[2] But my time was rather lazily spent. Evening at home till eight when we went to a small supper party at Mrs. A. H. Everett's. The persons were quite select, that is to say a compound of the most exclusive aristocracy and the most questionable people. The Sears, Thorndike, Ticknor, and the Inglises, Baldwins, J. S. Wright and J. E. Thayer—A very curious collection out of whom I knew but two or three. My evening was consequently one of the most stupid. I left in disgust and went home before the rest. It was tiresome enough.

[1] The meeting, occasioned by "the great political revolution achieved by the Whigs" in New York City, was held in State Street on the eastern front of City Hall because of a lack of capacity in Faneuil Hall, and was described as "one of the largest popular meetings ever assembled in this city" (*Columbian Centinel*, 16 April, p. 2, col. 2).

[2] The volume in Rev. Dionysius Lardner's *Cabinet Cyclopædia* was borrowed from the Athenæum.

WEDNESDAY. 16TH.

Morning fine but cool. I did intend to have started at once for Quincy but by going down to the Office and a few interruptions my time fell short so that I could only postpone to the Afternoon. Mr. Degrand called in upon business and one or two others upon various applications. Received a letter from my Mother mentioning the breaking of the Bank of Washington and the loss which would probably take place to the family—My brother being an owner of Stock in it.[1] Thus goes the world.

I rode to Quincy in the Afternoon, found the place looking much as usual—More done however, than I had expected. There was something a little cheerless in the appearance however, and I felt a failing in my interest in the place which is somewhat novel and surprised me. Perhaps it is not worth while to go far in quest of the causes of it. Gave directions and returned home by eight o'clock.

Mr. I. Barney, of Baltimore called in and spent the evening. He is here on a visit of a few days. He claims to be an old acquaintance, though I never respected him much.

[1] In reporting the failure of the Washington Bank, LCA gave Mrs. JA2's loss as $2,000; Walter Hellen's as "all or most of his inheritance"; and JQA's as "considerable" through his ownership of Franklin Insurance Co. stock, a creditor of the bank. She also reported the closing of the Farmers and Mechanics Bank of Georgetown and the Bank of Alexandria (to CFA, 12 April, Adams Papers).

THURSDAY. 17TH.

Very warm. I went to the Office. Occupied in various Accounts and lounging in the Insurance Offices reading Newspapers. The accounts are that the Patriotic Bank has stopped payment at Washington making the fourth in the District. The panic there seems to be general. Yesterday Kirk gave me a Note for $50 of the Union Bank of Georgetown which I sent on to be redeemed, today. It was a piece of imprudence in him. The people generally are the sufferers by a state of things like the present, through their ignorance. The better informed can guard against and take advantage of the distress.

Home, dinner. Afternoon, read the History of Maritime discovery and began Ovid with his first heroic epistle Penelope to Ulysses.[1] Evening quietly at home. Read part of Belinda, and German—Herder's sentimental mythology.

[1] A copy of the *Heroīdum epistolæ*, London, 1735, is in MQA along with three sets of the *Opera* of Ovid, 3 vols., London, 1815; 3 vols., Paris, 1762; and 5 vols., Oxford, 1825, two of which (1815 and 1825) were CFA's. His extensive reading in all the varieties of Ovid's works during the following months suggests that he was using one of the editions of the *Opera*.

FRIDAY. 18TH.

The thunder of yesterday chilled the air for today. I went out early and rode to Quincy. Passed the morning in superintending the garden and looking over some of my father's books and papers. Nothing material. The air was so cold that standing was not pleasant. Returned home to dinner.

Afternoon, at home read Maritime discovery, the first portion of which at least must be confessed to be dull. The author flies off to a dissertation upon the mythology of India. I sometimes wonder at the varied attainments of such a man as Sir James Mackintosh, and when I consider how little I have acquired and yet how much of my time is passed in literary occupation, I do not easily comprehend how men with four times the active occupation should have so many hundred times greater knowledge. I allow too for the difference of capacity and for the superior foundation of education.

Read Ovid's heroic, Phyllis to Demophoön. Evening at home, but my Wife having been out late on an excursion on horseback we read nothing. Afterwards, German.

SATURDAY. 19TH.

Morning Cloudy and towards night, rain. I went to the Office and was occupied in a variety of things—Accounts, calls from Mr. Spear and Thomas Doyle. The first about Quincy business, the other about his engagement as Coachman. I gave him a direction to be ready to start by Tuesday for Washington.[1] Wasted the remainder of my time. Walk, home. Afternoon, Maritime discovery, and half of an Epistle of Ovid, Briseis to Achilles. Evening quiet at home. Miss Edgeworth's Belinda and afterwards German. I am slowly going forward.

[1] Authorization to send Doyle on to Washington to accept employ as coachman had come from LCA in her letter of 12 April (Adams Papers).

SUNDAY. 20TH.

Morning cloudy after the rain but it cleared away before night. I read Basil Hall's visit to Loo Choo which I think is the most amusing of all his works.[1] He has less of the pretension of authorship and more good will to his subject which renders him extremely disposed to flatter. This sooths the pettish irritability of his natural temper and thus puts out of sight all rough and unsightly points.

I attended divine service and heard Mr. Frothingham preach all day, though without the power of clearly fixing my attention. His Texts were first from 1. Thessalonians 5. 14. "Support the weak," second from 2 Kings 2. 9. "And it came to pass, when they were gone over, that Elijah said unto Elisha, ask what I shall do for thee, before I be taken away from thee. And Elisha said, I pray thee, let a double portion of thy spirit be upon me." I must candidly confess I can say little about the discourses beyond what the Texts suggest. My mind will wander into fancies which are perhaps of very little service to any body.

Read a Sermon of Atterbury 1. Acts 3. "To whom also he showed himself alive after his passion by many infallible proofs being seen of them forty days and speaking of the things pertaining to the kingdom of God." The points discussed were three. 1. Why the Saviour remained forty days with his disciples. 2. Why he appeared only to his friends. 3. What was the employment of his time and consequent purpose of his return. I do not see that Atterbury strengthens the argument materially. When you discuss the motives of the Deity in governing the world, it is very natural, that you should be set afloat upon an unknown Sea. It is sufficient to me that the facts are duly authenticated.

In the evening I went with my Wife to spend the evening at Mrs. Frothingham's. Mr. and Mrs. Wales with their family were there and a Mr. and Mrs. Clement—She being one of the Phillipses of Andover.[2] Dry talk and return home at ten. Wrote some letters.[3]

[1] Capt. Basil Hall, *Account of a Voyage of Discovery to Corea and the Great Loo-Choo Island*, London, 1818.

[2] Phoebe Phillips, oldest of the children of Lydia (Gorham) and John Phillips of Andover, was the wife of Rev. Jonathan Clement (Henry Bond, *Genealogies of Watertown*, Boston, 1855, p. 886).

[3] One of the letters was to his mother (Adams Papers).

MONDAY. 21ST.

Cloudy with a thunder storm in the evening. I went to the Office and was tempted from thence to study General Jackson's new Protest against the usurpations of the Senate.[1] He is irritated by the vote of censure passed there and replies to them in a manner very well calculated to make the Nation awake. The paper is written with skill and ingenuity. It maintains that the Senate have prejudged his case and thereby violated their duties as final Judges in cases of impeachment, that he had a right to remove the Secretary of the Treasury and every other Officer but the Judges of the U.S., that he has the custody of the Treasury without control of the two Houses and that he is the representative of the People as contradistinguished from the Senate who do not, and who are an aristocratic body arrogating to themselves all the powers of Government. The intent of all this can hardly be misunderstood. It is a blow at the independence of the Senate, and the contest which will convulse the Nation for twelve months to come will be a final one between these two powers. The House of Representatives being divided so nearly in equal portions will not exercise much influence upon the result. Whatever it has will now be for the President. The times are growing fearful. This is a new ingredient in the political cauldron and may lead to results in comparison with which all that has gone before will be as nothing. The Country is certainly in a state of crisis.

Thomas Doyle called upon me and I despatched him to Washington. What the result of his mission will be I do not know. But I a little mistrust his capacity. Accounts and walk.

Afternoon, Maritime Discovery and the remainder of Briseis to Achilles. There is much beauty in the style of Ovid and he seems to have penetrated into the heart and been imbued with the feelings of a woman more perhaps than was perfectly appropriate. Evening at home. Miss Edgeworth's Belinda, and afterwards German.

[1] The President's Message protested against the Senate's resolutions "touching the constitutionality and expediency of the Removal of the Public Deposites ... from the Bank of the United States" (*National Intelligencer*, 18 April, p. 3, cols. 4–5). The Message itself, published simultaneously in the *Globe* with its dispatch to the Senate, was printed in the *Intelligencer* on the 21st (p. 1, cols. 1–7; p. 4, cols. 1–3).

TUESDAY. 22ND.

Clouds and chilly atmosphere. I went to the Office. Time rather wasted. Read a little of Jefferson's Letters which are not so interesting as one might expect. He seems to have been fond of the arts and desirous of introducing them into this Country, but his political ideas did not seem to obtain much more basis from the enlarged sphere in which he found himself.

Walk. I am interested in political affairs and wish I could do something in aid of the present excitement, but there are so many that I feel as if I could do but little. Why not try? and not be so confounded indolent as I now am. But I have been so indolent that I cannot wake up and so unsuccessful heretofore that I have no motive to wake up.

After dinner, Maritime Discovery and Ovid. Phædra to Hippolytus—

The shameless pleadings of criminal love. There is something disgusting in the argument and impudent in the tone which deprives the writer of all sympathy. Evening quietly at home. Belinda.

WEDNESDAY. 23D.

Day cloudy with rain. I went to the Office after reading for an hour the story of Gabriel Desodry or the Exalté a novel of Picard.[1] At Office engaged in writing and in conversation. Went to the Athenæum to get a book and from thence to the House of Mr. John Callender to see his Furniture, which is for sale. There was nothing very material. The house is purchased for Dr. Wainwright.[2] It is old fashioned, very much in the style of the two owned by my father at the bottom of the Common. Mr. Callender understood good living. He had things about him in fine condition—Not after the modern fashion but substantially good.

Home. Afternoon reading Maritime Discovery of which I finished the first volume. Ovid's Epistle Œnone to Paris. Mr. Brooks called for a few minutes. Evening, quiet at home. Belinda. I began a trial of a new Article for the Press.[3]

[1] A copy of Louis Benoit Picard's *L'exalté ou histoire de Gabriel Désodry,* 4 vols., Paris, 1824, is in MQA.

[2] The residence of John Callender, late Clerk of the Supreme Judicial Court, was at 26 Mt. Vernon Street, at the corner of Walnut Street (*Boston Directory,* 1833; *Columbian Centinel,* 24 April, p. 3, col. 5). Rev. Jonathan Mayhew Wainwright, later Protestant Episcopal Bishop of New York, was about to assume the pulpit of Trinity Church, Boston (*DAB*).

[3] The attempt came to nothing; see below, entry for 28 April.

THURSDAY. 24TH.

Fine day but cool. I went out early. Read the Newspapers and called at the Office. Then attended the Sale at Mr. Callender's for the purpose of purchasing by request of Mr. Brooks a set of China which was offered. I did not succeed but bought one or two articles for myself. This kept me until eleven and I wasted the rest of the time. This is too often my only record. Walk.

The President of the United States has sent to the Senate another Message explaining away the most offensive claim in his former one.[1] This is a curious Spectacle. The Chief Magistrate of the Nation does not know twenty four hours together what he does mean. Afternoon, I wrote busily upon my new undertaking. I do not know what the success of it will be. Probably another self delusion. At any rate it takes up my time.

In the evening, we went to the Theatre to hear Mr. and Mrs. Wood in Cinderella. The music of this piece is still charming although I have heard it so often. Mrs. Wood gives her part an effect which I have not seen equaled since Malibran. Yet some of Mrs. Austin's notes are sweeter. He is a very admirable singer although the compass of his voice is not great, and he has little or no rich melody, charming as Garcia did or the tremendous Angrisani.[2] Home late. The lower parts were performed in a very spirited manner—Although it is a little singular that there are no even tolerable voices.

[1] The supplementary Message in explanation was printed, along with an account of the debate in the Senate occasioned by it, in the *National Intelligencer*, 22 April (p. 3, cols. 2–3, 4).

[2] The adaptation of Rossini's *Cenerentola* had pleased CFA since he first heard it sung by Garcia's troupe in 1826. The singing of Manuel Garcia, of his daughter, Mrs. Malibran, and of Angrisani at that time, and of Mrs. Elizabeth Austin on later occasions, provided benchmarks for CFA against which the performances of others were customarily measured (vol. 2:54–60, *passim*; 4:ix, 263–264, 283; entries for 14 Jan., 12, 19 Dec. 1833, above).

FRIDAY. 25TH.

Cold morning. I went to the Office after writing for an hour. Time wasted in reading politics, writing Diary, Accounts and a little half hour of Mr. Jefferson's Letters. Nothing new.

Walk. Afternoon, wrote as industriously as if I was doing any thing remarkable. I find matter enough, and congratulate myself at least in this that my facility in writing does not decay for want of use. Began Beechey's Account of his Voyage through the Pacific to Behring's Straits.[1] Thus the day passed as days regularly pass with me.

Evening I accompanied my Wife to the house of the Misses Inches.[2] A small party. Tea and Ices. I found a much greater number of acquaintances than I saw at Mrs. Everett's and amused myself far more. Returned home rather late so that it was nearly twelve before I retired.

[1] Frederick William Beechey's *Narrative of a Voyage to the Pacific and Behring's Strait, 1825–1828*, 2 vols., London, 1831, was borrowed from the Athenæum.

[2] On the Misses Elizabeth and Susan Inches, see vol. 3:106–107.

SATURDAY. 26TH.

Fine day although the East wind prevailed. As I had asked a friend or two to dine with me, I was occupied first in providing the necessaries to entertain them, next in making up the party which cost me a great deal of trouble. Having delayed it so late, most persons had made their arrangements for the day. Read a considerable number of Jefferson's Letters which interested me in him somewhat. His character however is dreadfully artificial, warm words but nothing generous. The phrases always appear to outrun the man.

Walk. Messrs. T. Davis, E. Quincy, T. Dwight and J. W. Gorham dined and passed the afternoon with me. Conversation. Evening at home. I believe this is the last dinner of this description that I shall give. There is too great temptation to drink too much wine—And by barely saving appearances to escape the blame of excess, without escaping the error. In future, I shall mix a greater proportion of older persons. The conversation of convivial dinners is not overrefined, although I can boast that at my table it has never descended into coarseness. Literature and it's collateral subjects generally prevail, but it is not that which draws out the mind. Read the last Debates in the Intelligencer which are fiery enough—My father as usual in the midst of the fray.[1]

[1] The efforts of JQA to deliver a speech in the House of Representatives on 22 April are recounted in the *National Intelligencer* on the 24th (p. 3, cols. 3–4). The text of JQA's remarks, in his hand, is in the Adams Papers (8 p.).

SUNDAY. 27TH.

I both eat and drank too much for my wellbeing, yesterday. The consequence was that I did not feel in my usual good order today. My morning was taken up in reading the Exalté—An animated but rapid and rather superficial sketch of a French enthusiast placed in the midst of the scenes of the last Century towards its close.

Attended divine service and heard Mr. Frothingham all day. In the morning, a very good Sermon upon the virtues of patience. James 1. 4. "Let patience have her perfect work that ye may be perfect and entire wanting nothing." Perhaps there is no virtue which would require more of the lessons of religion than this, for a want of it very often distinguishes those who claim a very high position in the ranks of piety. Afternoon, Matthew. 10. 34, part of 35. "Think not that I am come to send peace on earth: I came not to send peace but a sword. For I am come to set at variance." This is one of those singular texts in the Bible upon which much miscon[s]truction can be put. Was it supposed that the Saviour meant that his great object in coming was to produce discord, it not only would make a startling doctrine but one entirely at war with every thing that otherwise distinguishes his character and precepts. He was looking rather to the consequences which would follow in point of fact, and which eighteen hundred years of the world have since developed. The preacher showed why the doubt that has been entertained of the benefits of the dispensation as compared with this mass of evil is groundless.

Read also a Discourse of Atterbury's. Mark 16. 20. "And they went forth and preached every where; the Lord working with them and confirming the word with signs following." The subject was miracles as being the most proper mode of spreading the truth, 1. by the common opinion of mankind respecting them, 2. by the general nature of them as evidence, 3. by the peculiar properties they possess for this purpose.

Evening quiet at home. Read the remainder of Desodry. It is an instructive book by presenting in strong contrast the two characters, one founded upon the practice of general principles without regard to system, the other upon the adoption with enthusiasm of particular theories.

MONDAY. 28TH.

Morning clear but uncommonly cold for the Season—A sharp frost. I read Helen, a novel by Miss Edgeworth. After a lapse of many years she has ventured with a new work. I am much pleased with the beginning of it and give her credit at once for maintaining her interest in the style.

Office, finished the first volume of Jefferson and was occupied with T. B. Adams' Accounts for the half year. Then a walk. Afternoon at home. Tried to work upon my new scheme but failed and concluded to give it up as a bad job. I must take Macbeth's motto and let chance crown me without my stir.[1]

Read Helen by way of relaxation from my graver studies which now turn out to have been disorganized without any sort of benefit to come from it. Evening, went down to Mr. Frothingham's where my Wife had taken tea. Mr. Brooks was there. Conversation upon the philanthropic schemes of the present day. Returned at ten.

[1] *Macbeth*, Act I, Scene iii, lines 143–144.

TUESDAY. 29TH.

Pleasant morning. I rode to Quincy. Found things much in the same State, but as there was nothing to be done, I felt my time heavy upon my hands. There is a sort of cheerlessness about the lonely appearance of an uninhabited Country house before vegetation bursts forth that discourages. And this old house without the large family which I have always seen in it, strikes me as peculiarly dismal. I have no schemes for it's improvement this year. No objects because I know not when we shall occupy it. The politics of the Country are as unsettled as ever.

Returned to town to dinner and as Abby had gone to Medford with her father, I dined at Mr. Frothingham's—Sociably and pleasantly enough. Home. Continued Beechy's narrative of his Voyage. His literary talent is not so good as that of Parry or Franklin.[1] My wife returned late. Quiet evening at home.

[1] On Sir William Edward Parry and Sir John Franklin, see vol. 4:6–7, 25.

WEDNESDAY. 30TH.

Day cloudy with heavy showers. I went to the Office and from thence to the Athenæum where I daudled away time reading little Essays in the English Periodicals of no sort of value to any body or thing. The running Literature of Great Britain is now all froth. Walk and home. Quiet afternoon. Continued and finished Helen—The interest of which story is exceedingly well sustained to the end. Miss Edgeworth is on the whole the best of novel writers because she connects a moral with her story and yet not disgusting or even fatiguing you. She goes also into the folds of the heart, exposes it's workings in the human family in their dearest domestic relations. A little too much display of reading perhaps but on the whole more diverting by its mass of happy allusion. I admire her works more than I do those of Scott. The latter had perhaps the most brilliant imagination, but he has not the pathos. Evening reading Belinda. Afterwards Göthe in the German reader.

THURSDAY. MAY 1.

A beautiful May day. I went out earlier than usual and was engaged much of my time in business affairs. Looked over my Accounts &ca. and afterwards took a walk. Nothing material took place.

Afternoon, Captain Beechey's Voyage. He seems to have been wanting in the conciliatory manners which are so necessary in a voyage of Discovery. I judge so because he gets into difficulty almost uniformly. He has contests with the natives of Easter Island, the Gambeis and the Esquimaux. He does not appear to have impressed them with a sufficient idea of his power, which is after all the only thing to keep the malicious propensities of man in subjection. He discovered but little. His merit seems to have been that of an accurate Officer. His losses by accidents amount to one eighth or ninth of the whole number of men. How will this compare with that of other Navigators?

Mrs. Adams went out to ride and did not return until late. In the evening, we went to a small family party at Mr. Josiah Bradlee.[1] It was excessively dull to me. Home at ten.

[1] Mrs. Josiah Bradlee was Nathaniel Frothingham's sister; see vol. 3:108; 4:365–366.

FRIDAY. 2D.

Morning fine although accompanied by an East wind. I rode to Quincy for the purpose of settling with Carr by his own request. But he was not ready and I lost my ride. The day was more cheerful and I therefore enjoyed it better. Looked over the garden and gave the necessary directions. Returned to dinner. My horse was not very well and I was somewhat delayed.

Afternoon finished Beechey and read Hypsypile to Jason being the sixth of Ovid's Epistles. There is too much sameness in them. All the ideas are prettily turned, most of them are feminine and appropriate, several quite pathetic but there is vastly little variety.

Evening, went to Mrs. Gorhams. A small party, very dull. Took refuge in Whist. Miss Edgeworth sneers at cards, but after all, if parties must be endured from civility why take away things which relieve the tedium. Home at ten.

SATURDAY. 3D.

Fine day. Morning to the Office. Occupied in business. Mr. Spear came in from Quincy and paid me the balance of his Note together with some other small sums. Conversation upon matters relating to Quincy affairs. Mr. Degrand came in about a transaction with the Market Bank, and I went with him afterwards to arrange it. This with my Diary completed my morning and I went to walk.

Edmund Quincy asked me to dine with him at Mr. Parker's, where he lives.[1] Nobody there but T. Davis. The wine was good. Mr. Parker was not present. He has gone to New York. There is a stiffness about a situation like Quincy's which is painful enough. He must have to put up with many things.

We left him before five and as there was only a remnant of an afternoon I proposed to Davis to take a ride. We accordingly went to the Nursery of the Winships in Brighton a place I have passed without ever visiting before. The two persons at the head of the Establishment received us very cordially and showed us the Greenhouse Mr. Cushing has been constructing for them. It is very pretty and quite expensive. We returned home by sunset. In conversation with Davis, I regretted to perceive a tendency as I thought to free opinions in matters of religion. He has been dipping into the free thinking works of the present day. This will not last long, and it is to be hoped that it should not. Young men generally have one moment of such trial. Quiet at home.

¹ Daniel P. Parker was Edmund Quincy's father-in-law.

SUNDAY. 4TH.

A fine day. I went to walk with my Wife and child before Meeting. Attended divine service and heard Mr. Frothingham from Job 29. 2. "Oh! that I were as in months past as in the days when God preserved us." The wish to go back as contrasted with that of future improvement. Psalms 92. 14. "They shall still bring forth fruit as in old age." My mind is not so settled as it was. I feel the difference more especially in the difficulty of catching the substance of these sermons. Mr. Frothingham is always refined in his speculations. He rarely writes the strait forward every day common sense which is more easily remembered from the fact of its being commonplace.

Sermon of Atterbury in vindication of the difficult passages of Scriptures. 2 Peter 3. 16. "In which some things hard to be understood, which they that are unlearned and unstable, wrest as they do also the other Scriptures, unto their own destruction." He first explains the text, next accounts for the obscurity of the passages and finally justifies the course of the Deity in allowing them. This is one of three Sermons from which I hope to get something valuable upon this interesting point. Evening quietly at home.

MONDAY. 5TH.

Morning pleasant. I was engaged for some time in disposing of the various little matters that have accumulated upon my table during the past winter. Office, where I finished the Leases which I had engaged to draw out for a new Tenant at Quincy, and read a little of Mr. Jefferson's second volume. Walk.

Afternoon. Began Mandeville's Fable of the Bees. A curious production which manifests the curious mechanism of the human mind, working to paradox as well as truth. The argument is ingenious though every thread of the web is rotten. Ovid, Dido to Æneas, not so much to my fancy. Ovid has a style which requires familiarity with it to be easy.

Evening. Theatre. A new opera, by Auber. Fra Diavolo.[1] An Italian Bandit disguised as a nobleman pursuing an English *Milord* with his Wife and plenty of Money and Jewels, travelling for pleasure. He is finally caught by stratagem. Mr. Wood was the robber. Mrs. Wood, the Innkeeper's daughter through whom the discovery takes place. The Music is lively, a little in the ballad way with occasional bursts of harmony. The Woods sing and perform almost equally well. His soft notes are perfectly enchanting, while her complete management of her voice and powerful compass give the requisite brilliancy of execution. We retired much gratified. It rained hard and we were caught. Luckily I could procure a Carriage. Home not very late.

[1] Not strictly a "new" opera, *Fra Diavolo* had been introduced in New York by Mrs. Austin in June 1833; its first appearance in the Woods' repertory was in November of that year (Odell, *Annals N.Y. Stage*, 3:624, 661). The present production promised for the first time all the original music without abridgment or mutilation (*Columbian Centinel*, 26 April, p. 2, col. 6).

TUESDAY. 6TH.

Heavy rain in the morning, and thick weather all day. I was engaged in details much of my morning, preparatory to change of residence. Took an Account of my Wine of which I have far more than I know what to do with. Arranged my papers &ca. At the office where I read very quietly some of Jefferson's Correspondence. One rigmarole Letter to a lady in the shape of a Dialogue between his head and his heart is a very curious specimen of gallantry of the heavy style.

Home. Afternoon, continued reading the Dissertation of Mandeville. As singular as any thing I ever knew. Ovid also, Hermione to Orestes. Evening finished Miss Edgeworth's Belinda. The catastrophe is disfigured by one or two awkward incidents. The idea of a girl's being in love with a picture is not a natural one. And the calm philosophy with which Belinda passes herself over from one betrothed to another, though it may be reason, is repugnant to the feelings.

My wife took tea with Miss Carter and I went in the evening. Two Miss Sigourneys from Hartford, Miss Julia Gorham and her brothers. Tedious. Returned at ten.

[*Medford*]

WEDNESDAY. 7TH.

It held up during the morning but by noon it set in as earnestly as ever and rained heavily all the rest of the day. This was peculiarly disagreeable as we had fixed upon this day for our removal to Medford. The House was in such a condition that it was deemed inexpedient to delay, although it was rather cheerless to start in such a Storm. My morning was passed in a variety of little occupations incident to this business. I saw my wife and the children fairly off in the Carriage, after which I made preparations to go myself. Mr. Brooks accompanied me. We were not materially wet. Dinner and afternoon quiet.

My arrangements could not be very methodical, and my books not being here, I was obliged to sit down with any book I could find. Took up Swift's four last years of Queen Anne. A compound of all bad passions. I wonder people admire his style so much. There is nothing in it but clearness. The graces and the virtues are all wanting. Evening got hold of a Novel, Esteban, a sort of personal biography of a Spaniard during the times of trouble. Read my Chapters of the Bible.

THURSDAY. 8TH.

Fine morning with the air mild and pleasant. I went to town accompanied by Mr. Brooks. Time occupied in commissions of various sorts. Called in at a sale of pictures,[1] from thence to my House which I found duly closed and at the office where I read a considerable part of the Report and Investigation by the Committee of the last Legislature upon the subject of Freemasonry. It is evidently from the pen of Mr. Hallett and very clear but rather dull. He often writes with spirit but not with that sort of vigor in his serious papers which makes them amusing.

Returned to Medford to dinner. Afternoon. Commenced Madame de Stael on Literature,[2] and read Ovid, Deianira to Hercules. I also took up Italian which with German I mean to make my occupation this Summer. Evening. Mirabeau, Considerations sur l'ordre de Cincinnatus, a translation of Burke's pamphlet which first attacked the order in this Country.[3] Began to feel more settled.

[1] The paintings were advertised as having been received from Antwerp and as the work of Rubens, Cuyp, Hobbema, Poussin, &c. (*Columbian Centinel*, 8 May, p. 3, col. 6).

[2] In CFA's set at MQA of Mme. de

Staël's *Œuvres complètes*, 17 vols. in 9, Paris, 1820–1821, "On Literature" is in vol. 4.

[3] A copy of the London, 1788, edition is at MQA. The author of the original pamphlet, published in 1783, was Ædanus Burke of South Carolina (*DAB*).

FRIDAY. 9TH.

Fine morning. I went to the Office after riding into town with Mr. Brooks. My time taken up for the most part in business matters. Conversation with Mr. Walsh and doing little or nothing.

Finished the Pamphlet relating to Freemasonry, in which I am a little disappointed. The refusal of the Senate to sanction a demand for the evidence defeated the Investigation. No Mason would attend or testify voluntarily thereby pretty clearly manifesting the indefensible nature of the Institution. The more I think of that question, the more I am amazed at it's character—That so much bad faith should have been found among men in the common relations of life, and that so much influence should be constantly and yet silently exerted over the Community.

Returned to Medford at noon. After dinner read Madame de Stael's book upon Literature. Ovid, Canace to Macareus—A disgusting story of incest. Ovid had no delicacy in his notions of Love. It is all desire.

SATURDAY. 10TH.

I had fixed upon this day to go to Quincy, but upon waking, I found it raining heavily which continued without intermission through the day. Consequently I sat down very quietly and deliberately to read and occupy myself at home. My time was not heavy at all. I began reading the Letters of Ortis in Italian,[1] a work of high sentiment apparently upon the plan of Werter. I do not much admire the Author's preface. My hours were divided between Mirabeau, Madame de Stael, Ovid, and this Italian, besides a Letter to my Mother which I completed and yet with nothing [in] it.[2] The air was so cold as not to make it perfectly pleasant to sit out of the reach of the fire, yet I could not very well do much in the room where the family assemble. Mr. Brooks though he has uncommon resources for a man who has led so active a life, yet flags a little. Evening quiet at home.

[1] CFA's copy of Jacob Ortiz, *Ultime lettere*, 2 vols. in 1, London, 1817, is at MQA. On its acquisition see vol. 4:278, 286.

[2] To LCA, 10 May (Adams Papers).

SUNDAY. 11TH.

Morning quite fine. Read some of Madame de Stael's fine theory of perfectability not a particle of which do I believe in. Attended divine service and heard Mr. Sargent preach all day. Psalms 126. 5 "They that sow in tears, shall reap in joy." Philippians 4. 5. "Let your moderation be known unto all men." The latter Sermon of these two was very clear in its simple way, but Mr. Sargent will not be likely to astound the world.

Read a discourse of Atterbury being No. 2 on the subject touched upon last Sunday, and following up the concluding point of that discourse, or in other words justifying the obscurity in the hard passages of the Testaments. This is a valuable subject and I think he treats it clearly.

Dr. Swan and Mr. Jonathan Brooks two Medford gentlemen took tea and passed the evening.[1] A sharp thunder storm towards midnight. I could not help moralizing a little when I was in the Meeting house today for it is some time since I was there and things look changed.

[1] On Dr. Daniel Swan, physician, see vol. 2:206; 3:163. On Jonathan Brooks, in whose visits CFA had earlier taken pleasure, see vol. 3:70, 232.

MONDAY. 12TH.

Cold, gusty day. I went to town and passed an hour there in business. Received a letter from T. B. Adams inclosing a bill in payment of his Note to me.[1] This required attention which I accordingly paid.

At ten, I started for Quincy in consequence of my being so much disappointed by the rain of Saturday. I might have saved myself my trouble on both days as the principal object I had in going was frustrated. I nevertheless saw Mr. W. Spear and transacted business with him. The remainder of the day until my time of starting to return was taken up in examining the garden and reading in the Library.

At three after dinner I set out to return to Medford which I did through the Country. I passed through Dorchester, Roxbury, Brookline, Cambridge and West Cambridge embracing the prettiest portion of the vicinity of the City. I was much struck with the great change and improvement in the appearance of things in these towns since the time when I was at Cambridge and frequented them more. The tide of wealth is certainly flowing into this quarter of the world. But in all the modern buildings I think I perceive a tendency to make things too small, which gives a contracted look to places. The Cottage form seems to be nicely calculated as our houses are to the smallest possible quantity of room.

Evening at home. I read aloud to Mr. Brooks, the speech of Mr. Clay in answer to the President's protest.[2]

[1] Letter missing.
[2] *National Intelligencer*, 8 May, p. 2, col. 1 – p. 3, col. 2.

TUESDAY. 13TH.

Quite cold and cheerless for Country life. My Wife has by imprudent exposure caught a violent cold which has fixed in her throat and makes her very uncomfortable. I accompanied Mr. Brooks to town. Received a letter upon business from my brother at Washington and was engaged in other money matters.[1] Called to see Mrs. Frothingham on some little commissions. The remainder of my morning wasted. Neither was the afternoon much better. After dinner, I rode down to see Mrs. T. B. Adams at Mr. J. Angier's and make her the payment usual in April but which from her absence was delayed. Saw Mrs. Angier and her brother Mr. Luther. Stopped about half an hour only. Then home, children and Madame de Stael. Evening, Mr. Lincoln's Speech aloud.[2]

[1] Letter missing.
[2] Levi Lincoln's speech in the House was in the *National Intelligencer*, 9 May, p. 2, cols. 1–5.

WEDNESDAY. 14TH.

Blustering, cold weather more like the month of March than May. There was a frost this morning which hazards very seriously the fruit for the year. I accompanied Mr. Brooks to town. Time taken up in various commissions, and making up my Diary and Accounts which my late absences have allowed to run backwards. Nothing new.

Surprised by the arrival of Thomas Doyle from Washington. I was at first fearful that I had sent on an unworthy character and he was therefore dismissed in disgrace. Yet I thought if that was the fact, he would hardly adventure to show himself before me. He showed me a very strong character given him by my brother John, and proceeded to explain his mortification at being dismissed to make room for a man and his Wife who were to come into the family. I was not a little mortified myself and resolved to be wiser in future. My notions are perhaps a little rigid upon these subjects, they certainly are very different from those held at Washington.[1]

Home to dinner. My wife suffers very severely from sore throat so as to make me quite anxious. The children however, thank Heaven, remain well. Madame de Stael, and Ovid, Medea to Jason. Evening. Read aloud to Mr. Brooks.

[1] The family's dissatisfaction with Doyle was owing to his incompetence as a coachman. "In every other respect he appears to be a worthy creature and had it been possible with any degree of safety to have trusted ourselves with him I should have kept him" (LCA to CFA, 17 May, Adams Papers).

THURSDAY. 15.

Weather cold and cheerless. We have frosts every morning which are likely to do great injury. I accompanied Mr. Brooks to town or rather he went with me. Time passed very quietly in reading Jefferson, whose letters as he goes on become more interesting. In one of them he gives the characters of several leading members of the Revolutionary party—My grandfather among the number, upon whom he is somewhat sharp. There is some justice however in a portion of his criticism. The letter gives some insight into the course of Jefferson's subsequent life.

Received a letter from my father giving me orders to transmit the sum of money I had nursed so carefully to pay Isaac Hull, to Washington.[1] Such is my compensation for taking care of his interest. Every thing that comes from Washington deeply mortifies me. Why should I take any pains to do any thing? Why should I not strive to turn my situation to my own account? There would be at least advantage in that? This heavy burden of debt is to continue the same.

Home to dinner. Afternoon, reading Madame de Stael, Ovid, Laodamia to Protesilaus. Evening the same. I pass about an hour of every morning reading Italian.

[1] JQA to CFA, 10 May (Adams Papers). CFA had succeeded in accumulating in JQA's account, $3,125, the sum due Isaac Hull Adams under his grandfather's will on Hull's twenty-first birthday. On 15 April JQA had written Hull at West Point (LbC, Adams Papers) offering him his choice of receiving the full sum in cash on his birthday or allowing the principal to be retained by JQA at 6 percent interest. To this Hull replied on 21 April, electing the latter with the quarterly interest to be paid to his mother. JQA carried out his wishes, executing a series of promissory notes (JQA to Isaac Hull Adams, 22 May 1834, LbC, Adams Papers). Without reference to his communications with Hull, JQA asked CFA to transfer to him in Washington $3,000 of the sum that had been earmarked. CFA expressed his regret over this course in his reply to JQA on 18 May (LbC, Adams Papers). See also JQA to CFA, 28 May (Adams Papers).

FRIDAY. 16.

Another frost and the day cold although much pleasanter than it has been. I accompanied Mr. Brooks to town, after reading an hour in Ortis, a sort of crazy book of Italian sentiment. The language is charming from its soft sounds notwithstanding. Engaged much of my morning at the house, copying a letter of mine to T. B. Adams[1] and finishing off the semi-annual Account which is on the whole a respectable one. I was also occupied in overlooking work for Agency. My Carpenter is a very clever man, but is fond of making new work when old will answer as well. Home to dinner notwithstanding a call to attend a Meeting of the Boylston Market Directors. I have got tired of this business and was elected on a tacit understanding that if not convenient I should absent myself. Madame de Stael and Ovid, Hypermnestra to Lynceus. Quiet evening. My Wife does not recover very rapidly from her cold. Mr. Calhoun's Speech.[2]

[1] LbC, Adams Papers. Lt. Adams was at Allegheny Arsenal in Pittsburgh. His reply of 25 May is also in the Adams Papers.

[2] Calhoun's speech on the President's protest to the Senate was delivered in the Senate on 6 May. It was printed promptly in several papers but did not appear in the *National Intelligencer* until 17 May (p. 2, cols. 1–5).

SATURDAY. 17.

Weather better today although still very far from warm. I went to town accompanied by Mr. Brooks. Walk to the Estate, corner of Boylston Street to examine the premises and see the necessity of repair. Concluded against any more work. The outlay is considerable already. Proper attention to an estate like my father's involves a vast deal of time requisite to be spent upon it. I take more interest in it than nine agents out of ten and yet, if I was myself the owner, I think I should improve upon my present amount. Mr. Carr came in from Quincy and made a settlement with me for his farm. I then arranged Accounts and returned with Mr. Brooks to Medford. Afternoon at home, reading Mandeville. Mrs. Palfrey and Miss Russell from Cambridge interrupted me. Ovid, Sappho to Phaon. Evening, Hume's Essays.[1]

[1] Two copies of David Hume's *Essays* are at MQA, one CFA's, 2 vols., London, 1788; one JQA's, 2 vols., Georgetown, D.C., 1817.

SUNDAY. 18.

The first day in character with the Season and very pleasant it was. I amused myself in sauntering about a little while and afterwards in reading Hume's Essays which are very interesting. His reflection and his style are attractive, though neither of them perfectly sound.

Attended Divine Service, Mr. Stetson. Prayer for Mr. Brooks upon the death of his only brother at Portland,[1] after a lingering illness which made life to him hardly desirable, and not at all to his friends. Sermon Luke 20. 36. "Neither can they die any more: for they are equal unto the angels; and are the children of God, being the children of the resurrection." This was incidental to the death of a little girl, the promising daughter of one of the parishioners, Mr. Furness. It was consolatory, in the usual course of reflection and I thought judicious and soothing.

Afternoon. 3 Philippians 13. 14. "Forgetting those things which are behind and reaching forth unto those things which are before, I press toward the mark for the prize of the high calling of God in Christ Jesus." The necessity of *future* improvement, the vanity of turning back to the past unless with some view of operating upon the future. This is the reflection of a young country but it debars one of the most pleasing though melancholy pleasures. Reflection upon the past has its pleasures instead of benefits and why should an innocent pleasure be sacrificed. Not in the spirit of repining should it be exercised, certainly, but in regret unavailing as it plainly is, or in gratification at success equally unfruitful. What is Europe with all its wealth and power, unconnected with the charm of memory. It is the same with the moral qualities of being.

Afternoon. Sermon by Atterbury. Text, the same as last Sunday and the third in the Series upon the difficult passages of Scripture. It related more especially to the last clause which states the punishment of a wrong construction of these passages. This seems hard measure, but he maintains that it applies only to the wilful who *wrest* the meaning to purposes of their own, inconsistent with the real objects of Christianity. Evening, Charles Brooks and William G., his brother, were here from Boston. These are sons of the Portland gentleman lately deceased.

[1] Cotton Brown Brooks (1765–1834).

MONDAY. 19TH.

A lovely day. I went to town with Mr. Brooks. Time taken up in some Commissions and at the House where I copied a letter to my father written yesterday and afterwards dispatched it.[1] Afterwards, Accounts. Nothing of particular consequence transpired. The probability seems now to be that Congress will sit until quite late, and very probably the family will scarcely come from Washington at all, or if a short time, not till our engagement at Medford shall be well closed.

Returned to dinner. Afternoon, a little of Mandeville, and Sappho to Phaon which I compared with Pope. Some passages seemed to me better and some poorer. But the general spirit well maintained. Evening, Hume's Essays. Tried to write a little.

¹ To JQA, 18 May (LbC, Adams Papers).

TUESDAY. 20TH.

Day pleasant although somewhat cooler. I read Italian for some time and then rode to town accompanied by Mr. Brooks. Passed some time in writing, reading from Mr. Jefferson's work and at my house. Nothing new. Returned to Medford and occupied in the Afternoon in reading Mandeville. Ovid, Paris to Helen, an epistle the authenticity of which is very much doubted. There are fine points in it nevertheless. The objection however still exists of the immoral character of the piece, an invitation to commit adultery. Evening, Hume's Essays.

We have now been two weeks at Medford and I find nothing to object to the residence except it's enervating character. I feel a languor, an inaptitude to exertion coming over me which will very probably in it's tendency be fatal to my success. I have tried to contend against [it] with some effort, but the influence of circumstances prevails. I may continue however to cultivate myself and enjoy the luxury of literature as a resource from the dangers of idleness and apathy.

WEDNESDAY. 21ST.

Very warm and pleasant day. I accompanied Mr. Brooks to town and not having much of any thing to do, I sauntered into the Artist's Exhibition for an hour. Four of the Boston Painters appear to have assumed the business of showing their works. Harding, Doughty, Alexander, and Fisher.¹ The pieces of each are of very unequal merit. Harding does not appear to me to improve. Alexander has. Fisher and Doughty being needy are obliged to paint too much for sale. Nothing that I saw counterbalanced the unpleasant feeling produced by the multitude of portraits of people who have themselves painted without rhyme or reason for the mere gratification of their beautiful selves— of this vanity comes all the support our poor artists get.

Home. Mr. Shepherd and P. C. Brooks and his Wife dined. Mr.

Stetson called in afterwards. Thus the afternoon passed and I only reviewed a little of the Epistle to Helen. Evening, Hume's Essays, and writing without profit or aim.

¹ Chester Harding, Thomas Doughty, Francis Alexander, and Alvan Fisher had recently banded together to establish at Harding's rooms on School Street an "Artist's Gallery" in which their works could be exhibited for sale. Unlike the annual exhibitions at the Athenæum Gallery, the proceeds of which were used to purchase paintings for the Gallery's permanent collection, the profits from the sale of tickets at the "Artist's Gallery" were shared among the four artists (Mabel M. Swan, *The Athenæum Gallery, 1827–1873*, Boston, 1940, p. 98–99).

THURSDAY. 22D.

Fine day but cold. I went to town with Mr. Brooks. Office. Jefferson's Journal of a Journey through the South of France and Italy. Not very interesting. House, thence idling at the Gallery and other places. My day not passed very creditably. Home in the Carriage with my Wife who was in town. Mrs. Frothingham and two children, and two children of Mrs. Everett. Quite a load and a pretty noisy one.

Afternoon. Mandeville and Ovid, Helen to Paris. A reply eminently well drawn. There is some doubt as to the original letter being of Ovid, but I think this shows his hand. Mr. Brooks was absent all day. Evening. Mr. Frothingham came out and after spending an hour, took his family home. Hume's Essay. Writing a little without aim.

FRIDAY. 23RD.

A cold, cloudy day. I accompanied by Mr. Brooks rode to town. Morning passed very quietly at my Office where I made progress in Mr. Jefferson's book. His Journal contains a good deal of interesting information upon a variety of subjects belonging to the cultivation, products &ca. of the Country he went through. Mr. T. Davis called upon me for an Autograph of my grandfather which I had promised him. He sat here conversing an hour or two.

Returned to Medford. Afternoon, Mandeville. Very drowsy. Ovid, Helen to Paris, and Leander to Hero. Evening, Hume's Essays. That on the Balance of Trade is worth considerable reflection. He rather inclines against our system of credit. And I do not know but with some justice. Hume is an agreeable writer. His thoughts are never commonplace, though not always very convincing. He gives an easy motion to his style which carries you along even when you feel disposed to withdraw your assent from the truth of his positions.

SATURDAY. 24TH.

Morning cloudy and warm. I accompanied Mr. Brooks to town. Time passed at the Office. Mr. W. Spear called and paid some money, besides discussing matters relating to Quincy. He seems likely to prove a very good Man to examine things and suggest improvements I cannot observe. I have made up the sum I expected in readiness for the 26th, Isaac Hull's birth day. But the point is lost and the money goes to pay other debts which are not calculated to relieve me from the payment of interest. Went to the House for one or two things. Return. Afternoon, Mandeville, and Ovid, Leander to Hero and the reply. Evening, Hume's Essays. A thunder shower. It is impossible to describe any thing more quiet and methodical than my present way of life.

SUNDAY. 25TH.

Morning cold and raw. The proportion has been very great of this weather during this month. The clouds seem to predominate. I read Italian before attending divine service. Heard Mr. Stetson, in the morning from Matthew 1. 21. "And she shall bring forth a son, and thou shalt call his name Jesus for he shall save his people from their sins." The mission of the Saviour, his people originally signified the Jews, but rejected by them extended to all men, who made themselves fit by a belief and practice of his commandments and in no other manner.

Afternoon. Matthew 11. 29 "Take my yoke upon you and learn of me; for I am meek and lowly in heart, and ye shall find rest unto your souls." The nature of the Communion, whether any difference is to be perceived in the injunction of Christian duty between those who partake of it and those who do not—the prevailing idea is erroneous. Notwithstanding this, I am of opinion that the Communion is a more solemn affair than all this would make it. A man is surely more criminal in violating an Oath than he is if he makes none. A man assumes a degree of virtue he is bound afterwards to sustain—the moral guilt of crime may not be greater, but the self degradation ought to be far more perceptible.

Read a Sermon of Atterbury. 2 Corinthians 13. 5. "Examine yourselves, whether ye be in the faith: prove your own selves." Subject. Religious sincerity which he considers to be proved by 1. obedience, 2. good conduct, 3. a wish to improve, 4. *private* devotion, 5. absence of interested motive, 6. self distrust, 7. Enjoyment in the study of the Scriptures. The discourse is a good one. Evening quietly at home. P. C. Hall came in for an hour.[1]

[1] On Peter Chardon Hall, see vol. 3:273.

MONDAY. 26TH.

Cold and cloudy. I went to town in the Carriage with Mr. Brooks and the two Everett children who were going home. Office where I remained very quietly reading Jefferson's Letters for the greater part of the morning. My present Life is even more monotonous than that in Boston. It is passed in riding and in study, in Accounts and in idling. I have become a mere vegetable but a very contented vegetable.

Home. Afternoon, Mandeville, and Ovid's Epistles, Hero to Leander which I read over with attention. There is so much sameness in all these that I have become pretty tired of them. It is all sugar and honey. Evening, Hume's Essays, the first volume of which I finished and began upon the other which contains the philosophical and more abstruse works. Italian with an hour of Essay writing.

TUESDAY. 27TH.

Morning cloudy with a cold Easterly wind, but it cleared away and became pleasanter in the afternoon. I went to town accompanied by Mr. Brooks. Called to see Mrs. Frothingham and from thence went round to the Athenæum where I stepped in for a moment to see the gallery. It is not so good as it was last year,[1] but will compare favorably with any other season. The proportion of good pictures is small, and I do not know that I was much struck with one of the new ones. Perhaps I may except from this remark the piece from Tristram Shandy by Leslie, and one or two copies from the old masters. Office. Nothing new.

Home. Afternoon Mandeville. Finished the Fable of the Bees. A system that recommends itself for nothing but its ingenuity. It is not worthy of an answer because it is as Hume calls it, almost a contradiction in terms. Ovid, Acontius to Cydippe—People whom I never had heard of before. It is much doubted whether the two Epistles are written by Ovid. Evening, read aloud to Mr. Brooks the report of the Committee of the House of Representatives upon the affair of the Bank.[2] Hume.

¹ The 1833 exhibition at the Athenæum Gallery had been rendered special by the importation from New York of a collection of paintings of the principal European schools exhibited under the management of an Englishman, John Watkins Brett, and referred to by his name (Swan, *The Athenæum Gallery*, p. 95–97).

² The Report of the Bank Committee appeared in the *Globe* on 24 May under unusual circumstances (*National Intelligencer*, 26 May, p. 3, col. 1). The *Intelligencer* was not able to carry it until the 27th (p. 1, col. 2 – p. 3, col. 4).

WEDNESDAY. 28TH.

Another cloudy, cheerless morning. I accompanied Mr. Brooks to town. Passed some time at the Office reading Jefferson's book and then spent an hour at the Artists Gallery. I paid some attention to the pictures of Doughty. His Landscapes are in a peculiar style and characteristic to a great degree of American Scenery. There is too much sameness in them. A sheet of Water, bright blue sky and vapoury clouds with high and peaked mountains are the main features. Most of them perfectly wild and almost solitary. He has a good deal of merit. His execution is good and his colouring though gay is not perhaps too much so for his scenes. But he wants the sunny warmth and fertile cultivation which gives one a fancy to dwell upon the spots that are represented.

Returned to Medford. Afternoon devoted to Mandeville. I felt some inconvenience from a cold. Ovid, Acontius to Cydippe and her reply which makes the last of twenty five heroic epistles. I shall be glad to get upon something of a different description, although it be only a variety of the same species. Evening, Hume's Essay upon the subject of the Human Mind. Liberty and Necessity that long disputed and never to be decided question. He defines necessity to be a power restraining human action in certain limits and is thus a Necessitarian.

THURSDAY. 29TH.

We are so accustomed to dark, cold, wet mornings now that we hardly expect any thing else. I accompanied Mr. Brooks to town. Passed part of the morning in reading, writing and Accounts, the remainder, I was at the Athenæum which is now reopened. Mr. Walsh sat some time in conversation also. Stopped in at the Gallery and was better pleased with it today than I was the other day.

Returned to Medford to dine. Afternoon, Mandeville, the first volume of whom I finished. His Essay upon Charity Schools I think has views which separated from his system may be held as true and capable of useful application. Ovid, Cydippe to Acontius. Finished it and the last of the Author's heroic Epistles. Evening quietly at home. Read Hume. The Chapter upon Miracles is one of the most ingenious pieces of reasoning I have ever seen. But it seems to me rather curious than sound as is much of the other writings of the same Author.

FRIDAY. 30TH.

Cold and rainy. I notwithstanding made up my mind to go to Quincy, which I accordingly did. The ride was a long one through the Country, but I came home by the way of the town. The moisture has given very great beauty to all the vegetation but it looks cheerless. At Quincy, found Mr. Spear, but did not find the man who was to execute the Leases. Thus my trip was wasted. Nevertheless I looked over the garden which generally looks well. The Peach trees however appear to be suffering exceedingly with some unknown disorder. Dined at Quincy, and returned. It is more than thirty miles to come and return the way I did. I had little or no time and no great inclination for occupation afterwards, but I skimmed along the pages of Horace Walpole's first volume. I read the third some time ago.[1] This being the one relating to his father's fall from power interests me much more.

[1] CFA, as he had six months earlier (see above, entry for 18 Dec. and note), had again borrowed from the Athenæum, Horace Walpole's *Letters to Sir Horace Mann.*

SATURDAY. 31ST.

Another cloudy day. I concluded to stay at home. Passed some of my time in reading Italian, then Hume, Dissertation of the passions.

Took a walk along the border of the Canal down to where it meets the road to Boston.[1] There is something exceedingly pretty and rural about it's banks which gives me a peculiar sort of pleasure. I am fond of the solitary but not the wild. I like to see the evidences of cultivation and industry but not the agents themselves.

Mrs. Gray and her daughter and son with Mrs. Hall came to dine here, and Mr. Brooks brought out with him for a few days the two eldest children of Mr. Everett. The Afternoon was consequently wasted. Evening short and I did nothing but idle over Walpole.

[1] For a description and map of the area, see vol. 3:xviii, following p. 314.

SUNDAY. JUNE 1ST.

Warmer but still cloudy and with occasional showers of rain. I passed much of my day in reading Horace Walpole with whose book I was much amused. He certainly writes with very great ease and not with the formality which is so clearly perceptible in the Correspondence of many great men. A formality which announces that the public and not any individual are addressed.

Attended Divine Service all day. Heard Mr. Stetson, all on a single Text. Acts 26. 9. "I verily thought with myself, that I ought to do many things contrary to the name of Jesus of Nazareth." Conscience, discussed as being the test of moral sensibility and the rule of judgment. He considers it as defective, brings instances in which the dictate of Conscience is not at all in proportion with the magnitude of the offence, considers it deficient as a rule of retribution in this world and thereby argues for a future state. The discussion involves the deeply metaphysical question whether there is any moral sense, or mode of distinguishing right and wrong which is not arbitrary. I do not reason upon it. I *feel* that there is.

Sermon of Atterbury upon the *Martyrdom* of Charles I. Luke 23. 28. "Daughters of Jerusalem, weep not for me, but weep for yourselves and for your children." That is, regret not his death for his sake but for the everlasting disgrace and judgments your posterity must endure. To all this, I have not a syllable to add. I do not admire Charles nor do I approve his execution. But there was no murder about it. Evening. Finished Walpole and began Brewster on Natural Magic.[1]

[1] CFA had borrowed from the Athenæum vol. 40 of Harper's Family Library containing Sir David Brewster's *Letters on Natural Magic*, London, 1832.

MONDAY. 2D.

Rode to town accompanied by Mr. Brooks. It cleared off and became a fine day. The sight of sunshine was quite a novelty. Office. Letters from Washington.[1] Congress appear likely to adjourn about the 1st of July. I wrote my Diary which had been by my absence falling into arrears a little. Artillery Election day, a holiday still kept up although deprived of many of its supports.[2] Home to dine in a high wind. Afternoon, Mandeville whose second volume appears to me to want genius and Ovid, Love Elegies—Free enough. Evening, Finished Brewster on Natural Magic. A curious work the beginning of which is better than the end.

[1] One of these was JQA to CFA, 28 May (Adams Papers).
[2] The 196th anniversary (*Columbian Centinel*, 2 June, p. 2, cols. 2, 4). For an account of the annual ceremonies held by the Ancient and Honorable Artillery Company, see vol. 3:255.

TUESDAY. 3D.

A fine day though cool and with a high wind from the Northwest. I went to town with Mr. Brooks in his Carriage and the children of Mr. Everett who return home. They are interesting. Nothing of any consequence. I was at the Office a little while and then went down to the Athenæum where I passed a couple of hours in reading the English Periodicals. An Article in Blackwood upon Lord Brougham,[1] evidently from one of the Bar who feels the effect of the Chancellor's new measures. It is difficult to draw the substance out of the mass of party violence in England. There is probably some justice in the complaints of both sides. Lounged a short time in the Gallery. This brought me to about my time to return to Medford. Mrs. Frothingham's two eldest boys went with us.

Read Mandeville after dinner, and Ovid's Elegies. There is no delicacy in the love of these. It is all sense. Evening, accompanied Mr. Brooks to his neighbor and connexion Mr. Jonathan Brooks'. Passed an hour. He was not as lively as I have known him. Home. Read two Lectures upon Political Economy by Whately of Oxford.[2]

[1] "Lords Brougham, Lyndhurst, and Local Courts," *Blackwood's Magazine*, 35:562–586 (April 1834).

[2] CFA had borrowed Richard Whately's *Lectures on Political Economy*, London, 1831, from the Athenæum.

WEDNESDAY. 4TH.

Fine day. I went to town accompanied by Mr. Brooks. Office, and to the House from whence I strolled to the Athenæum Gallery and reading room. I have got into such a habit of idling my time about that I can hardly sit down deliberately to read.

Coming into town I had a conversation with Mr. Brooks upon the subject of my Wife's fortune. He seemed desirous of knowing my feelings as to his retaining it. He offered to give it outright in some invested shape—An offer which flattered me extremely as I know he would do no such thing if he was not confident both in my honour and judgment. The best way in such cases is not to try them unnecessarily. I am satisfied that an outright grant of any invested property would scarcely give me a clear income of 6 per cent interest and keep the Capital secure in the long run.[1] I expressed my disinclination and the more strongly, as to make a difference between me and other daughters' husbands would scarcely be judicious. I mention this conversation because it gratified me with evidence that my labor for years had not been in vain.

Home to dinner. Afternoon Mandeville. Mr. Theodore Lyman called to see Mr. Brooks and took tea. Dr. Edward Warren [2] and Miss Julia Gorham also came out which prevented my reading Ovid. Mr. Lyman is old and failing. He seemed anxious to recur to old scenes but his memory did not equal his will. He is eighty one.[3]

[1] On the financial provisions which Peter C. Brooks had made for his daughters, see vol. 3:95.

[2] Edward Warren, a graduate of Bowdoin, had received his medical degree at Harvard in 1829 (*Harvard Quinquennial Cat.*).

[3] Theodore Lyman Sr., wealthy Boston merchant, a director with Mr. Brooks of the Massachusetts Society for Agriculture, and the owner of an extensive estate in Waltham, is identified at vol. 3:321 but is there partially confused with his son Gen. Theodore Lyman. His wife was a niece of the old foe of the Adamses, Timothy Pickering.

THURSDAY. 5TH.

Very unexpectedly we perceived the sky overcast this morning and it rained very heavily all day so that nobody went to town. I passed my time quietly enough. My difficulty is only in the coldness of the weather which prevents my sitting with comfort [away?] from a fire. Read German this morning, this being my month according to my plan of studying the languages alternately. Also Hume System of Morals founded upon Utility. Very questionable. Wrote part of an Essay upon our affairs. Afternoon Mandeville and Ovid. Evening, History of Maritime Discovery,[1] the early adventures in South America, very interesting, but a very black page in European History.

[1] Probably one of the three volumes on *Maritime and Inland Discovery* by W. D. Cooley in Dionysius Lardner's *Cabinet Cyclopædia* which CFA had borrowed from the Athenæum.

FRIDAY. 6TH.

Morning cloudy but it afterwards cleared a little. I accompanied Mr. Brooks to town. Nothing of material importance. Read some of Jefferson, conversed with Mr. Walsh, wrote my Diary. At Washington they have chosen a new Speaker in the place of Mr. Stevenson who has resigned.[1] The result betokens some shaking in the Councils of Washington. The Caucus system does not go down quite so easily as in the smaller limits of the State of New York. On the whole the political horizon shows some few spots of light.

Home to dinner. Afternoon, Mandeville whose book I finished. His second volume somewhat softens the intention of the Author, although it does not appear to me to deduct from its deformity. Ovid's Elegies.

He seems to have been pretty full of his desires. He reminds me of Byron, in a very different style however. Evening. Maritime Discovery. A very interesting Account of the Northern expeditions, in which so many men have lost their lives in the most fearful manner.

[1] On 2 June, following the resignation of Andrew Stevenson for reasons of health, John Bell of Tennessee was chosen Speaker of the House of Representatives (*National Intelligencer*, 3 June, p. 3, col. 4).

SATURDAY. 7TH.

Pleasant day. I rode to town accompanied by Mr. Brooks. Nothing of any consequence transpired. I was at the office sometime. Mr. Spear called in from Quincy and I settled with him for his services in collection. This was a pretty efficient measure. It secured to me a sum in a few days which would have taken me as many months and at a less price to my father. I lose something by it, but that ought not to be counted. One or two other persons called with demands after which I left town.

Edward Brooks and P. C. Brooks Jr. dined at Medford and we had a very pleasant time. I did little or nothing in the afternoon in consequence. That is an incident to a country life. Evening very quiet at home. Pursued the History of Maritime Discovery which continues to be exceedingly interesting.

SUNDAY. 8TH.

A fine day and in character with the season which has been a rarity heretofore. I passed my morning, partly in reading German and partly in Hume's Dissertation upon Morals. Attended Divine Service all day. Mr. Stetson preached. Job 27. 10 "Will he always call upon God." The character of men as manifested by his habits of devotion. The impossibility of adhering to a custom very long after the sincere desire to carry it on has ceased. The difficulty of the hypocrite. Afternoon, Mark 4. 14,15. "The sower soweth the word. And these are they by the wayside, where the seed is sown; but when they have heard, Satan cometh immediately, and taketh away the word that was sown in their hearts." The meaning of the word Satan in the passage, Sin and sinful ways. The seed is the word, the wayside, habits of inattention. Then a digression upon the habit of sleeping, and neglect of the Sermon, as well as the disposition to criticize in a literary point of view. All of which he discussed calmly and sensibly. Mr. Stetson is rather above the ordinary level of the Clergy.

Read a Sermon of Atterbury. 1. Timothy. 6. 1. "That the name of God and his doctrine be not blasphemed." Subject, Wickedness no proof against the truth of Christianity. He maintains first, that wickedness is no proof because it is not evident that there is so much of it, but if there was, it is yet no argument from its abuse 3. inferences. The argument might be summed up in the short question whether Christianity made men wicked by any thing peculiar to itself which might be pointed out.

Mr. Philip Hone from New York with his daughter Miss Hone and Niece Miss Anthon came out and took tea. I have not seen him for many years. He seems to me to have grown old and conceited.[1] Evening quiet at home.

[1] On Philip Hone, the diarist, whom CFA had last seen in 1826 in New York, see vol. 2:58–59.

MONDAY. 9TH.

A very warm day indeed. I accompanied Mr. Brooks to town. Passed my time at the Office reading Jefferson and also in the performance of several Commissions which I had been charged with. Nothing of particular interest in town. Returned to Medford to dinner. Afternoon. Continued the History of Maritime Discovery and Hume's Moral Dissertation, Utility, and not Self Love which system he combats more successfully than he builds the other. Ovid's Elegies. I do not turn my time to much profit. But the circumstances must excuse me. Evening at home. Maritime Discovery which is interesting though almost too brief.

TUESDAY. 10TH.

Warm day but not like yesterday. We are in general subject here to a rapid alternation from cold to hot without much of the middling weather which is so agreeable to the system. Went to town accompanied by Mr. Brooks. As my Office was not habitable under the process of purification I went to the Athenæum where I amused myself reading Blackwood upon Trade Unions.[1] Called for my Wife who was in town and we went to the Athenæum Gallery together. Then back to Medford. Afternoon not much employed. My place of occupation is too near the children. Read a little of Discovery, finished Hume's Moral Treatise, and two elegies of Ovid. Then took a walk with my child. Evening, read aloud to Mr. Brooks, Mr. Webster's late speech upon the Protest.[2] It is the next best thing to the reply to Hayne which he has done. Some parts are very fine.

[1] "Progress of Social Disorganization: The Trades' Unions," *Blackwood's Magazine*, 35:331–353 (March 1834).

[2] Webster's speech delivered in the Senate appeared in the *National Intelligencer*, 7 June, p. 2, col. 1 – p. 3, col. 6.

WEDNESDAY. 11TH.

Fine day. I accompanied Mr. Brooks to town and passed my time very quietly at the Office making up my Accounts which have fallen backward somewhat and writing my Diary. After which I read Jefferson, finishing the second volume of his Correspondence which embraces the period he passed in France. He perhaps enjoyed himself as much during that time as he ever did, and was probably engaged in as few bad movements. His religion seems to have been in a process of corruption at this time, and the evidence of it now and then peeps forth, but it was left for times afterwards to show it forth in all its ugliness.

Medford to dinner. Mr. and Mrs Frothingham with two children, Mr. G. M. Dexter, at dinner, and afterwards, Mr. C. A. Davis of New York, Mr. A. Belknap, a Mr. Cunard from Halifax, descended from a Philadelphia refugee, and P. C. Brooks Jr., Mrs. W. R. Gray and her daughter. These were more than enough. I dislike this influx of company. They are uninteresting people and I am in just such a position as to be "de trop" in all the companies.[1] Quiet evening. Maritime Discovery.

[1] Mr. Brooks in naming his guests offers little more by way of identification than does CFA. He does say that Mr. Dexter is "of Railroad" and gives Mr. Belknap's name as "Andrew" (Brooks, "Farm Journal"). Charles A. Davis was the business associate of Sidney Brooks (see vol. 4:147); and Mrs. W. R. Gray was the sister-in-law of Mrs. Samuel Gray, sister of Mr. Brooks. CFA's uncomfortableness in the social gatherings in Medford may have been due in part to his being essentially a stranger in a company made up otherwise of old friends and relatives, in part to political animosities generated by JQA, and in part to the absence of any persons of bookish tastes.

THURSDAY. 12TH.

Day cool and windy. I went to town accompanied by Mr. Brooks. Office. Nothing of any consequence. Read Jefferson's [Letters?]. Went to my House where I found Mrs. Fields quite comfortably settled. I presume it is rather an advantage to have a House kept open. On this principle it is that I give the use of mine to Mrs. Fields who has left us for the purpose of taking better care of her two sons. Found some books from the binder, but the last volume of the Spectator missing. Bad business. Returned to Medford.

Afternoon. Quietly at home. I could not help contrasting the pleasantness of this quiet with the disturbed day yesterday. In truth, though company is agreeable yet it is necessary that it should be of an interesting description. Hume, and Ovid and Maritime Discovery. Evening alone at home, Mr. Brooks being down in the village.

FRIDAY. 13TH.

The day was cloudy and as I had nothing to do, I concluded to remain at home. Divided my time, so that I read German, wrote[1] and began upon the life of Mr. Jay,[2] distributing equal portions to each. A peaceful and I hope not unprofitable way of consuming the morning. Afternoon, Mr. Brooks and my Wife rode to Cambridge. I was at home, read Ovid, and finished the last volume of Maritime Discovery. This is uninterrupted study to be sure. Congress have voted to adjourn on the 30th of this month and it remains to be seen what disposition must be made of the remainder of the Summer. I am fearful there will be some difficulty. Evening at home. Read the Letters of Jack Downing which are amusing enough. Mr. Davis is the author of them.[3]

[1] In the Adams Papers (M/CFA/24.3) is a draft in CFA's hand, dated 13 June 1834, "On a peculiar feature of our History as a Nation" (4 p.). CFA examines the division among Americans between those who favor a strong ruler and those who would have the power reside in the people. He states that the division has always existed in America, and probably will continue to do so. In the course of the argument, he maintains that those who champion power in the people, when elected to high office, generally find circumstances such that they must belie their theories by actions which strengthen the ruling position (i.e.

Jefferson and Jackson).

[2] William Jay's *Life of John Jay* had been published in New York in 1833.

[3] Probably, CFA was reading the *Letters of J. Downing, Major, to Mr. Dwight, of the New York Daily Advertiser* (N.Y., 1834). Charles Augustus Davis had brought them out in imitation of the letters of "Major Jack Downing," the creation of Seba Smith, which had first appeared in the *Portland Courier* and been widely circulated in the newspapers and published as a book, *The Life and Writings of Major Jack Downing of Downingville*, 1833. See DAB under Smith.

SATURDAY. 14TH.

Morning pleasant although uncommonly cool still. I went to town accompanied by Frank Frothingham who returns home from his vacation. Mr. Brooks intending to dine abroad went in his own conveyance. Morning taken for the most part at a wine sale which I attended for the purpose of procuring some for Mr. Brooks. There was a great deal of various sorts sold at reasonable prices. I bought White Hermitage and Rudesheimer. The rest of the day was spent at the Office quietly writing. Returned to Medford to dinner. In the afternoon, read part of Cowper's Correspondence as published after his death, Mr. Jay's book and Ovid. Nothing material. Evening quiet. Cowper.

SUNDAY. 15TH.

Morning clear but cool. I read German, finishing the extracts from Goethe in the reader and several of Hume's Dialogues upon Natural Religion. There is a sort of playing with truth in his writings which is not a little provoking. He seems to consider every thing as a fair subject for the reasoning powers and rather takes delight in throwing dust than clearing it away.

Attended divine service all day and heard Mr. Stetson in the morning from Romans 2. 4. "Despisest thou the riches of his goodness and forbearance and long suffering not knowing that the goodness of God leadeth thee to repentance." A sermon upon the necessity of repentance and amendment without which the goodness of God would not suffice to lead to immortal happiness. He seemed incidentally to express an opinion which was pretty decisive against the universalist doctrine. Afternoon 2. Timothy 1. 10. "But it is now made manifest by the appearing of our Saviour Jesus Christ, who hath abolished death, and hath brought life and immortality to light through the Gospel." Mr. Stetson's Sermons are very good.

Read a short one of Atterbury. Philippians 6. 1 "Work out your own salvation with fear and trembling." The fear of God a proper motive to holiness. Addressed to people who think too ill of themselves and depreciate this as their motive, when on the contrary they should regard it as a firm support and introduction to a higher feeling of love. Mr. Franklin Story, F. Gray and Mr. L. Angier were here in the course of the evening.

MONDAY. 16TH.

Heavy rain this morning so that I made up my mind very quietly to remaining at home. Read German, Muller, History of the Appenzel War which is interesting. But I find my progress exceedingly slow. The great difficulty in German is from the great number of compound words which are not to be found in Dictionaries and yet which represent shades of ideas different from any simple words. Read Hume, Dialogues upon Natural Religion. Tried to begin an Essay upon the character and influence of Mr. Jefferson but only succeeded in laying out what might be considered as the rough ground. Read some of Mr. Jay's book.

Afternoon Cowper's Correspondence. This opens to me a new view of character. It seems his morbid sensitiveness took the direction of religion. He believed himself everlastingly damned. The Deity appeared to him only as an avenger. At times this state of mind merged into insanity but it rarely rose into a better condition. Shocking enough—Yet with all this his letters and Poems show a sort of humour which betokens a mind at peace with itself and others. Flowers covering a precipice.

TUESDAY. 17TH.

Rode to town, accompanied by Mr. Brooks. Found myself in pretty active request, first by the necessity of attending to my purchase of wine, then to go to the Athenæum, then to call upon Mrs. Frothingham and then Office where I had Mrs. Relief Harris in quest of information about her claim for pension arrears.[1] Then an applicant for the office below and thus my morning passed. Out of town. Afternoon, reading Cowper which book I finished not I hope without having made some reflections of a profitable nature to myself. Poets seem to have some tendency to madness. Inspiration among savage nations is our madness. The Intellects brighten when reason fails. I accompanied Mr. Brooks to make some town visits. Mrs. Hall's, Mrs. Gray's and Mr. Stetson's the Clergyman of the Parish. We rode home.

[1] JQA had been enlisted, in the absence of a representative from her district, to present the claim of Mrs. Relief Harris, widow of Oliver Harris. CFA wrote to his father on the matter at once (17 June, LbC, Adams Papers). JQA replied that he had earlier notified her agent that the claim had been denied (26 June, Adams Papers).

WEDNESDAY. 18TH.

Very heavy rain again today. I did not stir out of the House. Read Muller and almost finished the lively Account of the Appenzel Insurrection. Then Hume whose Dialogues I finished. He was a Deist admiring to[1] exercise his capacity upon intricate subjects and scarcely possessing the foundation necessary to fix his judgment to sound conclusions. Wrote and copied a letter to my father and read a little of Jay. So much for the morning.

In the Afternoon, I read Walpole's Letters which are all of them amusing enough. He had the art of writing nothings admirably well. His life was the life of a humanist. His feelings do not appear to have been so strong as his expressions and His heart amazingly selfish. Ovid, Elegies. That upon the death of Tibullus is very pretty. Evening continued Walpole.

¹ In the sense of being pleased to.

THURSDAY. 19TH.

The day was cloudy with passing showers. I went to town in my own way. Time somewhat taken up with commissions after which I sat down and made up the record of my Diary which has been going backward this week—An inconvenience attending my absences from town. This and accounts took up my day. Returned in a shower. P. C. Brooks Jr. came out with his father. After dinner read Walpole, and Ovid.

My Wife this day received a letter from my Mother stating the probability that my brother and his family would in all probability come with her and spend the remainder of the Summer at Quincy.¹ She hints at losses of property and at our taking a separate house in case I should conclude to go to Washington next Winter. I am afraid things there are in a condition such as for a long time I have anticipated. The worst of it is that there is no remedy to that disease. A good pruning knife would have done the business long ago. The consequence of this immediate step seems to be probably to fix my family where it now is for the Summer.

¹ Letter missing. CFA, in his letter to his father of 17 June, had expressed the hope that JA2 and family would accompany JQA and LCA to Quincy as the happiest means of relieving CFA's and ABA's dilemma over their obligations both to Mr. Brooks and to CFA's parents, Mr. Brooks being particularly insistent that ABA remain with him. CFA proposed that if these arrangements could be carried out he and his family would come to Washington for the winter months.

FRIDAY. 20TH.

Morning pleasant. I went to town accompanied by Mr. Brooks who took me a long Journey round to deliver him in Chestnut Street. We did not reach it after all. In the course of it, I went into streets I had never seen before. Very good ones too.

Engaged at the Office in writing and reading. Nothing particular however. I sat down and tried to understand the science of bookkeeping according to the Italian method, but I made a very poor business of it. There is something puzzling in applying this to a small scale. Yet it is so necessary in a business community like this to be acquainted with it that on the first of July I intend to make an effort.

Home to dinner. Afternoon reading Mrs. Inchbald's Memoir by Boaden.[1] A poor thing. Ovid, Art of Love. Evening, Quarterly Review—June, a little.

[1] CFA had borrowed the *Memoirs of Mrs. Inchbald* by James Boaden, 2 vols., London, 1833, from the Athenæum.

SATURDAY. 21ST.

I did not go to town today. But Mr. Brooks and P. C. Jr. and my wife did go. My occupation was principally German, an extract from Schiller's Thirty years war which I found easy and agreeable, and an Article in the American Quarterly Review upon the Currency question[1] which required very deliberate examination. Few subjects are more intricate than the questions of political economy. We are as yet only in the infancy of the science. There has been a vast deal of superficial theory and false induction. The experiments require to be upon so great a scale that it is very difficult to observe them properly, and when observed, their correctness is endangered by the accidental occurrence of a thousand external circumstances. Life of Jay. Afternoon Mrs. Inchbald. P. C. Brooks Jr. did not return today. Ovid. Evening, Quarterly Review, very Tory, but not without a good deal of ability.

[1] "The Public Distress," *American Quarterly Review*, 15:498–531 (June 1834).

SUNDAY. 22D.

Pleasant day. I read more of Schiller which was interesting and gave me some encouragement for my German. This with a walk in the garden with the children took up my time.

Attended divine service. Heard Mr. Stetson preach all day. 1. Peter 3. 8. "Be courteous." The necessity of mild and pleasing manners to Christians not as a motive to selfish success [so much?] as to keep up the respect of the Christian character. Very good. Psalms. 77. 6. "I call to remembrance my song in the night: I commune with mine own heart, and my spirit made diligent search." The morning Sermon being upon courtesy to others, the afternoon's was upon self reflection, private thought to mould the heart and purify the affections. This was also very good.

Sermon by Atterbury—Matthew 14. 1, 2, 3, too long but relating to Herod's emotion at hearing of Jesus, from his impression it was the return of John. Subject. Conscience, its terrors, why not sometimes effective and a short admonition to his hearers. A very slight discourse. Such a one as would do injury to the reputation of many of our Clergy. Evening, a stroll along the bank of the Canal with my Wife and her father.

MONDAY. 23D.

Warm morning. Instead of going to town, I decided upon going to Quincy. I rode round the Country through Cambridge and Brooklyne and felt the fatigue more than usual. I have nothing very especial to do when I go, but Kirk and his Wife expect me out and I feel as if they may occasionally require my presence. Arrived at noon and as it was too warm to pay the visits intended I sat in my father's Library looking over his German authors and walked about the Garden. Dined and soon after started on my return to Medford through Boston. I was nearly six hours on the road this day and very much fatigued. The ride is too long for pleasure.

Abby received another letter from my Mother announcing a change of arrangement and that my brother and his Wife were *not* to come on this year at all.[1] This throws every thing up into the air again. It is a very singular feature of our family proceedings that we never know what is what.

Mr. Brooks and Abby went out in the evening but I staid at home. Mr. J. Angier and Price Greenleaf of Quincy called and I accompanied them round the garden.

[1] Letter missing.

TUESDAY. 24TH.

Morning warm but misty after which it cleared away. I went into town with Mr. Brooks. Time at the Office where I wrote my arrears of Journal which are constantly accumulating and then to the Athenæum to get Books. I looked into the English Newspapers which are quite full of notices of our affairs. They do not at all understand the action of our Government. But our troubles may have a good effect in checking the licentious tendencies in Great Britain. What is the world coming to.

In the mean time poor General La Fayette is dead.[1] His life has been a stormy one, but his character is highly honorable to him. There is no sort of guilt affixed to his public career, although he has lived in times of carnage and desolation. If he has not possessed the vigor which might have put him upon a level with Cæsar and Cromwell and Bonaparte, he has at least avoided the disgrace of their crimes. Our Country was very certainly indebted to him largely, but for its credit it may be said that it was not insensible to it. Never did man have a more splendid triumph than his tour in 1825.

Home. Afternoon, Mrs. Inchbald. Company, but I did not see them.

[1] The death of Lafayette on 20 May had been reported in the Boston press on 21 June (*Columbian Centinel*, p. 2, cols. 1–3).

WEDNESDAY. 25TH.

I remained very quietly fixed at home today. Passed my morning which went off very rapidly in reading Schiller. I accomplished ten pages being the whole of the Account of the Execution of Counts Egmont and Horn. It is easy and very interesting. This seems like progress in my German. Read also the little volume of Horace Walpole's Reminiscences,[1] a pleasant little book which I have gone over several times with much gratification. Very desultory and perhaps for that reason more agreeable to me.

Afternoon, Edinburgh Review upon the state of French Literature.[2] This and the Quarterly join in expressing their opinion of its unnatural state. The taste is for the horrible and the extravagant, for the unnatural and the infidel, for the disorganizing and levelling. Ovid, finished the first book of the Art of Love, and the first volume of my edition. Mr. Brooks dined in town. Quiet evening. Life of Mr. Jay.

[1] Borrowed from the Athenæum.
[2] Perhaps the review of *Tableau historique de l'état et des progrès de la littérature française* by Marie Joseph de Chenier in the *Edinburgh Review*, 35:158–190 (March 1821).

THURSDAY. 26TH.

Weather warm but pleasant. There was a thunder shower in the afternoon. I went to town accompanied by Mr. Brooks. Occupied at my Office in writing up Diary, then to the Athenæum and from thence to my house. Thus the time passed, then to Medford.

Afternoon, read Mrs. Inchbald's Life. A poor thing as ever was. Towards the latter part of the second volume the letters of Miss Edgeworth are introduced which are worth all the rest put together. The more I see of that lady, the more I admire her. She represents more fully the English character in its best condition than any body I know.

Ovid, Art of Love, second volume, which is prettier. One may trace in this book many of the notions which prevail with respect to women, as that deception is lawful, the modes of flattery, the excessive subjection to their will &ca. &ca. His particular fort lays in the [*illegible word*] the Grecian Mythology.[1] Nothing else material. Received a letter from my father conveying some disagreeable news respecting Joseph H. Adams.[2]

[1] Not only is the illegible word overwritten, but the sentence is probably otherwise defective.

[2] To CFA, 23 June (Adams Papers). Midshipman Joseph Harrod Adams had contracted debts and had drawn upon JQA for money. JQA, having declined to accept the draft, asks that Phineas Foster, Joseph's guardian, be approached to see if he feels authorized to order its payment. The upshot was that Foster, authorized by the judge of probate, agreed to pay the sum and asked that JQA honor the draft at maturity (CFA to JQA, 27 June, LbC, Adams Papers).

FRIDAY. 27TH.

A cool but very pleasant day with the wind from the Northwest. I accompanied Mr. Brooks to town. Office, thence to see Mr. Foster about this draught of Joseph upon my father, inquiring if he would pay it. He said he would consult Judge Leland and afterwards expressed his assent. To my House where I copied two letters to my father which took up most of my remaining time.[1]

Received a short letter from my Mother.[2] She seems to be in a rather unpleasant state of mind, about our absence. I regret it but scarcely know how to avoid giving pain somewhere. She gives more weight to Abby's inclination to stay at Medford than it deserves.

Returned to Medford. Afternoon, Mrs. Inchbald's Life which I finished without regret. Read several of Cowley's Poems, being resolved to revive my knowledge of the British Poets. Ovid also. Quiet evening.

[1] Only one letter to JQA of this date appears in CFA's letterbook. RCs of both letters are missing.

[2] To CFA, 23 June (Adams Papers).

SATURDAY. 28TH.

Pleasant morning but it clouded up afterwards. I went to the Office after carrying Mr. Brooks with me into town. My time much cut up. Attended a sale of stocks to make a purchase but did not succeed. I do not like to appear a dabbler upon so small a scale in competition with men of so much more extensive basis. Read more of Jefferson's Letters, but during the period for which he was Secretary of State, they are mostly official and uninteresting.

Return to Medford. Edward Brooks and Thomas K. Davis came out here and dined. Pleasant but consumed the afternoon. Evening I amused myself with Walpole's Castle of Otranto.[1] Political news— The battle between the President and the Senate waxing warmer. The latter have rejected the nominations of Mr. Taney and Mr. Stevenson.[2]

[1] CFA had borrowed a copy of the London, 1796, edition from the Athenæum.

[2] Although Roger B. Taney had served as Secretary of the Treasury and Benjamin F. Butler as Attorney General for more than six months by appointment of the President, he did not send their names to the Senate for confirmation until 23 June. On that day he also sent the nomination of Andrew Stevenson as Minister to England. On the next day the Senate voted to reject the nominations of Taney and Stevenson and to confirm that of Butler (*National Intelligencer*, 24 June, p. 3, col. 4; 25 June, p. 3, col. 6).

SUNDAY. 29TH.

Cloudy with a fine rain. I continue my shower baths in the morning begun in warm weather but now rather a trial. Read German. Schiller. He is on the whole rather an easy writer.

Attended divine service. Heard Mr. Stetson. James 4. 14. "Whereas ye know not what shall be on the morrow." Matthew 4. 1 and the following verses containing a history of the temptation of the Saviour. Both good Sermons.

Read a discourse of Atterbury. Acts 24. 25. "And as he reasoned of righteousness, temperance and judgment to come, Felix trembled." 3 divisions, first, the subject, *morals*, righteousness, temperance and judgment to come, second, the instrument he *reasoned*, third the effect, Felix trembled. This was a discourse of rather more value than the generality. Its practical character is one of it's merits. The necessity of moral excellence, and the use of reason are two points which can be illustrated to considerable advantage in our day.

The remainder of my day, I filled up with articles from the leading British reviews for a year or two past. Those in the Quarterly are very spirited but excessively partial and occasionally even coarsely abusive. I like to read it, while I feel at every step, as if the taste was hardly a creditable one. Rain.

MONDAY. 30TH.

Cold, cloudy morning. I accompanied Mr. Brooks to town and passed my whole morning very busily in Accounts. Drew up my Quarterly Statement for my father and prepared my own books on the system of Double Entry to make an experiment. I think I am getting a little insight into the matter. Nothing else material.

Returned and passed the afternoon in examining the Post Office Pamphlet which displays a sum of public corruption I would not have supposed possible to take place in so short a time.[1] My father's administration was attacked for its corruption by these very men. The truth was it was not corrupt enough for their taste.

Ovid. Finished the second book of the Art of Love. I long to get to something better. Evening, the Misses Brooks called. Read the Extract from Schiller's Ghost Seer in the German Reader. Very interesting.

[1] The Report of the majority of the Post Office Committee was severe in its judgment of the integrity with which the Post Office Department was administered.

TUESDAY. JULY 1.

A cloudy, cool morning. We have as yet had no summer. I went to town alone. And was very much occupied nearly all my time in Accounts. My first day of the Quarter is generally devoted to a variety of little payments which should be made. I also went to the Athenæum, and from thence to Mrs. Frothinghams. On my return transacted business with one or two Tenants and thus passed the time.

Returned to dinner. Mr. Brooks brought up his son P. Chardon with him. Afternoon read German finishing the interesting extract from the Ghost Seer. Ovid also. Evening. An article in the last number of the North American which is the smoothest piece of workmanship upon so difficult a subject as our party history, which I have seen. Alexander and Edward Everett are studious perverters of History.[1]

[1] The article in the *North Amer. Rev.*, 39:208–268 (July 1834), on "The Origin and Character of the Old Parties" was by A. H. Everett.

WEDNESDAY. 2D.

Morning rain so that I omitted my shower bath. Not however without regret as it was sultry. It cleared away so that I went to town. My time for the most part taken up with accounts, and payments.

Had a visit from Mr. New the eldest surviving son of the old barber upon whose Estate I administered.[1] He is a Sailor and appears to be a very respectable man. He intimated that he had risen to the command after long service. Yet there seemed something melancholy about him, which I could not get over. My account was briefly given and after sitting idly for half an hour, he left.

To Medford in the rain. Mr. and Mrs. Frothingham dined with us. Pleasant conversation which consumed the afternoon. Evening quietly at home. Looked over King's survey of Australia.[2]

[1] On Robert New, the father of CFA's visitor, see vol. 3:221–222; 4:77.
[2] CFA borrowed from the Athenæum, Capt. Philip Parker King's *Narrative of a Survey of the Inter-tropical Coasts of Australia, 1818–1822*, 2 vols., London, 1827.

THURSDAY. 3D.

Morning cloudy with a little drizzle. I accompanied Mr. Brooks to town and went to the Office where I passed much of my morning. Busy in Accounts although I had no visitors on the account of rent. The pressure for money is said to be considerable at which I wonder, for it seems very certain that no profits are now made upon undertakings.

We got the news today of the adjournment of Congress. A long and an interesting but not a profitable Session to the people. The struggle for victory between power and the people will now commence. But the prospect is very dubious.

Home to dinner. Afternoon reading King's Australia and the Ghost Seer the extracts of which in Follen's book I have read twice and mean to send for the book itself. I also read Ovid. Nothing further remarkable.

FRIDAY. 4TH.

This being the great Anniversary of the Nation I should have preferred to have remained quietly at Medford, but as Mr. Brooks and my Wife proposed to make a trip to Andover, I thought I would not stay alone and therefore would drive over to Quincy. Passed through town and noticed the diversified gaieties of the town. Came across the Trade's Union Procession which had a great ship upon rollers. Then a troop of truckmen in white on horseback. Then a boy's engine company. I got through all these things and finally reached Quincy. Found Kirk gone to town. This was bad but I sat down and read the Ghost Seer all day so that I made it up. Returned home. Quite fatigued. Although a novice in German, I read sixty pages of this book today.

Others were probably engaged in the noisy festivities of the day. I have no such fancies. Perhaps I am wrong. There may be public spirit in public eating and drinking and walking but I never could understand it.

SATURDAY. 5TH.

Morning pleasant but warm. I went to the Office and from thence after doing some business with William Spear who came in from Quincy I went upon several small commissions and accidentally dropped into an Auction where I purchased a shawl for my Wife taking it to be Indian Cashmere but what was my surprise on taking it out to find that it was French and that I had been imposed upon. I hardly know of any thing that could have happened in a small way, which was more mortifying. I had intended an agreeable surprise to my Wife and instead of it enjoyed a vastly disagreeable one myself. Afternoon read the Ghost Seer, and Ovid. Nothing remarkable of any sort.

SUNDAY. 6TH.

Morning at home. The weather exceedingly warm. I spent much time in reading the Ghost Seer, quite an interesting pursuit. I think in this way I shall make up my knowledge of the Language in a much more rapid manner than by a variety of short extracts in which I take no interest.

Attended divine Service and heard Mr. Stetson all day. John 11. 35. "Jesus wept." A Communion sermon upon the causes of the act described in the Text. Acts 20. 35. "It is more blessed to give than to receive." Upon the present tendencies to excessive charitable foundations where more beggars are made than are found. The discrimination of useful charities with a direct aim at the peculiar value of a Minister's fund, and the contribution to be levied for it after the Service. This was done, and with the liberality turned out tolerably.

Sermon of Atterbury. Galatians 6. 14. "But God forbid that I should glory, save in the cross of our Lord Jesus Christ, whereby the world is crucified unto me and I unto the world." Glory in the cross of Christ not in external advantages nor without purpose, but to sustain it against enemies. This is the whole substance of the Sermon.

There was company during the whole afternoon and evening. Mr.

Jon. Brooks, Dr. Swan, Mr. D. Hall, Mr. Bartlett, Col. Brooks,[1] Mr. L. Angier. Quite a number of Medford persons. The evening was warm.

[1] Perhaps Major Alexander Scammell Brooks, who did not actually become a lieutenant colonel until 1835.

MONDAY. 7TH.

Cloudy but very warm with a thunder shower in the middle of the day which did not cool the air much. I went to town accompanied by Mr. Brooks full of trouble about my shawl. Much of my time was consumed in attending to it. However by persuasion I at last induced Mr. Cunningham[1] to exert himself agreeing that if he would get me off the Shawl I would take at the same price a point Lace pelerine which he could not sell. Thus the matter was finally settled and my mind prodigiously relieved. For though I did not want the Lace, yet it is a representative of much more permanent value. It cost $200 at Brussels. No news from Washington. Returned to Medford. Afternoon German. Read Ovid also by snatches, for we had visitors. Mrs. Frothingham, Miss Wales and her brother and Mrs. Emmons. An uncommonly hot night.

[1] Joseph L. Cunningham, the auctioneer; see vol. 3:19.

TUESDAY. 8TH.

This is the first case of decided and extreme summer heat. I should not have gone to town with Mr. Brooks had I not supposed it probable that some of the Tenants might call to settle. My expectation was realized and I found I had determined wisely. Miss Oliver called. I was engaged in my Accounts much of my time. It was very advisable to keep as cool as possible. Returned to Medford. Afternoon passed as quietly as possible. Read some German and some of Ovid. Evening, it grew more sultry so that we could do nothing and afterwards, the Night was one of the hottest that I ever passed in this Climate. The same dead calm which is so often felt in Washington and leaves a man more tired in the morning than he was the night before.

WEDNESDAY. 9TH.

The perfect calm which prevailed until eleven o'clock seemed to me the most forcible example of the torrid zone I had ever perceived. I concluded not to go to town and tried to get some shade and air in the grove by the pond. But this was worse and worse. I retreated into the House and at the hour above mentioned a breeze arose which took off all oppression, leaving the atmosphere still very warm.

Read the Ghost Seer in which I made considerable progress and an article in the Christian Examiner upon the application of the Old Testament prophecies to the coming of Jesus. Liberal beyond all liberality and in my mind very abominable.[1] Mrs. Frothingham spent the day here and so did George M. Dexter who brought her out and dined here. Afternoon, Whately's Rhetoric.[2] Ovid. Evening, fine southerly breeze, but I could not read.

[1] The essay-review [by George Rapall Noyes] in the *Christian Examiner*, 16:321–364 (July 1834), of Prof. E. W. Hengstenberg's *Christology of the Old Testament, and Commentary upon the Prophecies relating to the Messiah* so inflamed feeling in the community that the charge of blasphemy was raised, and the institution of possible legal action discussed. See *Boston Courier* [semi-weekly], 10 July 1834, p. 2, col. 2. On Noyes, Harvard 1818, Divinity School 1822, see *DAB*.

[2] Richard Whately, *Elements of Rhetoric*, Cambridge, 1832, borrowed from the Athenæum.

THURSDAY. 10TH.

Very warm day although not quite so oppressive as it had been from the presence of some light, flying clouds which settled into a thunder storm, in the afternoon. I went to town accompanied by Mr. Brooks. No accounts from Washington. My time was passed at the office and in commissions part of which carried me to my house. A terribly warm walk. Took up a new book upon Political Economy I found in my office but could not read much of it. On the whole rather easy. Home. Several deaths reported to have taken place. Whately's Rhetoric and Ovid. Remedy of Love, contains at least one passage of admirable poetry and several of exceedingly pleasing character. Evening, North American Review.

FRIDAY. 11TH.

Morning cloudy and much more cool. I went to town with the idea of going to Quincy to meet my father whom I expected to see there, but upon arriving I found a letter dated at Philadelphia on Tuesday informing me of the probability that owing to the sudden illness of my Uncle Mr. Johnson, my Mother would not be able to come away for some time, so that they would not reach this quarter until the middle of next week.[1] This changed my plans and after spending my time much as usual, I returned to Medford.

Afternoon, Dr. and Mrs. Stevenson and their child called and spent the afternoon. Of course I could not do much. Read a little of the fourth volume of Puckler Muskau and found him amusing though this is the second perusal.[2] Evening quiet. Really a do nothing sort of a life.

[1] JQA to CFA, 8 July (Adams Papers). JQA had preceded LCA to Philadelphia in order to give a deposition in a suit at law arising out of the railroad accident of the preceding year (see above, entry for 10 Nov. 1833). He proposed to await her arrival in Philadelphia before proceeding to Quincy. On receipt of a letter from her written on the 10th (Adams Papers) announcing her decision to remain for some days at least with her brother, JQA resumed his journey on the 11th (JQA to JA2, 12 July, Adams Papers).

Thomas Baker Johnson's illness was of long duration. In late 1835 CFA became his agent and the manager of his funds, remaining so during Johnson's lifetime. On Johnson, see vol. 1:443; the entries for 8 Sept. 1835; 25 Feb., 19 April, 12 May 1836, below; and Adams Genealogy. A likeness of Johnson is reproduced in the present volume; see also p. xvi–xvii, above.

[2] As he had earlier (entry for 8 June 1833), CFA borrowed the *Tour in England* from the Athenæum.

SATURDAY. 12TH.

A cool day. I went to town with Mr. Brooks. At Office, where I was engaged with one or two Tenants, after which having received a Notification that I was appointed upon a Committee to make arrangements to do honor to the memory of LaFayette, I attended a meeting of the same at the Office of Mr. Austin but they being slow, I did not wait for the formation of a Quorum. This is a singular appointment from the fact that I never attend the occasions and have a very small number of acquaintances who do. My desire in similar cases is rather to go through all necessary and proper forms than to put myself at all in advance. I showed my willingness to do my part and that was enough. Attended a Stock Sale but purchased nothing.

We went out of town earlier than usual as Mr. Brooks was to have company at dinner. The Agricultural Society of which he is a Member and an Officer have a board of Trustees and these dine at each other's Houses once in each year. There being twelve, makes the dinner come monthly. In order to fill up the table, strangers are invited as guests. There were today, Messrs. J. Welles, E. H. Derby, Guild, Codman, J. Quincy Jr. and J. C. Gray, of the Society. And Messrs. Gorham, Sam. Welles, R. D. Tucker, Inches, Col. Baldwin, Rev. Mr. Stetson, Guests. Mr. Everett, Mr. Frothingham and Edward Brooks of the family. The dinner was quite pleasant and the Guests departed in good humor. Evening quiet. I could not do much so I retired somewhat earlier than my usual hour.

341

A cool, cloudy day. I read German in the morning and attended divine service where I heard Mr. Furness of Philadelphia.[1] 1 Corinthians 15. 32. "What advantageth it me, if the dead rise not? let us eat and drink; for tomorrow we die." The old subject of immortality as connected with the doctrines of the Epicureans. Acts 16. 31. "Believe on the Lord Jesus Christ and thou shalt be saved and thy house." Faith necessary to salvation. Mr. Furness is a good reader and a sensible writer, but he wants the higher attributes of Oratory.

Sermon by Atterbury. Psalms 95. 6. "O come, let us worship and bow down, let us kneel before the Lord our maker." External worship considered as a duty to God, to ourselves, and to others. By external worship is meant principally kneeling. I think it scarcely a duty for mechanically done it loses its value. Nevertheless it is sometimes very advantageous to the cultivation of feeling. Evening quietly at home. It rained heavily all night.

[1] On Rev. William Henry Furness, see vol. 2:2.

Misty and damp but it cleared away very warm by evening. I went to town with Mr. Brooks and kept myself vastly quiet at my Office. This was owing to an accident that befell my white Pantaloons which disabled me from appearing in the Street. I did not find that my father had arrived at Quincy nor had I any tidings of him. There was a call of the La Fayette Committee but I did not attend it. My morning was agreeable from it's perfect quietness.

Returned to Medford. Afternoon very warm. Read part of Whately's Logic and finished Ovid's Remedy of Love. One of the best things he has written but not without his usual admixture. Evening quiet at home but no reading from the heat. More idle than ever.

[*Quincy*]

Morning pleasant but very warm. I went to town alone, and finding that my father had really arrived at Quincy on Sunday night, after a hurried day I started for Quincy. My time was mainly engrossed by visitors. Mr. Hurlbert talking about the Lease of the House in Court Street and Isaac Hull Adams to see me.

I found my father looking very well and quite lively. We spent the afternoon in conversation about political affairs and home affairs. He explained his opinions upon various subjects. I did not find them very different from what I had anticipated. Evening passed quietly also in the same manner.

Medford

WEDNESDAY. 16TH.

A very warm day with light showers morning and evening. I was engaged to go to town, but as I did not know where to dine, and had some business in Quincy, I concluded to remain there until the afternoon.

Walked up to Mrs. Adams to settle with her as usual for the Quarter and found Louisa C. Smith and John Quincy with her. After some miscellaneous conversation she went into her private affairs more particularly connected with her unmarried daughter which were painful enough for me to hear and in which I sympathized with her more than has been customary with me in her troubles.[1] I could advise to nothing however. So much of my time was consumed there that I only had leisure to read the beginning of Goethe's Werter.[2] After dinner, I started on my return to Medford which I reached in due season and found Mr. Brooks and my Wife tired out with their day spent in the Theological Commencement at Cambridge.[3]

[1] "Elizabeth C. Adams has just returned from New Orleans and dismissed her admirer Mr. Gourgas whose conduct has been exceedingly offensive to her mother and whose reputation runs low. ... Of all misfortunes that can befall a woman I can scarce conceive of one more terrible than that of being the wife of an intemperate man" (JQA to LCA, 24 July; see also LCA to Mrs. JA2, 13 Aug.; both in Adams Papers).

[2] At MQA is JQA's set of Goethe's earlier works: *Schriften*, 8 vols., Leipzig, 1787–1790. *Die Leiden des jungen Werthers* is in vol. 1.

[3] Nathaniel Hall, Mr. Brooks' nephew, was in the graduating class at the Divinity School (*Harvard Quinquennial Cat.*).

THURSDAY. 17TH.

Morning to town with Mr. Brooks. The day was as warm as any we have had and it seemed to me as if I had not been so much called upon to be out for the whole season. I went to the House leaving my Key at home and trusting to Mrs. Fields' being there. But I found her out and had to repeat the hot walk. The transfer of some stock &ca. consumed a vast deal of time and I was excessively heated. My father also came in and called at my Office. He was to attend a meeting of the Overseers[1] and from thence go to Medford.

After a variety of occupations, I went for the Carriage, called at the State House and went in that manner to Medford barely escaping a thunder shower of some violence. There were at dinner today, Mr. and Mrs. Everett, Mr. McCracken a gentleman from New York, a friend of Henry Brooks, Edward and P. C. Brooks Jr. and Mr. Frothingham. It was tolerably and the company left us early. My father to spend the night here.

[1] The Harvard Board of Overseers met at the State House (JQA, Diary).

FRIDAY. 18TH.

A change in the Weather and much cooler. I went to town with my father in the Carriage. Time much occupied with commissions of various sorts. Called upon Col. Thayer of the Army with a Thermometer which my father was entrusted with at Washington. He has a small, pleasant house in Allen Street. My errand was to inquire if the fortifications in Boston Harbor were to be commenced immediately. He showed to me the official Letter which was pretty explicitly in the negative.[1] Thus goes the Government. A fear of a deficiency in the Revenue prompts this course.

I then joined my Wife and Mrs. Frothingham in a visit to Mr. and Mrs. Lothrop—He being now installed as Minister of the Brattle Square Church.[2] This done I was next busy in dispatching my father to Quincy after which I joined the party to dine at Mr. Frothingham's. This consisted only of Mr. Brooks, Mr. McCracken, my wife and myself. Pleasant enough. Then home to Medford. In the evening there was company. Miss Osgoods, Mr. and Mrs. Stetson and Mr. Furness and son.

[1] Col. Sylvanus Thayer, a native of Braintree, in 1833 had completed his long and distinguished term as superintendent of the Military Academy at West Point and begun his tenure as engineer in charge of fortifications at Boston Harbor entrance (*DAB*).

[2] On Samuel Kirkland Lothrop and his wife, the former Mary Lyman Buckminster, see vol. 2:262 and above, entry for 10 April 1833, note.

SATURDAY. 19TH.

Morning cool and pleasant. I went to town with Mr. Brooks. Office where I passed my time very quietly. Nothing of any particular importance. I was engaged in making up my Accounts. Conversation with Mr. Walsh &ca.

Returned to Medford. No news from Washington. The East wind made me exceedingly drowsy. I read some of the letters of Madame de Maintenon. Whately's Rhetoric, the small fragment, "Medicamina faciei" of Ovid, and some of the Life of Alexander Hamilton by his son.[1] A pretty miscellaneous collection and but little of each. Evening, Mr. Brooks, my Wife and self paying a visit or two. Mrs. Hall's and Mrs. Gray's. Return early.

[1] CFA borrowed John Church Hamilton's *Memoirs of the Life of Alexander Hamilton*, N.Y., 1834, from the Athenæum.

SUNDAY. 20TH.

Another very cool but clear day. So sudden are the changes of our atmosphere that it was now uncomfortable to be out of woollen. I read some of Madame Maintenon and of Hamilton. This is a very indifferent writer. There is labour and obscurity in it. It is also full of high party prejudice.

Attended divine service and heard Mr. E. B. Hall preach all day.[1] Malachi 1. 8. "And if ye offer the blind for sacrifice, is it not evil? And if ye offer the lame and sick, is it not evil? Offer it now unto thy governor; will he be pleased with thee or accept thy person? saith the Lord of Hosts." Afternoon 1. Corinthians 7. 31. "And they that use this world as not abusing it." Edward Hall is respectable as a preacher. He has no fine points, but he is not dull.

Read of Atterbury, from Lamentations 3. 14. "Let us lift up our hearts, with our hands unto God in the heavens." A sort of continuation of the last Sunday's showing that external worship was after all but a slight affair in comparison with the disposition to holiness without which all worship is worse than useless. A pretty good discourse. Evening quietly at home. Read Mr. W. T. Barry's Address to the People.[2]

[1] Rev. Edward Brooks Hall is identified at vol. 3:70.
[2] JA2 had sent the postmaster general's defense of his conduct in office to JQA with a letter on the 11th (JQA to JA2, 23 July, Adams Papers).

[*Quincy*]

MONDAY. 21ST.

I started for town alone this morning. Passed my time at the Office very quietly with the exception of a visit to the Athenæum. One or two Tenants called among others Mr. Hurlbert about the Lease of the building 23 Court Street. I agreed with him at an advanced rent to begin with the expiration of his present term. As a necessary consequence, I was obliged to give a warning to the present Tenants whom I am very glad to get rid of.

At noon I went to Quincy and found my father quite alone. Conversation much of the Afternoon, and I copied one or two Letters so that I only had time to read one or two of the Tristia of Ovid. There is a sickly sort of effeminacy about his thoughts and a servility even more striking than that of his brethren of the poetic brood in the days of Augustus. Yet his style has beauty and feeling. Evening quiet at home. Conversation.

Medford

TUESDAY. 22D.

I read a little of Goethe's Werter this morning before starting for town. My father's lonely situation gives me much pain as he seems to take it patiently. My mother does not talk of coming on yet[1] and I like to take no decisive step until I see the ground before me.

My arrival in town being late, I made a short stay. Mr. Thomas Davis came in and sat with me so that I did nothing. At one there being a call of the La Fayette Committee I attended. The object seemed to be merely to appoint subcommittees for the necessary arrangements. I left in the middle and returned to Medford.

Afternoon interrupted. I read some of Hamilton's book however and several of the Lamentations of Ovid. Mr. and Mrs. Everett paid an afternoon's visit here.

[1] In letters to JQA, LCA reported her inability to leave Washington because of the illnesses of her brother, T. B. Johnson, and of JA2 and his wife (JQA, Diary, 18, 21 July).

WEDNESDAY. 23D.

The weather is now very steadily cool and pleasant with cloudless days. I accompanied Mr. Brooks to town and was occupied much of my morning in business at the Office.

I had little or no interruption and had on that account some opportunity to pursue the reading of the Letters of Jefferson. Those written from 1793 onward are steeped in the very gall of party. He seems to have lost his temper and his feelings and indulges in the most ungenerous strictures upon his opponents. Even my grandfather does not escape insinuations although he affected in his case to display a moderation he certainly did not feel. The violence of both parties is to be examined narrowly by any one who wishes to form an impartial judgment and one side may correct the other.

Returned to Medford where there was company for the rest of the day. Mr. and Mrs. Frothingham dined with us, and after dinner there was Mr. G. M. Dexter and his sister Catherine, Mrs. Hall and her son Edward, and Mr. J. C. Gray. They did not go until late and I did nothing afterwards. Mrs. Frothingham staid.

THURSDAY. 24TH.

The day being cool and pleasant I thought I would stay at home. Accordingly I spent the morning down in the Grove which was cool and quiet. My occupation was so constant that I executed a good deal. Finished the Life of Hamilton, a book full of party feeling antipodal to Jefferson's, and good to read at the same time on that account. Finished Whately's Rhetoric the last chapter of which on Elocution is worth all the rest of the book. I hope I have strengthened some of my notions in case (which is very doubtful) I ever should exercise my powers. Finished also the life of John Jay. A good though rather a heavy book. He was one of the most conscientious, highminded patriots of the Revolution, and guided by a strong religious feeling which exalts him far above some of his co-temporaries. Thus the time was filled up.

After dinner, I accompanied Mr. Brooks and my Wife to Cambridge. Called upon Mrs. Parks,[1] and took tea at Mrs. J. C. Gray's. Mr. and Mrs. Lothrop there. We went into Mount Auburn which is far more tastefully laid out than I had expected. It was quite late when we got home.

[1] On Mrs. Warham Parks, sister of ABA's mother, see vol. 2:266.

[*Quincy*]

FRIDAY. 25TH.

It was quite warm again today. I went to town. Found a letter from my father for me inclosing two to be copied.[1] One of these to my brother is a little remarkable as disclosing a painful state of feeling in respect to him.[2] The prosperity of the Presidential days completely unnerved him for exertion, and the climate of Washington together with his sanguine temperament may be considered as the causes of his misfortune. This letter is an attempt to bring round a removal to this climate. Will that better the matter? There is in the Cranch and Johnson blood an apparent inactivity which has weighed heavily upon our house. If I have ⟨in any degree⟩ escaped from utter prostration it has been only through the divine goodness aiding my effort. There was a moment when I was in very great danger.

I went to the Athenæum and thence round to call for my Certificate in the Merrimack Manufactory. On my return I procured Insurance upon it at the National Office. I then rode to Quincy, dined and passed the afternoon with my father. Miscellaneous conversation. Read a little of Ovid and some of Jefferson's Letters. Mr. Price Greenleaf took tea and passed the evening. Conversation but not interesting.

[1] The letter to CFA is missing. Of the other letters JQA wished CFA to copy, perhaps as a means of informing him of their content, one was to LCA (24 July), the other to JA2 (23 July, both in Adams Papers).

[2] Writing to JA2, JQA urged that he and his family spend the remainder of the summer and the autumn in Quincy and that he give the most serious consideration to breaking up the Washington establishment and moving permanently to Quincy. For himself he proposed disposing of all his Washington property "and totally to dissolve all connections that I have in the District. ... It is doubtful whether after the close of the next Session of Congress ... I shall ever see it again." Should JA2 agree to fix his abode in Quincy, JQA proposed that he undertake the management of JQA's landed estate: "A large portion of it I intend shall pass to you or your children."

That letter and its sense of crisis were provoked by the most recent of LCA's distressed communications from Washington to JQA (16 July, Adams Papers), in which she had written:

"John has again been sorely threaten'd with loss of sight and I am convinced that it is entirely owing to the dreadfully debillitating effect of this climate. Would to God we could find some lucrative and advantageous scheme of business that would place him in a more social sphere of action. For here all his powers even his qualities are lost for the want of action.... You cannot reproach yourself in this respect as far as intention can go but assuredly there has been great want of judgment in all our plans which has caused great disappointment and I fear serious if not irremediable evils. The convenience resulting from the residence of our children in this place for political purposes has blinded us to the truth of its difficulties in so far as it regards any possibility of promoting their personal interests or the fitness of the business in which they were engaged and this has caused a lavish expenditure resulting in loss. In no way as you know have I ever been consulted or have I even participated in the settlement of my Children but it is impossible for me any longer to remain a silent spectator when I think timely and judicious exertion might save them from years of misery. You have some friends and perhaps might procure some Agency business which would furnish active occupation and a suffi[cient] degree of responsibility to ensure its performance.

"Let me entreat you carefully to deliberate on these suggestions as I really think that the perfect nonchalance exhibited by you as it regards your own affairs has the most fearful effect upon your Sons the more especially as it is a departure from the peculiar characteristic which has been a marked feature of your former life."

Medford

SATURDAY. 26TH.

An excessively hot day. After despatching my business, I returned to town. These visits are short but necessary to keep up my father's spirits which sink upon the return to quiet and solitude.[1]

At Boston I was very busy, first in Accounts, then in copying a Letter for my father to John following up the other. He wishes to bring him to settle in Quincy. I do not know but this is the only course in which he might do good.[2] But if he accepts the invitation my position is most essentially changed and many of my views disappear. Not with any great regret on my part indeed, for I can easily adapt myself to the new circumstances. My time was so much engrossed that I did not execute all my work.

Returned to Medford. Afternoon quiet. Read Puckler Muskau Volume 1 which is more German than the rest. Ovid, and Madame de Maintenon. It was so warm that I was very languid.

[1] "The thoughts of the future haunt me in my dreams; of which I had a cruel one last Night" (JQA, Diary, 26 July).

[2] In this new "supplicatory letter" (Diary, 26 July), JQA wrote: "You have met with severe disappointments, but let them not overcome your resolution or your perseverance. There are prospects incomparably more favourable for you here than any that it is possible should arise for you in Washington.... Washington is no place for enterprize. Here so long as I live and have a house over my head, it shall be yours and your children's and when I depart it may with prudence, industry, and frugality secure to you and them an independent existence.

"Here my father began his career upon nothing, he lived a long life of vicissitudes but always a life of honour, always with a modest competency.... Here he found a refuge from the Hurricane of Political conflict. I have done the same. The ruin of all his fortunes and the destruction of his family would have been inevitable after his Presidency if he had taken his residence in any of our cities. My own situation has been similar to his. My preservation from ruin hitherto has been my retirement here, and here is a last resort for my children to maintain their independence when they meet with nothing but disappointment elsewhere." (To JA2, 26 July, Adams Papers.)

SUNDAY. 27TH.

Another hot day. I passed the morning reading Puckler Muskau whose Style amuses me very much. His modes of thinking are curious, but he *does* think. Nor does he confine himself like the Duke of Saxe Weimar to follow the bill of fare of every Table d'hote he finds. The Germans are a singular people. Without much solidity in their opinions they indulge in a considerable range of thought, and combine with

349

it a sense of refined enjoyment of the essence of beauty in the world both moral and physical which makes them as writers generally pleasing, sometimes unintelligible.

Attended divine service in the morning but not in the afternoon, Mr. Muzzy of Cambridge, a young man in College with me.[1] He hit upon the same Text with Mr. Stetson's on the 6th [July:] Acts 20. 35. "It is more blessed to give than to receive." The present was a theoretical view of charity. Mr. Stetson's was a coarsely practical one. Neither of them touched upon the sources which make Charity the greatest of three with faith and hope. Neither of them considered the moral duty in its operation both on others and on one's self. It was too warm to listen well today.

Read A Sermon of Atterbury's. Psalm 57. 7 and 8. "My heart is fixed, O God, my heart is fixed: I will sing and give praise. Awake up, my glory! Awake psaltery and harp! I myself will awake right early." It was upon the usefulness of Church music, by fixing the attention and producing a proper state of feeling. One head was upon the *superior* adaptation of the music of the Church of England. And it closed with an exhortation. I once heard Dr. Kirkland[2] preach upon the same subject but his was a historical sketch of sacred music. I am much of a believer in its efficacy. Read Madame de Maintenon's Letters. And in the evening Mr. Hall and Dr. Swan were here. Conversation tedious.

[1] Artemas Bowers Muzzey, Harvard 1824, later an Overseer.
[2] John Thornton Kirkland was president of Harvard College during CFA's undergraduate years (vol. 1:12; 2:226).

[*Quincy*]

MONDAY. 28TH.

The morning was cool and clouds came up from the Eastward which soon produced a strong contrast to the yesterdays temperature. I went to town alone, and was occupied all the morning, first in a visit to my House where I put away my Certificates &ca. and then in copying for my father and writing for myself.

At noon I went to Quincy. Found my father at dinner, not expecting me much. He seemed in better spirits than he was. Conversation. In the afternoon, I finished the third volume of Jefferson. A change and a very bad change came over his spirit in 1794. His letters are after that period very full of bad passions. Read Madame de Maintenon and a little of Ovid very superficially. Two visitors were here to see my father but I did not go down. A. H. Everett and B. F. Hallett. Quiet evening.

TUESDAY. 29TH.

Another cool morning. I remained here doubtful about returning in the afternoon when a heavy thunder shower came up and settled the question. Our day was quiet and uninterrupted. I read Madame de Maintenon and a little of Goethe besides Ovid.

Had some conversation with my father respecting his situation and my brother John's. He talked very fully and materially altered the impressions I had previously obtained. Perhaps there is no better subject for constant reflection to me, than the history of our family from the middle of the last Century, and it may profitably extend itself into all the branches. *My* duties are fearfully heavy. The continuation of the respectability of our name depends much upon me and its distinction entirely. I feel myself unlikely to do much for the latter. My habits are too speculative, my feelings not at all inclined to court the public gale. In all these reflections, I have only to sustain my courage the idea that I have been much blessed by the goodness of the Deity hitherto, and a consequent hope that he will continue the same in future. What a fallible creature is man, and how much he needs protection from himself as well as from others!

[*Medford*]

WEDNESDAY. 30TH.

Fine day. I arose and immediately after breakfast returned to Boston. Passed my morning very quietly at the Office writing and making up Accounts. There is no time flies so fast with me as the morning and yet there is none in which I do so little.

Returned to Medford at noon. Found my Wife with Mr. and Mrs. Frothingham, and soon after came Mr. R. D. Shepherd and a Mr. Harrison from Louisiana, a relation of Gorham Brooks' partner at Baltimore. The dinner was dull, and I felt very dull myself. So that I did hardly anything for the afternoon.

As Mr. Brooks and Abby went out in the evening, I made up a little of my allowance of Ovid and read some German—Part of one of Augustus Lafontaine's familiar Historys in German.[1] Also two Cantos of Chaucer's Knight's Tale modernized by Dryden.

[1] CFA was to use the novels of August Heinrich Julius Lafontaine (1759–1831) for his German studies during the remainder of 1834, and in 1835 as well. Two sets of his *Familien Geschichten*, one in 2 vols., Berlin, 1797, the other in 8 vols., Berlin, 1800–1801, are at MQA.

Quincy

THURSDAY. 31ST.

I came into town with Mr. Brooks and found my father at the Office when I got there. He had made such arrangements as necessitated my going to Quincy with him in the evening. Much of my morning was passed at the Athenæum in reading a new book upon Railroads that struck me very much. If the statements of the Author whose name is Grahame are true, Railroads must cease to be private property.[1]

I went into the Athenæum Gallery and saw two marble busts, one of Mr. Webster and the other of Mr. Bowditch, by Frazee of New York.[2] They are certainly admirable. I think far superior to any thing of Greenough's excepting perhaps the bust of Mr. Quincy. I do not speak of his works of imagination.

My father returned to the office from a meeting of the Overseers of Harvard University. He seemed unwell and out of spirits. He complained of head ache and resumed the conversation of the other day.[3] I shall have to reflect well upon my course in this matter, and especially refrain from the expression of individual opinion.

I went over to Charlestown and dined with Mr. Everett. Nobody but Mr. Brooks and myself. The dinner was not pleasant. I *cannot* like that gentleman. My efforts have been great and they have been perpetually defeated. His public popularity is to me unaccountable.

Returned to town to ascertain the arrival of the mail and with it my father's horses and carriage which had been sent to Dedham for the contingency of my Mother's arrival and if she did not come, to return to town. I saw nothing of them so that at seven o'clock I hired a Chaise to take my father who had dined at Dr. Parkman's to Quincy.

In the interval however, I observed the ascension of Mr. C. F. Durant in a balloon. He rose from the bottom of the Common at about 6 o'clock and moved rapidly to the North East gradually rising until he appeared like a mere speck in the horizon. The day was so clear that it was a beautiful spectacle and the whole town and it's vicinity were alive to witness it.[4] Such is the daring of man in pursuit of mere pelf, for the idea of philosophical advancement is pretty nearly given up. He was last visible directly over the Ocean. Evening fine. I arrived at Quincy at nine but no horses or carriage there.

¹ Perhaps Thomas Grahame's *Treatise on Internal Intercourse and Communication in Civilized States*, London, 1834.

² The marble busts of Webster and Nathaniel Bowditch by John Frazee were the first of seven for which he was commissioned by the Athenæum between 1833 and 1835 and which remain there. Frazee, originally a stone-cutter, at about the time of his sculptural commissions became the architect of the New York Custom House (Mabel M. Swan, *The Athenæum Gallery, 1827–1873*, Boston, 1940, p. 143–147;

Groce and Wallace, *Dict. Amer. Artists*).

³ Probably that in regard to JA2 on the 29th. JQA recorded in his journal: "I was very unwell almost the whole day, with a severe feverish headache, and a load upon the Spirits, almost beyond my strength to bear" (31 July).

⁴ JQA and the guests at Dr. George Parkman's dinner rose from the dessert to witness the event from the top of the house (JQA, Diary, 31 July). A contemporary print of the ascension appears in the present volume; see also p. xix–xx.

Medford

FRIDAY. AUGUST 1ST.

I returned to town this morning and found Wilson with the Carriage there. He had come in before I left town but gone to another Stable so that he missed me and waited for orders until this morning. At Office I found Mr. T. K. Davis and Mr. Walsh and we sat conversing for some time so that I had only leisure to do my writing labor.

We hear of Mr. Durant this morning, that he was picked up in the bay near seven last evening. He was in the water a considerable time but not injured. I am glad of it and yet such wantonness deserves little sympathy.¹

Returned to Medford. Afternoon pretty quiet. I read the beginning of Lord Nugents Life of John Hampden.² Also finished the second book of the Lamentations of Ovid. His defence is a pretty ingenious one and leaves it to be supposed that the other incident to which he barely alludes was the true moving cause of his banishment. Miss Gray and her brother Francis were here to tea. He sails for Russia in a day or two. German.

¹ The rescue won JQA's comments also: "I rejoice to hear that Durant was saved. It made my heart ache when I saw him suspended between Earth and Heaven, to think how needlessly men will be prodigal of Life, and how wan-

tonly they will defy the Laws of Nature" (to CFA, 1 Aug., Adams Papers).

² CFA borrowed G. N. T. Grenville, Baron Nugent's *Memorials of John Hampden*, 2 vols., London, 1832, from the Athenæum.

SATURDAY. 2D.

Pleasant morning. I went to town accompanied by Mr. Brooks. Received a letter from my father¹ stating that my Mother had not yet arrived so that I remained in town. Time taken up at the Office in Accounts. Looked over and summed up my general expense for the fifth year of my marriage and found it exceeded any preceding one in a ratio of nearly one third. This is large but not in proportion to the rate of the other side. Thus far I have been exceedingly fortunate in my private affairs. Conversation with Mr. Walsh. Rather idle.

Returned to Medford. Afternoon, I could do little on account of visitors. Mr. and Mrs. Everett, and T. K. Davis, W. E. Payne and Edward Blake. The influx of people here upon Summer Afternoons is such that my time is rarely at my own disposal. My views of self improvement are perpetually disappointed and I believe I go backward rather than forward. Evening, went to Mrs. Gray's with my Wife and Mr. Brooks. He sails tomorrow,[2] wind and weather permitting.

[1] 1 Aug. (Adams Papers).
[2] That is, Francis A. Gray.

SUNDAY. 3D.

Morning hazy with a warm day. I amused myself reading German for some time. I find I make progress in the particular book which I read without however being at all able to understand any other I happen by chance to open. Read a few of the Letters of Madame de Maintenon and some of the Life of Hampden.

Attended divine Service all day and heard a discourse running through both parts of it, upon the text 1 Timothy 2. 5. "For there is one God, and one mediator between God and man, the man Jesus Christ." I thought Mr. Stetson leaned a good deal to the stricter faith in his explanation of the passage. He explained his idea of a mediator as distinct from the notion of atonement, and yet clearly maintained the divine character of the Saviour and his unity of purpose if not of person with God. I am glad to hear opinions which do not all strain to absolute infidelity.

Read an excellent Sermon of Atterbury upon an anxious mind. Matthew 6. 34. "Take no thought for the morrow." He considers excessive anxiety an evil as well as a folly. The first because it destroys energy, the second because it implies distrust of a divine providence. He yet does not understand the injunction literally for this would not agree with other portions of the Bible. I think so too and quote the parable of the faithful Servant, which he does not. Quiet afternoon and evening. Read a little more of Hampden and Maintenon. Also Mr. Dew's Pamphlet on Slavery.[1]

[1] Thomas Roderick Dew's *Review of the Debate* [on the abolition of slavery] *in the Virginia Legislature of 1831 and 1832*, Richmond, 1832, later incorpo-

rated in the volume of essays entitled *The Pro-Slavery Argument*, 1852, was long regarded as the definitive economic justification of the institution (*DAB*).

[*Quincy*]

MONDAY. 4TH.

Morning pleasant. I went to town alone. At the Office where I was occupied in my usual manner. Finished Professor Dew's Pamphlet upon Slavery which has effected a considerable change in my opinions upon the subject. He mixes a great deal of fallacy, much narrowness of mind and Virginia bigotry, with clear and forcible views. The argument against the practicability of deportation strikes me as conclusive, that against emancipation as very forcible. I think the most expedient course is to leave the matter for those to settle who are most deeply interested in doing so.

Hull brought a message from my father informing me of my Mother's arrival, so that I went to Quincy. Found her with her granddaughter Louisa and Walter Hellen.[1] She looks better than I expected to see her. Nearly the whole of the remainder of the day was passed in conversation. I went out and rode with her, stopping for a few moments at Mrs. T. B. Adams'.

[1] LCA's nephew (1814–1850), son of her sister Adelaide, the second of the Johnson sisters married to Walter Hellen (d. 1815). See Adams Genealogy.

TUESDAY. 5TH.

A warm morning. I remained at Quincy throughout the day and passed it in uncommon indolence. Much of it was taken up in conversation with my Mother and Walter Hellen and Isaac H. Adams who passed the day here. I did make considerable and encouraging progress in my German book nevertheless and read my usual portion of Ovid in the third book of the Tristia. Also took a bath at Mr. Greenleaf's wharf at noon with my father. Thus I have a pretty thorough analysis of my day.

My father did not converse much as he is engaged in writing A Report upon the Harvard University Affairs.[1] My Mother seems in far better spirits than I anticipated, but she gives an Account of Washington affairs which is truly bad enough—An immense sacrifice of property to negligence and fraud.

[1] See below, entry for 23 Aug. and notes there.

WEDNESDAY. 6TH.

A succession of clear, warm days. I went to town after a not very early breakfast. Office where I was engaged in copying for my father several letters and this with making up my Diary consumed my time. Thus passes the most valuable portion of the time, which I do not profit by.

To Medford—The day becoming rather oppressive. Afternoon passed rather languidly. I read a little of the Life of Hampden which contains much of plain good sense without much ornament. Also made considerable progress in the reading of Ovid. I do not think I have ever so wasted a Summer. But the spring of exertion is much relaxed with me. I am fond of literature and of luxury—Attached to my family and I hope a tolerably moral man. The rest is *in* me but I do not know whether circumstances will ever be favourable or my courage great enough to bring it out. Evening, Mr. and Mrs. Angier, not her husband but her brother.[1]

[1] That is, Mrs. John Angier and one of her husband's brothers, Joseph or Luther.

THURSDAY. 7TH.

A very warm day. Perhaps as oppressive as any which we have had. I went to town with Mr. Brooks and after I got there regretted very much my going. I was not much occupied. Time engrossed by trifling occupations and a conversation with Mr. Walsh. Returned to Medford. P. C. Brooks Jr. and his wife at dinner and in the afternoon. She has just returned from a visit with her father and mother to the Sulphur Waters of Western Virginia. This is a pleasant trip enough for those who love some interruption to the humdrum of life. The Afternoon was unemployed. Evening very warm. Mrs. Gray and her daughter Henrietta spent the evening.

FRIDAY. 8TH.

The weather changed from warm to cool in the course of the night. I went to town accompanied by Mr. Brooks. My time was pretty much taken up in attending to my Mother and Walter Hellen who came in to meet my Wife and her children. I took him as a young Stranger about the Streets showing him the principal objects of attention. This was fatiguing, and killed all my morning. Returned to Medford with

Mr. Brooks. We dined alone and very quietly—My Wife having remained in town until evening.

I read a good deal uninterruptedly, Madame de Maintenon's Letters. These were collected and published by a French writer, La Beaumelle, who is thought to have introduced a good deal of his own to animate the style.[1] Nevertheless there is much that is interesting and valuable in the work. She rose from extreme wretchedness. Born in a prison, the sport of adversity in her younger life, married for a home to a wretched piece of deformity, she became the wife of the first monarch of Europe and the ruler of many events. Yet she was scarcely happier in her later than in her early days. Ovid also. I read German in my spare moments, especially in the Evening.

[1] L. A. de La Beaumelle, *Mémoires pour servir à l'histoire de Mme. de Maintenon,* 6 vols., Amsterdam, 1755-1756.

SATURDAY. 9TH.

Cool morning. I went to town in my own way, Mr. Brooks being about to dine abroad to day. Went to the House to obtain the Keys and some books. Also on several Commissions. Conversation with Mr. Walsh and Mr. Odiorne.[1] The latter called upon me to inquire if I would accept the nomination as one of the delegates to the Antimasonic Convention on the 10th of September. I asked him what the probable course of the party would be. He said to nominate my father, but in case of his refusal, Mr. Everett and should he decline, then to join in the nomination of Judge Morton. This at least seemed to be the feeling of the State Committee. I told him that my opposition to Judge Morton was so determined, it ought to be known before I was chosen a Delegate. I should go there mainly to oppose a nomination. If it was thought fit to select me as one with that understanding I should accept the appointment. We then went into an examination of the difficulties of the case and it's probable effect upon general affairs. He left me, intimating that he should report my acceptance with the condition to the contrary nevertheless. Returned home to dine. Afternoon the reading of German and of Ovid. Evening, a visit with my Wife at Mrs. Hall's and Mrs. Angier's.

[1] On George Odiorne, see Darling, *Political Changes in Mass.,* p. 87.

SUNDAY. 10TH.

Pleasant morning. I went to Meeting all day and during the remainder of it occupied myself with German. Mr. Burnap of Baltimore preached.[1] Matthew 5. 3. "Blessed are the poor in spirit; for their's is the kingdom of heaven." And 1. Peter 5. 5 "Be clothed with humility." The same general subject. He managed it tolerably but gave nothing new or particularly striking. His own manner and his general character are somewhat at variance, in appearance at least with his general character.

Read a Sermon of Atterbury upon that remarkable text Genesis 49. 4 in which the patriarch addressing his eldest son prophecies of him "Unstable as water, thou shalt not excel." No language can express more distinctly the character of a wavering mind and it's fatal consequences. The Preacher considers it in two lights as losing all probability of advantage in this life, and forfeiting every pretence to happiness in the next. True indeed, instability of mind is perhaps the greatest punishment which can be inflicted upon man. It ruins his best laid plans, it vitiates his morality, it destroys his reliance upon himself. Perhaps Miss Edgeworth has embodied the effects of it as powerfully as any one in her little story of Vivian. I met with a living instance of it in the character of my poor brother. Quiet evening. Continued August Lafontaine's German story.

[1] On Rev. George Washington Burnap, see vol. 3:53.

[*Quincy*]

MONDAY. 11TH.

Morning warm after the east wind was over. There were clouds which threatened rain but they passed off. I went to town alone. Office with little or nothing to do. Conversation with Mr. Walsh upon political affairs. I partially disclosed to him my quandary but it produced only an argument about Masonry and I regretted I had said so much. I must draw my conclusions for myself. Yet it does me no injury to hear the incidental reflections of others.

Went to Quincy to dine. Found the family as usual and had much conversation with my father upon the general subject of the state of political affairs at present and incidentally discussed the College matter. In this way I managed to do little or nothing, a little of Ovid was all. Evening, an interesting conversation about the Old Testament and the present character of religious opinions in France.

TUESDAY. 12TH.

The weather was so warm I concluded to postpone my departure until Afternoon. My morning was not very profitably spent. Conversation and a little German with La Beaumelle's Life of Madame de Maintenon, which is a spirited work enough. After dinner, just as I was getting ready to start a heavy thunder cloud in the South threatened so fearfully that I concluded to remain until after it passed over. This was so late that I concluded to remain. Mr. Townsend of Boston, Mr. Courtney a gentleman from South Carolina and Price Greenleaf were here.[1]

Walter Hellen who went to town this morning, brought intelligence of the destruction of the Ursuline Convent at Charlestown by a mob who went up by concert late last night and after warning out the defenceless female inmates to the number of fifty or sixty, deliberately set fire to all the premises and burnt them to the ground. This has been occasioned directly by a story of the abduction of a girl which has been circulating for a day or two. What a comment upon our free institutions! What an indelible disgrace to the famed liberality of New England! The town of Boston being much excited about it, there was a meeting today at Faneuil Hall to express public opinion.[2] Townsend stayed until late and for a wonder, conversed with considerable force and clearness.

[1] J. C. Courtney, "keeper of a female School at Charleston South Carolina" (JQA, Diary, 12 Aug.), subsequently wrote an account of the visit he and Alexander Townsend made to JQA and published it in *Niles' Register* for 11 Oct. 1834. It has been reprinted in *The Adamses at Home*, Boston, 1970, p. 41–43.

[2] The burning of the Ursuline Convent seems to have been the first major expression of a spirit of lawlessness and violence that would characterize the social scene in Boston for the next thirty years. The waves of immigration had begun to rise. By 1830 Boston and Charlestown had a Catholic population estimated at 10,000. The Ursuline Convent was one of the institutional expressions of the influx. Rumors of suasions and constraints practiced within its walls had built up for a year, fanned by allegations made by two unbalanced communicants who had sought refuge outside. Public authorities failed to heed warnings of trouble and provided no protection against the mob of native laborers or "Boston Truckmen."

When news of the destruction spread, there were strong public fears of acts of retaliation by the angered Irish. Provisional arrangements were made to call out the militia when needed, and in order to reassure the aggrieved Catholic population that official and law-abiding Boston shared their sense of outrage, the meeting of prominent citizens in Faneuil Hall was promptly arranged. Resolutions were passed deploring the act; Mayor Lyman appointed a committee to investigate and to employ "every suitable mode" of bringing the offenders to justice. But JQA found "a singular inertness in the public authorities" (Diary, 13 Aug.). The committee's report made subsequently was an able one. Several persons were identified and brought to trial, but only one conviction was obtained, and that of a minor participant, later released at the instance of the Bishop. (Winsor, *Memorial History of Boston*, 3:238–240, 519, 521–524; for an account of the affair in its broader setting of anti-Irish and anti-Catholic feeling stimulated by rising immigration, see Darling, *Political Changes in Mass.*, p. 162–166, and the works cited there.) A contemporary view of the Convent is reproduced in the present volume; see also p. xviii–xix.

Medford

WEDNESDAY. 13TH.

My child is this day three years old. May God bless her and preserve her. I returned to town after breakfast.

The Community seemed to be in great agitation and alarm, nothing else being talked about but the outrage. Yet no clue seems to have been afforded to solve the mystery. The prejudices against the Institution appear to be very general in the County and the act to have resulted from the coarse prejudices of the ignorant and little principled. These repeated outrages in our Country are alarming indications of our condition. The idea that justice must be done by direct violence is becoming familiar to all and the lower part of the population are the persons who think themselves perfectly fitted to administer it. Soon there will be no toleration of any expression of opinion contrary to the popular one. This is the freedom of America. Heavens! what a thought—That man can not be trusted with power. I am afraid it is so.

Much engaged in Commissions. To Medford to dine. Afternoon. Company, Commodore Hull, Mr. Goldsborough of the Navy board and a Mr. Cumming from Georgia.[1] The two former I knew in Washington. Quiet evening, read the third volume of Puckler Muskau. Amusing enough.

[1] On Commodore Isaac Hull, see vol. 2:130. C. W. Goldsborough was secretary of the Navy Board (*Mass. Register*, 1833, p. 212). Mr. Cumming of Georgia may have been the Col. William Cumming, partisan of W. H. Crawford, who fought a duel with George McDuffie, Calhoun's protégé, in 1822 (JQA, *Memoirs*, 6:76; *DAB*, under McDuffie), or perhaps Alfred Cumming, later the territorial governor of Utah (*DAB*).

[*Quincy*]

THURSDAY. 14TH.

I went to Boston this morning in my own way, and passed by the blackened walls which are all that remain of the Convent. The feeling that came over me was one of the most affecting I ever experienced. The illiberality of our people has always been known to me but I had always supposed their love of order such that it would prevent any public exhibition of it. It seems I was mistaken and that there stands now a monument far more striking than that of Bunker hill to call up emotions of horror and disgust.

My father came into town with the Carriage which is to return with my Wife and family to Quincy. Mr. Odiorne and Mr. Henry D. Ward called to see him but he had gone. At one, I went to Quincy. Found my mother in good health. Afternoon quietly at home. Read much of Mr. Jefferson's Letters which grew more malignant as he grew older. The passions of the man did not soften nor did he arrive at any of those good feelings in human nature which attach us to character. Read Ovid and a little of German. Evening. Conversation. There was a very severe thunder shower which lasted some hours during the night and made us quite uncomfortable.

FRIDAY. 15TH.

I remained at home today and passed much of my time in making a rough draught of what I might have to say in case I should attend the Antimasonic Convention. It is difficult to foresee precisely what the contingency may be and I wish on that account only so to methodize my thoughts as to enable me to make use of them in train if I should have occasion. A new element appears to have entered into the composition of our politics. The Antimasonic Committee of Worcester have addressed a letter to Governor Davis which he has answered. With a prodigious multitude of words and a tone of timid anxiety, he has ventured to express an opinion that the Masons should dissolve. What the operation of this will be, remains to be seen, but it does something to relieve me from my difficulties.[1]

Read some of Jefferson. Afternoon, J. H. Foster and his Wife paid a visit.[2] He has become inoculated with the prejudices of the coarse, ignorant mob. He says that one of the leaders is, thank God,[3] taken, and has confessed. Read Ovid. Conversation with my father. Jefferson and Hamilton, the funding system and their general quarrels. Story that Hamilton wrote anonymous Letters to Washington accusing him which was the cause of Jefferson's bitterness.

[1] The Antimasons were currently torn between the opposing wings of the party composed of those who were normally either National Republicans or Democrats. The Democrats among the Antimasons had been making considerable progress in their efforts to swing Massachusetts Antimasonry in the Democratic direction and to effect an alliance in support of Judge Marcus Morton for the governorship. Their success stemmed from the uncompromising way the National Republicans in the Massachusetts House of Representatives had denied the claims of Antimasons to a share of the vacant seats in the Senate following the election of Gov. Davis with antimasonic help, and from the National Republican majority's action in causing the report of the joint committee investigating Freemasonry to be tabled.

The National Republicans in or allied with the antimasonic party sought to counter the drift toward the Democrats by persuading Gov. Davis that he should issue a statement declaring his support for the dissolution of Freemasonry as an institution. The fruit of their labors was the equivocal statement from Davis which did not prove as satisfactory to the Antimasons as CFA seems to have hoped, but probably served to prevent the endorsement of the Democratic ticket by the Antimasons (Darling, *Polit*

ical Changes in Mass., p. 118–123).

[2] Mrs. James Hiller Foster was a niece of AA. See vol. 1:155 and Adams Genealogy.

[3] The parenthetical exclamation is clearly an expression of CFA's position, not Foster's.

SATURDAY. 16TH.

Morning cloudy but it afterwards grew warm. I went to town and was occupied for considerable time in business and commissions. We hear today that several of the leaders are taken and the investigation in the affair goes on successfully. So much the better. Nothing else material. Returned to Quincy.

Afternoon. Took a walk with Walter Hellen to Mount Wollaston to look at the Orchard. The trees purchased by my father look pretty well and bear some fruit this year, but the Baldwins do not succeed very well. The frost of two years ago seems to have had a very bad effect upon that particular tree every where. On my ascent of the hill, I had a feeling which is always pretty strong with me that I wish I had a house on the spot all ready, but I do not think I should ever have the enterprise to build one. Nor am I sure that I should ever like it after I had got it. The spot is nevertheless decidedly beautiful.[1]

Home. Read Ovid as usual. Evening some visitors, Mr. Beale and his daughter Anne with Mr. Emmons[2] and his Wife of Boston who are staying there.

[1] For other statements of the same theme see vol. 3:268; 4:362–363. The notion of "a mansion house" on Mount Wollaston, long cherished, came closest to fulfillment in 1845 when, upon CFA's bidding, an architect, Alexander Jackson Davis of New York, had plans "in study," and with CFA visited the site

to explore the question of "placing the house." Davis' brief account is printed in *The Adamses at Home*, Boston, 1970, p. 46.

[2] Perhaps John L. Emmons, merchant, who lived at 11 Beacon Street (*Boston Directory*, 1834).

SUNDAY. 17TH.

Pleasant day. I read a good deal of German. La Fontaine's style is so easy and his stories are so interesting that I make great progress. Attended divine service all day and heard Mr. Eliot of Washington preach two sensible Sermons. The one from 1 Romans 7 "called to be Saints," the other from 2 Corinthians 4. 4 "the glorious gospel of Christ," the subject the nature and perfection of Christianity as evinced in its principal doctrines of atonement or reconciliation, regeneration and eternal life. He is a young man, just out of Cambridge and to be a Missionary.[1]

Having accidentally left Atterbury at Medford of whom but a single Sermon remains unread, I was obliged to look elsewhere and pitched upon a discourse of Warburton.[2] John 18. 38. "Pilate saith unto [him] What is Truth? And when he had said this, he went out again." He considers men's prejudices against general truth, and their objections in particular to religious truth. His style is nervous and reflections sound. The remainder of the day passed in reading Jefferson and conversation.

[1] On Rev. William Greenleaf Eliot, see below, entry for 7 June 1835.
[2] See vol. 4:363.

MONDAY. 18TH.

I am this day twenty seven years old. My youth may now be said to be complete. I have observed that this has frequently been the particular age at which men famous for talent have begun to develope it to the world. This was the age at which my father began his public career, and at which Cicero made his defence of Roscius of Ameria. This was the age at which Demosthenes entered upon the public business. I mean to compare myself with none of these but I have long been impressed with the idea that if I made no reputation at all at this age, I should never make any. My hopes have sustained themselves until now, and this will be the date of their decline.[1] In other respects I have to thank God for all his mercies. Health for myself and mine, prosperity far beyond my deserts, and the most encouraging of all, a pretty good conscience. If it is his will, I remain in obscurity, I shall regret it only on account of my family whose previous reputation will in the world's eye contrast with my "fainéantise," deeming it far more for my own happiness to keep myself in quiet. Such is the fallibility of man, such is my own weakness that an exposure to the public will diminish my claims to my own esteem.

I remained at Quincy all day. Morning taken up in arranging my thoughts upon Antimasonry. I am quite doubtful whether my frank exposition of my thoughts to Mr. Odiorne may not have the effect of depriving me of a seat at the Convention. Considering the difficulties that surround me, I should prefer this to any other result, as the one which would save me most clearly from harm. But if it should turn out that wanting *names* they still cling to mine, and that nevertheless the leaders adhere to the determination to amalgamate with Jacksonism, it becomes me thoroughly to reflect upon that course which shall redeem me from any similar servitude. The Advocate throws off Mr. Davis, and the course seems to be to nominate Judge Morton as the Antimasonic Candidate, the Jackson party to fall in without making a distinct nomination. The consequences of this course are manifest. At all hazards, I will avoid them.

In the Afternoon, I went with my father to see Mr. Price Greenleaf's nursery which he has made out of a rocky and marshy swamp. His labour has been prodigious and he is only beginning after the lapse of two years to perceive results. This is better than idleness or vice, but at this work a wild Irishman would do as well as Newton or Bacon. Home. Ovid. Evening quiet. Conversation.

[1] JQA in noting in his Diary CFA's arrival at the age of twenty-seven called it "A short time to look back." The substantial amount of writing on political subjects that CFA completed over the next several years is probably to be related to the resolve here made. See, for example, the entry for 18 Aug. 1835, below.

TUESDAY. 19TH.

I went into town this morning accompanied by Walter Hellen. My time was very much taken up in running around with him to show him the town. This with half a dozen business Commissions made the hours slip away fast enough. Returned to dinner. The day was cloudy, and threatened rain.

Afternoon. I finished Mr. Jefferson's works. The impression they leave is not favourable. You cannot think the man great. His ideas were all refinements and his benevolence had so theoretical an aspect that it never touches the heart. On the other hand, his malignity seems to have grown with his age, and his last Letters breathe the discontents of a mortified man instead of the softened exultation of a uniformly prosperous one. His irreligion gives the last deep shade to the picture. Read several of the Lamentations of Ovid which are another and a different but an equally discreditable picture of human life.

Evening, quiet, finished the first volume of Madame de Maintenon's Memoirs which are well written.

WEDNESDAY. 20TH.

The rain fell heavily almost all day with a cold north east wind. I remained quietly at home, and thinking I could employ my time to a useful purpose, I began again upon my last year's design, assorting my Grandmother's papers. Selected my father's correspondence in order to get that put into a more durable shape. By reading the Letters I get into the whole of the History of the family far more thoroughly than I could do by any other means, and after all, this is knowledge which may become the most essential of all. But besides the information, the Letters are themselves remarkable both in the peculiar style of the writer and in the developement of the feelings which were operating. I continued the work all day with the exception of an hour of Ovid. Evening, we played a game of Whist in the family.

THURSDAY. 21ST.

A North Easterly mist still so that I thought I would remain at home. My father nevertheless went in the Stage to an Overseers Meeting of Harvard University. I continued my labour of assorting Letters assiduously and pursued the History very assiduously through the periods of 1794 to 1800, 1803 to 1812, and 1815 to 1817, all periods for the most part spent abroad, and all of them deeply affecting the general history of the world as well as the more particular career of the writer. I read these papers and unavoidably contrast my own situation with his. Mortifying enough. The world however is now a different one. The same regard is not now paid to education and all are more uniformly as well as superficially instructed, which breeds great self opinion. A much smaller disposition to concede superiority and a greater one to control it. After all the excuse is not satisfactory. Read a little of Ovid. Evening, a game of Whist.

FRIDAY. 22D.

Morning warm. I went to town. Morning consumed in making up the Arrears of my Diary and in arranging my Accounts. My frequent absences from town make my time when there more in request. I was also engaged in several Commissions for the family.

A residence at Quincy is vastly a more anxious one to me than one at Medford. The want of responsibility at the former place by which a great many things go on neglected or ill attended to, the desire to correct met by the difficulty of doing any thing that is not radical altogether make a very unpleasant state of feeling to me. Yet as an exercise of the intellect Quincy has corresponding advantages. My father's society is worth that of a hundred common minds.

Back to dinner. Afternoon, continuing the Letters of which I have collected all immediately within reach. Read also a little of Ovid. Evening, Whist.

SATURDAY. 23RD.

My father wanted a long report of his upon the affairs of Harvard University copied today so that I was obliged to sit down early and work almost without cessation in order to accomplish it. The only relaxation I allowed myself was a bath at Mr. Greenleaf's wharf with my father before dinner and an hour in the evening. The consequence was that my wrist was very tired. My father has become very much interested in the present condition of the College and has in consequence assumed the defence of the Government at the present crisis. This has brought him into conflict with several of his acquaintance and will probably cause him much anxiety. His report is a severe one upon the Circular of the Senior Class undoubtedly the most injurious step taken to the discipline of the College.[1] Evening, Whist.

I confess I feel a very mixed sort of sensation when I reflect upon Cambridge. I remember days of slavery to disagreeable studies and of loneliness in feeling. Among all the young men I met there, not one did I find with a character at all congenial to mine. They were either dull, or riotous. Jolly companions or studious drones. My *studies* were considerable but not of that sort to gain mere rank. What might I not have been made had I had even but a single teacher who had felt one grain of interest in my success. Why should I feel interested in the College?[2]

[1] The report of which JQA had CFA make a fair copy had been accepted unanimously the preceding day by the Overseers' committee (Richard Sullivan to JQA, 22 Aug., Adams Papers) and when submitted to the Board of Overseers on the 25th would be adopted and ordered published. (In the Adams Papers is a corrected draft in JQA's hand, Aug. 1834. It was printed, together with all relevant exhibits, as *Proceedings of the Overseers of Harvard University relative to the Late Disturbances in that Seminary*, Boston [1834].) This final Report conformed essentially to what JQA, following his appointment at the Overseers' meeting on 31 July as chairman of the committee, had submitted at its first meeting on 8 August. In the in-

terim, however, his draft report had been subjected to numerous vicissitudes. When he first read it to the committee (1¼ hours), "it did not meet the approval of any other member" and was judged "much too severe upon the Students." Joining other members in opposing its harshness of language, ex-Governor Levi Lincoln and A. H. Everett had also objected to its substance (JQA, Diary, 8 Aug.). The committee's own substitute, a patchwork acquiesced in by JQA, when submitted to the Overseers was ordered referred to a new committee (on which JQA was the only holdover) along with JQA's original draft which the Overseers had requested to hear (Diary, 21 Aug.). The action of the new committee next day was to accept JQA's draft, minimally modified, as its report. (CFA when much later selecting from his father's diary for publication chose to include all the passages bearing on the matter without abridgement. JQA, *Memoirs*, 9:157–186 *passim*.) Although the report concerned itself only with recent disorders and with the means taken to restore order, at issue were matters of much greater significance and complexity. Because those matters bear upon so many relationships, both intrafamily and interfamily, of importance in CFA's diary, an extended discussion of the report in its larger frame has been thought necessary. Despite its length, the discussion makes no effort to deal more than tangentially with the student rebellion itself.

The immediate difficulties which President Quincy was experiencing with the students had begun in May, triggered by an altercation between a Freshman and an inexperienced and unpopular tutor of Greek. In the course of the ensuing and ever-widening conflict between the Immediate Government and the students, protests and petitions were followed by severe retaliatory punishments; destruction of college property and the concomitant signs of rebellion were met with the dismissal of the Sophomore class for the year, rigorous action against the Juniors, and, in an effort to identify individual culprits, the invocation of the civil arm by referral to the Middlesex Grand Jury. Drawn in reluctantly, the Seniors issued a printed "Circular" which undertook to give a full report of the rebellion from the student point of view, thereby evoking wrath and fear in large and influential sections of the community and resulting in the signers being deprived of their degrees. (The events are recounted in Robert A. McCaughey, "The Usable Past: a Study of the Harvard College Rebellion of 1834," *William and Mary Law Review*, 2:602–605 [Spring 1970], and more fully in the same author's *Josiah Quincy, 1772–1864: The Last Federalist*, Cambridge, 1974, ch. 8.

Despite Quincy's strengths in a number of facets of administration, strengths that would be abundantly evident in the eleven succeeding years of his presidency

(McCaughey, *The Last Federalist*, ch. 9; Morison, *Three Centuries of Harvard*, p. 254–267), his endowments were not such as would make him successful in imposing discipline upon a student body accustomed to laxness and indulgence. The judgment from a later perspective that he showed a "complete misunderstanding of youth," that his government was characterized by "alternate cuffing and caressing," by abruptness and tactlessness in conferences, is probably justified (*Three Centuries of Harvard*, p. 251–252). Quincy's manner with students seemed even to his admirers open to objection. The reservation is evident in the otherwise eulogistic memorial tributes to Quincy from his colleagues in the Massachusetts Historical Society. Rev. George E. Ellis, to Quincy's qualities of ardor and impetuosity, added "severity of sarcasm and rebuke" and remarked that "the question . . . was often discussed, whether he had real strong sympathies for young men, — could deal with them by wise allowances and gentle tolerances." R. H. Dana Jr., himself rusticated by Quincy in 1832 but later an admiring friend, posed the problem neatly by admitting that if bigotry meant an "undue confidence in and devotion to our opinions" and was "consistent with entire kindness and desire to do justice," Quincy might be so called, and concluded, "We need not fear to meet complaints from those who have encountered him front to front, — that he was severe, and even bigoted. . . . Perhaps his temperament did not admit of his dealing with men and measures as the policy of political management requires" (MHS, *Procs.*, 1st ser., 7 [1863–1864]:387–388, 402–404). Emerson's remark (*Journals and Notebooks*, ed. Gilman, 9:381) that Quincy, despite "a sort of violent service he did the College, was a lubber and a grenadier among our clerks," differed from these judgments chiefly in tone. Nor was there substantial difference in the list of his attributes drawn up by an anonymous and unfriendly critic at the time, though to those already noted were added a "general tendency of . . . mind to . . . inaccuracy," a "lamentable want of memory," and manners, "to those students, in particular, who have come ... from the southern states ... any thing but conciliating" (*Remarks Occasioned by the Publication of a Pamphlet Entitled Proceedings of the Overseers ...* [pamphlet], Boston, 1834, p. 18, 31, 33). John Langdon Sibley in his "Private Journal" a few months after Quincy's retirement (12 Jan. 1846, MH-Ar) also recorded that, along with abruptness in manners, "His memory, especially respecting people, was bad." Even JQA, Quincy's kinsman and staunchest of defenders ("my intimate friend for nearly fifty years; without interruption even by the most earnest and ardent opposition of political opinions ... unwavering"), with "the most unbounded confidence in his integrity," and with a predisposition to find "among the Students a contumacious and insurgent Spirit," admitted to his journal his "fear that from some of the peculiarities of [Quincy's] temper, and from a hesitancy in his elocution the Students have lost the feeling of reverence for his character which is essential to the preservation of authority" (JQA, Diary, 26 July, 8, 19 Aug. 1834). See also Adams Genealogy.

Opposition to President Quincy within the College, however, had a longer history and was of greater extent than the student disorders in 1834. From the inception of his administration in 1829 his academic policies met with strong student resistance (McCaughey, "The Usable Past," p. 597-601), and there were powerful forces in the faculty bent upon bringing him down. This opposition had multiple origins: the younger faculty, of whom Tutor Henry S. McKean was in the forefront, tended to take the student view; another group, of whom John Farrar, Hollis Professor of Mathematics, was one, had been strong partisans of President Kirkland, remained bitter over the circumstances of his resignation, and expressed it by an antagonism to his successor. Another element of opposition was composed of those who wished more emphasis given to curricular and instructional reform than the non-academic Quincy seemed interested in. The leader in this cause, as he had been in the Kirkland days, was George Ticknor, who wrote on his re-

tirement in Jan. 1835: "I have been an active professor these fifteen years, and for thirteen years of the time I have been contending against a constant opposition to procure certain changes.... As long as I hoped to advance them, I continued attached to the College; when I gave up all hope, I determined to resign.... In my whole connection with it I ... [have been] actuated by a sense of duty to improve the institution.... So, I doubt not, are those who have the management of the College, and pursue the opposite course.... We differ, however, very largely, both as to what the College can be, and what it ought to be." The most active figure among the faculty opposed to Quincy was Charles Theodore Follen, whose differences with Quincy, brought in to be a president who was a "business man," were of several kinds. Wives too entered the fray. By 1836, when Quincy had reestablished a hold, not one of those whose names have been mentioned remained on the faculty. (McCaughey, *The Last Federalist*, ch. 9; George Ticknor, *Life, Letters and Journals*, 2 vols., Boston, 1877, 1:400-401; Edmund Quincy, Journal, 7 July 1834, MHi:Quincy Family Papers; JQA, Diary, 24 Aug. 1834; Charlotte Brooks Everett to Edward Everett, 8 April 1828, MHi:Everett MSS.)

However much opposition had been generated within the student body and faculty by Quincy's personal attributes and policies, his unassailable confidence in his own course caused Quincy and members of his family to remain convinced that the rebellion was "encouraged systematically by external discontent"; that "those troubles were fanned from without, if not enkindled there" (Josiah Quincy, Journal, 8 Nov. 1846, 3 Nov. 1855, quoted in Edmund Quincy, *Josiah Quincy*, p. 491, 505; see also same, p. 454, 464; Sibley, Private Journal, 28 May 1868).

That there was widespread dislike of Quincy outside the College and that there were those ready to take advantage of any opening that presented itself is of course true. Quincy's long political career as an ardent Federalist in Congress and as an activist mayor of

Boston, coupled with a social manner which tended to make his political opponents become his enemies, had left a residue of ill-wishers including a substantial section of the Boston press. The same condition obtained in the sector more strongly motivated by religious considerations. There, disaffection for the Quincy administration resulted both from the failure of the College in the choice of Quincy as president to adhere to the long tradition of a clergyman in the office and from the occupancy of the chair by a Unitarian rather than an orthodox Trinitarian (Winsor, *Memorial History of Boston*, 3:231–233; Edmund Quincy, *Josiah Quincy*, p. 430; James Walker, "Memoir of Josiah Quincy," MHS, *Procs.*, 1st ser., 9 [1866]:125).

Those in opposition to the College administration, including those whose purpose was to unseat Quincy, found in the meetings of the Board of Overseers the forum for the expression of their discontents. This was in natural consequence of the heavy *ex officio* representation on the Board from the State Senate and from the Congregational clergy. When early in 1829 the Corporation, dominated by Boston business interests in the persons of Nathaniel Bowditch and Ebenezer Francis and fearful of choosing a clergyman from either wing of a divided church, seized upon the opportunity presented by the unexpected termination of Quincy's mayoralty to break the eight-month stalemate, the assent of the Overseers to Quincy was anything but certain. When confirmation came it was by a vote of 40 to 26. (McCaughey, *The Last Federalist*, ch. 8. Edward Everett to A. H. Everett, 20 Jan.; to ——, 21 Jan.; to Isaac Parker, 22 Jan. 1829, LbC [all in Everett MSS]. Edmund Quincy, Journal, 29 Jan. 1829, Quincy Family Papers.) A negative attitude toward Quincy and his policies persisted among Overseers, ready for expression when there was opportunity. One such was provided by the controversy in the Overseers over procedure in the award of an honorary degree to Andrew Jackson. On that occasion James Trecothick Austin, attorney general of the Commonwealth, and A. H. Everett had made common

cause against Quincy (see above, entry for 27 June 1833, note; McCaughey, "The Usable Past," p. 606–607).

When the handling of the student disorders of 1834 was scheduled for hearing before the Overseers, JQA, correctly sensing that another effort to bring Quincy down was imminent, while promising his full support had warned the President to be prepared to defend his course and that "his present situation is very critical." Quincy, however, characteristically felt there was nothing for discussion: "the Law was plain" (JQA, Diary, 26 July). But his old adversaries, J. T. Austin and A. H. Everett, joined by George Blake (whom Quincy had twice defeated for mayor), and supported in a large section of the Boston press, were prepared to settle for nothing less than Quincy's resignation.

Much later, Quincy on reading JQA's journal entries for the period recognized fully the perils of his position: "a number of political rivals thought they had me at disadvantage." He and his family, echoing JQA, continued to think that A. H. Everett, "this vermicular enemy," was animated in his leadership by a determination to win for himself the presidency he had eagerly sought and been denied by Quincy's election five years before. (JQA, Diary, 26 July, 8 Aug. 1834; Josiah Quincy, Journal, 3 Nov. 1855, quoted in Edmund Quincy, *Josiah Quincy*, p. 505; J. L. Sibley, Private Journal, 28 May 1868; McCaughey, "The Usable Past," p. 605–606.) It seems unlikely, however, that A. H. Everett was looking to the office for himself in 1834. His own fortunes and reputation had declined markedly in the years since 1828 (see above, entries for 27 Sept. – 6 Nov. 1833 *passim*) when his brother Edward, then unwilling to foreclose a young political career that seemed to carry infinite possibilities, had stepped aside to support Alexander's candidacy. (Charlotte Everett to Edward Everett, 14 April; Edward Everett to ——, 9 May; to A. H. Everett, 11 June, 15 Sept., 15 Oct.; to J. E. Sprague, 11 Sept., LbC; to George Bancroft, 11 Sept., 6 Oct., LbC; to Joseph Story, 3 Oct.; to JQA, 30 Oct., LbC, 1828 [all in Everett MSS].) In 1834 Edward's political advancement seemed estopped, a prestigious academic post was more alluring, and the chance a welcome one to unseat Quincy. Quincy it is true had offered to support Edward for the presidency immediately following Kirkland's resignation (Peter C. Brooks to Edward Everett, 14 April 1828, Everett MSS), but when Quincy had been named by the Corporation Edward had opposed his confirmation to the last as "a 'Notion' of the first magnitude," an insult added "to the injuries which the Corporation has so freely done the College" (Edward Everett to A. H. Everett, 20 Jan.; to ——, 21 Jan.; to Isaac Parker, 22 Jan., 1829, LbC [all in Everett MSS]). CFA was correct in identifying for his father the likely successor to Quincy in the probable event of his fall — Edward Everett (17 June 1834, LbC, Adams Papers).

To the offers of support for the vacancy that seemed to all to impend, Everett offered no discouragement this time. His father-in-law, expressing his own gratification at such a prospect, summarized, "The thing would, I believe, make Charlotte happy.... The college is in a sad state, and the common opinion seems to be that Mr. Quincy will not be happy in long remaining. There seems to be stilness now ... but it is of that sulky and silent kind that evidences discontent.... Your name and yours only, in one connection, have I heard mentioned.... I am somewhat aware of what the feelings of some were in times past. But I do not believe that things and opinions are now as they once were. ... I am glad however at finding your own way of thinking somewhat different from what it once was" (Peter C. Brooks to Edward Everett, 25 June; see also Joseph E. Worcester to same, 23 June 1834 [both in Everett MSS]). On 16 Aug. Everett took a step he had been considering for almost a year. He resigned his seat in the current Congress and announced that he would not be a candidate for reelection. Neither Everett attended the meeting of the Overseers on 25 Aug. to hear and act on JQA's Report (JQA, Diary, 26 Aug.; Everett, Diary, 16 Aug. 1834, Everett MSS).

The adoption by the Overseers of the Report was a distinct vindication of Quincy and essential to him in his fight to retain his post. Quincy and his family, however, tended to take the acceptance of the Report as concluding the whole matter. Both JQA and CFA recognized the Quincy response as perhaps too unqualified and premature. CFA, on Commencement Day, noted their "state of considerable elation and on the whole I did not wonder although perhaps I may differ in my opinion of the degree in which it was justified"; and JQA, when Quincy called on him with proof sheets of the Report, recorded Quincy's "very high Spirits at the issue thus far of his troubles, and I hope understands that he is not yet out of them" (below, entry for 27 Aug.; JQA, Diary, 30 Aug.; see also McCaughey, "The Usable Past," p. 607–609).

There were signs that suggested the Adamses were right. Edward Everett recorded in his Diary that he did not attend the exercises on Commencement nor the ΦBK exercises the next day, both abstentions contrary to his custom. There may have been significance in the fact noted in the *Columbian Centinel* that on Commencement afternoon *two* Cambridge residences, that of the President and that of J. T. Buckingham (editor of the *Boston Courier*), "were thrown open ... for the reception of their friends and the friends of the University" (28 Aug., p. 2, col. 2). Those committed to the effort to induce Quincy's resignation did not allow the publication on 8 Sept. of the Report in the *Proceedings of the Overseers* to go unanswered. Some opponents, seeking to make capital of the political unpopularity of JQA, attempted to blunt the effect of the Report by assailing its author as possessed of a "malignant heart." "The mortifications and disappointments of his life have soured the old man's temper — and he must needs disgorge his venom." His Report is called a "fulsome eulogy of his relative, President Quincy"; characterized as "misrepresentations ... seasoned with caustic bitterness" (*Remarks on a Pamphlet Entitled "Proceedings of the Board of Overseers of Harvard University, 1834"* [printed leaflet without place or date, attached to Benjamin Waterhouse to JQA, 15 Oct. 1834, Adams Papers], p. 2, 4, 7). An opposite approach was adopted by another pamphleteer cited earlier in this note. This was "a Son of Harvard," who treated the Report minimally ("written hastily," "perchance penned by the Honorable Chairman during a few moments of leisure from the bustle of political life, with a prompter at his elbow") while praising its author ("so profound a scholar, so skilful a rhetorician, so great a man") and proceeded to his avowed object: "To show in as few words as may be, the entire unfitness of the present occupant of the Presidential chair for the station which he now holds." Having concluded his case with an invocation of the names of Kirkland, Hedge, and Popkin, he becomes the advocate to urge that Quincy step down for a successor readily identifiable as Edward Everett: "In the late difficulties [Mr. Quincy] has come off conqueror. We advise him to retire in the moment of victory, to repose upon the laurels he has gained. He must have already discovered ... 'that he is not in his right niche.' Or, if he ... is not yet convinced of this fact, we will tell him plainly, that it is the belief of all, even of his greatest friends.... What else can the constant inuendos of the public journals, in regard to his expected resignation, mean?... The man must be short-sighted, indeed, who cannot perceive their purport. The fact is, the public eye is resting upon one, who will undoubtedly be chosen to fill the presidential chair, the moment the resignation hinted at takes place. A son of Harvard — he is one of her greatest boasts. Known throughout the Union for his profound learning and his heart-thrilling eloquence; beloved for his dignified yet conciliating manners, honored for his independence, and revered for his purity of character. Every task that has yet been entrusted to his care ... has been performed ... to the admiration of the public. Every public act of his life reflects credit ... and every station that he has occupied he has adorned. Add to all this, his well-known domestic character. For the sake of his family he

leaves the high seats of honor, preferring the enjoyment of domestic felicity to the flattering triumphs which awaited him in political life." (*Remarks Occasioned by the Publication of a Pamphlet Entitled Proceedings of the Overseers*, p. 3, 4, 34–35.)

The storm did subside, however, and within a month Quincy's tenure seemed safe to JQA, though he saw it incorrectly as not a happy one nor of long duration: "President Quincy ... called upon me. He spoke of the present condition of the University as satisfactory; but while his words were cheering, his tone was dejected. He can never regain his popularity with the Students, and the public treat him as they treat all old men, with cold neglect and insulting compassion. He is not made of stuff to struggle long against this" (JQA, Diary, 15 Oct. 1834). Everett's announcement a week later that he had reconsidered his earlier intent to resign his seat but was firm in his decision not to seek reelection may suggest that he saw the situation similarly. In the following January he announced for governor, and he did not become president of Harvard until 1845.

Twelve years after the Rebellion and following his retirement from the presidency he had held so long, Quincy took occasion to express to JQA "my sense of obligation for the manner in which in 1834–35 ... he had come forward in an unqualified spirit in my defence. I told him I had never ceased to be grateful for the aid he afforded me on that occasion. He said he was conscious of the service he had rendered me, and had always considered the opportunity then afforded him of doing me justice as one of the happiest of his life." Still later, after JQA's death and when CFA had allowed Quincy the use of JQA's Diary in preparing the *Life of John Quincy Adams*, published in 1858, Quincy reflected that rivals "would probably have given me great trouble had not Adams had the courage and the friendship to interpose in my behalf.... Until I had the reading of this diary, I never understood the malignity with which I was assailed, nor the laborious zeal with which I was defended by Mr. Adams"

(Josiah Quincy, Journal, 8 Nov. 1846, 3 Nov. 1855, quoted in Edmund Quincy, *Josiah Quincy*, p. 491, 505).

² CFA's remarks here on his memories of his Harvard education echo similar sentiments he expressed elsewhere (see above, entries for 5 and 28 Aug. 1833) and also what Harvard's historian asserts to have been the general view of alumni of the time: "Almost every graduate of the period 1825–60 has left on record his detestation of the system

of instruction at Harvard.... The Faculty were not there to teach, but to see that boys got their lessons" (Morison, *Three Centuries of Harvard*, p. 260).

Despite CFA's asserted lack of interest in Harvard and its problems, he did address himself to the subject in an essay early in the next year; see below, entries for 11 Feb. – 4 March 1835 *passim*.

SUNDAY. 24TH.

Morning warm but we had a thunder storm in the evening. I read German in order to keep up my little idea of it which a few days may have weakened. Attended divine service and heard Mr. Lunt preach from Romans 2. 12 "For as many as have sinned without law shall also perish without law: and as many as have sinned in the law, shall be judged by the law." He took up the idea of natural propensities as urged by disbelievers to contradict the restraints imposed upon them by christianity. He affirmed that the argument was drawn from an unfair view of the parts which make the sum total of man's nature— By giving undue consideration to one passion in a state of inflammation at the expense of the rest. That man was to be judged as a whole, and according to the distribution of passions, and affections, it would not be unfair to set down as a rule of judgment nature alone. The afternoon's discourse from Titus 2. 11, 12. "For the grace of God that bringeth salvation hath appeared to all men. Teaching us that denying ungodliness and worldly lust we should live soberly, righteously, and godly in the present world." After service Mr. Lunt dined with us. T. B. Adams who has just arrived was also here. I barely had time to read a Sermon of Warburton's upon the moral government of God. Psalm 144. 3. "Lord what is man that thou takest knowledge of him? or the son of man that thou makest account of him." A text differently construed by the religionist and the freethinker. The one making it the foundation of humility the other of debasement. Then to the proof of God's moral government drawn as well from the moral as the natural attributes of the Deity and from both together. I was much struck with a figure illustrative of the mode by which men can only approach to an idea of God's perfection. The sun not visible to the common eye, but its light refracted into distinct shades of colour can then be in parts susceptible of examination. Mr. Quincy was here in the evening.

MONDAY. 25TH.

My father accompanied me to town this morning being engaged with the business of the College. I went to the Office and engaged as usual in my various avocations. These consist mainly of Accounts and the Diary which by intermissions becomes something of a tax. I had also some little Commissions to perform. At the regular period returned to Quincy.

Afternoon somewhat wasted. Managed to read an Epistle of Ovid from Pontus which varies only from the rest by being addressed to persons by name. The same general tone, querulous and servile. Read more of the Memoires de Mad. Maintenon.

The family were quite interested in the ascent of the balloon although no one went into town to see it. Mr. Durants was a brief ascension, coming down safely in half an hour at Mount Auburn.

Mr. P. Whitney called and paid a short visit after which my father and I joined him in a walk to Mrs. T. B. Adams's. There were several of the Quincy people. Mr. and Miss Beal, Dr. Woodward, Miss Whitney and Mrs. Hill together with Mrs. Angier, Miss Harrod and Mrs. Boyd who are staying at the house at present. Mrs. Adams took me aside to ask a question or two about Mr. Gourgas and my father in connexion with the Administration Account. I could give but little satisfaction in answer. Home.

TUESDAY. 26TH.

Fine day. My time was consumed in reading German, until my Mother was ready to go to Boston where I accompanied her, in the Carriage. I had not much leisure from the necessity of attending to her, but had enough to accomplish two or three small objects for which I most particularly came in. Office and Accounts. Returned home early.

Afternoon, finished the assortment of the Letters remaining of my father, but I have not succeeded in laying my hands upon them all. Read a little German and my usual portion of Ovid. Mr. Webster, with Messrs. Mangum, Tyler, and Ewing being the Senate's Committee of Finance came out this afternoon but I did not go down to see them. Read Ovid as usual and came across two or three of his beautiful passages which interspersed with his tediousness relieves it materially.

Evening a family tea party. Mrs. Angier and Mrs. Boyd, Mrs. Adams with her two sons Thomas and John, and Miss Harrod. Cards which have become a great subject of amusement to my Wife and the family.

WEDNESDAY. 27TH.

Having agreed to go with Walter to Commencement today we arose and started betimes. I thought he would like to see a little of the Country so I took him round through Roxbury and Brookline until I missed my way and struck Newton and Watertown instead of going through Brighton. However we reached Cambridge at eleven and heard quite enough of the performance.

The day passed off far better than had been anticipated. The refractory students divided, one portion returning to their duty the rest being punished by the Government. Thirty nine out of fifty eight took degrees. The performances were very mediocre both in composition and delivery. The Master's Latin Oration was far the best in both respects which I heard. The House was thin. I dined in the Hall with Richardson but the dinner was dull. After we rose it was announced to us that there was a Meeting of Alumni to take into consideration the state of the College. Judge Story made a Speech in support of a plan to raise $100,000 to assist in paying the expenses of young men. Mr. J. T. Austin opposed it with his usual tartness. In the course of his speech he touched at two or three of the places where the real canker of the University lies but the places are so sore, and they were so roughly handled that it produced nothing but furious irritation. The debate was carried on by Mr. Saltonstall, Mr. J. C. Park and others until it became late and I left.

After a short visit at Mr. Quincy's to deliver him a letter from my father and making a bow to the ladies we left Cambridge and got home to Quincy before nine o'clock. Mr. Quincy and his family appeared in a state of considerable elation and on the whole I did not wonder although perhaps I may differ in my opinion of the degree in which it was justified.

THURSDAY. 28TH.

I remained at home all day—My father going to Cambridge to the exercises of the ΦBK. My day was not very usefully spent. Arranged and put away the Manuscripts as far as I had gone with them, then read German, the Story of the Halden Family becomes so interesting that I pursue it whenever I take it up. La Fontaine's style is now easy but I cannot read any body else's. This is a difficulty greater in German than in any other language apparently. I pursued my usual study of Ovid. This is my beggarly account of my summer exploits. I do nothing but luxuriate in the indulgence of reading. Evening, Cards. Interrupted by a visit from Mr. and Miss Beale, Mr. and Mrs. Emmons.

FRIDAY. 29TH.

Arose early and set off with Walter Hellen for Boston so as to be in time for the boat which goes to Nahant. As this is one of our greatest curiosities I thought it would be an act of kindness to let Walter Hellen see it before he left this part of this Country. We were extremely fortunate in our day which was clear and calm—The wind from the Eastward so as to make it quite cool. We started at nine and reached Nahant by eleven. There were few people on board the Boat or at the Hotel with whom I was acquainted so that we spent our time in rambling about to see the Swallow's cave, the spouting horn and the other curiosities of the place. This with a game at billiards killed the day. At dinner we met with Mrs. Gorham and Mrs. Chadwick, and Col. S. Swett who had been in the Boat was very civil to us. These were all with whom I was acquainted. My luck was not so great today as upon the last occasion when I was here with Robert Buchanan. But perhaps I was as well off. Nahant is a fatiguing place to spend a day. There is such a seeking after amusement and so little freshness and seclusion. Sun and rocks strike at first but soon grow tiresome.[1] We reached Boston shortly after Sunset, and Quincy after eight o'clock, heated and tired. E. C. Adams at the House. Family as usual.

[1] For the earlier occasion on which CFA visited Nahant and for an engraving and account of the place, see vol. 3:x–xi, following 218, 305–306.

Quincy–Medford

SATURDAY. 30TH.

This was the day fixed for the termination of our visit at Quincy and return to Medford. I started as usual shortly after breakfast. Engaged most of the day at the Office in making up the arrears of my Diary which the voluminous occupations of the week have thrown into the background. I wrote pretty constantly but did not quite succeed in finishing all I had to do.

Rode to Medford—The day feeling like Autumn. The place as quiet

375

as usual. I passed my afternoon not very usefully but still quietly and in the pursuit of my usual studies. Read Madame de Maintenon and Ovid. But I must get higher game than all this amounts to.

My Wife conversed with me about the prospects for a winter arrangement. It will soon be necessary to reflect well upon this subject, and make some definite choice. Mr. Brooks is troubling his mind about it at present as he does not know what to do. I must think well about it, and decide soon. In the evening, quietly at home. Read in the Quarterly Review the article upon Sir Jas. Mackintosh.[1]

[1] An essay-review of Sir James Mackintosh's *History of the Revolution in England in 1688* (*Quarterly Review*, 51:493–534 [June 1834]).

SUNDAY. 31ST.

I resumed my shower baths this morning although the passage of the season makes it much more trying to take than when I left. Read German in continuation. I find it now pretty easy to read familiar conversation in this Language.

Attended divine service all day and heard Mr. Stetson from 15 Luke. 18–20 or rather generally the parable in that Chapter of the prodigal son—Treating in the morning of the character of the prodigal as an object of mercy, and in the afternoon, of the attributes of the Creator as a dispenser of justice. They were good Sermons, occasionally commenting upon the controverted subjects of election, innate depravity and atonement.

Read the last Sermon of the Collection by Atterbury. Romans 12. 18. "If it be possible as much as lieth in you, live peaceably with all men." An exhortation upon his leaving the Parish of St Bride's to a quiet election of a successor. He treats of the extent, of the difficulties in the way and of the helps to the practice of the precept. And the Sermon is generally a very good one. On the whole I think not much of a sermon writer. Occasionally he is sound and practical, never great and often exceedingly meagre and poor.

Evening at home. Pursued the reading of the Quarterly Review. Several amusing articles upon what I should consider likely to be amusing works. I also read a little German in which I persevere.

[*Quincy*]

MONDAY. [SEPTEMBER] 1ST.

The morning looked dark and threatening. Nevertheless I went to town. My time partly taken up in writing arrears of Diary, partly in a

visit to the Athenæum and partly in several little Commissions necessary but not pleasant. I went to Quincy in the midst of an Easterly
rain at one o'clock and found the family dining. I felt a little unwell
without knowing precisely wherein—A sort of indefinite uneasiness
which is not pain and yet prevents the sense of health.

Afternoon quietly passed in reading a new book called the Doctor
written anonymously but supposed to be by Southey.[1] It is rambling
but quite amusing, a sort of receptacle of old quotations and loose ideas
which cannot find their place in other writings. Now and then there is
a sound reflection but the weaving makes up a great proportion of the
whole. Read Ovid as usual. Evening, we sat down to Whist, four of us
and played two rubbers, after which I spent another hour in reading.

[1] *The Doctor*, by Robert Southey, ultimately published in 7 vols., 1834–1847, was
borrowed from the Athenæum.

TUESDAY. 2D.

It rained in the morning and the weather looked threatening all
day. I sat quietly at home all the time it was doubtful and read German, Goethe's Werther by which, and a volume of Lessing's Laocoon
which I opened, I can test the progress I have made. It is greater than I
had anticipated. Read also the Doctor &ca., and had half an hour's
conversation with my Mother, respecting my future plans for the
winter. I must bethink myself rather sooner than I had expected to as
my decision is very likely to affect that of others. I laid before her the
precise state of the case and requested her to ascertain what the probable cost would be of spending some months in Washington. She said
she would try.[1]

As it seemed to hold up at one, I accompanied my father and Walter
Hellen to Squantum—It being the day of the regular meeting for
choice of Directors &ca. of the Neponset Bridge Corporation. They
usually have a dinner and invite all the gentlemen in the town. Mr.
Beale, Messrs. Danl. and Thos. and E. Price Greenleaf, Mr. Miller,
T. B. Adams, Dr. Woodward, Mr. Emmons and a certain Capt. Quincy
made the Company. Two years since on a similar but worse day I had
been foolish enough to commit an excess in drinking bad wine. I remembered it upon this occasion to advantage.[2] I do not know why I
derived so much satisfaction from my this day's moderation unless it
was that I felt as if the Quincy people present might be looking with a
little attention to my conduct. Our family has been so severely scourged
by this vice that every member of it is constantly on his trial. I hope I

377

am *now* properly aware of the necessity of avoiding even the shadow of suspicion.[3] Nothing passed, the weather cleared up and we returned home before sunset. Evening. Cards, and the Dr. &ca.

[1] LCA inquired of JA2 on 5 Sept. (Adams Papers) about the availability and cost of a four-room establishment in Washington.
[2] For the earlier outing, see vol.

4:357.
[3] On an addiction to alcohol as a prevalent vice in the Smith-Adams line, see above, entry for 9 Aug. 1833 and note.

Medford

WEDNESDAY. 3D.

A lovely morning after the rain. I went to town and upon arriving received an invitation to dine at Mr. Everett's which I accepted. My time passed pretty actively. I made up the Arrears of my Diary and finished a volume of the Doctor &ca. Mr. N. Curtis called upon me with a piece of business as a Lawyer. I have so much given up business that I feel a little doubtful about undertaking it. On the whole, my morning was fully taken up until two o'clock when I walked over to Charlestown. Met at dinner Mr. and Mrs. Sidney Brooks who are now here, Mr. Edward Brooks, my Wife and her father. Quiet enough. And dull.

I returned to Boston, got my Gig, took Mr. Brooks up from Charlestown and reached Medford at sunset. My Wife in the Carriage with Sidney and his Wife. On her arriving, she gave me a notification of my election as a delegate to the Antimasonic Convention. This is dated August 16, and was left at the house. I was there on the 26th when it was not given me and was probably not left. It becomes necessary for me to reflect now what I must do. I endeavoured to digest my thoughts this evening. My prevailing inclination is to decline. The Worcester men upon whom I relied have left the party, and the Boston men have obtained a complete control by the new organization of the State Committee to include several of the then dissatisfied members. Evening, conversation. I read a few Chapters of the Life of Maintenon.

THURSDAY. 4TH.

A fine day but exceedingly warm. I accompanied Mr. Brooks to town. My first business was to reflect calmly upon the subject alluded to yesterday and to prepare a letter in case I should conclude to decline. In affairs of party it is always a hard thing to know what to do and yet it is worse to stand still. It is evident to me that the object of the Boston men is to join with the Jackson party, this by force of organization they will carry. The candidate of Antimasons for the Governorship will be the candidate of the present dominant party in the Nation. The result must inevitably be the union of these two parties in all subsequent measures, and in the submersion of the weaker in the stronger. Now with my present feeling to Jacksonism I cannot bring my mind even indirectly to give it any aid. On the other hand Governor Davis and a considerable number of Masons in various parts of the State are lending their aid to dissolve the Institution, the results of which exertion are not yet visible. I think the duty of Antimasons is to suspend action until the hope of any effect from it has expired. And not to rush into violent measures which will only exasperate and defeat the object in view. This will not however be the opinion of active Politicians who live upon organization.[1] I finally settled down upon these latter considerations as motives for my declining, wrote them out fairly and sent them to Dr. Phelps, Chairman of the meeting,[2] under cover to Mr. Hallett. Thus finishes this business with me. My Antimasonry has not been a discreet measure but it was based upon what I believe to be solid principles and the same is the case with my retirement. There is no other safety for a person taking part in political affairs. My mind was easy when I had done it.

The remainder of the morning was taken up in the usual way. Returned to Medford. Mr. Brooks had expected some of the family but none came. Sidney and Wife passed the day. In the afternoon read Maintenon, and Ovid. Evening it was so warm I was idle. Did not touch German today.

[1] JQA had at the same time arrived at similar conclusions as to the proper course for Antimasons to take and as to the unlikelihood that the party would adopt such a course. JQA, Diary, 6 Sept. 1834.
[2] LbC, Adams Papers.

FRIDAY. 5TH.

A warm hot cloudy day with a southerly wind and rain. I went to town in the Carriage with Mr. Brooks and Sidney and Wife. Time passed very quietly at the Office in writing Diary and setting down some thoughts which I have entertained an intention of communicating to the world. Whether I shall do it, or this will prove only one of a thousand abortive attempts I am as yet puzzled to know.

Sidney Brooks came in for half an hour to inquire if my father could give him any letters of recommendation to Europe whither he proposes to sail on the 1st of next month. I told him exactly how I believed my father stood in those respects, that he had been long at home and that most of those persons whom he knew were dead. He said he was aware of the fact. I promised with this understanding to state the case.[1]

Home in the rain. I have for several days been suffering with a great oppression upon the chest caused by a cold and today felt particularly unwell. Afternoon quietly at home. Read Madame de Maintenon and Ovid. Evening, German.

[1] On 24 Sept. JQA wrote letters introducing Mr. and Mrs. Sidney Brooks to Edward Livingston, U.S. minister to Paris, to Daniel Brent, American consul there, and to Aaron Vail, chargé d'affaires at London. LbC's of these letters and a draft of JQA's covering letter to Brooks, dated 26 Sept., are in the Adams Papers.

SATURDAY. 6TH.

This being the day fixed for the delivery of the Eulogy of La Fayette by Mr. Everett, Mr. Brooks, my Wife and I went to town in the Carriage. The day was very fine and the town seemed to be all in motion. I went to my house where I found my father, mother and Walter Hellen who had come from Quincy for the occasion. Thence to the State House. Being a member of the Committee of arrangements I enjoyed its privileges, though it must be confessed I have not troubled myself much with its pains. We were kept waiting for nearly two hours, but at last started upon a very long procession, the length of half the town. This took us until two o'clock. We reached Faneuil Hall and obtained seats not far from the Speaker—Being within one on his right. The Hall was appropriately decorated and the ceremonies effective.

Mr. Everett fulfilled the public expectation. It is now many years since the last time I heard him in the House of Representatives. He has gained in manner by throwing off the formality which still remained to him from the pulpit and by perfect ease and self possession. His modes of hitting the audience remain the same, brilliant contrasts, happy allusions, striking anecdotes, but there is no *depth* or maturity of thought, no greatness of view, no ingredients that make the Statesman or the Philosopher. As a popular festival Orator he will be unrivalled, but I doubt his success as a name for futurity. He appeared very much exhausted by his effort to speak, and closed sooner than he had intended.[1]

At four o'clock the ceremonies were through. I joined my father and father in law, and Walter Hellen to go to Mr. Frothingham's to dine. My Mother and Wife, Edward and Sidney Brooks with his wife made up the company. We had a tolerably pleasant time and returned home quietly to Medford. But I was so very much fatigued that I could not remain long up.

The standing and walking and hearing and seeing in such a day fatigue me more than the hardest work. I am not fond of this over-turn of life, not all the distinction in the world could make me think it more than a heavy tax one pays to society. The happiness of life is the quiet enjoyment of the pleasures of the world—The *moderation* of man's desires, the peace of his conscience, the blessedness of his social relations. I hope that my aim will be good, that I shall be seduced by no jack a' lantern to injure so much of those ingredients of happiness as I already possess.

[1] "A splendid Oration of an hour and fifty minutes was delivered by Edward Everett. He ... for lack of time abridged his discourse perhaps nearly an hour.... It was delivered every word from Memory—his manuscript lying on the table, and he never once recurred to it" (JQA, Diary, 6 Sept.).

SUNDAY. 7TH.

The day was cloudy with so much rain that in the afternoon Mr. Brooks did not attend Church. We went in the morning and heard from Mr. Stetson a Sermon from 1 John 3. 2. "Beloved, now are we the sons of God and it doth not yet appear what we shall be; but we know that when he shall appear we shall be like him for we shall see him as he is." He discussed as his subject for one half the day the question what we *are*, and how the sons of God; leaving the residue for the afternoon.

I read a Sermon by him preached lately upon the outrages at Charlestown. Text from 1 Peter 2. 13 to 16. "Submit yourselves unto every ordinance of man for the Lord's sake, whether it be to the king as supreme or unto governors, as unto them that are sent by him for the punishment of evil doers and for the praise of them that do well. For so is the will of God, that with well doing ye may put to silence the ignorance of foolish men; as free and not using your liberty for a cloak of maliciousness but as servants of God." He maintained the doctrine of Christianity to be a submission to the law, violence more especially to be foreign from it. Governments were either of men or of Laws, those of men were dangerous and despotic, those of law peaceful and moderate. Nobody here ought to complain of government for he had a right to a voice in changing it if unsatisfactory. The doctrine is sound but man is made blind by prosperity.

The remainder of the day I passed in reading German. This novel grew so interesting I could not leave it until after reaching the crisis.

MONDAY. 8TH.

I went to town this morning alone. Nothing material. Busy all the morning in making up arrears which continue to press upon me. Also in accounts. Went up to my father's buildings in Tremont Street to collect some rent of a Tenant, thence to my own house where I copied into my Letter book my missive to the Antimasons, thence again to the Office to write. Thus my time went. Home. Showery with heavy rain towards evening.

Afternoon, just as I was sitting down coolly to my reading, a Carriage drove up with company. Mrs. Sidney Brooks with Mr. and Mrs. Barclay of New York and a daughter about nine years old, and a Mr. Hood, a very Ignorant Englishman. I took no great pleasure from the visit and was glad when it was over.

Finished the German story. We were invited to spend the evening out this evening but the rain and the company prevented. Louisa being taken sick in the night made it very uneasy to us.

TUESDAY. 9TH.

This being a sultry morning and my child suffering severely from an attack of Cholera Morbus and subsequent fever, I arose early and took the bath to refresh myself. My spirits rather heavy from the anxiety always attendant upon sick children.

Went to town with Mr. Brooks. Received a Note from my father informing me of my mother's sickness, and her change of intention respecting her journey this week.[1] Occupied at office. Wrote arrears of Diary, and accounts, after which I tried to draught something for the Newspapers. Just as I was getting in the vein, it was time to return to Medford.

Quiet afternoon for once. Read Madame de Maintenon and Ovid. The Child's fever appeared very much subdued though not completely. I accompanied my Wife this evening to see the Miss Osgoods, a few persons, Mrs. Angier, Elizabeth, &ca. Only an hour. Read the last Essays of Elia.[2]

[1] JQA to CFA, 8 Sept. (Adams Papers). LCA had planned to go on an excursion to Lowell on the 9th.

[2] Lamb's *Last Essays of Elia* in the London, 1833, edition was borrowed from the Athenæum.

[Quincy]

WEDNESDAY. 10TH.

Cool and clear. A fine day. The Child had a very uneasy night but seemed on the whole to be better this morning. Although my anxiety is by no means quieted yet it is considerably diminished by the quickness with which the fever has abated.

I went to town early and was busily occupied all the time, first at Office, then in some Commissions and finally in an investigation of Title in the Office of the Register of Deeds. This is a serious Affair and will require a longer time than I could give to it today. I spent some time in writing upon the Antimasonic question. This is the day of assembling of the Antimasonic Convention and it now only remains to be seen what they will do.

Rode to Quincy today to see my father. My Mother has been very ill, far more so than I had supposed, and even now suffers severely from a very violent cough.[1] Nothing particularly new but the house seemed very dull. Thomas B. Adams passed some hours and took tea. Conversation. Nothing of importance.

[1] "The Gates of Death have been wide open to receive me" (LCA to JA2, 10 Sept., Adams Papers).

Medford

THURSDAY. 11TH.

A cold morning but fine weather. My Mother suffered much from a restless night and coughing and seemed not so well this morning.

I returned to town after breakfast. Learnt that the Antimasonic Convention had nominated Mr. Bailey for Governor. This is on the whole well enough. The sound principles of the party have been maintained at least and the introduction of Jacksonism as a branch of the party repudiated. It is nevertheless probable that the Jackson party will drop Judge Morton and come in to the support of their own interest under the new shape of Antimasonry. We must now see what the game will be. For my part, I rest quietly on my Oars. My course has been one strictly correct in principle and that is my foundation.

Busy at Office all the morning excepting what was spent in Commissions for my Mother. At one o'clock attended a Meeting of the La

Fayette Committee. Very few present. Question, Money. One of the number Mr. Codman raised a doubt whether any thing could be taken for general expenses from the fund in the hands of the Treasurer collected for the Cenotaph. The Majority did not doubt and proceeded to vote the money. I was inclined to their opinion from a misconception of the character of the fund. But on reflection I believe in Mr. Codman's objection. There was such a vagueness and bluster in the talk of Col. Baker who appears to be Chairman upon this occasion that I foresee difficulty and above all I see the necessity if I take part here of controlling my temper. The adjournment was sine die, and this is the way young men do business. No wonder they are so often caught in difficulty.

Rode to Medford. The child seemed much better but still weak from reduction. Mr. and Mrs. Everett dined here. Nothing new. Read Madame de Maintenon and Ovid. Evening Elia. Quite cool.

FRIDAY. 12TH.

I accompanied Mr. Brooks to town this morning. Passed my time very busily at the Office in writing until T. B. Adams came in. His object appeared to be inquiry into the matters relating to the settlement of his father's Estate, and also to consult me about his own affairs. He goes away in a few days and wishes to make a thorough disposition of his business before he goes.

Afterwards, walk. Rather idle. Returned to Medford. Afternoon I was just sitting down very comfortably to read when Mr. Augustus Thorndike and Mr. Eckley called to see Mr. Brooks. They did not see him as he was out upon his place. I was therefore obliged to do the honors and accompany them over the grounds. This was wearisome.

In the evening I determined to make up the deficiency in Ovid which is so frequently taking place and read two long Epistles in the third book from Pontus. I am tired to death of these for their sameness, their servility and their whining tone. Read German also and one or two Essays of Elia but it was so cold and there being no fire, I did not enjoy them much.

SATURDAY. 13TH.

Cool morning with probably a slight frost. I persevere in taking the shower bath although it is now pretty trying. Went to Boston alone as Mr. Brooks was going to Salem.

I had intended to have devoted my time to the investigation of title of the Boylston Estate but my father came in with bad accounts of my Mother's condition and with commissions which kept me pretty busy the remainder of my morning. He saw me only for a minute, then disappeared with a promise to see me again, but he did not and when I went to look after the Carriage, an alarm of fire in the Stable had put every thing in such confusion as to render it impossible for me to find out any thing positively but that the Carriage was safe, and gone.[1]

Home to dinner. Quiet afternoon finished the fourth volume of Madame de Maintenon, and the third book of the Epistles from Pontus. He says in the beginning of his fourth book that his correspondents complain of uniformity, and *I* think justly enough. Evening, German.

[1] "At half-past one, I went to Charles's Office. The key was in his door but he was not there. Just then the Bells were ringing for a fire; and the Engines were rattling over the pavements; and the People were running to and fro in the Streets with much confusion. The fire was in a Blacksmith's shop next door to Foster's Stable where my Carriage and Horses were put up. . . . I was a full half-hour approaching it . . . before I could reach it. . . . When I came to the Stable, the man told me that at the first cry of Fire, my Coachman Wilson had gone off with the Carriage and Horses, without saying where" (JQA, Diary, 13 Sept.).

SUNDAY. 14TH.

Fine day. I passed the morning in reading German. Attended divine service and heard a young man Mr. Briggs just commencing his profession.[1] In the morning from John 14. 21. "He that hath my commandments and keepeth them he it is that loveth me; and he that loveth me shall be loved of my father and I will love him and manifest myself in him." The nature and force of love, as explained by the Saviour. In the afternoon Hebrews 13. 18. "For we trust we have a good conscience." The intricate question of conscience is rather trying to a young beginner. However he managed it judiciously insisted only upon the necessity of enlarging it's power by knowledge and especially by religion and of listening to it as the dictate of a judge not of a reasoner. He has considerable power. A degree of eloquence in his manner, and a fervor of style which might (I should think) raise him quite high in public estimation.

At home, read a Sermon of Warburton, upon the love of God. 1 John 4. 20. "If a man say, I love God and hateth his brother, he is a Liar, for he that loveth not his brother whom he hath seen, how can he love God whom he hath not seen?" He traces Religion up to Love,

385

Love up to benevolence and benevolence to selfishness. This appearing to be the origin with him of the moral sense. Benevolence being the general Law which prompts to Love, it extends both to that for God and man and cannot easily be found where both of these its natural consequences do not exist. I do not at present entirely assent to this derivation of our moral sense, and of our virtues. The Sermon has nevertheless some merit.

In the evening, I read to Mr. Brooks at his request a Sermon of Sterne's upon the text of this afternoon. It is a mixture half facetious, half profound with occasional touches of nature, like every thing else of that author. German. A new story in which I do not succeed so well.

[1] George Ware Briggs had received his degree in divinity only in the preceding month (*Harvard Quinquennial Cat.*).

[*Quincy*]

MONDAY. 15TH.

Fine day. The air milder than it has been. I went to Boston alone. My time partly wasted, partly taken up in Accounts and partly in investigations at the Office of the Register of Deeds, as yet without fruit. My father wrote me a letter [1] requesting some things which I procured and then went to Quincy. Found my Mother still exceedingly ill. She has been suffering now for ten days without apparent amendment. A lung fever of great violence. I sat with her much of the afternoon but she was unable to talk much. The house seemed disconsolate enough. In the evening I sat up in my room and read German.

[1] 14 Sept. (Adams Papers).

Medford

TUESDAY. 16TH.

My Mother was still very ill and I recommended the sending for Dr. Holbrook as consulting physician with Dr. Woodward which was accordingly agreed to be done. As I was of no service and a little in the way, I concluded to go and take Walter Hellen with me to Medford for a day or two.

Boston. Athenæum where I remained an hour and afterwards to the Office. T. K. Davis came in to see me and he talked for a couple of hours, after which Walter came in so that I had little or no leisure to do any thing. My business is trifling and yet my interruptions are so numerous that I can hardly find any leisure to do it.

386

To Medford at the usual time. Dinner and Afternoon walk round the Garden. On our return, we found Mr. and Mrs. Everett, and Mr. and Mrs. Lothrop. Mrs. Everett was quite lively. Mr. Lothrop with the peculiar manners which one sees in him always and which betray the hypocrite by the force of circumstances.[1] Mr. Everett looked in better spirits but careworn. They remained until after tea, and I was not sorry when they went. We had a game of Whist in the evening very quietly at home. Read for half an hour afterwards from Southey's first volume of the Doctor. How my Summer has slipped through my hands. Doing nothing at all. And giving myself up to the course of circumstances.

[1] On CFA and Rev. Samuel K. Lothrop of the Brattle Square Church, see above, entry for 10 April 1833.

WEDNESDAY. 17TH.

Fine morning. Instead of going to town I went with my Wife and Walter to Mount Auburn in Cambridge to show it to the latter. We rambled round while Mrs A. went to see her Aunt Mrs. Parks who is quite sick. I saw only one or two Monuments that were new to me and none that struck me. The day was one of our hazy Autumn ones, not favourable to a view but very much so to the senses of feeling. The spot is a delightful one and shows only how much might have been made of it as a residence for the living instead of a repose for the dead. I am pleased with it's quiet and when it becomes thickly strewed it will be interesting by association, although it will hardly possess many known to fame.

Returned to Medford. Dinner. Afterwards, Walk to Mrs Angier's with Walter to pay her a visit. She was not at home at first but came in afterwards. Saw Mr. Angier and two brothers, Chas. and Joseph. Home. Evening. Whist. I felt very much fatigued from my rather unusual quantity of exercise.

[*Quincy*]

THURSDAY. 18TH.

Cloudy and slight showers of rain. I went to town accompanied by Walter. But I had little leisure to attend to any thing. I first went to an Auction Room where some Engravings were sold. Purchased one. Then to Mrs. Frothingham's, then to the Exhibition of the Horticultural Society at Faneuil Hall. This was a very pretty collection of things from the gardens in the vicinity of the town. A great display of grapes, peaches, pears and apples, together with flowers of many varieties. The hall was decorated with these in very good taste. I found a great many people whom I knew, and was engaged in conversing with them. The birds and the gold fish added much to the effect of the scene. I hurried away and accompanied Walter to the North end for the purpose of going over to East Boston but not readily finding the ferry and it becoming late I desisted. Returned with him to Quincy to dine.

Found my Mother pronounced a little better. She seemed to me however still suffering very much. In the evening after the visit of the physician I thought she improved and was quite lively. Indeed this activity betokens to me some remainder of fever. Conversation with my father who is dull, and after all retired, Goethe's Werther, and dipped into the Pensees Ingenieuses of Bouhours.[1]

---

[1] Dominique Bouhours, *Pensées ingénieuses des anciens et des modernes.* A copy of the Paris, 1707, edition is in MQA.

Medford

FRIDAY. 19TH.

I remained at Quincy until four or five o'clock. My time was not passed very usefully and yet agreeably. There is a great deal of pleasure to be derived from the desultory reading in a Library. It prevents the necessity of continued thought and yields a variety that is inspiriting. I read some of Antoine Hamilton's rambling stories which are told with a good deal of volatile humor.[1] Also Werther the other extreme of sentimentality. My father's library is a treasure from which I scarcely draw enough.

In the afternoon as it seemed to threaten rain I concluded to start for Medford. My Mother seemed better, and yet she has more fever and consequent strength than I perfectly confide in. I did not reach home until evening. Finished the Essays of Elia which have on the whole disappointed me.

---

[1] Copies of two editions (1749) of the *Œuvres mêlées* of Charles Antoine Hamilton, along with copies of three of the *contes* published separately, are in MQA.

SATURDAY. 20TH.

Morning to town with my Wife and Mr. Brooks in the Carriage. My first business was to call upon Miss Oliver the Tenant in Hancock

Street and see the house. She pointed out several things to be done which I made a memorandum of and then announced the increase of rent from the 1st of January, upon which I left. Occupied at my Office, but Sidney Brooks came in about his Letters and made me an interruption for some time. I did not even finish the arrears in my Journal which are now perpetually occurring. Never was a man more occupied about nothing than I.

To Medford to dine. Afternoon not entirely useless. Read more of the Doctor and several epistles in the *last* book of Ovid. I am glad of it for I am almost tired out. The Metamorphoses come next to which I hope to pay attention. W. G. Brooks and his Wife came in and took tea. Quiet evening. I read another of Lafontaine's Novels, Herr von Lange. Very much pleased with it.

SUNDAY. 21ST.

Our weather for several days past has been charming, uniting the ingredients of a pleasant temperature. Morning reading German. These Novels of Lafontaine delight me very much. There is a high tone of morality in them combined with masterly touches of nature.

Attended divine service and heard Mr. Briggs again. He did not please me quite so much today. He adopted more of the mere visionary enthusiasm of the Unitarian school of the present day. Morning text 1 Corinthians 2. 2 "For I determined not to know any thing among you save Jesus Christ and him crucified." Afternoon 2 Corinthians 13. 5 "prove your own selves." On the whole, the young men of the present day *generally* write and preach better than their predecessors but there are fewer exceptions of excellence. The character of the whole Community is changing to a state of calm mediocrity. Is not this for the better?

Read a Sermon from Warburton from Proverbs 17. 5. "Whoso mocketh the poor reproacheth his Maker." A superfluous text one would at first think, but in the world perhaps there is no more frequent vice. The distinctions of Society are shocking to an unartificial mind and yet they have their compensations. All good is mixed, all evil is mixed. Civilization compounds the [*illegible word*] more variously as it becomes more refined but the ingredients existed with the world.[1]

P. C. Brooks Jr. came out with a Mr. Davis nephew to C. A. Davis of New York. In the evening Dr. Swan and Jonathan Brooks. Tiresome.

---

[1] The illegible word, overwritten, seems to be *dress* or *dross*. Although either reading presents difficulties, the drift of the thought can be discerned through the cloudy figures.

[*Quincy*]

MONDAY. 22D.

Fine day. I went this morning to town. My boy is this day one year old. I always think of the passage of time as it respects the children with gratitude to God. One year ago, the day was one of immense and trying anxiety to me—My mother taken ill fearfully in the morning, and my wife in childbirth before night. I am, thank God, easier now, although a man after he acquires his relations in life is rarely free from anxiety. My Mother is now very ill and my daughter is ailing. Yet my lot is a blessed one in having health myself and in my Wife as well as uncommonly healthy children. Let me trust every thing to the Deity.

Busily occupied this morning with my arrears. Then to the Carpenter's who was not there and to the Athenæum. Attracted by two numbers of Jacob Faithful a story in the Metropolitan Magazine, which appear to me far superior to the rest.[1] Remained there longer than I had intended. Received from my father for my son, a silver cup as a birthday present.

Went to Quincy. Found my Mother a little better but still apparently quite ill. Passed much time with her, the remainder in reading the second volume of La Fontaine's Novel. T. B. Adams came in. J. Q. Adams his brother has got an appointment in the Navy and sails in the Potomac. This is the fourth appointment to the United States Service in that family and two of them with reasonable ground for doubt of their propriety.[2] But I say nothing. Evening. Conversation with my father upon the prospects of this Country. Afterwards, sat up until late deeply interested in Herr von Lange.

[1] *Jacob Faithful*, like a number of the other novels of Capt. Frederick Marryat, appeared serially in the *Metropolitan Magazine*, of which Marryat was the editor, 1832–1835.

[2] An appointment in the Navy for Joseph H. Adams and one to West Point for Isaac Hull Adams had been obtained by the intervention of LCA and JQA. See vol. 4:76, 197, 235. JQA had also used his good offices in behalf of young J. Q. Adams' appointment (JQA, Diary, 22 Sept. 1834). On these sons of TBA, see also Adams Genealogy.

Medford

TUESDAY. 23D.

I left Quincy this morning finding my Mother much the same. In Boston engaged constantly in something or other without making profitable progress in any thing. Accounts. Copying letters. Diary arrears. Agency business. I find no time to execute my purpose of examining the Registry of Deeds, nor for going to my House. J. Q. Adams called for a few minutes. He has been to the Potomac, but the Captain was not there.

Went to Medford at noon. Afternoon pursued the reading of Herr von Lange, and the Epistles of Ovid, which I have now very nearly closed. My time is principally devoted to this German, for I mean to be acquainted with their Literature. The child Louisa is very drooping, we do not know what the case is.

WEDNESDAY. 24TH.

Louisa looked so poorly this morning that I recommended to her Mother to act decisively with her. I never think it worth while to nurse[1] a diseased state of the body. With children, it leads to serious sickness.

I accompanied Mr. Brooks to town and was occupied as usual. Passed an hour or more making an investigation at the Record Office. Then to the House for some Papers. Writing Diary, and some affairs for Agency completed my time.

Home. Quiet afternoon. Pursued the reading of Herr von Lange, a book which pursues the history of two generations. This is always a mistake. It parts the interest, and lengthens too much the trial of patience of a reader. It ceases to be novel and becomes history. Finished the Epistles of Ovid very much to my satisfaction. For they have tried my patience as they did that of all his friends and acquaintants. On the whole they show no great merit in the man. Evening at home.

[1] In the sense of attempting to cure an illness by taking care of oneself, or to drive it away by nursing (*OED*, vb. 5b). In general, CFA was inclined to call in a physician upon the first sign of a child's indisposition.

THURSDAY. 25TH.

A pleasant day. I continue my shower baths in the morning and as yet do not find them unpleasant. My child was better this morning but seems yet to be hardly herself.

I went to town accompanied by Mr. Brooks. Received a short Letter from my father covering the requisite Letters for Sidney Brooks which I copied and returned for him to frank.[1] Thomas B. Adams and his brother John Q. called in by whom I sent them. Their report of my Mother's condition is little different from what it has been heretofore.

I look to the close of this week for an improvement. Other occupations consumed the remainder of my time. It is a little singular what small chance there is for me to read at all. I have hardly looked into a book at my Office for months. Today I took up a German one to see what progress I made, and the attempt discouraged me.

Home. Afternoon, Herr von Lange which I finished in the course of the evening. It does not appear to me to be equal to the Halden family, and yet perhaps it's moral tone was superior. Redding's History of Modern Wines and John Bowring's Minor Morals. He is a disciple of the Bentham school and talks of the greatest happiness of the greatest number.[2]

[1] See 5 Sept., above, and note.
[2] Sir John Bowring's *Minor Morals for Young People*, London, 1834, was borrowed from the Athenæum.

FRIDAY. 26TH.

It is very seldom now that I do not go to Boston, and it is exceedingly seldom that I find I improve my time in doing so. I had made an appointment this morning with the Carpenter to go and inspect Miss Oliver's house for the purpose of making the repairs I contemplate. On examination, I find them greater than I expected. But the property has been neglected and it is a good investment to bring it up again. Having done with this business I was then obliged to go to the other side of the Common to see Mr. Kauffer my Painter and from thence to see the Clerk of the Boylston Market, so that it was nearly noon before I got home to the Office. Mr. Walsh then came in and talked until it was the hour for returning.

I have felt quite unwell for a day or two from too great indulgence in fruit. The temptation is rather powerful, but it becomes soon satiety. Afternoon a new German book of La Fontaine's, Karl Engelmann's Tage Buch, and the Preface to Ovid's Metamorphoses.[1] Quiet uninterrupted day and evening. A little of Mr. Bowring.

[1] Although it would appear that CFA's reading of the *Metamorphoses* was in one of his sets of the *Opera* of Ovid (see above, entry for 17 April 1834), there are at MQA seven copies of the *Metamorphoseon* published separately at various times and places.

SATURDAY. 27TH.

Fine day although we had a few clouds and slight showers. I went to town with Mr. Brooks, found at my Office my father who told me my Mother was better. Yet he speaks very discouragingly of her situation and seems to adhere to his belief that she will never entirely recover. I do not like to think so. Nor do I yet think there is occasion if any faith is to be put in medical advice.

My time was taken up at a sale of engravings where I purchased a few, also at the Office as usual. Returned to Medford—Mr. Brooks' horse Squire being much indisposed. He is a veteran in the service and came in in the morning very briskly. But his strength was exhausted and barely brought us home.[1]

After dinner there was company. Mrs. Adams, Mr. and Miss Soley with her lover Mr. D'Wolf,[2] with Mr. and Mrs. Everett from Charlestown. I felt exceedingly unwell and unable to exert myself. A hearty dinner which I made upon saltfish increased the indisposition I had experienced before. Quiet evening. Continued La Fontaine.

[1] On the 29th in his "Farm Journal," Mr. Brooks recorded the death of "The 'Squire": "He had been sick since Saturday . . . and from that time scarcely eat or drank. He died of old age. He was, I think, about 26. . . . He has been one of the best and most powerful animals I ever had. As I do not sell my old horses, I should probably have ordered him killed this fall and therefore do not regret his loss. I only regret that I used him on Saturday and drove him down faster than usual. . . . Had the poor old fellow buried in the orchard . . . taking off his shoes."

[2] Mary Russell Soley, daughter of John Soley, would marry William Bradford DeWolf in a month (*Columbian Centinel*, 24 Oct.).

SUNDAY. 28TH.

I arose this morning feeling extremely unwell, and omitted my usual bath. By starvation however I recovered the tone of my stomach and felt as well as usual before evening. I did not attend divine service in the morning.

After dinner, heard Dr. Follen 43 Psalm 5. "Why art thou cast down O my soul? and why art thou disquieted within me? hope in God": He reviewed the miseries of life, the uncertainties of this world, and considered them as yielding to the desire which improves upon experience. A little touch at politics, the late liberation of slaves in the West Indies, as a sign of this great improvement. A poor sermon.

Read one of Warburton's which struck me much. 1 Corinthians 1. 30 "Jesus Christ who of God is made unto us wisdom and righteousness and sanctification and redemption." One part of the Sermon seemed to be intended to form Christs character as a divine Messenger foretold, the other to show the purposes of his coming as explained in the two latter terms of the text. The argument upon the nature of the prophecy and the fulfilment of it by the Saviour seems to me very strong and embodies many floating thoughts which I had in reading Mr. Noyes' Article in the Christian Examiner.[1]

I read and finished La Fontaine's third story. It has perhaps Passages more eloquent than either of the others, but I like it as a whole the least. Yet there is a moral tone pervading all his works which renders them charming to me. Minor Morals, which I do not like at all or believe in.

[1] See above, entry for 9 July.

[*Quincy*]

MONDAY. 29TH.

A cool morning but a beautifully clear one. We were again in some anxiety respecting our child who droops in an inexplicable manner. I went to town in my own way and was occupied in a variety of things. Drew up my Quarterly Account which is by far the smallest I ever presented. This with going round in various directions for one thing and another took my time. Finding myself so unable to pursue the investigation of title with the closeness I ought to, and perceiving that Mr. Walsh really wants business and I do not, I thought it an act of Kindness in me to give it over to him to do.

Dined at Mr. Frothingham's. Conversation not interesting. He has the strong prejudices of the sphere in which he lives and when they come in contact with mine which are as strong and as peculiar, there follows constraint. I have of late acquired the wisdom in general to hold my tongue.

Attended a meeting of the Directors of the Boylston Market where they made a good Dividend and debated the rest of the afternoon without coming to any conclusion, as usual. We have one or two *great* Speakers upon these occasions. Rode to Quincy. Found my Mother rather better and the rest of the family as usual. Miss Louisa Foster staying out there.[1]

[1] Louisa Catherine Smith Foster was a daughter of the James Hiller Fosters and thus a grandniece of AA.

TUESDAY. 30TH.

A cold morning. I remained at Quincy today. Most of my time spent with my Mother who was better and sat up some hours in conversation. I also read through Goldsmith's charming little story of the

Vicar of Wakefield,[1] in consequence of my purchase the other day of Newton's picture engraved by Burniè. There is a most fascinating union of shrewdness and simplicity, of genuine feeling and drollery developed in it's natural forms. No exaggeration, no straining after strong lights and gaudy shows.

We dined early in order to accommodate Dr. Waterhouse who came over on his annual visit. He is now eighty years of age but time is heavy upon his intellect. He begins to repeat and to talk without object. The change is a painful one.[2] It prefigures what we may all come to. It shows the dark side of this world. The Dr. is now a child under direction of no mild Mistress and perhaps that may have contributed to his decline. I left him to sit with my Mother.

Evening, a conversation with my father upon the subject of the old controversy with the federalists which has been revived by a private letter from old Mr. Pickman of Salem calling upon him for private explanation, in a friendly way.[3] This has affected my father, and although he gives up nothing yet I think I see a little regret at his position. We discussed the opposed characters of Mr. Lowell and Mr. Otis, and the probable actors in the scheme of an Eastern confederacy—Col. Pickering one of the main pillars of it.

[1] The Edinburgh, 1822, edition is at MQA.

[2] JQA's reactions after Dr. Waterhouse's visit were similar: "His Spirit still lively, but his memory much decayed of which he is conscious, and his judgment, more than ever under the ascendancy of his Passions. It amounts to little short of dotage" (Diary, 30 Sept.). Nevertheless, there seems no loss of powers evident in his letters to JQA, 24 Sept. and 3 Oct. (both in Adams Papers). On Waterhouse and the Adamses, see also note 2 to entry for 27 June 1833, above.

[3] Benjamin Pickman to JQA, 27 Sept. (Adams Papers). On JQA's charges against the Massachusetts Federalists and the protracted controversy which followed, see vol. 2:297, 311, 312, 317; 3:63, 332, 418–420; 4:144, 423.

Medford

WEDNESDAY. OCTR. 1.

I did not mention Walter Hellen's leaving us yesterday morning as he only started for Boston. Today he goes home. I have been pleased with his unassuming manners and amiable disposition, and regret that he is now obliged to leave the family to whom he has much recommended himself.

I returned to town this morning with John Quincy in company who appears all agog with his appointment. Office where I was busy with Accounts and Money—Copying letters and some general commissions.

This was Quarter day and therefore attended with the usual payments. Returned to Medford. Found that poor old Squire was dead. Quite a pathetic close to a long service of usefulness. Poor fellow. It was time.

Afternoon. Began a new German story and read a little of the Preface to Ovid. Nothing further. Evening, notwithstanding a heavy blow from the Southward, we went down to attend a party at Mrs. Dudley Hall's. The Medford people. It was exceedingly dull and tiresome to me. Home by ten. The relation in which Town people and those of the Country stand to each other is always a stiff one. They have few common topics of conversation and yet the one expect a great deal from the other with little to give in exchange.

THURSDAY. 2D.

Cloudy and with a high Southerly wind but exceedingly warm. I went into town with Mr. Brooks. Time consumed in Office, business—Rents, Money, Athenæum &ca. I barely read a few lines in the new Number of the North American and did not much like those. How fast time flies in a morning.

Home. Mr. and Mrs. Frothingham dined with us and we had a pleasant time. There has been much conversation about an arrangement for Mr. Brooks this Winter. He has been inclining very much to ask me to sell my House and take the Lease of his, provided that he remain in the House as Winter tenant. He has been much inclined to ask my Wife to go there, and spend the Winter without reference to further measures. There are difficulties in all the arrangements. My intention has been and is, if I can get good accommodations to go to Washington. But if my Wife inclined to accommodate her father, I would consent to her going and I was to go merely to Washington and home again for a month. In the meantime Mr. Brooks hit upon another arrangement with his Sister which suits him in many respects far better. But he remains balancing and undulating like a pendulum. In the mean while I am waiting for information from Washington.[1]

Evening quietly at home I read a good deal of the criticism upon Ovid and was pleased with it, also German.

[1] CFA's plan to take his family to Washington for the winter, or, failing that, to install his wife and children with Mr. Brooks and spend some time in Washington himself was changed by the circumstance that ABA had become pregnant (LCA to JA2, 10 Sept., Adams Papers). CFA2 would be born in May 1835.

FRIDAY. 3D.

A beautiful day. I went to town accompanied by Mr. Brooks. Office where I was engaged with business and Accounts my whole time. Mr. Walsh came in about the case of the title for the trustees of Boylston, and we discussed it pretty fully. It goes on so slowly I hardly think I made a mistake in giving it away. I am now pretty much of a useless drone. I have for many years nourished the idea that I might do something to add to my reputation, but I have failed and being above the necessity of labouring for a living, I have only to be idle, my powers which I *know* to be somewhat respectable notwithstanding. With respect to these however I feel that it will be advisable to think rather more humbly of them than I have done. The world wants great powers, and when I reflect that I have none to turn to account in any line which I [can] point out above what many others possess, I think I may as well retire within my shell of modesty. My grandfathers papers are my only resort and to that I must fix myself. Home. Afternoon, German and Ovid. Evening out. A visit at Mr. Jonathan Brooks' and one to Miss Mary B. Hall.

SATURDAY. 4TH.

Morning cloudy with a Southerly wind which brought a storm of rain before night. I went to town with Mr. Brooks and was busy at my office much of the day. My father sent me a long letter, the answer to Col. Pickman to copy. I think with the exception of one or two passages, it is very well. The subject is a painful one to all parties and should be treated with the gentlest language.[1] T. B. Adams came in just before I left town, and I was obliged to hurry in order to complete my business with him. He wants an advance as usual with him when he comes to this Quarter.

Home. Afternoon quiet at home. Read German. The Life and Adventures of Quinctius Heymerau von Flaming. A work by La Fontaine, but more comical than his others. Read in the evening, two hundred lines of Ovid's first book of the Metamorphoses and was much charmed with them—Incomparably superior to all the rest of his works, by the nobility of it's thought. The versification is as easy as usual. A little of Mrs. Austin's Characteristics of Goethe.[2] Very German. I have a notion, I shall not like him. The boy was quite unwell with his new teeth today.

[1] JQA to Benjamin Pickman, 4 Oct. (LbC, Adams Papers). The interchange had

a happy conclusion in a warm reply from Pickman, 8 Oct. (Adams Papers).

² CFA borrowed Mrs. Sarah T. Austin's *Characteristics of Goethe*, 3 vols., London, 1833, from the Athenæum.

SUNDAY. 5TH.

The weather changed to cold with a high North westerly wind. I passed the morning in reading German and laughing over the story, then attended Divine Service and heard Dr. Follen preach morning and afternoon from the same text. 4 Ephesians 28 "Let him that stole steal no more, but rather let him labour, working with his hands the thing which is good that he may have to give to him that needeth." The virtues described in the text are honesty, industry and charity, the force of each he discussed in one, and their union and harmony in the other Sermon. There is a curious mixture of good sense and practical wisdom with flighty, unreal visions in this man. It is in character with his Nation whose Literature has reacted upon them to heighten these ill assorted mixtures.

Read a Sermon of Warburton's or rather two thirds of what made in preaching several Sermons but were afterwards condensed into one. John 14. 16. "And I will pray the father, and he shall give you another comforter that he may abide with you for ever; even the *spirit of truth*. He dwelleth with you and shall be in you which is the *Holy Ghost* whom the Father will send *in my name*. He shall teach you all things." The subject, the process of sanctification by the mission of the Saviour, in whom the Holy Ghost acted as an instrument to extend the spirit of truth. He incidentally discusses the objections made by the Sceptics, to one great sign of this operation, the gift of tongues to the Apostles, and to the incorrect style of the Scriptures. These Discourses are strongly imbued with reasoning and are worth reading even by me who am no doubter. Evening, Mr. Jon. Brooks, his two daughters and Mr. L. Angier.

[*Quincy*]

MONDAY. 6TH.

This was one of the most beautiful days I ever remember in our climate. The air was pure and the sky so clear that the outlines of all the distant hills seemed distinctly defined to the eye. I went to town accompanied by Mr. Brooks who was afterwards to dine at Mr. Everett's, visit the Potomac [1] and return in the Carriage which was to come down with my Wife. I was engaged [during] my morning as usual.

Obliged to go to my House which I found Mrs. Fields had left. Two or three Commissions and my regular work consumed the remainder of the time.

Rode to Quincy. Found my Mother still improving, but a good deal depressed by information from Washington of the illness of both my brother and his Wife.[2] I had a good deal of conversation with her during the afternoon. It is the first time she has ever spoken freely to me, and I have always avoided it myself. I do not know, but I always experience a strange mixture of fearful sensations when I reflect upon the relations of life in which I stand and have stood. I do not feel as if it would be prudent to commit these to paper.

In the evening I went up on my usual errand to see Mrs. Adams and Elizabeth. Thomas, and Louisa C. Smith there. We chatted quite agreeably for an hour after which I returned. Family all retired and as I was sleepy, so did I.

[1] The frigate *Potomac*, Capt. Nicholson, to which young J. Q. Adams had recently been assigned, was lying near the Navy Yard (Brooks, Farm Journal).

[2] News of the illness of JA2 and of his wife with chills and fevers had reached LCA in a letter from her sister, Mrs. Frye (JQA, Diary, 6 Oct.).

Medford

TUESDAY. 7TH.

A pleasant morning although it clouded in the course of the day. I returned to town this morning and was engaged a considerable part of my time collecting Dividends and making up Accounts. The remainder in conversation with Mr. Walsh and in reading the last number of the North American. There is a rather remarkable article in it upon Coleridge's Poetry,[1] but no criticism. Indeed the art of criticism both in England and in this Country is almost entirely neglected.

Home to dinner. Afternoon, pursued assiduously my German which I admire in this book. There is great distinctness of delineation in the pictures drawn and the moral is excellent. Evening at home alone. Pursued the reading of Ovid with which I am charmed. The Metamorphoses restore to me the good humour, his whinings had disturbed. Nothing material occurring.

[1] The article on Coleridge's poems in the October issue (39:437) is by Robert C. Waterston.

WEDNESDAY. 8TH.

Another fine day although it clouded up before evening. I went with Mr. Brooks into town, and was busy for some time in Accounts, and collecting my semi-annual Dividends. These are this year quite favorable. I have been tolerably successful so far in the little circle of my own affairs, and have reason to be grateful for this as for all my benefits. Read a little of the North American Review and nothing further. Returned to Medford and passed the afternoon in reading German.

Evening, Ovid. Finished the first Book of the Metamorphoses with which I have been very much pleased. He has written fifteen books of these and my wonder will be, if he can sustain himself equally well to the end.

The change in the Season makes some reduction in the amount of our visitors and for this I am not entirely sorry, but the same change operates again unfavourably by driving me from my little study, as there are no accommodations for winter quarters. We remain in a state of painful suspense respecting our future residence this winter.

THURSDAY. 9TH.

As Mr. Brooks was to dine out, we had fixed upon this day for my Wife to ride with me to see my Mother at Quincy. The morning looked cloudy with a warm southerly wind but I thought the probabilities were that it would clear away. It rained a little on the road to town where I changed horses, but becoming tolerably clear, we determined to proceed and got safely there. After our arrival it set in and rained extremely hard for several hours.

My Mother was looking better and seemed to be slowly reviving. I talked a little with my father, but passed most of my time reading Werther. Mr. William Plumer of New Hampshire dined with us. Conversation dull as my father appeared fatigued.

After dinner, I decided to return, knowing that as the rain was precisely behind us, we should probably be as dry as if we were riding on the fairest day. It was a just conjecture, the rain stopped before we reached town and we arrived at Medford in good season for tea. Mr. Brooks did not return for an hour. Evening, German.

FRIDAY. 10TH.

Morning clear with a high wind from the North West. I went to town accompanying Mr. Brooks. Time wasted, excepting a little in business.

Mr. Brooks has made his children another present—Dividing among them the amount which his son Henry had remaining of his property at his death. This comes to my Wife and myself in the shape of three shares in the Lawrence Manufacturing Co. and is another evidence of the beneficence of my father in law,[1] as well as of the goodness of the Deity. My means are now more than sufficient for my living and mere property can add little more to my happiness. It must be my endeavor that it shall not take off from it by giving me a spirit of uneasy restlessness or vague ambition. I am blessed as much as man ever is in this sublunary state. May God be merciful to me and keep me humble and sensible of the extent of his goodness.

Athenæum. John Quincy made me a visit. He is not to sail for some days. Home to Medford. Afternoon German and in the evening read Ovid's Metamorphoses. Also Mrs. Austin's Characteristics of Goethe.

[1] Peter C. Brooks to ABA and CFA, 6 Oct. (Adams Papers). In acknowledging the gift, CFA wrote: "Our stock of words is quite used up.... Your bounty has given us a superfluity which we are perfectly aware is beyond our merits" (18 Oct., Adams Papers).

SATURDAY. 11TH.

A cold clear morning. I took a shower bath but it is so cold that I believe after this I shall give it up. With but one intermission since I have begun in June last, I have when at Medford constantly taken it and I think my health has been very much aided by it. Mr. Brooks being about to be absent from home all day, I went into town accompanied by my Wife who wished to see and to consult her sister. Time at the Office. My father came in on some commissions of his. Nothing new.

Called for my Wife and returned to Medford to dinner. Afternoon quiet. Read the second volume of Quinctius Heymerau von Flaming and was amused by it although I do not think it equal to the first. Evening Mrs. Gray and Miss Henrietta called. I managed notwithstanding to read a good deal of the second book of the Metamorphoses.

SUNDAY. 12TH.

Mild autumn day. I passed my morning reading German. Attended divine service and heard Mr. Stetson preach. Genesis 18. 26. "And the Lord said, if I find in Sodom fifty righteous men within the City then I will spare all the place for their sakes." Matthew 22. 37 "Thou shalt love the Lord thy God with all thy heart and with all thy soul and with all thy mind." I am ashamed to say that I could not fix my attention sufficiently upon these Sermons to be able to give any definite account of them. My mind would wander into those rambling paths of thought in which I felt myself running on a string of words in a supposable case. It is of no use.

Read in the afternoon and evening the remainder of Warburton's Sermon commenced last Sunday. He considers the mission of the Holy Ghost in the Saviour here as a comforter, and also the point of the duration of the gifts of grace. I did not admire this portion of the discourse. Read another short Sermon upon the character of the Apostles as Messengers of the truth. Matthew 10. 16 "Behold I send you forth as Sheep in the midst of wolves. Be ye therefore as wise as serpents and harmless as doves." Evening Mr. Chardon Hall came in and spent considerable time.

MONDAY. 13TH.

Mild morning, but it clouded up to rain in the latter part of the day. I went into Boston with Mr. Brooks. Morning passed rather indolently. I was obliged to go and make several commissions which led me down to the Athenæum. There I was fascinated with another number of Jacob Faithful and remained some time.

Then back to the Office where Thomas B. Adams called to see me. His Mother accompanies him to stop at Mr. DeWint's at Fishkill for a short time.[1] Thus that family is at last utterly scattered. The vicissitudes of this world are wonderful. My Grandfather who collected around him in 1817 as many descendants as fall to the lot of most persons, is gone and this winter the scene of his residence will probably not be marked by the tread of a single one of them.

Home to Medford. Afternoon German, but interrupted by the visit of Mr. Henderson Inches, his two sisters[2] and daughter. These are pleasant people who have seen something of the world and accommodated themselves to it easily. Perhaps above the common average of women and apparently inclined to remain single from a fancy for independence. A rare thing in this Country. Evening alone at home. Read Ovid but with less pleasure than usual. I did not feel quite well today.

---

[1] On John Peter de Windt, his wife Caroline, and their home, "Cedar Grove," see vols. 1:389, 2:71–72, and Adams Genealogy.
[2] The Misses Elizabeth and Susan Inches; see vol. 3:107.

TUESDAY. 14TH.

The morning was cold, cloudy and with a little snow, but as the wind promised a clear day I went to town. Time taken up at Office and in Commissions for my father, my Agency and myself. Called upon my father's Tenant, Fuller for a settlement of rent and was hurried in doing nothing. Rode to Quincy to dine. Found my Mother better but still unwell and hardly able to move from her sofa. I passed the afternoon in desultory conversation. My plans continue very unsettled. I hope to receive such definitive intelligence in a few days as will set at rest the mere question between my going to Washington or taking my own House. Evening, a very pleasant conversation with my father, upon Alexander Hamilton, Jefferson and Knox. T. B. Adams there at tea. Quiet evening. Werther.

Medford

WEDNESDAY. 15TH.

I arose very early this morning and went down to fish for smelts. The air was sharp and I thought would probably be very favorable but I hardly had a bite. After three hours expectation I returned home. Morning in consequence pretty short. I read a little more of Werther finishing the first part. A very curious book with some very powerful passages in it, and others that are perfectly burlesque. Afternoon, I started shortly after dinner and reached Medford by six o'clock. The evening quite sharp. Mr. Price Greenleaf called and conversed in a very lively manner. I read German.

THURSDAY. 16TH.

As my Wife was going to town in the Carriage, Mr. Brooks and I accompanied her. Morning engaged in several Commissions. Went to the House and from there to several other places with my Wife. Time short.

Mr. Devereux and Walsh called and consumed some of it in their schemes. They are unsettled by the present motion in Offices and wish to make hard bargains out of me.[1] I do not know whether it is wise to resist them or not. I hope these revolutions will cease with the present completion of the Street. My father's property here ceases to be productive in one part when it begins in another. So that on the whole things remain pretty even.

Home by the way of Cambridge to enquire after Mrs. Parks' condition which is very bad. Afternoon, I did not feel at all well. But I pursued my usual avocations which hardly need recapitulating as I do so often. Evening read Ovid Metamorphoses, which do not, I think, hold out quite so well as I had anticipated. More conceit and less beauty.

[1] John Devereux and John Walsh were the current tenants at 23 Court Street (M/CFA/3).

FRIDAY. 17TH.

Mild but cloudy. I felt quite unwell this morning but it afterwards passed off. Rode into town accompanied by Mr. Brooks, by way of Cambridge, to inquire into the condition of Mrs. Parks. She was not better. Time taken up as usual. I am ashamed of my Diary and of myself. Never was my Diary so perfectly uninteresting and never was I so much tempted to close its pages forever. Nothing of any consequence but rumors of violence at the elections in Pennsylvania. My interest in political affairs is failing very much. Indeed I am becoming a piece of vegetation.

Afternoon at home. German. Mr. Brooks is again in great embarrassment respecting his winter arrangements. His intended one has unexpectedly failed. This operates upon my own. I do not incline to live with him, and yet I wish to do every thing that is consistent with my relation to him. The pecuniary advantages attending such an arrangement are considerable. But the love of money is becoming a thing to be guarded against by me. I will not encourage it wantonly. Should Mr. Brooks think proper to ask me, I should feel it right to accept, but I will take no step to offer myself.

In the evening I accompanied Mr. Brooks to pay a visit to Mr. Jonathan Brooks. His son the Minister there who has just returned from Europe. No assumption about him though.[1] Home at 8 after which I read Ovid and Flaming.

[1] Rev. Charles Brooks of Hingham. The comment would seem to relate to CFA's observation of affectation in other returned European travelers.

[*Quincy*]

SATURDAY. 18TH.

A very beautiful day such as we rarely have so late in the Season as this. I went to Boston with Mr. Brooks. My morning rather wasted.

Went to the Athenæum and from thence to the gallery to see some Paintings of Rome. They are of the middle of the last Century and painted by Sigr. Panini. Two of them are views of the inside and the outside of St. Peter's. The other two contain a great number of smaller ones in which all the principal objects of curiosity in ancient and modern Rome are given in small. There was also a small collection of cabinet pictures—One or two of which were quite pretty. There was also a small collection of pictures for sale.

At Office writing. Just as I was going back to Medford I called at the Post Office and received by Mail a letter from Walter Hellen giving such very alarming intelligence of the condition of my brother John that I felt it my duty to proceed directly in a chaise to Quincy and apprise my parents of it.[1] I accordingly arrived at Quincy before three and communicated directly with my father. He was very much agitated. Then came the most trying part of it, the disclosure to my Mother. Barely able to move after so severe an illness we expected a terrible effect. She was very deeply affected[2] and the operation of it was to bring on a return of sickness, but the Dr. assured us her personal health had not suffered and we prayed for calmness.

My father and mother are to a certain extent prepared for this blow. They have watched his gradual decline for two years past and have seen that he cannot continue long in this condition. But this attack is rather sudden to them. May God have mercy upon them and all of us.

[1] Letter missing.

[2] JQA recorded her distress as "agonizing, and ... though unable to walk across her chamber long insisted upon going immediately, herself to Washington. . . . Dr. Holbrook ... assured my wife that ... the attempt would be at the hazard of her life. She became herself convinced it would be so and was partially tranquelised" (Diary, 18 Oct.).

Medford

SUNDAY. 19TH.

I spent most of this day in the company of either my father or mother. The former was making preparations to go off to Washington tomorrow morning and leaves me with the care of the family upon my shoulders, to go on with my Mother whenever the opportunity will permit. They were both very much affected and in conversing with me seemed to derive their main support. I promised to do everything I could to relieve them, which God knows, is less than I could wish. My mother was pretty quiet on the whole.

I did not attend divine Service or in short do any thing at all. At about 4 I started to take my father to town. We arrived and I left him at the Tremont House. I then went down for letters and got one dated the 16th from Mr. Johnson.[1] It is not so discouraging as Walter's. It expresses Dr. Huntt's opinion that the case is critical without entirely depriving us of hope. I felt a little relieved by it. I remained with my father and Mr. Degrand until nearly eight. This gentleman poked himself into the business without invitation and yet I felt glad he was there as he turned my father's thoughts from gloomy subjects.

It rained heavily all the evening. I went down and got into the Medford Stage, which runs in the evening, reached there at nine o'clock precisely. From the tavern the man sent me in a Chaise and at half past nine I surprised Mr. Brooks and my wife by my presence. I sat down and we had some conversation upon our intentions. My going to Washington will take place probably early in next month, and Mr. Brooks will take my Wife to his house for the winter. This will relieve me very much from anxiety about my own family, which I could not reconcile myself to leaving alone.

[1] Letter missing.

[*Quincy*]

MONDAY. 20TH.

I left Medford this morning in a very heavy rain which did not appear encouraging to my father's progress, but it soon stopped and before evening became very clear and bright. In turn, occupied much in Commissions, and copied some letters for my father, this with other things engrossed much time and I found myself soon called upon to start again for Quincy. The weather growing colder.

Arrived at Quincy, found my Mother more quiet, but suffering from faintness consequent upon the reaction of her system. I was in the mean time, beginning to suffer under one of my head achs which I resisted as long as I could but which I was finally forced to give way to and go to bed although only eight o'clock. Elizabeth C. Adams and Louisa C. Smith still here.

TUESDAY. 21ST.

A beautiful morning with a fine North west breeze. I think my father must have had a favorable passage. I went to town. My Mother was quiet although she did not pass a very quiet night. Her head is now running upon ever so many things and she worries herself out of trifles. We had no letters by the Mail of this morning, nor by yesterday's, which I consider in my brother's case as a favorable omen.

At the Office engaged in writing. Called at Mr. Frothingham's to see my Wife and occupied in a variety of Commissions for my Mother. Returned to Quincy to dinner. Afternoon passed with my Mother and in planting some of the seeds left by my father. Evening I managed to make use of some hours to read some pages of Ovid and my German.

My occupations grow less and less and my anxiety greater and greater. When I reflect upon the future I think I perceive much to be gone through before we reach again a clear sky. My brother may if he has energy enough left and survives this attack, yet recover. But the probabilities must be admitted to be against the first even more than the second condition. My father is daily becoming more helpless in his private concerns and there is nobody but me who takes interest enough in them to attend to them properly. I foresee much sacrifice and after all, but it is useless. My ideas are perhaps those of a croaker. And it is better for me to trust implicitly to a superior being who guides us all, only keeping myself properly prepared to execute whatever it may fall to my lot to do.

Medford

WEDNESDAY. 22D.

A southerly wind blew up a great quantity of clouds but it did not rain. I went to the Office and was engaged there in overlooking my papers and making some disposition of them. They seem to overflow me every little while and yet I appear to be among the most quiet and retired beings in the Community. Perhaps one reason of my difficulty is that I keep almost every piece of paper.

At noon I received a letter directed to my father and dated Sunday Evening, from Mr. Frye,[1] repeating almost literally the preceding letters. The delirium is in addition only. That it should continue without abatement is an unfavourable sign. Indeed at first I felt almost without hope, but afterwards (such is man's nature) I thought it presented nothing new. The word is still *critical* which is ambiguous. We shall now soon know from my father who will, in hope, be on the spot this evening.

I retained the letter and went with it to Medford where we enjoyed a pleasant and quiet afternoon and evening. I was rejoiced to see my children well and my Wife. How much I have to be grateful for.

[1] Letter missing. On Nathaniel Frye Jr., brother-in-law of LCA, see vol. 1:4 and Adams Genealogy.

THURSDAY. 23RD.

I left Medford this morning for the purpose of taking up my residence generally at Quincy until the time should come for me to go with my Mother if she wishes. It is the first time since my marriage I have been separated for any time from my family and it appears odd and uncomfortable. At Office in town. Received a letter from my father at New York giving us an Account of his favourable passage across the sound.[1] No advices from Washington. I feel relieved for each day is a little gain.

I was again busy at the office in making all my clearances which are numerous enough. Small commissions. On the whole I made very good progress. To Quincy to dine.

Afterwards, Conversation with my Mother. So differently do we take things that what I considered as so discouraging seemed to inspire my Mother with hope. I was glad of it and think it probable she is right.

Read Flaming and some more of Ovid's Metamorphoses. Elizabeth C. Adams has now left us and we are reduced to a very small number. This may serve to keep the House more quiet.

[1] To CFA, 21 Oct. (Adams Papers).

FRIDAY. 24TH.

A fine cold morning. I went to town and to the Office, from thence to the House where I wished to procure some things. This with my occupation at the Office in writing letters to my father[1] and to Mr. Jones the Auctioneer at Weston to proceed as usual with the sales of Wood there notwithstanding my absence.[2] I try to think of every thing before hand as my Mother begins to talk of next week for starting. Perhaps if things are favorable, it may be the week after.

I propose to change my Office this winter to the one directly below mine and am putting into it grates which will I hope make me comfortable for the first time. I have heretofore been able to let all the rooms in this building for my father, but as this winter, they will be empty and one of them contains the article which is becoming daily more important to me, a safe for the preservation of papers, I have concluded to fit it up. This will be the *third* of the Offices I have fitted up in this building, for myself.

No further news from Washington but a letter from my father who has got as far as Philadelphia.[3] Tomorrow we hope to hear his account from Washington. Returned to Quincy. My Mother seemed better today. I went down to fish and caught one smelt for her. Conversation. Ovid and Quinctius Heymerau von Flaming which has become dry.

[1] Letter missing.
[2] To Col. John Jones, 24 Oct. (LbC, Adams Papers).
[3] To CFA, 21 Oct. (Adams Papers).

SATURDAY. 25TH.

A fine day but quite cold. I went into town in the morning and was busy most of my time in my affairs. I got the Mason to be busy about the grates in the lower room and shall probably be in preparation to move in next week. Mr. Curtis called to see me about the deeds which are not done. I went to the Athenæum and returned the remaining books belonging there. Thus most of the morning was consumed. But the main business of my day, the arrival of letters from Washington, I was disappointed in. It is now a week since the date of the last. My Mother did not seem so well, probably owing to the bracing herself up to bear the expected letter and to the disappointment and suspense. In the afternoon I went down and tried to catch a few fish, without much success. Evening quietly at home. Read Ovid and Flaming without much cessation.

SUNDAY. 26.

I cannot go through a detailed Account of this day. Stormy as it was, the confusion of the elements was little to me compared to the trouble of the mind. We had spent a quiet day entirely at home, interrupted by nobody but a short and ceremonious visit from Mr. Southard[1] and his daughter. My Mother under her anxiety sent in Wilson to Boston in order to get the letter so fearfully expected. We had just done tea and were patiently expecting his return when a rap at the door startled me and I went. It was Mr. W. S. Smith and his wife just from New York.[2] They had received a letter from Mr. Johnson, at New York, and hurried on instantly to this spot. My poor brother had ceased to breathe on the night of the 23d just four hours after my father reached the House.[3]

After I had in a degree recovered from the shock, the next thing was to communicate the tidings. And it devolved upon me to be the bearer of them. Agitated as I was, it was not the easiest thing to tell what I knew would bring upon my Mother distress perhaps more than she could bear. But it must be done. I went up and upon her inquiry who came in, I was obliged to tell her. The announcement of Mrs. Smith's arrival was enough. She lay in a state of almost stupor for some time, followed by violent and indefinite emotion.

Notwithstanding the rain, we sent for Dr. Woodward who was visiting here some time since in the absence of Dr. Holbrook when it is not possible for him to come. He gave her an opiate under which she soon became quiet and found relief in tears and in conversation. The crisis was over for the night and on the whole far better than we could have anticipated. Mr. and Mrs. Smith proved invaluable auxiliaries in the case. This is the fourth time only in my life that I have been exposed to these fearful scenes. They have all been in connexion with my Mother and they will remain forever engraved upon my Memory. Thank God, it was no worse. Thank God that my Mother was so much prepared by timely and seasonable reflection that the blow came with but half it's force. I retired after all was quiet at about midnight although my sleep was restless and broken.

[1] Samuel Lewis Southard, a cabinet member in JQA's Administration (vol. 2:104).

[2] On William Steuben Smith, son of AA2, and his wife Catherine Johnson Smith, sister of LCA, see vol. 1:3 and Adams Genealogy.

[3] "I went to his bed-side twice and saw and heard him; he had no consciousness of any thing on Earth" (JQA, Diary, 22 Oct.).

[*Medford*]

MONDAY. 27TH.

The Storm howled through the night, but the morning was fair and bright and Autumnlike. After a good deal of conversation with my Mother in which she appeared calm and reasonable, I thought it safe to leave her for the sake of going to town, and from thence to Medford to communicate this intelligence to my Wife.

In Boston, I passed the greater part of my time at my Office in reflection and in writing to my father.[1] Upon this trying occasion, it seems as if an opportunity was presented for consideration. The family of my father must assume a new position and upon that position will depend very much it's future happiness. Knowing as well as I do the particular characters of it's members, I cannot say that I have any great hope in futurity. It seems to me as clear as fate makes any thing future that my father has not the energy necessary to do what is absolutely requisite. And yet he will not suffer any body else to have that complete control which will answer the purpose.

I went to Medford with Mr. Brooks. Enjoyed for the remainder of the day, the prodigious luxury of the company of my Wife and children—A comparative absence from care in my own family for which I feel particularly thankful at this time.

[1] Letter missing.

[*Quincy*]

TUESDAY. 28TH.

I left Medford this morning in the Carriage with my Wife and Mr. Brooks. My morning was too much taken up in running about and trifles. Mr. Walsh came in and worried me a good deal, for I received two letters from my father both of which needed special attention which I was unable to bestow.[1] The Carriage came in with Louisa C. Smith and to be left for repairs. I called to take her to Quincy to dinner.

Found my Mother much as I left her yesterday. She does not appear to me to suffer under this much. My brother had turned the rise of the hill and his progress was downward at a pace so accellerating and she was so aware of it, that I do not believe she feels as if it was a blow for which she had any complaint to make against Providence.[2]

For myself, I may be called cold in heart, and I have often thought with possible justice, but I cannot regard the loss of either of my brothers as a calamity either to their families or to themselves. They were saved much misery which would have been otherwise inevitable, and their friends the harrowing anxieties of witnessing a remediless evil. A calm judgment could come to no other conclusion. Conversation with my Mother about her plans. Ovid and German.

[1] To CFA, 23 and 24 Oct. (both in Adams Papers). The immediate charge was to arrange for a loan of $15,000 to meet the joint and several debts in Washington contracted by JQA and JA2.

[2] "My dear Son had been in a declining and drooping state of health more than three years. Several times afflicted with severe and acute disease; often so far recovered as to be out — able to travel and attend to business but never well.... His case did not however present symptoms of danger, till Sunday the 12th of this Month, from which time there has been no rational hope of his recovery" (JQA, Diary, 23 Oct.). The exact nature of the fatal illness remained undiagnosed, or at least undisclosed (same, 28 Oct.). In the family correspondence of the preceding months are references to intermittent fevers, to threatened loss of eyesight, to stiffening of limbs and joints, to an involvement of the feet, and to some loss of memory (LCA to JQA, 16, 25 July; to JA2, 31 July; to Mrs. JA2, 12 Oct.; all in Adams Papers).

Beyond the physical decline, CFA's words are to be understood as referring to a declination of another kind. See below, entries for 18 Nov., 31 December.

WEDNESDAY. 29TH.

I went to town with the design of doing a great deal. But I was so much deranged by the process of moving from my old Office to my new one that I could accomplish very little. I wrote a short letter to my father and that was all.[1] His scheme is a plain one and if carried through will answer, but I distrust his perseverance.[2] Returned to Quincy. My Mother appears inclined *now* to make the Journey. But I much fear her ability. She does not get up as she used to do.

Conversation with Mrs. Smith. Not the most discreet person to confide in but my Mother with her intimates never had secrets. My father wishes me to go on, attending to the House for the whole Winter. This is changing my object entirely and making me serve a purpose which I certainly do not intend. I offer to go, to put his affairs on a footing so that they may go on for the winter, and then to go again if necessary in the Spring and attend to the breaking up of the Establishment and its removal to Quincy. In this I can be useful but not in any other capacity. After that we are again independent and I imagine from that time permanently, for with this new arrangement, my family is excluded from the mansion, and this I do not for my own sake regret. Ovid in the evening.

[1] Letter missing.

[2] JQA's intent was to install Mrs. JA2 and her children in the Old House at Quincy as soon as possible, to remain himself at Washington through a last winter in the Capital, to be joined there by CFA who, with him, would undertake to sell all the Washington holdings prior to final removal of family and possessions to Quincy. JQA to CFA, 24 Oct. (Adams Papers).

[*Medford*]

THURSDAY. 30TH.

Nothing but the power of habit keeps up my fancy for Journalizing. For I have now little worth recording. Even my reading is disappearing and I am becoming the common place animal like all the others, in the world. It rained in the morning but I went to town notwithstanding. Time taken up at the Office in writing Diary and a letter to my father[1] in which I spoke plainly my opinions for the last time. Things after this must take their course. I then went to Medford with Mr. Brooks to spend the night. Disagreeably surprised by company. Mr. Shepherd, Mr. Harrison from Baltimore, Mr. Stetson, Jonathan Brooks, Edward and Chardon were here, some to dine and the remainder afterwards. This spoiled my day which I wished to devote to quiet and my children. I did nothing and felt very much depressed. My anxieties are now particularly numerous. I must hope and trust for the best.

¹ Letter missing.

Quincy

FRIDAY. 31ST.

I had intended going over with my Wife and children to Quincy this morning, but after studying out the weather I thought the probabilities were against us and having been so caught the time before, concluded to leave them behind me and go with Mr. Brooks.

At Boston, I was occupied at the Office and begin to enjoy the comfort of my new situation very much. It is more quiet and warmer than my former position. One or two called upon business and I was so engaged in commissions that the time flew.

Went to Quincy. Found my Mother sitting up but not very amiable. Just in the irritable state which a particular stage of strength or weakness creates. I nevertheless feel encouraged in the hope of her more rapid recovery. The whole force of this last blow being now suffered, I am now entertaining a better feeling than I have had about it for weeks.

My father writes me but as yet without any method.¹ I spent the afternoon in my Mother's room and the evening with the exception of only about an hour of Ovid in conversation with Mrs. Smith upon many very painful scenes of the past, reviewing the late misfortunes of the family and it's bitter disappointments. Lessons of wisdom to those who remain—Purchased dearly and perhaps not duly profited by.

¹ 25 Oct. (Adams Papers).